*New Beacon Bibl

MARK

A Commentary in the Wesleyan Tradition

Kent Brower

BEACON HILL PRESS

OF KANSAS CITY

Copyright 2012
by Beacon Hill Press of Kansas City

ISBN 978-0-8341-2409-7

Printed in the United States of America

Cover Design: J.R. Caines
Interior Design: Sharon Page

Library of Congress Cataloging-in-Publication Data

Brower, K. E. (Kent E.)
    Mark / Kent Brower.
        pages cm — (New Beacon Bible commentary)
    Includes bibliographical references.
    ISBN 978-0-8341-2409-7 (pbk.)
    1. Bible. N.T. Mark—Commentaries. I. Title.
    BS2585.53.B76 2012
    226.3'07—dc23

                                                                                    2012017863

10 9 8 7 6 5 4 3 2 1

DEDICATION

In memory of the late Dr. Hugh Rae:
Colleague, Mentor, Friend

COMMENTARY EDITORS

General Editors

Alex Varughese
Ph.D., Drew University
Professor of Biblical Literature
Mount Vernon Nazarene University
Mount Vernon, Ohio

Roger Hahn
Ph.D., Duke University
Dean of the Faculty
Professor of New Testament
Nazarene Theological Seminary
Kansas City, Missouri

George Lyons
Ph.D., Emory University
Professor of New Testament
Northwest Nazarene University
Nampa, Idaho

Section Editors

Joseph Coleson
Ph.D., Brandeis University
Professor of Old Testament
Nazarene Theological Seminary
Kansas City, Missouri

Robert Branson
Ph.D., Boston University
Professor of Biblical Literature
Emeritus
Olivet Nazarene University
Bourbonnais, Illinois

Alex Varughese
Ph.D., Drew University
Professor of Biblical Literature
Mount Vernon Nazarene University
Mount Vernon, Ohio

Jim Edlin
Ph.D., Southern Baptist Theological
Seminary
Professor of Biblical Literature and
Languages
Chair, Division of Religion and
Philosophy
MidAmerica Nazarene University
Olathe, Kansas

Kent Brower
Ph.D., The University of Manchester
Vice Principal
Senior Lecturer in Biblical Studies
Nazarene Theological College
Manchester, England

George Lyons
Ph.D., Emory University
Professor of New Testament
Northwest Nazarene University
Nampa, Idaho

CONTENTS

GENERAL EDITORS' PREFACE

The purpose of the New Beacon Bible Commentary is to make available to pastors and students in the twenty-first century a biblical commentary that reflects the best scholarship in the Wesleyan theological tradition. The commentary project aims to make this scholarship accessible to a wider audience to assist them in their understanding and proclamation of Scripture as God's Word.

Writers of the volumes in this series not only are scholars within the Wesleyan theological tradition and experts in their field but also have special interest in the books assigned to them. Their task is to communicate clearly the critical consensus and the full range of other credible voices who have commented on the Scriptures. Though scholarship and scholarly contribution to the understanding of the Scriptures are key concerns of this series, it is not intended as an academic dialogue within the scholarly community. Commentators of this series constantly aim to demonstrate in their work the significance of the Bible as the church's book and the contemporary relevance and application of the biblical message. The project's overall goal is to make available to the church and for her service the fruits of the labors of scholars who are committed to their Christian faith.

The *New International Version* (NIV) is the reference version of the Bible used in this series; however, the focus of exegetical study and comments is the biblical text in its original language. When the commentary uses the NIV, it is printed in bold. The text printed in bold italics is the translation of the author. Commentators also refer to other translations where the text may be difficult or ambiguous.

The structure and organization of the commentaries in this series seeks to facilitate the study of the biblical text in a systematic and methodical way. Study of each biblical book begins with an *Introduction* section that gives an overview of authorship, date, provenance, audience, occasion, purpose, sociological/cultural issues, textual history, literary features, hermeneutical issues, and theological themes necessary to understand the book. This section also includes a brief outline of the book and a list of general works and standard commentaries.

The commentary section for each biblical book follows the outline of the book presented in the introduction. In some volumes, readers will find section *overviews* of large portions of scripture with general comments on their overall literary structure and other literary features. A consistent feature of the commentary is the paragraph-by-paragraph study of biblical texts. This section has three parts: *Behind the Text*, *In the Text*, and *From the Text*.

The goal of the **Behind the Text** section is to provide the reader with all the relevant information necessary to understand the text. This includes specific historical situations reflected in the text, the literary context of the text, sociological and cultural issues, and literary features of the text.

In the Text explores what the text says, following its verse-by-verse structure. This section includes a discussion of grammatical details, word studies, and the connectedness of the text to other biblical books/passages or other parts of the book being studied (the canonical relationship). This section provides transliterations of key words in Hebrew and Greek and their literal meanings. The goal here is to explain what the author would have meant and/or what the audience would have understood as the meaning of the text. This is the largest section of the commentary.

The *From the Text* section examines the text in relation to the following areas: theological significance, intertextuality, the history of interpretation, use of the Old Testament scriptures in the New Testament, interpretation in later church history, actualization, and application.

The commentary provides *sidebars* on topics of interest that are important but not necessarily part of an explanation of the biblical text. These topics are informational items and may cover archaeological, historical, literary, cultural, and theological matters that have relevance to the biblical text. Occasionally, longer detailed discussions of special topics are included as *excurses.*

We offer this series with our hope and prayer that readers will find it a valuable resource for their understanding of God's Word and an indispensable tool for their critical engagement with the biblical texts.

Roger Hahn, Centennial Initiative General Editor
Alex Varughese, General Editor (Old Testament)
George Lyons, General Editor (New Testament)

AUTHOR'S PREFACE

On reflection, the shape of this commentary began in my first year as an undergraduate through a little book by Paul and Elizabeth Achtemeier. Their narrative approach to Scripture, as I would now describe it, led to my work on Markan intertextuality in a Ph.D. thesis (1978) under the supervision of Professor F. F. Bruce. A narrative approach to Scripture is fully compatible with the conviction that the central point of Scripture is God's reconciling work in the life, death, resurrection, and ascension of Jesus of Nazareth. This cannot be clearly understood without beginning with Abraham and God's response to the human plight. This conviction shapes my thinking.

In more than thirty years of working in NT studies and biblical theology, the debt I owe to scholars is huge. Conversation partners for this commentary simply add to it. It extends well beyond those names in the bibliography. They are only those whose works have been cited directly. Several recent commentators have been almost constant companions. The influence of Collins, Donahue, Evans, France, Guelich, Hooker, Marcus, Stein, and Wright may be detected on almost every page. Indeed, each one of them would recognize influence on my work in ways about which I am no longer even conscious.

Most of my academic life has been at Nazarene Theological College-Manchester. I have been blessed by its generosity in providing support for serious academic work. My faculty colleagues over the years have contributed to a lively scholarly and interdisciplinary community. The exceptional resources available in the college and through its partnership with the University of Manchester have been a boon. The privilege of teaching postgraduates and supervising some very bright research students have kept me engaged. Particular mention should be made of those who have worked with me on Mark (Rob Snow, Arseny Ermakov, and Gabrielle Overduin-Markusse). Thanks also go to the patient people at NPH. George Lyons' attention to detail and sharp editorial skills have improved this commentary at innumerable places. He has asked appropriate questions at key points, pressing me to make my points more clearly and effectively. Thanks, George.

My spiritual home for some time now has been the Longsight Community Church of the Nazarene, a place where the love of Jesus is manifest in extraordinary ways. Few of my brothers and sisters there would be interested in reading this commentary. But the remarkable flavor of the Longsight family escapes description by mere words. I am deeply indebted to the wonderful range of people there. They put flesh on Jesus' pronouncement in Mark 3:35.

Special gratitude goes to my wife, Francine. In the midst of her own career as a specialist in autistic spectrum disorder, she has been constant in her support and encouragement. She alone knows how much I owe her. My children have also maintained a lively interest in this project.

More than thirty-five years have passed since one of the earliest sentences developed by my son Derek was "Daddy–thesis?" That has been replaced in the household vocabulary by "working on his commentary." No longer! I can now move on to other projects!

ABBREVIATIONS

With a few exceptions, these abbreviations follow those in *The SBL Handbook of Style* (Alexander 1999).

General

→	see the commentary on
‖	Synoptic parallel to
2TP	Second Temple period
2TJ	Second Temple Judaism
ad loc.	*ad locum*, at the place discussed
A.D.	anno Domini (precedes date) (equivalent to C.E.)
B.C.	before Christ (follows date) (equivalent to B.C.E.)
B.C.E.	before the Common Era
C.E.	Common Era
ca.	circa, approximate time
ch	chapter
chs	chapters
DSS	Dead Sea Scrolls
e.g.	*exempli gratia*, for example
esp.	especially
ET	English translation
etc.	*et cetera*, and the rest
Gk.	Greek
Heb.	Hebrew
i.e.	*id est*, that is
LXX	Septuagint (Greek translation of the OT)
MS	manuscript
MSS	manuscripts
MT	Masoretic Text (of the OT)
n.d.	no date
n.p.	no place; no publisher; no page
NT	New Testament
OT	Old Testament
s.v.	*sub verbo*, under the word
v (vv)	verse (verses)
vs.	versus

Contemporary Sources

AB	The Anchor Bible
ABD	*The Anchor Bible Dictionary*
BDAG	*Greek-English Lexicon of the New Testament and Other Early Christian Literature* (see Bauer)
BibInt	*Biblical Interpretation*
BTB	*Biblical Theology Bulletin*
BZNW	Beihefte zur Zeitschrift für die neutestamentliche Wissenschaft und die Kunde der älteren Kirche
CBQ	*Catholic Biblical Quarterly*
ExpT	*Expository Times*
ICC	International Critical Commentary
JBL	*Journal of Biblical Literature*
JSNT	*Journal for the Study of the New Testament*
JSNTSup	Journal for the Study of the New Testament: Supplement Series
JSOT	*Journal for the Study of the Old Testament*
JSOTSup	Journal for the Study of the Old Testament: Supplement Series
JTS	*Journal of Theological Studies*
LNTS	Library of New Testament Studies
NIBC	New International Bible Commentary

NICNT	The New International Commentary on the New Testament
NIGTC	New International Greek Testament Commentary
NovT	*Novum Testamentum*
NSBT	New Studies in Biblical Theology
NTS	*New Testament Studies*
SBL	Society of Biblical Literature
SBLDS	Society of Biblical Literature (Dissertation Series)
SBLMS	Society of Biblical Literature (Monograph Series)
SBT	Studies in Biblical Theology
SCM	Student Christian Movement
SJT	*Scottish Journal of Theology*
SNTSMS	Society for New Testament Studies Monograph Series
SPCK	Society for the Promotion of Christian Knowledge
TS	*Theological Studies*
TynBul	*Tyndale Bulletin*
WBC	Word Biblical Commentary
WUNT	Wissenschaftliche Untersuchungen zum Neuen Testament
ZNW	*Zeitschrift für die neutestamentliche Wissenschaft*

Modern English Versions

KJV	King James Version
NIV	New International Version
NKJV	New King James Version
NRSV	New Revised Standard Version

Print Conventions for Translations

Bold font	NIV (bold without quotation marks in the passage under study; elsewhere in the regular font, with quotation marks and no further identification)
Bold italic font	Author's translation (without quotation marks)

Behind the Text: Literary or historical background information average readers might not know from reading the biblical text alone

In the Text: Comments on the biblical text, words, phrases, grammar, and so forth

From the Text: The use of the text by later interpreters, contemporary relevance, theological and ethical implications of the text, with particular emphasis on Wesleyan concerns

MARK

Old Testament

				New Testament	
Gen	Genesis	Hos	Hosea		
Exod	Exodus	Joel	Joel	Matt	Matthew
Lev	Leviticus	Amos	Amos	Mark	Mark
Num	Numbers	Obad	Obadiah	Luke	Luke
Deut	Deuteronomy	Jonah	Jonah	John	John
Josh	Joshua	Mic	Micah	Acts	Acts
Judg	Judges	Nah	Nahum	Rom	Romans
Ruth	Ruth	Hab	Habakkuk	1—2 Cor	1—2 Corinthians
1—2 Sam	1—2 Samuel	Zeph	Zephaniah		
1—2 Kgs	1—2 Kings	Hag	Haggai	Gal	Galatians
1—2 Chr	1—2 Chronicles	Zech	Zechariah	Eph	Ephesians
Ezra	Ezra	Mal	Malachi	Phil	Philippians
Neh	Nehemiah		(Note: Chapter and	Col	Colossians
Esth	Esther		verse numbering in the	1—2 Thess	1—2 Thessalonians
Job	Job		MT and LXX often		
Ps/Pss	Psalm/Psalms		differ compared to	1—2 Tim	1—2 Timothy
Prov	Proverbs		those in English Bibles.	Titus	Titus
Eccl	Ecclesiastes		To avoid confusion, all	Phlm	Philemon
Song	Song of Songs / Song of Solomon		biblical references follow the chapter and verse	Heb	Hebrews
				Jas	James
Isa	Isaiah		numbering in English	1—2 Pet	1—2 Peter
Jer	Jeremiah		translations, even when the	1—2—3 John	1—2—3 John
Lam	Lamentations		text in the MT and LXX is	Jude	Jude
Ezek	Ezekiel		under discussion.)	Rev	Revelation
Dan	Daniel				

Apocrypha

Jdt	Judith
1—2 Macc	1—2 Maccabees
3—4 Macc	3—4 Maccabees
Sir	The Wisdom of Jesus Son of Sirach
Tob	Tobit
Wis	Wisdom of Solomon

OT Pseudepigrapha and NT Apocrypha

1 En.	*1 Enoch* (Ethiopic Apocalypse)
4 Ezra	*4 Ezra*
Jub.	*Jubilees*
Prot. Jas.	*Protevangelium of James*
Pss. Sol.	*Psalms of Solomon*
T. Dan	*Testament of Dan*
T. Iss.	*Testament of Issachar*
T. Sol.	*Testament of Solomon*

Dead Sea Scrolls and Related Texts

CD	Cairo Genizah copy of the *Damascus Document*
Q	Qumran
1QH	*Thanksgiving Hymns*
1QM	*Milhamah* or *War Scroll*
1QS	*Rule of the Community*
1QSa	*Rule of the Congregation* (Appendix a to 1QS)
4Q174	*Florilegium*
4Q242	*Prayer of Nabonidus*
4Q417	Instruction (*olim* Sap. Work A^c)
4Q521	*Messianic Apocalypse*
11QT^a	*Temple Scroll^a*

Philo

Spec.	*De specialibus legibus*

Josephus

Ag. Ap.	*Against Apion*
Ant.	*Jewish Antiquities*
J.W.	*Jewish War*

Rabbinic Texts

b.	Babylonian Talmud
'Erub.	*'Erubin*
Giṭ.	*Giṭṭin*
Ḥag.	*Ḥagigah*
Mak.	*Makkot*
Nid.	*Niddah*
m.	Mishnah
Šabb.	*Šabbat*
Sanh.	*Sanhedrin*

Apostolic Fathers

Did.	*Didache*

Greek and Latin Works

Ep.	Pliny the Younger, *Epistulae*
Haer.	Irenaeus, *Against Heresies*
Hist. eccl.	Eusebius, *Ecclesiastical History*
Vit. Apoll.	Philostratus, *Vita Apollonii*

Greek Transliteration

Greek	Letter	English
α	alpha	a
β	bēta	b
γ	gamma	g
γ	gamma nasal	n (before γ, κ, ξ, χ)
δ	delta	d
ε	epsilon	e
ζ	zēta	z
η	ēta	ē
θ	thēta	th
ι	iōta	i
κ	kappa	k
λ	lambda	l
μ	mu	m
ν	nu	n
ξ	xi	x
ο	omicron	o
π	pi	p
ρ	rhō	r
ρ	initial rhō	rh
σ/ς	sigma	s
τ	tau	t
υ	upsilon	y
υ	upsilon	u (in diphthongs: au, eu, ēu, ou, ui)
φ	phi	ph
χ	chi	ch
ψ	psi	ps
ω	ōmega	ō
ʾ	rough breathing	h (before initial vowels or diphthongs)

Hebrew Consonant Transliteration

Hebrew/Aramaic	Letter	English
א	alef	ʾ
ב	bet	b
ג	gimel	g
ד	dalet	d
ה	he	h
ו	vav	v or w
ז	zayin	z
ח	khet	ḥ
ט	tet	ṭ
י	yod	y
ך/כ	kaf	k
ל	lamed	l
ם/מ	mem	m
ן/נ	nun	n
ס	samek	s̱
ע	ayin	ʿ
ף/פ	pe	p; f (spirant)
ץ/צ	tsade	ṣ
ק	qof	q
ר	resh	r
שׂ	sin	ś
שׁ	shin	š
ת	tav	t; th (spirant)

16

BIBLIOGRAPHY

Annen, Franz. 1976. *Heil für die Heiden: Zur Bedeutung und Geschichte der Tradition vom Besessen Gerasener (Mk 5.1-20 parr.).* Frankfurter Theologishe Studien 20. Frankfurt am Main: Josef Knecht.

Barrett, C. K. 1947. *The Holy Spirit and the Gospel Tradition.* New York: Macmillan.

Barton, Stephen C. 1994. *Discipleship and Family Ties in Mark and Matthew.* Society for New Testament Studies Monograph Series 80. Cambridge: Cambridge University Press.

Bauckham, Richard. 1994. The Brothers and Sisters of Jesus: An Epiphanian Response to John P. Meier. *Catholic Biblical Quarterly* 56:686-700.

————, ed. 1995. *The Book of Acts in Its First Century Setting: Palestinian Setting.* Grand Rapids: Eerdmans.

————, ed. 1998. *The Gospels for All Christians: Rethinking the Gospel Audiences.* Grand Rapids: Eerdmans.

————. 2002. *Gospel Women: Studies of the Named Women in the Gospels.* London: T & T Clark.

————. 2006. *Jesus and the Eyewitnesses: The Gospels as Eyewitness Testimony.* Grand Rapids: Eerdmans.

Bauer, Walter, William Arndt, and Frederick W. Danker. 2000. *A Greek-English Lexicon of the New Testament and Other Early Christian Literature.* 3rd ed. Chicago: University of Chicago Press.

Beasley-Murray, George R. 1954. *Jesus and the Future: An Examination of the Criticism of the Eschatological Discourse, Mark 13, with Special Reference to the Little Apocalypse Theory.* London: Macmillan.

————. 1993. *Jesus and the Last Days: The Interpretation of the Olivet Discourse.* Peabody, Mass.: Hendrickson.

Beavis, Mary Ann. 1989. *Mark's Audience: The Literary and Social Setting of Mark 4.11-12.* Journal for the Study of the New Testament Supplement 33. Sheffield: JSOT Press.

Best, Ernest. 1990. *The Temptation and the Passion: The Markan Soteriology.* 2nd ed. Cambridge: Cambridge University Press.

Betsworth, Sharon. 2010. *The Reign of God Is Such as These: A Socio-Literary Analysis of Daughters in the Gospel of Mark.* Library of New Testament Studies 422. London: T & T Clark.

Bird, Michael J. 2003. The Crucifixion of Jesus and the Fulfillment of Mark 9:1. *Trinity Journal* 24:23-36.

Blomberg, Craig L. 2005. *Contagious Holiness: Jesus' Meals with Sinners.* New Studies in Biblical Theology 19. Leicester: Apollos.

Bock, Darrel L. 1998. *Blasphemy and Exaltation in Judaism and the Final Examination of Jesus.* Wissenschaftliche Untersuchungen zum Neuen Testament 2 106. Tübingen: Mohr-Siebeck.

Bolt, Peter G. 2004. *The Cross from a Distance: Atonement in Mark's Gospel.* New Studies in Biblical Theology 18. Leicester: Apollos.

Bond, Helen K. 1998. *Pontius Pilate in History and Interpretation.* Cambridge: Cambridge University Press.

Bonhoeffer, Dietrich. 1959. *The Cost of Discipleship.* Translated by R. H. Fuller. London: SCM.

Borg, Marcus J. 1998. *Conflict, Holiness, and Politics in the Teachings of Jesus.* Harrisburg: Trinity.

Brooke, George J. 2005. *Dead Sea Scrolls and the New Testament: Essays in Mutual Illumination.* Minneapolis: Augsburg Fortress.

Brower, K. E. 1978. "The Old Testament in the Markan Passion Narrative." Ph.D. Thesis. The University of Manchester.

————. 1980. Mark 9:1: "Seeing the Kingdom." *Journal for the Study of the New Testament* 6:17-41.

————. 1983. Elijah in the Markan Passion Narrative. *Journal for the Study of the New Testament* 18:85-101.

————. 1997. "Let the reader understand": Temple and Eschatology in Mark. *"The Reader Must Understand": Eschatology in Bible and Theology.* Leicester: Apollos.

————. 2005. *Holiness in the Gospels.* Kansas City: Beacon Hill Press of Kansas City.

————. 2007a. The Holy One and His Disciples: Holiness and Ecclesiology in Mark. Pages 57-75 in *Holiness and Ecclesiology in the New Testament.* Edited by K. Brower and A. Johnson. Grand Rapids: Eerdmans.

————. 2007b. "We are able": Cross-Bearing Discipleship and the Way of the Lord in Mark. *Horizons in Biblical Theology* 29:177-201.

Brower, K. E., and M. W. Elliott, eds. 1997. *"The Reader Must Understand": Eschatology in Bible and Theology.* Leicester: Apollos.

Brower, K. E., and Andy Johnson, eds. 2007. *Holiness and Ecclesiology in the New Testament.* Grand Rapids: Eerdmans.

Brown, Raymond E. 1994. *The Death of the Messiah Vol. 2: From Gethsemane to the Grave—A Commentary on the Passion Narratives in the Four Gospels.* London: Geoffrey Chapman.

Bruce, F. F. 1969. *New Testament History.* Nelson's Library of Theology. London: Nelson.

————. 1984. Render to Caesar. Pages 249-64 in *Jesus and the Politics of His Day.* Edited by E. Bammel and C. F. D. Moule. Cambridge: CUP.

Bryan, Steven M. 2002. *Jesus and Israel's Traditions of Judgment and Restoration.* Society for New Testament Studies Monograph Series 117. Cambridge: Cambridge University Press.

Burridge, Richard A. 2004. *What Are the Gospels? A Comparison with Graeco-Roman Biography.* 2nd ed. Grand Rapids: Eerdmans.

Capper, Brian. 1995. The Palestinian Cultural Context of the Earliest Christian Community of Goods. Pages 323-56 in *The Book of Acts in Its First Century Setting: Palestinian Setting.* Edited by Richard Bauckham. Grand Rapids: Eerdmans.

Charlesworth, James. 1985. *The Old Testament Pseudepigrapha.* Vol. 2. New York: Doubleday.

Collins, Adela Yarbro. 2007. *Mark.* Hermeneia. Minneapolis: Fortress Press.

Crossley, James. 2004. *The Date of Mark's Gospel.* Library of New Testament Studies 266. London: Continuum.

Culpepper, R. Alan. 2007. *Mark.* The Smyth & Helwys Bible Commentary 20. Macon, Ga.: Smyth & Helwys.

Danker, F. W. 1966. The Literary Unity of Mark 14:1-25. *Journal of Biblical Literature* 85:467-72.

_____. 1970. The Demonic Secret in Mark: A Re-examination of the Cry of Dereliction (15:34). *Zeitschrift für die Neutestamentliche Wissenschaft* 61:48-69.

Deasley, A. R. G. 2000. *Marriage and Divorce in the Bible and the Church.* Kansas City: Beacon Hill Press of Kansas City.

Deming, Will. 1990. Mark 9:42—10:12, Matthew 5:27-32, and *B. Nid.* 13b: A First Century Discussion of Male Sexuality. *New Testament Studies* 36:130-141.

Donahue, John R. 1992. Tax Collectors. Pages 337-38 in vol. 6 of *The Anchor Bible Dictionary.* New York: Doubleday.

Donahue, John R., and Daniel J. Harrington. 2002. *The Gospel of Mark.* Sacra Pagina 2. Collegeville, Minn.: Liturgical Press.

Downing, F. Gerald. 1988. *Christ and the Cynics: Jesus and Other Radical Preachers in First-century Tradition.* JSOT Manuals. Sheffield: JSOT Press.

Edwards, James R. 2006. The Servant of the Lord and the Gospel of Mark. Pages 49-63 in *The Gospel of Mark.* Vol. 1 of *Biblical Interpretation in Early Christian Gospels.* Edited by Thomas R. Hatina. Library of New Testament Studies 304. London: T & T Clark International.

Eusebius. 1942. *The Ecclesiastical History.* Translated by Kirsopp Lake. The Loeb Classical Library. London: Heinemann.

Evans, Craig A. 1989. *To See and Not Perceive: Isaiah 6.9-10 in Early Jewish and Christian Interpretation.* Journal for the Study of the Old Testament: Supplement Series 64. Sheffield: JSOT Press.

_____. 2000. Mark's Incipit and the Priene Calendar Inscription: From Jewish Gospel to Greco-Roman Gospel. *Journal of Greco-Roman Christianity and Judaism* 1:67-81.

_____. 2001. *Mark 8:27-16:20.* Word Biblical Commentary 34B. Dallas: Word.

Evans, Craig A., and W. Richard Stegner, eds. 1994. *The Gospels and the Scriptures of Israel.* Journal for the Study of the New Testament: Supplement Series 104. Sheffield: Sheffield Academic Press.

Foskett, Mary F. 2005. *Virginity as Purity in the Protoevangelium of James.* Pages 67-76 in *A Feminist Companion to Mariology.* Edited by Amy Jill Levine and Maria Mayo Robbins. New York: Pilgrim Press.

Foster, Richard J. 1985. *Money, Sex and Power: The Challenge of the Disciplined Life.* San Francisco: Harper & Row.

France, R. T. 1971. *Jesus and the Old Testament: His Application of Old Testament Passages to Himself and His Mission.* London: Tyndale Press.

_____. 2002. *The Gospel of Mark: A Commentary on the Greek Text.* The New International Greek Testament Commentary. Grand Rapids: Eerdmans.

Freyne, Sean. 1980. *Galilee from Alexander the Great to Hadrian, 323 B.C.E. to 135 C.E.: A Study of Second Temple Judaism.* Edinburgh: T & T Clark.

Geddert, Timothy J. 2001. *Mark.* Believers' Church Bible Commentary. Scottdale, Pa.: Herald Press.

Goodacre, Mark. 2002. *The Case against Q: Studies in Markan Priority and the Synoptic Problem.* Harrisburg, Pa.: Trinity Press International.

Guelich, Robert A. 1989. *Mark 1—8:26.* Word Biblical Commentary 34A. Dallas: Word.

Gundry, Robert H. 1993. *Mark: A Commentary on His Apology for the Cross.* Grand Rapids: Eerdmans.

Hanson, K. C. 1997. The Galilean Fishing Economy and the Jesus Tradition. *Biblical Theology Bulletin* 27:99-111.

Hart, H. StJ. 1984. The Coin of "Render unto Caesar . . ." (A Note on Some Aspects of Mark 12:13-17; Matt. 22:15-22; Luke 20:20-26). Pages 241-48 in *Jesus and the Politics of His Day.* Edited by E. Bammel and C. F. D. Moule. Cambridge: Cambridge University Press.

Hatina, Thomas J. 2002. *In Search of a Context: The Function of Scripture in Mark's Narrative.* Journal for the Study of the New Testament: Supplement Series 232. Sheffield: Sheffield Academic Press.

_____. 2005. Who Will See "The Kingdom of God Coming with Power" in Mark 9:1—Protagonists or Antagonists? *Biblia* 86:20-34.

_____, ed. 2006. *The Gospel of Mark.* Vol. 1 of *Biblical Interpretation in Early Christian Gospels.* Library of New Testament Studies 304. London: T & T Clark.

Hay, David M. 1973. *Glory at the Right Hand: Psalm 110 in Early Christian Literature.* Society of Biblical Literature Monograph Series 18. Nashville: Abingdon.

Hays, Richard B. 2005. Christ Prays the Psalms: Israel's Psalter as the Matrix of Early Christology. Pages 101-18 in *The Conversion of the Imagination: Paul as Interpreter of Israel's Scripture.* Grand Rapids: Eerdmans.

Head, Peter M. 1991. A Text-Critical Study of Mark 1:1. "The Beginning of the Gospel of Jesus Christ." *NTS* 36:621-29.

Hengel, Martin. 1985. *Studies in the Gospel of Mark.* Translated by John Bowden. London: SCM.

_____. 1986. *The Cross of the Son of God.* Translated by John Bowden. London: SCM.

Hoehner, Harold W. 1972. *Herod Antipas: A Contemporary of Jesus Christ.* Grand Rapids: Zondervan.

Hooker, Morna D. 1991. *A Commentary on the Gospel According to St. Mark.* [New ed.] London: A. & C. Black.

_____. 1994. *Not Ashamed of the Gospel: New Testament Interpretations of the Death of Christ.* The 1988 Didsbury Lectures. Carlisle: Paternoster.

_____. 2005. *Isaiah in Mark's Gospel.* Isaiah in the New Testament. The New Testament and the Scriptures of Israel. London: T & T Clark.

Hurtado, L. W. 2009. The Women, the Tomb and the Ending of Mark. Pages 427-50 in *A Wandering Galilean: Essays in Honour of Sean Freyne.* Edited by Zuleika Rodgers and Margaret Daly-Denton. Leiden: Brill. Cited from http://larryhurtado. wordpress.com/essays-etc: 1-45 (accessed January 11, 2011).

Instone-Brewer, David. 2002. *Divorce and Remarriage in the Bible: The Social and Literary Context.* Grand Rapids: Eerdmans.

Jeremias, Joachim. 1966. *The Eucharistic Words of Jesus.* New Testament Library. Translated by Norman Perrin. London: SCM.

Johnson, E. S. 1978. Mark 8:22-26: The Blind Man from Bethsaida. *New Testament Studies* 25:370-83.

Juel, Donald. 1977. *Messiah and Temple: The Trial Narrative in the Gospel of Mark.* Society of Biblical Literature Dissertation Series 31. Missoula, Mont.: Scholars Press.

Kee, Howard Clark. 1986. *Medicine, Miracle and Magic in New Testament Times.* Society for New Testament Studies Monograph Series 55. Cambridge: Cambridge University Press.

Kernaghan, Ronald J. 2007. *Mark.* IVP New Testament Commentary Series. Downers Grove, Ill.: InterVarsity Press.

Klassen, William. 1996. *Judas: Betrayer or Friend of Jesus?* London: SCM.

Klawans, Jonathan. 2000. *Impurity and Sin in Ancient Judaism.* Oxford: Oxford University Press.

Kloppenborg, John S. 1987. *The Formation of Q: Trajectories in Ancient Wisdom Collections.* Studies in Antiquity and Christianity. Philadelphia: Fortress Press.

_____. 2006. *The Tenants in the Vineyard: Ideology, Economics, and Agrarian Conflict in Jewish Palestine.* Wissenschaftliche Untersuchungen zum Neuen Testament 195. Tübingen: Mohr-Siebeck.

Kunene, Musa Victor Mdabuleni. 2010. *Communal Holiness in the Gospel of John: The Vine Metaphor as a Test Case with Elements of Comparative Ethnography and Implications for the Contemporary Church.* Ph.D. Thesis. The University of Manchester.

Lane, William L. 1974. *The Gospel According to Mark: The English Text.* The New International Commentary on the New Testament. Grand Rapids: Eerdmans.

Lee, Dorothy. 2004. *Transfiguration.* New Century Theology. London: Continuum.

Lightfoot, Robert Henry. 1935. *History and Interpretation in the Gospels.* Bampton Lectures. London: Hodder & Stoughton.

_____. 1950. *The Gospel Message of St. Mark.* Oxford: Clarendon Press.

Manson, T. W. 1935. *The Teaching of Jesus.* 2nd ed. Cambridge: Cambridge University Press.

Marcus, Joel. 1993. *The Way of the Lord: Christological Exegesis of the Old Testament in the Gospel of Mark.* Studies of the New Testament and Its World. Edinburgh: T & T Clark.

_____. 2000. *Mark 1-8: A New Translation with Introduction and Commentary.* Anchor Bible 27. New York: Doubleday.

_____. 2009. *Mark 8-16: A New Translation with Introduction and Commentary.* Anchor Bible 27A. New York: Doubleday.

Marshall, I. Howard. 1980. *Last Supper and Lord's Supper.* The 1980 Didsbury Lectures. Exeter: Paternoster.

_____. 1990. Son of God or Servant of Yahweh? A Reconsideration of Mark 1:11. Pages 121-33 in *Jesus the Saviour: Studies in New Testament Theology.* London: SPCK. Reprinted from *New Testament Studies* 15 (1968/69):326-36.

_____. 2002. The Meaning of the Verb "Baptize." Pages 8-24 in *Dimensions of Baptism: Biblical and Theological Studies.* Journal for the Study of the New Testament: Supplement Series 234. London: Sheffield Academic Press.

Martínez, Florentino García, ed. 1994. *The Dead Sea Scrolls Translated: The Qumran Texts in English.* Leiden: Brill.

Mauser, Ulrich. 1963. *Christ in the Wilderness: The Wilderness Theme in the Second Gospel and Its Basis in the Biblical Tradition*. Studies in Biblical Theology 39. London: SCM.

Metzger, Bruce M. 1975. *A Textual Commentary on the New Testament*. London: United Bible Societies.

Meyer, Ben F. 1979. *The Aims of Jesus*. London: SCM.

Middleton, Paul. 2006. *Radical Martyrdom and Cosmic Conflict in Early Christianity*. Library of New Testament Studies. London: Continuum.

Moyise, Steve, and Maarten J. J. Menken, eds. 2005. *Isaiah in the New Testament*. The New Testament and the Scriptures of Israel. London: T & T Clark.

Muddiman, John. 1992. Fast, Fasting. Pages 773-76 in vol. 2 of *Anchor Bible Dictionary*. New York: Doubleday.

Mullen, J. Patrick. 2004. *Dining with Pharisees*. Interfaces. Collegeville, Md.: Liturgical Press.

Murphy-O'Connor, Jerome. 1990. John the Baptist and Jesus: History and Hypotheses. *New Testament Studies* 36:359-74.

Myers, Ched. 2008. *Binding the Strong Man: A Political Reading of Mark's Story of Jesus*. 2nd ed. Maryknoll, N.Y.: Orbis Books.

Neale, David A. 1991. *None but the Sinners: Religious Categories in the Gospel of Luke*. Journal for the Study of the New Testament: Supplement Series 58. Sheffield: JSOT Press.

Neyrey, Jerome H. 1986. The Idea of Purity in Mark's Gospel. *Semeia* 35:91-122.

Nolland, John. 2005. *Gospel of Matthew: A Commentary on the Greek Text*. The New International Greek Testament Commentary. Grand Rapids: William B. Eerdmans.

Oden, Thomas C., and Christopher A. Hall, eds. 1998. *Mark*. Ancient Christian Commentary on Scripture: New Testament 2. Downers Grove, Ill.: InterVarsity Press.

Öhler, Markus. 1997. *Elai im Neuen Testament. Untersuchungen zur Bedeutung des altestamentlichen Propheten im Frühen Christentum*. Beihefte zur Zeitschrift für die neutestamentliche Wissenschaft und die Kunde der älteren Kirche 88. Berlin: de Gruyter.

Porter, Stanley E., ed. 1999a. *Baptism, the New Testament and the Church: Historical and Contemporary Studies in Honour of R. E. O. White*. Journal for the Study of the New Testament: Supplement Series 171. Sheffield: Sheffield Academic Press.

_____. 1999b. Mark 1:4, Baptism and Translation. Pages 81-98 in *Baptism, the New Testament and the Church: Historical and Contemporary Studies in Honour of R. E. O. White*. Journal for the Study of the New Testament: Supplement Series 171. Sheffield: Sheffield Academic Press.

_____. 2002. *Dimensions of Baptism: Biblical and Theological Studies*. Journal for the Study of the New Testament: Supplement Series 234. London: Sheffield Academic Press.

Rainer, Reinhold. 1987. "Bethany Beyond the Jordan" (Jn 1:28). Topography, Theology and History in the Fourth Gospel. *Tyndale Bulletin* 38:29-64.

Reinhardt, Wolfgang. 1995. The Population of Jerusalem and the Numerical Growth of the Church in the Book of Acts. Pages 237-66 in *The Book of Acts in Its First Century Setting: Palestinian Setting*. Edited by Richard Bauckham. Grand Rapids: Eerdmans.

Sanders, E. P. 1992. Sinners. Pages 40-47 in vol. 5 of *Anchor Bible Dictionary*. New York: Doubleday.

Schürer, Emil, Geza Vermes, Fergus Millar, and Martin Goodman, eds. 1973. *The History of the Jewish People in the Age of Jesus Christ (175 B.C.—A.D. 135)*. Vol. 1. Edinburgh: T & T Clark.

Schweizer, Eduard. 1971. *The Good News according to Mark: A Commentary on the Gospel*. Translated by Donald Madvig. London: SPCK.

Shiner, Whitney Taylor. 1995. *Follow Me!: Disciples in Markan Rhetoric*. SBL dissertation series 145. Atlanta: Scholars Press.

Smith, Mahlon H. 2008. "Capernaum." No pages. Cited January 18, 2011. http://virtualreligion.net/iho/capernaum.html.

Snodgrass, Klyne. 2008. *Stories with Intent: A Comprehensive Guide to the Parables of Jesus*. Grand Rapids: Eerdmans.

Snow, Robert E. 2010. "Let the Reader Understand": Mark's Use of Jeremiah 7 in Mark 13:14. Paper presented to the 2010 British New Testament Conference, Bangor.

Stein, Robert H. 2008. Mark (Baker Exegetical Commentary on the New Testament). Grand Rapids: Baker Academic.

Taylor, Joan E. 1997. *The Immerser: John the Baptist Within Second Temple Judaism*. Studying the Historical Jesus. Grand Rapids: Eerdmans.

Taylor, Vincent. 1966. *The Gospel According to St. Mark: The Greek Text*. 2nd ed. London: Macmillan.

VanderKam, James C. 1998. *Calendars in the Dead Sea Scrolls: Measuring Time*. The Dead Sea Scrolls. London: Routledge.

_____. 2001. *The Book of Jubilees*. Guides to the Apocrypha and Pseudepigrapha. Sheffield: Sheffield Academic Press.

Vermes, Geza. 1961. *Scripture and Tradition in Judaism: Haggadic Studies*. Studia Post-Biblica, v. 4. Leiden: Brill.

_____. 1983. *Jesus the Jew: A Historian's Reading of the Gospels*. London: SCM.

Watts, Rikki. 1997. *Isaiah's New Exodus and Mark*. Wissenschaftliche Untersuchungen Zum Neuen Testament 2, 288. Tübingen: Mohr.

Webb, Robert L. 1991. *John the Baptizer and Prophet: A Socio-Historical Study*. Journal for the Study of the New Testament: Supplement Series 62. Sheffield: JSOT Press.

Wenham, J. W. 1991. *Redating Matthew, Mark and Luke: a Fresh Assault on the Synoptic Problem*. London: Hodder & Stoughton.

Wesley, John. 1979. *The Works of John Wesley*. Vol. 11. Jackson Edition. Grand Rapids: Baker.

_____. 1986. *The Works of John Wesley*. Vol. 3. Bicentennial Edition. Edited by Albert Outler. Nashville: Abingdon.

Westermann, Claus. 1974. The Role of the Lament in the Theology of the Old Testament. *Interpretation* 28:20-38.

Wieder, Naphthali. 1962. *The Judean Scrolls and Karaism*. London: East and West Library.

Williamson, Lamar. 1983. *Mark*. Interpretation. Atlanta: John Knox.

Wrede, William. 1901. *Das Messiasgeheimnis in den Evangelien: Zugleich ein Beitrag zum Verständnis des Markusevangeliums*. Göttingen: Vandenhoeck & Ruprecht. English edition, 1971. *The Messianic Secret*. Translated by J. C. G. Grieg. Cambridge: James Clarke & Co.

Wright, N. T. 1992. *The New Testament and the People of God*. Christian Origins and the Question of God 1. London: SPCK.

_____. 1996. *Jesus and the Victory of God*. Christian Origins and the Question of God 2. London: SPCK.

_____. 2003. *The Resurrection of the Son of God*. London: SPCK.

_____. 2007. *Surprised by Hope: Rethinking Heaven, the Resurrection and the Mission of the Church*. London: SPCK.

Zimmerli, Walther, and Joachim Jeremias. 1957. *The Servant of God*. Translated by Harold Knight and others. Studies in Biblical Theology 20. London: SCM.

INTRODUCTION

A new religious movement of surprising vigor emerged from a troublesome and obscure part of the Roman Empire. It started in Galilee and Judea during the reign of the Emperor Tiberius and in the latter part of the Herodian period (40 B.C. to A.D. 70). But thirty years or so later, it had spread to all parts of the empire. The movement started as part of the Judaism of the late Second Temple period (about 520 B.C. to A.D. 70). Judaism was viewed by many as the strange and unaccommodating religion of a Semitic people who populated part of the Roman administrative province of Syria. Jews also lived across the empire but retained their pattern of life to the extent that was possible. The Jews believed their God was the only true God and that they were his special people, but their current circumstances belied this belief.

Many Jews longed for the restoration of the nation as promised by the prophets. Some believed that God would only act when the people obeyed the Torah. Several holiness movements sprang up, recalling the people and their leaders back to their calling as God's holy people. The Pharisees were one such movement, seeking to live lives of purity and holiness within society, through maintaining strict boundaries. The Dead Sea community at Qumran also sought to be God's obedient holy people, but they withdrew from society, seeing themselves as the righteous remnant through whom God would act. John's call for Israel to repent and be forgiven of sins is part of this context.

This new religious movement started as a holiness renewal movement within Judaism. Jesus shared the essential beliefs of his fellow Jews. He called people to join on his mission of announcing and effecting the reign of God. But he was calling and creating a renewed holy people on rather different terms. Ethnicity was no longer the prime criterion. This was good news for all nations. All that was required was wholehearted commitment to following the Messiah.

The story is more complicated than that, however. Jesus' disciples only gradually grasped his identity and the significance of his mission. Jesus Messiah was Jesus of Nazareth, a man rejected by the religious authorities and crucified on a Roman cross in Jerusalem. Were it not for their unshakable conviction that God had raised Jesus from the dead, this would have been just one of the many tragic stories of misguided people claiming to be "the messiah" and aspiring to lead Israel back to God's way. But the resurrection of Jesus and the experience of the Spirit in their community changed their time perspective. These were indeed the last days: the promised gift of the Spirit had been fulfilled and the resurrection of God's people had been signaled in the resurrection of Jesus Messiah, the representative of Israel. God's big purposes for his entire created order were now unfolding.

If we only had Mark, we would know very little of Jesus' life before he begins a short ministry of one year. Mark tells us nothing about Jesus' birth or early life. But Matthew and Luke both have stories of Jesus' birth; John sets Jesus in the divine activity culminating in the Word becoming flesh. John has Jesus' ministry extending over three years. Even these details give a limited picture of the historical Jesus.

For two hundred years scholars have wrestled with this limited evidence and attempted to reconstruct a reliable picture of Jesus, with limited success. Too often the results of investigation looked more like a modified self-portrait than a plausible portrayal of Jesus. But while we lack many specific details about Jesus himself, we are increasingly well-placed in our understanding of late 2TP Judaism itself. The discovery of the Dead Sea Scrolls and refined critical methodologies have given new impetus for historians to reread the ancient texts and interpret them afresh in light of new evidence. A more sympathetic reading of 2TJ, free from the nasty anti-Semitism that has plagued much of Christianity for centuries, has also helped us place the story of Jesus in a clearer context.

The story of Jesus is cast against the sociopolitical backdrop of the empire and the small Jewish temple state of Judea and Galilee. Roman hegemony is the ever-present context of Jesus' life. It is also the backdrop of Mark himself. But far more significant is the reality of late 2TJ, a form of Judaism forever lost with the destruction of the temple in A.D. 70. Set within the context of the late 2TP as part of the larger Greco-Roman world of the first century, Jesus emerges more clearly, enabling today's readers to understand better how Mark's (and others') portrait of Jesus has been framed and illuminated.

Mark begins his Jesus story with the announcement by a prophetic figure in the wilderness, John the Baptizer. Mark also tells of the descent of the Spirit upon Jesus and forty days fast in the wilderness before Jesus came into Galilee. Jesus announced the arrival of the good news of God's reign. Many Jews expected God to act decisively in the future, but Jesus' proclamation told them that the time had arrived—they should prepare for the kingdom of God.

The reign of God was celebrated in worship and song, and it shaped the longings and hopes of the people. People longed for God's deliverance, for a new Exodus and a full spiritual return from exile. The promises of the prophets fired imaginations and sustained hope. But this hope became postponed further and further into the future. Of course, God would act—that conviction remained firm. But hope seemed so distant, especially after the all too brief century of independence was brought to an abrupt end in 63 B.C. with Pompey's intervention in a Jewish civil war, and his entrance into the temple.

When Jesus was making his announcement, everyone was under the control of the vast Roman Empire. Roman hegemony spanned the whole Mediterranean basin and the entire hinterland to the Black Sea, the Euphrates, the Sahara, and southern Europe. In such a context, Jesus' announcement that the reign of God was at hand was, therefore, welcome and risky—and humanly implausible. Unless God were to act, things could not change. And that is exactly what Jesus was announcing: The reign of God was arriving in his life and mission; and people were being invited to join in with God's new thing.

Roman Empire

Shortly after the first Easter, stories about Jesus almost certainly began to circulate orally as this movement spread from Jerusalem and Galilee to the outer fringes of the empire. By the time Mark was written, these stories had spread through this whole region. They were likely circulating primarily in oral form—used to spread the "good news," the gospel, across the empire. Some of Jesus' teaching may have been written down in one form or another, but if so, we no longer have any hard evidence for this possibility. And if Jesus himself ever wrote anything, it is no longer extant.

Jesus lived in a predominantly Jewish culture where Aramaic was the primary language of home. Jesus may have been able to speak Greek, but his teaching was almost certainly in Aramaic. Indeed, according to a fragmentary note from Papias, "Matthew composed the oracles [ta logia] in the Hebrew dialect [dialektos] and everyone interpreted them as he was able." There are numerous uncertainties about this statement, but it may suggest that the words of Jesus may have originally circulated in Aramaic. This was the common language of the Levant including Galilee, Samaria, and Judea as well as southern parts of the Roman province of Syria, of which Judea was a part.

Even if the stories originally circulated in Aramaic, they were soon translated and told in Greek, the lingua franca of the Greco-Roman world. Sometime after these events, probably while some of those who had been with Jesus were still alive, the stories began to be written down. By the time we come to Luke, it is clear that written and oral material was available to him to use in writing his Gospel (Luke 1:1-4). No doubt Mark also had access to some similar material.

A. Genre, Authorship, and Location

The vast majority of scholars now agree that Mark's Gospel is the earliest of the four Gospels, all of which tell the story of Jesus from the perspective of the author. That raises the question about its literary form. Does it fit in with other examples of ancient literature in Jewish or Greco-Roman history, or is it the first of a unique kind of document? Earlier scholars argued that the Gospels were unique—and that Mark is the first example of this literary form.

That view dominated until the late twentieth century. But the uniqueness of the Gospels does not depend on their form. It lies much more in the theological content of the stories. More recent studies have returned to an older view that the Gospels share many of the characteristics of the ancient form of *bios* or biography (see Burridge 2004).

This term should not be confused with modern biographies—Mark shows little interest in vast swathes of Jesus' life. Rather, it means that all of them have Jesus as the central character. Everything revolves around Jesus. Literarily, he is the most fully formed character, with others being less well-rounded. He also shares with the narrator a wider perspective and level of understanding than the other actors in the story. Particularly in Mark, the other actors are frequently befuddled, sometimes even obtuse. The Markan Jesus alone understands the significance of the path he is taking, even predicting his death and vindication beforehand. Other characters play significant parts in the story, but each plays it as part of Jesus' story.

None of the Gospels has a title as such: "The Gospel according to Mark" forms no part of Mark's text. Rather, the term serves as a classification and probably did so from the first century (see Hengel 1985, 65-84), especially if the Gospels circulated widely (see Bauckham 1998). This document, along with the other three Gospels, is distinct within the NT canon.

The appellation "Gospel" assigned to the four Jesus stories in the NT probably comes from the opening lines of Mark. But it is much more than a title. "Gospel" gives the content of the story. The term is used by Paul frequently to describe his message. (Of the ninety-one occurrences of the word in the NT, seventy of them are in the Pauline corpus.) Mark's Jesus story is the good news about God's redemptive purposes finding their fulfillment in Jesus' life and ministry.

"Gospel" has roots deep in Scripture. The prophets proclaim to the oppressed people in exile that God's rescue is underway (see esp. Isa 52:7; 61:1; Nah 2:11; *Pss. Sol.* 11:1). The announcement of good news heralds the redemption of God's people from exile or oppression. Mark begins his story of Jesus by announcing that it is "good news" and thereby firmly ties the Jesus story to the purposes of God already announced in the prophets, and now coming to fulfillment in the story he is about to tell. The prophetic hopes of liberation and rescue are underway—God's new thing is occurring.

But who is this Mark? All of the Gospels are anonymous. The first identification of Mark as the author of the Gospel that bears his name comes from Papias, bishop of Hierapolis (probably flourished in early to mid-second century A.D.). According to Eusebius (*Hist. eccl.* 3.39.15), Papias makes this identification in the introduction to a now lost five-volume book titled *Exposition of the Dominical Oracles.*

Eusebius quotes Papias as writing,

"And the presbyter used to say this: Mark became the interpreter of Peter and wrote accurately all that he remembered, not, indeed, in order, of the things said or done by the Lord. For he had not heard the Lord, nor had he followed him, but later on, as I said, followed Peter, who used to give teaching as necessity demanded but not making, as it were, an arrangement of the Lord's oracles, so that Mark did nothing wrong in thus writing down single points as he remembered them. For to one thing he gave attention, to leave out nothing of what he had heard and to make no false statement within." This is related by Papias about Mark. (Eusebius, *Hist. eccl.* 3.39.15)

The Papias tradition is weighed variously by scholars. Problems occur in determining precisely the extent of Eusebius' quotation and the translation of key words. Some are inclined to dismiss it, partly because elsewhere Eusebius expresses a low view of Papias' reliability and partly because they doubt the connection Papias makes between Mark and Peter. But recent detailed reconsideration of this and related evidence is giving more credence to the Papias claim that Peter's testimony stands behind Mark's account (see especially Bauckham 2006, ch 9).

In fact, Papias' statement can be read as pointing to the reliability of Mark because of his connection to Peter and that Mark thus "puts readers into direct touch with Peter's oral teaching" (Bauckham 2006, 208). If this is so, then the survival of Mark's Gospel and its standing as one likely source of Matthew and Luke is more easily explained. Early in the period of transmission, Mark's Gospel was recognized by the other evangelists as resting on eyewitness tradition from Peter even if, according to Papias, it did not have the chronological order of the Fourth Gospel. If the first three Gospels are related in some way, they may offer a Petrine tradition, while the Fourth Gospel offers a Johannine tradition.

Clement of Alexandria (ca. A.D. 150-215) locates the work of Mark and Peter together in Rome. Eusebius (*Hist. eccl.* 6.14.5-7) quotes Clement as writing, "As Peter had preached the Word publicly at Rome, and declared the Gospel by the Spirit, many who were present requested that Mark, who had followed him for a long time and remembered his sayings, should write them out." Clement is manifestly dependent upon Papias, probably deducing that Rome was the location about which Papias wrote. That has led to the conventional view that Mark wrote in Rome for the Romans. A minority of scholars have argued for a Galilean location for Mark's audience. Michael Bird represents a growing view that "if a Markan community did exist it is impossible to identify its situation and location with any degree of certainty" (2006, 474). Hooker opines that Mark could have been written almost anywhere in the Greco-Roman world (1991, 8).

The exact date of Mark's Gospel is equally difficult to determine. The vast majority of scholars place its composition sometime between A.D. 60 and 70, with Martin Hengel offering the most precise date (see Hengel 1985, 28). The arguments are complex and the evidence is slender. But the likelihood that Mark is composed near to but before the destruction of the temple is strong, if not incontrovertible. For this reason, dates as early as the mid- to late-30s and mid-40s (Crossley 2004, 208) and A.D. 45 (Wenham 1991, 223) have been offered. Neither Crossley nor Wenham has persuaded many.

This meager information does not tell us much about Mark's identity, however. The name Mark (or John Mark) occurs in Acts 12:12, 25; 15:37; Col 4:10; Phlm 1:24; 2 Tim 4:11; and 1 Pet 5:13. There is no way of proving that Mark the Evangelist is one of these. But a very plausible case for Mark being the John Mark of Acts 12:12 can be made, especially if his connection with Peter is as close as Bauckham and Hengel think. Further, a Jerusalemite could plausibly have the facility in Aramaic and Greek that the Gospel seems to warrant.

Even with this information, details of "the historical Mark" are sketchy. But to what extent does this matter? The actual author, plausibly identified as the John Mark of Acts, is of less importance for interpretation of the Gospel than the "implied author." This is the Mark who is revealed to readers on the pages of the Gospel and who tells us the story of Jesus. Thus, this commentary will use the name "Mark" to refer to the implied author and phrases like "the Markan Jesus" to indicate that this is the portrait being painted by this author.

The text of Mark we are interpreting is itself composite. It is the earliest recoverable form that we have. But no one claims that it is the actual text, even before translation, that the "real" author wrote. That is irretrievably lost. Rather, attention is given to the text that we have in front of us—the text as text. Readers read the text from a variety of social locations as well. Thus, readers may hear the text in polyvalent ways that could be beyond the intention of Mark. Nevertheless, the text does reveal a great deal about the intentions of the implied author.

This implied author, "Mark," has a sociohistorical location, of course. He (or she—we will follow the convention of using "he") is an itinerate believer in Jesus Messiah writing somewhere in the Greco-Roman world to an audience located in that first-century world. This indeterminate location coupled with the Papias tradition makes it more rather than less likely that he was in contact with the living tradition of Peter, Paul, and probably others.

Once we acknowledge our limited access to the actual author of Mark, we discover that we can say a great deal about the implied author. This Mark has a detailed and deeply embedded dependence upon the LXX Scriptures. The good news is steeped in, illuminated by, and announced through careful attention to this intertextual relationship with his scriptures. He demonstrates facility in Aramaic as well as Greek and possibly Latin. He assumes that his readers do not share his detailed and insider knowledge of Judaism but nevertheless asks a great deal of them in reading or hearing the text. It is possible that he himself has experienced persecution.

Mark takes for granted that the story of Jesus he tells actually "happened" in Galilee and Judea—this is no pious fiction. But his interest is much more on the significance of the events he narrates. He tells his readers "what was going on in what happened." And he does this through what he selects from the resources available to him, how he weaves them together, how he shapes them.

Mark knows more than he tells us, but he tells us what he considers important. He uses conventional literary skills profusely to great effect. Literary techniques such as bracketing and sequence are important. Mark may write the Gospel with an eye to oral performance, or, possibly may commit an oral performance to writing. He may have deliberately enhanced the literary structure in committing the oral performance to written text.

Most of all, he has a profound sense of the ultimate significance of the Jesus story. He believes that this story of Jesus is the story of God and that Jesus is the fulfillment of God's promises. It is both the expression of and the focal point of the story of God's rescue plan for his created order as told in Israel's scripture. Indeed, the story of Jesus makes sense out of the grand narrative he reads in his scriptures.

The story of Jesus is thus soaked with OT echoes, themes, and quotations. Through these the implied author illuminates for his readers the portrait of Jesus he paints. He crafts the story in such a way as to lead his implied readers inexorably to the conclusion that Jesus is the Son of God, and never more so than at the crucifixion. Through the skill of this master storyteller, readers then and now see Jesus. And in doing so, this story becomes the word of God illuminating and revealing the Word of God. It is inspired and inspiring.

B. Mark and the Others

Readers of the Gospels have always noted the similarities between the first three Gospels and the differences of these three from the Fourth Gospel. Reflection on the possibility of a literary relationship between the first three raised the so-called synoptic problem. The most widely accepted answer to this problem has been called the two-source hypothesis. Its major tenet is that Mark was the first Gospel and that it was one of the sources for the Gospels of Matthew and Luke, who also used a source called Q.

All parts of this hypothesis have been contested. The evidence in favor of Markan priority, that is, that Mark is the earliest of the written Gospels and is used by Matthew and Luke, is robust and convincing (see Goodacre 2002, 19-45). This commentary assumes Markan priority but does not depend upon it. The alternative, the so-called Griesbach hypothesis, in which Mark is an abridgment of Matthew, is held by very few; it is also rejected in this commentary.

The Q-hypothesis is far less secure. If there is a direct literary relationship between the Gospels, then Q may be an eloquent postulate demonstrating how Luke and Matthew agree with each other in many places. But the problems with the hypothesis are numerous enough to lead an increasing number of scholars to question it (see Goodacre 2002; for a defense of Q, see Kloppenborg 1987).

C. Mark's Theology: Jesus and His Identity

Mark's theological purpose is primarily to reveal the identity and meaning of Jesus as Messiah, Son of God. He does this by telling Jesus' story as an overlay of the story of Israel that, in turn, gets its meaning from the revelation of God's good purposes from the beginning (see Exod 19:1-6). Like Paul, his fellow early believer and, perhaps, his companion on occasion, Mark is convinced that Israel's story makes sense in the light of Jesus, and when viewed through the mission of Jesus, reveals God's big purposes.

But Jesus' story is more than a recapitulation of Israel's story. Mark pictures Jesus as the locale of the divine presence among his people (1:10-11, 25). Mark makes the daring inference that Jesus acts as God acts—indeed, is the presence of God amongst his people. While he does not have the explicit language of John 1:14, "The Word became flesh and made his dwelling among us," the same point is made implicitly in a number of ways throughout this narrative. This is an incarnational story.

Mark uses two primary means to do this: narrative composition and scriptural intertextual citations, allusions, and echoes. Hence, those who wish to hear Mark's story afresh need to be attuned to Mark's narrative technique and to listen carefully to the intertextual links he provides. Mark's narrative style and use of Scripture invites this reading strategy. Listening to the text in this way takes its interpretation one step further than "authorial intention."

Mark gradually unveils Jesus' identity through the interaction of the various players in the drama with Jesus. Readers, of course, know from the outset who Jesus is: "Messiah" (1:1 NIV 2011). This is only gradually revealed to the other actors in the story, however. Mark is reticent to unveil it, not because Jesus' ministry was unmessianic and only later viewed in that light, but because the title was heard in a variety of ways in the late Second Temple period. Almost always it carried militaristic baggage in the popular imagination. On this view, the Messiah, God's anointed, would come at some point, defeat the enemies of God (which were the same as the enemies of Israel), and rule over a re-created and restored Israel.

The disciples almost certainly share this popular view. But the Markan Jesus resists it. Their own proclamation of the kingdom may well have dangerous overtones (→ 6:12, 13, 45). The fact that he is Messiah only becomes clear to the disciples half-way through the story (8:27-30).

So Jesus is Messiah. But Messiah on its own scarcely does justice to Jesus' identity. Jesus accepts the identity, but immediately redefines messiahship in a way that is different from expectations. Similarly, the term "Son of David" features in Mark. In 2:25, Jesus compares himself to David; in 10:47-48 Bartimaeus cries out insistently for mercy from the Son of David. At the entry, the crowds seem to acclaim Jesus as Son of David. Here again Jesus does not reject the identification, but he does relegate it to a subordinate role (12:35-37).

Thus, Jesus' messiahship, although fulfilling the hopes for a son of David, is different. Jesus is a "Son of Man must suffer" kind of Messiah. And that is hard for the disciples to grasp. They initially reject the view out of hand, and thereby place themselves in the category of opposition to God's purposes (8:33). Only as they continue "on the way" do they begin to understand (9:32; 10:32).

Jesus is also introduced as Son of God in the incipient (1:1). Although it is uncertain whether the phrase is included in the earliest recoverable form of the text (→ 1:1), the narrative is enhanced by it. Jesus is Son of God. This, however, is not revealed immediately to others in the story. Only Jesus, the narrator, and the readers see the heavens rent apart and the Spirit descending in the form of a dove (1:10). Only Jesus hears the voice from heaven confirming to him his identity as the beloved Son, on the mission of the triune God (1:11). This identity and commitment to the mission is tested immediately when the Spirit drives Jesus into the wilderness.

Ironically, the identity as Son of God is known and noted repeatedly by the demons (see 3:11). For Mark, this confirms Jesus' true identity and places him in the realm of deity. Mark takes for granted that the demons know because they are part of the spiritual realm. Their witness is reluctant but true.

"Son of God" is used in key OT texts as well to describe the seed of David or the people as a whole (see 2 Sam 7:14; Hos 11:1). In 2 Sam 7:14, Yahweh says, "I will be his father, and he will be my son." This is part of Yahweh's promise to build the house of David and establish his throne forever. The verse is used in 4Q174 where it is interpreted as a latter-day Davidic liberator of Israel.

Clearly, then, the term includes this human dimension, but in Mark "Son of God" is far more than that. In 9:7, the voice from heaven speaks again, this time to the three disciples. They are told that Jesus is the beloved Son, confirmation of Jesus' identity and the divine origin of his path to the cross.

In the trial scene, the high priest asks Jesus the question "Are you the Messiah, the Son of the Blessed One?" and Jesus' response is "I am" (14:61-62 NIV 2011). This is another indirect confirmation of Jesus' identity. Nevertheless, the only human voice to make this confession explicitly is the centurion at the crucifixion (15:39). This confession is highly significant because it serves as the literary conclusion to the narrative. With 1:1, it serves to bracket the whole gospel story, so that the story itself unveils the identity of Jesus as Son of God, seen most clearly—and paradoxically—as he dies on the cross.

There are also a number of other clues to Jesus' identity as Son of God on the side of the divine throughout the narrative. Three stand out: The stilling of the storm and the walking on water (4:35-41; 6:46-52) are portrayed by Mark as parallel to the action of Yahweh in Scripture. The disciples recognize the extraordinary character of this action but remain puzzled (4:41) or hard-hearted (6:52). The exorcism in 9:14-29 is told in such a way as to contrast the authority and power of Jesus with that of the disciples. They fail to exorcise the demon from this poor child and when they ask Jesus why they failed, he tells them that this kind only comes out through prayer (9:29). Significantly, however, Jesus exorcises the demon *without* prayer—the implication being that he is acting as God acts. He is indeed the beloved Son.

It would be pressing Mark too far, however, to treat "Son of God" as if the later formulation of Jesus' divinity by the Greek fathers could be read directly off Mark's text. Nevertheless, Mark, together with the other Gospels, provides clear and unequivocal support for these later formulations of the doctrines of incarnation and Trinity.

Significantly, the first identity that the disciples hear about Jesus is that he is "the Holy One of God," a confession on the lips of the demon in the first exorcism story (1:24). That title assumes disproportionate importance in Mark because it points to the presence of Jesus as the Holy One in the center of the re-created holy people. In Scripture, the holiness of people, things, and places is always a derived holiness, never inherent within them. Only God is inherently holy. Therefore, God is the source of all other holiness.

Thus, this identification of Jesus as the Holy One of God is, for Mark, an essential prerequisite for the re-creation of God's holy community. Jesus is creating a holy people centered on himself. He is the source of their holiness. It evokes the whole Exodus story with God's call of his people and signals a new Exodus and the re-creating of the covenant community. That in itself is a clue that Jesus is more than simply another earthly figure who could be delusional. Once again, those from the spirit world know his identity—an identification that Mark thinks is important enough to be the first designation the disciples have in Mark's narrative.

The "Son of Man," used twelve times, is Mark's most frequent identification for Jesus. But the question "Who is this 'Son of Man'?" that was on the lips of the crowd in John 12:34 exercises scholars. The phrase is not a ready-made title in the late 2TP that can be applied to Jesus. Rather, Mark fills the phrase with content through its intertextual echoes in 2TJ (especially Dan 7:13) and its narrative settings in the Jesus story. In the narrative the Son of Man has authority (Mark 2:10, 28) and is a suffering figure (8:31; 9:12, 31; 10:33, 45; 14:21, 41) who is vindicated through suffering (8:31; 9:9, 31; 10:33) and who exercises power and authority in the end (8:38; 13:26; 14:62).

The phrase, therefore, points to Jesus as the representative figure for the people of God, a theme that develops from Dan 7:13, 27. Jesus, as Son of Man, embodies the hopes of the suffering people of God. And in some sense, they are included within the mission of the Son of Man (see esp. Mark 10:45 below). The answer to the vexed question, "Is the son of man a human or a divine figure in Mark?" is probably "yes" in both cases. As Mark uses it, it contributes to his incarnational perspective.

The theme of the righteous sufferer is particularly important in the Passion Narrative but occurs throughout. Jesus' death is illuminated through frequent references to OT suffering figures, particularly in the psalms of lament and echoes from the Isaianic Servant of Yahweh passages. He goes to his death as God's righteous sufferer, a term that includes a whole range of figures from Scripture including the one like a Son of Man and the servant of Yahweh from Isaiah.

Jesus' ministry is characterized by conflict with evil. The confrontation with the Satan (Mark 1:13) sets the scene and probably lies behind the binding of the strong man (3:22-27). The opposition to Jesus' ministry is understood in human, but also in supramundane, terms. The hegemony of Rome as oppressor is viewed by Mark as a symptom of the far more sinister opposition to Jesus by the powers of evil. The exorcisms and the healings indicate that the oppression being suffered is beyond that of political oppression.

Conversely, the exorcisms and healings are pointers in Mark to Jesus' announcing and effecting the reign of God. They are part of the good news being proclaimed (see 1:27). Liberation of the oppressed in mind, body, and spirit is demonstrated throughout Mark. The story of Legion—this possessed, fragmented, and marginalized man—shows the effect of the good news. Jesus releases him from his oppressed condition—he is left by Jesus, Mark tells us, clothed and in his right mind, restored to his community (5:16).

D. Mark's Theology: Discipleship and Identity

A secondary but significant element in the revelation of Jesus' identity is how Mark shapes the story of the disciples. They are neither the primary focus nor the central characters in Mark, but their presence throughout in juxtaposition to Jesus—sometimes as learners, sometimes as foils—is one essential ingredient to Mark's technique. It is not by accident, then, that the first act of the Markan Jesus is to call the first four disciples (1:16-20).

Within the big purposes of God in redeeming his created order, he chose to act through his people. Israel's vocation as a kingdom of priests and a holy nation was the reason behind their election. Israel's story, however, was fraught with failure and disappointment, leading to exile. The prophets promised that God would restore his people to their purpose and mission. So they returned from exile, but the return was neither as glorious nor as complete as they had hoped.

Mark ties the story of Jesus and his disciples directly to that hope and expectation (scholars refer to "restoration eschatology"). The whole Jesus story begins with the work of the Baptist—with citations and allusions to the return-from-exile motif of Isaiah. The Baptist calls for repentance, and all of Jerusalem and Judea come to the Jordan to be baptized by John. By this means the people are prepared for the Coming One.

When Jesus begins his ministry, he immediately selects four to be with him (1:16-20). Their first clue to his identity is the defensive confession of the unclean spirit: Jesus is "the Holy One of God." The gathering of followers continues. They come from the marginalized and the unclean. Jesus eats with the tax collectors and sinners, with his very presence transforming them into participants in this new holy community centered on him.

In a particularly dramatic event, Jesus goes to the mountain and calls to him those whom he wants to appoint as the representatives of this new people (3:13-15). There are overtones of Moses on the mountain (Exod 24), but it is much more than that. Jesus acts as Yahweh does in gathering Moses and the seventy elders to the mountain. Now Jesus gathers the Twelve and appoints them as apostles to be sent out to proclaim the good news and to have authority over unclean spirits. The Twelve are now the vanguard of the new people of God. And they are to be with Jesus. This is significant, since a few verses later, those gathered around Jesus are called Jesus' family, because they are doing the will of God (3:32-35).

But the picture is far from triumphant or smooth. The disciples are a mixture of incredible stupidity and breathtaking insight. They can be effective healers and teachers (6:30-31). And they can participate in miraculous feedings—twice. But they still cannot grasp fully who they are following. In fact, like those who reject Jesus from the religious establishment, it seems that their hearts are also hardened.

With a remarkably skillful design, Mark has Jesus teaching the disciples on the journey between Caesarea Philippi and Jerusalem (8:27—10:45). This journey "on the way" is set between two stories of the healings of blind men (8:22-26; 10:46-52). Details are in the commentary. But this section is concentrated teaching on the meaning of discipleship. It is not enough to know Jesus' identity; confession involves wholehearted commitment.

Jesus, therefore, invites any who would follow him (8:34) along with the Twelve, to take up the cross after him. The sanitized version of the cross in the Western world is far removed from the horror of a humiliating public execution on a major thoroughfare in Jerusalem. Cross-bearing is not an inviting prospect. Dying as a follower of Jesus, of course, is not just a sacred memory of past martyrs. It is the grim potential prospect of those who call Jesus Lord in too much of the world today.

Despite the teaching of Jesus on the way, however, the disciples seem to miss the point repeatedly. After three explicit predictions of his own death (8:31; 9:31; 10:32-33), they are still vying for prominence in the kingdom (10:34-45). Readers today are tempted to disdain the disciples for their stupidity until we examine our own tendency to be self-serving.

The disciples are not prominent at all when Jesus is teaching in the Temple, although their presence is assumed. But they return in the Passion Narrative. Some of Mark's most important teaching occurs there. The Last Supper is a covenant-making meal. Its association with the Passover meal celebrating the Exodus gives it profound significance. The disciples are the new community.

But the dark specter of betrayal haunts the entire story, adding to its somber and contrasting colors. The work of Jesus is nearing fulfillment, as he goes as it is written of him. But one of his followers will precipitate his death; and all of them will fail, despite their loud protests of unshakable fidelity (14:28-31).

Mark tells the story of Peter's denial of Jesus with consummate skill. He interweaves it with Jesus' trial before the Sanhedrin, drawing a stark contrast between Jesus' strength and Peter's failure. The haunting words at the end of the story, describing Peter's bitter remorse, capture something of the depths of Peter's own experience, perhaps even as he himself recalled it.

But this story is gospel—good news. Jesus predicted that the disciples would collapse under pressure (14:27-28) and they have done so. But he also promised that after he was raised he would gather the scattered flock together again. The scene at the empty tomb concludes with the words of the young man to the women: "Go, tell his disciples and Peter, 'He is going ahead of you into Galilee, . . . just as he told you'" (16:7). The message of the gospel to the first disciples and to readers (then and now) is that there is hope for failed disciples.

E. Mark's Theology: Discipleship and Holiness

Mark does not deliberately set out to formulate teaching on Christian holiness. But neither is it merely an appendage. The quest for holiness was a central identity issue in the late 2TP. It was a live issue for Jesus and the other holiness movements of his day. Read against this backdrop, Mark's perspective can be seen more clearly. He makes a contribution to the NT picture that needs to be heard.

Mark shares the biblical premise that God alone is holy in essence and that he has called a holy people as "a kingdom of priests and a holy nation" (Exod 19:6; see 1 Pet 2:9). All human holiness is a derived holiness. It depends on responding to the call of God and being drawn into a relationship with the holy God.

This is foundational for Mark as he tells the story of Jesus and his disciples. Their holiness is predicated on their relationship to Jesus. Discipleship and the call to be holy are inextricably linked. To be disciples of Jesus implicitly requires people to be holy. To be holy requires the presence of the Holy One. And Jesus is actually the Holy One in their midst (Mark 1:24). His disciples follow him on the journey through the Gospel. The hallmarks of their journey give some clue to Mark's view of the life of holiness for all followers of Jesus.

Mark begins by telling of the descent of the Spirit on Jesus (1:10). Through the subtle use of OT allusions, Mark shows us that Jesus is now the locale of God among his people. This initial Trinitarian scene sets the stage for Mark's portrayal of the renewed holy people of God. Jesus' work is that of God—Father, Son, and Spirit.

The Spirit drives Jesus into his mission (1:12), but unlike Luke, Mark does not speak extensively about the Spirit. Rather, the presence of the Spirit in the transforming work of Jesus is assumed. Only two passages refer directly to the Spirit. First, those who fail to attribute to God the work and mission of Jesus blaspheme against the Spirit who is at work in this mission (3:29). Second, those who are arraigned before authorities will be able to answer through the Spirit's aid (13:11).

If the holiness of disciples is dependent upon their relationship with the source of holiness, in Mark it has a starting point in the call of the first disciples. This involves full commitment right from the start (1:20; 10:28): there is no partial discipleship in Mark (see 10:17-27). Full commitment does not require full understanding, however. Rather, discipleship is an open-ended journey (see 1:16-20; 16:8), full of surprises and challenges. Progression happens, but the disciples show time and again that this is not constant, even in the presence of Jesus, the master teacher and model.

Mark is also quite clear that discipleship is not an individual pursuit. Individuals respond to Jesus' invitation, but this is always an invitation to join a people. The disciples are in it together with Jesus on his mission.

The Twelve represent the (re)new(ed) people of God. When they are on Jesus' mission, they are acting as the holy people of God. But they are not alone. All are invited to take up their crosses after Jesus (8:34). The possibility of participation in this holiness renewal movement is open and inclusive. That bothers the religious leaders, especially those for whom holiness is maintained by separation. They resist the announcement and effecting of the kingdom because they fail to recognize the presence of the kingdom in Jesus. Those originally inside, including Jesus' family, move outside, while those originally on the outside—the sinners, the blemished, the demonized, the crowds, and the disciples—are gathered around him. Jesus states with great potency: "Whoever does God's will is my brother and sister and mother" (3:35).

The heart of Mark's teaching on Christlike discipleship occurs on Jesus' journey with his disciples from Caesarea Philippi to Jerusalem. The journey is theological and geographical. He explained the significance of his identity as Messiah, by teaching and demonstrating what it meant to be followers of the Messiah, to be like him.

The disciples also need to learn that they are not the focal point; Jesus is. Disciples do not determine the parameters of the people of God. The determining criterion for discipleship is simply being part of God's holy people, in relationship to Jesus, the Holy One of God (9:38-41). As God's holy people, the holiness of disciples is social and personal, not an individual relationship with the Holy One.

Mark's story gives a poignant reminder that even the most committed disciples may fail, even after being on the journey with Jesus for some time. This may be Mark's most important lesson to his readers, then and now. Failure remains a lamentable possibility for committed disciples. It is not inevitable; but it can occur if disciples don't "keep awake" (13:37; 14:34-41). But the good news of Mark is that forgiveness and restoration are offered to failed disciples. Grace and restoration, not failure and rejection, are Mark's last words to Jesus' sometimes feeble followers.

Jesus' teaching comes to its high point with the reiteration of the Great Commandments (12:28-34). He summarizes them by citing the Shema of Deut 6:4 and the call to love of neighbor from Lev 19:18. These two commandments, the heart of Second Temple Jewish piety, are central to Jesus' kingdom teaching. But because Jesus proclaims that the kingdom has arrived, the teaching has a much more radical and daring conclusion. The center of God's good purposes are to be found in the inward, in-the-heart Torah promised by Jeremiah and Ezekiel. That time has arrived. No wonder Mark tells us, "From then on no one dared ask him any more questions" (12:34b).

For Jesus, for Mark, and for Wesley, these two commandments sum up God's good purposes and Christian holiness. There is no hint, of course, that the disciples are able to fulfill these commands in their own strength. Discipleship in Mark is pictured as a human impossibility (10:27); holy living is possible only through the power and presence of God. But Jesus' disciples still follow, still are committed to Jesus and his way, still trust in his promise that God's good purposes will ultimately prevail for them and for God's entire created order.

Jesus' redefinition of holiness is an underlying motif throughout all the Gospels. This redefinition returns the conception of holiness to its source in the very being of God. The result is that holiness is no longer construed primarily as separation from neighbor but expressed as love of neighbor. For the Markan Jesus, holiness is contagious, outgoing, all-embracing, and transforming.

This does not mean that God's holy people no longer are concerned with holy living. On the contrary, holy living is the fruit of the new covenant relationship being established by Jesus himself through his life, death, and resurrection. This holiness is a dynamic power emanating from the source of holiness, the Holy One.

But one word of caution: Those who would seek to derive their understanding of Christian holiness and the holy life solely from Mark will have a rather truncated picture. A proper account of Christian holiness will listen to all the NT voices. But Mark's voice must be heard as well (see Brower 2005 and 2007a).

F. The Perspective of This Commentary

I assume that Mark makes sense as a whole and needs to be read that way. Mark is also manifestly part of a larger scriptural picture. Great illumination comes from careful reflection on Mark's literary and historical setting within the late 2TP. These perspectives may be described as intratextual and intertextual readings.

It follows that this commentary does not contribute to any quest for the historical Jesus. Nor does it attempt to uncover the history of the pre-Markan tradition. The commentary thus gives little attention to the historicity of events, source of the tradition, or the history of its transmission. These discussions may be of interest in their own right. Whether the tools of source, form, and redaction criticism are up to the task of addressing them is a matter of dispute. In any case, application of these tools has provided very limited illumination to the text in front of us. Readers will have to go elsewhere for these discussions (Donahue and Harrington 2002, 1-2, take a similar approach).

Any claim by any writer to objectivity needs to be treated with extreme caution. All writers have a point of view from which they approach a topic. The same applies to commentators. Commentators strive to read the text faithfully using the tools available to them, but they cannot escape their own perspective. Readers read the text in front of them as they are situated in their own context. Any reading of a text thus becomes a contextual interpretation of that text. Texts are also read within an interpretative community.

This commentary is unapologetically written from the perspective of one who reads Mark in a Wesleyan community. Mark has also been read alongside scholars who do not share this perspective. This reading has profited greatly from that conversation, especially from other commentators. But the Wesleyan perspective is crucial. This is not with a sense of its superiority but rather the conviction that this reading needs to be heard along with others so that Jesus is more clearly seen.

Wesleyans read Mark as Scripture, as part of the collection of texts in which the supreme revelation of God's big purposes for his whole creation in Christ is narrated. Scripture's authority is dynamic. The Holy Spirit is active throughout the process of Scripture formation and interpretation. The Spirit inspired the writers and is active in Scripture's preservation, collection, transmission, translation, and interpretation within the community of believers. The inspired story of Mark matters, not because of the intrinsic sacredness of the words, but because it reveals Jesus, the complete and final revelation of God to his creation.

The commentary is written from the perspective of a believer in the Jesus who is met in Mark and in the rest of the NT. I stand humbly and gratefully within the Wesleyan tradition. The work has been completed within a community of scholars that shares the view that a Wesleyan theological reading of Scripture makes a valuable contribution to the human attempt to hear the voice of God in the story of his Son, Jesus of Nazareth. That context includes a worshipping community of believers committed to living their lives in a way that bears witness to the love of God poured out in their hearts through the Holy Spirit.

May all of us, as users of this commentary and Mark's readers almost two millennia after he penned the words, see and know Jesus just a little more clearly, and be transformed on our journey together into his likeness.

COMMENTARY

I. THE ANNOUNCEMENT OF THE GOOD NEWS: MARK 1:1-15

A. The Opening Line (1:1)

BEHIND THE TEXT

The earliest evidence associating Mark with this Gospel dates from about A.D. 110 and depends on the witness of Papias, preserved in the fourth-century church history by Eusebius (→ Introduction). No other name has ever been attached to this Gospel. Mark's name was probably attached before the end of the first century. As soon as the Gospels began to circulate (and widespread early circulation is likely; see Bauckham 1998, 9-49), they would have to have had a name attached (see Hengel 1985, 64-81) if only as a shorthand means of identification.

41

The fact that about 96 percent of Mark is reproduced in the other Gospels raises the question about its survival. The early link with Peter's name may well be important. According to Papias, Mark was Peter's interpreter in Rome. Like so much else in the history of the early Christian community, any involvement of Mark with Peter in the earliest days is shrouded in mystery. Later tradition has Peter in Rome—and its widespread currency suggests that there is some substance to that view. But it is unlikely that Peter planted the church in Rome any more than Paul. Tradition reports that Peter and Paul were martyred in Rome under Nero. But again the hard evidence is slender. Richard Bauckham (2006, 155-82) has shown that the tradition of a connection with Peter is stronger than has sometimes been thought.

Papias on Mark and Peter

The earliest evidence for a connection between Mark and Peter comes from a quotation in Eusebius' *Ecclesiastical History* (3.39.14-16) from Papias, bishop of Hierapolis. Papias wrote near the beginning of the second century, cites "the elder" named John, quite possibly referring to a period about A.D. 80 (so Bauckham 2006, 14).

Scholars do not agree on Papias' reliability. On the one hand, some discount the connection between Mark and Peter (Marcus 2000, 21-24). Others think the evidence is strong (Bauckham 2006, 155-82, 202-39; Hengel 1985, 50-52). In addition to the Papias reference, Bauckham notes the frequency of references to Peter and the literary signals that Peter is the main eyewitness source and that Mark tells the story predominantly from Peter's perspective.

Mark's story of Jesus needs to be understood within two historical contexts. First, Jesus' life is set geographically in Galilee, Judea, and occasionally in the surrounding territories. Jesus lived during the era of 2TJ, in the late 2TP. The people of Judea and Galilee (along with the rest of the ancient Near East) were under foreign occupation. Since 63 B.C., the Romans have been occupying the land, with ruthless efficiency. Judea was under the direct rule of a procurator and a client king (→ 6:14-29 BEHIND THE TEXT sidebar, "Herod Antipas").

For the majority of the population, the deliverance to their homeland and the return to the glorious time of peace that was promised by the prophets of the exile seemed to be, at best, disappointing. There was a sense in which they saw themselves as still in exile, still longing for the restoration promised by the prophets. Most people, of course, probably just got on with life. Others longed for the day when, once again, God would dwell in the midst of his people, the temple would again be God's earthly dwelling place, and his holy people would thrive.

Some considered a serious willingness to be obedient to God's call to be a holy people to be the only conditions under which God would once again dwell in their midst. For many, the big problem was the Romans—a Gentile occupying force. For others (the Sicarii), the situation was so intolerable that they engaged in guerilla warfare against the occupying forces. Still others (the Dead Sea sect) completely withdrew from the society. Others (the Pharisees) believed this purity was to be maintained within society at the same time as they sought to extend priestly levels of purity to all of Israel. For a minority (the temple authorities), the situation worked to their advantage.

The second setting of Mark's Gospel was that of the author and his first readers. It was probably written and read in Rome (but see Marcus 2000, 33-39) before it circulated throughout the known world. Within that setting, the language Mark used in his Gospel at key points was brought into sharp relief by the Imperial cult that dominated the religious marketplace in Rome and, indeed, the empire.

Jesus' ministry was conducted in an occupied land, subdued and pacified by the Romans. The Pax Romana, the peace of Rome, was sustained under the feet of the legions who kept problems in this small Jewish client state under control. And it might have been heard with particular sharpness in Rome, in the physical shadow of the imperial power. Religion and politics were inextricably bound together in this context.

In most Bibles, a footnote at the end of verse 1 draws attention to a significant textual issue. Most modern translations include the words **Son of God.** But while the majority of Greek manuscripts include the words **Son of God** (*hoiou theou*), some of the oldest manuscripts do not. The decision to adopt the longer reading is reached by considering textual evidence as well as literary and theological grounds.

Son of God in Mark 1:1

All extant Greek NT manuscripts (about six thousand) are handwritten copies of the original text (called autographs). These autographs no longer exist, so scholars compare existing copies, which are not identical. By doing this they hope to get as close to the text written by Mark (and other NT writers) as possible.

In reaching their conclusions on Mark 1:1, scholars weigh evidence differently. Those who think the shorter reading (omitting *hoiou theou*) is closer to the original argue that it is easier to explain why scribes would add the words "Son of God" than why they would delete them. Furthermore, it explains why one of our earliest major manuscripts (A = Alexandrinus from the fifth century) includes the phrase but only in a corrected form (see Collins 2007, 130).

But those who consider the longer reading the original argue that the words were omitted by a copyist because of homoeoteleuton. This refers to the repetition of words with identical endings, causing the copyist's eye to skip the final phrase (France 2002, 49; Guelich 1989, 6).

On textual grounds alone, the evidence is finely balanced, perhaps tipping toward the shorter ending. But other factors cast doubt upon this conclusion, including the literary and theological significance of this phrase in Mark's narrative, especially the conclusion to the crucifixion in 15:39. The inclusion of the phrase is wholly consistent with Mark's perspective.

IN THE TEXT

Opening lines matter. Classic literary lines like Dickens' famous "It was the best of times; it was the worst of times" etch themselves on the memory. Mark's opening line is like that: it captures in one pithy sentence the entire theological direction of his story of Jesus. Careful attention to these words gives significant clues to the rest of the narrative.

■ I The opening word translated **The beginning** already tells us something of Mark's perspective. The basic meaning is clear enough: Mark is saying that God's good news, **the gospel,** has its beginning with the inauguration of the mission of Jesus. This in itself is noteworthy. Unlike the other Gospels, Mark does not begin with birth narratives (see Matthew and Luke) or a prehistory (see John). Some suggest that Mark does not know any details of Jesus' life before his baptism. This view has little to commend it. However, it does imply that the birth stories are not essential for this telling of the story of Jesus. For Mark **the gospel** has to do with the long-standing purposes of God as set out in Scripture. So he starts by establishing the identity of Jesus and the character of his mission.

If the opening few words of Mark are clearly an introduction, it is less clear what is being introduced. Since the ministry of John the Baptist is the precursor to Jesus' own work, it could be argued that **the beginning** refers primarily to the work of the Baptist and thus points to 1:1-8.

A stronger case can be made for arguing that it includes all that occurs up to 1:13, concluding with the wilderness test. The voice from heaven, the descent of the Spirit, and the challenge of the Satan are all part of establishing Jesus' mission and identity.

A third alternative points to everything up to the end of 1:15, Jesus' appearance in Galilee, the beginning of his ministry, and the proclamation of the good news (Collins 2007, 131). This final suggestion has the advantage of allowing **gospel** in 1:1 and 1:14-15 to form a literary bracket around this initial section. All of these suggestions are plausible.

Another possibility is that Mark has a bigger picture in mind as he writes. That is, Mark sees the coming of Jesus and his ministry as the beginning of God's previously announced purposes that are now coming to fulfillment. The beginning of the good news thus includes the whole story. It reaches back into Scriptures, and then on to the preparatory work of John, the proclamation in word and deed by Jesus as well as his passion, his resurrection, and his reconstitution of the scattered disciple band in Galilee, those who would continue the mission. This view does not exclude any of the others. Indeed, Mark is frequently polyphonic, that is, the message of the narrative is almost always more than the sequence of events shown in the narrative.

That Mark chooses the same word that opens the LXX in Gen 1:1 (*en archēi*) may signal that this story is a new beginning of God's good purposes. It evokes the same anticipation as Genesis. The same God who brought order out of chaos was doing a new thing in the face of Roman occupation and the disastrous spiritual leadership that Mark thinks is given by the temple elite.

Allusions to the OT Scriptures are deep and all-pervasive in Mark, and at least as significant as the direct citations. For Mark, Isaiah is a particularly important intertextual source for illuminating the story of Jesus and explaining exactly what God is doing. According to Isa 43:19, God announces his purposes through the prophet in the context of exile: "See, I am doing a new thing! Now it springs up; do you not perceive it? I am making a way in the desert [*poiēsōen tēi erēmōi hodon*] and streams in the wasteland."

This activity of God in Mark is, therefore, not the first. Rather it is in continuity with what God has already done, a perspective that is confirmed by the rich intertextuality that we find in these opening lines. But it is also a "new thing." The beginning words thus have a dual referent—the Gen 1:1 opening of Scripture with God's completely new thing and an allusion to Isa 43:19, again linking to the citations from the OT in the next two verses. Isaiah, in turn, echoes Exodus language.

The word **gospel** translates *tou euangeliou*. This could also be translated as "good news" (so NRSV). In favor of **gospel** is the fact that Mark uses the noun form of the word six more times (1:14, 15; 8:35; 10:29; 13:10; 14:9). Mark's reception history in the early church (see Bauckham 2006, 12-38) shows that very early the term becomes a word that encapsulates the whole story of God's action in Christ.

Paul in particular used this term as a noun. If Paul's usage of the term was already commonplace by the time Mark wrote, there is every reason to suppose that it influenced Mark here. Mark, however, appears to be the first one to have used the term to describe the narrative of the life, death, and resurrection of Jesus. Although none of the other books we call Gospels used this designation internally to identify itself, their similarity to Mark caused them very early also to be called Gospels.

The Genre of Mark

Scholars of an earlier generation argued that the gospel form itself is one of a kind. But more recent study (Burridge 2004) has called that into question. Rather, the gospel form is a subset of ancient *bios* ("life," as in "biography"). Burridge notes several generic features in common between the Gospels and *bioi* including opening features, the dominance of Jesus as subject of a large number of verbs, and similar internal and external features. The Synoptic Gospels fit in the overall genre of *bioi*. This means that the interpretation of Mark needs to focus on Jesus.

This denotation as the good news about Jesus must not obscure the deep OT roots of the word. In Isa 52:7, the prophet used the participial form (*euangelizomenou*) when lauding those who announce good news. Those who announce the good news proclaim peace (*shalōm*), salvation, and the reign of God. Mark undoubtedly uses **gospel** here due to Isaiah (see Guelich 1989, 13-14).

But how would this term be *heard* during the chaos and fear of Rome in the mid to late 60s? Although the Priene Inscription may be more explicitly reflected in Luke 2, the language and tone of this inscription may also be relevant for Mark 1:1. This is the context in which Mark "dared to put forward the Christian gospel and declare that the true son of God was Jesus, the Messiah of Israel and 'king of the Jews'—not some would-be Roman emperor" (Evans 2000, 79; but see Guelich 1989, 14).

The dubious claims of the Imperial cult in which the emperor is hailed as divine and Caesar is lord are contrasted with Mark's perspective that Jesus is actually the beginning of God's shalom, God's peace. Salvation is in him, not in Caesar. Jesus, not Caesar, is Lord. Despite the divine claims of the Roman emperors, this could scarcely be the meaning of Isaiah's good news: peace, salvation, and of the reign of God. All of this would certainly have been a challenge to the hegemony of Rome.

Mark is quite clear, of course, that this is more than a battle against the Romans. In Isaiah, the beautiful feet are those "who proclaim peace, who bring good tidings, who proclaim salvation, who say to Zion, 'Your God reigns!'" (52:7). Some scholars hear a military nuance of victory in battle here, and think this is important for Mark (Marcus 2000, 146). But Mark's perspective is that violence is not the way of Jesus (see Wright 1996). Violent opposition to the empire only leads to the scenario behind Mark 13, in which the destruction of the temple is the disastrous consequence of the current direction in political thinking and activity.

Rather, this is indeed good news: The gospel of God's redemptive activity in Jesus Messiah. His activity transcends, but does not exclude, the flesh-

46

and-blood world. Throughout the subsequent narrative there is clear evidence that God is indeed acting in strength.

This good news is **the gospel about Jesus Christ.** The precise translation of the genitive in Greek here yields different nuances. Is this the gospel *about* Jesus in the sense that the good news tells the story of Jesus? Or is it that the content of the good news *is* Jesus? That is, Jesus himself is the good news from God. Either is possible. This is likely an instance where both nuances are present. It is even possible that the genitive is used by Mark deliberately to include both nuances.

Jesus is a very common name. **Christ** becomes almost a proper name in Paul. But Mark probably intends readers to hear *Jesus, the Messiah* (see 8:27-31).

A particularly difficult decision faces translators of the next phrase, **the Son of God.** If this is read (see textual discussion), then it coheres well with an important theme (1:11; 3:11; 5:7; 9:7; 13:32; 14:61; 15:39). Second, the phrase does not have an article—so it could be translated simply as "son of God." But this anarthrous form is more likely to mean "the son of God," just like *archē* is translated using "the" even though it does not have the article in Greek. Whatever the conclusions reached on textual grounds, the absence or presence of these words in this line make no difference to the overall theology of Mark: this is *the good news about Jesus Messiah, Son of God.*

MARK

B. As It Is Written (1:2-3)

1:2-3

BEHIND THE TEXT

The importance of Scripture, and particularly of Isaiah, to Mark is difficult to exaggerate (see Marcus 1993, who titles a chapter "The Gospel according to Isaiah"). His first direct reference to Scripture is introduced as **it is written in Isaiah the prophet.** Mark believes that what God is now doing in Christ is the new thing promised in Isaiah but also in continuity with God's announced good purposes in the past. Marcus notes that "each of the initial five pericopes in Mark's Gospel has strong connections with the second half of the book of Isaiah" (Marcus 2000, 139). This sense of looking to Isaiah goes well beyond these first direct citations or even the first few verses. Isaiah is cited or alluded to elsewhere (1:11-12; 7:6; 9:48; 10:45[?]; 11:17; 13:24-25; 14:24[?]), but the influence extends beyond citations and allusions to themes.

These first citations are not only from Isaiah, however. Mark 1:2*b* and *c* are a combination of Exod 23:20 (LXX), which is verbally closer, and Mal 3:1 (MT), contextually closer to Mark's citation, and 1:3 to Isa 40:3 (LXX) (see Guelich 1989, 7-8). Why, then, does Mark say **in Isaiah the prophet?** This problem was noted early, with three major MSS (A, L, W, and the Textus

Receptus) reading "in the prophets." The earliest MSS, however, read **in Isaiah the prophet** and is certainly the more likely.

At least two solutions are on offer. First, Mark is unaware of the combination because he simply takes over already combined material from a source. He could well have used an already existing combination; it seems unlikely that he would be unaware of the fact, since he uses the wider context of Mal 3:1 to develop the picture of John.

Second, Mark himself has woven together Isaiah with these texts and subtly modified them for his purposes. Mark, of course, does not always identify his sources for citations. But where he does, it is probably an important clue as to how the citation ought to be understood. It is also likely that Mark would note that the judgment motif of Malachi is close to that of the Baptist's announcement. Malachi is important for explaining John's role and mission *in Israel* (see Öhler 1997, 31-37; Taylor 1997, 8).

But Mark's purpose here is to focus on the good news, and that has to do with Jesus, predominantly taken from Second Isaiah. But all of this would be seen in light of Isaiah since the Baptist's ministry *with respect to Jesus* is best explained in terms of Isaiah. Mark has other combined citations (1:11; 12:36; 14:24, 27, 62). More likely is Isaiah's critical role in Mark's theological purposes (so Marcus 1993, 12-47). This introduction is the fullest in the Gospel and is far more likely in view of Mark's evident skills as a writer (see Marcus 1993, 17).

Isaiah 40:3 at Qumran

Isaiah 40:3 is also important at Qumran—the site of the discovery of the Dead Sea Scrolls. The vision for the community, set out in IQS includes the hope that it will be "the most holy dwelling . . . a house of perfection . . . in order to establish a covenant in compliance with the everlasting decrees and . . . atone for the earth . . . and there will be no iniquity . . . And when these exist as a community in Israel . . . they are to be segregated from within the dwelling of the men of sin to walk to the desert in order to open there His path. As it is written, 'In the desert . . .' and then follows a citation of Isa 40:3 (IQS 8:8-14). All of this is predicated upon full compliance with the Law. This community also sees itself as the initial stage of fulfillment of Isaiah's prophecy.

IN THE TEXT

■ **2** The Jewishness of Mark's initial statement is clear with the phrase **it is written** and signals a citation from Scripture. In common with other NT writers Mark thinks that Scripture, written in the past, has continuing impact on the present. This is a connecting phrase (*kathōs gegraptai*), showing that the previous words are an opening line, not a title (see Guelich 1989, 7).

Thus, the beginning of the good news is connected to Isaiah. And the story of Jesus is grounded firmly in God's big purposes. These were announced beforehand in Scripture in general but particularly in Isaiah. And they are now coming to fulfillment in Jesus' story. The Scripture cited is **in Isaiah the prophet**. The importance of Isaiah has already been noted. However, of the quotations that follow, only 1:3 comes from Isaiah.

I will send my messenger ahead of you. This comes almost word-for-word from Exod 23:20 (LXX), but the Exodus context has little to do with Mark's. In Exodus, Yahweh is the One who will send an angel. The word **messenger** (Heb.: *mal'ak*; Gk.: *angelos*) can be either a human or a heavenly figure. Yahweh's angel will lead the people in the wilderness. They, in turn, are to heed his voice.

In Mark, almost all agree that **my messenger** refers to John. The messenger is to **prepare your way.** The notion of "way" (Heb.: *derek*; Gk.: *hodos*) assumes great importance in Mark as the way of the Lord, a journey with Jesus on mission, to the cross and then again in mission on which the disciples are invited to embark (see Marcus 1993).

This part of the citation is clearly related to Mal 3:1, where the messenger is preparing the way for Yahweh to come in judgment to Israel (Mal 2:17—3:5). But Mark has made a subtle but significant alteration. Instead of **prepare the way before my face** as in Malachi, Mark changes "my" to "your." As a result, the words point to Jesus. On one level, the change simply made the text fit with the historical narrative. That is, John would prepare the way for Jesus. But at another level, Mark is saying that Jesus Messiah is linked to God, and what is attributable to God in Scripture is attributable to Jesus Messiah, Son of God.

■ **3** Mark follows the LXX form of Isa 40:3, highlighting that John is **a voice of one calling in the desert.** John is in the wilderness crying out, **Prepare the way for the Lord, make straight paths for him.** Once again, the quotation is not exact and the changes matter.

In Isaiah, the call is to prepare the way *for Yahweh* and to make the paths straight *for our God.* Mark follows in preparing the way for the Lord, but changes the last word to **for him,** making a direct equation between Lord (*kyrios*) and Jesus, who is the likely antecedent of him (*autou*). Thus Mark states indirectly but clearly that "to prepare the way of Jesus as Lord is also to prepare a way for the Lord God" (Collins 2007, 137).

The implications of this for Mark's Christology are important. As Hooker notes, "God's advent in salvation and judgment has taken place in Jesus" (1991, 36). Such an astonishing claim fits both the Second Temple and Roman contexts that we noted earlier. Evans argues that

49

in mimicking the language of the Imperial cult and in quoting Isa 40:3 Mark appears to have welded together two disparate, potentially antagonistic theologies. On the one hand, he proclaims to the Jewish people the fulfillment of their fondest hopes—the good news of the prophet Isaiah. But, on the other hand, he has boldly announced to the Roman world that the good news of the world began not with Julius Caesar and his descendants, but with Jesus Christ the true son of God. (Evans 2000, 77)

The conflation of these OT citations is important for Mark. While Isaiah functions as the controlling interpretative framework, the use of Mal 3:1 in particular brings the motif of purifying the people in preparation of the coming of the Lord more clearly into the frame. Thus, the voice is not only announcing that the time of the exile is over but also expecting the people to be prepared for the mission of God. "In essence, as the immediate context bears out, he is calling the people of Israel to prepare themselves not only for the visitation of God, but also for following his commands" (Hatina 2002, 182). This, as we shall see, is a journey with the Holy One of God, on his mission, with his authority and proclaiming his message, the message set out in 1:14-15.

C. John the Baptist (1:4-8)

BEHIND THE TEXT

The location of the wilderness where John was baptizing is probably in the southern part of the Jordan Valley east of the river a few kilometers north of where it empties into the Dead Sea. The term translated as **desert** (*erēmos*) may give the impression of a bleak place without vegetation. But the term is better translated as "wilderness" (so NRSV), meaning an uncultivated place some distance from human habitation. That description fits Bethany in Jordan, which is today widely accepted as the site of Jesus' baptism. And it suits Mark's claim that people from Judea and Jerusalem came to be baptized by John in the Jordan.

Jesus came there as well. Murphy-O'Connor speculates that Jesus encountered John while on pilgrimage to Jerusalem. Despite the vegetation near the site with wild boar and vipers in the dense reeds, the area in general is inhospitable (see Murphy-O'Connor 1990, 359, 361).

The location also has symbolic significance since Mark links John with Elijah, the eschatological prophet who is the voice in the wilderness. Thus, "John appeared exactly where Elijah had disappeared (2 Kings 2:4-11)" (Murphy-O'Connor 1990, 360 n. 7). Taylor thinks this location helps explain 1:13 (1997, 46).

Another textual problem occurs in this passage. Should we read **John came, baptizing** (so NIV and Collins 2007, 133) or "John the Baptizer appeared" (so NRSV and France 1971, 60, 64)? Elsewhere in Mark (6:14, 24 NRSV) it is "John the Baptizer" (in 6:25, "John the Baptist"). If Mark writes "the baptizer," then the emphasis falls upon John's proclamation, in keeping with the voice in the wilderness (so Hooker 1991, 37).

The meaning behind the simple translation of the phrase *baptisma metanoias*, **a baptism of repentance,** is difficult. Is John preaching repentance that leads to baptism or baptism that leads to repentance? Grammarians and linguistic theorists offer contradictory and confusing responses. Although Porter does not think a new translation is possible, he argues that the grammatical structure shows that the genitive *metanoias* is dependent upon the noun *baptisma*. The grammar and syntax, therefore, require that John proclaimed "a baptism . . . that is restricted by the concept of repentance, as opposed to other restricting factors (here unspecified). Although not specified, either baptism or repentance, or both, seem to lead . . . to forgiveness of sins" (Porter 1999b, 98).

Baptism

The link between living water and cleansing is firmly rooted in the Pentateuch. Cleansing from ritual impurity (ritual impurity and sin are not synonymous), which prevented participation in the cult, required water (see Lev 14:9; 15:13, 16, 18; 16:4, 24, 26; Num 19:7-8). By the late 2TP, archaeological remains in Palestine of cisterns and pools for purification show how important ritual cleansing was for observant Jews (see John 2:6). The Qumran community gave particular attention to purification (see 1QS 4:18-23) as seen in the elaborate system for water collection and distribution.

John's baptism and Qumran practice have some similarities, but the differences are more significant. Both may have involved immersion (but see Marshall 2002). But at Qumran this was self-administered and repeated, presumably following the Levitical code for purification. John's baptism was neither self-administered nor repeated.

John's baptism was likely an innovation in line with prophetic symbolism (see Barrett 1947, 32). That is, it was a prophetic representative action in which the actual action participated in the effect (see also 14:22-25).

Later rabbinic texts show that baptism was the means of incorporating proselytes into Judaism. But scholars are uncertain whether Jewish proselyte baptism was practiced in the 2TP. If proselyte baptism is the model for John, the irony in Mark is that it was Jews, not Gentiles, who were coming to be baptized by John. By the time of Paul, baptism seems to have been the Christian sacrament of initiation into the new people of God.

The mass movement led by John is noted in Josephus (*Ant.* 18.116-19). This text describes Herod Antipas' fear about John's influence, his arrest of

John and Antipas' subsequent defeat by Aretas as a punishment from God for killing John.

John's clothing is mentioned in Mark. But he adds nothing more about his ascetic lifestyle. The description is very close to that of Elijah in 2 Kgs 1:8 (but see Guelich 1989, 21). His diet of **locusts and wild honey** may indicate his dependence upon natural foods (see Taylor 1997, 32-42). Eating locusts did not incur uncleanness (Lev 11:22).

The **thongs** of the sandal were the leather strap that fastened the sandal to the foot. John's comparison emphasized his humble position vis-à-vis Jesus. Untying this strap was the duty of a slave; it was beneath the dignity of a disciple (see Marcus 2000, 152).

According to Mark and John, the Baptist announced that Jesus **will baptize you with the Holy Spirit.** Matthew 3:11 and Luke 3:16 add "and fire." Literary solutions to this difference have been proposed by appeal to synoptic relationships and Q. But none is wholly convincing. More plausible is the suggestion that the words on the lips of John are "with wind and fire," since pneuma can mean either "wind" or "spirit." Wind/spirit and fire are associated with judgment (see Isa 4:4).

Thus John predicted, "I am baptizing you with water, but the one who comes after me will exercise the judgment of wind and fire" (Mark 1:8 paraphrased). The advantage of this reading is that it coheres nicely with John's preaching of coming judgment according to Matthew and Luke (see Hooker 1991, 42). But John could also have considered himself the prophet of the age to come. In this case he looked for the future outpouring of the Spirit (so Hooker 1991, 42). In light of the picture Mark has been constructing already, this likely has its primary reference to Ezek 36:25-26. The messianic figure in Isaiah is the spirit-bearer (Isa 11:2; 44:3; 61:1).

IN THE TEXT

The description of the activity and message of John is crucial for understanding the good news of Jesus Christ. John is the voice in the wilderness, announcing the good news of God's action. Hence, the conflated OT citations (1:2-3) serve as the framework within which John's work is to be considered. This is the good news as announced in Isaiah that the time of the eschatological restoration of the people of God has arrived. Mark's citation of Isa 40:3 evokes the entire holy remnant notion, immediately creating a context of heightened expectation. The hopes, so long in abeyance, are being fulfilled; the new exodus/new return from exile is underway. The interweaving of Mal 3:1 with Isaiah allows Malachi to be read within the Isaianic framework. This is the beginning of the re-creation of the people of God. The arrival of the kingdom of God is *now*. This is a point Jesus makes explicit in his proclamation; and John's work is the opening scene (see Hooker 1991, 37).

John's geographical location is noted above. But the significance of this location lies beyond geography. The wilderness itself is part of the restoration theme that runs through Isaiah, not only in Deutero-Isaiah, but also Isa 11 and 35. It is tied to the notion of the returning remnant (Isa 11:11) in a kind of second exodus (Isa 11:16). According to Isa 35:8, the Lord makes a way of holiness on which the redeemed return to Zion. The call by John in the wilderness recalls the narrowing process that always attends the wilderness with God's people being renewed. "John is in the wilderness because that is where he must be if he is to play his role in the unfolding drama" (Brower 2007a, 61).

■4 The NIV makes the connection between John and the previous verses obvious: **and so John came, baptizing in the desert region.** As suggested above, the NRSV reading makes better sense of this passage: John the Baptizer comes **preaching a baptism of repentance for the forgiveness of sins.** This brief statement leaves many questions unanswered. What is John's message? Is this baptismal regeneration? That is, does the baptism itself effect the forgiveness of sins? The wording was considered awkward enough that the other Evangelists made subtle but significant changes that avoided this possible misunderstanding.

Matthew 3:2-6 omits the words and emphasizes the call to repentance after which the people are baptized. Luke's description of John's message is identical (Luke 3:3) to Mark's. But through the addition of John's preaching, he makes it clear that acts of repentance are required (Luke 3:8) before baptism.

Although Cyprian wrote, "The Holy One who was destined to grant remission of sins did not himself disdain to submit his body to be cleansed with the water of regeneration," Tertullian, Chrysostom, and Jerome see the remission of sins as future, depending upon the death of Christ (see Oden and Hall 1998, 4-5). But Mark makes no such concessions.

Our difficulty is to hear these words within their Second Temple context. N. T. Wright argues that a first-century Jew would hear them, not merely as a private blessing, but would put them in the context of the nation as a whole. It refers to the inauguration of "the redemption for which Israel was longing" (Wright 1996, 271), possibly along the lines of Jer 18:7-10.

Collins notes that the phrase **baptism of repentance** could imply that God changes his mind toward the people (Collins 2007, 140-41) as he did in Jonah. In line with the conflated citation in Mark 1:2-3, John's call is an invitation for the people to prepare themselves as a purified people ready for the coming of God and his reign and to participate in God's mission through Jesus Messiah, Son of God.

Unlike Qumran and other ritual washings, John's baptism is not primarily for removal of impurity. Rather, it is "a transformation of the Levitical type of immersion in light of eschatological expectations based on prophetic texts" (Collins 2007, 140). The conflation of Isaiah and Malachi, together with the description of John's clothing and diet, invite reflection on Mal 4:5-6, where God sends "the prophet Elijah before the great and terrible day of the LORD . . . [to] turn the hearts of parents to their children and the hearts of children to their parents" (NRSV).

Similar motifs occur in Zech 12:10—13:1. God pours out "a spirit of compassion" (NRSV); mass repentance follows. God opens a fountain for the house of David and the inhabitants of Jerusalem to cleanse them from their sin and impurity (see Marcus 2000, 155-56). Mark undoubtedly had a variety of OT passages and motifs in mind, not least the outpouring of a new spirit (Ezek 36).

■ **5** Although the widespread impact of the Baptist movement should not be underestimated, the arrival of **the whole [***pasa***] Judean countryside and all [***pantes***] the people of Jerusalem** is hyperbolic. By this statement, Mark signals that God is initiating a mass movement and re-creating his holy people to be who they are intended to be.

The people come **confessing their sins.** There may have been personal confession. But this is likely a public, communal confession analogous to a similar annual confession in Qumran (1QS 1:18—2:19) signifying "acceptance of John's prophetic mission and a plea for forgiveness and thus for being spared from or in the eschatological judgment and punishment of God" (Collins 2007, 144-45). The fact that the people **went out to him** from Jerusalem, where the temple is, and at which there is an annual Day of Atonement suggests that John is subverting the conventional—and biblical—pattern of confession, offering, and forgiveness.

The people are **baptized by him in the Jordan River;** the river itself was a highly symbolic place for Israel as the scene of the crossing into Canaan, where God drove out their enemies. Some no doubt wondered if this new movement would inaugurate another conquest in which the Romans would be driven out.

■ **6** Mark tells us that **John wore clothing made of camel's hair, with a leather belt around his waist, and he ate locusts and wild honey.** This interesting information does more than add color to the passage. In itself, this does not establish the John-Elijah link. But Mark considers it vital that the voice crying in the wilderness, John the Baptizer, is fulfilling the role of Elijah. Malachi 3:1, cited in Mark 1:2, has a wider context of purification and judgment. But God promised to send "the prophet Elijah before the great and terrible day of the LORD comes. He will turn the hearts of parents to their children and the hearts of children to their parents, so that I will not come and strike the land with a curse" (Mal 4:5-6 NRSV).

Malachi called the people to turn from their covenant unfaithfulness. John called the people to repent and be baptized, thus creating a holy people fit for a holy God (see Mal 3:7). If Mark sees John as the eschatological prophet of Mal 4:5-6, then he also shows that John's work of preparing the people is the fulfillment of the expectation of what Elijah will do (see also 1 Kgs 18:21).

In Mark's view God was doing a new thing (see Isa 43:3, 19): "in and through the remnant of Israel God reconstitute[d] his holy people" (Meyer 1979, 118). They were to be the purified people of God, whose sins were forgiven. The renewal movement was underway. John's role was "to assemble by baptism the remnant of Israel destined for cleansing and acquittal and so, climactically, for restoration" (Meyer 1979, 128).

■ 7 But John is clearly not the main act. In Mark's view, John's own testimony, the only words attributed to him, points to Jesus: **After me will come one more powerful than I.** But at the level of the "historical" John's expectation, the case is less clear. Of the suggestions that have been put forward, the two most plausible are that John expected God to come or that he expected God's agent, the Messiah, to come (see Guelich 1989, 22-23).

The first option coheres with the view that John is the Elijah of Mal 4:5-6 preparing God's way, that the term "more powerful one" in the OT points to God, and that God pours out his Spirit on the last days (see Isa 44:3; Ezek 36:26-27; 39:29; Joel 2:28-29). It runs into difficulty, however, with the comparative **more powerful than I** and untying **sandals.** John and God are simply not comparable in this way.

The second option is, therefore, better (see Marcus 2000, 151). As Mark tells the story, there is no doubt that the stronger one is Jesus. What is remarkable, as France points out, is that Mark takes language usually pointing directly to God to refer to the human Jesus. "For him, apparently, the coming of Jesus *is* the eschatological coming of God" (2002, 70). In starkest terms, John is the forerunner of Jesus who, in turn, is acting as God acts, rather than the forerunner of God's messianic agent who awaits the arrival of God. John is already restoring the people of God in preparation for God's returning to his people. And Jesus is indeed "Son of God."

■ 8 John's second contrast has to do with the baptism itself. **I baptize you with water, but he will baptize you with the Holy Spirit.** The passage is full of interesting points.

First, it continues the contrast that John has been making between himself and the One who comes after him: my baptism is **with water;** he will baptize **with the Holy Spirit.** This contrast is between the work of the human John and the work of God (see Ezek 36:25-28—God puts his Spirit in the people).

55

Second, the contrast is between water baptism and Spirit baptism. But the fact that cleansing and purification are linked with putting God's Spirit in the people in Ezek 36:27 raises a note of caution. The repentance associated with John's baptism as the eschatological prophet is linked with the eschatological action of baptizing with the Holy Spirit.

Third, while Ezekiel holds the cleansing and outpouring of the Spirit together, Mark thinks of the reception of the Spirit as separated from his baptism. In Ezekiel,

> the cleansing with water and the gift of the Holy Spirit are two aspects of the same event or process. Mark 1:8, however, divides the eschatological renewal into two stages. The cleansing with water has become a preparatory rite of repentance in the public activity of John, whereas the gift of the Holy Spirit is reserved for a second stage, the activity of Jesus. (Collins 2007, 146)

Jesus was to be the agent of this postresurrection baptism (see Marcus 2002, 158).

Finally, Mark used the verb form *baptisei* here, not the noun *baptisma* (**baptism**). The preposition *en* is likely to be instrumental here. However, the attention in this passage is not on the verb nor the preposition, but on the contrast between water and Holy Spirit (see France 2002, 72).

Sprinkling, Pouring, or Immersion?

Many Christians assume that immersion is the only biblical mode of baptism. But is this assumption justified? Marshall thinks not. Most NT passages that use the term "baptize" (including Mark 1:8) require a more flexible approach to mode.

"Baptize[d] . . . with fire" (Matt 3:11) uses "fire" in metaphorical terms as a liquid either poured from on high or engulfing as a river. In OT texts that influence the NT, the Spirit is frequently poured out from on high (Isa 32:15; Ezek 39:29; Joel 2:28-29; Zech 12:10), again in metaphorical terms as a liquid. Drenching, rather than immersion, therefore, is the better implication for "baptize[d] . . . with the Holy Spirit."

If that is so, Marshall argues,

> then the same can also be true when ["baptize"] is used in relation to water. For John the Baptist, "baptize" cannot have referred purely to dipping or plunging in water. The verb must imply being drenched with water from above as well as from below. . . . What John meant was "I have drenched you with water, but he will drench you with the Holy Spirit," or "I have cleansed / purified you with water, but he will cleanse / purify you with the Holy Spirit." . . . The reference is not so much to the *mode* of the action (whether immersion or effusion) but to the *result* of being drenched . . . and in the case of the Spirit the imagery of effusion is clearly more appropriate. (Marshall 2002, 22-23)

John's baptism was given to people who were already part of Israel, the elect people of God. This, then, was not an initiatory rite through which people who were outside the covenant were brought into it; covenant entry was signaled by circumcision of all males on the eighth day. Nor should this be confused with proselyte baptism; this was the incorporation of Gentile converts into Judaism. While some evidence may exist for this in Diaspora Judaism, Mark says nothing about Gentiles coming to be baptized. These baptizands were Jews.

This is a specific preparation for the coming of God into their midst. They must be holy people to be the dwelling place of the Holy God. This purification involves the forgiveness of sins. But this is not to be understood primarily in terms of individual sins. For those sins, the Levitical code made appropriate provision. This forgiveness is preparation for the return of Yahweh. Mark transforms this into preparation for the arrival of Jesus. He will inaugurate the age to come through his life, death, and resurrection.

This is now the second signal that Mark gives through the Baptist that Jesus is acting as God. Here John promises that Jesus will enact God's promises to pour out the Spirit and place the Spirit within the hearts of the people, thus allowing the dry bones to live (Ezek 37). Mark does not take the Jesus story beyond the empty tomb, but were he to do so, it is likely that the pattern would be similar to Luke's.

Two useful points may be drawn from this. First, it is doubtful whether this passage should be used to support a two-stage salvation paradigm with water baptism to be followed by Spirit baptism. Nor should it be pressed in the direction of a first blessing (water baptism) and second blessing (Spirit baptism). In the teaching and experience of the people of God, such a rigid pattern would be difficult to sustain. For Christians, the triune God is active through the Spirit in all of human salvation, from beginning to end. The sacrament of baptism as practiced in the church always includes the Spirit. This recognizes that the Spirit has been poured out on the holy people of God at the inauguration of the church.

Second, this is a reminder that the people of God are to be a holy people so that the holy God may dwell in their midst.

D. Jesus the Son of God (1:9-11)

This is probably the most significant point in the opening fifteen verses. The process of identifying Jesus comes to its high point with the combination of Jesus' baptism, the descent of the Spirit, and the crescendo of the voice from heaven confirming to Jesus his identity and mission.

After he baptizes Jesus, John's function in Mark is finished. His arrest signals the beginning of Jesus' mission (1:14); and there is a lengthy section on his death (6:14-29). But he only figures in the discussion in 11:28-33 (where Mark notes that everyone held that John really was a prophet).

But the importance of Elijah in the drama continues right up to 15:35-36. All of this is intertwined in Mark's view that John fulfills the role of Elijah. By 1:14, Elijah's role as the restorer of the people to covenant faithfulness has been accomplished; John has completed his task of setting the stage for the Coming One, Jesus Messiah, Son of God, the Holy One of God. Now the restored and forgiven holy people of God are ready for the mightier One to baptize them with Holy Spirit and lead them on his mission. That mission begins, Mark tells us, when Jesus arrives in Galilee after John is arrested (1:14).

BEHIND THE TEXT

All four Gospels refer to Jesus of Nazareth (1:24; 10:47). Mark tells us nothing about Jesus' earlier life apart from this information. Nothing is known of Nazareth before the Gospels—it seems simply to have been an insignificant village in Galilee where Mary and Joseph live. Matthew 2:23 states that this is to fulfill prophecy: "He will be called a Nazarene." But this is not picked up by the other Evangelists. Nazareth features in Mark only as a place of some hostility (see 6:1-6). Indeed, Nathanael's comment in John 1:46 seems entirely appropriate: "Can anything good come out of Nazareth?" (NRSV). The antipathy between Galilee and Judea only adds to the insignificance of Nazareth.

John's baptism is "a baptism of repentance for the forgiveness of sins" (v 4). Why, then, is Jesus baptized by John? The NT is unanimous in its picture of a perfectly obedient Jesus. Thus, this is not an idle question and is addressed by the other Gospels in varying ways. Matthew 3:14-15 notes that "John tried to deter him . . . [from being baptized but] Jesus replied, 'Let it be so now; it is proper for us to do this to fulfill all righteousness.' Then John consented."

Luke gives little attention to Jesus' actual baptism. Rather he describes the work of John in 2:3-18. Then he interjects the arrest and imprisonment of John by Herod in 3:19-20. Only in 3:21 does he add, "When all the people were being baptized, Jesus was baptized too." John's Gospel does not refer to Jesus' baptism. The issue was addressed in the early church fathers as well. Gregory of Nazianzus simply states that "as a man he was baptized, but he absolved sins as God. He needed no purifying rites himself—his purpose was to hallow water" (Oden and Hall 1998, 11). Ephrem the Syrian goes further, paraphrasing Jesus' words in Matthew: "by my baptism the waters will be sanctified" (Oden and Hall 1998, 15).

IN THE TEXT

■ **9** The importance of this section is signaled by Mark with the opening words **at that time.** The Greek phrase (*kai egeneto en ekeinain tais hēmergais*) could be translated, ***and it came to pass in those days.*** It is very similar in form to Luke 2:1, itself a significant marker for Luke. This is OT style (see Judg 19:1; 1 Sam 28:1). "Mark stands in the tradition of the great chroniclers of the acts of God in the OT" (France 2002, 75). This shows that Mark sees the gravity of the event as a new and significant beginning as well as linking it securely to the story of God's activity as set out in Scripture.

Mark gives the impression that Jesus made the three-day trip **from Nazareth in Galilee** specifically for this event. But he may well have been in Jerusalem for festivals on other occasions. He tells us nothing more. He offers no hint of what Jesus was doing during the previous years. He gives no clue about his age, no suggestion that John and Jesus knew each other, much less were related (see Luke 1:36, 56).

The only contact between John and Jesus in Mark is summed up in these words: he **was baptized by John in the Jordan.** Mark makes no attempt to explain this. The most plausible suggestion is that this is Jesus' identification with the people. However, Mark explicitly has Jesus come from Galilee, not Judea and Jerusalem. His attention is on the next two verses.

■ **10** According to Mark, Jesus is the only witness to the next part of the story. He alone hears the voice from heaven directly speaking to him. After his baptism, Jesus **saw heaven being torn open** (*schizomenous*). This picture is particularly vivid. Mark uses the same word in 15:38 (*eschisthē*) to describe the tearing of the ten-meter-high (eleven yards) temple veil from top to bottom. This expression does not occur elsewhere in either LXX or NT Greek. But it strongly echoes the Hebrew of Isa 64:1: "Oh, that you would rend the heavens." If this is so, then this hope of Trito-Isaiah is being fulfilled.

But "the key point is that **the Spirit [is] descending on him.** Through this gracious gash in the universe, he has poured out his Spirit into the earthly realm" (Marcus 2000, 165). The speculation on the Spirit descending **like a dove** is rife. The most probable solution refers to the Gen 1:2 hovering of the Spirit. Thus, it emphasizes the new creation (see Marcus 2000, 165; Hooker 1991, 46).

■ **11** The climax of this pericope is the **voice . . . from heaven.** Some commentators explain the voice in terms of the *bath qôl* (***daughter of a voice***). But this is unlikely, since it was considered to be inferior to God's direct voice (see Hooker 1991, 47; and France 2002, 79 n. 71). There is no hint of this whatsoever: this voice from heaven is the voice of God.

MARK

1:9-11

This is the first of two times when the voice comes in Mark. On this occasion, Jesus is the only auditor. The second occasion is in 9:7, where Peter, James, and John hear the voice as well. That Jesus alone hears the voice in 1:11 is important. Readers know who Jesus is from the beginning and are privileged to hear the voice from heaven. But no one else in Mark's narrative hears these words. The identity of Jesus is disclosed to the characters in the drama during the course of the next eight chapters culminating in 8:27-33.

The words **You are my Son, whom I love** ["the Beloved" (NRSV) is a better translation]; **with you I am well pleased** echo the language of the OT—but scholars have not agreed which OT texts. That should not trouble us. Hatina considers the search for *the* one textual background myopic. A plurality of voices and echoes are appropriate (Hatina 2006, 98-99).

Scholars of a previous generation considered Isa 42:1 the central text (see, e.g., Zimmerli and Jeremias 1957, 81). More recent study has called this into question. An allusion to Isa 42:1 depends either upon a link between son (*huios*) and servant (*pais*) as synonyms, or a link with the second half of the verse, "I have put my spirit upon him" (NRSV), which inevitably draws attention to Isa 42:1. Neither of these is wholly persuasive, since verbal parallels to the LXX or MT are almost absent.

But that does not mean that neither Isa 42:1 nor the Isaiah servant passages more generally are unimportant. Marshall argues, "Granted that the baptismal saying contains a reference to the messianic Son of God, it is entirely fitting that it should develop this thought with the aid of language from Isaiah 42:1" (1990, 129). The difficulty leads Hatina to suggest that Mark has in mind the wider Isaianic servant tradition rather than a specific citation. This is far more likely, given other echoes of the servant passages in Mark 10:45; 14:24; and other possible allusions. If this is so, then Jesus' baptism would signal his "vocation as the one who recapitulates the Isaianic servant of God by giving his life for the sake of the nation" (Hatina 2006, 88).

In fact, Marshall has shown conclusively that the first allusion, **You are my Son,** is to Ps 2:7 (1990; see Hatina 2006, 94-98). Although the word order in the LXX of Ps 2:7 (*huios mou ei su*) is different from Mark's, this is not significant.

Psalm 2 is sometimes called a "royal psalm," perhaps one of those recited at an annual festival for the Davidic king. Thus, the psalm has been interpreted messianically. The text is used at Qumran (4Q174 1:10-13) in a midrashic combination with 2 Sam 7:14: "I will be a father to him, and he shall be a son to me" (NRSV). Mark sees this clearly in messianic terms (Collins 2007, 150) and confirms the designation in 1:1 of *Jesus Messiah*.

Some early Christians "could have conceivably understood Jesus' baptism as a type of Davidic coronation" (Hatina 2006, 97). The fact that Ps 2:2

speaks of opposition, "The kings of the earth take their stand and the rulers gather together against the LORD and against his Anointed One," should not go unnoticed given the context of hostility from rulers in the subsequent narrative (see Marcus 2000, 166). "The point is that the designation 'son of God' as king conforms to the portrayal of Jesus in both the broader narrative and the socio-religious context" (Hatina 2006, 98). Ambrose is among the early fathers who guard against any adoptionist use of this text (see Oden and Hall 1998, 12).

But where does "the Beloved" (NRSV; Gk.: *ho agapētos*) fit? Hooker notes that this is normally used of an only child and goes on to note that the phrase "denotes Jesus' unique status" (1991, 50). Attempts to link this verse to Isa 42:1 through the word *agapētos* have been largely unconvincing. But it could be linked to Gen 22:2, 12, 16. The idea of Isaac as the beloved and obedient son developed into the "Binding of Isaac" tradition that was widespread in the 2TP (see Vermes 1961; Best 1990). This motif may have had some influence on Mark's theology, but the evidence is limited. Furthermore, it is not used directly in other places where it might have provided some support.

A concentration on any one of these putative echoes to the exclusion of the others denies the richness of allusions to the OT that is clearly present in Mark (see Marshall 1990). Each individual part is interesting in itself, but the combination of these three in the voice from heaven gathers together some significant points for Jesus' identity and mission, according to Mark. First, it confirms, on divine authority, that he is the Messiah who is the Son of God. Earlier we heard the voice in the wilderness; now we hear the voice from heaven.

Second, this stronger One is also taking on the role of the servant of Yahweh from Deutero-Isaiah. This role not only entails suffering on behalf of his people but also shows that the servant embodies in himself their suffering. The combination of Messiah and Servant is rich in connotation. Jesus' messiahship is a "Son of Man must suffer and be killed" kind of messiahship. In this Jesus embodies the role of the suffering figures in the OT in their God-given mission. That becomes clear in the subsequent narrative, but here, the combination prefigures that direction.

Third, this mission is God's mission—the voice from heaven is well pleased with Jesus. Finally, although it is not particularly available on the surface of the text, the underlying theological thrust has Jesus Messiah, Son of God, as the bearer of the Spirit of God who hears a voice from heaven confirming his identity and mission. Readers are privy to a private event—the voice is heard by Jesus and he is addressed in the second person—and so we are invited to listen in on the conversation of the Holy Trinity.

E. The Temptation (1:12-13)

The story of Jesus' temptation in each of the Synoptics no doubt refers to the same event. But the way the story is told by Matthew and Luke is quite different from Mark. Mark's account is brief, simply stating that Jesus was in the wilderness for forty days tempted by Satan and that the angels served him. The other accounts are more elaborate, clearly being the testing of God's Son in the wilderness during which Jesus' identity and mission are challenged. That theme is present to a degree in Mark. But there appears to be a different emphasis. The temptation for readers of Mark is to interpret his account in terms of the others, rather than letting Mark speak for himself.

BEHIND THE TEXT

One of Mark's key literary devices is the use of the word *euthys* or *eutheōs*, which he uses over forty times, here translated **at once** ("immediately"—NRSV). He has already used it in 1:10, where it was translated by the rather weak **as**. Its use gives Mark's narrative a sense of flow, sometimes even conveying urgency. Here the term makes a clear connection between the descent of the Spirit and the immediate departure into the wilderness.

Satan is not prominent in the OT. The most well-known passage is the story of the Satan who tests humans at the behest of God (Job 1—2; see Zech 3:1-3). The one exception is 1 Chr 12:1, where Satan incites David to take a census of Israel against the command of the Lord. The 2TP saw a significant rise in attention to angelology and demonology based loosely on the OT but heavily influenced by other religious cultures. The emphasis in Mark is upon Jesus being in the wilderness, not so much on Satan's temptations (see Guelich 1989, 37).

IN THE TEXT

■ **12** The connection between the descent of the Spirit and this next episode is obvious. Mark notes that this incident immediately follows—**at once** ("immediately" [NRSV]). But **the Spirit** and **the desert** are also linked. The wilderness context has been crucial: vv 3 and 4 as well as this one have this setting. Hooker surprisingly suggests that the Jordan cannot have been in the wilderness, because the Spirit sends Jesus into the wilderness from the Jordan, but there is no need for the wilderness to be distant from the river.

The Greek for **sent him out** (*ekballei*) is the first use of the historic present form of the verb in Mark. This is characteristic of his narrative style, conveying pace and immediacy, especially when combined with the adverbs *euthys* or *eutheōs*. It is used more often than the NIV translation implies. Mark uses it elsewhere in connection with exorcisms (see 1:39; 3:15, 22, 23; 6:13; 9:38) as well as to describe Jesus' action in the temple (11:15).

The NRSV translates "drove him out." Guelich suggests that the context indicates that the Spirit took control of Jesus and impelled him to go into the wilderness (1989, 38).

But why? France notes that *ekballein* often implies some possibility of resistance (2002, 85). This could be why the term is avoided by the other Evangelists. But Mark's combination of images in v 11 may imply suffering messiahship. If so, the Markan Jesus may have a sense of foreboding as he embarks on the mission that leads to 14:32-42 on the way to the cross. In any case, Mark is clear that Jesus, upon whom the Spirit descends, goes immediately into the wilderness equipped with the Spirit to begin his mission.

■ 13 Jesus spends **forty days** in the wilderness. The reason is less clear. Here, perhaps as much as anywhere, exegetes need to let Mark be Mark, rather than read this story in the light of Matthew and Luke. Mark does not say that Jesus fasted for forty days. Had he wished to do so, no doubt he would have; he does note fasting in 2:18-20. But Mark draws our attention elsewhere.

The forty days may simply mean "a long period"; it could also echo Moses on Sinai (e.g., Exod 24:18) or Elijah in the wilderness (1 Kgs 19:8). Israel's forty-year-long wilderness wanderings (Num 14:34) may also be in view (France 2002, 85).

But some recent studies have argued that the story of Adam is the primary background here. Marcus (2000, 169) suggests that the *Life of Adam and Eve* in the pseudepigrapha casts some illumination. The statement **he was with the wild animals** could have hostile associations (see Isa 13:21; 34:14; Ps 22:12-21). This may reflect the integrated order of creation that Adam enjoyed before Gen 3. In Isa 11:1-11 the Spirit of the Lord is promised to come upon the root of Jesse who rules in righteousness and peace. The picture of order and peace that comes from his rule, including the animals, has a strong claim to background here. If so, Jesus fulfills the intended role of Adam within the created order, which also fulfills Isaianic hopes.

That **angels attended him** does not give the impression of a forty-day fast (the Greek for **attended** [*diēkonoun*] is imperfect: *were attending*), perhaps suggesting God's provision for Jesus throughout the forty days, rather than a one-time service at the conclusion. The presence of Satan, angels, and wild beasts draws attention to Ps 91:11-13 (Collins 2007, 151-53). This evokes images of a battle between Satan, wild beasts, and, by implication, demons vs. Jesus, the Spirit of God, and the angels.

But what does **being tempted** mean? If Adam is at least partly in view here, this is Gen 3 revisited, but with a different outcome. Adam was tempted and yielded; Jesus (it is implied) did not. Thus, the story of Jesus and the conflict on which he is about to embark is far beyond the level of the mundane. The opposition to God is cosmic in scale; the battle is far greater than that perceived by those who thought the Romans were the only issue. They turn out to be ciphers for the wider opposition to God's big purposes, his announcement of the good news of the kingdom. And that is precisely what happens next.

F. The Time Has Come (1:14-15)

The identity of Jesus and his mission has been established, and the time for its inauguration has arrived. The preparatory work of John is finished. The mission and identity of Jesus have been confirmed by the voice from heaven. God's Spirit impels and empowers the Son of God in the mission of God, directing him to fulfill the role of Adam. Furthermore, Jesus has been tested, and while we are not directly told the outcome, Jesus appears in Galilee proclaiming the good news of God.

BEHIND THE TEXT

The story sequence is clear in Mark: it is only after John is **put in prison** that Jesus begins his ministry. Mark does not imply any overlap between the ministry of John and Jesus (as in the Fourth Gospel). Rather, in Mark the sequence of "after me will come one" (v 7) depends on the passing of John from the scene. Nothing is told of John's ministry after Jesus' baptism, apart from the explanation for his imprisonment (6:17-20).

The verb translated **was put in prison** (*paradothēnai*) is used repeatedly in Mark in a variety of forms, including key passages like 9:31; 10:33; 14:21, 22, 41. There, it means "is handed over," describing Jesus' arrest and betrayal. On the one hand, it can simply mean, as translated here by NIV: after John **was put in prison.**

Mark knows Herod arrested and executed John. But the verb in the passive voice leaves the implied actor(s) unstated. Thus, a translation that preserves this ambiguity and better fits the context would be: after John *was handed over.*

The Isaianic background also contributes to our understanding. The LXX of Isa 53:6, 12 uses the same verb (*The Lord handed him over for our sins; his life was handed over to death*). Once these points are recognized, especially in light of the wider context, it becomes clear that "behind the human scenario at the end of John's and Jesus' ministries stands God's purpose and activity expressed by the divine passive" (Guelich 1989, 42).

The second tricky translation is of the word *ēngiken.* The meaning of the verb *engizein* is usually "come near" or "draw near," as reflected in the translation **is near.** Scholars have debated whether this means "has arrived" or "is near, but not yet arrived." Mark's only other use of the word is in 14:42. There it means that the betrayer is about to betray him "immediately" (14:43 NRSV). Lexical approaches have limited value, however. This word takes its nuance from the context and depends upon the phrase **the time has come** on the one hand and the meaning of **the kingdom of God** on the other.

IN THE TEXT

■ **14** The conclusion to the introductory sequence comes in these two verses. They also summarize all that Mark will explain from 1:16—16:8. **After John was put in prison** his activity, but not his significance, draws to a conclusion. Although John's Gospel has some overlap in ministries, Mark does not. The attention now shifts fully to **Jesus.**

The opening summary is that Jesus is **proclaiming the good news of God** (see 1:1). This phrase also epitomizes the mission of the people of God. This is both good news about God, that is, his reign, and the good news God is bringing. Jesus' message is the good news about God (1:14); but after Easter, the story is the good news about Jesus Christ, Son of God (Marcus 2000, 172).

Jesus went into Galilee. "The geographical contrast suggests a thematic and qualitative distinction between the time of repentance and asceticism in the wilderness and the time of good news, fulfillment and trust in Galilee" (Collins 2007, 154). John works in the wilderness and at the Jordan, two geographical settings that echo the exodus-conquest motif.

Jesus is in Galilee. There are other similarities and contrasts between the ministry of John and Jesus. According to Mark, Jesus is not baptizing— that was a preparatory rite for Israel for the coming of the Lord. John's message is preparatory; Jesus' message reflects Isaiah's announcement: the good news of God is being proclaimed, not just promised and anticipated.

■ **15** The opening words summarizing Jesus' message are joyous and pregnant with significance: **The time has come** (*peplērōtai ho kairos*). The NRSV translation, "the time is fulfilled," captures more clearly the thrust of this statement. Both key words (*kairos* and *plēroō*) in this context have connotations well beyond their usual usage. *Kairos* used here in combination with **has come** signals that a decisive time has arrived, a time that brings to fulfillment the purposes of God as announced in the prophets.

The perfect tense (*peplērōtai*) indicates that the time of waiting has now been fulfilled and has an ongoing current effect on the present. "This is not an announcement of something future, even imminent; the state of fulfillment already exists" (France 2002, 91).

If that is so, what is the meaning and significance of the following statement, **the kingdom of God is near?** The debate about the meaning of **is near** cannot be resolved on philological grounds (→ BEHIND THE TEXT). Rather, the key to understanding this is based upon the phrase **kingdom of God.**

Immediately to be excluded is an understanding that suggests the **kingdom** is "just over the horizon," as it were, as if God's decisive action would

1:14-15

only be occurring sometime in the future. Mark can hardly mean that—as other passages confirm (see 9:1; 13:30). Something that is perpetually in retreat just over the horizon soon loses its significance. Rather, this verse announces that God's reign in strength is already arriving.

But it cannot mean fully "arrived" either, if that implies that God's good purposes have been entirely realized.

> It is therefore not appropriate to ask whether "the kingdom of God" is past, present, or future, as if it had a specific time-reference like "the day of Yahweh." God's kingship is both eternal and eschatological, both fulfilled and awaited, both present and imminent. . . . To declare that God's kingship has come near is to say that God is now fulfilling his agelong purpose, rather than to point to a specific time or event which can be defined as either present or still in the future, but not both. (France 2002, 93)

In the light of the good news, people are called to **repent.** This is the same message as John's; and the call is essentially the same: They are called to turn from their current direction and become the people God intended for them to be, namely, "a kingdom of priests and a holy nation" (Exod 19:6).

Essentially, Jesus called Israel to return to covenant faithfulness and obedience. This turning to God's way includes the invitation to **believe the good news.** This unusual construction, **Repent and believe,** summarizes the call to discipleship. It is a reordering of life and direction away from a self-centered or self-absorbed direction toward the good news of God's big purposes. The call is answered both corporately and personally. Not surprising, then, the next episode in Mark's story is the call of the first four disciples.

II. ANNOUNCING AND EFFECTING THE GOOD NEWS: MARK 1:16-45

The remainder of ch 1 builds upon the introduction of the identity of Jesus set out in 1:1-15. The proclamation of the good news begins. Significantly, the first episode is the calling of four disciples, followed immediately by an exorcism in which the identity of Jesus is revealed in a semipublic, albeit ambivalent fashion. Other mighty deeds signaling the rule of God in strength follow, which rapidly lead in turn to spreading news about Jesus in the area of Capernaum. Jesus withdraws from the crowds and readers are reminded of Jesus' ministry focus. Finally, he heals a leper, restoring the leper to his place within the people of God.

At this stage, there is no sign of conflict, although the dispatch of the leper to the priest might have triggered a response. In fact, all seem to be impressed by him—**people still came to him from everywhere** (v 45). Jesus is taking them by storm!

A. The Call of the Four (1:16-20)

The first episode in Jesus' ministry is the call of the four fishermen to follow him. This may seem slightly surprising. Should we not have expected some teaching and mighty deeds? But from Mark's perspective, the announcing and effecting of the kingdom includes the active participation of the people of God in God's mission. Indeed, the disciples are Jesus' constant companions throughout his mission. Thus, before any events are noted, Jesus calls Simon, Andrew, James, and John. Two other call/commissioning events occur (3:13-19; 6:7-13). "The creation of community has primacy over both teaching and christological confession" (Shiner 1995, 191).

The call is crucial for Mark's developing narrative. On the one hand, the proclamation of the good news of God is a mission involving Jesus and those who follow him, the re-created people of God. Discipleship is a major theme in Mark; Jesus spends considerable time and energy in teaching the disciples and preparing them for their role in the mission of God. On the other hand (remembering that the voice from heaven is addressed to Jesus, not to those around him), it is essential that the disciples are present from the beginning (see Acts 1:22) for the gradual disclosure of Jesus' identity to them.

BEHIND THE TEXT

We might ask how four fishermen could abandon their nets without any apparent prior hint of who Jesus is. According to John 1:35-51, the call of the first disciples was rather more involved. These disciples were part of the Baptist's entourage. John pointed them to Jesus. Luke does not describe the call of these disciples until after reporting several impressive events (Luke 5:1-11). Matthew tells us that Jesus left Nazareth and lived in Capernaum (4:13) before beginning his proclamation of the good news (4:17). Only at that point did he call the four. They presumably already knew him from living in the same village. But Mark does not answer our question.

The Sea of Galilee, Capernaum, and Fishing

The Sea of Galilee (also called Tiberias, Gennesaret, and Lake of Galilee) is a tear-shaped freshwater lake about twenty-three kilometers by thirteen kilometers (fourteen miles by eight miles) at its largest dimensions. The Jordan, which descends from Mount Hermon in the north, and other lesser streams feed the Sea of Galilee. It lies over two hundred meters (six hundred feet) below sea level. On the south it empties into the Jordan, which continues to the Dead Sea.

Capernaum was a flourishing fishing village, about four kilometers (two miles) from Bethsaida. Between 4 B.C. and A.D. 37, its location on a trade route between Damascus and Egypt made it "the most likely site on the west side of the lake for a toll station with a military garrison. This temporary strategic importance as a border post disappeared, however, when Galilee was united to the kingdom of Agrippa" (Smith 2008).

The Gospels make no mention of Jesus visiting the two major cities of Tiberias (Antipas' capital), on the southwest shore of Galilee, or Sepphoris, in the hill country near Nazareth. Apparently, Jesus gradually gathered followers who were "socially insignificant people from an insignificant corner of provincial Galilee" (France 2002, 94; see 14:70).

IN THE TEXT

■ **16** According to Mark, much of Jesus' ministry is centered around the Sea of Galilee. Capernaum (probably meaning "village of Nahum"), on the northwest shore, was likely Jesus' home. This may help account for the readiness of these four fishermen to follow Jesus. But if so, Mark does not tell us. Rather, Mark seems more interested in the pattern of this call, probably 1 Kgs 19:19-21 (so Marcus 2000, 181-84; see Collins 2007, 156-60). God's call of his people is well known in the OT (Isa 41:9 and 42:6 explicitly refer to God's call of his servant).

As Jesus walked beside the Sea follows immediately after Jesus' proclamation. That **Simon and . . . Andrew . . . were fishermen** is not surprising, given their home in Capernaum (or Bethsaida, John 1:44). **Simon**—the name Mark uses until the Twelve are appointed (3:13-16; see 14:37)—is given prominence in this story as the first disciple called, a position that continues in Mark (see Bauckham 2006, 155-82).

■ **17** The call to **Come, follow me** (*deute opisō mou*) emphasizes that they are not called as Jesus' equals (→ 9:38). They are "being called to follow Jesus as their leader, a relationship that went beyond mere formal learning to full-time 'apprenticeship'" (France 2002, 96).

Their occupation as fishermen gives Jesus the opening to describe their mission in an understandable metaphor: if they follow him, he **will make** (*poiēsō*) them "fish for people" (NRSV). Marcus gives five possible options for explaining this metaphor. He concludes that the metaphor is multivalent and should be taken as referring to future teaching, missionary preaching, and exorcism, all in God's holy war (Marcus 2000, 184). Several scholars draw attention to the possible allusion to Jer 16:16-18, in which fishers are given the task of gathering Israel from afar (see Meyer 1979, 118). But this is unlikely (see France 2002, 96-97; Collins 2007, 159).

■ **18** The attachment of the disciples to Jesus should not be confused with the Jewish rabbi-teacher relationship. Pupils selected their rabbi; Jesus calls his disciples. This call is a radical call, more connected to a prophetic call. **At once** [*euthys*] **they left their nets** gives an indication of the seriousness and level of commitment required of the disciples right from the beginning, and **followed**

him. The verb *akolouthein* is used repeatedly by Mark to describe the relationship of Jesus to his disciples (2:14, 15; 8:34; 9:38; 10:21, 28, 32, 52; 14:54[?]; 15:41) but not always with the same connotation. Hooker (1991, 60) reminds us that a boat was readily available throughout Jesus' Galilean ministry (3:9; 4:1, 36; 5:21; 6:32, 45; 8:13), suggesting that the break might not have been quite as radical as sometimes pictured (see 1:39; but also 10:32).

■ **19** While the call of James and John is somewhat separated from that of Simon and Andrew, it follows the same pattern. Jesus is still by the sea and sees **James son of Zebedee,** who was martyred by Herod Agrippa in A.D. 43, **and his brother John in a boat, preparing their nets.**

■ **20** Again, the call is abrupt and the response instant. **Without delay** [again *euthys*, "immediately"] **he called them, and they left their father Zebedee in the boat with the hired men.** This statement suggests that Jesus' first followers would be called middle-class businessmen in modern Western terms. They traded in the flourishing fishing industry centered on the abundant fish in Galilee. But they still **followed him,** leaving **their father Zebedee with the hired men.**

The grammatical structure of this section has the disciples as subjects only after following Jesus. This might indicate that "authentic human identity is found only in discipleship to Jesus." This idea contrasts with the restoration of the distorted humanity of the following episode (Marcus 2000, 185).

FROM THE TEXT

Isolated from the other Gospel accounts, this story strains credulity. But read in its narrative flow, a variety of ideas emerge. First, the call is a continuation and extension of the ministry of John, who calls out a remnant from all Judea and Jerusalem. But Jesus' call is to those outside the heartland of Jerusalem and Judea. This remnant, then, is an "open remnant" (Bryan 2002, 121 n. 97). The implications of this open call to discipleship are readily apparent for ministry today. Jesus invites any and all who will to become his disciples.

Second, this section shows the radical nature of discipleship. To follow Jesus on his way is to make a complete commitment. The point is not so much that everything is abandoned (the disciples do seem to retain boats and homes), but that everything else pales into insignificance compared to this call.

Third, there is no two-stage discipleship portrayed here. While it is clear that the disciples do not understand from the beginning and, indeed, later fail, this is no half-commitment. These men leave their nets and their families to follow Jesus. Later (8:34-38) we will see that radical discipleship is not limited to a select few.

Fourth, following Jesus means identifying fully with his mission, God's great purposes for the world. Finally, the disciples are always disciples, never masters themselves (see Brower 2005, 83-102, on holiness and discipleship).

B. The Holy One of God (1:21-28)

This first episode after the call of the four begins a hectic twenty-four-hour period. Mark's redactional activity can be seen throughout. There is no opposition to Jesus from people; but demonic opposition points to the cosmic significance of Jesus' ministry. The structure of the day is likely Mark's as well, compressing into it a great deal of typical activity: teaching, exorcism, and healing. Mark draws together this series of stories, organizes them, and shapes them in order to make several important points.

BEHIND THE TEXT

Mark includes four exorcisms (1:21-28; 5:1-20; 7:24-30; 9:14-29). Their prominence shows how crucial they are for Mark's theology. The identity of Jesus is stated by demons. Their witness is reliable but antagonistic to his spiritual reality. But exorcisms matter also because they signal the cosmic scope of God's big purposes, particularly of transforming the created order distorted by evil.

Mark uses his language carefully to distinguish demonic possession from mental illness. While modern medical diagnosis of the conditions described in Mark might, in some cases, be different from Mark's categorization, he does not naively assume that all illness is demonic. Whatever else these exorcisms tell us, at the very least they signal that the opposition to God is far greater than the sum of its human manifestations. In short, it is cosmic in scope. So the solution must be cosmic in scope and significance.

This first episode is shaped by "bracketing." Mark begins and ends this story emphasizing Jesus' authoritative teaching (vv 21-22, 27-28). Into this story he inserts the exorcism (vv 23-26). Mark usually uses this technique to illuminate some particular aspect of either part by bringing the two together in this way.

Scholars have debated whether synagogue worship was actually practiced in Galilee before the destruction of the temple in A.D. 70. Recent discussions favor the view that it was in existence. Archaeological work in Capernaum has uncovered the remains of a large synagogue dating from as early as the third century A.D. But "underneath the central nave, a large floor of basalt stones was found which dates to the beginning of the first century C.E. . . . This floor may have belonged to an earlier synagogue building or to a large home that was used as a gathering place for the Jewish community" (Collins 2007, 162). This could have been the synagogue in this story.

■ 21 The first episode follows from the call—perhaps the next day—and occurs in **Capernaum** on the **Sabbath**. Jesus' Sabbath practices are not an issue here, but they soon will be (2:23-28). The synagogue was "a communal institution that served the full range of needs of a community" (Collins 2007, 164). Synagogues were run by a group of elders. The work of priests seems to have been limited to temple worship. Any competent male could be asked by the synagogue ruler to teach. Reading and interpretation of Scripture was a feature (see Luke 4:16-21). Mark apparently distinguishes **teaching** (*didaskein*) from "proclaiming" (*kēryssein*). He confines **teaching** to Jesus, but others also preach in Mark (France 2002, 102).

■ 22 Jesus is now accompanied by his disciples. Like the people, they are **amazed at his teaching** (see 6:2; 7:37; 11:18). We are not told the content of his teaching, only its character, **as one who had authority** (*exousia*). This follows from Jesus being Spirit-possessed (1:10). We are told later that his was "a new teaching" (v 27). Not only is his teaching with authority, but he also has authority over the unclean spirits and he gives his disciples this authority (3:15).

His teaching is different from **teachers of the law** (*grammateis*) who studied and interpreted Torah. Although usually pictured as hostile to Jesus, their role is acknowledged in 9:11 and 12:35. If the later rabbinic pattern was followed this early, these scribes would cite tradition to reach an authoritative interpretation rather than offering fresh insight. Jesus' teaching, however, undoubtedly reflected the announcement that the good news of God's deliverance was already taking place. "They represent the old régime, challenged by the fresh new teaching of Jesus" (France 2002, 102).

The disciples' amazement is implicit. Although readers already know that the whole narrative is about Jesus, Son of God, the beloved Son (1:1, 11), the disciples do not. There is something compelling about Jesus, to be sure, but they follow "without knowing his identity or his important role in the divine drama of the end of the age" (Shiner 1995, 193). Most significantly, these disciples are now with Jesus.

■ 23 Jesus' authoritative teaching is linked directly to the exorcism. This man was possessed by "an unclean spirit" (NRSV), a better translation of *pnemati akathartōi* in this context. Unexpectedly, this man was **in their synagogue**. His unclean condition would normally exclude him from worship. Perhaps, then, he just appears suddenly (Mark uses *euthys*, perhaps deliberately rather than rhetorically). The phrase *en pnemati akathartōi*, **by an evil spirit**, could mean that "the man's personality has been so usurped by the demon that the demon has, as it were, swallowed him up" (Marcus 2000, 192). This may be so. Clearly he has an "unclean spirit." This highlights the clash in identities between the unclean spirit and the Holy One of God.

■ **24** Once the unclean spirit sees Jesus, he cries out. Each part of the cry is important. The first is a sign of fear and surprise, **What do you want with us?** Note the plural **us,** perhaps implying that he speaks here in a general sense of opposition between the demonic world and Jesus.

The second part of the cry expresses alarm at the power of Jesus, perhaps alluding to his earlier confrontation with Satan. Here the demon speaks again in the plural, possibly for the demonic realm, **Have you come to destroy us?** Marcus considers this the most important part, because it shows that Jesus is no ordinary exorcist—exorcism was common in this period—but One who is bringing all opposition to God's rule to an end (Marcus 2000, 192).

But in terms of the identity of Jesus, the third part in which the demon seeks mastery over Jesus through his knowledge of him, is the most important. **I know who you are—the Holy One of God!** (*ho hagios tou theou*).

The identity of Jesus is crucial for two reasons. First, it is accurate because it comes from the spirit world. This is the first explicit identity of Jesus that the disciples learn in Mark's narrative (see Brower 2007a). Second, Jesus is the Holy One of God. He is the embodiment of the holy in the midst of the people in confrontation with the unclean.

The definite article, **the Holy One** (emphasis added), is significant because "it exalts Jesus over Enoch and all other mere human beings as the holiest of God's elect. . . . [His holiness] is the polar opposite of the uncleanness of the spirit" (Collins 2007, 170). We already know that Jesus possesses the Holy Spirit. Thus, he is able to act in the power of the age to come. But for those with eyes to see, Mark is signaling that Jesus is the unique Son of God. This identity is important for understanding critical passages later.

■ **25-26** Jesus' response is to rebuke the unclean spirit (*epitmēsen autōi*). Mark uses the same word in 8:33, so it is not a technique or a formula (so France 2002, 104; but see Marcus 2000, 193). He simply forbids the demon to speak and orders him to **"Come out of him!"** The demon does not depart quietly: the unclean spirit **shook the man violently and came out of him with a shriek.**

■ **27** The conclusion to the story emphasizes the authoritative teaching of Jesus as demonstrated by the obedience of the unclean spirit. The words and deeds of Jesus together signal the coming of the kingdom. Jesus wins the first skirmish in the battle. **The people were all so amazed** probably because no exorcism of which they were aware had been accomplished with only a word. It is likely, as well, that Jesus' teaching announcing and explaining the good news, perhaps even an invitation to follow him on his way, was **a new teaching—and with authority!** This translation follows the best of three possible punctuations (considering the bracketing technique of Mark in 1:22, 28). His authority is confirmed by the unclean spirits who **obey him.**

This is important for the identity and authority of Jesus as a teacher and exorcist effecting the kingdom of God. But "the key point for the disciples is that Jesus is identified by the unclean spirit as the Holy One of God. What does occur is that the disciples are in the company of Jesus, the one with *exousia* who is the Holy One of God. They are part of God's holy people because they are with the Holy One" (Brower 2007a, 65-66).

■ **28** As a consequence, word about Jesus spreads immediately. As the teacher with authority, he announces God's good news. And this authority is exercised against the oppressive power of evil by freeing this man from the distortion of his being. He is a teacher with authority and the news spreads **over the whole region of Galilee.** No wonder, then, that he gets no rest. But, significantly, his identity as the Holy One of God goes unremarked. Only gradually does the reality of Jesus' true identity dawn on the disciples, much less on the people in Capernaum (see Matt 11:23; Luke 10:15).

FROM THE TEXT

Two points emerge from this short text. First, the confrontation between good and evil is not merely a human conflict. The description and personification of evil in terms of the developed demonology in this period was widespread in many cultures and societies of that day. At the least, this story is a grim reminder that beneath the surface of this conflict lies systemic evil that feeds upon the wickedness of humankind but is greater than the sum of its parts. This story and the other exorcism accounts in Mark give notice that evil cannot ultimately rule in God's sphere.

Second, Jesus is the Holy One of God—and all human holiness derives from the holy God. Those around Jesus, then, are being re-created as the new holy people of God, with Jesus, the Holy One, in their midst.

C. The Spreading Fame (1:29-45)

BEHIND THE TEXT

The story continues with two specific healings (1:29-31, 41-45), growing popularity (1:32-34, 39, 45*b*) and withdrawal by Jesus followed by a restatement of his mission (1:38-39). One emerging feature is Jesus' command to silence. These demands are strange in themselves; some are impossible to fulfill. How likely is it that a leper who has been restored to the community will be able to keep quiet about his cleansing (1:44) or that questions would not be asked about others who were healed or who were freed from demonic possession? At the end of this section, readers have a clear idea of Jesus' identity, his mission, his authority, and the nature of the kingdom. Whether the people in the story have the same understanding is doubtful.

The Messianic Secret in Mark

For over a century, scholars have noted the widespread requirement for silence about Jesus' identity: of the demons (1:25; 3:12) and of the healed (1:44; 5:43; 7:36; 8:26). There are similar commands not to reveal his identity (8:30; 9:9). William Wrede (1901) proposed that Jesus was unmessianic in his actual life and ministry, but that after the resurrection, the early church came to believe that he was also Messiah during his lifetime. So Mark devised the motif of a secret messiahship, which he wrote back into the story of Jesus. Thereby, he transformed the historic reality of an unmessianic Jesus into a messiah whose messiahship was secret and unknown. Few scholars today accept Wrede's theory without modification. Without canvassing all the options, the most plausible explanation depends upon recognizing that Mark's narrative functions on two levels: the level of the actors in the story (except Jesus) and the level of Mark, his readers, Jesus, and occasionally, others.

At the first level, for the most part, the participants just don't get it: Their eyes are blind. But those at the second level do. Mark used this literary device to draw attention to the real significance of the story. Thus, "the truth about Jesus is at once hidden from view and yet spelt out on every page of the gospel" (Hooker 1991, 69). Jesus is Messiah during his lifetime, but it is only after the resurrection that the disciples actually "get it"! (see Hooker 1991, 66-69; Collins 2007, 170-72).

IN THE TEXT

I. Simon's Mother-in-Law (1:29-31)

■ **29** Although the two stories are different in detail, Mark connects this single healing directly to the synagogue exorcism. This also occurs on the Sabbath. But, again, he makes no mention of a Sabbath violation. The language **as soon as they left the synagogue** is awkward because the antecedent of "they" is unclear. Had Mark written "he," it would have referred to Jesus. Perhaps, Mark refers to Jesus and Simon, who go **with James and John to the home of Simon and Andrew.** That Mark's first healing story depends upon Peter's reminiscence is attractive, but beyond proof (Hooker 1991, 70).

This is the only explicit identification of a home for Jesus or his disciples. But unspecified later references to a house as a place of retreat and private teaching (2:1; 3:20; 7:17; 9:33) may point to this house. An excavation next to the site of the uncovered synagogue in Capernaum has been called "Peter's House." Again, this is plausible but unprovable (see France 2002, 107). If it is

Peter's house, Mark's *immediately* (untranslated here) may imply proximity, rather than simply one more example of his characteristic style.

■ **30** The story of the healing of **Simon's mother-in-law** (Peter also has a wife—see 1 Cor 9:5) is told in classic healing narrative form. The healer arrives; the illness is described (she **was in bed with a fever**); a request is made **(they told Jesus about her)**; the healing event occurs; the result is reported; and its effect on the eyewitnesses is noted.

Form, of course, tells us nothing about the historical reliability of the story, nor its significance in the narrative. Simon's mother-in-law was prostrate with fever; fever was sometime considered an illness itself rather than its symptom (see Guelich 1989, 62). Recognition of Jesus' authority meant that they turn to him immediately.

■ **31** Jesus **went to her, took her hand and helped her up.** Two interesting points: First, the Greek word order is *coming to her he raised her taking her hand.* This perhaps emphasizes that he raised her (Matt 8:15 emphasizes Jesus' touch). Mark's story is told in very minimalist fashion—no spoken word is noted—simply the fact that she was raised up (see 5:41-42) and that **the fever left her.**

Second, Marcus draws attention to "raised" in connection with resurrection from the dead as well (2000, 199). The close link between these stories reminds readers that sickness and the demonic are both distortions of human wholeness. As a consequence of her healing, she began to wait on them. The verb *diēkonei* is in the imperfect tense, one Mark often uses. So it may or may not mean more than serving one meal. It is the same verb describing the angels' service of Jesus following his temptation (1:13). Perhaps Peter's mother-in-law served the group on more than one subsequent occasion (see 15:41).

2. The Mission Expands (1:32-39)

■ **32** The transition from private to public space for healing and exorcism is noted by two phrases: **that evening** and **after sunset.** This duality is a Markan characteristic, but here it deliberately emphasizes that the people of Capernaum waited until the end of Sabbath (**after sunset**) to bring people to Jesus, to avoid breaking the Law. The meaning is *in the evening after Sabbath.* This reminded Gentile readers that there was no incompatibility between the piety of observant Judaism and recognition of Jesus. But Mark has already noted that Jesus is not restricted by these laws on Sabbath observance. **The people brought [** *epheron = were bringing;* i.e., *were queuing up to bring***] to Jesus all the sick and demon-possessed.** Note that Mark distinguishes these two groups from each other.

■ **33-34** Mark uses hyperbole here, having **the whole town** (v 33, *holē hē polis*) and "all" (*pantas*) in v 32 come to Jesus (→ 1:5). This stylistic device emphasizes the rapid effect of rumor in a small town and the impact of the exorcism in the synagogue. **Jesus healed many** and **drove out many demons** (*pollous*), perhaps implying "but not all." The continued clamor in vv 36-37 may confirm this.

But the summary emphasizes the widespread effect of Jesus' authority over sickness and the demons (see Matt 11:23, "the miracles that were performed in you"). It is particularly focused on his refusal to allow the demons to speak **because they knew who he was** rather than on the numbers. Mark has already established Jesus' identity through a demon's witness. But here the command to silence is more likely due to Jesus' reticence for this knowledge to be widespread lest it be misunderstood (see 8:28).

■**35-37** At the end of this day in Capernaum, a new step is taken in Jesus' mission. Mark again uses a double statement: *Before sunrise the next morning* Jesus **went off to a solitary place, where he prayed.** Mark does not tell us what Jesus prayed. Literarily, this statement parallels his description of the prayer in Gethsemane (14:32-42). This might suggest that both concern the Father's will.

A clue may come in the next verse: **Simon and his companions** find Jesus and tell him that crowds are still looking for him. There is great potential for him to take a different path, if he comes back to Simon's house.

■**38-39** Jesus' response is clear.

His activity of proclaiming is not to be confined to Capernaum. He will not make his headquarters in Simon's home and wait for the people to come to him. He will go out to them, but he leads his followers to perceive the scope of his mission gradually. He asks them simply to go out with him to the neighboring market-towns, for that is why he has left Simon's house. (Collins 2007, 177)

The NRSV translates *eis touto gar exēlthon* (**That is why I have come**) "for that is what I came out to do." This gives a better sense of the two-level response: "that is why I left Capernaum this morning" and "that is my whole mission." The mission is not local—at this point it is **throughout Galilee, preaching in their synagogues and driving out demons.** But it will expand beyond Jewish territory. Interestingly, healing is not mentioned, although the next episode is a healing story.

3. The Cleansed Leper (1:40-45)

BEHIND THE TEXT

Leprosy in the Scriptures refers to a wide range of scaly skin diseases. This may include what we call leprosy today (Hansen's disease). All of these rendered their sufferers ritually unclean. Leviticus 13 had extensive regulations for determining whether the condition was likely to be temporarily contagious with recovery expected, or the virtually incurable (until recent times) Hansen's disease. Leviticus 14 provided the ordinances and offerings for purification of those deemed to be unclean and put outside the camp.

This story implies that the sufferer has a serious form of the disease, has been unclean for some time, and is therefore isolated from normal society. "Sufferers were regarded as, in effect, corpses, and physical contact with them produced the same sort of defilement as touching dead bodies (see Num 12:12 and especially Lev 13:45-46)" (Marcus 2000, 208).

Mark gives no particular location for this story. Most scholars conclude that he brought it to this setting. If so, then a literary reason could well be the transition from the wide acclamation of the Capernaum day to the increased attention from the religious authorities.

Jesus has already healed on the Sabbath. But the respect for the Sabbath given by the people is mirrored in Jesus' order to the cleansed leper to show himself to the priest. We get a hint of the controversy that will deepen in the next stories. The actions of Jesus show an interesting contrast between strict Torah observance (the priest is to pronounce the healed leper clean) and nonobservance (Jesus touches the leper, thereby rendering himself unclean according to Torah).

IN THE TEXT

■ **40** There are a number of aspects of this story that challenge the Levitical codes. This **man with leprosy came to him;** he should not even approach other people. That he **begged him on his knees** suggests that he is also touching Jesus. France (2002, 117) rightly notes that Mark's series of participles (*parakalōn, gonypetōn, legōn*) heightens the urgency of the leper's plea: **If you are willing, you can make** [*dynasai*] **me clean.** Mark can use *dynamai* to refer to the humanly impossible (see 10:27). This nuance seems to be the nuance here. The leper was confident that Jesus could do the impossible and make him clean. Perhaps, the good news had reached this outcast. He asked to be made clean—not for healing. Being clean would bring him reintegration into society. But, of course, that would presuppose being healed.

■ **41-42** Jesus is **filled with compassion** (*splanchnistheis*). A variant reading here is *orgistheis*, **filled with anger.** Most translators follow the majority reading **compassion.** But several scholars prefer "filled with anger." It is the more difficult to explain as an error arising from "filled with compassion" than the opposite. But what does Mark mean? Some have suggested that Jesus is angry due to the implication of doubt behind *ean theleis*, **if you are willing.** Others think Jesus is annoyed that the man touched him, rendering him unclean.

Neither suggestion is satisfactory. More likely Jesus was angry with the physical and social effects of this disease. His compassion was evident in his willingness to cleanse and heal—he **touched the man** and stated, **I am willing. . . . Be clean!** Again the simplicity and the authority of Jesus are noted.

There is no hint that Jesus becomes unclean by touching the leper. In each of his encounters—unclean spirit, disease, leper—according to the Law, contact would have incurred one degree of impurity or another. But the Holy One transforms the impure and the unclean into the pure and the clean.

This is exactly what happens here: **Immediately** [the word here implies this was not a gradual recovery] **the leprosy left him.** Clearly, the man **was cured,** but Mark's point was that the leper was "made clean" (NRSV; *ekatharisthē*), a transformation that would enable him to rejoin society.

■ **43-44** It is, therefore, surprising that Jesus immediately sent him away (*exebalen*—the word used of exorcisms) **with a strong warning.** He told him to "say nothing to anyone" (NRSV; → 1:29-45 sidebar, "The Messianic Secret in Mark"). Guelich's (1989, 75-76) suggestion that the background to the command arises from possible exorcism formulae in Mark's source offers no assistance.

Much more helpful is Hooker's two-level approach (1991, 81; followed by Collins 2007, 179). On the one hand, the command stresses the urgency of going directly to the priest. On the second level, it fits in with the view that telling this story would only lead to incomprehension. Thus, it is part of the messianic secret.

The cleansed leper is to **offer the sacrifices that Moses commanded for your cleansing.** The usual significance of the **testimony to them** would be to signify to the priests and people that the person has been deemed to be clean, but the antecedent is ambiguous. Since this phrase may be translated as ***testimony against them*** (see 6:11; 13:9), it might have hints of antagonism. At the readers' level, however, it could have the implication of the witness to the people concerning Jesus and his authority to cleanse, an authority authenticated by the priests.

■ **45** We are not told whether the man eventually went to the priests. Most translations assume that he was unable to keep his cleansing secret and instead begins to proclaim the word (*kēryssein . . . ton logon*). Grammatically, **he** could apply to Jesus. But that creates some difficulty with the following statement that because of this Jesus **could no longer enter** a city (*polis*) but stayed in rural areas. That did not stem the flow of people who **still came to him from everywhere.**

This section ends the first chapter, in which Mark sets out his major ideas about Jesus. He is announcing and effecting the kingdom of God. Already at this stage, readers know that Jesus is more than one of the prophets. And we can observe another theme—those with eyes to see and ears to hear now can see who Jesus is. He is the Messiah, Son of God, beloved Son and servant, and the Holy One in the midst of the people. He has a core of disciples gathered around him. Opposition is looming—already it is seen in the demonic response to Jesus' presence and his healings and exorcism.

79

III. MISSION, CONFLICT, AND REJECTION: MARK 2:1—6:6A

The opening two sections in the Gospel set out the essentials of Jesus' identity and mission. God's good news in Jesus has already been challenged, however. If opposition from Satan in the wilderness to Jesus was not directly stated (1:12-13), the first demonic confrontation makes explicit the problem facing Israel. And it is more than Roman occupation. The demons symbolize the larger conflict of good and evil that Jesus has come to engage.

The seeds of Jesus' conflict with the religious establishment are sown early. People notice how starkly the scribes' teaching contrasts with Jesus' authoritative teaching. This assessment of Jesus seems to have spread. And if the leper actually does not go to the priest, and instead declares that he has been made clean outside the prescribed system, the issue is only compounded.

This next major section has two parts. The first part consists of five controversy stories (2:1—3:6a). These indicate how the progressive anxiety of the religious authorities concerning Jesus gradually became open hostility. The section is remarkable for its sense of movement. Initially, the scribes are seated around Jesus (2:6). By the end (3:6), the Pharisees have gone out and are conspiring with the Herodians on how to kill Jesus. The tone of the debate hardens. The scribes debate the proper way to keep the Sabbath holy with Jesus, who challenges their halakah (oral law). The irony is unmistakable: The people of the leading holiness movement, the Pharisees, move away from the Holy One of God and align themselves with the secular forces against Jesus.

81

In the second part (3:6*b*—6:6*a*), opposition arises from Jesus' own people. His family is concerned for his sanity. By 3:22, scribes from Jerusalem accuse Jesus of working with Beelzebub. His family is situated outside the inner circle (3:31-32). By 6:1-6*a*, he meets with almost complete indifference from the Nazarenes in his hometown.

But Jesus' mission continues. Earlier Mark noted that Jesus was traveling throughout Galilee, "preaching in their synagogues" (1:39). This section concludes with Jesus traveling about "teaching [*didaskōn*] from village to village" (6:6*b*). Each episode further defines Jesus and his mission.

At the same time, there is also movement toward Jesus. He gathers around him many disciples who are of the wrong sort, according to the Pharisees (2:15-17). He calls the Twelve to be with him, on his mission and acting on his authority (3:13-15). Gradually it becomes clear that proximity to Jesus and joining him in doing the will of God is crucial (3:33-35). The family of God is redefined outside of blood lines: those who do the will of God are the brothers and sisters.

It is not too surprising, then, when Jesus' first parable confirms the hardness of heart of those who are outside (4:10-12). The parables of the kingdom follow, showing the kingdom's ultimate triumph despite obscure beginnings. He teaches the disciples in private. But they prove to be almost as dull as the religious authorities: they find themselves terrified during a storm and puzzled by Jesus, asking the question, "Who is this?"

The answer to that question is repeated in the second exorcism story. This takes place outside Jewish territory. Jesus' reputation has reached there as well: he is the Son of the Most High God. The healing of Jairus' daughter and that of the woman with an issue of blood are set just before Jesus goes to Nazareth where the faith of Jairus and the woman stand in stark contrast to the unbelief of the Nazareth crowd.

A. The Paralytic (2:1-12)

BEHIND THE TEXT

Extensive archaeological excavation has been done on the traditional site of Peter's house in Capernaum. Typical houses in Capernaum during this period likely consisted of small roofed rooms around a large courtyard, suggesting that more than one family lived together in rooms around the same courtyard. In general this supports the picture in Mark that this house would have space for people to gather at the door as well as being home to others besides Peter.

The passage alerts us to a key debate between Jesus and the Pharisees concerning the grounds on which God forgives sins and Jesus welcomes sinners. Most 2TP Jews would know about the established means of atonement for sin through the God-given sacrificial system in Torah (see the extensive discussion of the "sin offering"—Heb.: *ht't* in Lev 4 and 5). The temple and priests are a central part of this system. Instances in which people ask God to forgive sins occur in Scripture (see Exod 32:32; Num 14:19; Job 42:10). Because they considered the temple to be hopelessly corrupt, the Qumran community withdrew from society and the temple system. They saw themselves as living lives that made atonement for sin (1QS 8:6, 10; 9:4). One reason for doing so was to offer atonement for the sins of the people. Later Christian readers would note John 20:19-23.

The forgiveness of sins as distinct from pronouncement of sins forgiven is another matter. In one Qumran text (4Q242) a Jewish diviner may forgive the sin of King Nabonidus (Marcus 2000, 217), but that seems to be unusual. Hence, this statement in Mark is shocking to the scribes but entirely consistent with Mark's emerging portrait of Jesus as the One who speaks God's word, acts as God acts, and is identified as the Holy One of God.

IN THE TEXT

■ **1-2** After the healing of the leper and a period outside the cities, Jesus returns to Capernaum. This sets the stage for the next few episodes that seem to occur in and around Capernaum. The tightness of the time in 1:21-39 is resumed. Despite the summary statement in the previous story in which Jesus is prevented from going into the cities, Mark reports his return only a few days later. Capernaum seems to continue to be the base from which Jesus' mission work occurs: **the people heard that he had come home** (*en oikōi*).

There is nothing to tell us whose house this is—it could have been Jesus', although it is likely Peter's. Jesus' reputation is obviously spreading rapidly. This episode has people gathered at the door after presumably filling the room. Jesus continued to preach the word to them (*elalei . . . ton logon*, "speak the word" [NRSV]). The NIV translation **preached** is curious, given that the word usually translated "preach" was rendered as "talk freely" in 1:45.

The word seems to be Mark's term describing the good news of the kingdom, the word of the Lord Jesus announces and that the leper spreads. Its most concentrated use in Mark is in Jesus' explanation of the parable of the sower in 4:14-20. This is followed by a general summary of Jesus' use of parables to the disciples (4:33).

■ **3-5** The arrival at the door of four men **bringing to him a paralytic** poses a problem. Jesus is teaching with people crowded into the small room and no one wants to move. The ingenuity of these men is remarkable and well known.

They gain access to the roof probably via a wooden ladder or an outside staircase. This is itself quite a feat while carrying a paralyzed man on a stretcher. Then they dig a hole in the roof and lower the man to the floor in front of Jesus. The roof would likely have been constructed of wooden beams covered with beaten mud mixed with reeds or straw. Removal would have been relatively easy, but scarcely inconspicuous.

The picture is vivid; the spectacle amazing, given the great potential for accident and embarrassment. Jesus **saw** [*idōn*, perhaps with the implication of spiritual insight—see 4:12] **their faith.** Their disruptive intrusion is praised. We are not told whether it was the faith of the paralytic or his bearers. The point is not their faith but Jesus as the object of their faith. "Faith breaks through barriers to bring a person to Jesus" (Donahue and Harrington 2002, 99).

Faith in Mark

The noun "faith" (*pistis*) and the verb "to believe" (*pisteuein*) occur in 1:15; 2:5; 4:40; 5:34; 5:36; 9:23; 9:24; 9:42; 10:52; 11:22-24; 15:32. Unbelief occurs in 6:6; unbelief and faithless generation in 9:19.

The first instance is Jesus' summary call to believe the good news of the kingdom. Other instances appear in healing stories, in which the people trust or hope in the power and authority of Jesus to heal. Some, like 9:42, have the implication of loyalty or fidelity to Jesus, implying some christological focus.

Guelich believes the meaning in Mark goes further, especially in the miracle stories, because "it always involves actions that transcend human obstacles or limitations and cross social boundaries. . . . Faith denotes an attitude expressed in conduct" (Guelich 1989, 85).

Thus for Mark, "faith is not so much a precondition for healing (see 1:34; 6:5-6), but rather it demonstrates the willingness of suffering people to break through physical and social boundaries in order to approach Jesus" (Donahue and Harrington 2002, 98). Thus the excluded and the needy dare to exercise their belief that the good news of God is for them as well.

Jesus **said to the paralytic, "Son, your sins are forgiven."** This is completely surprising. Why does Jesus announce the forgiveness of sins? The biblical understanding of sin is more related to what should not happen than to the modern notion of individual or subjective sin, which helps explain the link between sin and illness: "both disease and sin mar God's creation" (Donahue and Harrington 2002, 94-95). Belief in a connection between illness and sin was widespread in antiquity. By extending forgiveness to the paralyzed man, Jesus perceived that for this man forgiveness would cure his paralysis (Hooker 1991, 86).

The concept of psychosomatic illness is well known. This connection may be the issue here. But other healing stories do not draw this link. On the contrary, Scripture deliberately puts an end to this popular notion of an automatic cause-and-effect between sin and illness (see John 9:2-3).

Apart from the unexpectedness of this response, the meaning is somewhat unclear. **Are forgiven** is the passive *aphientai*. Jesus did not directly forgive the man. He pronounces that God has forgiven him his sins. This might be compared to the priestly absolution mentioned in Lev 4:20. In that case, Jesus gives assurance to the man and acts as a priest.

If at least some of the scribes are members of priestly and Levitical orders, as seems likely (see Marcus 2000, 519-24), the tension is increased: this nonpriestly person usurps a priestly function. But even priestly assurance only followed from the appropriate cleansing rituals. It is even more concerning if Jesus merely forgives the sins of the man, usurping God's prerogatives.

■ **6-7** Those who were **teachers of the law** are in no doubt: Jesus is **blaspheming**! **Who can forgive sins but God alone** [*heis ho theos*, **the one God**]? Jesus challenges God's authority, perhaps even the Shema (see Marcus 2000, 222). Some scholars comment on the artificiality of the scribes being on the scene. But for Mark they are an essential part of his story. They are **sitting there** around Jesus as part of the group who is listening to the word. Mark has those who know the Scriptures better than anyone else at the center. They have every opportunity to hear the good news and confirm God's new thing.

But the scribes are not impressed by Jesus (*ti houtos* = **why does this fellow?**). When they hear his pronouncement that the man's sins are forgiven, they are outraged. As far as the scribes are concerned, this is a blasphemous statement. A mere human is arrogating to himself the sole prerogative of God.

■ **8** The inner spiritual perceptiveness of Jesus continues: he knows instantly (*euthys*) exactly **what they were thinking in their hearts**. Mark may be echoing an OT theme in which God is the One who knows the heart (see Guelich 1989, 88). If so, this gives further support for the view that Mark is deliberately painting Jesus in divine hues.

■ **9** Jesus' question to the scribes is as intriguing as the answer is puzzling: **Which is easier: to say to the paralytic, "Your sins are forgiven," or to say, "Get up, take your mat and walk"**? On the one hand, it could be argued that the forgiveness of sins is the harder, since that is God's prerogative only. On the other, it is easier *to say* "Your sins are forgiven" because there is no way to prove that this is so. Thus, by walking, the paralytic demonstrates that his sins are forgiven—the easier (forgiving his sins) confirmed by the harder (healing his paralysis). "Since the scribes clearly regard Jesus as having used empty words, he will now demonstrate that for him, as for God, to speak is to act" (Hooker 1991, 87). From the scribes' perspective, the question, **Which is easier . . . ?** is unanswerable (see 11:29-33).

■ **10** This verse is full of theological significance for Mark. First, Marcus suggests that the phrase **that you may know** (*hina eidēte*) may be an echo of God's word of judgment through Moses to Pharaoh (Exod 8:6, 10; esp. 9:14). "If

Mark is aware of these echoes of Exodus, it is significant that he has transformed divine oracles against the ancient, archetypical Gentile enemy of Israel into a prophetic judgment against Israel's own religious leaders" (Marcus 2000, 218).

Second, this healing is to show that **the Son of Man has authority on earth to forgive sins.** The complexity of the Son of Man (*ho huios tou anthrōpou*) sayings in the Gospels is well known. Here our questions are simply, how would the scribes and other auditors in the scene hear this phrase? (The awkward Greek suggests a preservation of an Aramaic phrase.) And then, how would Mark's readers hear it?

At the basic level, the phrase could be heard as another way of saying "someone like me" or "a person like me" rather than "I." Or it could mean someone else, perhaps humanity in general (see Matt 9:8). The scribes, well-schooled in Scripture, might well hear an echo of Dan 7:13-14. There, in a celestial temple, the one like a Son of Man comes before the Ancient of Days and receives dominion and authority. But this occurs only after he has suffered and been oppressed under the beasts from the sea (Dan 7:1-12).

The phrase **on earth** implies that the authority granted in the celestial temple to the Son of Man is now being exercised on earth. If so, it would confirm their view that Jesus is blaspheming because he is claiming that his authority is given directly from God. It could also alarm them if they were to perceive that by opposing the Son of Man, they exercised the same opposition as the pagan rulers against the people of God, but that could be too subtle even for the sophisticated scribes.

The second hearers, Mark's Christian audience, would be in no doubt: Jesus has authority to forgive sins, not just to pronounce sins forgiven. Even if the phrase is not a messianic title in the 2TP, it is filled with content by the Markan Jesus. Mark presents Jesus as the Son of Man who suffers, is vindicated, and exercises authority. Furthermore, he embodies in himself the vindication of the holy ones of the Most High (see Dan 7:22-27).

■ **11-12** The Greek syntax of these verses is difficult, but the meaning is clear enough. **Get up** is again (→ Mark 1:31) the same term used for resurrection. The three commands—**get up, take your mat and go home**—are followed exactly. The man got up and immediately walked out **in full view of them all.** The result is that all are **amazed . . . and . . . praised** [*doxazein*] **God.** Mark does not distinguish the scribes from the people, since all are **amazed.** Some scholars point to this as an indication that Mark has put two separate stories together (see Guelich 1989, 94). But it is conceivable that the scribes are also amazed and do glorify God. Although opposition has been mounted, it is not yet implacable. Dialogue is still happening, but the movement away from Jesus is soon to occur. The authority of Jesus as Son of Man is explicitly derived from God, to whom the people give glory. Something new is happening: **We have never seen anything like this!**

B. Controversy and Conflict (2:13—3:12)

BEHIND THE TEXT

The next two stories, the call of Levi and the meal in his house, have been crafted into a four-part scene. Jesus is again beside the lake, recalling 1:16. He is followed by a large crowd, not necessarily those from the previous episode since these people come to him. Characteristically, Jesus begins to teach them. Then he sees Levi and invites him to follow.

So far, the story is similar to the earlier call of the four (1:16-20). But Levi is a tax collector. Tax collectors—whether royal appointees, supervisory officials (such as Zacchaeus), or toll collectors—were in a despised occupation (but see Neale 1991, 75). This was perhaps because they were in the service of the Romans. But more likely, it was due to their reputation for dishonesty.

Levi was likely a toll collector for Antipas, the Jewish client king of Galilee. He apparently collected customs duty, perhaps on the main road between Damascus and Egypt that passed through Capernaum during this period. Thus, the fifth named person Jesus calls is not a middle-class fisherman, but a tax collector—marginalized from society.

The problem of Levi's identity is notorious. He is not mentioned again in Mark (the list of the Twelve in 3:18 does not include him, although there is a *Iakōbos* who is the son of Alphaeus). The lists in the other Gospels are unhelpful for sorting this problem—indeed, all have some variation in names, suggesting that the group of twelve was more significant than the individual members, most of whom do not feature in the subsequent story. The parallel story in Luke also calls this person Levi; the Matthean parallel (9:9) has Matthew. Both Mark and Matthew have a "Matthew" in the list of the twelve. Matthew calls him Matthew the tax collector. He also has a James the son of Alphaeus; Mark just names a Matthew.

Several solutions have been proposed to this problem, including the possibility that the names are just not remembered accurately. A simple answer would be that Levi and Matthew were alternative names for the same person, but this is unlikely. Bauckham proposes that Matthew has simply taken Mark's story of Levi and applied Matthew's name to it (see Bauckham 2006, 108-12). Since Mark is very concerned that the call to discipleship extends to all (see 8:34), Hooker makes the intriguing suggestion that Mark may well be including "someone who was called to be a disciple but was *not* one of the Twelve" (1991, 94).

The conflict that arises in this section initially has to do with Jesus' dining companions. Some scholars have explained the importance of meals with reference to Greco-Roman *symposia*. But a more appropriate background occurs in Judaism itself. Evidence from the 2TP shows just how important meals were as occasions when boundaries were drawn. The elaborate strictness and protocol practiced at Qumran takes this boundary-setting agenda extremely seriously. "Dining created an intimate setting in which one nurtured friendship with the right kind of people, eating the right kind of food. . . . [And] unclean people and objects constantly threatened to corrupt God's holy, elect nation and individuals within it[;] . . . we may think of ritual impurity as contagious" (Blomberg 2005, 93).

The problem is, therefore, that Jesus is eating with tax collectors and sinners. The term "sinners" is not the equivalent of the impure, nor is it limited to prostitutes. It is more likely a collective term of "those who represent a whole complex of behaviour that is opposed to God and his ways" (Neale 1991, 95). Thus the phrase "tax collectors and sinners" probably means that the people concerned were considered wicked or immoral (Blomberg 2005, 23) and alienated from God. Of course, as sinners they were also impure and their impurity, it was thought, would be contagious to this holy person.

So why could Jesus countenance such a risk? He "defies the conventions of his world by his intimate association with a group of people deemed traitorous and corrupt in his society. Still, he does not condone their sinful lifestyles but calls them to repentance, transformation and discipleship" (Blomberg 2005, 102). Or, in Jesus' words, **I have not come to call the righteous, but sinners** (2:17).

IN THE TEXT

1. Tax Collectors and Other Sinners (2:13-17)

■ **13-14** The transition from the house to the lakeshore draws us back to the call of the first disciples. Jesus is **once again . . . beside the lake.** The implied time break suggests that this **large crowd** is not identical to those in the house. Rather, the flow of the story suggests that these **came to him** because of the universal acclaim that has been following him: "new teaching" (1:27). In effect, they were saying they had never seen anything like this before. The crowd (*pas ho ochlos*) is part of the story—they are those that hear him gladly (see 12:37). So **he began to teach them.**

The call of Levi follows the pattern of the earlier call. Jesus **saw Levi** at his work as a toll collector. Levi's presence in the group of followers is not defiling: Mark has just told us that the Son of Man has authority to forgive sins. Once again, no clue about any previous meeting is given, although the narrative sequence would tell us that it would have been hard for Levi to avoid knowing about Jesus. The call **Follow me** becomes almost synonymous with a call to discipleship. The response of Levi is as with the first four: **Levi got up and followed him,** but after the next story, he disappears completely from Mark's view.

■ **15-17** The next part of the story shifts quickly from the lakeside to his house (*tēi oikiai autou*). Mark is not clear about whose house this is—Levi's or the house in 2:1. Luke 5:29 assumes it is Levi's. If so, it explains why this story is placed here. The fact that Jesus is eating here is interesting because of the highly symbolic character of meals.

While (*kai ginetai*) may signal a period of time that has passed since Levi responded to the call. Mark does not say how long, but it requires enough time for **many tax collectors and "sinners"** to be welcomed in his presence, and that Jesus already has **many who followed him. Jesus was having dinner** (*katakeistai*). ***Reclining at table*** gives a sense of the intimacy and importance of the meal (see Mark 14:3).

The meal context is crucial for the reasons noted above. If this is Levi's house, the presence of Jesus is significant. The conventional views of table fellowship protected the purity that boundaries ensured. On that view, if Jesus is a holy person, he is at risk.

But this is not a private meal with Levi: **many tax collectors and "sinners"** are there. Jesus is continuing to attract the impure and welcomes the outcasts right into an intimate relationship with him and the rest of his followers. Mark's repetitive wording emphasizes the welcome and the welcomed.

Mark's sequence of stories is important here. In the healing of the leper, Jesus removes impurity; in the healing of the paralytic, Jesus forgives sins. Now, in this story, he is in intimate fellowship with tax collectors and sinners. Thus, instead of excluding sinners from his followers, the One who has authority to cleanse impurity and forgive sins welcomes them, and does so outside of the prescribed system. By their response to him they signal that they have repented and believe the good news, a point Mark makes clear later in this section.

Luke turns this story into a great banquet, an image that conjures up the messianic feast (see Isa 25:6-9). While Mark does not make this explicit, the implication is present in the following debate. This also is part of the new teaching—that God is creating a new people by bringing those on the fringes into the circle of Jesus' fellowship.

The Pharisees

For casual Gospel readers, the Pharisees are by far the best-known Jewish group in the Gospels even if the picture is limited. They probably arose sometime during the Maccabean revolt and were very influential in the Hasmonean period (164-63 B.C.). Although after 63 B.C. they no longer exercised direct political power, their influence was significant. Some may have favored active violent revolutionary opposition to Roman rule (see Wright 1992, 190-92). Others concentrated on the study of Torah. After A.D. 70, the Pharisaic tradition became essentially mainstream Judaism.

The Pharisees were an important holiness movement within 2TJ. Torah obedience was essential. Indeed, they seemed to live according to the standards of purity required of priests. If God's people were called to be a kingdom of *priests*, then the purity rules for temple service should be expanded to include the whole of Israel and the whole land.

Three key areas were important: first, the food rules laid down for priests were extended to the lay Pharisaic community. The preparation of the food, as well as their meal companions, were carefully controlled to avoid impurity. Hence, they were highly critical of Jesus' own meal practices.

Strict Sabbath observance was another key point. The Sabbath was to be kept holy, wholly free from work. But what was "work"? The answer to that question developed into a series of prescriptions and prohibitions. This was another area of controversy with Jesus, whose Sabbath observance, they thought, was at best lax and at worst blasphemous. Tithing, a third major issue, does not feature prominently in their conflict with the Markan Jesus.

Holiness, they believed, was best maintained by separation. Since God is holy and separated from all that defiles, they too must be separate. Some holiness groups separated *from* society (the Qumran community). But the Pharisees advocated separation *within* society. "In the face of social, political and cultural pollution in society as a whole, they concentrated on personal purity and cleanness in such a way as to maintain an area of personal purity—an island of purity in a sea of pollution" (Brower 2005, 32; see Wright 1992, 181-203).

Jesus had his most sustained and serious clashes with the Pharisees. Some of these are reflected in the Gospels. But it is important to note that there was never any debate over whether holiness was essential. It was. The disagreements were over the means and the meaning of holiness.

Jesus' breach of convention is of great concern to the scribes who were Pharisees. The Synoptic Gospels portray the Pharisees as the major antagonists of Jesus; they occupy this role in the first part of Mark. They, like Jesus and John, are seeking the holiness of the people of God. Since a key element for them is the strict adherence to the food rules of the Torah, they treated mealtimes as boundary-marking occasions. In their view, holy persons would keep themselves pure from potential impurity and particularly so at mealtime. This gives rise to their question, **Why does he eat with tax collectors and "sinners"?**

The "scribes of the Pharisees" (v 16 NRSV) are interpreters of the Torah who have adopted the Pharisaic view of holiness. They disagree with Jesus' interpretation of Torah; he seems habitually to eat with the outcasts, welcoming them into his fellowship. In contrast to the preceding story, the scribes are no longer seated around Jesus. Instead, they distance themselves from him, speaking to him through intermediaries—his disciples.

Jesus' response explains the radical character of his mission and the big purposes of God. The hoped-for re-creation of Israel promised by Isaiah is being enacted in these meals. Announced by John and Jesus and coming into effect with the good news of God, the meals are signs of the ingathering of God's people. The outcasts represent an inclusive and reconfigured Israel surrounding Jesus, the Holy One of God. They follow him on the mission of God. These newly gathered people include those formerly excluded—the wicked of society who are transformed by the presence and call of the Holy One. As Jesus explains: After all, **it is not the healthy who need a doctor, but the sick.**

Jesus is self-conscious about what he is doing. He is not naively entering into compromising situations that would deny the need of those he calls or adversely affect his holiness. On the contrary, his openness to outcasts is a sign of the mission of God: **I have not come to call the righteous**—those already following the ways of God. He reaches out to **sinners**—those alienated from God and his purposes. "Holiness does not need a defence from the contagion of evil. Instead holiness itself is contagious. Jesus does not acquire impurity. He touches the unclean; . . . he shares meals with sinners. And by doing so, he imparts cleanness and wholeness" (Brower 2007a, 72; see Neyrey 1986, 112).

2. The Old and the New (2:18-22)

BEHIND THE TEXT

Questions about fasting are not new. The prophets offer scathing critiques of fasting and public piety that is not rooted in justice (see esp. Isa 58:3-6; Zech 7:1-14). In addition to the compulsory fast on the Day of Atonement, during the 2TP there was "widespread approval of voluntary fasting as a mark of religious devotion" (Muddiman 1992, 774). A similar pattern is followed in the early church without being "formalized in its own discipline" (Muddiman 1992, 775).

Fasting is also connected with mourning. The Markan form of Jesus' response curiously forbids fasting until the mourning fast at his death. *Psalms of Solomon* 3:8 pictures the righteous one making expiation for (the sins) of ignorance by fasting. This Pharisaic text supports the practice of the Pharisees and John (see Collins 2007, 198).

IN THE TEXT

■ **18-20** This is the first indication in Mark that John has disciples. One can flesh out the picture by reference to the other Gospels; but like so much else in Mark, this is stated without explanation. It is not surprising that **John's disciples and the Pharisees were fasting.** They are both part of movements concerned with the renewal of Israel and for them, fasting may have been

91

penitential. But **some people** wondered why Jesus' disciples were not doing the same, since they too are part of a renewal movement. **Jesus answered** with a metaphor that says two things.

First, weddings are feasts, not fasts. The announcement of the good news of God should be a time of rejoicing, not mourning or penitence. Jesus' words and deeds are a time to glorify God (v 14). Second, and more importantly, **the guests of the bridegroom** [perhaps *groomsmen*] . . . **cannot** fast while **the bridegroom** remains **with them.** This draws attention to Jesus as the groom, echoing the metaphor of God's marriage to Israel in Hosea and especially Isa 62:5*b:* "as a bridegroom rejoices over his bride, so will your God rejoice over you" (so Collins 2007, 199).

But there is also an ominous note: **the time will come when the bridegroom will be taken from them.** This hints at the fate of Jesus, when his followers will hold a mourning fast. It is a reminder that opposition to him is already present and will lead to his death: **on that day they will fast.** Mark's use of "days" (*hēmerai*) and "on that day" (*en ekeinai tēi hēmerai*) place Jesus' death in the context of the fulfillment of time announced in 1:14-15.

■ **21-22** This is a new day that cannot be contained by the old system. John, a transitional figure, is part of the old system, as are the Pharisees. Common sense dictates that **No one sews a patch of unshrunk cloth on an old garment.** The problem is that the unshrunk **new piece will pull away from the old, making the tear worse.** Mark's phrase **the new from the old** (*to kainon tou palaiou*) invites readers to make the application: Jesus' authoritative new teaching cannot simply be grafted onto the old interpretation of Scripture. It announces God's new arrangements in light of what he is doing in Christ.

To that is added the potent metaphor of new wine in old wineskins. The continuation of the fermentation process will burst the old, hardened leather. The new wine of the kingdom requires a fresh and flexible way of being the people of God and hearing the word of God. Both metaphors express concern about the old garment and the old wineskins. But both imply that neither the teaching of the scribes nor the piety and boundary markers of the Pharisees can simply add on the new message of the kingdom Jesus teaches.

3. Lord of the Sabbath (2:23-28)

BEHIND THE TEXT

Sabbath observance was probably a live issue in the post-Easter church. How should Gentile and Jewish Christians treat the Sabbath? The next two stories about Jesus may well have addressed this issue. But the primary issue again has to do with Jesus' identity, his relationship to Torah, and the authority of his teaching. Two questions are of interest:

First, what are the Pharisees doing in the grainfield on a Sabbath day? The scene appears to be artificial, since "it seems improbable that the Pharisees would be shadowing Jesus and his followers in Galilean wheatfields" (Donahue and Harrington 2002, 112). Mark, however, is not particularly interested in chronological connections. Theological concerns dominate his narrative throughout. Hence, this story has more to do with the theological location of the Pharisees vis-à-vis Jesus than their physical location. Within this chapter significant movement has taken place. From being around Jesus, to querying his eating companions, and now to checking on his Sabbath observance—the keeping of Torah itself—an underlying sense of growing distance is present.

Second, careful readers will note that details of the story Jesus tells are at variance with 1 Sam 21:1-6. First, the actual actions of David are different from Jesus'. David's companions are hungry; Mark makes no such claim for Jesus' disciples. David feeds his companions; Jesus doesn't. David's deed is not done on the Sabbath so far as we are told in 1 Samuel. Second, the priest in Nob is Abimelech, father of Abiathar, not Abiathar.

Explanations for this discrepancy range from reading the text *epi Abiathar* as **in the lifetime of Abiathar,** or noting the confusion in the OT parallel accounts where Abimelech is son of Abiathar in 2 Sam 8:17 and 1 Chr 24:6, to a Greek mistranslation of the Aramaic "in the days of Abiathar" (see France 2002, 145-46, esp. n. 52). Marcus thinks this could be a deliberate generalization on Mark's part to evoke the wider "holy war" context of 1 Sam 15 (2000, 242). None of these solutions is particularly helpful.

In fact, the inexactness of detail indicates that the point of the story lies elsewhere. The name of the priest is clearly incidental to the story, so nothing is at stake except a particularly modernistic or Islamic view of Scripture that is troubled over such discrepancies. Perhaps the simplest solution is that Mark shares the confusion of his sources (see France 2002, 146).

Sabbath Observance

Along with circumcision and food rules, Sabbath observance, as a perpetual sign of the covenant, was a key identity marker of Judaism in this period (Exod 31:14-17). The command to keep the Sabbath holy was fulfilled by resting from labor. All work was excluded (Exod 20:8-11). But what is "work"? Several OT texts give an indication of forbidden activities (Exod 16:22-30—collecting manna; 34:21—harvesting; 35:2-3—building a fire; Num 15:32-36—gathering wood, etc.). The written law (Torah) contained 613 commands—365 negative and 248 positive, according to the rabbis. But it did not definitively define work.

The development of oral law (halakah), Torah-based case law, upon these commandments was an attempt to address such questions. Although the oral law was not finally systematized and written down in the Mishnah until sometime after A.D. 200, discussions about how to keep the commandments were ongoing (see *Jub.* 50:6-13; CD 10:14—11:18, both predating the NT). One entire tractate of the Mishnah, *b. Šabbat,* is devoted to ways to protect the holiness of the Sabbath and enable holy people to avoid profaning it. Another (*b. ʿErubin*) is a rabbinic discussion of the ways of ameliorating the more onerous effects of the rules while maintaining Sabbath sanctity. Thirty-nine categories of prohibited work are defined (see *b. Šabb.* 7:2), the first six connected to harvesting and fields.

Thus, debate over Sabbath observance between Jesus and the Pharisees is to be expected, since both are concerned with holiness. Jesus is considered too lax in his practice by the Pharisees. Ironically, the Pharisees themselves may have been criticized for the same thing in the Dead Sea Scrolls (see Collins 2007, 202).

IN THE TEXT

■ **23-24** The simple statement, **one Sabbath Jesus was going through the grainfields,** obscures Mark's Greek *kai egeneto.* This echoes the language of scriptural narrative in the LXX (see Marcus 2000, 244). The KJV translates "and it came to pass," a phrase that captures Mark's gravitas. This signals a new story significantly reminding us of the escalating disclosure of Jesus on the one hand, and the mounting opposition on the other.

That the disciples are *making their way through the field* functions at two levels. Walking through a wheat field requires pushing grain to the side by hand—as any farm child would know. But the idea of preparing the way for Jesus is not too farfetched on the deeper level of significance (see Marcus 2000, 239).

It is, however, the action of the disciples who **began to pick some heads of grain** that precipitates debate. While Deut 23:25 distinguishes "plucking" and "reaping," the later Mishnah provided extensive clarification on what was considered reaping and what was not, and therefore, what was acceptable to do on Sabbath while avoiding work. Plucking was a subset of reaping according to *Šabb.* 7:2. From the Pharisees' perspective, the disciples are reaping, thereby profaning the Sabbath.

■ **25-26** Instead of disputing the halakic point over whether plucking is really reaping, Jesus' response points to **David . . . and his companions.** The specifics of the story are irrelevant. But a number of motifs are possible within the story.

First, by his allusion, Jesus makes an unmistakable comparison between himself and David. Jesus as Son of David does not figure prominently in Mark, but is not rejected. It is inadequate for a full identity (see 10:46-52; 11:10; 12:35-37). In the 1 Samuel story, David assured the priests that his companions were ritually pure. But Mark makes no mention at all of ritual purity.

In Mark's telling, David breaks explicit Torah: **he entered the house of God and ate the consecrated bread,** the loaves of the presence (see Exod

25:30; Num 4:7). These twelve loaves were placed on the golden table each Sabbath near the holy of holies where only priests were permitted to enter. Because it was in such proximity to the holy of holies, it was the holiest part of the offering, **which is lawful only for priests to eat** at the end of each week (see Lev 24:5-9). Furthermore, David gave it to his companions who **were hungry and in need.**

Second, Jesus not only assumes the prerogatives of David but also defends his disciples because they are with him. Thus, Mark makes the point made explicit in the Matthean parallel—"one greater than the temple is here" (Matt 12:6). The emerging identity of Jesus as the Holy One of God whose touch cleanses the impure, whose word exorcises the unclean spirit, and whose presence transforms sinners into intimate table companions is greater than the holiness of the bread of the presence.

■ **27-28** The second response Jesus makes to the Pharisees builds upon the first. It has two parts: *The Sabbath was created for humans, not humans for the Sabbath.* The general nature of this comment suggests that Sabbath rest is part of God's good created order made for the good of humanity (Gen 2:2-3; see Deut 5:14-15). Thus, this general statement is another demonstration of the authoritative interpretation of the Torah by Jesus—he goes behind the halakah to the intention of the lawgiver in giving the Sabbath. Thereby he frees it for its intended good purposes for humanity. This statement is missing in the parallel versions in Matthew and Luke. Did they consider Mark's rendering too radical and sweeping (→ Mark 7:19) in their context of debate between Christian Jews and Christian Gentiles (so France 2002, 146)?

The second part moves from the anthropological to the christological level: **the Son of Man is Lord even of the Sabbath.** Some suggest that this is simply another way of saying that humankind has the right to decide what to do on the Sabbath. Others point to the personal lordship of Jesus over all things including the Sabbath.

But the most likely explanation is given by Hooker (1991, 105): "If the sabbath was made for man (i.e., Israel), then it is to be expected that the Son of man (representing obedient Israel, restored to dominion in the world), should be Lord even of the sabbath: the original purpose of God, set out in v 27, is fulfilled through him." This flows from the earlier "how much more" in the comparison with David and Jesus; here is its "how much more" with respect to Israel (see France 2002, 148). It forms part of the increasing revelation of who Jesus is and his re-creation of the holy people of God around him.

4. The Man with the Withered Hand (3:1-6)

BEHIND THE TEXT

There is no good reason for the break between chs 2 and 3, since this episode continues the debate about the way to keep the Sabbath holy. It also continues the disclosure of Jesus' identity. Mark allows readers to imagine that the two episodes occur on the same Sabbath.

The whole debate about healing on the Sabbath was, like the definition of work (→ 2:23-26), a live issue in 2TP Judaism. In this story, a man with a shriveled hand appears—so we know a healing will occur. But the focus is on the confrontation between Jesus and the Pharisees.

This story has something of a formulaic look: location, description, witnesses, question, action, healing, and consequence. In many ways it is similar to the first controversial healing story (2:1-12). It has a heightened sense of conflict, however, indicating the increasing disenchantment of the religious authorities with Jesus. This culminates in the conspiracy between the Pharisees and the Herodians (3:6).

IN THE TEXT

■ 1 Jesus' first confrontation on his mission occurs in a synagogue (1:22-28). There he exorcises a demon who gives the hearers, including the disciples, the first clue to Jesus' identity. This could be in the same Capernaum synagogue—Mark does say **the synagogue,** although some MSS omit the article. The story does not say anything about the disciples—**he went into the synagogue**—although we presume they were with Jesus.

This man has a **shriveled hand.** The condition may be due to some sort of paralysis or it may be a condition of "dryness" (see *zēran* in v 6) that would be treated by a traditional healer (see France 2002, 149 n. 1; Collins 2007, 206). Whatever the condition, it is scarcely an emergency that could not wait until the end of Sabbath. But it was a condition that would exclude the person from priestly service (see Lev 21:16-20).

The combination of this story with the previous one shows that Jesus' halakah is not expressed in a way to put a fence around the Torah, even as a means of ensuring its sanctity is not breached. Rather, Jesus' teaching focuses on what to do on Sabbath. Here, as elsewhere, Jesus gets back to the intention of the lawgiver, and thereby intensifies the direction of holiness. The healing of the man's hand is not wholly incidental, however, since it restored him to wholeness, perhaps even for service.

■ 2 The real point of this story in Mark's narrative now becomes clear: **Some of them were looking for a reason to accuse Jesus.** Mark does not tell us who they are, but the sequence suggests that these are Pharisees, perhaps even the same ones who were raising questions in the field. The NIV changes the word order from the Greek, giving a smoother sentence in English but changing its nuance slightly. In Greek, the sentence focuses upon whether Jesus' Sabbath practice followed their Pharisaic interpretation of Torah, leading to a potential accusation. The NIV emphasizes the hostility to Jesus that would be confirmed by a breach of Sabbath observance. The statement begins with *kai pareteroun*, a verb with negative overtones of lying in wait to catch him breaking the Law (see Luke 14:1; Acts 9:24).

The question is whether Jesus **would heal him on the Sabbath** or not. Later rabbinic halakahs "make it clear that it is the intention of healing and the performance of any activity for the purpose of healing that are forbidden on Sabbath. . . . anything done with the intention of healing is defined as work, even if the same activity done without the intention of healing would not be classified as work" (Collins 2007, 207). The only exception was for saving a life (see France 2002, 149).

The Pharisees intend **to accuse Jesus** of profaning the Sabbath, presumably to the local council or court. Herod Antipas probably placed local government in the hands of local priests, Levites, and elders (Collins 2007, 208).

Penalty for Breaking the Sabbath

According to Exod 31:14, "Anyone who desecrates it [the Sabbath] must be put to death; whoever does any work on that day must be cut off from his people." Whether these penalties were exacted during the late 2TP is doubtful. Collins draws attention to texts in *Jub.* 2:25-27 and 50:6-13, which call for death by stoning. But the *Damascus Document* (CD 12:3-6) imposes exclusion for seven years. According to the Mishnah (*Mak.* 3:15a), "cutting off" from the people may be fulfilled by a scourging of thirty-nine lashes. If this interpretation were current during the time of Jesus, it could suggest that the Pharisees "intended to accuse Jesus of deliberately profaning the Sabbath. In principle, the penalty for this offense was death. In practice, a scourging was the more likely outcome" (Collins 2007, 206-8).

■**3-4** There is no mention of faith in this story. In fact, the man does not seem to be seeking Jesus for healing at all. Rather, the focus is on Jesus and the Pharisees. And Jesus is aware of the impending confrontation. So he **said to the man . . . , "Stand up in front of everyone."** The scene is easy to imagine, with this man being asked to *stand in the middle* (*egeire eis to meson*). Jesus' provocative request indicates no interest in healing him quietly away from the crowd (see 5:37, 40).

The purpose of the confrontation is clear: How does Jesus understand keeping the Sabbath holy? He has already declared that the Son of Man is Lord of the Sabbath. Jesus does not shy away from confrontation, addressing his antagonists specifically on a point of Torah interpretation. He uses language that frames rabbinic-style debate: **Which is lawful on the Sabbath: to do good or to do evil?** The question is deliberately provocative. All Jews would agree that obedience to Torah is good. So Sabbath observance itself is "good." Any breach of observance must either be evil or for a greater good.

But Jesus escalates the debate to the general principle: is it lawful on Sabbath **to save life or to kill?** The question presupposes that the Pharisees would agree that to save life was permissible on the Sabbath. The parallels in the passage set up the equations of "doing good" = "save life"; "doing evil" = "to kill." Since Mark implies that Jesus knows ("supernaturally"—so Marcus 2000, 252) why the Pharisees are watching him, the implication is that his opponents intend to do harm, to take life. Jesus' intent is to do good, to save life. His question, then, "is a powerful indictment of the motives of his opponents and also a highly polemical reflection on the tradition that the need to save a life overrides the prohibition of work on the Sabbath" (Collins 2007, 208).

But they remained silent, refusing to engage in debate about their Sabbath halakah or the implications that flow from Jesus' pronouncement in 2:28. Were this man actually dying, it may be that the Pharisees would have been prepared to intervene. But this is clearly not the case here.

■ **5** Instead of restoring the man's hand, Jesus' first response is to look **around at them in anger.** Jesus' response of anger has already featured in the variant reading at 1:41 and in 1:43. Here the reason for Jesus' anger (*orgēs*) is clear: they refuse to change their views on the meaning of doing good on Sabbath and refuse to understand who he is. So Mark tells us that he is **deeply distressed.** This description completely removes the connotation of petulance from Jesus' anger. He is grieved **at their stubborn hearts.**

The motif of hardness of heart is an important one in Mark (see 4:12; 6:52; 8:17), drawing heavily on the OT story of Pharaoh as well as the prophets' theme of Israel's refusal to follow Yahweh (see Isa 6:10). Hardness of heart is also prominent in Rom 11:7, 25; 2 Cor 3:14. "The phrase is almost a stock expression in the NT for those who cannot or will not perceive the truth" (France 2002, 150). If Mark does allude to the Pharaoh story, the irony is unmistakable: "Pharaoh is the proto-typical enemy of God's people and representative of ungodliness, whereas the Markan Pharisees present themselves as the spiritual guardians of the nation" (Marcus 2000, 253).

The tension between human responsibility and divine purpose in hardness of heart runs through the entire biblical use of the motif. In many instances, the metaphor, if not the language, echoes Exod 7:3, where God hardens Pharaoh's heart even in the face of miracles. The language suggests that Pharaoh's hardness is divinely ordained. But Pharaoh's choice is also noted.

The same tension is found in Mark. Jesus grieves at their sinful hardness of heart, but God's ultimate purposes are not thwarted by human stubbornness.

The healing is described briefly: **"Stretch out your hand." He stretched it out, and his hand was completely restored.** While the healing can scarcely have been incidental to the man, this story is told to emphasize another point: Jesus, the Son of Man, Lord of the Sabbath, transforms the meaning of Sabbath observance in the direction of God's good purposes. Furthermore, the presence of Jesus, the Holy One of God, in their midst makes the Sabbath a joyous occasion celebrating the restoration of God's good creation. And this is a time of restoration of the people of God, symbolized by the wholeness given to this man. "If Jesus is 'the holy one of God' whose holiness implies the apocalyptic destruction of demons and disease (cf. 1:24), then his Sabbath-day healing of the man with the paralyzed hand is a fulfillment rather than an infraction of the [Sabbath] commandment" (Marcus 2000, 252-53).

■ **6** There is, however, also a more sinister undertone. Immediately after the event, **the Pharisees went out and began to plot with the Herodians how they might kill Jesus.** This simple statement is full of irony. First, the debate, as Jesus has framed it, is centered on which is lawful on Sabbath: to do good or to do evil; "to save life or to kill" (v 4). Now, on Sabbath, the Pharisees are plotting how to **kill Jesus.** Instead of fulfilling the good intentions of the Sabbath, they are plotting to do evil.

Second, they are plotting **with the Herodians,** presumably the local officials to whom this accusation of profaning the Sabbath would be made. Because it is impossible to separate the religious from the secular in this period, some think the joint plot unremarkable (so France 2002, 151). But Hooker is quite right to observe that "an alliance between such men and the Pharisees, who were completely opposed to them in attitude and interest, is extraordinary" (1991, 108). The Herodians were supporters of the Roman client king Antipas. The Pharisees, by contrast, as one of the leading holiness renewal movements, believed Roman rule compromised Judah's holiness.

Third, note the direction of movement: the Pharisees immediately **went out** (*exelthontes*), away from Jesus, and joined **with the Herodians.** The theme of movement away from Jesus by the religious people continues.

FROM THE TEXT

The continuing disclosure of the identity of Jesus now includes direct and organized opposition to him. The conspiracy to get rid of Jesus by the Pharisees (people primarily concerned with a renewal of holiness) with the Herodians (people primarily concerned with the administration of power) is surprising. But a concentration on their definition of holiness and the way in which it should be practiced blinded the Pharisees to the presence of the Holy

One in their midst. This led them to align with people who do not share their desire.

Their concern to keep the Sabbath holy led them to develop many safeguards so that they would not inadvertently profane the Sabbath. It made some, who could not get beyond their narrow interpretation of God's will, into legalists. They could not engage with the heart of the lawgiver, for whom the purpose of Sabbath was for the good of humanity. The slope from "helps to holy living" to hard-hearted legalism is slippery. Holiness people always need to go back to the basics, that is, sensing the direction of God's heart through the Spirit.

Healing this man's shriveled hand was not a matter of life or death. He did not need to be healed on Sabbath. He could have waited for another few hours. His inclusion in those restored to health seems not to matter in terms of the numbers who are following Jesus.

But the restoration of the broken, bleeding, and excluded individuals to the people of God is not a matter that should be postponed. Return to the place where they too can be a part of the holy people, the kingdom of priests, should not be forbidden for the sake of the rules on how to keep the Sabbath holy. No one is unimportant.

The transforming and healing power of Jesus for the marginalized characterizes the ministry of his followers, then and now. And they need to be careful that their anxiety to keep the rules does not affect their ministry to the marginalized who desperately need the transforming touch of Jesus.

5. You Are the Son of God (3:7-12)

BEHIND THE TEXT

This text functions as a Markan summary and transition. But it also contributes to Mark's developing themes. It starts with a retreat to the lake (see also 4:1; 5:21) and highlights the diversity of the crowds who are now coming to Jesus. Then it reminds readers of the identity already established as well as the conflict his work engendered. It concludes with a repetition of the impossible plea for secrecy. Neither in terms of escape from the crowds nor from rapidly spreading news will there be any respite.

Crowds followed him to the lake before, but now they are larger. The names of places are interesting. Although there were some Jewish populations in each of them, they were predominantly in Gentile territory.

We have been informed of other exorcisms, but no details have been given. But this summary pointedly notes that the demons always confess that Jesus is the Son of God, clearly a reminder that for Mark, this identity is precisely what he wishes his readers to remember. The identity is to remain secret, however, continuing Mark's curious motif of a secret that cannot be kept.

■ **7-8** The Greek text of this section has many variant readings. Both France (2002, 152) and Collins (2007, 211) suggest that copyists were attempting to make sense of a long sentence and one in which *poly plēthos* is repeated. The result is that some MSS read **followed** after **Galilee** (so NIV; the NRSV adapts another MS reading that adds *autōi*, "him," after "followed"). Despite the complexity of the Greek MS tradition here, the meaning is clear enough.

Jesus' escape from the previous scene is noted: **Jesus withdrew** [*anechōrēsen*: a "tactical withdrawal"; France 2002, 153] **with his disciples.** To this point only five disciples have been called to follow him. But Mark gives the impression that there are many others who follow. Clearly, the lakeshore gives the crowds greater access to him. Vital points emerge:

First, the **large crowd from Galilee** that is following Jesus is larger than the crowds in 2:13. Already there is a distinction between the crowds who listen to Jesus and the religious officials who reject him.

Second, Jesus' ministry is far more wide-ranging than that of John's. In John's ministry, all of Judea and Jerusalem come to him. Now Judea and Jerusalem are included in a range of places surrounding Galilee from where people come.

Third, while the crowds that follow are initially from Galilee, **when they heard all he was doing, many people came to him from Judea, Jerusalem, Idumea, and the regions across the Jordan and around Tyre and Sidon.** Perhaps Mark intends to show that those from Galilee already **followed,** while those from elsewhere are making the first move to become followers. Galilee occupies a central role in the early parts of Jesus' story and is the implied place of continuation after the resurrection.

But Mark's point is larger than this: The impact and the ministry of Jesus extends well beyond its beginnings in the predominantly Jewish territory of Galilee. It now comprehends the whole range of Jewish and mixed territory (**Judea, Jerusalem, Idumea, and the regions across the Jordan**) and explicitly Gentile territory (**Tyre and Sidon**).

Jesus is on the Isaianic mission of gathering the scattered people of God (see Isa 43:5; 45:20; 49:5, 18; 56:8; 60:7; 66:18) *and* is gathering the Gentiles to himself. If so, the picture emerges of a growing movement of people who **came to him.** This identifies Jesus and the character of the kingdom he is proclaiming.

Matthew does not include Tyre and Sidon in his parallel summary (see Matt 4:25). He emphasizes Jesus' mission to Israel (see Matt 10:5-6). Mark's inclusion here of explicit references to Jesus' work in Gentile territory is noteworthy. Gentiles come because **they heard all he was doing.**

The picture summarizes all of Jesus' previous activity. It also gives some clues as to what is to follow. From the crowds that are following him, Jesus chooses twelve. His mission is to gather the people of God from the far corners of the earth so as to restore the remnant of God's holy people for the mission of God. If so, the Twelve represent the scattered remnant who return as harbingers of the kingdom of God Jesus is proclaiming.

■ **9-10** The pressure of the crowds has been a feature from ch 1. Now Jesus tells his **disciples to have a small boat ready for him,** anticipating his need to get away. Boat trips are an important literary feature of Mark. It does not mention Jesus' teaching from the boat here, but elsewhere significant teaching about Jesus and his mission occur on boats. Here, the boat is simply a means of escaping the crowds: **to keep the people from crowding him.** Mark chooses the verb *thlibōsini*, which typically describes oppression or tribulation. Here Jesus is concerned that the physical reality of crowd-pressure might necessitate escape.

The reason is clear. Jesus **had healed many.** As a result, people are pressing to touch him. We might imagine a scene similar to those surrounding celebrities or sports stars or papal visits. But these are needy people—more like those crowding around vehicles delivering water or food from relief agencies to desperate people following a natural disaster. Mark clearly sees a connection between touch and healing (see 5:25-34; 6:56). So it is not surprising when people are pictured as *falling over* Jesus (*epepeptein autōi*) in an attempt to make contact with him.

The language Mark uses to describe **those with diseases** (*mastigas*) may better be translated as *torments.* In its concrete form, it refers to *whips* or *lashes.* The word may mean simply suffering the torments of illness. But lurking behind the word is the description of disease as oppression. Luke 7:21 distinguishes "diseases" (*noson*), "sicknesses" (*mastigon*), and possession by "evil spirits" (*pneumaton ponērōn*). Mark here treats illness different from demonic possession (France 2002, 155), but the boundaries between the two are not always so clear.

■ **11-12** The reaction of human sufferers is paralleled by that of the *unclean spirits* (not **evil spirits**; Marcus 2000, 258-62). Their identification of Jesus is important for Mark. It explicitly states that Jesus is the Christ, the Son of God in 1:1. And his death elicits the exclamation from the centurion, "surely this man was the Son of God!" in 15:39. But the term is not otherwise used by human characters in the story. In fact, of those who do ascribe this epithet to Jesus, the unclean spirits and the Gentile centurion appear to be hostile or, at least, unexpected witnesses to Jesus' identity.

Nevertheless, the phrase remains structurally significant for Mark. He opens with the phrase (1:1), and his narrative reaches its climax in the crucifixion (15:39). The voice from heaven (1:11; 9:7) combined with the testimony of unclean spirits witness to Jesus' true identity. In fact, **whenever the unclean spirits saw him,** not only did they cry out, **"You are the Son of God,"** but **they fell down before him.**

Collins represents scholars who see this confession as indicating that "Jesus is the messiah of Israel, the eschatological king" (2007, 213). Marcus takes a different view, noting that the term "is not simply a title for Jesus as the human Messiah . . . but a designation suggesting that he participates in God's sovereignty over evil supernatural forces" (2000, 261). In Mark's view, the demons know who Jesus is (1:34), despite their hostility to him. It is possible that they attempt to gain mastery over him through their cry, **You are the Son of God.** But if so, Mark uses it for his own purposes. That they **fell down before him** signals their reluctant recognition of his sovereign authority over them. Mark uses this expression elsewhere for worshipful submission (see 5:33; 7:25).

Once again, Jesus **gave** those he exorcized **strict orders not to tell who he was.** This seems difficult to envision on the historical level. If the unclean spirits attempt to name Jesus in order to have control over him, onlookers would hear the phrase. Perhaps this is Mark's way of signaling that the confession is inappropriate because of its timing (Guelich 1989, 149).

Mark does not think Jesus' identity becomes clear until the end of the narrative in light of the crucifixion—and then only for those who have ears to hear. Thus, at the story level, the confession by the centurion in 15:39 is scarcely beyond Luke's parallel "righteous man" (Luke 23:47). But for Mark, it encapsulates the entire story about Jesus. The unclean spirits know who he is, but they are forbidden to reveal it. Despite this open secret, only rarely does anyone come close to knowing who Jesus is. It emerges only to submerge again in blindness and hardness of heart.

FROM THE TEXT

Mark's summary reminds readers that Jesus' identity is established in word and deed. They confirm the voice from heaven and the testimony of the unclean spirits. Readers know that the work of announcing the kingdom of God, the reign of God, suffers opposition from the powers of evil.

Some rather fruitless debate over whether or not there is "a personal devil" detracts from the reality that opposition to God's good purposes continues but the victory is assured. The exorcisms of Jesus remind us of the cosmic character of the struggle between good and evil. But this and the previous section illustrate that the main opposition to God's good purposes is human. The unclean spirits know who Jesus is and prostrate themselves before him;

the human opponents of Jesus deny his identity and resist the message at every opportunity.

The two sections also remind us that opposition can come in the very potent mix of religious piety and political power. The Pharisees, the holiness people, sell out to the Herodians. They serve the Herodians' ends of maintaining the Pax Romana—where power and authority are vested in the empire and Caesar is hailed as Lord.

The people of God lose their prophetic voice when they collude with a political entity that arrogates to itself the prerogatives of God. They unwittingly align themselves with the forces of evil, disguised in the partnership of piety and patriotism, not with righteousness and peace.

C. The Appointment of the Twelve (3:13-19)

BEHIND THE TEXT

On the face of it, the story is simply about Jesus calling his twelve apostles and giving them their names. But it is laden with significance in light of its narrative setting and the intensity of its intertextual echoes.

First, its place in the narrative flow is important. The story so far has included the appearance of John in the wilderness announcing the coming of the kingdom while proclaiming a baptism of repentance. The response has been extensive—all Jerusalem and Judea have come out to be baptized by John in the Jordan. Israel is invited to experience the reality of the new thing that God is about to do.

Jesus comes from Galilee and is baptized. In response, the heavens open and he is confirmed as God's beloved Son, the messianic servant. After confronting Satan in the wilderness, and the arrest of John, Jesus appears in Galilee proclaiming the arrival of the kingdom of God. He invites people to repent and believe the good news. God is doing the new thing promised in the Prophets, particularly in Isaiah. He is restoring the people of God, or, at least, the holy remnant of the people of God.

Jesus' first act is to call four disciples, who witness the first exorcism and hear the first public identification of Jesus as the Holy One of God. The healings, exorcisms, forgiveness of sins, and exercise of sovereign authority over the Sabbath round out Jesus' identity. Finally, we are reminded that all the unclean spirits know who Jesus is—the Son of God.

Second, the intertextual echoes that have been such a prominent theme in Mark to this point are particularly strong here. Here, Jesus, narratively identified as the Holy One of God, the Son of God, calls people to himself. From among those who respond, he chooses twelve people to be with him, under his authority, and on his mission. The narrative points to the re-creation of Israel as a holy people fit for God to dwell in their midst.

Now this passage confirms the extent of the re-creation of this people: Jesus calls people from the four directions and creates the Twelve to represent God's holy people, on the mission of proclaiming and effecting the good news Jesus is announcing. Without that picture based upon the narrative flow and its intertextual links, the implications of the call of the Twelve are reduced to a story about when the twelve disciples are called and who they are.

IN THE TEXT

■ **13** The Greek here simply reads *he went up the mountain.* Since Jesus is not named, *he* requires an antecedent from the previous passage. It is Jesus, Son of God, who ascends the mountain. The link is important. Mark includes the definite article with *mountain* (*to oros*).

The mountain can be understood in different ways. France, along with the translators of the NIV, sees this reference simply as "a journey 'into the hills,' apparently to escape the crowds" (2002, 160). Jesus escapes the crowds in Mark by going to the wilderness (see 1:35). But here he actually calls people to come to him on *the mountain.*

If, however, translators give full value to Mark's article, the translation is *the mountain.* This connotes more than a retreat in a mountainous setting. Several scholars think this suggests "the mountain of God." Exodus 24:9-11, the occasion on which Moses and the elders meet God, is the most likely allusive background (Collins 2007, 215). If this is the mountain of God, what picture is Mark painting for his readers?

Marcus (2000, 266) suggests a Moses-typology as part of the background. Moses ascends Sinai several times to meet God (Exod 19; 24; 34; Num 27; Deut 9—10; 32). In Exod 19:3-6 Moses is called up to the mountain of God, where God sets out the terms of his covenant relationship with Israel and announces their status as "a kingdom of priests and a holy nation" (Exod 19:6). In Exod 24:1-11, God invites Moses together with the elders to the mountain to meet with him. When they return from the first meeting, they erect twelve pillars (24:4). Moses institutes the covenant by offering a sacrifice and sprinkling the blood of the covenant sacrifice on the altar and the people (24:8). Then they return to the mountain to eat and drink with God (24:11).

But does Mark present Jesus as a new Moses? If so, this is the first time we have seen it in Mark. Or is the focus elsewhere? Exodus 24 is particularly instructive. God calls Moses and the leaders to come to him. They descend from the mountain and act on God's mission of instituting his covenant. Then they return to have fellowship with God on the mountain. The picture may more accurately be seen as the Holy One of God, gathering his leaders around

105

him so that he dwells in their midst and they then descend from the mountain to be on his mission and to proclaim his message.

The likelihood of a new-Moses motif is diminished by Mark 9:2-9. There Mark excludes both a new-Moses and a returned-Elijah identity for Jesus. Both Elijah and Moses appear (9:4) along with the transfigured Jesus. Jesus is designated the beloved Son by the voice from heaven (9:7).

Up to this point in the narrative, Mark's focus has been on Jesus actually acting on behalf of God and as God's agent, as Son of God. Here, Jesus is the Holy One on the mountain in the midst of the people, calling the representatives of the people to himself and thus re-creating the holy people of God centered on himself.

Jesus **called to him those he wanted.** But who are they? We cannot tell from Mark's language here whether this refers to the Twelve or to the wider group of followers from whom the Twelve are selected. Mark could focus only on the Twelve, although this requires reading the text in a less than natural way. But in light of 8:34, when Jesus calls the crowd with the disciples, it seems likely that here he is calling a wide range of people, not just the Twelve. Here, the initiative of Jesus is stressed, mirroring the sovereignty of God. He calls to himself those whom he wants.

This is not necessarily a call that implies an exclusion of others. The echoes of Exod 24 suggest that those called by Jesus are representatives of the wider renewed people of Israel. This is a call to a group that represents all who have followed him. Together this is the renewed righteous remnant. This flows naturally from the immediately preceding summary of those who come to Jesus from the four directions.

Another echo of Isaiah might be here. Isaiah 41:9 notes that God gathers his servant "from the ends of the earth" and "from its farthest corners" he called them. And **they came to him.** Marcus (2000, 266) suggests that *apēlthon* (**came**) might imply that they are leaving their previous pursuits. If so, it fits with Mark 1:16-20; 2:14; and 3:31-35 (see also 10:28).

■ **14-15** From those he called and who came to him, Jesus **appointed twelve.** The Twelve clearly are a special group in the early church. While a few scholars in the past argued against the historicity of such a group during the lifetime of Jesus, recent scholars are less skeptical. The theological significance of the Twelve is critical in Mark.

The verb translated **appointed** (*epoiēsen*) could be translated **made** or **created.** The Twelve is "the creation of the new people of God" (Guelich 1989, 157). The argument is not decisive either way, but this verb heightens the significance of this group.

Second, the creation of the Twelve symbolizes God's newly reconstituted people, which fulfills the promises through the prophets (see Isa 49:12;

Ezek 45:8; Sir 36:10 [LXX]; 48:10 [LXX]). The eschatological role of the Twelve is picked up by Matthew (19:28) and Luke (22:30). But for Mark, the creation of the Twelve is wholly in line with the announcement and effecting God's good news now (1:14-15).

The phrase **designating them apostles** is missing in some MSS. Most scholars see it as an assimilation to Luke 6:13. Luke uses the term "apostles." **Twelve** is likely synonymous with "apostle" for Luke (see Acts 1:25-26).

The threefold reason for the appointment is set out. They are called to **be with him.** This first point is crucial. God's people are holy only in relation to the holiness of God; theirs is a derived holiness. Being with the Holy One of God is central to their identity. Second, he will **send them out to preach.** They are on his mission, announcing the good news that he announces, and they are given **authority to drive out demons.** They thereby are called to enter into the cosmic dimension of the struggle that Jesus himself enters.

■ **16-19** Mark lists the names of **the twelve he appointed.** There are some differences in the order of the names in the other accounts (Matt 10:2-4; Luke 6:14-16). And whereas Mark has Thaddaeus, Luke has Judas, son of James. First on the list is **Simon.** The grammar here sets Simon/Peter off from the rest. The importance of Peter to Mark's Gospel has been highlighted recently by Bauckham. He gives substantial support for the traditional view that Peter's eyewitness tradition stands behind Mark (see Bauckham 2006, 155-82). Whether or not that is the case, the prominence of Peter in Mark is a characteristic of the Gospel. He is one of the first called (1:16-20) and he features in crucial scenes (8:27-33; 9:5; 10:28; 11:21; 14:29, 37, 54-72; 16:7).

Simon is one of the most common Jewish names in the 2TP. But Jesus gives Simon a new name, **Peter.** This name means "rock." The name is probably *Kēphas* in Aramaic, which Paul uses in Galatians and 1 Corinthians. *Petros* is the Greek translation. Neither name is widely used in Aramaic or Greek before this usage.

A change of name is sometimes connected to nodal points in the life of the person: for instance, Abram to Abraham and Sarai to Sarah (Gen 17), Jacob to Israel (Gen 32:28; on the Philadelphians' new name, see Rev 3:12). Matthew explains the change in name around Peter's confession of Jesus' identity as the foundation of the church (Matt 16:18). Mark's placement here suggests that "Simon Peter is to be the foundation of the community anticipated by Jesus, namely, the restored Israel" (Collins 2007, 218).

The next two names were also among those first called in Mark 1:16-20. The Zebedee brothers are also given a nickname—**Boanerges, which means Sons of Thunder.** The derivation of the term *boanērges* is difficult to explain. That it is not used again (unlike Simon/Peter) in the Gospels is even more surprising. Mark's translation, **Sons of Thunder,** does not help much. Collins sug-

MARK

3:14-19

107

gests that the phrase might suggest to those who were familiar with Homer's story of Zeus sending thunder and lightning, "the epithet 'Sons of Thunder' might have suggested that James and John were prophets" (2007, 221). But if so, the connection is obscure. Guelich's admission seems more likely: "we remain at a loss to explain its occasion and significance" (Guelich 1989, 162). The fact that they are given nicknames may signal their place within the inner circle who are given names: Peter, James, and John. These three do figure regularly in the rest of the narrative.

The final person of the original four, **Andrew,** starts the rest of the list to which little detail is added. **Andrew** and **Philip** are Greek names. **Bartholomew** (son of Talmai), **Matthew, Thomas, James son of Alphaeus,** and **Thaddaeus** follow. **Simon the *Cananean*** (*simōna ton Kananaion*) is called "Simon . . . the Zealot" in Luke 6:15. The NIV follows Luke because the meaning of the term ***Cananean*** is likely "derived from the Aramaic *qanʿānā,* 'enthusiast,' 'patriot' . . . in a religious rather than a political sense" (France 2002, 162). The Zealot party did not exist until the beginning of the Jewish War in 66-67 (see Collins 2007, 222). However, by the time Mark is written, the name would have had political connotations as well, especially if Mark is composed around the time of the Jewish War.

Judas Iscariot (*Ioudan Iskariōth*) probably means Judas, a man from Kerioth, possibly a village in Judea Kerioth Hezron south of Hebron (so Collins 2007, 223; but see France 2002, 163). The important point in the tradition is that Judas **betrayed him** (*hos kai paredōken auto*). Mark's choice of language here is a reminder of the ambiguity of Judas' action, a point that Mark bears out in 14:21. Mark also uses the verb *paradidōmai* in 1:14 and in the passion predictions, all of which give the impression that the focus is on the death of Jesus in light of God's plan and purposes rather than the act of betrayal itself. Mark is restrained in his depiction of Judas. The later Gospels have far more elaborate depictions of Judas' dubious character and culpability.

This is, however, also a very sobering reminder that even those called by Jesus to be with him, who proclaim the message and are given authority to engage in the mission, may ultimately betray Jesus. It is one of the Twelve who betrays Jesus. Indeed, Mark bluntly reports that all of the disciples forsake Jesus and flee (14:50). Failure and betrayal in Mark are linked to the failure to continue to be with Jesus.

FROM THE TEXT

This section provides a summary of Mark's view of discipleship. It includes being with Jesus, on his mission and under his authority. Because human holiness is always in relation to the source of holiness, coming to and being with the Holy One of God is what makes these people God's holy people.

The point is important: our holiness is only and always as we are in relationship to the Holy One. It is not a possession that is given to us to be preserved like a treasure. God's people are his sanctified ones, devoted to him, because he dwells in their midst and within them.

Second, this is God's mission, not ours. Followers of Jesus are at risk of assuming that they are the focal point of the mission of God. Indeed, the danger is that disciples can sometimes think they are gatekeepers (see 9:38-40; 10:13-14). But disciples are called to enter into the mission of God, the redemption and restoration of his alienated creatures and his marred creation. Disciples take their eyes off their own individual fulfillment and self-actualization to find their identity in God's grand purposes. By this means anxieties about finding the personal plan "God has for you" and worries that it might be missed evaporate.

Third, the authority and power to carry out this mission come from God—once again, not a personal possession as if we were given a finite amount of power for our own use. All authority is vested in Christ, and ours to use only in direct relationship with God and his mission. The dangers for disciples come to the fore in the remarkable botched exorcism of 9:14-29. We are never independently empowered exorcists or ministers of the gospel.

Fourth, this section reminds us that the call of God to individuals is to join the people of God. The naming of the Twelve reminds us that they follow Jesus in a personal way. But they do so as the Twelve who are the representatives of the wider restored and renewed remnant of God's holy people. Following Jesus as a disciple is a group exercise: with the Holy One and forged into his holy people.

Conversely, this reminds us that God chooses to fulfill his good purposes through Jesus and those he calls to be with him, his holy people, not independent from the holy people. The reminder of the corporate or communal character of our discipleship is a serious challenge to the individualism in all areas of life, including religion, which has affected Western social relationships since the Enlightenment. The biblical picture in general complements Mark's reminder of the corporate nature of our existence as the people of God.

D. The Insiders and Outsiders (3:20-35)

BEHIND THE TEXT

This section brings to an end the first cycle of stories that set out Jesus' identity and the identity of those who follow him. Two narrative points aid in the interpretation of the passage.

First, this concludes the narrative movement of some of the central figures: the scribes, the Pharisees, the crowds, the disciples, and Jesus' family.

From the opening scene in 2:1-9, those around him were the scribes. By the end of the section, the opposition to Jesus from these same people is implacable. This time, however, it is scribes from Jerusalem, the center of religious authority and piety, who accuse him of sorcery. Once again, as with the earlier charge of blasphemy, this is punishable by stoning. Even Jesus' family is involved in this sequence. They have been introduced at this last stage, not particularly for their own sake, but to show that the only relationship that really matters is nearness to Jesus. Those around him are his fictive family, those who are doing the will of God as announced by Jesus.

Second, this narrative clue comes in the form of Mark's writing style. He introduces Jesus' family in 3:20. He tells the story of the scribes from Jerusalem, severely warning those who fail to see the Spirit at work in his ministry and mission. Then, he returns to the family in the final section. As always in Mark, the A-B-C-B'-A' (*inclusio*) pattern contributes to the interpretation of each part.

The section also contains the notoriously treacherous passage on the "unforgivable sin." Taken from its context in its narrative sequence, it is an extremely difficult saying. Within the context of the debate Mark brings together, however, it warns those who refuse to see that Jesus acts as the One full of the Spirit and as the Holy One of God. That puts them on the side of opposition to the will of God, a place that can lead only to ultimate defeat and exclusion from the purposes of God. As such, it serves as a warning especially to the scribes from Jerusalem. By opposing Jesus and accusing him of acting by the power of Beelzebub, they are actually denying the activity of God in Jesus. Despite their religious credentials, they align themselves with Satan, not God. From that settled position there is neither retreat nor hope.

IN THE TEXT

■ **20-21** These opening verses are full of difficulties. First, the beginning is different in the English versions. The NIV starts with **then Jesus entered a house.** But other versions attach this to the close of 3:19. Chapter and verse divisions appeared well over a millennium after Mark wrote. The NIV follows the sense of the passage even if it does not agree with the majority of English versions, which follow the older order.

Second, the text simply states that *he entered the house.* It does not indicate whether the disciples were with him, although 3:31-35 indicates that they were. Neither does the text give any clue as to the location of this house. However, the phrase *eis oikon* could mean *his house* or home. It probably was in Capernaum. But the appearance of the family of Jesus on the scene could point to a setting in Nazareth (so Marcus 2000, 279).

The continuity running through these stories is somewhat obscured by the translation **and again a crowd gathered.** The Greek is better translated as in the NRSV: "and the crowd came together again." This emphasizes that the people following Jesus continued to stay with him.

The crowd in Mark is that group of people who hear Jesus. They are often compared favorably with those who reject Jesus (see esp. 12:12, 37). Here the contrast is obvious between the family and the scribes—those who ought to have been closest to Jesus and the crowd. At the end of this sequence the crowd will be gathered around Jesus (3:32). Mark again reminds us of the popularity of Jesus: The crowd so crowds around him that **he and his disciples were not even able to eat.** Mark emphasizes this by means of a double negative (*mē dynasthai autous mēde arton phagein*).

The third challenge is the translation of *hoi par'autou.* The general meaning is *those with him.* It can mean *relatives* or **family.** If the phrase means **his family,** then it seems likely that at the time Mark writes, the level of embarrassment about the rejection by Jesus' own family runs strong. The parallel traditions in Matt 12:24-32 and Luke 11:15-22 omit this short statement. The embarrassment likely explains why some later textual variants read "the scribes and the rest." Some early copyists also found this offensive. They identified "the standard opponents of Jesus, rather than his family," as those who "said that he had lost his senses" (Collins 2007, 225). Older translations also opt for this approach. They translate the phrase "his friends." A minority of recent scholars interpret the passage as if it says that the Twelve go outside to control the crowd.

None of the alternatives does justice to Mark's narrative structure. The introduction of the family here is essential for the point he wishes to make later, and forms part of his typical bracketing structure. Mark's point is that even Jesus' own family, those who ought to have known him best, have not really understood who he is or what is happening.

When his family hear **about this,** perhaps about the crowds and the healings and exorcisms, they are concerned for his sanity. It could also have to do with rumors about the mountain scene. They may have heard that Jesus was arrogating to himself the very role of God by calling people to himself on a mountain, in selecting Twelve apostles to be with him as his representatives and as representative of a re-created Israel. To objective or skeptical observers, even those who know him, Jesus seems to be delusional.

So, **they went** [*exēlton,* **went out**] **to take charge of** [*kratēsai,* **seize, restrain**] **him.** This rather bland reading suggests that they treat him as someone liable to do himself harm. While this translation is possible, the connotation of *kratēsai* is rather more sinister (see 6:17; 12:12). Their intent was hostile. That they *went out* becomes more important later in the narrative.

All attempts to lessen the impact of this sentence fail. Those nearest to Jesus, his family, go out to restrain him because they believe **He is out of his mind.** Although Mark can use *exestē* to mean "amazed" or "astonished" (2:12; 5:42; 6:51), the meaning "insane" is widely known. Juxtaposed to the following story, in which the scribes posit that Jesus is demon-possessed, the reference here to some sort of mental disorder is inescapable.

Collins draws specific attention to the theme of rejection, a motif common in the Psalms of Lament. According to Ps 69:8-9, the righteous sufferer endures "misunderstanding of his charismatic activity. This misunderstanding is tantamount to a rejection of his divine mission" (2007, 227). Collins and others before her have drawn attention to the importance of these psalms in telling the story of Jesus. The image of the righteous sufferer drawn from the Psalms of Lament is crucial for interpreting the Markan Passion Narrative. This prominent feature has been explored in depth (Brower 1978 and 1983).

■ **22** The sequence now moves to the second stage. Jesus has already been opposed by the **teachers of the law** (see 2:6, 16). But this time, the scribes **came down from Jerusalem.** This clearly heightens the opposition to Jesus. Scribes from Jerusalem would be more weighty opponents than their provincial counterparts. This foreshadows the significance of Jerusalem (really the temple establishment) in the final scenes in the drama. Coming down from Jerusalem carries sinister overtones: The highest religious authorities arrive to pass judgment on Jesus.

They do not deny that Jesus is healing the sick or exorcising demons. Nowhere in the Gospels is Jesus accused of fake healings or exorcisms. Their accusation is rather different. And it fits with the idea that "he is out of his mind" (v 21). Jesus **is possessed by Beelzebub!** If this accusation were true, Jesus would be liable to death by stoning as possessing a "familiar spirit" (Lev 20:27 KJV), or excluded ("cut off") from the community as in the case of Legion in Mark 5.

But Mark's readers know Jesus is the Holy One of God and Son of God, because unclean spirits bear reluctant witness to that (1:24; 3:11). Nevertheless, as Marcus notes, "it is an understandable charge given the moral ambiguity of miracles and other charismatic phenomena; Old Testament and Jewish traditions, therefore, attempt to provide criteria for distinguishing divine charismata from demonic ones." The basic criterion is whether or not the action is consistent with the Law (2000, 281). Once again, the apocalyptic theme of the cosmic struggle between good and evil that marks the coming of the kingdom of God in power lies behind this statement.

Beelzebub

The MS tradition has a variety of spellings for this term: *Beezeboul, Beelzeboul, Beelzebub*. Collins argues that the earliest form is *Beelzeboul*. The first reading likely arises from the difficult Greek combination of *lz*, while the form *Beelzebub* follows the Latin Vulgate and Syriac versions in assimilating this passage with 2 Kgs 1:2, 3. Collins argues that the 2 Kgs 1:2 "'Baal Zebub,' which means 'Lord of the Flies' . . . is likely . . . a mocking play on the name of a well-known Semitic deity . . . 'Baal Zabul,' which means 'Baal the prince'" (2007, 229). The NIV consistently follows MSS that read *Beelzebub*, while the NRSV prefers "Beelzebul" on stronger textual grounds.

Collins argues that the evidence supports the view that a demon given the name Beelzebul was widely known in this period, especially from the *T. Sol.* 3:1-6, where he is a fallen angel.

■ **23-26** Mark interprets Beelzebub as the equivalent of Satan, who is widely regarded as the ruler of the forces opposed to God. So, the response of Jesus does not mention Beelzebub at all. Instead, **Jesus called** the scribes with the language suggesting that he summoned them in a quasi-legal sense to hear his statement. But the response he makes is **in parables,** that is, comparisons or similes.

These two short parables are the first in Mark. As Marcus notes, "these parables are not timeless maxims but weapons of warfare" (2000, 281). As is also the case in the next chapter, the parables are tools to determine who is inside and outside the people of God.

Jesus poses the question: **How can Satan drive out Satan?** Clearly Satan is here a personal name for the ruler of his kingdom—and if Satan is exorcising his serving unclean spirits, then the division inevitably leads to collapse. **If a kingdom is divided against itself, that kingdom cannot stand.**

This is parabolic language, but it suggests "that Satan has a kingdom opposed to the kingdom of God although permitted as part of the divine plan" (Collins 2007, 232). The logical outcome, then, if the scribes are correct, is that Satan's civil war brings his reign to an end. Clearly, that is not the case; the flawed logic of their proposition is established.

■ **27** But lest this give the impression that Satan's kingdom is not under threat, the second, and climactic, parable excludes that possibility. This parable argues that actually Satan's kingdom is crumbling, but not of its own division. It is being defeated in cosmic battle by the One who is the exorcist and healer, who comes announcing and effecting God's reign. "Internal revolution is not the only way to topple a regime; an alternative method is invasion" (Hooker 1991, 116).

3:22-27

Jesus reminds the scribes that **no one can enter a strong man's house and carry off his possessions unless he first ties up the strong man. Then he can rob his house.** The implication is clear: Jesus himself is the strong man who has already bound Satan and is plundering his house. The binding of the strong man may have intertextual connections. Collins draws attention to the link through *deō* (**bind**) with God's binding of Leviathan in Job 41:1-2 (2007, 234). If so, the divine authority of Jesus is implied.

The exorcisms and healing are the dispossession of the kingdom of Satan. This is possible only because he has already been bound. That is, he is already a defeated foe. Perhaps this alludes to the confrontation with Satan in 1:12-13. However, as in NT eschatology in general, while Mark knows that the outcome of the war is never in doubt, battles on the cosmic and the mundane scale continue until that time when all God's purposes are accomplished and evil is banished forever (see Rev 21:1-7).

■ **28-30** Taken from their context, these next three verses are some of the most fearsome texts in Scripture—the so-called unpardonable sin. But they can only be interpreted properly in the context. The gravity of the pronouncement is indicated by the opening words: Jesus addresses the scribes, **I tell you the truth** (*Amēn legō hymin*), a phrase that also indicates his authority.

First, he announces that all sins will be forgiven, perhaps a positive fruit of the binding of Satan, the accuser (so Marcus 2000, 283). **All the sins and blasphemies of men** [that is, *of people in general* = *tois huiois tōn anthrōpōn*] **will be forgiven them.** Guelich thinks that **the sins** (*ta hamartēmata*) refers to those against other human beings (1989, 179), while **blasphemies** refers to those against God. France (2002, 175) does not take **blasphemies** here in the technical sense. It refers rather to the more general idea of slanderous talk (as in 7:22). Hence, all sins are forgivable.

But then Jesus enters a massive caveat: **but whoever blasphemes against the Holy Spirit will never be forgiven.** The caveat is very specific. Attributing the work of Jesus through the Spirit to Satan, instead of recognizing him as the Spirit-bearer, announcing and effecting the kingdom of God, treats him as the agent of Satan. This is no casual or hasty assessment, however. Jesus speaks here of the ultimate fate of those who reject God's good news in Jesus. France thinks the phrase means "will be guilty of a sin with eternal consequences" (France 2002, 176).

This, then, is a warning to the scribes from Jerusalem. They should consider carefully the source of the work of Jesus. "While Jesus' words do not in themselves directly accuse the Jerusalem scribes of this ultimate spiritual defection, Mark's v. 30 does make them, and any who share their attitude to the ministry of Jesus, *enoxoi aiōniou hamartēmatos*" (France 2002, 177). The danger for the scribes is that this hardness of heart, this resistance to the will of God in Jesus, can become so entrenched that it cannot be overcome. This theme will be explored more fully in ch 4.

Interpreted in its narrative sequence, then, this warning is a reversal of the accusation of blasphemy leveled against Jesus by the scribes in 2:1-9. Instead of Jesus being guilty of blasphemy, their refusal is blasphemy. They do not see his ministry as the work of the Spirit of God renewing and re-creating his people. If the scribes continue to hold this view, they are doomed.

"Ironically, therefore, it is actually Jesus' enemies, who accuse him of demonic collusion, who are permanently wedded to Satan" (Marcus 2000, 284). Mark is careful to make clear the reason why Jesus made the statement, lest there be misunderstanding: **He said this because they were saying, "He has an evil spirit."**

■ **31-32** Jesus' family now returns to the scene. The irony of the opposition to Jesus continues. Between the two phases of opposition from Jesus' family, Mark has inserted the opposition by scribes. Those who are meant to be the guardians of the tradition and the truth for the people are completely wrong about Jesus. And so are those who are closest to him—his blood relations. Mark is not interested in where they have been during the dispute with the scribes.

But now **Jesus' mother and brothers** arrive. Jesus' family has only been introduced briefly in Mark. But who are Jesus' brothers? Are they his biological siblings? Three usual answers have been noted by commentators, all variously supported from the second century onward.

First, they are his biological siblings, that is, younger children of Mary and Joseph, a view held widely in the early church. Two other hypotheses are that "brothers" refers here to Jesus' cousins, or possibly stepbrothers, that is, children of Joseph by a previous marriage. Marcus (2000, 276) succinctly highlights the weaknesses of the latter two views. Donahue and Harrington (2002, 187-88) simply note that none of these views would compromise the doctrine of the virginal conception of Jesus. But they do not commit themselves more fully to one view or the other. Bauckham (1994) eliminates the cousin hypothesis but argues that the evidence is not strong enough to eliminate the stepbrother view. Nevertheless, the more natural reading probably makes Mark's point clearest—these are Mary's children and, therefore, Jesus' brothers.

Significantly, his mother and brothers are **standing outside** (*exō stēkontes*). Earlier they were outside seeking to restrain Jesus. Now they are standing outside, away from Jesus. Furthermore, rather than going inside to him, **they sent someone in to call him.** The symbolic nature of the separation from Jesus is highlighted not only by their location but by their calling him to leave those gathered around him.

They want him to return with them to their family home. This is a reversal of his radical call of the first disciples to leave their father in the boat (1:20). The NRSV captures the tone when it translates, "Then his mother and his brothers came; and standing outside, they sent to him and called him."

A crowd was sitting around him. Again, the location is important—it is the crowd who is with him (*peri autou*), those who have followed him to the house. They told Jesus, **Your mother and brothers are outside looking for you.** The phrase "and your sisters" is inserted after "brothers" in some early MSS, but omitted by others. The MS evidence is too balanced to decide (see Guelich 1989, 168; Collins 2007, 225; Marcus 2000, 276).

The crowd sitting around Jesus notes that his family is **outside looking for** him. In light of the tone of 3:21, this is rather more sinister than a social call. They are there to take him away from the crowd and the overexcitement of his own apparently delusional views. They want to save him from himself. And so they are **seeking** him (*zētousin*), used elsewhere to describe the plans of his opponents.

■ **33-35** The response of Jesus to the summons of his family is blunt, even shocking: **Who are my mother and my brothers?** Jesus questions the social reality in which the closest relationships are blood kinship. His is a new social reality. The restored people of God are now able to do the will of God because they are cleansed, healed, called, entrusted with the mission and message of Jesus, and, most importantly, are with him. This relationship with Jesus transcends the closest of kinship ties. So, it is not accidental that Jesus **looked at those seated in a circle around him.**

This may be a description of the seating plan in the house—in a circle around Jesus to hear his teaching. But it is also metaphorical. That is, these are the people who are circled around the Holy One in their midst. Given the recurrent themes of restoration and renewal already established by Mark, particularly in intertextual reflection on Isaiah, this circle is now the restored people of God, the remnant called to proclaim God's good news. This intimacy with Jesus is the closest possible relationship: **Here are my mother and my brothers! Whoever does God's will is my brother and sister and mother.**

The scene is graphic. Called to leave **those seated in a circle around him** (see Isa 49:18; 60:4) to see his family outside, he perhaps gestures and says, **See—my mother and my brothers** (*ide, hē mētēr mou kai hoi adelphoi mou*). He calls into existence "the eschatological family . . . by a gaze that takes possession of people and thus decisively routs the power of the Devil" (Marcus 2000, 286).

Jesus is gathering around himself a disparate group: the Twelve, the crowds, the cleansed, the healed, the forgiven, the formerly demonized. And he transforms them into his holy community—the restored kingdom of priests and the holy nation. They are reminiscent of those God first called—a collection of slaves. Their core characteristic is doing **God's will.**

This is Mark's only use of the phrase *the will of God.* So its meaning here cannot be determined from his direct use elsewhere. But the narrative setting helps. The debate with the family and scribes from Jerusalem about the origin of Jesus' mission and ministry, whether from God or another source, has been answered by Jesus. He is on God's mission (Mark 1:14-15) as the Holy One of God (1:27), obedient to God's purposes as the beloved Son (1:11).

His work is restoring the righteous remnant of Israel to fulfill the purposes for which God called them: to do the will of God. Those in the circle around Jesus, therefore, are not only those who follow him for their own purposes but also those who follow him in full identification with his mission.

For Jesus, doing the will of God has already encountered opposition from Satan. Opposition will continue and lead to his death, already prefigured in the story of the bridegroom (2:19).

The final statement Jesus makes is important for its inclusiveness. In his social context, the role of women would not have been prominent in the mission of God. Jesus states that **whoever does God's will is my brother and sister and mother.** His deliberate inclusion of women implies that women as well as men are seated in the circle around Jesus (see 15:41). It also contrasts with his statement in 3:32: his mother and brothers are outside looking for him. The inclusion of women in his inner circle is characteristic of the Jesus movement and represents a countercultural approach to women.

If Jesus is doing the will of the Father as the obedient Son, then his followers will also do the will of God by following Jesus. The will of God for disciples turns out to be remarkably similar to the will for Jesus (see 8:34-38).

At this point, however, the contrast is described in terms of outsiders vs. insiders. Those who began on the inside—scribes, Pharisees, and family members—have moved to the outside. Those on the outside—the unclean, marginalized and demonized, tax collectors and sinner—have been brought into the circle of the restored people who do the will of God.

FROM THE TEXT

This section makes some important points about God's purposes and the character of his people. The people of God are determined rather straightforwardly: They are those who do God's will.

Mark's story has dispelled several mistaken notions. The people of God are not determined by their intellectual acumen. The scribes from Jerusalem would have been the foremost interpreters of the Law in Judaism—temple-centered interpreters. They would know whether or not Jesus was of God—and they get it spectacularly wrong. Nor is membership in the people of God determined by family lineage. The people gathered around Jesus may well have included Gentiles—after all, Gentiles were already part of the crowd who came from a distance (→ 3:8).

The reminder that family connections are inconsequential in the kingdom of God challenges Evangelical Christianity's current emphasis on family values. If we recovered old-fashioned family values, so the argument goes, we would fix what is wrong with society. So attention is given to biological families. But Jesus subtly warns against an idolatrous fixation on families—especially "normal" families (Dad, Mom, two children, and a dog). The new fictive family gathered around Jesus takes precedence over natural families. Jesus emphasizes that the purposes of God take priority—those who are brothers and sisters on the way are the true family.

Donahue and Harrington note that this passage stresses "the radically communal nature of discipleship" (2002, 135). Following Jesus includes a willingness to act in solidarity with Jesus. At this point, the will of God is only vaguely pointed to the suffering of Jesus—in the oblique reference to the bridegroom's departure (2:20), the conspiracy of the Pharisees and the Herodians (3:6), and his identity as the beloved Son in ways that echo the Suffering Servant of God (1:11). To this point, those who follow Jesus do not know that this is a call to take up a cross (8:34-38). That will change soon enough. In the well-known words of Dietrich Bonhoeffer, "When Christ calls a man, he bids him come and die" (1959, 89).

Finally, the careless or thoughtless use of the "unpardonable sin" passage in sermons must be resisted. It is safe to say that anyone who is worried about this passage is unlikely to have committed such a sin. But the dangers of abuse are evident. Christians of all periods have struggled to understand this particular part of the story in a way that preserves the good news of forgiveness while retaining its challenge. It behooves preachers and teachers to exercise great care in interpreting this passage, especially for those of a sensitive conscience or for children who might be catching parts of a sermon intended for adults. Sadly, experience over the generations has shown that such care is not always taken.

But that is not to say this warning is unimportant. The warning is given to the scribes, those entrusted with teaching God's people. Donahue and Harrington follow Cranfield in suggesting that those who most particularly need to heed this warning are church leaders—theological teachers and official leaders (see 2002, 136). Great reticence needs to be exercised when pronouncing on whether or not some particular phenomenon or practice is of God, lest we be found opposing the work of the Spirit.

E. Kingdom Teaching (4:1-34)

Jesus came into Galilee announcing the good news that God's kingdom was at hand. But the expression **kingdom of God** has not been used again in the story until this section (vv 11, 26, 30). The crowd marvels that Jesus teaches with authority, heals the sick, and exorcises unclean spirits. But Mark has reported little actual teaching apart from the opening summary. Jesus' identity has been established in the narrative for the readers—the Son of God, the Holy One of God. Disciples have followed Jesus.

But Jesus' mission has also encountered opposition from the beginning. Resistance from unclean spirits is not unexpected (→ 1:24). But the opposition from the scribes and Pharisees is more surprising. Those closest to him in their desire to see Israel become God's holy people again, the Pharisees, have conspired with the agents of the state to find a way to kill him. The scribes, the guardians of the Law above all others, ought to know the Scriptures. They might have been expected to receive the message of the kingdom with anticipation, but they have rejected Jesus. Instead of seeing the will of God being accomplished in Jesus and his mission, they accuse him of being on the side of the enemies of God. Even his family has rejected him.

Why has the good news received such a mixed reception? The parable chapter offers a partial explanation. It also prepares the way for the increasingly polarized reception of the good news in the following chapters, and explains Jesus' activity in Gentile territory.

The overall narrative flow is relatively clear. But there are indications that Mark has brought this material together from a variety of sources and constructed it carefully to achieve his literary purposes. The passage includes a narrative introduction and conclusion (4:1-2, 33-34), both indicating that Jesus used parables in his teaching. But the internal structure is problematic. The literary seams have not been ironed out, leading to the suggestion that Mark is combining two sources.

Many scholars note that Jesus first addresses the crowds, then the disciples privately. There is no indication when the crowds again become his audience, although this is presumed by the conclusion of the section (see, e.g., Marcus 2000, 289). Collins thinks an oral tradition underlies the three parables (vv 3-8, 26-29, 30-32) and the conclusion in v 33. A different source portrays Jesus' parables as riddles (vv 3-9, 11-20, 34; Collins 2007, 240).

I. The Parable of the Sower (4:1-9)

BEHIND THE TEXT

This parable is at home in the agrarian setting of Galilee. A story of a sower scattering seed would make an immediate connection. Detail is missing, however. Is this sower broadcasting the seed? Does this fit with standard practice? Is this sower slightly extravagant? What prudent sower would spread precious seed on the path? These questions remain unanswered but may give clues as to the meaning of the parable.

There are important intertextual links, particularly the story of God's vineyard in Isa 5:1-10 (see Mark 12:1-9). Isaiah's parable about an unfruitful vineyard (Isa 5:10) pictures Judah and its failure to respond to God's care. This is expressed in his planting of the "vineyard on a fertile hillside" and his tender cultivation of it (Isa 5:1-2). Following the parable, Isaiah describes God's execution of judgment on Judah (Isa 5:16) as "the Holy One of Israel" (Isa 5:19, 24). Isaiah 6:1-6 has the prophet in the temple, where he sees the Lord's holiness in contrast to his own unworthiness and that of his people.

But God commands the prophet to go to the people on a strange mission: "Make the heart of this people calloused; make their ears dull and close their eyes. Otherwise they might see with their eyes, hear with their ears, understand with their hearts, and turn and be healed" (Isa 6:10). The sequence will be important for understanding the private teaching of Jesus in Mark 4:10-12, where Isa 6:11 is cited.

IN THE TEXT

■ **1-2** The continuity of this long teaching section with the preceding activity is noted: **Again Jesus began to teach.** The location is the same as earlier teaching (2:13; 3:7): **by the lake.** Mark notes that Jesus' teaching has authority (1:22, 27) but has not included much. He summarizes the content of Jesus' ministry as "the kingdom of God is near. Repent and believe the good news!" (1:15). But he offers no elaboration until now. Rather, he has focused on the identity of Jesus and the character of his mission. Readers could fill some gaps by reflecting on the Scriptures, particularly Isaiah (Hooker 2005, 49).

The numbers of people coming to Jesus are growing—even greater crowds (*ochlos pleistos*). Mark uses **crowd** in a variety of ways. In the preceding narrative a serious crowd of those doing the will of God sits around Jesus as his true family. But most follow him only superficially. The large crowd here almost certainly consists of a kind of mixture of serious and superficial followers.

This crowd **was so large that he got into a boat** (see 3:9). Here, however, the boat is not to escape the crush; it is his podium. Assuming the usual posture for a teacher, Jesus **sat in it.** His teaching is stressed by its threefold repetition: **Jesus began to teach . . . he taught them . . . in his teaching.**

Mark's Greek says (lit.), Jesus gets into the boat *to sit upon the sea* (an allusion to Ps 29:10? so Marcus 2000, 291). The Greek continues to be awkward, but the translation, **the people were along the shore at the water's edge,** adequately captures the sense. Jesus sits in a boat, from which he teaches the people standing on the shore, specifically **by parables.**

Parables

The popular definition of a parable as "an earthly story with a heavenly meaning" does not fit the parables in Mark. That definition owes more to Aristotle than to Jesus. Aristotle conceived of parables as serving a rhetorical function of persuading an audience. Collins (2007, 240) thinks that the parable of the sower may originally have had a rhetorical function, which is now unrecoverable. But that is not persuasive.

In the LXX, *parabolē* translates the Hebrew *mashal*. It is used in a variety of contexts referring to what we would call proverbs, riddles, wisdom sayings, and prophetic warnings. The word in 3:23 introduces Jesus' illustrative stories used in his debate with the scribes.

Parables often have hooks in their tails—surprises that jolt the perceptions of the hearer. The meaning of parables, "when discovered, is not likely to lie at the purely cognitive level, but will include (indeed, may even simply be) a call to response at the level of attitude, will, and action. To understand a *parabolē* is usually to be changed (or, at least challenged to change), not just enlightened" (France 2002, 183).

After the NT period, parables became almost synonymous with allegories. Interpreters expected every aspect of parables to signify something else. Origen wrote: "Not even the whole world itself could contain the books that might be written to fully clarify and develop the parables. But . . . a receptive heart might grasp something of them" (Oden and Hall 1998, 50). Clement of Rome moved easily from the parable of the sower to the fable of the Phoenix to illustrate Jesus' resurrection (Oden and Hall 1998, 50).

But allegorization of parables became unfashionable in the late nineteenth century. This gave rise to the equally inadequate view held for much of the twentieth century that parables have only one meaning.

Not all parables are allegories, but many parables have allegorical elements. Recent scholarly approaches to parables seek to understand them within their literary contexts as well as self-contained stories. The Markan Jesus interprets the parable of the sower as an allegory.

This is not all Jesus teaches (**many things by parables**). But the parable of the sower (and its interpretation) is the first of just two lengthy stories by Jesus included in Mark. Significantly, the other is a reworked version of the song of the vineyard from Isa 5 (in Mark 12:1-9).

■ **3-8** This parable has a fourfold pattern that speaks of four kinds of soil and what results from seed being planted in each. The open-endedness of the parable form requires hearers to interpret them in their context.

Thus, Jesus' teaching starts with the command to **Listen!** Listening should enable listeners to understand, if they are open to hearing. The word **Listen** signals the importance of what follows. It is linked to a Hebrew word that means both hear and heed. Thus, understanding should lead to an active response (Hooker 1991, 122). That is confirmed by the conclusion: "Let anyone with ears to hear listen!" (NRSV). Hearing is a main theme of this section.

The story starts with a common picture: *the sower went out to sow.* There is nothing extraordinary about the scene. Yet, there can be little doubt that Jesus intends his hearers to identify with the sower who has *gone out* (see 1:38; 2:13; 2:17) to proclaim the message of the kingdom. But the concern in the parable is with the fate of the seed, not of the sower. **As he was scattering the seed, some fell along the path** (*para tēn hodon*).

The seed falls on the edge of the path, *the way.* Readers already know *the way* of the Lord is important in Mark. But this seed is at risk because it is *beside the way.* In agricultural terms, it might not be covered over when the sower cultivates again. Quite naturally, **the birds came and ate it up.**

The description of the seed that **fell on rocky places** is longer than the others. Hearers would be familiar with rocky soil in Galilee. The fate of the seed fits into a realistic agricultural framework (but see France 2002, 191). Germination occurs quickly **because the soil was shallow** and warmer. But the new shoots **withered** in the hot sunshine over a period of days, **because they had no root** development due to the lack of soil and water.

There is no problem with the soil for the **seed** that **fell among thorns.** These seeds did not die; they just **did not bear grain** because the already established thorns provided too much competition for scarce moisture and nutrients.

Finally, **still other seed fell on good soil.** Where the soil was properly prepared, the seed **came up, grew and produced a crop.** Here the Greek changes from singular **seed** to plural; and the verb tense changes from the aorist (suggesting completed action) to imperfect (suggesting continuous action). "These subtle changes suggest both a multiplicity of sowings and a continual process of growth. The triadic pattern of sprouting, increasing, and giving fruit is in contrast to the three previous failures and suggests the ultimate 'triumph' of the good seed" (Donahue and Harrington 2002, 139). In the literary sequence, this emphasis on repeated sowing and continual growth is a reminder that the announcement of the kingdom has not been a one-time event. Jesus has proclaimed it repeatedly to the crowds, and it has been producing good fruit already.

The shock in this parable is the productivity of the seed: **multiplying thirty, sixty, or even a hundred times.** Some scholars now discount Jeremias' view that this yield is extraordinary (e.g., Collins 2007, 246). But they tend to depend on literary references to ancient crop yields. In fact, "the yield of the seeds in good ground represents what a farmer might reasonably hope for in a very good year" (France 2002, 193). Under modern agricultural conditions in a good year, thirtyfold or sixtyfold yields would not be unusual. But most farmers would consider a hundredfold yield extraordinarily fortunate.

■ 9 The conclusion to the parable ties it to the opening words—**Listen**. Jesus challenges those who are listening to reflect on the story and to make the appropriate application. His teaching implicitly announces the good news—the word that "the kingdom of God is near" (→ 1:15). But why has it not been heard?

The parable gives the impression that the problem is with neither the sower nor the seed. Rather, the condition of the soil makes the difference. There are, of course, massive crowds following Jesus, which indicates that some of the seed has fallen on good ground and produced abundant harvest already. The challenge to hearers, then, is to heed: "Let anyone with ears to hear listen!" (NRSV).

Despite the call for all to "Listen!" in v 3, this statement implies that only those with **ears to hear** will listen and discern in the ambiguities of their historical context that the kingdom of God is arriving.

Marcus notes the similarities and differences between 4 Ezra 4:26-29 (a late first century A.D. text) and this passage. He argues that "Mark is drawing on a standard apocalyptic metaphor: the new age will be like a miraculously fruitful field" (2000, 296). But in Mark the miraculous harvest produced by good soil coexists with the fruitlessness of the seeds sown on bad soil. Thus, to see the presence of the kingdom requires discernment. The mystery of the kingdom is only perceived by those with eyes to see and ears to hear. "For Mark this secret something is the cross, for it is there that the believer looks to see God's victory in an apparent defeat" (Marcus 2000, 297).

2. The Secrets of the Kingdom (4:10-34)

BEHIND THE TEXT

This section consists of five parts:

- a short response by Jesus to a question from those around him about the parables (4:10-12);
- a detailed interpretation of the parable of the sower (4:13-20);
- two short parables (4:21-25) that include the refrain "let anyone with ears to hear listen!" (NRSV);
- two parables directly illuminating the kingdom (4:26-32); and
- a summary of Jesus' use of parables (4:33-34).

The whole section forms a coherent piece, despite a number of places where gaps have to be filled in by readers.

The first section, sandwiched between the parable and its explanation, is relatively clear. It simply has Jesus tell the group around him that they, in contrast to others, have the privilege of having the mystery of the kingdom explained. But this is one of the most difficult passages in Mark. The reasons are not hard to find.

First, it raises enormous theological questions. Read as a propositional statement about the purpose of parables, it seems to claim that Jesus deliberately teaches in parables so that outsiders will not understand and so remain outside the renewed people of God. Apart from the theological challenges this reading poses, it does not cohere with the picture of Jesus and his announcement of the kingdom that has been emerging in Mark or with the flow of Mark's narrative to this point.

Second, why does Mark cite a part of Isa 6:9-10 at this point, but modify the wording of both the LXX and the MT (see Mark 8:17)? And what does the text mean in Isaiah? Does this meaning affect Mark's usage?

Such questions have occupied scholars for years. A previous generation of scholars concentrated on the source of individual units of the tradition that Mark may have used to try to explain this difficult section. Some argued, for instance, that Mark inserted vv 11-12 into the parable and its interpretation (see Guelich 1989, 199-203). But that merely invites more questions, since the attempt to separate tradition from redaction in Mark is notoriously difficult.

Recent Markan scholarship has examined the individual parts of the Gospel as a whole in light of its place in the narrative. It assumes that, whatever the *source* of the material, the key question has to do with Mark's *use* of the material. That approach is far more fruitful. Full answers to these questions are well beyond the scope of this commentary. The path charted here through these difficulties lets Mark speak for himself. However uncomfortable this may be at times, it makes sense within the narrative structure of the Gospel as a whole.

The next two parts of this major section are less fraught with difficulties. The interpretation of the parable of the sower provides illumination both to the parable and to the verses between them. The two parables of the kingdom will have encouraged Mark's first audience. Surely, they heard the words of Jesus to insiders as referring to them. And the summary of Jesus' parable teaching brings the whole section to a suitable close.

IN THE TEXT

a. Parables and the Mystery of the Kingdom (4:10-12)

■ 10 After Jesus finishes the parable of the sower, the scene changes. Jesus withdraws from the great crowd. There is no real time indication here. Mark could imply that Jesus left the boat and returned to the house. The close connection between the parable and its explanation, which follows immediately after this section, supports this view. But Mark's use of the imperfect tense may suggest that this questioning occurred on more than one occasion. This is not the only time Jesus teaches his followers away from the wider crowd. He taught those around him with the Twelve as they traveled. The tense could indicate that this was the regular pattern of Jesus' teaching. A pattern of public teaching and private explanation is not unusual in the 2TP. This reflects rabbinic practice (e.g., Beavis 1989, 75). Those around Jesus with the Twelve were taught by him, often on the journey itself.

Jesus does not explain the parable to the crowd. Rather, **when he was alone** (*kata monas*), he entertained the questions of his disciples. This is the only use of this Greek idiom in Mark. But a similar phrase (*kat'idian*) is used five times to describe Jesus' private teaching of the disciples away from the crowds (France 2002, 194 n. 31). Most of the teaching on discipleship in the central section (8:27—10:52) is private. Significantly, however, his earliest explicit invitation for followers to take up the cross is given to the disciples and the crowd (8:34).

The Twelve and the others around him need an explanation of the parables. They are not as perceptive as Jesus hopes (see v 13, noting his exasperation). Mark identifies them carefully: "those who were around him along with the twelve" (NRSV). This puts the emphasis where Mark does—upon those around Jesus. Mention of **the others around him** (*hoi peri auton*) also links directly to the previous story. They are those near to Jesus, his true family, because they do the will of God (3:31-35). Now they are privileged with the mystery of the kingdom (4:11). Mark's attention is on Jesus and his followers, not just the Twelve (→ 3:13).

An important narrative point needs to be made here. Without it the following statement can be misunderstood. These people **around him** are at the end of the process that has seen insiders move to the outside and outsiders become insiders. Proximity to Jesus determines who are insiders and outsiders. The spatial relationship makes a theological point.

From 1:16 on, Jesus has been gathering people to be with him and shaping them into his holy people. At the same time, others have been rejecting his message and his mission. Mark does not see insiders and outsiders as predetermined or fixed groups. Movement from one to the other is possible and has already occurred in the narrative. A person's place within God's people—either closer to Jesus or away from him—is based solely on one's response to him and his announcement and effecting of the kingdom of God. The boundary between insiders and outsiders is porous. "The group of those *peri auton* is self-selected, rather than predestined" (France 2002, 195, citing C. F. D. Moule).

125

Those around Jesus **asked him about the parables.** Their questioning is a sign of eager followers. Jesus' use of parables as his principal method of teaching (4:34) makes him distinctive. But this leaves him vulnerable to a variety of interpretations and multiple meanings. Parables, like other stories, are polyvalent. They are inevitably heard differently by different listeners. Hence, Jesus' parables are sometimes misunderstood; on other occasions, they are understood all too well (see 12:12). They are a risky way of teaching, because hearers fill in the gaps from their own preunderstanding or frame of reference—"that is the nature of parables!" (France 2002, 195-96).

■ II Jesus' explanation for telling parables has occasioned considerable debate. The chief question is, Can exclusion and confusion really have been the purpose of Jesus' parabolic teaching? In response to the question of his followers about parables, **he told them, "The secret of the kingdom of God has been given to you. But to those on the outside everything is said in parables."**

Jesus' statement contrasts two groups: those around him and those outside. This contrast has been taking shape since ch 2. At the close of ch 3, Jesus calls those closest to him those who do the will of God. That is, they participate with Jesus in the mission of God, announcing and effecting his kingdom.

This separation process is a scriptural pattern. Obedience to the will of God separates the remnant of God's holy people from those who refuse to honor God fully. A remnant returns from exile. The known holiness movements of Jesus' day, the Pharisees, the Dead Sea community, and the followers of John all separated from others because of their desire to live lives of purity in obedience to Torah.

In Jesus' case, the call has been first to be with him, and then to share in his mission (3:13-15). Healing, exorcisms, and cleansing touches have all been part of Jesus' teaching about the kingdom. By such means he re-creates a holy people of God, fit for the mission of God. Central to all of this is proximity to Jesus, the Holy One of God. To be sure, his call brings separation (see 1:16-20); and his teaching also leads to separation. But the insider/outsider contrast that emerges in the ministry of Jesus does not oppose Jews and Gentiles. Nor does it reflect the extended standards of priestly purity. It depends solely on one's response to Jesus.

The secret . . . has been given (*dedotai*) to the circle around Jesus. The perfect passive implies that the secret is a gift from God, not a consequence of the inductive reasoning of disciples. It is also a reminder that the mystery of the kingdom has already been disclosed to them through the gradual unveiling of Jesus as the Holy One through whom the good news of God is happening. This is not a new secret. Nor is it best understood in terms of the so-called messianic secret, although the suffering-son-of-man character of Jesus' messiahship is yet to be disclosed.

The secret (*to mystērion*), better translated ***the mystery,*** is used only here in the Synoptic Gospels (Matt 13:11 and Luke 8:10 have "secrets"). The term has deep roots in late 2TP literature. It translates the Aramaic and Hebrew term *rāz*, which is used in both singular and plural to refer to the mystery of God's purposes. In Dan 2, it refers to the hidden purposes of God that are revealed in visions.

It is used at Qumran to describe the mystery of God's purposes set out in Scripture but now revealed to the community in their *pesharim*. Thus, in the 2TP, the mystery is essentially eschatological. That is, it focuses on God's plans for the end times (see 4QInstruction [4Q417]). In Mark 4:11 "the divinely willed way in which the rule of God will manifest itself and come to fulfillment through the agency of Jesus' is the meaning" (Collins 2007, 248). The mystery is already being revealed in Jesus. That is, the purposes of God are already being revealed in Jesus' word and deeds to those who have ears to hear.

This points forward to the revelation of God's purposes in the rest of Mark. They are seen in the cross-bearing servanthood of Jesus and the disciples, the relentless journey to the cross, and the bleak future of the temple. The mystery is revealed to the followers of Jesus on the journey. They gradually begin to see the big picture of God's purposes more clearly, revealed in Jesus. Finally, on the cross, the purposes of God become focused in the death of Jesus. Those who look at Jesus on the cross are invited to see and believe. The words of the chief priests and the scribes in 15:31-32 are dripping with irony.

But while the mystery is revealed, it is by no means comprehended fully even by those around Jesus. Because it is the mystery of **the kingdom of God,** it is "so paradoxical, so totally opposed to natural human insight, that it takes nothing less than divine revelation to enable people to grasp it" (France 2002, 197).

Here, Jesus speaks in parables (4:2). Later in the chapter he tells as many parables as his followers can grasp and explains everything to them (4:33-34). The misunderstanding of those who should be closest to Jesus continues throughout the narrative.

By the time we come to 8:32, Jesus no longer speaks in parables. There he gives an explicit prediction about the fate of the Son of Man—and immediately meets resistance from his disciples, particularly from Peter (see Collins 2007, 249). The coming of the kingdom is a mystery that can be comprehended only by revelation.

Jesus explains the mystery to those around him. **But to those on the outside everything is said in parables.** The key question here is, Who are **those on the outside**? Taken in isolation from its narrative context, this might refer simply to those not around Jesus. That is, some of those in the crowds who come to see and hear him, perhaps for healing or cleansing, are outside the inner circle. They receive (*ginetai*) **everything** (*ta panta*) in parables without explanation. Thus, **everything** may mean words and deeds of Jesus, as well as parables. The plural **in parables** has the adverbial sense of parabolically (Donahue and Harrington 2002, 140). Perhaps this is why even insiders need the parables explained to them (v 13).

■ **12** Verse 12, taken in isolation, is bleak and uncompromising. Few texts have received more scholarly attention (see Evans 1989 and Beavis 1989). The NIV translation, if anything, is bleaker than the Greek text. It focuses upon the idea of always seeing and hearing but never perceiving and understanding. From that perspective, there is no hope for outsiders (see 3:29). But is this the only way to read this passage?

Are misunderstanding and obduracy the intention or the consequence of Jesus' teaching and ministry? The answer hinges on the translation of two key words: *hina*, **so that**, and *mēpote*, **otherwise** ("in order that" and "so that" [NRSV]). Evans offers six alternatives, finally deciding that these words indicate the *purpose* of the parables. Jesus tells parables "to prevent them [the outsiders] from understanding, repentance and forgiveness" (1989, 92-96, 98).

Four alternatives that avoid this conclusion are offered by France (2002, 199):

- *hina* introduces a citation;
- *hina* is a mistranslation of an Aramaic word meaning "who";
- *hina* may be used to express result (like *hōste*) rather than cause;
- *hina* is a Semitic way of expressing first causes that bypass human decision.

France favors the fourth possibility. If this idea is behind the statement, the point is that "the ultimate outcome falls within the overall purpose of God" (France 2002, 199). These alternatives make it clear that the meaning cannot be determined by translation only.

As noted above, the citation comes from Isa 6:9-10. Mark has replaced "be healed" in Isa 6:10 with "be forgiven" (*aphethēi*). That change is reflected in the later Targum of Isaiah. Thus, it might be the Aramaic form used during the time of Jesus (Donahue and Harrington 2002, 141). This is possible. But "be forgiven" in Mark's usage is linked with **turn** (*epistrepsōsin*). It implies a reversal of one's present direction and being purified in order to become a part of the renewed holy people (see Mark 1:4-5).

More important for understanding the text is the extent to which the sequence of Isaiah's story is echoed in Mark's sequence and plays a role in its use of the text. In Isaiah, the obduracy pronouncement comes at the end of a sequence in which the people of God are invited repeatedly to return to God. It follows the parable of the vineyard (→ 4:1-9 BEHIND THE TEXT).

MARK

4:11-12

Thus, in Isaiah it concludes a lengthy wooing by God of the wayward people of Judah through his prophet. This clearly parallels the sequence of movement from insider to outsider and vice versa in Mark.

If this is what is implied, then misunderstanding and obduracy are the result of the ministry of Jesus, not its purpose. The scribes from Jerusalem, the Pharisees, and his own family have put themselves outside. This is no surprise to Jesus. It has been the historic response to the good news: Some receive it gladly; others stubbornly reject it. They do not have ears that hear—they just don't get it.

Read in isolation, this text is deterministic and bleak. But in its narrative sequence and with an awareness of the Isaianic sequence, the inability to hear—hardness of heart—is the inevitable and tragic consequence of rejecting the announcement of the kingdom.

b. The Interpretation of the Parable of the Sower (4:13-20)

■ **13** Despite their proximity to Jesus, even those around him do not understand the parables. They ask Jesus to explain them. He responds to their question with another question: **Don't you understand this parable?** The question is odd, since it focuses only on the parable of the sower and since he has just told them that they have been given the mystery of the kingdom. It carries an overtone of criticism, perhaps anticipating the disciples' frequent misunderstanding (see esp. 8:14-21; 10:35-45).

Donahue and Harrington suggest that Jesus' response is given on a number of levels. It might refer to the parable of the sower or to the statement just given or to the interpretation that follows. Their paraphrase captures Mark's perspective: "If you don't understand that the mystery of the kingdom is the paradox of the cross you will not understand the failure of the seeds and you will misinterpret the paradoxes of the reign of God that emerge in the following parables" (2002, 141). In effect, Jesus is saying, if you cannot understand the parable of the sower, **How then will you understand any parable?** or, indeed, the whole paradoxical coming of the kingdom?

■ **14-20** Jesus explains the parable. But he leaves the identity of *the sower* unexplained. It could refer to God, who speaks the divine word; to Jesus, who announces the good news; or to Mark's readers, who proclaim the good news (Marcus 2000, 311). The proclamation of the word continues as the sower sows (*speirei*). The seed that is sown is **the word,** without further description; but it likely means the gospel (see 1:45; 2:2).

Greatest attention is given to the fate of the sown seed. **Some people are like seed** sown beside **the path, where the word is sown.** Although the construction is difficult, the meaning is clear enough. The seed beside the way is quickly devoured by birds. In *Jub.* 11:11-14, the Satan figure (Prince Mastema; see VanderKam 2001, 128-29) is pictured as a bird devouring the seeds of the farmers in Babylon. This seems a plausible background for the link between the birds and Satan here.

The conflict between Jesus and **Satan** already taking place in Jesus' ministry should be kept in mind. The parable explanation gives no indication how Satan devours the sown seed. Jesus implies that those who oppose the good news he announces are doing the work of Satan (see 8:33). This is not without irony. Recall that the scribes from Jerusalem accused Jesus of working in league with Satan (3:22-25), thereby warning the people against Jesus. But, on the contrary, they are doing Satan's work. In their opposition to Jesus, **Satan comes and takes away the word that was sown in them.**

The **seed sown on rocky places** refers to those who **hear the word and at once receive it with joy.** They initially respond to Jesus with great enthusiasm. This refers to the fate of many in the great crowd following him, who by the end call for his crucifixion (15:13). It is also a painful reminder to readers of those who start on the way but fall away in the face of opposition (see esp. ch 13 and the Passion Narrative). The concern would not be lost on Mark's first readers.

The reason they fall away is that their commitment is shallow. They have **no root** (*rizan en heautois*). This, perhaps, implies a weakness of character or lack of courage in the face of **trouble** [*thlipseōs* = **tribulation**] **or persecution.** Persecution **because of the word** need not refer to state persecution. It applies equally well to low-level hostility on social or religious grounds that is the precursor to the official persecution that follows in the history of the church (see also 10:30). Without roots, disciples **quickly fall away** (*skandalizontai*). This same word describes failed discipleship in 14:27.

The third group is **like seed sown among thorns.** This is not a failure of soil or seed. The focus is on the thorns that deprive the seed of nutrients and light. Mark gives a threefold elaboration of these in terms that resonate with readers, then and now. These secondary concerns that hamper discipleship are elaborated on in the three stories in ch 10, where the issues of power (10:1-12), status (10:13-16), and security (10:17-22) are addressed by Jesus.

Jesus implies that these people do have ears to hear and do **the word.** But their commitment to following Jesus is hampered by three things:

- *the anxieties of the present times* (*hai merimnai tou aiōnos*). These are the temporal concerns of people living in the "real world." In NT eschatology in general, this age is passing away. The issues of this age can refer to legitimate concerns (2 Cor 11:28). But the best commentary on this might be Matt 6:25-34. There the cognate verb *merimnaō* is used. Jesus' command not to worry is linked to confidence in the care of their heavenly Father (see 1 Pet 5:7) and the conviction that the present age is temporary. Matthew concludes this instruction with the command to seek the kingdom of God.

- **the deceitfulness** [*apatē* could have the slightly less sinister sense of *lure*] **of wealth.** Here the language has a particularly strong meaning (see France 2002, 206), implying that wealth has a deceptive, entrapping power. The story of the rich man in 10:17-22 illustrates this issue. The language has overtones of idolatry. The man prefers retaining his wealth to serving Jesus. Matthew adds a comment on this: "You cannot serve both God and Money" (Matt 6:24).

- **the desires for other things.** Desires (*epithymiai*) is sometimes used in the NT in a neutral sense, of natural desires. But more often, they are misguided cravings. Paul uses the term to mean covetousness (Rom 7:8). **Desires for other things** (*hai peri ta loipa epithymiai*) captures the focus on secondary issues. Far from being "a rather lame conclusion" (France 2002, 206), this is a powerful warning against preoccupation with the peripheral and the ephemeral. The best commentary is Matt 6:33, where the focus is to be upon the kingdom, not "all these things."

Jesus is not concerned about wealth or things per se, but about one's inner disposition toward them. He uses the "thought"-words (France 2002, 206) anxieties, deception, and desires for the secondary concerns that **come in and choke the word.** Ephemeral interests can take hold of people and become the idolatrous focus of their lives.

By contrast, the single-minded devotion of God's holy people to him and his mission is the source of their fruitfulness. Devotion to anything else leads to **making** the word **unfruitful.**

In contrast to the three kinds of unproductive soil, Jesus refers to the **others** who **hear the word, accept it, and produce a crop—thirty, sixty or even a hundred times what was sown.** Jesus does not explain the metaphorical crop, nor what constitutes its astonishing growth. But *karpophorousin* in Col 1:6, 10 refers to the growth of the gospel, which is probably the implication here.

The threefold pattern of **hear . . . , accept . . . , and produce** contrasts the fate of the three soils that do not produce fruit with that of the good soil. Although the quantity of fruit is uneven, the good soil produces fruit. Throughout this parable, there is an organic connection between good seed and good soil. "This verse becomes an extravagant promise in contrast to the predicted rejection and failure of vv 11-12" (Donahue and Harrington 2002, 142).

c. Four Short Sayings (4:21-25)

Four short sayings continue the theme of hiddenness and disclosure that has been a narrative subplot since ch 2. The good news of the kingdom has been announced and effected by Jesus. Many are following him and those gathered around him are doing the will of God. But to those who refuse to hear or see, the good news remains a mystery. Indeed, those who look and hear but do not see and listen, lose the possibility of seeing and hearing, and align themselves with the opposition to God's rule.

■ **21** The first statement is written in the form of a rhetorical question that expects a "No" answer. It posits a commonsense absurdity: **Do you bring in a lamp to put it under a bowl or a bed?** Of course not. If a lamp were placed under a large measuring basket (*modios*) **or a bed,** these not only would obscure the light but also would probably catch on fire.

The **lamp** might be an allusion to Jesus—the light of the world, a metaphor used in John. Or, it may refer to the message of Jesus, which had to be announced widely and publicly, not squelched. If so, it continues the theme of the preceding parable: The seed is scattered widely, but it takes root and produces good fruit only in receptive soil.

■ **22-23** The point of the saying is this: **whatever is hidden is meant to be disclosed.** The good news of God's purposes, unknown in the past, has been **brought out into the open** in the words and works of Jesus. This saying counters any reading of vv 10-12 that might imply that the teaching of Jesus is esoteric knowledge disclosed only to the inner circle. On the contrary, the mystery of the kingdom is openly explained so that the disciples might participate in of the proclamation of the good news.

This is particularly seen in the supramundane character of the conflict in which Jesus is engaged. The true character of rebellious Israel and the world is now out in the open. And the true identity of Jesus will be revealed finally at the crucifixion (see 15:39). But the mystery, even at the cross in a scene full of irony, is only revealed to those who are prepared to hear it: *let the one with ears to hear, hear.*

■ **24-25** Jesus warns those who are listening, inviting them to *observe* what they **hear** (*blepete ti akouete*). The word **hear** is a connecting motif with the parable of the sower and the preceding stories. The language of seeing and hearing is often important (e.g., 8:15). *Pay attention* captures the meaning better than **Consider carefully.** The precise literary link of the saying to the context is unclear here (see Matt 7:2 ‖ Luke 6:38). It probably refers back to the previous scenes. If so, the implication is that those who ought to have known what was happening in Jesus' work—the scribes and his family—get it badly wrong. By rejecting Jesus "even what they have will be taken away" (Mark 4:25c NRSV).

But those who hear the word produce an abundant harvest: **whoever has will be given more.** "These verses emphasize the positive message of vv. 12-20: the word is meant to be heard, the seed to grow, the lamp to give light; ultimately God's purpose will be victorious. But the responsibility of men and women to respond remains: anyone with ears to hear may hear; therefore everyone must take care how he hears" (Hooker 1994, 135).

d. The Seed (4:26-29)

The following two parables describe the kingdom of God. They follow nicely from the parable of the soils and further explain the pattern that has been emerging in Mark about the teaching of the kingdom.

The first parable is the more elaborate of the two with a sower who plants a seed, who cannot explain its growth, but who harvests the crop when it produces fruit. In literary terms, the different stages are similar to the various kinds of soil in the earlier parable. But their description is also true to a farmer's observations of crops: planting, germination, growth, filling, ripening, and harvest. At each stage, the crop's development wholly depends on factors outside the farmer's control.

■ **26-27** That **he also said** gives the impression that this is one of several parables Jesus uses to describe **what the kingdom of God is like.** Some identify Jesus as the **man** who sows the **seed.** But there is no allegorical interpretation of this parable. The sower could be God or Jesus or those who announce the mystery of the kingdom. If the sower is Jesus, the remainder of the parable does not cohere with the picture of him that emerges in Mark. It seems more likely to refer to any who proclaim the good news of the kingdom. In Mark's narrative this includes the Twelve and others who are doing the will of God. In this Markan context, therefore, it almost certainly continues the polyvalent images already in this section. The parables are capable of a range of meanings within the Markan setting.

Night and day reflects the Semitic sequence where a day is from evening to morning (see Gen 1). It does not matter whether the farmer **sleeps or gets up.** He can do nothing to make the crop grow. This implies that the advance of the kingdom is entirely under God's control. He alone ensures that **the seed sprouts and grows** (see 1 Cor 3:7).

■ **28** Clearly, this is the good soil of 4:8, because **all by itself the soil produces grain.** The kingdom has not arrived in its fullness. The growth pattern—**first the stalk, then the head, then the full kernel in the head**—is a reminder that the kingdom is dynamic. It is in the process of arriving; it has not come to its consummation. Completion is assured because it is within the promise of the new thing God is inaugurating in the work of Jesus.

■ **29** At harvest, however, the farmer springs into action: **As soon as the grain is ripe, he puts the sickle to it.** Harvest comes when the grain is ripe. Impatience does nothing to hasten it. The primary image is joyous—a good harvest is always a blessing to a farmer.

But a judgment motif may also be here; the language at the end of the verse is similar to Joel 3:13, which refers to the eschatological judgment of God. That possibility is strengthened by the inclusion in the harvest metaphor of the separation of wheat from chaff (see Matt 3:12 ‖ Luke 3:17) or wheat from weeds (Matt 13:30).

e. The Mustard Seed (4:30-32)

The concluding parable in this chapter is less elaborate. With ironic hyperbole the smallest seed becomes the largest plant, allowing the birds of the air to use its branches. This parable paradoxically contrasts inauspicious beginnings with amazing results. Jesus has proclaimed the kingdom of God. But its beginnings have been difficult—acclamation mixed with rejection. After all, this good news is being announced by a Galilean peasant (see the distain implied in 14:70) thought to be acting in the power of Beelzebub by the authoritative teachers from Jerusalem.

Insignificant beginnings do not determine the final results, because this is the good news of God. The previous parable showed that the proclamation of the word by Jesus and his followers is essential. But this in itself does not produce the fruit. This parable offers great encouragement that God's ultimate purposes will be accomplished despite inauspicious beginnings. The whole chapter will be heard by Mark's readers as a word of encouragement.

■**30** The parable opens with a double introduction: **What is the kingdom . . . like, or what parable shall we use to describe it?** This short parable is a simile—a particularly brief form of parable familiar to modern readers. The double introduction is similar to Isa 40:18, but that introduction is in a rather different context (France 2002, 215). Rabbinic parables often have a double introduction (Donahue and Harrington 2002, 151).

■**31-32a** The comparison is with **a mustard seed.** Mustard is a common plant in the area, but the precise variety of mustard is unclear (France 2002, 216; Donahue and Harrington 2002, 151). This seed was proverbial for being **the smallest seed** (commentators regularly cite *m. Nid.* 5:2). The simile is used in Matt 17:20 and Luke 17:6 to describe a minuscule amount of faith. Here, the small seed must be planted on the ground—the good news must be announced, despite the risk. But that which falls on good soil produces **the largest of all garden plants.**

■**32b** So far, the simile is coherent. Mustard is a large garden plant. But when the parable says that this mustard plant has **such big branches that the birds of the air can perch in its shade,** the story becomes extraordinary. The main point is clear: The good purposes of God will come to fruition. These are beyond the imagination of those who are planting the seed and watching it grow. Marcus (2000, 330) calls attention to the intertextual links with Ezek 17:23; 31:6; and Dan 4:12. In Ezekiel, God's planting becomes a cedar and "birds of every kind will nest in it; they will find shelter in the shade of its branches."

If this is the background here, the irony is important. Instead of a splendid cedar, referring to the renewed kingdom of David, and therefore a mighty messianic vision, this picture of the kingdom of God is compared to an extraordinary mustard plant—one that provides shelter for the nations. Ezekiel 31:6 and Dan 4:18 describe Egypt and Babylon respectively.

Significantly, the birds of the air in these intertextual links refer to Gentiles. Mark

> would expect his readers . . . to conclude that, as the seedlike hiddenness of Jesus' earthly ministry and ignominious death has now given way to the plantlike revelation of the Christian mission, so the seedlike hiddenness of the present situation of suffering will soon give way to the plantlike revelation of the parousia. . . . [N]ot only is [the word] the means of *describing* the new creation, the dominion of God, but it is also the very instrument for *bringing it into being.* (Marcus 2000, 331)

The challenge to God's reign manifest in the parody of power that is the Roman Empire is a subtle backdrop to this parable. The paradoxes in the parable: small beginnings and mustard plant vs. the mighty cedar and Rome's imperial status is seen historically in the crucifixion of Jesus. Imperial Rome and its servants seem to defeat the pathetic crucified Messiah. Some of Mark's readers may well be alert to the irony that the kingdom of God is established in the face of the blatant and grotesque manifestation of imperial power symbolized in a Roman cross.

f. Teaching Summary (4:33-34)

■ **33** The parables conclude with a Markan summary. The parables included 4:32b-34 in this chapter are only part of **many similar parables.** But use of parables is characteristic of Jesus' teaching: **Jesus *was speaking*** [*elalei*] **the word,** again without qualification. But it must mean the good news of the kingdom.

The parables are told to all who would listen, but only "as they were able to hear it" (NRSV). Some argue that this contradicts 4:11-12. But it actually helps clarify how Mark understands this difficult passage. It reflects on the varieties of receptions the word has. Others see this as the conclusion to one of the two collections combined by Mark to make this section, with v 34 being the second ending (Collins 2007, 256). But even if this is so, these two verses do not contradict each other.

■ **34** This reiterates the use of parables as Jesus' preferred teaching method to the crowds. Not all will understand, however, so **he explained everything** to his disciples. Although it is possible that **his own disciples** refers just to the Twelve, it more refers to those gathered around him (→ 3:33-35; 4:10). The Twelve do not receive private teaching here in Mark.

FROM THE TEXT

This section is full of important theological motifs. We have already noted that the parables come at the end of a sequence in which the identity of

Jesus has been gradually revealed and in which he has gathered people to himself. At the same time, the inexplicable rejection of Jesus by those who ought to have known him best lies behind this section as well.

First, Mark's readers would be encouraged by these parables. They would have identified themselves with the good soil and the expected fruitful seed. But they may have been puzzled by the persecution they were experiencing and the apparently slow progress of the good news. This section explains that the good news is not accepted by all. Some simply do not understand. To them everything is in opaque parables that they hear but do not grasp.

Nevertheless, Mark encourages his audience to continue to proclaim the good news in word and deed. After all, if this is the light shining in the darkness, it needs to be allowed to shine. They must be patient. They can announce the good news, but they cannot determine the rate of its progress. They sow the seed, but they cannot cause it to germinate, sprout, fill, or ripen. God will bring his kingdom to its fullness, not human effort.

Second, the stories are a reminder that blindness and rejection occur even in the people who ought to know best who Jesus is, and who ought to align themselves with God's purposes. People can move from the "inside" to the "outside." When that happens, they no longer see God at work in the mystery of the kingdom. They miss the working of God in the small beginnings of his renewed people gathered around Jesus. This helps explain the rejection of the Jewish Messiah by most Jews and the shameful death of Jesus as the Messiah. They may be God's people by birth. But holiness is not a birthright or an heirloom. It is the consequence of being near the Holy One.

Third, Mark's readers are challenged to announce the good news to all, even while recognizing that sometimes the word will not take root. And even if it does, it may sometimes not produce the desired results. There is no restriction of the announcement of God's good purposes. They are all-embracing. There are no preconditions of who should be told. At the same time, this proclamation is not universally received or accepted.

Fourth, one key lesson arises from the lengthy description of the things that prevent the word from being productive. This has an uncanny contemporary ring. Sadly, experience has, time and time again, confirmed the reality of these dangers. For some, the cares of the world occupy both time and attention. Even legitimate concerns—family, health, education, the good things of life—can take precedence over the kingdom of God. When our ultimate focus is on the family or any other worldly concerns, the attention the kingdom requires can be compromised.

Especially in the wealthy West, delight in money and the things it can buy can take on a demonic character. It can become an idol, usurping the worship of God and obedience to his commands. The pursuit of money and the desire for things can squeeze the very life out of Christians, causing them to wither and die. For others, these pursuits do not entirely squeeze out the life of the Spirit. But they make persons and families fruitless in kingdom terms.

Ironically, the larger people's homes become and the more affluent they are, the less hospitable and generous they become. They no longer have time for the marginalized. They lose their generosity of spirit. Hence the possibility of fruit-bearing can be compromised by the subtle creep of idolatry in the tacit allegiance given the things of this age. The most tragic aspect of this is that the peril is recognized too late.

Fourth, the kingdom comes to fulfillment in the future. Miracles and exorcisms are signs pointing forward to the mystery of the coming kingdom. Paradoxically, the kingdom of God comes through the death of his Messiah.

Fifth, the mystery of God's good purposes is not an esoteric or exclusive message for the few. It is good news for all. Nevertheless, not all who hear the good news accept it. There is a cost to following Jesus; he is unlike the Messiah most expect.

F. Who Is This Person? (4:35—6:6a)

The unveiling of Jesus' identity to his followers continues. Although Mark has included some miracles in the narrative, the greatest concentration of them occurs in 4:35—8:26. A series of journeys on the Sea of Galilee is included. Jesus' ministry has been concentrated around this symbolic boundary between Jewish and Gentile territories. Hence, the crossings are also theologically significant. Although there is residual opposition to Jesus in these sections (6:1-6a; 7:1-13; 8:15), the concentration is elsewhere.

In this section the disciples continue to be with Jesus and participate in his mission. Nevertheless, their understanding of Jesus remains sketchy. Mark even describes their hearts as hardened (6:52) and has Jesus ask them: **Are your hearts *still* hardened?** (8:17).

I. Stilling the Storm (4:35-41)

BEHIND THE TEXT

This is the first of the so-called nature miracles. Their distinction from other miracles and exorcisms is somewhat artificial. Rational explanations have been attempted for healings as involving psychosomatic illness and exorcisms as epilepsy in the interests of reducing modern incredulity. But ending a storm on the lake is not amenable to such rationalization. Mark makes no distinction between these events. They all reveal the kingdom and the true identity of Jesus. Explanations, therefore, ought to be sought within Mark's narrative world rather than other alternatives.

This story is particularly rich in intertextual links. The picture of Yahweh in Ps 107:23-29 includes language that echoes here:

> Others went out on the sea in ships; . . . they saw the works of the LORD . . . he spoke and stirred up a tempest that lifted high the waves. . . . in their peril their courage melted away. . . . they were at their wits' end. Then they cried out to the LORD in their trouble, and he brought them out of their distress. He stilled the storm to a whisper; the waves of the sea were hushed.

Other OT accounts of Yahweh's mastery over the sea create a context for understanding Jesus' calming the sea. The story of Yahweh's deliverance of the Israelites at the Sea of Reeds (Exod 14:21-31) was embedded deep in the identity of all Jews. Verbal parallels to the story of Jonah are indirect, but the situations are similar (Jonah 1:1-16; Guelich 1989, 266). These and many other OT stories of Yahweh's mastery over the sea create a context in which the action of Jesus in calming the sea is a significant point of revelation.

The Sea of Galilee is little more than a lake. But its location and topography make it particularly vulnerable to Mediterranean-brewed storms, which can arise quickly. Even on a small but deep body of water a boat can be easily capsized or swamped. An unexpected nighttime storm can cause anxious moments even for experienced sailors. That these fishermen are at their wits' end, however, is surprising. This is no ordinary boat trip. Thus, like the parables, a routine story has an astonishing (Hooker [1992, 139] thinks intrinsically improbable) dimension.

In 1986 during a period of low water on the lake, an ancient fishing boat, dating from the time of Jesus, was discovered buried in the mud along the northwest shore of the Sea of Galilee. Soon dubbed "the Jesus boat," it probably resembles the kind of fishing boat that plied the fishing trade in Jesus' day. Its dimensions are about 8.2 meters (27 feet) long, 2.3 meters (7.5 feet) wide with a depth of about 1.25 meters (4 feet). It originally had a sail and places for four oarsmen and a steersman (Hanson 1997). Such a shallow boat would be at risk in a gale.

This is the first of several journeys Jesus makes across the sea, going from Jewish to Gentile territory. These boat trips are particular points of revelation in which significant teaching takes place. Mark tells this story with great care: The historic present tense provides the framework; five aorist verbs indicate Jesus' decisive actions and the fear of the disciples; an imperfect tense verb describes their continuing discussion. "The tenses are far from haphazard; rather, they demonstrate the natural ability of the storyteller to focus his audience's attention appropriately on the different aspects of the story as it develops" (France 2002, 222).

■ **35** Two time designations, **that day** and **when evening came,** provide the temporal setting (compare 1:32, 35; 2:20). This narrative marker may indicate that 4:1-34 is to be read as a literary unit. Perhaps this is "an anthology of Jesus' more extensive parable teaching" (so France 2002, 222). More probably, it merely draws attention to the time of the crossing. A night-crossing makes the subsequent squall more frightening, signaling that this is no ordinary crossing. If the seasoned seamen had no misgivings before they embarked, they may have questioned their judgment later.

In the story Jesus takes the initiative: **Let us go over to the other side.** Does he deliberately take a journey to Gentile territory at this risky time of day? At first glance, nothing in the story suggests that. But, as it turns out, the sole purpose of the journey is the exorcism of Legion (5:1-20). People from "the regions across the Jordan" (3:8) have come to Jesus; now he deliberately goes to their territory.

■ **36** Several points tie this story to what has gone before. **The crowd** refers to those who have been listening to Jesus throughout this chapter. Jesus is, once again, in the boat, although the language—**they took him along, just as he was, in the boat** (*paralambanousin auton hōs ēn tōi ploiōi*)—is awkward. It is better translated *they took him since he was already in the boat* (France 2002, 223). This was the boat in which Jesus had been teaching in 4:1 on the day of parables.

Not all who listened to Jesus follow him across the lake. But Mark tells us **there were also other boats with him.** More than the Twelve accompanied him, but they immediately drop out of the story. What happened to them?

■ **37** **A furious squall** (*lailaps megalē anemou*) probably means something like "a sudden tornado-like whirlwind" (Donahue and Harrington 2002, 158). In a craft like the "Jesus boat," that **the waves broke over the boat, so that it was nearly swamped** might be expected.

This aspect of the story is, of course, open to many metaphorical interpretations. Readers may well have seen the sudden rise of opposition that would threaten to overwhelm the fragile people of God. That was Matthew's reading, and it could be a legitimate lesson here. But the focus of this story is elsewhere.

■ **38** That **Jesus was in the stern, sleeping** is plausible and also reminiscent of Jonah. But there the similarities end. Jonah serves as an antitype in early Christian tradition (Collins 2007, 260). Jesus' sleep is probably due to exhaustion. Perhaps, as a part of the conflict with evil in which he is engaged, the storm arises because he is in the boat. If so, the storm is symbolic of opposition

MARK

4:35-38

to God and his rule. In this context, his mastery over the sea and the storm appear to be important for the subsequent story.

The contrast between Jesus and the disciples, who are in a state of panic, is evident. Significantly, **the disciples** turn to him in desperation, wakening him from sleep (see Ps 44:23—"Awake, O Lord! Why do you sleep? Rouse yourself! Do not reject us forever").

The disciples' question, **"Don't you care . . . ?"** (*ou melei soi*) is actually an accusation arising from their panic. They address him as **Teacher** (*didaskale*), not "Lord" as in the parallel story in Matt 8:25 or "Master, Master" as in Luke 8:24. This describes their characteristic relationship with Jesus (see Mark 1:27).

■ **39** If the Jonah story is an intertextual link, Jesus' behavior is exactly the opposite of Jonah's. Instead of an indirect or direct appeal to God (Jonah asks to be thrown overboard), Jesus **rebuked** [*epetimēsen*] **the wind and said to the waves, "Quiet! Be still** [*pephimōso*]**!"**

This is not an appeal to God. Rather, this language describes Yahweh's control over the sea in passages like Pss 65:7 and 107:28-29. "Thus, Jesus is portrayed not so much as a human being who has trust in God's power to save, but as a divine being" (Collins 2007, 260). This is a significant addition to the revelation of the identity of Jesus: He acts as God acts and exercises the power and authority God exercises over the mythic forces of the sea.

There is a clear link in this passage to the first exorcism. The verbs used to describe Jesus' rebuke of the demon in Mark 1:25 (*epetimēsen* and *pimōthēti*) are repeated here. These verbs regularly occur outside the context of exorcisms, but the similarities here are remarkable (but see France 2002, 224). And the response of the crowd to the exorcisms (1:27) is similar to that of the disciples here (4:41).

These similarities suggest that Mark takes the storm as more than a natural phenomenon. The idea of the sea as personified is present in Ps 106:9: "He rebuked [*epetimēsen*] the Red Sea." Similar references to the mastery of Yahweh over primeval sea monsters in other OT passages (Isa 27:1; 51:9; Job 9:13; 26:12; Pss 89:9-10; 74:13) suggest that the storm itself is personified in this story. Jesus demonstrates mastery over anything the sea can do: *the wind stopped and there was a great calm*—the opposite of a great storm. Whatever the occasion of the storm, Jesus is master. If it has overtones of cosmic conflict, is it incidental that the next story has the swine go into the sea (5:13)?

■ **40-41** Jesus is quite critical of **his disciples, "Why are you *scared*? Do you still have no faith?"** At one level, the question is odd: they feared they were going to drown. This implies a contrast between Jesus and the disciples. His confidence in God's purposes allows him to sleep in the midst of the storm. But the deeper question is: Do his followers not know who he is? They have witnessed exorcisms and healings. God has revealed to them the mysteries of the kingdom. Jesus has explained everything to them privately (4:34). But they still do not grasp fully his identity and the scope of God's action in Jesus. Even for those who are with Jesus, the path of discipleship seems to include a gradual coming to terms with who he really is.

The picture of the disciples that emerges is not flattering. Mark implies that they had no answer to Jesus' question—they are **terrified.** This is not the fear of drowning—Mark uses a different word here (*ephobēthēsan phobon megan*). Now they are ***awestruck*** in the face of this display of divine authority. That is why they **asked each other, "Who is this?"** The disciples do not yet grasp his identity. And when they finally do, in 8:27-30, they do not comprehend its significance.

The confirmation of Jesus' divine authority is that **even the wind and the waves obey him.** This response closely resembles that of the crowds after the first exorcism (1:27). Both the unclean spirit and the waves are rebuked; both obey his command; Jesus silences both.

FROM THE TEXT

This story is the clearest example so far in the narrative that Jesus has the same authority and power as Yahweh. If this is so, it confirms that Jesus really is the Holy One of God in the midst of his people. He is the One who gathers his people and who is Lord of all.

Fear is a natural response to grave threats outside our control. When waves threaten to overwhelm their boat and take their lives, the disciples are naturally terrified. But when Jesus acts to still the storm, they find themselves asking about this strange person with them. This will not be the last time they miss his identity on a boat trip (see 8:13-21).

4:35-41

At one level, the disciples stand in awe of Jesus, responding to his action in exactly the same way the synagogue crowd does to the exorcism in 1:27. At another level, their response is the appropriate one in the face of God's action. But Mark does not suggest this is the reason for their response. At this stage, any such response goes beyond their comprehension.

This story should not be used in a facile fashion that minimizes the very real storms of life that can bring fear to individuals, as if sufficient faith calms every storm. The great distress the disciples experience at the prospect of drowning is the kind Jesus faces in Gethsemane when the cost of obedience to the will of God threatens imminent death on a Roman cross. God's people are not immune to fears that threaten to overwhelm them. But in the face of catastrophe, this story reminds us that the good purposes of God will ultimately triumph. Sometimes it is through the immediate calming of the storm, as happens here. At other times God gives the courage and hope to face the storm, as with Jesus in Gethsemane.

There are other lessons about discipleship here. The disciples gather around Jesus, the Holy One of God. But their closeness to Jesus and the commitment of their lives to him does not mean that they fully comprehend. Indeed, they only gradually come to know who Jesus really is—the lessons are many and the progress slow.

We may be tempted to be dismissive of the disciples because of their "hardness of heart" until we take a closer look at ourselves. Then we are reminded that being God's holy people who are with the Holy One, on his mission and with his authority, is a journey of challenge, discovery, and deeper insight into the mystery of God's purposes.

2. The Healing of Legion (5:1-20)

BEHIND THE TEXT

The connections between the stilling of the storm and this story are strong. First, Mark uses his inclusion technique here, sandwiching the story of Legion (5:1-20) between two crossings of the sea (4:35-41; 5:21). Thus, the crossings, Legion story, disciples' question, calming of the sea, drowning of the swine in the sea, and calm return to Jewish territory are all interrelated.

Second, some scholars draw attention to a possible intertextual connection with Isa 65:3-4. There the idolatry of Judah is noted in language that resonates with this story. While the context is different, the echo may suggest that the impurity in this story could be linked to idolatry. Certainly the scene that confronts Jesus on his arrival is one that would be avoided by anyone concerned with Torah standards of purity and holiness.

Third, Mark goes into considerable detail in this story, much more than the parallels in Matthew and Luke. His reasons seem to be essentially theological. This story continues the theme of demonstrating the authority of Jesus. It adds to the mounting evidence about his identity. It is Jesus' first foray into Gentile territory and marks the extension of his mission, through the liberated demoniac, to the Gentiles.

An earlier generation of scholars concentrated on the development of this story to its present form, attempting to trace Mark's redaction of the tradition he received (see Guelich 1989, 272-75). Such efforts achieved limited agreement and limited exegetical significance.

More agreement has resulted from discussions of the textual variant in Mark 5:1. Where did this event occur? Three possibilities exist: The earliest texts of Mark have the story occur in the *vicinity of Gerasa* (*tēn chōran tōn Gerasēnōn*). Second, the majority text reads Gadarenes (*Gadarēnōn*), the reading of older versions like the KJV. Finally, a later correction of the early texts reads Gergesenes (*Gergesēnōn*).

The NIV adopts Gerasa, which scholars agree is the most probable reading. Identification of the best text is comparatively straightforward. But a problem arises when these places are identified on a map. Gerasa refers to a major Roman city nearly sixty kilometers (thirty-five miles) southeast of the lake (modern Jerash).

The second reading, Gadara, is improbable for Mark. This appears to be an assimilation to Matt 8:28. If Matthew used Mark at this point, he may have changed Gadara for Gerasa, since it is closer to the sea (Nolland [2005, 374] prefers Gerasa in Matt 8:28). But Gadara is still eight kilometers (five miles) away from the sea. And there are no steep slopes in its vicinity, leaving the historical problem unresolved.

The third reading, Gergesa, refers to a place unknown to us. Some identify it with the ruin called El Kursi. Origen first proposed this alternative: "An old town in the neighbourhood of the lake. . . . On the edge of it there is a steep place bordering the lake from which the pigs could have been driven down by the demons" (cited in Oden and Hall 1998, 67). But Origen gives no textual evidence for his proposal.

None of the scholarly solutions is entirely satisfactory (see Guelich 1989, 275-77). Origen's conjecture may be correct, "if only because no other suitable site exists" (France 2002, 227). Collins suggests that when the oral tradition of this story was committed to writing, the event was mistakenly linked to Gerasa, one of the better known cities of the Decapolis, "by someone who did not know how far Gerasa was from the sea" (2007, 266).

This exorcism has several similarities to the first (1:22-27), which occurred in a synagogue. This one occurs in Gentile territory, a location considered congenial to demons. The initial cries of the demons in both stories are virtually identical. They resist, but acknowledge who Jesus is. Both, therefore, make highly significant christological confessions, which contribute to the unveiling of Jesus' identity. But whereas silence is required of the liberated one in the first instance, here the person is told to tell everyone what the Lord has done.

IN THE TEXT

■ 1 A few MSS read "he came," but the plural, **They went,** ties the previous story to this one. Some commentators find an artificial seam between the two, because the crossing would have taken just two hours. After a nighttime crossing, Jesus and his disciples would have reached land during that night. This story better fits a daytime crossing. But this requires the precision of a travelogue Mark does not give. His point is that the journey, which started in Galilee and intended to cross the lake, was completed. They arrived in **the region of the Gerasenes.**

This information raises questions. The actual setting of the event cannot have been near Gerasa (→ FROM THE TEXT). The later variant reading **Gergesenes** is geographically more probable, but textually suspect. The best texts read **Gerasenes.** If this is what Mark wrote, the flawed geography does not affect the point of the story—that Jesus is in Gentile territory.

■ **2** *When Jesus disembarked, immediately he was met by a man from the tombs with an unclean spirit.* This episode is focused on the man *with an unclean spirit* and what this reveals about the identity and mission of Jesus. Mark reports nothing else between the two crossings of the lake, which form brackets around this episode. Once the man is liberated from the demons, he announces the good news in his own territory and Jesus returns to the other side of the lake.

When Jesus disembarks, *immediately he was met* by this desperate man. This is strikingly similar to the synagogue exorcism story (→ 1:21-28). Mark shows that the immediate opposition to Jesus' ministry is supramundane in Gentile as well as Jewish territory. The language describing the man is identical to the first exorcism: *en pneumati akathartōi*, once again indicating the helplessness of the victim. Later we discover that his situation is even more desperate.

He lived in **the tombs,** probably caves for burials hewn from the cliff. This emphasizes his dire straits—excluded from his community and, as far as Jews were concerned, living in perpetually unclean circumstances in tombs and under the control of an unclean spirit (but see v 9).

■ **3-5** Mark then elaborates further on his circumstances—he *had his home in the tombs,* the haunt of demons. Mentally and physically he is in torture. Previous attempts to restrain him, apparently to prevent self-injury (he **cut himself with stones**) and perhaps out of fear for his violence, failed. No human **could bind him any more.** Even chains failed to restrain him—he simply **tore the chains apart and broke the** *shackles binding* his feet.

He is, of course, completely bound by unclean spirits. And this captivity is well beyond human ability to control. The picture is relentlessly bleak, expressed in a series of negatives. He is isolated, completely out of human- and self-control, a danger to himself and others.

■ **6** The story resumes with a recapitulation of the opening line. **When he saw Jesus,** the demon-possessed man **ran and fell on his knees [***prosekynēsen***] in front of him.** Collins notes that this act "expresses the demon's recognition of Jesus' power and status" (2007, 267). This is not an act of worship by the man, who is under the control of the demon(s). Instead, he cowers in fear. There is a fatal attraction to Jesus as far as the demons are concerned.

■ **7-8** The demon, rather than the man, **shouted at the top of his voice.** The words are almost the same as in 1:24, **What do you want with me?** ("us" in

1:24). The point of this idiomatic expression is: ***What we are doing is no concern of yours.*** The **me** seems disingenuous, given the rest of the story. Was it a futile attempt to deceive Jesus?

The unclean spirit then names **Jesus.** This is an attempt to control Jesus. But for Mark, this truly identifies Jesus as from the realm of the supernatural. He calls Jesus the **Son of the Most High God.** This is significant in two ways.

First, it answers the disciples' question in 4:41 (see Donahue and Harrington 2002, 165). This supplements the demonic identification of Jesus given earlier in 1:24 and 3:11.

Second, the designation "Most High" (*hypsistos*) regularly translates the Hebrew *Elyon* in the LXX. It occurs on many synagogue inscriptions from Diaspora Judaism (see Marcus 2000, 344). This adjective emphasizes the sovereignty of God over all the earth, including supernatural opposition. Clearly this is of primary importance here.

This same divine name applies to Zeus in non-Jewish, non-Christian Greek texts (Collins 2007, 268, who draws attention to an inscription from A.D. 22 or 23 that "attests a temple and cult of Zeus Olympius in Gerasa"). If the unclean spirit identifies Jesus as only a "son of Zeus," it is a double-edged attempt to control him by naming him and reducing him to the category of one of the pantheon of Greek gods. His attempt to name Jesus is clearly a power play. But Mark sees it as a genuine, if begrudging, identification of Jesus.

The unclean spirit attempts to prevent Jesus from acting by using the language that an exorcist would use to expel a demon: "I adjure you by God, do not torment me" (NRSV). This has "an element of deliberate parody" (Marcus 2000, 344). It also signifies that a struggle is taking place between Jesus and the demon (Collins 2007, 269). Matthew 8:29 adds ***before the time*** (*kairos*), referring to the final fate of demons (see Rev 20:10).

Only now does Mark explain why the demon addresses Jesus: Jesus has already taken action. **For Jesus had said to *it,* Come out of this man, *unclean* spirit.** France suggests this may imply "that Jesus' 'success' in both healing and exorcism . . . was not always as instant as most of the narratives suggest" (2002, 229). In contrast to 8:22-26, this does not seem to be the point here.

■ **9-10** The exorcism starts with Jesus' question, **What is your name?** The use of a demon's name was a common technique of exorcists, but there is no hint of Jesus employing any technique. Jesus says little in this story. His exorcisms are simply done through a command. The answer by the demon evasively avoids giving a name: **My name is Legion.**

This is not a proper name. Instead, the demons warn Jesus that he was no match for them: **for we are many. Legion** is a Latin loanword that can refer to a legion of Roman soldiers. A legion consisted of 5,400 men plus 120 cavalry (a massive and menacing military machine) or simply a large body of

5:7-10

men (Collins 2007, 268). Here it is used as an imprecise description of the multiple possessions of the man. The response is intended to be sinister and intimidating.

Jesus does not use the name **Legion** in the exorcism itself. Apart from historical reminiscences, Mark may have had several reasons for including it: Clearly, it emphasizes the man's dire condition as multiple possession. Consequently, it heightens the authority of Jesus, ready to take on an army of demons gathered in this one unfortunate person and arrayed against Jesus. It also prepares for the story of the two thousand swine who rush into the sea following the exorcism. But this says nothing about the number of unclean spirits possessing **Legion**.

The primary meaning of this story is the restoration of this man to normal life. But some recent scholars draw attention to the possible political overtones of the designation **Legion**. Collins suggests that the name expresses anti-Roman sentiments (2007, 269). Marcus thinks it might be "a satire on the Roman military presence in the east . . . which fits into the overall Markan concept of the Messiah as God's holy warrior" (2000, 351-52).

If Mark is written just before or during the Jewish War in 66-70, Caesar's tenth Roman Legion stationed near Jerusalem would have made the connection possible. The presence of an occupying force in Judea and administered from Syria was a continual reminder that the empire was in charge. If Mark's first readers were in Rome, they could scarcely avoid hearing allusions to the Roman military, the basis of Rome's domination of the Roman Empire. "It would be a culturally logical step for the audience to link the kingdom of Satan with Rome and the healing activity of Jesus with the restored kingdom of Israel" (Collins 2007, 270). The link between the Roman Empire and opposition to God is writ large in Revelation.

Some scholars go further than this. They think the story alludes to Jesus' mission to liberate Palestine from Roman military occupation (e.g., Myers 2008). The political overtones are inescapable in my view. But few scholars are persuaded to go as far as Myers. France wryly comments: "This theory suffers from the apparent inability of virtually all readers of the story until now to have grasped the point Mark allegedly intended to make" (2002, 229 n. 12).

There is no doubt about the eventual outcome of the confrontation, despite the number of unclean spirits. The next statement has **Legion** in complete submission, recognizing that this possession was over. So the demon **begged** [*parekalei* is third person singular] **Jesus again and again not to send them out of the area** (*chōras*). The reason for this repeated request is unclear. Luke understands this as a plea not to be sent to ultimate destruction in the abyss (Luke 8:31). This perhaps builds on Matthew's accent on torment "before the appointed time" (Matt 8:29). But this is not Mark's point.

146

Perhaps the demons had a territorial assignment; they considered this their place to wreak havoc and destruction, near a center of idol worship. It could simply be a plea not to be sent to a remote place in the land, as if the tombs were not remote enough. Probably people thought the spirits of the ancestors inhabited such places.

It is possible to read *chōras* as **dry land.** If so, the demons beg not to be cast into the sea. They have a premonition of their future banishment in what was then considered the repository for the opponents of God.

■ **11-13** The presence of **a large herd of pigs** is not surprising, given this is Gentile territory. The unclean spirits live in an unclean place within an unclean man. Wishing to escape banishment from the land to the sea, and now completely under the control of Jesus, they beg him: **send us *into* the pigs; *let us enter them.*** Collins (2007, 271) notes that this kind of bartering was common in contemporary stories of exorcism. Jesus grants their request **and the evil spirits came out and went into the pigs.** The result for them is unforeseen, however.

The unclean spirits entered the swine and the whole **herd . . . rushed *headlong over the cliff into the sea* and were drowned.** The story does not suggest this as Jesus' intention. His purpose is to restore the man to wholeness by sending the demons away. But the entrance of the possessed swine into the sea gives the impression that the demons are now confined to the sea.

Several Qumran texts support the idea that demons are confined to the abyss in the time of the eschatological battle between good and evil (Collins 2007, 271-72). Collins concludes that the exorcisms Jesus conducts are "not the definitive manifestations of the kingdom of God. Rather, they constitute a struggle with Satan that prefigures and anticipates the final, full manifestation of the kingdom of God that will take place with the coming of the Son of Man" (2007, 272).

Jesus has just demonstrated his mastery over the sea (4:35-41). The implication seems clear: These demons too are completely powerless in the face of Jesus and are being confined to their appropriate home.

The picture is vivid. In addition to the lemming-like stampede of the swine into the sea, the formerly possessed man is "sitting there, dressed and in his right mind" (v 15). This confirms the control Jesus has. Mark does not claim that the demons themselves are drowned or destroyed.

It seems for a moment the two parties have come to a mutually amicable agreement; the demons will leave the man, as Jesus wants, but they will not have to leave the Gerasenes "land," as they want. But the comedy concludes when the demons, upon entering the pigs, find themselves incapable of controlling them and send them careening over a cliff into the sea. This gruesomely funny conclusion emphasizes the destructiveness of the demons as well as their shortsightedness; incapable of restraining their brutal rage, they unintentionally destroy their new lodgings and so thwart their own desire to stay on Gerasene soil. (Marcus 2000, 353)

■ **14** The swine herders *fled* from the scene, no doubt in disarray and fear. Mark does not address the ethical question of many modern readers of this text about the wanton destruction of these animals or the economic loss suffered by **those tending the pigs.** But this loss does seem a major concern of the characters in the story. The contrast with those who speak in praise of Jesus after other miracles is noteworthy. But some commentators underestimate the anxiety this loss of livelihood would cause those who owned the pigs or the unemployment of the lowly swineherds. The people may have commented positively about the deliverance of the possessed man. But their first concern was undoubtedly the fate of the swine. After all, this was an extraordinarily large herd—**about two thousand** pigs (v 13).

They *announced this in both town and country, and the people went to see what was going on.* Certainly there is evidence that pigs were used in cultic practice for sacrifice even in NT times (see Annen 1976, 162-67, drawn to my attention by Dr. Arseny Ermakov). Could this large number have been akin to the flocks of sheep kept near Jerusalem for slaughter in the temple cult?

■ **15** The first thing the townspeople saw **when they came to Jesus** was **the man . . . sitting there, dressed and in his right mind.** Now the emphasis shifts away from the swine to the one who had been demonized (*ton daimonizomenon*). This man was probably well known in both town and country. So they would have been amazed to see him sitting, rather than raving and bursting every restraint; and dressed, rather than naked; and acting normally. In response **they were afraid.** This is the same response as the disciples' in 4:41—an overwhelming mixture of terror and wonder at what they had witnessed. This was beyond any human capacity. They are in awe of the divine power in their midst.

■ **16-17** The first people to confirm what has happened presumably returned to the city and **told the people what had happened to the demon-possessed man.** There may well have been rejoicing at the news that he was liberated from the oppression of unclean spirits. But Mark says nothing of this. He pointedly notes that they **told about the pigs as well.**

The exorcism caused alarm (see Luke 8:37). In addition to their economic livelihood and food supply, the action of this Jewish exorcist leaves them wondering what might be next. Was he about to cleanse their region of all that was unclean? Should they fear for their lives?

Consequently **the people began to plead with Jesus to leave their region.** Jesus has been welcomed elsewhere, but he has also faced opposition. This theme continues here.

■ **18** This episode occupies the entire journey to the other side of the sea (4:35). It leaves the impression that curing Legion was the sole purpose for Jesus' decision to cross. The stilling of the storm—control of the forces of the sea—was the necessary prelude to the exorcism of the unclean spirits in this story. Significantly, no storm or disturbance arises as Jesus immediately makes his crossing of the sea (5:21).

Jesus complies with the Gerasenes' request that he leave. But Mark leaves open the possibility that this is what Jesus was going to do anyway. His purpose in crossing the sea is accomplished, as the rest of the story makes clear. But France (2002, 232) thinks Jesus' original purpose has been "overtaken by events."

As Jesus was getting into the boat to leave, **the man** he had exorcised *pleaded with Jesus that he might be with him* (echoing 3:14).

■ **19** But *Jesus sent him away.* At first glance, this seems odd, but Jesus also did not allow some others to follow him in his specific itinerate ministry (see 8:26; 10:52). In 3:13-19, Jesus' appointment of the Twelve to be with him was symbolic of the restoration of Israel as the holy people of God. The Twelve were chosen from among those who came to him, but not all had the same symbolic role or significance.

Instead of allowing **Legion** to follow, Jesus told him to **go home to your** *people.* Two points are made. First, through the work of Jesus this man is being restored to the normal life of home and community from which he has been excluded. "The liberation of the man from the destructive power of evil leads to a restoration of those familial relationships that were most prized and regarded as essential in antiquity" (Donahue and Harrington 2002, 168).

Second, Jesus instructs him: **tell them** *everything* **the Lord has done for you** *and his* **mercy** *shown to you.* There is no command to silence. On the contrary, the good news of God's liberation of people outside of Galilee is to be told. The good news knows no ethnic or national boundaries. Jesus' authority is not restricted to predominantly Jewish territory.

Jesus' initial refusal of the exorcised man's request has a positive purpose: "this man has an opportunity, which is uniquely his, to spread the news of what God is doing through Jesus of Nazareth among those who have known what he was before, and who therefore cannot ignore the dramatic change which has resulted from his encounter with Jesus" (France 2002, 232).

Jesus' command is to tell what **the Lord has done.** Mark does not explicitly use "Lord" as a title for Jesus, although that implication may be inescapable in 11:3; 12:11, 36-37. Here Jesus points to God as the source of the mercy the man has experienced. But the man credits God's representative.

■ **20** The man *goes away and begins to proclaim the good news in the Decapolis, everything that Jesus did for him.* First, Mark's language is deliber-

149

ately crafted to coincide with the good news announced by Jesus, and by those such as the cleansed leper who proclaimed to anyone who would listen exactly what Jesus had done (*kēryssein*; see 1:4, 7, 14, 39, 45; 3:14).

The cleansed man is not allowed to join the group following Jesus. But his mission is the same as theirs: proclaiming the good news. Jesus does not tell him to be silent. The man interprets Jesus' command to go to his own home and people in the broadest possible sense. He tells it in the whole area of the Decapolis, the region of the ten predominantly Hellenistic cities east of the Jordan.

Second, he also reinterprets Jesus' command to tell what the Lord has done. Mark tells us that he proclaims **how much Jesus had done for him.** On the lips of this liberated man, this could simply be a report that a Jewish exorcist had unexpectedly come to his country to perform this miracle. But in Mark's view, the work of God and the work of Jesus are the same. He makes this point by telling the story this way. Mark's Christology is rather more elevated than some imagine. The result of the good news is that **all the people were amazed,** just as was the case in Galilee.

FROM THE TEXT

The story of the deliverance of this man has several implications. First, the gospel is not restricted to the people of Galilee. Jesus crosses into Gentile territory solely to deliver this possessed man from the power of evil. Significantly, he does not tell him to remain quiet but sends him to his own people to tell the good news of what God has done for him. God's good purposes are universal in scope. It includes Gentiles as well as Jews.

Second, the organized forces of evil cannot withstand the power of the kingdom. Jesus is confronted with a legion of opposition. But the power of the kingdom prevails even against this organized evil. The condition of this person could scarcely have been more desperate, nor his plight more hopeless. But the liberating word of Jesus transforms him from a dangerous opponent serving the forces of evil into a witness to the work of God in Jesus.

Third, the exorcism of the legion has a political undertone. Evil in the disguise of the Pax Romana is symbolized by Legion. Its ruthless exercise of overwhelming military power under the lordship of Caesar will not triumph. This is a word of hope to all of us that the powers of states that claim the authority of God are a mere parody of the ultimate lordship of Christ.

Fourth, the liberation of people from the tyranny of evil powers is significant. The oppression of evil that afflicts humans is contrary to the good purposes of God. The liberating word of Christ sets people free from this tyranny. Jesus crosses the sea to rescue one person—and returns to the other side.

This deliverance symbolizes that even insignificant and marginalized persons are important. No one is beyond the pale.

Fifth, we see in the combination of these two stories that Jesus' authority is over all of creation—land and sea. The calming of the sea, the exercise of authority outside of Jewish land and the smooth return journey on the sea just after the demon-possessed swine had plunged into it reminds us that God's kingdom is over all. This is the foundation of Paul's affirmation that nothing in creation can separate us from God's love (Rom 8:38-39).

Finally, this story reminds us that the holiness of the Holy One of God is not affected by the worst imaginable context of impurity: swine, idolatry, oppression, unclean spirits. This is a recurring theme in the ministry of Jesus: his holiness does not need to be protected as a polished possession. It is his intrinsic character as the Holy One of God. His followers, who are holy in relation to him, are invited to participate in his mission, to share in his authority. They can enter into the haunts of evil and oppression and, through the derived power and authority of the Holy One, transform them by word and deed.

3. Jairus' Daughter (Part One) (5:21-24)

BEHIND THE TEXT

The raising of Jairus' daughter to life is the third of four miracle stories in this sequence. The narrative structure of these stories is an obvious example of Mark's inclusion technique. Mark starts and concludes the story of Jairus' daughter, inserting the story of the woman who touched Jesus' garment in between. The bracketing of the story of Legion by two sea crossings is a similar device. But this one is much tighter, in that one event is split in two in order to enclose the second story. This interweaving of stories strongly encourages readers to interpret each story in light of the other. Several points are of importance in these two stories:

First, the key element lying behind both is the issue of impurity. Purity/impurity and its connection with holiness has been an underlying theme throughout Mark. Jesus' table fellowship, for instance, has been questioned. The story of Legion also involved purity issues: swine, tombs, Gentiles. Now, the theme continues as an implicit undercurrent. In both cases, these females are a source of Levitical impurity.

In the first instance, the woman with the twelve-year gynecological disorder has been ritually impure for that entire time. She is a constant, potential source of impurity (see Lev 12:7; 15:19-33, esp. v 25; 20:18). Leviticus devotes considerable space to the impurity of the menstruant (*niddah*), who is considered unclean for seven days (Lev 15:19-24). But women with vaginal bleeding outside their normal cycle (*zabah*) remain unclean for as long as the condition persists (Lev 15:25-29).

The extent to which a woman would be quarantined during the Second Temple period is uncertain. But the probability of some separation is strong (see Marcus 2000, 357-58; Collins 2007, 283-84). Among those whose concern for ritual purity was high (e.g., at Qumran), some separation was likely. In 11QTemple XLVII.14-17, menstruants are categorized as those that defile alongside lepers and those with infectious diseases, including scabies and gonorrhea. Therefore, they were to be separated from society.

The case of Jairus' daughter is similar in that she is dead; and touching a corpse conveys impurity. Jesus again demonstrates that his holiness cannot be overwhelmed by impurity, either of this twelve-year-old girl or this twelve-year constantly impure woman. His holiness is a contagious, transforming power that overcomes both impurities.

Second, the Markan Jesus has compassion for both of these women. These stories have undoubtedly been selected from many that could have been told. In the case of the woman, Jesus acts well outside the bounds of conventional behavior between women and men—speaking to this woman in public (see also 7:24-30), calling her **daughter,** and exercising effusive concern about her. Mark allows us to listen in to the internal thoughts of the woman, developing our understanding of her in a fuller characterization.

The significance of Jesus' reference to both women as **daughter** deserves special attention. This is a family term. In the first instance, the woman is depicted as separated from her family. In the second, the beloved daughter is dead. Jesus restores both. The woman is potentially restored to her family; Jairus' daughter clearly is. But by addressing them in this family term, the Markan Jesus welcomes both of these into his fictive family (see 3:35). The point is clear with respect to the older woman. "When Jesus calls the woman 'daughter,' he does not merely address her affectionately; rather, Mark is making a significant statement regarding the inclusive nature of the Reign of God. All types of daughters are included in God's rule, even older, impoverished ones who were formerly chronically ill" (Betsworth 2010, 107).

Third, the element of faith is central in both stories. Both Jairus (who exercises faith on behalf of his beloved daughter) and the woman who exercises faith by risking social humiliation and failure to touch Jesus' garment are models of the faith in Jesus displayed by true followers.

There is no connection, however, between the size of the woman's or Jairus' faith. Mark does not make a crass calculation that implies their quantity or quality of faith heals them. Mark's point is about the signs of Jesus as the One who is effecting the good news. It is because of who he is, not the size of their faith. Mark is interested in the contagiousness of Jesus' purity and that he is even able to give life to the dead. These two stories are set up to contrast with the following story in 6:1-6*a* in which Jesus' own people seem unwilling to accept Jesus' identity, putting themselves on the side of the scribes in ch 3.

■ **21** This section closes the story of Legion by bringing Jesus back **to the other side of the lake.** At this point, the mission in Gentile territory is ongoing through the witness of the former demoniac. Now, on his return to Jewish territory, once again **a large crowd gathered around him while he was by the lake,** virtually a repetition of 4:1. Mark gives no location. Was it in Capernaum? Jesus' coming again attracts a large crowd. *En tō ploiō* (*in the boat*) is missing from some early manuscripts. But the best reading is likely to be *Jesus in the boat* (so Collins 2007, 274).

■ **22** Opposition to Jesus from the religious establishment has been strong since ch 2. But this story has **one of the synagogue *leaders,*** a man **named Jairus,** join the crowd. The synagogue ruler was the "president" of the synagogue, a layperson in charge of the nonpriestly functions within the synagogue. That Jairus is **one** of the leaders suggests that he is not the president. He would, however, have been an important person in the community. This story is a reminder that the notion of relentless opposition to Jesus from the Pharisees, scribes, and other religious leaders is wide of the mark. **Seeing Jesus, he fell at his feet.** Given his social status, this is probably a sign of desperation, not worship. He is begging for help.

■ **23-24** When he approaches Jesus, he pleads with him fervently: **My little daughter** [*thygatrion*] **is dying** (*eschatōs echei* = *facing imminent death*). Jairus' affection for his daughter is noted in the diminutive of *thygatēr*. But she is twelve, not a toddler.

Jairus' faith in Jesus' touch could have come from firsthand observation. The request to **put your hands on her** is used in Mark regularly in healings. Jairus pleads for Jesus to act before death comes: **so that she will be *saved*** (*sōthēi*) from death (Donahue and Harrington 2002, 173) **and have life** (*zē ᷄sēi*). **So Jesus went with him.** Mark's note that **a large crowd followed and pressed around him** (see 3:9) prepares for the following story.

4. The Woman with a Flow of Blood (5:25-34)

■ **25-26** The details of this story are important for Mark. He begins with an elaborate sentence containing seven participles (***being, suffering, spending, not benefiting, becoming, hearing, coming***). He builds a picture of a woman stripped of all social standing and living in semi-isolation for as long as Jairus' beloved daughter has been alive. Ironically, the story of this perpetually unclean woman is juxtaposed with that of a leader of the synagogue, a place from which she would have been excluded (but see France 2002, 235 n. 20).

This woman has been suffering from a gynecological disorder (*ousa en rhyse haimatos*, **being in a flow of blood**) for twelve years. The NRSV translation, "suffering from hemorrhages for twelve years," unless it implies an intermittent problem, seems mistaken. A nonstop hemorrhage would have been potentially fatal. The euphemistic language here (and in v 29) resembles that used in Lev 15:19 and 28 for vaginal bleeding. This has made her ritually unclean and childless for twelve years. This probably affected her standing at home and in the community. She may even have been divorced from her family over childlessness (Donahue and Harrington 2002, 180).

She has "endured much under many physicians" (NRSV). The double criticism—"much under many" (NRSV)—heightens her plight and negatively assesses physicians. Jews viewed physicians along a spectrum from positive to negative (see Sir 38:1-5; Tob 2:10). Here they are not praised. She had exhausted whatever wealth her social standing may have included. After all this, "she was no better, but rather grew worse" (NRSV).

■ **27** This woman, **hearing about Jesus,** joins the crowd. But instead of approaching Jesus, falling before him, and begging for healing, she **came up behind him in the crowd.** The contrasts are significant:

male	female
synagogue leader	excluded from the synagogue
named	nameless
sees Jesus	hears about Jesus
approaches him about his daughter	dares only approach him surreptitiously

The woman **touched his cloak.** After the string of participles, this main verb becomes the focus of attention in the story. Jesus does not touch her; she reaches out to touch him. The touch itself was potentially risky. Under normal circumstances, this would convey impurity to the holy person, annulling his power (Marcus 2000, 358, 366).

■ **28** Healing by touching Jesus' garments is also noted in 6:56, so this is not unusual. Healing through touch occurs throughout Scripture (e.g., 1 Kgs 17:17-24; 2 Kgs 4:25-27) and widely in the Greco-Roman world (see Collins 2007, 281-83). Healing through contact with clothing or even the shadow of a holy person occurs in Acts 5:15 and 19:12.

What is unusual is the attention Mark gives to her rationale: **If I *can* just touch his clothes, I will be *saved from my plight.*** Mark allows us to listen in as she talks to herself. She is desperate. "She needs Jesus in the depths of her isolation" (Betsworth 2010, 105).

Hers is an almost magical view of healing that fits very well within its period. "Mark's Jesus," says France (2002, 237), "is less bound by correct procedures, and even correct theology, than some of his followers." In this view, there is a "sort of power resident in the holy person's body that can be stored, tapped, or even transferred to other physical objects. . . . [here this] has been extended from the holy person's body to his garment" (Marcus 2000, 359).

■ **29** In contrast to the failed healing from twelve years of medical attention, **immediately** *the flow of blood* stopped. "Jesus extends God's protection to her" (Betsworth 2010, 105). Collins suggests that she became immediately menopausal with eschatological significance (2007, 282). But this seems unlikely.

Most importantly, instead of her impurity being transmitted to Jesus, she *knows in her body that she was healed from her affliction* (*mastigos;* → 3:10). Now, we are privy to the woman's inner sensations. She has been transformed by the power of the kingdom in being saved from her dire condition. Her impurity is gone; her isolation, over. She can now function as a normal part of the people of God. For Mark, she is the paradigm of those who come to Jesus and are transformed by his power and welcomed into God's family.

■ **30-31** Simultaneously, **Jesus** *knows* **that power** *has* **gone out from** *himself.* This is the first use of **power** by Mark to describe Jesus' authority to heal. In the next pericope, Jesus is unable to do any deeds of power in Nazareth because of the people's lack of faith. In 9:39, the disciples try to stop an unnamed exorcist doing works of power in the name of Jesus.

Jesus' response to the knowledge that power has gone out is to turn sharply around to the crowd pressing in on him and ask an absurd question: **Who touched my clothes?** Mark's scene is comparable to a crowded marketplace. That people are touching Jesus constantly seems to be ignored by Jesus, and the disciples give the commonsense answer: "You see the crowd pressing in on you; how can you say, 'Who touched me?'" (NRSV). They see the crowd, they see the situation, but they do not perceive who Jesus really is. So, they offer a sarcastic, mocking response.

The implication is that merely touching Jesus is not the point, since many people are touching him. In this case "only touch with the intention of being healed and with trust that Jesus is the bearer of power to heal creates this phenomenon" (Collins 2007, 283). There is no implication that everyone in the crowd who happened to press against Jesus is miraculously healed. In fact, the opposite is the case. This healing is extraordinary, not a matter of ordinary touch as the disciples think.

■ **32 Jesus kept looking around to see who had done it** (*poiēsasan*, feminine participle). Marcus notes the "extraordinary pileup of epistemological language and the concentration on Jesus' perception; Mark's grammar, moreover, suggests that Jesus supernaturally perceives the gender of the person who has touched him" (Marcus 2000, 359, see 368). But on the face of it, this attempt to see who touched him is as absurd as the earlier question.

■ **33** The woman was already disappearing, but when she hears Jesus' question, she returns. She is *fearing and* **trembling** because she knows **what had happened to her.** Donahue and Harrington (2002, 175) suggest that this is a deeper understanding of what Jesus has done for her.

But she also knows that she has touched Jesus and, therefore, has made him ritually unclean. If Jesus knows she has touched him, she fears he knows he has been made impure by her touch. Her response may reflect her natural fear of discovery. But it is also the awe occasioned by the presence of divine power (Donahue and Harrington 2002, 175). That is the implication of her action: she "fell down before him" (NRSV, NIV 2011). She confesses that she is the one who touched him and, presumably, that she has been healed.

■ **34** Jesus' response to her is lavish and significant. First, he breaks convention by speaking to a woman who is not his wife in a public place. Second, he calls her **daughter,** "and thereby draws her into his family" (Betsworth 2010, 105). The term indicates familial connection (→ 3:35 and BEHIND THE TEXT above). Third, he tells her that her **faith has *saved her.*** Her trust and confidence in Jesus, even though she has only heard about him, has been exemplary. The irony is that the disciples, despite witnessing all the mighty works, seem not to get it.

Then Jesus tells the healed woman to **go in peace.** Unlike the cleansed leper in 1:41-44, Jesus does not prescribe the ritual requirements. He does not tell her to wait the requisite seven days and on the eighth day to go to the priest with the offering prescribed in Lev 15:29. She is no longer unclean; she can go in peace, in wholeness, and in health.

The last part of Jesus' statement, **be freed from your suffering** (*isthi hygiēs apo tēs mastigos sou*), "makes it clear that her cure is not a merely temporary remission. *Hygiēs* . . . relates to physical health, not to 'cleanness'; the effect of the cure will be, however, to remove her impurity and restore her to a normal place in society" (France 2002, 238). The affliction that tormented her for twelve years is gone.

5. Jairus' Daughter (Part Two) (5:35-43)

BEHIND THE TEXT

This story takes Jesus' redemptive activity to another level—raising a dead girl. Although there are reports of healers in pagan circles raising the dead (see Philostratus, *Vit. Apoll.* 4:45), Mark's story is focused upon this act in the context of the wider words and deeds of Jesus in announcing and effecting the kingdom.

There are several variants of the Aramaic phrase *talitha koum,* probably due to the unfamiliarity of copyists with Aramaic. Some texts read *tabitha,* a confusion from the name in Acts 9:40. The variation between *koum* and *koumi* is due to gender in Aramaic. Thus *koum* is masculine but is used here without reference to gender. But *koumi* is imperative feminine singular and is probably a later correction (France 2002, 234 n. 41). The earliest text is likely *talitha koum.*

IN THE TEXT

■ **35** The connection between the two stories is made clear by the resumptive words: **While Jesus was still speaking.** The Greek could mean while Jairus was still speaking, which would be the case if the stories have been brought together by Mark. But in this context, it is Jesus who is speaking to the woman.

The news that interrupts the conversation is not good—some ***people came from the house of Jairus*** *with the terrible news,* **"Your daughter is dead. . . . Why bother the teacher any more?"** There appears to be no tone of reproach in their voices, as if they were dismayed that Jesus had allowed himself to be interrupted by this episode with the woman. After all, the narrated event would occupy a very short time and would have no effect on whether or not the girl remained alive until Jesus' arrival.

But that is scarcely the point of this story. Rather, the point is that the messengers arrive while Jesus is confirming the restoration of this woman to full physical and social health. Jesus' power to heal is not in doubt. But this is a different matter—this young girl is dead. Healers might be able to restore the ill to health, but raising the dead is of a different order. Hence, they seek to bring closure to the request. Their reference to Jesus as **the teacher** is not disrespectful. Rather it is in keeping with Mark's picture of teaching with authority that has already included an exorcism and healing (1:27; 2:10).

■ **36** Jesus overhears what was likely a quiet word to Jairus, and ignores it (see Luke 8:50). His response is instead to tell Jairus to ***stop being*** **afraid** (present imperative) and **just believe.** The verb **believe** has no object. The context suggests this is belief in Jesus' mastery of the situation rather than any exhortation to just believe more.

Whether Jairus is comforted by these words, we are not told. But the narrative sequence of stilling the storm and exorcising Legion when intercalated with the restoration to full health of a woman beyond expensive health care helps readers to expect more than a funeral oration.

■ **37** Why Jesus **did not let anyone follow him except Peter, James and John the brother of James** is unexplained. Perhaps this follows the pattern of narrowing the witnesses to the key events. Perhaps it was the size of the house or the room that limited the numbers. If so, the statement is curiously dislocated,

5:35-37

since Jesus is not yet at the house. It is more likely that these three are key disciples on other occasions (→ 9:2; 14:33; see 13:3), all momentous points of revelation about Jesus and the purposes of God.

■ **38-39** The arrival at **the home of the synagogue ruler** confirms the report that the girl is dead: **people** are **crying and wailing loudly.** Quite possibly these are professional mourners as well as family members (see Jer 9:17-20). But Jesus makes an astonishing statement: **Why all this commotion and wailing? The child is not dead but asleep.** Although *katheudō* occurs as a metaphor for death in Ps 88:5 and Dan 12:2, it is an unusual choice. The usual word in the NT is *koimaō.*

Some rationalistic interpreters suggest that Jesus is making a perceptive diagnosis of her condition—she is not really dead, only in a comatose state. Thus, this is not so much a resuscitation of a dead girl as a story of Jesus' perception. But if this is an attempt to reduce the miraculous elements in the story, it is misplaced. This girl is dead (Matt 9:18).

Jesus' statement to the contrary, then, has to be read against two contexts. First, **asleep** is regularly used as a euphemism to signal death (see John 11:11-14). But more specifically, this particular word has intertextual overtones that link this story to the hope for resurrection expressed in Dan 12:2. Belief in resurrection was gaining currency during this period. This is an eschatological statement—of the kind Martha could affirm in John 11:24. Jesus' action is the zenith of his demonstration that the eschatological future is already at work. Death is not the end, and Jesus' action here is a symbolic reminder of that.

■ **40** The response of the professional mourners is predictable: **they laughed at him.** This is the response of Abraham and Sarah (Gen 17:15-17; 18:12) in the face of the promise of a child. But it is also a signal that their hearts were hardened. The mockery of the mourners only added to the sarcasm of the disciples (Mark 5:31). To this point, the response to Jesus by the crowds in Galilee has been positive—only the religious leaders have rejected him. But this response sets the stage for the next story in which Jesus' lineage is the source of disbelief and mockery. And mockery will be the fate of Jesus in the Passion Narrative. The crowd here is also among those who would not believe even if they were to see (see 15:29-32). So Jesus puts **them all out** (*ekbalōn*—the word usually describing exorcisms). Instead, he takes the child's parents and the **disciples who were with him . . . in where the child was.**

■ **41** Throughout this sequence (Legion, the woman, this girl) the issue of purity/impurity has been a subtext. Here Jesus expressly **took her by the hand,** thereby putting himself at risk of corpse-impurity by crossing this boundary. He then **said to her, "Talitha koum!"**

Two views could be taken of this preservation of an Aramaic phrase. First, in two of the healings away from the crowds (this one and 7:34) the Aramaic verbal command is preserved. Some commentators argue that this story preserves the typical technique of healings employing foreign incantations, formulas, and techniques as in the magical papyri.

But these words are not foreign to Jesus' context nor to the early Aramaic-speaking church. In fact, the preservation of the Aramaic may imply that Jesus did *not* use a foreign formula. He simply spoke in the ordinary tongue of the girl. The touch and the word of Jesus effects the restoration to life, not any invocation of a magical formula. The phrase is so ordinary that any notion of a magical formula is baseless (France 2002, 240). Mark makes no attempt to preserve the secrecy of the phrase. Instead, he offers a straightforward translation, **Little girl, I say to you, get up!** for the sake of his Greek-speaking audience.

The preservation of the Aramaic words reflects Mark's penchant for vividness, not an incantation. Hooker (1991, 150) translates Jesus' words, "Lamb, get up," offering a glimpse of the tenderness of Jesus that parallels Jairus' reference to "my little daughter." This goes beyond affection; this is family language. This twelve-year-old is part of Jesus' fictive family. Perhaps Jairus and his family are or become followers of Jesus.

■ **42-43** The restoration is immediate and obvious: the young lady arises and begins to walk around. The story is told without drama. But the language evokes the resurrection of Jesus. Mark only now notes that **she was twelve years old.** This may be another indication of the vividness of Mark's narration. But it also links this story to that of the woman with an issue of blood for twelve years. She is of marriageable age—at the beginning of a fruitful life.

Of course, the disciples and the parents **were completely astonished.** Despite their nearness to Jesus throughout the preceding narrative, the disciples still seem not to understand who Jesus is.

As with earlier miracles, Jesus **gave strict orders not to let anyone know about this.** The reason for this command is probably that people would not be able to understand what this was all about. For Mark, the disclosure of Jesus' identity and the significance of this event take place later in the narrative—when the three disciples in the inner circle are with Jesus on the mount and in Gethsemane. All of this becomes clear only after Easter (see 9:9-10). The complete improbability of keeping this secret is again evident—especially since the professional mourners have already been engaged.

The story closes with the puzzling command: **give her something to eat.** France (2002, 240) calls this "remarkable bathos"—trite and anticlimactic, but it could also be to show that she is really alive rather than a phantom (see Luke 24:37-43; Tob 12:19). This provides a transition from the raising of this dead girl to the rejection of Jesus in Nazareth. Collins thinks this is due to

5:41-43

Mark's source, where the next story is the multiplication of the loaves (2007, 286), but this is unnecessary.

FROM THE TEXT

This collection of miracle stories (4:35—5:43) has some vital lessons. Here we see Jesus exercising power "over chaotic nature, destructive demons, debilitating illness and death itself" (Donahue and Harrington 2002, 179). The clearest lesson is connected to the theme of purity. Jesus encounters three distinct sources of impurity but is never made impure. Rather, the impure people are transformed into people able to reenter society, effectively restored to life. Legion is no longer living in the tombs and possessed by unclean spirits. The woman with the gynecological disorder is no longer perpetually impure, but able to participate in normal society and synagogue worship. And the girl is raised from the dead, her corpse-impurity completely gone.

The language describing Jesus' sensing power going out from him in 5:30 captures the view that Mark has of Jesus and his holiness. Instead of being rendered impure by the contagion of impurity, Jesus' holiness restores the unclean man to his community, the unclean woman to society, and the dead girl to her parents.

The lesson for holiness people of all ages is important: holiness is not preserved by cutting oneself off from the marginalized and the needy, but is demonstrated precisely in the contact with the unclean and the excluded. Thus, holiness is not a thing to be protected but a relationship to be shared in the mission of God. Are people transformed by contact with us, by touching us? To what extent do we sense the power of God at work in our contact with the unclean in our crowded lives?

A second theme emerges particularly in the interlinked story of these two women. Donahue and Harrington (2002, 181) call attention to the links: both are in life-threatening situations, both are called daughter, in both stories faith in Jesus' identity is important, and both are unable to have children. The woman with the flow of blood breaks through the barrier of her condition and the religious boundaries to connect with the source of wholeness. Her faith is strong and resolute. And Jesus' response to her demonstrates clearly that societal oppression of women for religious or social reasons is not part of the way the new people of God are called to display their holiness before the world.

The raising of a dead girl to life is another clear demonstration of the importance of this girl. This girl is more or less of marriageable age, and would soon be able to bear children. "In these two narratives Jesus not only rescues the two women from death but also restores to them their life-giving capacity. Both can bring forth life from their bodies, one once racked with disease, the other deprived of life itself" (Donahue and Harrington 2002, 181).

A subsidiary theme has to do with the fact that Jesus heals the daughter of a synagogue elder. Opposition to Jesus from the religious establishment was not universal.

6. Rejection at Nazareth (6:1-6a)

If the pinnacle of Jesus' kingdom-effecting power is reached in the raising of Jairus' daughter, the story takes a downward turn in this episode. Rejection has been part of the pattern since ch 2; it culminates in the dark saying in 4:11 about the effect of the parables. Jesus' message has not always fallen on good soil. Jesus' family has also been in the picture, trying to persuade him to abandon his mission and return to his life as a carpenter (3:20-21, 31-35). But people have also been coming to him in droves. The press of the crowds provided the hoped-for obscurity sought by the woman with an issue of blood. Now Jesus returns to Nazareth for the first time in Mark's Gospel.

BEHIND THE TEXT

The inauguration of Jesus' ministry in Luke occurs in the synagogue at Nazareth (4:16-20) where he gives his electric interpretation of Isa 61. The setting here is also the synagogue in Nazareth. As in the Lukan story, at first the Nazarenes' response is amazement and wonder. But their initial enthusiasm soon gives way to questioning. And, as in Luke, it turns to violence.

There are two interesting points to be noted here. Jesus is identified as **Mary's son.** Since this is unusual, it leads to several explanations. Some suggest that this is because Joseph has been dead for some time and the family is known locally as the family of Mary. Another suggestion is that Mary's extended family is well known, while Joseph's is not. But that suggestion founders on the genealogies in Matthew (ch 1) and Luke (ch 3) in which the Davidic descent of Jesus is traced through Joseph. Others suggest that this reflects the hint of scandal surrounding the birth of Jesus and, hence, is a slur on Jesus.

An even more debated question is whether or not the brothers and sisters in this passage are the biological siblings of Jesus. Three responses have been given throughout church history. First, these are the biological children of Mary and Joseph. This is the usual view of contemporary Protestant scholars and some recent Roman Catholic NT scholars. Second, Joseph had other children by a previous marriage. Thus, Jesus is called Mary's son to distinguish from his half-siblings, the children of Joseph. On this reading, the brothers and sisters were not biological siblings of Jesus. The third view is that these are Jesus' cousins, perhaps the children of a sister of Mary's.

These last two suggestions are particularly attractive to those who argue for the so-called perpetual virginity of Mary. Although a robust defense has been mounted for the second view, which is first set out in the *Protevangelium of James*, the most natural reading of this text is that these are the biological siblings. Mary's perpetual virginity is a primary focus of the *Protevangelium of James*, a mid-second century A.D. apocryphal gospel. But the picture drawn of Mary in this document bears little resemblance to the infancy narratives in Matthew and Luke. Nothing in the NT actually supports the dogma of Mary's perpetual virginity (see, e.g., Foskett 2005, 67-76). None of the views matters one way or the other for the doctrine of the virginal conception of Jesus.

IN THE TEXT

In the last two stories, belief in Jesus' power to heal has been emphasized. The theme of faith continues, but this time it is the lack of faith that is noted.

■ I Jesus leaves Capernaum and *comes to his hometown and his disciples are following him.* The family has earlier come to the house in Capernaum to attempt to take him in hand (3:21, 31-32) leading to Jesus' redefinition of family (3:33-35). Now Jesus leads his disciples on the journey to his hometown. Nazareth is not named here (but see 1:9), allowing the literary parallel to the latter part of this story to be made clear.

■ 2 In a scene reminiscent of the opening story of the teaching in the synagogue in Capernaum (1:21), **when the Sabbath came, he began to teach in the synagogue.** This may suggest initial approval of Jesus, but that is at best implied both here and in 1:21. Perhaps the word of Jesus' teaching here by the sea has spread. Nazareth is roughly thirty kilometers (eighteen miles) from the sea of Galilee. The response by **many** [= "everyone"] **who heard him** is also similar—they are **amazed** at his teaching.

Mark does not tell us what Jesus taught (as does Luke 4:16-20), nor does his teaching follow a mighty work (as in Mark 1:21-27). But the people are obviously aware of both. The crowd's response here is ambiguous, whereas in the earlier instance it was clear.

They pose a question, **Where did this man get these things?** and then exclaim, **What's this wisdom that has been given him, that he even does miracles!** or, "What deeds of power are being done by his hands!" (NRSV). They do not quite share the same satanic assessment of Jesus as the scribes from Jerusalem (in 3:20-30). But neither do they praise God for him (2:12). The further development in the story confirms that their comments are essentially negative, even sarcastic.

■ 3 The crowd's response soon turns hostile. Jesus is nothing more than a local boy. The first ironic question, **Isn't this the carpenter?** is an insult. "Criticism of social background was a standard mode of invective in antiquity" (Collins 2007, 290), not always left behind in modern politics. Artisans were not high on the social scale in Greco-Roman societies. So a comment on his trade as **the carpenter** is simply another put-down (but see France 2002, 243). In this context, the intent is negative—***Isn't he just a carpenter?*** A variant reading has, "Is this not the son of Mary and the carpenter?" But this is probably an assimilation to Matt 13:55 (see Metzger 1975, 88).

The question, **Isn't this Mary's son?** yields a range of answers (→ BEHIND THE TEXT). Collins sees it as an insult (2007, 290). France (2002, 242) takes it as an indication that Joseph is dead or that it is simply a colloquial designation—"Mary's boy."

Of the four brothers named here, **James** later became the leader of the church in Jerusalem, while tradition identifies **Judas** as the author of Jude. The other two, **Joseph** and **Simon,** are such common Jewish names that further identification is impossible. If Jesus' mother is the "Mary the mother of Joses" in 15:40, 47, then a fifth brother is mentioned. But this is unlikely. No names are attached to his sisters.

In their view, there is nothing special about Jesus. **And they took offense** [*eskandalizonto*] **at him.** As Collins (2007, 291) notes, "All other instances of the verb in Mark refer to the apostasy of those who have previously had faith or trust in Jesus (4:17; 9:42, 43, 45, 47; 14:27, 29)." The irony of this situation is clear. The people who know Jesus cannot accept him. This is an extension of the rejection by his biological family.

■ **4** Disbelief in a local boy who has made good is commonplace. France (2002, 243-44) equates Jesus' response to them as equivalent to the well-known English proverb "familiarity breeds contempt." He considers the reference to a prophet as proverbial as well. This is a common enough saying repeated in a variety of ways elsewhere (see Matt 13:57; Luke 4:24; John 4:44). But there is more here. Jesus exclaims that *a prophet is dishonored only in his hometown, among his own extended family and in his own house.*

The theme of rejection of the prophets by their own people is a continuing theme in Scripture. It clearly stands behind 4:10-12. But as a backdrop for the response to Jesus' work, the designation "prophet" turns out to be an inadequate understanding of who he is (see 8:27-30).

■ **5-6a** The result is that the activity of Jesus in Nazareth is curtailed because of their rejection of him. But the power of Jesus cannot be completely thwarted. So, although **he could not do any miracles there,** he did **lay his hands on a few sick people and heal them.** France says that there is "a delightful irony in the juxtaposition of the two clauses of this verse: for most people the healing of a few invalids by laying hands on them would hardly constitute *oudemia dynamis*" (2002, 244). "Jesus still retains the power to do mighty works in the face of disbelief. What he cannot do is compel acceptance" (Donahue and Harrington 2002, 186).

In Mark, there is a link between believing in Jesus and the works he does, but there is never a one-to-one relationship between faith and healing.

6:3-6a

Mark does not think that Jesus' power is dependent upon the belief or unbelief of the people as if somehow his power could be manipulated by them if they just had enough faith. Jesus' healings are part of establishing his identity and proclamation of the good news. That message is as relevant today as at any time.

Mark alone tells us that Jesus **was amazed at their lack of faith.** Perhaps this was considered inappropriate by the other Evangelists, but if so, Mark does not see a problem. The language is interesting. Just as the people in the Decapolis were amazed at the deliverance of the demonized man (5:20), Jesus is **amazed** at their refusal to believe. The contrast between belief and unbelief is set out in Mark in a variety of ways. It is specifically tied to an "unbelieving generation" in 9:19.

FROM THE TEXT

Neither mighty works nor wise teaching compels belief. Nothing in Mark indicates that all who were healed by Jesus became believers, even if there was widespread acceptance of him. In fact, obstacles to the gospel come in many forms. Perhaps it is hostility to the genuine demands of the gospel because it challenges a strongly held conviction that has become simply part of the religious culture. That seems to have been the case in 3:20-30. At other times, it is simply dismissed because of familiarity with the messenger, as seems to have been the case here. They have eyes to see but fail to get beyond their pettiness and parochialism. And so they cannot see, because they refuse to—the same problem that occurs in ch 4.

In this case, they are so scandalized by Jesus' failure to meet their expectations that even he is **amazed** at their unbelief (6:3, 5). Nazareth seems to be rather stony ground—few, if any, Nazarenes (including his family) actually believed in Jesus at this point. Significantly, however, for Mark's readers, the prominence of Jesus' family in the post-Easter church would be a reminder that unbelief need not be permanent.

The second critical point to learn from this narrative is in the fact that while there is a connection between belief in Jesus and effecting the good news of the kingdom, the ultimate power and direction of God's good purposes cannot be thwarted by the resistance of those who refuse to believe.

IV. FROM MISSION TO MISUNDERSTANDING: MARK 6:6*B*—8:21

This major section in Mark builds on the story of Jesus' mixed reception in Nazareth. It begins with a commissioning of the disciples to participate in the work of Jesus, virtually relaunching his mission: first, Jesus has called the two pairs of brothers to follow him (1:16-20); then, he created the Twelve (3:13-19), calling them to be with him and giving them authority to exorcise demons and proclaim the good news.

But nothing in the story to this point indicates that the disciples or the Twelve specifically were actually active in the mission. They are with Jesus, of course, but he is the exorcist, healer, and proclaimer. They were present when he was identified by and acknowledged as having authority over unclean spirits. They have seen evidence of his contagious holiness, mastery over the sea, and defeat of death. The disciples should now have an appropriate understanding of who Jesus is. The good news of the kingdom is poised to advance.

Only now are they sent by Jesus to expand his mission. Throughout this section the disciples actively participate in the mission. They are successful healers and exorcists and assist in two miraculous feedings. They are with Jesus on his further incursions into Gentile territory.

But any hopes that this advance of the good news would be serene are dispelled immediately by the story of John's death. The announcement of the kingdom, which calls for repentance, can be costly. And expectations that the disciples might now have a clear understanding of Jesus' identity (4:41) are proven to be premature. In fact, like the Pharisees before them, their hearts are hardened (6:52); they don't understand his teaching (7:18); they can't understand how he will feed the four thousand (8:4) despite being with him when he fed the five thousand; and at the end of the sequence, they still don't understand (8:21).

But the disciples are not the focus of this section. That remains on the identity and mission of Jesus. The disciples' mission is an extension of Jesus' mission. John's role as Elijah is finished. News of his death prefigures Jesus' death (see 9:13). The emphasis upon Jesus' feedings of the multitudes in two settings connects with OT expectations. The healings draw attention to the Scriptures, while their location signals the deliberate extension of the gospel beyond Jewish territory. The lengthy discussion of food and purity is a reminder of the nature of holiness. Jesus' pronouncement on clean and unclean food would have been read with great relief by Mark's predominantly Gentile readers. In all these stories, the disciples participate, but Jesus is the central figure.

A. The Twelve on Mission: Part One (6:6b-13)

BEHIND THE TEXT

The mission of the disciples is divided into two parts separated by the story of John's death. This bracketing technique is typical of Mark's style, used most recently in the healing of Jairus' daughter.

This is the first mission of the disciples apart from Jesus. The parallels in Matthew and Luke have similarities and differences. Their message and mission is identical to that of Jesus—including the call to repent, the authority to cast out demons, and the power to heal the sick. Between their dispatch and their return after a successful mission, Mark inserts the story of the death of John.

Complications arise in the Synoptic accounts of the disciples' mission. First, the Markan Jesus permits taking a staff; Matthew and Luke do not. Second, the Markan Jesus permits the wearing of sandals; not so Matthew and

Luke. Third, Matthew includes elaborate instructions about their conduct in the villages (Matt 10:5-15). Fourth, Luke reports two missions—one with the Twelve (Luke 9:3-6) and another with the seventy (Luke 10:2-12), with slightly different instructions.

Attempts to harmonize these accounts are unconvincing. A source-critical explanation, which seeks to establish a literary link involving Q, Mark, Matthew, Luke, and L is possible. But it depends upon the prior acceptance of Q—no longer a scholarly consensus (but see Marcus 2000, 386-87). The so-called Q mission is more elaborate and prophetic than Mark's. But there is no direct evidence Mark knew Q as a fixed tradition (Donahue and Harrington 2002, 192).

Mark undoubtedly uses traditional material here, as do Matthew and Luke. But the story as told is shaped by Mark. And Q is an unnecessary postulate for interpreting Mark. Reconstructing a reliable text of the common material in Matthew and Luke that is normally not used in Mark is fraught with insurmountable difficulties. Source-critical analysis may help exegete Matthew and Luke. But even if the Q-source did exist, its value for interpreting Mark is limited. Neither Mark nor Q give details as to what happened, only that the mission occurred. Mark encourages us to ask only why it happened (Guelich 1989, 320).

Scholars see a variety of parallels to other traditions of mission. Collins (2007, 298-99) sees analogies to Josephus' account of Essene customs, but thinks the analogies provide only similar values of simplicity. She also draws attention to the similarities and differences with Cynics, but concludes: "There is little in the mission instruction of vv 8-9 to link those sent with the Cynics" (2007, 300). In fact, the contrasts are as important as the parallels. If there were any Cynic background here, it would be to contrast the mission of Jesus' disciples and the peripatetic activity of Cynics (against Downing 1988). Marcus finds a link to the Exodus story, in which clothes, bread, and sandals (Deut 29:5-6) suggest that Mark implies that the disciples embark upon a journey of liberation with Jesus, who will sustain them along the way (2000, 389-90). If this is the background, it is subtle indeed.

IN THE TEXT

■ **6b-7** The rejection of Jesus at Nazareth did not thwart the wider mission. Instead, **Jesus went around teaching from village to village.** Elsewhere in Mark, teaching includes healing and exorcisms; there is no reason to suppose it is different here. Jesus calls **the Twelve to him.** This is the third time disciples have been called specifically to him, but it is the first time they have been commissioned to participate in the mission. Their initial enthusiasm should not be confused with adequate preparation.

6:6b-7

Jesus **sent them** (*ērxato autous apostellein* = ***began to send them***). Mark's language implies that they are sent with a commission and the authority to act. This is an ongoing pattern that extends beyond the Twelve into the period of Mark's readers. They go **two by two,** which seems to be regular post-Easter practice as well (see, e.g., Acts 8:14; 13:2; 15:2). The pairings may have been for safety; it could also have been because two people are needed for credible witness and official business (see Marcus 2000, 383). Jesus **gave them authority over *unclean* spirits.** His mission in Mark always involves confrontation with unclean spirits. Earlier he summoned and appointed the Twelve to be with him, to have authority, and to be sent on his mission. Now they actualize that appointment.

■ **8-9** The **instructions** Jesus gives them are **for the journey,** language used in Mark to describe the life of discipleship. It becomes important in 8:22—10:52. They are allowed to take with them only minimal provision. This evokes the wilderness provision of God for his people. They are to take nothing **except a staff.** Explanations for this range from protection and support to the symbol of authority like the staff of Moses and Aaron's rod.

The parallels in Matthew and Luke forbid a staff and sandals. Is this an added provision reflecting the needs of later missionary journeys (so Hooker 1991, 156)? Explanations for the disparity between the Synoptic accounts vary. All agree that the missioners are to take **no bread, no bag, no money** in their **belts.** They are to rely on the provision of God; the mission may be intended to be time-limited or reflect the urgency of the mission (so Donahue and Harrington 2002, 191). They are to **wear sandals,** evoking preparation for the Passover meal (Exod 12:11). They are **not** to wear **an extra tunic,** the one normally worn next to the skin. This may lend further support to the new exodus motif in Mark (see Watts 1997).

■ **10-11** Jesus advised the Twelve to stay in the homes where they are welcomed. The theme of hospitality runs deep throughout all the Gospels. Although it has its roots in Middle Eastern culture, it also has theological roots in the character of God. Here the missioners could expect to be welcomed. If they are, they are to **stay there until** they **leave that town.** The prohibition in *Did.* 11-13 of staying more than two or three days may have arisen from abuse of Jesus' saying by later traveling evangelists (so Marcus 2000, 384).

There might well be a **place** (*topos*—perhaps referring to villages rather than *oikia,* **houses**) that **will not welcome . . . or listen** to them. This might imply a general refusal to accept them, paralleling Jesus' experience in Nazareth. He does not stay when rejected, but moves on. They too are to move on, and when leaving, to **shake the dust off** their **feet.**

Two explanations are usually given for this. It might symbolize a break in fellowship. That is, the disciples are to have nothing more to do with those who will not listen (see Acts 13:51; 18:6; so Marcus 2000, 384). Or, the gesture may function as a curse (see Neh 5:13), a pronouncement of judgment (so Collins 2007, 301-2). A refusal to welcome guests, a breach of cultural practice, was symbolized by a failure to wash the guest's feet. Hence, shaking off the dust, which should have been removed by washing, is **a testimony against them.** (The Greek *eis martyrioun autois* could also mean a testimony that would lead to repentance, but the context here is rather a pronouncement of judgment.)

■ **12-13** The message and activity of the Twelve is identical to the message and mission of Jesus. They **preached that people should repent.** The proclamation of the gospel has been the pattern of Jesus since 1:14. But it reflects the earlier message of John in 1:4, and it serves as a literary reminder of the connection of this section with John's life and death. The disciples' message is that of Jesus (see 1:15), announcing the arrival of the kingdom.

But the summary of their activity is also important—they proclaim the good news as agents of Jesus. They announce the good news and call on people to turn to God, exactly as Jesus did (1:34, 39): *they cast out many demons.*

Mark adds that they **anointed many sick people with oil.** Jesus is never described as anointing with oil, but it was practiced in the church (see Jas 5:14). The use of oil in medical treatments during this time is widely attested. The anointing is not the key element in the healing. As the oil "contributed physically to the healing," it symbolized "God's care for and restoration of the patient" (France 2002, 251). Mark's statement might reflect the later practice of Mark's readers. Healings and exorcisms are separated in this statement of the disciples' activity, as they are in Jesus'.

FROM THE TEXT

Rejection of the message of Jesus by the Nazarenes does not thwart the work of Jesus. He continues traveling from village to village. And, for the first time, he sends the disciples on a mission away from his presence.

The mission of God announced by Jesus is the mission of his followers. They are sent out under Jesus' authority and with his message. From the start, the mission of God has been to call a new people to be the agents of the good news, who announce and effect the kingdom of God. They are able to do this only because they are sent by Jesus and under his authority, empowered by him as effective agents.

The mission is never ours. We always proclaim God's kingdom. That is a sober reminder to those tempted to believe they are the key to a church or ministry. It is also a great relief. This is God's mission, not ours.

The progression from the beginning is important. The way has been prepared by John. Jesus, the beloved Son, begins his mission and actively engages the powers of evil, defeating even death. There is, of course, opposition. Sadly, the vested interests of the religious establishment join the cosmic opposition to God.

B. The Death of John (6:14-29)

BEHIND THE TEXT

The question facing interpreters is always the link between two stories. Here, first, Mark reminds readers that the announcement of the arrival of the kingdom and its attendant call for repentance are fraught with potential danger. He gives no evidence that the disciples suffered on their mission in this instance. But juxtaposing the story of John's death story with their mission highlights what could and does happen to God's messengers. John is put to death for speaking against the wickedness and corruption in the court of Herod Antipas. This fate could befall disciples—and Mark's readers—in their proclamation of the good news.

More importantly, however, the Baptist's execution prefigures the death of Jesus. The literary connections to later parts of the Gospel are numerous. John announces the kingdom; so does Jesus. Both John and Jesus have disciples who follow them. John is a righteous and just man; Jesus dies as a righteous sufferer; John draws the role of Elijah into his identity and is put to death; Jesus, as Son of Man, is put to death just as John-Elijah is.

Mark obviously considers this story vital to the Gospel. Its length alone, compared to the abbreviated accounts in the other Gospels, indicates this. His language is carefully chosen; the setting is given greater elaboration than might be expected; the details are gruesome. It is apparently located here for narrative reasons.

First, John has been arrested and put into prison. But until now, Jesus has not drawn much attention to himself within political circles. But his ever-widening influence and the mission of the Twelve multiply his notoriety until the interest of Herod Antipas is aroused. Mark suggests that his guilty conscience over the execution of John plays on his mind.

Second, in Mark's view, the work of John-Elijah has been completed. This is vital for Mark's narrative in 9:2-13 and 15:33-39. A widespread belief persisted, probably based on Mal 3 and 4, that Elijah, the prophet who had been taken to heaven in a whirlwind (2 Kgs 2:11), would return in the last days. Some looked for him as the one who would deliver the righteous from death (Wis 2:10-18). In Mark's narrative, this reference to Elijah paves the way for the definitive appearance of Elijah with Moses in 9:6.

Third, a popular religious idea persisted that especially good or evil people could come back from the dead. This revived figure was thought to have powers beyond ordinary humans (Collins 2007, 304). Although the Gospels attribute no miracles to John, his return from the dead would explain the miracles associated with him in popular legends. Later in the first century, the myth of Nero redivivus was widespread. Mark reports that instead of Jesus being Elijah redivivus, Elijah appears with Moses and Jesus. John-Elijah's work is done.

Herod Antipas

The family tree of Herod the Great (37-4 B.C.) is complicated. Josephus devotes a whole section in *Ant.* 18.5.4 to sort out the details. Herod the Great had ten wives, and his children intermarried. Here is a brief summary of leading Herodian characters in John's story:

- **King Herod** here is Herod Antipas, tetrarch of Galilee and Perea from 4 B.C. to A.D. 39. Although Mark calls him king, the Roman Emperor Gaius refused him that title. He was the son of Herod the Great's fourth wife, Malthace, a Samaritan woman.

- **Herodias** was the granddaughter of Herod the Great and daughter of Herod's son Aristobulus, half-brother of Antipas. Mark claims Herodias had been married to her uncle, **Philip** (6:17). Josephus calls him Herod (*Ant.* 15.7.1). Some scholars call him Herod Philip, to remove the conflict. This is just possible, but unlikely. Since Herod had ten wives and many sons and grandsons named Herod, confusion is understandable. **Herodias** divorced her first husband to marry Antipas [**King Herod**], another uncle.

- Salome, not named in the NT, was the daughter of **Herodias** and Herod/**Philip,** the niece and stepdaughter of Antipas. She later married **Philip** the tetrarch of Traconitis, who died childless. She then married Aristobulus, her cousin and the son of her mother's brother, Herod Chalcis (for details, see Hoehner 1972).

IN THE TEXT

■ **14-16** Although 6:13 mentions the mission of the Twelve, from Mark's perspective the focus is still on Jesus. When **King Herod heard about this**—presumably the mission of the Twelve, he raised questions. This is Mark's first mention of Herod; the Herodians were the conspiratorial partners of the Pharisees in 3:6. However, this is his territory and the growing public awareness of Jesus' preaching and activity needs to be watched. If Antipas is aware of any of the teaching about the arrival of the kingdom, he could be concerned, although his level of paranoia seems to have been lower than his father's. The work of the disciples is a subset of the mission of Jesus. By expanding his mission **Jesus' name had become well known** (see earlier 1:28; 3:7-8).

The mission of Jesus seems to have led to several speculations. Rumor has it that in Jesus **John the Baptist has been raised from the dead, and that is why miraculous powers are at work in him.** Mark says nothing about miracles attributed to the Baptist. Rather, it seems popular belief held that a righteous person who returned from the dead had extraordinary powers.

The popular belief (see 8:28) that Elijah would return (see Mal 3 and 4) led some to say of Jesus, **He is Elijah.** Elijah was a miracle-working prophet. But a link in identity between Jesus and Elijah is, in Mark's view, mistaken. From his opening chapter, allusions to John's activity, locale, and garb give a clear indication that Mark believed John the Baptist fulfilled the role of Elijah. John died as a consequence of his fearless confrontation of Antipas over his unlawful marriage. This is reminiscent of Elijah's confrontations with King Ahab in 1 Kgs 17—19. Elijah has come as the Baptist (see 9:13).

Others say of Jesus, **He is a prophet, like one of the prophets of long ago.** The hope for a prophet like Moses (Deut 18:15, 18) seems to be reflected here and in Mark 8:28. Note the irony that Jesus is popularly known as a prophet, but not in his hometown of Nazareth (Donahue and Harrington 2002, 196).

Herod's response could be ironic: **John, the man I beheaded, has been raised from the dead!** He could have meant no more than, "And just when I thought my problems were over, along comes another one just like the last" (see Collins 2007, 304). But more likely this is terror based on a guilty conscience—"John has come back to haunt me because I executed this just and righteous man" (see 6:20).

Confusion about the identity of Jesus runs throughout these chapters. Some reject him completely; others see him in terms of figures from the past—Elijah or another prophet. This is no surprise; even his disciples are confused. When the confession of Peter (8:27-30) comes shortly after this story, the same range of identities is extended: Elijah, one of the prophets, or John the Baptist redivivus. All of these are either wrong or reductionist.

■ **17-18** Mark launches into a lengthy explanation of why Herod thought Jesus was John come back from the dead. His source is probably a court anecdote about the extravagances and debauchery of the powerful oppressor of this righteous person (Collins 2007, 304-5). There is plenty of evidence of intrigue, excess, and ostentation in the accounts of the dynasty of Herod the Great reported by Josephus in his *Antiquities*.

Mark uses this story for his own purposes. He reports that **Herod himself had given orders to have John arrested, and he had him bound and put in prison.** He does not specify the location. The impression is given that it is in Galilee. But Josephus places the imprisonment in Machaerus, the hilltop site of a palace of Herod the Great located about twenty kilometers (twelve miles) south of Madabah, Jordan, overlooking the Dead Sea. It was considered impregnable. During the final siege of Jerusalem in A.D. 66-70, Jews who fled there were not conquered by the Romans until A.D. 72.

Herod did this because of Herodias, his brother Philip's wife, whom he had married. Mark pictures Herodias as a particularly odious and power-hungry woman, a picture confirmed by Josephus (*Ant.* 18.5.4). She is willing to divorce Philip under Roman law, which allowed a woman to divorce her husband (→ 6:14-29 BEHIND THE TEXT sidebar, "Herod Antipas") and marry Antipas.

The problem, according to Mark, is that **John had been saying to Herod, "It is not lawful for you to have your brother's wife"** because it would violate Lev 18:16 and 20:21. The issue here is not Herod Antipas' divorce of his first wife, the daughter of Aretas. A man could divorce his wife under Jewish law. Mark fails to mention the political and popular support for John (→ 1:5), although Josephus (*Ant.* 18.5.2) notes this.

■ **19-20** Herod feels the guilt, but the scheming of **Herodias,** who **nursed a grudge against John and wanted to kill him,** lies behind the story. The echoes of the Ahab-Jezebel story in the Antipas-Herodias account enhance the Elijah-John motif Mark has already established. But John seems to have enjoyed a measure of protection from Antipas. According to Mark, the reason is that **Herod feared John** because he is **a righteous and holy man** (*andra dikaion kai hagion*). This language evokes the imagery of the righteous sufferer, unjustly persecuted by his enemies, in the Psalms.

John's execution as a righteous and holy man prefigures the execution of Jesus (9:13). This is one of many intratextual connections between this story and Jesus' passion. Arrest, plot, fear, innocence, a leader yielding to pressure, and a note on burial figure in both stories. Guelich notes that "by having Herod identify Jesus with John and relating the latter's death during this interlude for the mission of the Twelve, Mark ironically allows Herod to make the connection necessary for ultimately understanding Jesus" (1989, 328).

Herod has an almost morbid attraction to John. He is "greatly perplexed [*polla epoei*]; and yet he liked to listen to him" (NRSV). This is reminiscent of the fascination the demons have for Jesus (Marcus 2000, 401).

■ **21-28** Mark's skillful storytelling is at its best in the next section. **Finally the opportune time came.** He implies that Herodias (not named, but clearly the conspirator) is hatching a plot. That this coincided with Antipas' **birthday** has an ironic twist. Birthdays were not celebrated in Judaism, but Herod's birthday would now be remembered as the day of John's death (Donahue and Harrington 2002, 199). The guest list at this party includes the administrative leaders of Galilee, who would enjoy some suitable entertainment. The location of the party poses a problem: It would almost certainly be in a palace in Galilee (Sepphoris or Caesarea?). But Machaerus, where Josephus (*Ant.*

18.5.2) reports John is imprisoned, is far from Galilee. If Herod hears John regularly, and if the leading courtiers are present, a Galilean location is likely.

The entrance of **the daughter of Herodias** is the first part of the plot. The best MSS here read *tēs thygatros autou Hērōidiados*, "his daughter Herodias" (NRSV). But others read *autēs tēs*, *her daughter* (presumed by the NIV). In the remainder of the story the girl takes orders from her mother, whom Matthew clearly understands to be Herodias' daughter. It appears that the best MSS preserve an early error (France 2002, 258). If this is the Salome of tradition, she is likely between nine and nineteen (see Collins 2007, 308).

She **came in and danced.** Although the language is restrained (Collins 2007, 308-10), the implication is that the dance is sensual. That she **pleased** [*ēresen*] **Herod and his dinner guests** in some LXX contexts has sexual overtones. His language and oath to give her **up to half** his **kingdom** echoes the story of Esther (see Esth 2:9; 5:3).

The promise is sealed with an oath, a serious matter since it invokes a self-curse, if not fulfilled. An example of a tragic oath is that of Jephthah (Judg 11:31-35). Acting because of social pressure links Herod with Saul (1 Sam 15:15, 21, 24) and Pilate (Mark 15:15).

The scheme works: **she went out** [respectable women did not attend male banquets] **and said to her mother, "What shall I ask for?"** Herodias replies, **the head of John the Baptist.** The daughter is portrayed as equally as despicable as her mother. Mark's two previous stories of women called "daughter" presented them in a wholly positive sense. This daughter is the antitype, quickly obeying her mother's evil request: **I want you to give me right now the head of John the Baptist.** She wants his head **on a platter,** outdoing her mother in this outrageous act. Despite his great distress, Herod complies in a moment of "Gothic horror" (Marcus 2000, 403).

■**29** Mark mentions "John's disciples" in 2:18 in connection with fasting. In Matt 11:2 ‖ Luke 7:18, John's disciples take a message from prison to Jesus, indicating their continued activity, but probably not in Galilee. Now, **on hearing of** John's death, his **disciples came and took his body and laid it in a tomb.** This prepares for a contrast with Jesus' disciples, who are nowhere to be found when he is buried (15:40-47).

FROM THE TEXT

The story of John's death is a reminder that the announcement of the good news of the kingdom of God is never good news for the secular powers who seek to dominate and arrogate power to themselves. Here, as always, when religion and politics mix, there are dire consequences. The story reminds us that the message of liberation from sin is not restricted to the spiritual realm. John's fearless confrontation with Herod cost him his life.

C. The Twelve on Mission: Part Two (6:30-32)

IN THE TEXT

■ **30** Meanwhile, the disciples have been on a successful mission. In addition to the exorcisms and healings detailed in 6:12-13, they have been teaching—proclaiming the good news in what **they** have **done and taught.** Sent on a mission by Jesus (6:7), they are now designated **apostles,** a noun derived from the verb (used only here in Mark and in some MSS at 3:14).

The juxtaposition of these two stories is important: The proclamation of the kingdom and the mission of Jesus is costly. At the story level, however, the disciples have reason to be pleased, so they **reported to him all they had done.** The narrative contrast between the reception of Jesus in Nazareth and the subsequent success of Jesus and his disciples is to be noted.

■ **31-32** The positive note continues—the popularity of the mission of Jesus and the disciples continues to mean that they are pressed by the crowds, so much so that **they did not even have a chance to eat** (see 3:20). Jesus invites them to retreat to **a quiet place,** an echo of Jesus' own practice in 1:35, 45. Perhaps, they are called to join him so that they, like he, can keep their focus on the reason for the mission (see 1:35-38). Together they follow by boat **to a solitary place.** This scene offers a useful literary transition to the next story, in which the people have nothing to eat.

Mark does not identify this solitary place, but the parallel in Luke 9:10 locates it in Bethsaida, hardly a solitary place. This creates a problem for 6:45, where the next boat trip is toward Bethsaida. "Mark's geography cannot easily be harmonized with Luke's, except by deleting *pros Bēthsaidan* from v. 45, but surprisingly there is no MSS evidence for this convenient emendation" (France 2002, 264; → 6:45-52 BEHIND THE TEXT).

D. Feeding the Five Thousand Men (6:33-44)

BEHIND THE TEXT

This is the first of two feeding stories in Mark. This one is the only miracle story told in all four Gospels. Mark and Matthew have a second feeding of four thousand (8:1-10 and Matt 15:32-39). Explanations for why Mark has two are many. The stories themselves have, of course, raised questions.

The first question is historical and has two parts. First, what is the likelihood of this event occurring? This multiplication of bread is yet another step-up in the series of improbable miraculous occurrences in Mark. None of the rationalistic explanations has much to commend it. One popular suggestion has proposed that Jesus' teaching moved the heretofore selfish crowd to share with their neighbors. To their amazement, they discovered that there was more than enough to go around. Such explanations are unsatisfactory, arising as they do from a worldview that excludes anything other than "the laws of nature" from the "real world." Whatever its explanation, the probability of this feeding actually occurring is of no interest to Mark. He sees this as a miraculous event and simply uses it to build on the growing unveiling of Jesus' identity.

The second part of the historical question is more interesting. Assuming that Mark gives a picture that goes back to a historical event, the question is, What were all these people doing here? In the narrative, it could simply be a continuation of the great crowds who come to see Jesus. But this seems different.

If one reads between the lines and places the events in the cauldron of Zealot-like resentment and violent opposition to Roman rule that marked Palestine in this era, the gathering of five thousand men in the wilderness may have political overtones. Some of the narrative details support this reading. These men are organized with military precision into hundreds and fifties, perhaps in preparation for an insurgency. The parallel account in John 6:1-15 concludes with the clamor of the crowd wishing to make Jesus king, a temptation from which Jesus flees.

The sequence of stories also adds to the impression. Jesus is on a wide-ranging mission, announcing and effecting the kingdom of God. He sends the disciples out with the same mission and message. Inserted into this report is the story about the political confrontation between John and Antipas. Josephus' account (*Ant.* 18.116-18) adds a wider context to Mark's account and gives much more prominence to the political dimension of John's preaching. The disciples' successful mission, including their teaching about the kingdom, may have contributed to or even encouraged this militaristic picture. Their own understanding of Jesus and his mission is sketchy, to say the least. According to Acts 1:6, their association of the kingdom and political power persists even after the crucifixion and resurrection. Could these men be gathering in the wilderness for Jesus to become the military Messiah who would lead the revolt?

If this was the historical undercurrent, Mark dispels any sense that this begins a messianic revolt against the Romans. The political overtones in the story of John's death are muted. And Jesus dispatches "the disciples before they could be infected by the popular enthusiasm (6:45) [which] would be in keeping with the consistently anti-Zealot stance in which he is depicted in the gospels" (France 2002, 261).

Although rich OT background lies behind this story, it does not draw from any one text. Rather, it alludes to the imagery of several stories. This allows the feeding to contribute to Mark's ongoing disclosure of the identity of Jesus and his creation of the renewed people of God. First, the story evokes the wilderness tradition in which God provides food for the people (Exod 16:1-26; Num 11:4-9). If there is a subtext of a new Exodus in in Mark, this action complements it. Second, the language reminds us of a miraculous feeding in the Elijah-Elisha cycle in 2 Kgs 4:42-44. Third, Mark's description of the crowd as helpless and harassed sheep without a shepherd reflects the prophecy of Ezek 34 against the false shepherds.

The narrative location of the story simply adds to the description of who Jesus is and isn't. He is not Elijah or Elisha, not one of the prophets, and not John redivivus. Rather, he is the One who gathers and cares for his people who are no longer scattered and chaotic, abused by their leaders and hopeless.

IN THE TEXT

The story begins with the familiar scene of great crowds coming to Jesus. There is no escape from crowds, except, it seems, on the water.

■ **33** The theme of crowds following Jesus continues. Even when he and his disciples leave by boat for the desert place, **many . . . recognized them and ran on foot from all the towns and got there ahead of them.** If they are on the east side of the lake as some suppose, how could the crowd have arrived on foot before the boat? This seems possible only if their destination is Capernaum and they embark from farther down the western shore. More people seem to have gathered, awaiting Jesus' arrival, than might have been expected. Mark is not overly concerned with such details.

■ **34** Upon reaching land, Jesus **had compassion** [*esplanchnisthē*] **on them.** The other uses of this term are in 8:2 and 9:22 (and in most MSS of 1:41). The noun form refers explicitly to the visceral organs, the seat of emotions in first-century physiology. It is metaphorically equivalent to being "sick at heart" in the English idiom. The depth of Jesus' compassion is emphasized by this word, which is virtually synonymous with ***merciful*** (*oiktirmōn*), a prime characteristic of God (Luke 6:36; Exod 34:6). Jesus cares for his people.

Mark's explanation for Jesus' compassion is the state of the people: **they were like sheep without a shepherd.** The metaphor of sheep and shepherd is regularly used in the OT to describe the people of God and their leaders, whether Yahweh or the king. Sheep without a shepherd are people without leaders. Several passages merit particular attention as a conceptual background here. In Num 27:15-18 Moses appoints "a man . . . so the LORD's people will not be like sheep without a shepherd." He is "Joshua [Gk.: *Iēsous* = Jesus], a man in whom is the spirit."

The prophet Micaiah ben Imlah uses this metaphor in 1 Kgs 22:17, describing Israel as "scattered on the hills like sheep without a shepherd." He predicts the death of the kings of both Israel and Judah in battle if they continue their path of war with Aram, leaving them without leaders. As the story unfolds in 1 Kings, the leaderless people disperse and "go home in peace." This is the solution the disciples propose for dealing with the hunger of the crowd in this story. Of course, the people have a titular leader—the narrative irony of Mark is clear. He calls Herod "King Herod," but despite his ostentatious claim, his rule is a parody of true kingship. The people of God are effectively leaderless.

These intertextual connections are linked to the prophecy against the false shepherds in Ezek 34:7-16. In this passage the "flock lacks a shepherd and so has been plundered and has become food for all the wild animals, and . . . [the] shepherds . . . cared for themselves rather than for [Yahweh's] flock" (v 8). Again, the irony is clear. Juxtaposed to the story of the extravagant but grotesque birthday feast of Herod, this story tells of the hungry and helpless people of Israel. But this problem is deeper than Herod's profligacy; the people of God are leaderless because the Jerusalem authorities have rejected Jesus (Mark 3:22-30). Jesus implies a similar critical stance toward the Jerusalem elite as do the people at Qumran—they are bereft of spiritual leaders.

Significantly, in Ezekiel, Yahweh himself will come to look after his flock: "I will tend them in a good pasture . . . I myself will tend my sheep and have them lie down" (34:14-15). The LXX of this passage adds, "And they shall know that I am the Lord" (*kai gnōsontai hoti egō eimi kyrios*), an apropos background for the revelation of Jesus' identity.

■ **35-36** The disciples, who themselves had no time to eat (v 31), realize that it is **late in the day** (*hōra pollē*), the normal time for the afternoon meal. They are in **a remote place,** so they come to Jesus to alert him to the needs of the people. But they do nothing about it beyond telling Jesus to **send the people away.** They see no need to care for the crowds. Nor do they see themselves as caregivers; they have little sense of the significance of their appointment as the Twelve (3:13-15) and the authority they have just exercised (6:6*b*-13).

Instead the disciples think the people should **go to the surrounding countryside and villages and buy themselves something to eat.** There is a clear contrast between Jesus, who has compassion on the crowd, and the disciples, who do not. Jesus' instinct is to gather people together and care for them; the disciples' is self-preservation. They themselves need to eat because **it's already very late.**

■ **37-38** To the disciples' surprise, Jesus orders them: **You give them something to eat *yourselves.*** The human impossibility is obvious. They themselves have not had time to eat, and have certainly not brought enough provisions with them on the boat for five thousand men. The irony here shows their continued misunderstanding, especially in light of their earlier success at exorcising unclean spirits and healing the sick. Jesus gives them opportunity; they don't seize it.

They respond with a rough estimate of the cost of feeding such a crowd: This would take **eight months of a man's wages!** The Greek refers to two hundred denarii, a common laborer's pay for two hundred days of work. And even that might have been an underestimate, given the massive crowd.

The disciples are incredulous, even sarcastic, in their response: **Are we to go and spend that much on bread and give it to them to eat?** Jesus responds to their incredulity with another question: **How many loaves do you have?** This does not help, when they find out that they have only **five [loaves]—and two fish,** a surprisingly meager amount even for the disciples on their own journey.

■ **39-40** The feeding proper begins with Jesus directing the disciples **to have all the people sit down** (*anaklinai*). The verb is used elsewhere to describe people reclining at a banquet. This has led to the suggestion that the eschatological messianic banquet may be the imagery behind the story. It also has the connotation of seating a guest. They are placed **in groups** (*symposia symposia*). The phrase is used in distributive fashion (**group by group,** like "two by two" in 6:7). "A *symposion* is a group of people eating or (more commonly) drinking together, and suggests a relaxed, even convivial atmosphere" (France 2002, 267). Ordinarily, this would refer to a small, intimate party. But Mark pictures an extraordinary banquet, with Jesus as the host. Collins (2007, 324) notes the contrast with Herod's dinner in the preceding story: a lavish menu and upper-class guests vs. Jesus' simple fare for ordinary folks. Another contrast pits Jesus against the Jerusalem elite (12:38-40).

The people are **on the green grass.** This episode takes place near the time of Passover. Only during the springtime would the **grass** be **green.** This may intentionally connect the feeding and the Eucharist (→ 14:12-26). The Passover connection is important. It could also be a reminder of Lord as shepherd leading his sheep "in green pastures" (Ps 23:2).

The disciples organize the guests in groups (*prasiai prasiai*). Since *prasiai* refers to garden plots, Mark pictures the men arranged row by row, **in groups of hundreds and fifties.** Again OT allusions are important. The scene is reminiscent of the people of God in the wilderness, organized around the tabernacle of God (Exod 18:25). "More pertinently, the Qumran community adopted these groupings for enhancing their community identity as the true Israel (1QS 2:21-22; CD 13:1; 1QM 4:1—5:17) and specifically for the messianic banquet (1QSa 2:11-22)" (Donahue and Harrington 2002, 206; see Collins 2007, 324-25).

■ **41-44** The distribution of the food to the hungry can be understood at two levels. It may be read as a miraculous feeding comparable to the story of Elisha in 2 Kgs 4:42-44, in which twenty loaves feed one hundred men. There, Elisha announces the word of the Lord: "They will eat and have some left over" (2 Kgs 4:43). Jesus does not make a similar statement; but Mark's story closes

179

with the words: **they all ate and were satisfied, and the disciples picked up twelve basketfuls of broken pieces of bread and fish** (6:42-43).

Jesus is thus more than the prophet in three ways: First, the scale of the provision is far more miraculous. Second, the number of basketsful of food is greater than "some left over" (2 Kgs 4:43). Third, this is clearly an action of God. Jesus does not promise plenty; he simply distributes the food and there is more than sufficient. Fourth, the twelve basketsful of provision may have significance beyond simply abundance. These people represent the scattered people of Israel, and the provision for them is enough for all the gathered and reconstituted people.

The second level is the possible Eucharistic overtones. The language of **looking up to heaven, he *blessed* [*eulogēsen*] it and broke the loaves** (*artous*) is similar to the language at the Last Supper (Mark 14:22). This may reflect the Jewish pattern of the *halah* prayer before eating bread on Shabbat: "Blessed are you, LORD, our God, King of the universe, who brings forth bread from the earth." It is unclear here whether Jesus is blessing God or the bread. In 14:22, he blesses the bread.

The comparison with the Eucharist is tantalizingly close, but far from exact. There are too many missing elements for it to be explicitly Eucharistic. Fish do not feature in the Eucharist, wine is absent here, and Jesus says nothing about the broken bread being his body (but see John 6).

After breaking the loaves **he gave them** [*edidou*—the perfect tense might signal continual giving, but this is overly subtle] **to his disciples.** They are his agents in setting the meal before the people. They share in his mission. They also divided and distributed the fish.

Following the meal, **the disciples picked up twelve basketfuls of broken pieces of bread and fish.** Perhaps each disciple uses the basket (*kophinos*, a large peasant basket) from which the fish and bread were distributed to collect the leftovers. There is no historical reason why we are told about these leftovers. The action here and in 8:8 is likely more than ornamentation.

Like the other numbers in the story (**five, two, five thousand**), **twelve** is probably important. At the very least, it signifies the abundance of the leftovers—far more than the meager beginnings. But the narrative suggests more for several reasons.

First, the later feeding of the four thousand (8:1-9) also includes an abundance of food, with seven basketfuls of leftovers collected. Unlike twelve, seven cannot be linked to the disciples.

Second, the gathering of the scattered people of Israel—the dispersed twelve tribes—is an eschatological theme in the Prophets. Jesus' appointment of Twelve apostles is clearly linked to this theme (see 3:13-15). The story, then, means that Jesus cares sufficiently for the needs of all of the reconstituted people of God, with abundance to spare. The text explicitly states that *everyone ate and all were fully satisfied* (*echortasthēsan*). This was not a token meal. **The number of the men who had eaten was five thousand,** possibly reflecting a fighting group; presumably women and children were in addition.

FROM THE TEXT

The compassion of Jesus for the physical needs of the multitude is an important reminder that compassionate ministries are not an extraneous addition but are at the heart of proclaiming the good news of the kingdom. The disciples seem to think that teaching is enough; Jesus doesn't. Indeed, compassion has always been central to God's purposes. Closely associated with this is the lesson on the abundant provision of God. God cares for the hungry and the leaderless out of inexhaustible resources. He can meet the needs of all.

Second, the kingdom is not about achieving power. Both the story of John's death and the immediately following story of Jesus' dismissal of the crowd who may well have been thinking of political power are reminders that temporal power is not the goal of the mission of God. Indeed, God's mission is most at risk when the people of God find themselves so closely aligned with the temporal powers that they lose their prophetic voice in calling for justice at the heart of power or, more worryingly, seek to gain power and impose their will on others by force. Political power must never be the goal of the church, no matter how often the church has yielded to the temptation of power.

Third, that Jesus involves the disciples in this feeding should remind us that the proper pursuit of Jesus' followers should be to participate in his mission. Here, they organize the crowds, distribute the bread and fish, and collect the leftovers. They deliver the direct care that Jesus ultimately provides. That is precisely the call of all ministers today, whether lay or clergy.

E. Jesus Walks on the Water (6:45-52)

BEHIND THE TEXT

This complicated story raises a range of questions:

First, was the link between it and the previous feeding story due to Mark's redaction, or was it already combined before Mark uses it? Elsewhere Mark seems to have taken stories that existed separately and brought them together for his narrative purposes. But this story is told in the same sequence in three of the four Gospels, including the Fourth (widely considered an independent tradition). Thus, the combination of the two incidents seems to have been early. Luke may omit this story because he thinks it makes essentially the same point as the calming of the sea (France 2002, 269).

Second, the geographical sequence of the miraculous feeding and of Jesus walking on water is confusing. Mark has Jesus tell the disciples to go toward Bethsaida. This village on the east side of the mouth of the Jordan on the northeast side of the lake (6:45) had recently been made a fortified city and renamed Julias by Herod Philip (see 6:14). But in the next story, they arrive at Gennesaret (6:53), on the northwest side of the lake. Stein (2008, 330) offers several explanations for this apparent discrepancy:

1. Because the same sequence is found in John 6:1-21, the link may be pre-Markan.
2. Perhaps Mark 6:32-52 was followed by 8:22-30 in Mark's source. His insertion of the material in 6:53—8:21 disrupted the geographical sequence in which the healing of the blind man in Bethsaida followed the walking on water (Hooker 1991, 171). But John mentions neither Bethsaida nor the healing there.
3. Third, Jesus sends his disciples toward Bethsaida, but they land at Gennesaret. Grammatically, Mark's *pros* (vs. *eis*) in 6:45 indicates direction, not destination (Guelich 1989, 348).
4. Fourth, the disciples were blown off course by the wind mentioned in 6:48. They came ashore at Gennesaret instead of their intended destination.
5. Fifth, the reference to Gennesaret in 6:53 applied to a subsequent journey, following their arrival and embarking from Bethsaida.
6. Sixth, Mark has conflated two stories, inadvertently creating the geographical difficulty.

Stein considers the third and fifth explanations above as the more plausible (2008, 331).

One early textual variant in 6:45 omits the words *eis to peran* (perhaps in an attempt to smooth out the difficulties). But this does not help much (see Stein 2008, 329). The best solution may be to acknowledge that Mark seems uninterested in precise historical settings. He is interested in Jesus' ministry in the environs of the lake, but mentions only a few place names. We assume that Jairus was a leader in the synagogue in Capernaum, but Mark does not say. He reports that after the episode in Jesus' unnamed hometown (6:1-6a), the disciples have a wide-ranging ministry. But he mentions no villages by name. Nor does he locate either of the miraculous feedings. This one may occur somewhere on the western side of the lake. The location of the second is disputed.

Third, what is the connection between the earlier story of the calming of the sea and the present story of Jesus walking on water? Is this, too, a nature miracle revealing the identity of Jesus to the disciples? Or, is this an epiphany story or a rescue story? An epiphany seems more likely than a rescue story, as the account unfolds. But the decision makes little difference to its meaning. In this story, the disciples do not seem to be in peril. More likely, this story draws to a conclusion a sequence Mark uses to unveil Jesus' identity and to show the mixed level of understanding and activity of the disciples. Mark is able to conclude at the end of this story that the disciples have hardened hearts because they do not understand about the loaves (see 6:51-52).

While these questions are historically interesting, they are not particularly of concern to Mark. He seems far more interested in the interrelations between the stories, as the text will show.

IN THE TEXT

■ **45-46** Mark uses **immediately** to connect the feeding story with that of Jesus walking on water. There is urgency in the story because **Jesus compelled** [*ēnankasen*, only here in Mark] **his disciples** to leave immediately (but see Stein 2008, 322). There is no obvious reason for this compulsion within the story itself. But if we consider its context after the feeding of the five thousand, the mission of the Twelve, and the beheading of John, the meaning becomes clearer.

If the feeding has messianic overtones of a militaristic hue (→ 6:33-44 BEHIND THE TEXT), then Jesus may be anxious to get the disciples out of the situation. This is how the parallel in John 6:15 understands the consequences of the feeding: Jesus escapes from the crowd that **intended to come and make him king by force.** This motif may be present here as well. But in Mark, the disciples need to be whisked away. Jesus hurries them out of this charged situation in which they might be swept up with misguided messianic fervor. The revelation of Jesus' identity through the narrative indicates that he is Messiah. But that confession does not come until 8:27-30. The risk is that the disciples will make the wrong kind of messianic identification.

Jesus has the disciples go . . . **ahead of him** *to the other side,* to Bethsaida (→ BEHIND THE TEXT above on the geographical issues). As they embark, Jesus **dismissed the crowd** (thirty-four times in Mark). Mark says no more about this—but the sequence of sending the disciples away and dispersing the crowd by Jesus may point to Jesus' control of the situation. It may hint that he does not trust the disciples in this situation.

After leaving them—both the crowd and his disciples—Jesus **went** *to the mountain* **to pray.** The location of *the mountain* is of less importance to Mark than that Jesus goes there. The mountain location has intertextual significance as the place where God appears to Moses and the people (see Exod 19:3, 20; 24:15) to establish the covenant with Israel. It is also important for Mark: The call of the Twelve (3:13) and the transfiguration (9:2) both occur on the mountain. Mark implies that this is a crucial meeting of Jesus with God. He gives no explicit details about his prayer. But it is noteworthy that this escape to the mountain also concludes the feeding in John 6:15, although John makes no reference to prayer. Matthew 14:23 makes it explicit that Jesus is praying alone.

The only other instances of Jesus praying in Mark are in 1:35 and in Gethsemane (14:32-42). All three seem to be connected to temptation. Here the temptation is to capitalize on his widespread reputation and the effect of the feeding miracle on the masses as a means to fulfill the purposes of God to restore his holy people. But this would be to avoid the suffering Jesus has already anticipated (2:20). That certainly is the case in Gethsemane, where the prayer of Jesus is that God will remove the cup and allow fulfillment of his task in a different way.

■ **47-49** If one is looking for historical improbabilities, the rest of this story is fraught with them: First, if the boat is in the middle of the lake at evening and Jesus is on the shore, how is he able to see the disciples? Second, how does Jesus walk on water? Third, how do all of these events (the feeding and its aftermath, the crossing of the lake, and the journey to the mountain) occur within Mark's time frame?

None of these historical problems is addressed by Mark; apparently they are irrelevant to his story. He uses the story to enhance the revelation of Jesus' identity and show the mixed understanding the disciples have of Jesus. There are numerous affinities between this story and a range of biblical, Hellenistic, Roman, and Jewish traditions. These make it difficult to determine whether the story was intended to represent an actual event or consciously composed as a symbolic narrative (Collins 2007, 328-32). On either view, this is just the most recent in a series of stories in which Jesus' extraordinary activity is used by Mark to place Jesus' identity within the divine sphere.

The key elements in the description are that it was **evening** and the disciples are in a **boat** that **was in the middle** [*en mesō*] **of the lake.** Thus, they were about five or ten kilometers (three to six miles) from the shore. And Jesus **was alone on land.**

The story unfolds with the first extraordinary aspect. Jesus **saw the disciples straining at the oars, because the wind was against them.** Mark makes no attempt to explain how Jesus could see them, whether because of a particularly clear and moonlit night or remarkable eyesight. His whole point is that Jesus has the extraordinary ability to see them even from a mountain. This story does not necessarily depict a storm—only a contrary wind.

The time setting, **About the fourth watch of the night,** on the Roman dividing of the night into four watches, would be between 3:00 and 6:00 A.M. Then Jesus **went out to them, walking on the lake** (*epi tēs thalassēs*). Some commentators in the modern era have proposed rationalistic explanations of

Jesus walking on the water. Some have translated *epi tēs thalassēs* as "by the sea," that is, on the shore. Thus, they presume Jesus was actually walking on a sandbank or mudflat. But seasoned fishermen would be unlikely to mistake a figure walking beside the sea on a mudflat with one walking on water (France 2002, 270). None of these explanations persuasively assists in understanding the story in Mark. He has Jesus walking on water for reasons that become apparent through an intertextual reading of this story.

If Jesus is concerned about the disciples, it is puzzling why **he was about to pass by them** (*ēthelen parelthein autous*). Explanations include that this reflects the disciples' thinking, that is, that they thought Jesus was about to pass by them or that Jesus was trying to test their faith or that he intended to walk alongside his disciples to lead them.

But none of these explanations is persuasive. It is doubtful that Mark would have thought his readers should understand an unstated "and the disciples thought that" before "he wanted" (so Stein 2008, 324). This is a test of faith, but the test is not so much to be found in Jesus passing them by, but in their understanding of his identity. The idea that he would lead his disciples to safety does not feature in the story. If it did, Mark could have made this point much more clearly in the earlier stormy sea story in which Jesus is in the boat with the disciples than is the case in this story (see 4:35-41).

If this story is understood in terms of the revelation of who Jesus is, then the phrase may best be understood as an intertextual allusion to the revelation of God. In Exod 34:5-6, "the LORD passed before him [Moses; *parēlthen kyrious pro prosōpou autou*] and proclaimed, 'The LORD, the LORD, a God merciful and gracious, slow to anger, and abounding in steadfast love and faithfulness'" (NRSV). In 1 Kgs 19:11 Elijah is told to "stand on the mountain before the LORD, for the LORD is about to pass by" (*idou pareleusetai kyrios*; NRSV). "The language of 'passing by' suggests that Jesus appears to his disciples in a way analogous to the appearance of God to Moses and Elijah" (Collins 2007, 334). Stein supports this view, even if he is skeptical that Mark's readers would have understood this technical meaning (2008, 324-25). But this cannot be the criterion for determining whether Mark consciously used this echo. The motif of walking on water was widely known in the Hellenistic world (Collins 2007, 332). Mark's diverse readership would have been capable of making a range of intertextual connections to biblical as well as Greco-Roman stories. And he seems to make use of these traditions.

Strictly in terms of the phenomenon, it is not surprising that when the disciples **saw him walking on the lake, they thought he was a ghost** (*phantasma*—used only here and in the Matthean parallel story) and **cried out** in fear. People do not walk on water; the only explanation would be a terrifying ghost. But in terms of Mark's narrative sequence, this should not have been a surprise to the

6:47-49

disciples since they have just participated in the miraculous feeding of the five thousand.

■ **50** This was not the nightmare of one bone-weary fisherman: **They all saw him and were terrified.** This natural response is also a response to the epiphany at a deeper level. But Jesus **immediately . . . spoke to them and said, "Take courage!"** They are to cheer up, take heart, and stop being afraid. The same word of encouragement (*tharseite*) is spoken by Moses to the Israelites when they are in utter fear of Yahweh (Exod 20:20), and they plead with Moses not to let Yahweh speak directly to them. But Jesus identifies himself, **It is I** (*egō eimi*), and tells them, **Stop being afraid.** This command is not exclusively used in epiphanies, but it often is.

But the most important part of the statement is the identification. At the one level, this is a simple assertion that it is Jesus, the human being; they are not seeing a ghost. But given the sequence of disclosure of Jesus' identity through the stories to this point, the words may well take on a deeper level meaning (against France 2002, 273). *Egō eimi* is the self-designation of Yahweh in Exod 3:14 (LXX—*Egō eimi ho ōv*). The same phrase is used in the Septuagint of Deut 32:39 and Isa 41:4. When combined with the OT portrayal of God as walking on or through the waters (Job 9:8; 38:16; Ps 77:19), the phrase enhances the sense of theophany (Stein 2008, 326). The "awareness of these intertextual connections is not necessary for the audience to realize that Jesus is being portrayed here as divine in a functional, not necessarily in a metaphysical sense" (Collins 2007, 335).

Mark's story often has a two-level significance (→ 14:62). He may not be thinking in later metaphysical terms about Jesus as divine. But his comment on the disciples' failure to perceive who Jesus is through their hardness of heart would apply by implication to his readers who had not yet discerned through the developing narrative that Jesus has a divine identity.

■ **51-52** In the previous episode of a difficult sea crossing, Jesus rebuked the wind and the waves (→ 4:39). This time Mark links the presence of Jesus with calm: **he climbed into the boat with them, and the wind died down.** This wind was under divine control. Perhaps Mark intends us to see this wind as a divine means of delaying the disciples so that Jesus could manifest his identity. But that might press the story too far.

Some suggest that this story ended at this point in the pre-Markan tradition with the rest of this story being Markan commentary (see Matt 14:32; 14:33 is a Matthean comment; so Stein 2008, 327). Clearly Mark's comment conveys his purposes. The disciples are **completely amazed** (*lian ek perissou en heautois existanto*). Mark's doubling of **very** and **exceedingly** is characteristic Markan stylistic redundancy for emphasis. The phrase **and they marveled** emphasizes their wonder. Amazement is usually positive in Mark (2:12; 5:42;

but see 3:21). But amazement at this extraordinary event does not indicate understanding.

Collins suggests that this story presents another opportunity for the disciples to exercise their faith along the pattern she observes in 4:40, in which the disciples could have stilled the storm; and in 6:37, in which they could have fed the crowds. Here, they could have stopped the wind, but they fail to do so. So Jesus acts again and uses this as another teaching moment (2007, 336). But that is far from clear in these stories.

In fact, this amazement here is cast in a negative light, because the disciples **had not understood about the loaves.** Despite their experience of being with Jesus, they saw no possibility of feeding the five thousand, nor any possibility of mastery over the sea. They simply failed to take on board the significance of the events in which they have participated and the secrets of the kingdom to which they are privy (4:34).

This leads Mark to describe their condition in the starkest possible language: **their hearts** [*hē kardia*, in the singular, suggests their corporate resistance] **were hardened.** The shocking conclusion Mark draws is that the Twelve can be described in the same language used to describe the opponents of Jesus (3:5; see 4:13). Collins notes that the advance in this story is that "the disciples are outsiders too; or at least, if they are insiders, they are not significantly different from the outsiders" (2007, 336). They exclude themselves from the inner circle around Jesus (see 3:20—4:13).

Their hardness of heart is subsequently linked to their failure to understand the significance of the two miraculous feedings. Both should have been particularly revelatory of Jesus' mission and identity. Here the comment is Mark's. In 8:17, Jesus himself asks, "Are your hearts hardened?" Mark does not consider hardness of heart to be a permanent, incurable condition. The disciples continue to follow Jesus. And, despite failure, they are reconstituted after the discovery of the empty tomb (16:7).

FROM THE TEXT

This second story of Jesus' mastery over the elements is important for the fleshing out of his identity. It teaches Mark's readers some important lessons.

First, following God's call and pursuing his mission, even successfully, does not exempt disciples from temptation to take an easier path. This is probably the temptation Jesus faces, which drives him to prayer. Following the miraculous feeding, he dismisses the crowd and goes to the mountain to pray. This may be the test Jesus faces in the wilderness (1:12-13). It is in Matthew's and Luke's temptation stories. And it likely explains his need to escape in John 6:15. If Jesus needs to maintain his focus on the will and purposes of God in the face of success, how much more do we? We need the constant reminder to keep in contact with God and keep our eyes fixed on the Father's will.

Second, the picture of the disciples straining against the contrary wind evokes the image of a struggling community getting nowhere. But the struggle is not hidden from Jesus, who comes to them even in the darkest hours of the night, gets into the boat with them, and through his presence calms the wind. That image must comfort those whose battles seem unwinnable. Jesus sees, comes, and gets in the boat.

Third, "In the OT-saturated atmosphere of our narrative" the passage of Jesus through the sea evokes the crossing of the Red Sea, which occurred in the morning watch (Exod 14:24; Marcus 2000, 431). The hardness of heart of the disciples is reminiscent of Pharaoh and of the people of Israel in the wilderness. But Mark explains their hard hearts as due to their failure to understand the loaves, not their inability to grasp the significance of his walking on water. Jesus' conquest of the chaos of the sea anticipates his triumph over death (Marcus 2000, 435). This helps explain Mark's puzzling comment that the disciples' hardness of heart is due to their failure to understand the loaves. Jesus' walking on the water foreshadows his conquest of death. Thus "Jesus miraculously makes himself present to the Markan community across the gulf of death" in the Eucharist (Marcus 2000, 435).

Fourth, the people of God can be encouraged that Jesus will rescue them even in the worst of circumstances. It may appear that disciples are out of Jesus' sight. But this narrative points to the extraordinary sight of Jesus, who perceives the struggle of his people and comes to rescue them in the darkest night.

F. Landing and Crowds (6:53-56)

This passage is used by Mark to bring this series of stories to a conclusion. It may form a bracket with 3:7-11 around stories related to the growing disclosure of Jesus to the crowds and to the Twelve. But because of the variety of teaching and activity, it may also simply be a second general statement about Jesus' ministry marking a change in the story. In either case, it gives a general description of the continuing mission of Jesus in healing and effecting the kingdom. It also summarizes past stories. In these, the crowds clamor after Jesus for healing. Even the touch of his garments (see 5:34) is generalized.

IN THE TEXT

■ 53-56 The previous story is linked to this one with the words, **when they had crossed over.** This refers either to leaving Bethsaida or completing their sea journey. But **they landed at Gennesaret,** a fertile plain between Tiberias and Capernaum, **and anchored there** rather than in Bethsaida, which seems to be their intended destination in 6:45 (→ 6:45-52 BEHIND THE TEXT).

The widespread word about Jesus is evident: **As soon as they got out of the boat, people recognized** [*epignontes*; see 2:8; 5:30; 6:33] **Jesus.** It is ironic that the crowds recognize Jesus immediately, while the disciples in the previous story do not. The crowds are particularly interested in Jesus as a healer, the focus of this summary. So the depth of their recognition is not that expected of the Twelve.

Their sense of urgency, the breadth of Jesus' reputation, and his itinerant mission are all seen in the statement: **they ran throughout that whole region and carried the sick on mats** [*krabbatois*; see 2:4] **to wherever they heard he was.** It didn't matter where he was—**villages, towns or countryside—they placed the sick in the marketplaces.**

Mark seems deliberately to bring the marketplace into the conversation. In this setting, with crowds of sick people everywhere, impurity is a constant threat for temple-purity. Jesus is an observant Jew, as illustrated by reference to **the tassel on his garment.** But his holiness is contagious. He does not contract impurity in marketplaces.

Begged (*parekaloun*) is used by Mark in healing and exorcism stories (1:40; 5:10, 12, 17, 18, 23; 7:26; 8:22) to convey the earnestness of the request. Here **they** ask **him to let them touch even the** *tassel* [*kraspedou*] **of his cloak.** This tassel refers to the four twisted braids the men of Israel are commanded to wear on their garments (see Num 15:38-39; Deut 22:12). That Jesus followed this cultural practice indicates that he is an observant Jew.

Mark has already indicated the importance of physical contact with Jesus. In 3:10 people crowd in to touch him. The woman with the gynecological disorder was anxious to touch him, because she believed that he would heal her. Here the progression is even greater—just the touch of one of his tassels would be sufficient.

And all who touched him [or *it*] **were** *being* **healed** (*esōizonto*). Once again, Mark uses *saved* (→ 5:27-28) to describe healing. For Mark, this healing is part of the bigger picture of God's saving purposes being announced and effected by Jesus in the proclamation of the kingdom. The good news must be proclaimed in the marketplace as well as in the synagogue.

G. Clean and Unclean (7:1-23)

This section follows a series of episodes in which the identity of Jesus has been disclosed through his deeds (4:35—6:56). His reception by the crowds has been extraordinarily positive. Except in his hometown, opposition has been confined to demons and the personified sea. But after a three-chapter hiatus (see 3:22-28), debate with scribes and Pharisees resumes, here over purity.

Apart from the declaration in 7:19, the debate seems irrelevant to modern Gentile readers of the Gospel. For us, washing hands before meals is simply a matter of personal hygiene. Even in the Torah (Exod 30:18-21), hand washing for purification was the concern of priests only, not laypeople, although Lev 15 extends ritual washings to deal with discharge-impurity. But the debate is still important in light of the identity of Jesus, the reconstituting of God's holy people, and the redefinition of holiness. This explains the prominence Mark gives it.

BEHIND THE TEXT

Scholars have given considerable attention to the origin and shape of this section (see Collins 2007, 342-43; Stein 2008, 335-36). Mark does not offer geographical information as to where Jesus and his disciples are, or when. They must be in Galilee, since the dispute is with scribes from Jerusalem. The lack of setting leads many to suggest that Mark combines two independent traditions here. The first deals with the traditions of the elders; the second, with inward and outward cleanness. This commentary treats them separately but will show how they function together.

It is important to place these stories in the Markan narrative sequence. Jesus debates the religious authorities only over central issues: his authority to speak as he does, his practice and teaching in Torah observance, and his understanding of the issues surrounding purity and holiness (see 2:7-12; 2:16—3:6, 22-30). He is an observant Jew (→ 6:56). But his less than strict adherence to the Torah and misgivings about the traditions of the elders (see 10:2-9) cause some to question his teaching and practice.

The overall theme is clear: ritual purity and clean and unclean foods. Both issues were important for his Gentile readers in Rome. But they also reflect live issues in the late 2TP of Jesus' day. There is nothing historically improbable about the general terms of the debate. But the shaping, wording, and placement of the material is Mark's doing.

Mark's explicit editorial comments in vv 2b-4 and 19 give a hint of his intended readers. They are probably only vaguely familiar with the purity issues in this passage, so Mark provides a rather general summary of them. The interpretation of Jesus' words in v 19 almost certainly would have been heard by both Jews and non-Jews as an abrogation of Jewish food rules. This explanation may suffice at a more general level, but it cannot fully explain why Mark devotes so much space to these issues. Nor does it explain why the Corban regulation is not clarified more fully. It would be, if anything, more obscure to Gentile readers than kosher laws.

The controversy over hand washing is more complex than first appears (→ IN THE TEXT below). The Mishnah requires that hands be rinsed before eating unconsecrated food. But "before one eats holy things, one's hands must be immersed in a valid immersion pool containing forty *seahs* of undrawn water" (Collins 2007, 345, citing *m. Ḥag.* 2.5). Mark's account makes this a practice that involves ordinary food, not just holy things. Furthermore, Mark says that this is the practice of **all the Jews,** not just Pharisees. Thus, many scholars think this "is an incorrect statement. . . . One must allow for some hyperbole or generalization at this point on the part of Mark" (Stein 2008, 339). But the Mishnah did not come to written form until hundreds of years after the time of Jesus. And we do not know precisely the practice of the Pharisees during his time. Two other points need to be considered.

First, even before the Roman destruction of the temple in A.D. 70, the Pharisees exercised an influence well beyond their numbers. Their concern for holiness led them to develop regulations to govern their own lives and the lives of all who shared their pursuit of holiness. "They were dedicated to the sanctification of everyday life in a manner that touched all aspects of experience" (Donahue and Harrington 2002, 228). If Judea and its people were to be God's holy people dwelling in God's holy land as a kingdom of priests, the biblical purity regulations for priests serving in the temple needed to be extended to all Jews.

Second, archaeological evidence for the presence of immersion pools (*miqvot*) dispersed widely over Judea adds credence to the view that concern for ritual purity as necessary for holiness was not the preserve of just the Pharisees in Jerusalem or the Qumran community. If this is so, then this whole section is part of the intense halakic debate within late 2TJ over how people should live as God's holy people. Mark's picture of the debate over **the tradition of the elders** between Jesus and the scribes and Pharisees from Jerusalem is not surprising at the historical level. Mark gives it prominence because it is important for his readers. Furthermore, it fits into the ongoing and developing implications of the Holy One among his people.

I. Controversy over Tradition (7:1-13)

■ **1-2a** The **Pharisees** have not appeared in the narrative since they decided to conspire with the Herodians concerning how they might destroy Jesus (3:6). Here they join **some of the teachers of the law who had come from Jerusalem.** Earlier, scribes from Jerusalem accused Jesus of acting in the power of Beelzebub (3:22-27). These two symbols of opposition to Jesus (see Brower 1997, 122-23) are **gathered around Jesus.**

The language itself is not particularly sinister. The verb **gathered** is used positively elsewhere (see 2:2; 4:1; 5:21; 6:30). But their hostility to Jesus expressed earlier and separately in the narrative gives the scene an ominous tone. The question they ask in 7:5 is not particularly hostile on the surface. It resembles the question posed in 2:18 on a point of Jesus' halakah about fasting. But the hostility to Jesus expressed earlier and separately by these two groups gives the scene an ominous tone.

The scene is set abruptly and awkwardly, with no explanation of why this group from Jerusalem is present or where or when they **saw some of his disciples eating** with *defiled* hands. There is nothing historically improbable about the presence of the Jerusalem scribes in Galilee (see Collins 2007, 344). That they observe **some . . . eating** with unwashed hands does not mean that others were purifying before meals because of this tradition.

It is possible that some post-Easter Jewish Jesus followers did observe this practice. On the surface and to a Gentile audience, the scribes' observation seems trivial at best. But Mark says that they are eating the bread with *defiled* [*koinais*] hands. The word simply means *common,* but in this context the implicit contrast is with "holy" or "cleansed" hands (see Acts 10:14, 28; 11:8).

■ **2b-4** Mark then adds a lengthy explanation of the Jewish practice of ritual cleansing. Far from being a trivial concern with poor hygiene, hand washing is directly related to purity and holiness. Jesus' teaching (his halakah) on how the holy people of God are to maintain their purity in a profane environment is profoundly different from that of the Pharisees.

Mark explains defiled hands as **unwashed** hands. They are *eating the loaves* (*tous artous*) without appropriate purification. It is unclear why Mark uses the plural here and the singular in v 5 (*ton arton,* **the loaf,** food). The whole explanation is for Gentile readers. At first glance, the claim that the practice applies to **the Pharisees and all the Jews** seems exaggerated (Stein 2008, 339). But evidence is emerging that this practice was more widespread than earlier supposed (→ BEHIND THE TEXT above). Collins offers evidence from Josephus, the *Letter of Aristeas,* and other extrabiblical sources that support Mark's application of the practice to **all the Jews** (2007, 345-46). Such dietary regulations served as "boundary markers" (Marcus 2000, 441) distinguishing Jews and Gentiles.

The translation of *pygmēi nipsōntai* as **ceremonial washing** is unclear, since *pygmē* literally means *fist.* Marcus (2000, 441) notes three possibilities: "up to the wrists," "with a fistful of water," or "with a cupped hand." But it may mean something like *washing up to the elbows,* which may better fit the idea of immersing the hands before handling holy things (Collins 2007, 347). The NRSV opts for the variant reading *pykna* (*often*) and translates it "thoroughly" (Metzger [1975, 93] defends the more difficult reading *pygmē*).

A key phrase here is **the tradition of the elders** (*tēn paradosin tōn presbyterōn*). This refers to oral regulations on purity and other matters of observance. These were not in the written Torah but were the oral interpretations or halakah on the Torah. Much of this was codified only centuries later. This represented the elaboration and teaching of the Pharisees on Torah. They attempted to protect people from inadvertent covenant violations. At the time of Jesus, the Sadducees refused to follow oral tradition (or even the Writings and Prophets).

Mark elaborates further on the Jewish practice, which includes purification after they have **come from the marketplace** (*ap' agoras*). He gives no explanation why he singles out **marketplace.** His summary in 6:53-56 reports that all of the sick are brought to Jesus in the "marketplaces" (→ 6:56). Perhaps he points to a contrast between Jesus and the Pharisees. Unlike them, Jesus is not rendered impure by contact with the diseased. Instead, the unclean are healed (***saved***). Mark's narrative sequence may help illuminate this otherwise unexplained comment.

When they come from the marketplace they do not eat unless they wash (*baptisōntai*). This could refer to ***purification by immersion,*** the preferred method at Qumran. But washing to the elbows could have been an acceptable alternative to bathing the whole body.

They also purified **cups, pitchers and kettles.** Kosher food entails not only what one eats, but its source, and where and how it is prepared. Some MSS add ***couches*** (*kai klinōn*). This may reflect Lev 15:4-6, where purification from bodily discharges is treated.

■**5** After the explanatory parenthesis, Mark returns to the story without finishing the sentence he interrupts in v 2. The question from **the Pharisees and teachers of the law** is not particularly hostile. But the preceding narrative (3:22-28) prepares readers for a confrontation. The question has to do with halakah: **Why don't your disciples live according** [*peripatousin* = ***walk***; halakah regulates the way one walks, i.e., conducts one's life] **according to the tradition of the elders?**

The question has this sense: If Jesus is a teacher concerned with holy living, why do his disciples not walk according to the traditions of the elders? The purpose for halakah is to insure holiness by following Torah.

Mark pictures Jesus as gathering around him disciples, forming a community that re-creates the holy people of God. So Mark takes the scribes' question as an attack on Jesus' identity. His questioners think his teaching and the practice of his followers ought to reflect the expectations of the holy God established in Torah and preserved through the halakah of the elders. They thought the halakah came to them by unbroken tradition from Sinai. Mark thinks Jesus has a superior halakah. By his divine identity, he gets to the heart of Torah (see 10:2-9).

■**6-8** Given the neutrality of the question, Jesus' response seems particularly hostile: **Isaiah was right when he prophesied about you hypocrites.** But read in connection with the earlier story that features scribes from Jerusalem and a citation from Isa 6 (→ 3:22-28; 4:11-13), the statement links the two confrontations (see Watts 1997, 210-20).

In the earlier story, "Jesus' deliverance of demonized Israelites had been met, not with thanksgiving, but censure. Here, Jesus' healing the sick is met, not with joyful praise, but with renewed criticism" (Watts 1997, 211). This is the only time Mark uses **hypocrites** to describe the Pharisees (compared to thirteen times in Matthew). "In ancient Jewish and Christian contexts, a hypocrite is a person whose interpretation of the Law differs from one's own" (Marcus 2000, 444).

Jesus cites Isaiah with a formula implying that for Mark this is an authoritative text (Scripture): **as it is written.** The Pharisees would have agreed with this assessment, but not Jesus' application. They would have argued that Jesus is *not* following Torah. But Jesus' (and Mark's) view is that the Scripture applies to Jesus' opponents as it did to the religious and civic authorities in Isaiah's time. That some of Jesus' opponents were scribes from Jerusalem and that the Pharisees had earlier conspired with the Herodians sharpens the applicability.

The citation from Isa 29:13 is a fair description of hypocrites: **These people honor me with their lips, but their hearts are far from me.** Watts points out that the picture of Isa 29:13 is of "a national leadership and a people, already under the effects of the judicial blinding pronounced in Isaiah 6" (1997, 215). Mark uses Isa 6 in ch 4 to describe the effect of the movement away from Jesus by the religious establishment (chs 2—3), epitomized by the confrontation with the scribes from Jerusalem in 3:22-28.

Jesus quotes Isaiah to charge that "their teachings are merely human rules" (v 7 NIV 2011). This sets up a contrast between inward and outward obedience, which follows. The Pharisees' problem is that they have "let go of the **command** [*tēn entolēn*] of God and are holding on to *human traditions*" (v 8 NIV 2011). That is, they have abandoned the Torah (the point of the singular ***command***). The Pharisees, of course, would reject the premise of Jesus' argument.

Clearly, the immediate focus of this passage has to do with the specific, and somewhat narrowly conceived, issue of the correct approach to purity. Jesus' approach is that holiness is better understood in terms of mercy, compassion, healing, and deliverance. People are saved in the marketplace when he is there (6:56; see Borg 1998).

In the wider narrative setting, the issue turns out to be greater than simply following the traditions of the elders. Mark pictures the Pharisees as fundamentally opposed to God's purposes in Jesus (so Watts 1997, 216-17). Those who follow Jesus and his teaching do the will of God (see 3:31-35). Those who do not are opposed to God. This idea gains further support later.

Jesus rebukes Peter for thinking human rather than divine thoughts when he attempts to dissuade Jesus from a suffering-Son-of-Man kind of messiahship (8:33).

■ **9-10** The opening words, **And he said to them,** suggest that we have an ongoing conversation here. Scholars who think two independent traditions have been brought together here find support in these introductory words. There is a measure of repetition of the earlier statement from Isaiah. But the language here intensifies the criticism. The Isaiah citation has them *abandoning* (*aphentes*) the command. Mark has them *nullifying* [*atheteite*] *the commandment* of God **in order to observe** their **own traditions!** The contrast is intended to be stark. By *nullifying* God's *commandment,* they have upheld their **own** human **traditions.** Thus, we have opposed divine vs. human and command vs. tradition.

The command Jesus cited to illustrate their hypocrisy comes from the heart of the Ten Commandments in the Torah. He picks it up because the word **honor** (*timai*) is used in both the Isaiah citation and in the commandment. This highlights the seriousness of their rendering of the command of God null and void.

The first citation, **Honor your father and your mother,** comes from Exod 20:12. But its form is closer to the LXX of Deut 5:16. Exodus 21:17 gives the severe penalty for breaching the command: **Anyone who curses his father or mother must be put to death.**

■ **11-13** Mark heightens the contrast between the command of God and Pharisaic tradition with the opening phrases of vv 10 and 11: "Moses said" . . . **But you say** (*hymeis de legete*). This is made all the more emphatic by its placement (at the start of the sentence) and its use of the redundant *hymeis*. "Moses" is more than a name. It is shorthand for the Torah, the books of Moses. Again, the emphasis is that Moses speaks the command of God. But the Pharisees elevate their human tradition above Moses. The contrast is stark.

This particular tradition of the elders is puzzling. Mark only briefly explains the **Corban** as **a gift devoted to God.** Whether or not this is a real-life situation is a moot point. It is difficult to imagine the Pharisees (or anyone else) *encouraging* the disreputable practice Jesus accuses them of sponsoring.

All biblical vows were dedicatory, that is, a sacred promise to give something or someone to God. **Corban** is an additional, prohibitive vow. Moshe Benovitz shows that in the rabbinic prohibitive vow, "property is often *likened* to an offering, prohibiting its use *as if* it were actually an offering" (cited in Collins 2007, 351). In the Corban vow, one promises certain property to the temple. But the "property is not dedicated to the temple unless and until the person mentioned in the vow derives benefit from it" (Collins 2007, 352). In this case, the portion of property that would be used to support one's parents is dedicated to the temple. Because it is Corban, it could never be used for the

7:6-13

benefit of the parents. Any such use would trigger the dedicatory vow to the temple.

If this is the kind of vow Mark refers to here, it effectively allows adult children to avoid any obligation to their parents as an act of apparent piety. The example illustrates the cynical hypocrisy of those who honor God with their lips but whose hearts are light-years removed from God's purposes. In this way **you nullify the word of God.** And this is not the only example he could offer: **you do many things like that.** Mark mentions no further examples, however.

In the later rabbinic period, a mechanism to fulfill or annul dubious vows was available. Whether this mechanism existed during the late 2TP is unknown. If it did, this dialogue ignores it. Jesus' point is that the Pharisees' manipulation of tradition for their personal gain is wrong in itself and should be overridden. Stein claims that a practice of dishonoring parents prohibited by the Torah was "not only permitted but even required by the Pharisaic tradition" (2008, 342). But this is too harsh. The cynicism behind taking this vow was not *required* by the traditions of the elders even if it was *allowed* until this abuse was corrected.

Jesus' own practice on Sabbath observance has already been shown to be at variance with the Pharisees. The Markan Jesus sees purity and holiness in rather different ways, with the implication that this tradition of dedicating something to the temple should never get in the way of providing for the needy.

2. Inward and Outward Cleanliness (7:14-23)

■ **14-15** On two occasions, Mark signals an important pronouncement from Jesus with a summons to the crowd (see also 8:34). It is emphasized here by Jesus' imperative, **Listen to me** [*akousate mou*], **everyone.** Jesus makes the implied claim out of the immediately preceding story. He claims to speak for God in a way that the tradition of the elders does not. That the authoritative character of Jesus' teaching is to be taken seriously is confirmed in 9:7 by the voice from heaven. God identifies Jesus as his **beloved Son** and commands, "Listen to him" (*akouete autou*). In this instance, the Greek tense suggests that the command is for the specific occasion. In 9:7, the tense suggests a continuous command to listen to Jesus.

Jesus refers to the specific issue of the demands of a holy people. Mark implies that his teaching on defilement identifies the problem as deeper than external adherence to a code of holy conduct. Jesus insists: **understand** [*synete*] **this** (see also 4:12; 6:52; 8:17, 21).

In the context of the holiness agenda of the 2TP, Jesus' teaching that *nothing from outside can defile* sets him at odds with the Pharisees and, indeed, one reading of Torah. This is a general pronouncement by Jesus for his followers and would-be followers. He calls the crowds and emphasizes its generality by using the term *anthrōpos* four times for **person** in these pronouncements. Defilement remains an issue. Mark's Jesus' picture of humanity is less optimistic than that of some of his contemporaries: ***it is what comes out of a person that defiles.***

■ **16** If anyone has ears to hear, let him hear (NIV margin). This verse is added to older translations (e.g., KJV and NKJV). The majority of Greek MSS include this verse. But it is absent from the important Alexandrian witnesses. Metzger (1975, 95) considers it an apropos but later scribal gloss in response to the call to listen in v 14. It is correctly omitted in most recent translations.

■ **17-19a** Jesus' pronouncement has been made in a public setting. But here he addresses his disciples specifically. Private teaching featured prominently in 4:10, 34. There Jesus explained everything to his disciples, as they were able to understand (4:33). Here again, **his disciples asked him about this parable.** Jesus' response, as in ch 4, is that of an exasperated teacher, who has been explaining things all along.

Mark gives no teaching on clean and unclean per se. But he emphasizes that Jesus is never defiled by any touch of the ritually impure, the sick, or the dead. His contagious holiness makes him impervious to all external sources of impurity. So his rhetorical **Are you so dull?** is less impatient than it might appear. The evidence has been clearly there for those with eyes to see. But the disciples continue to lack understanding in several places. This is illustrated most recently by their failure to understand the significance of the miraculous feeding in 6:52.

Jesus' point is made with a rudimentary physiological observation that then mixes with a more subtle analysis. Nothing that is eaten can defile because it simply enters the digestive tract and is excreted into the toilet. It simply does not enter into the **heart,** the center of emotion and understanding. It is hearts that are hardened, not stomachs. So defilement does not come from food.

This is a radical teaching, clearly in contradiction with the Levitical code. This leads many interpreters to propose that Mark has deliberately elaborated and generalized this episode for his Gentile readers. If Jesus is not focused on external purity, Mark's readers need not focus on it either.

■ **19b** Modern translators place this part of the verse in parentheses, indicating that this is Mark's comment. It interrupts the flow of the discussion. It is a possible implication from Jesus' dispute with the scribes and Pharisees, but it is not the main point of the debate. That has to do with their refusal to recognize who is announcing God's good purposes and their failure to understand that he is redefining holiness in his teaching and ministry.

These few words were clearly important in the discussion between Jews and Gentiles over Jesus' identity. The heat of the debate is reflected in Gal 2 and Rom 14. Mark's Gospel certainly comes later than Paul's Epistles. Acts 8—9 may reflect a similar wrestling with this issue in the early church. In Acts, Peter required a vision to change his mind about clean vs. unclean. In Mark, clarity comes as the outcome of Jesus' dispute with the elders: **Thus Jesus declared all foods clean** (*katharizōn panta ta brōmata*). Marcus notes that "this proleptic abrogation of the OT food laws, laws that divided Jews from Gentiles, is very significantly placed before a section of the Gospel in which Jesus feeds Gentiles (7:24—8:10)" (2000, 458).

■ **20-23** The central point Jesus is making is resumed with the words, **He went on,** another signal that v 19b is Mark's comment. Defilement comes out of a person. In Jesus' view, defilement "comes . . . from within, from the human heart" (NRSV). "Heart" is understood in scripture as a metaphor for people as they essentially are. It is not just a simple contrast between external and internal. The point is that people manifest who they essentially are in their behavior.

Thus, the inner life of people generates the community-destroying behavior described in the following list, not what they eat. Jesus heads the list with "evil intentions" (NRSV, *hoi dialogismoi hoi kakoi*). "The heart is the battleground between good and evil. People give praise and thanksgiving to God from their hearts (Isa 30:29; Pss 9:1; 13:5; 16:9; 19:8; 28:7) yet from the heart flow evil inclinations and rebellion (Gen 6:5; 8:21; Pss 55:21; 66:18; 78:8)" (Donahue and Harrington 2002, 224). All of what follows flows from the essence of people whose thought patterns or inclinations are turned toward evil designs. **Evil thoughts** are patterns that could issue in action against other people, were the circumstances right.

Evil intentions issue in evil actions. The first six actions in the list are plural in form, while the last six are singular, but this mixture seems to be simply stylistic (compare Gal 5:19-21 and 2 Cor 12:20; so France 2002, 293). While the form of virtue and vice list has its origins in Stoicism, their contents are rooted in Hellenistic Judaism (Collins 2007, 357-58).

The first, **sexual immorality** (*porneiai*), may be more narrowly construed as sexual intercourse between unmarried partners or more broadly as any form of immortal sexual behavior. In this list it should probably be translated as "fornication" (NRSV), since **adultery** comes later in the list, but the choice is not significant. **Sexual immorality** is defilement "in a moral sense, not a ritual sense. . . . and lead[s] to the expulsion of the nation to which the offenders belong (Lev 18:24-30; Ezek 33:26b)" (Collins 2007, 358).

Theft, murder, and **adultery** are explicit breaches of covenant law (see Exod 20:13-15). The translation of *pleonexiai* as **greed** has the connotation of desire for more beyond what is necessary and, therefore, **covetousness.** It could, therefore, imply the tenth commandment. Jesus does not list that command among those that the rich man knows in 10:17-21 (→). But the conclusion of that story shows that the tenth commandment was his problem. Greed defiles because it issues from a heart that is missing the inner direction of the commandments. It, therefore, fits with the stinging criticism of the Pharisees above (see also 12:38-40). **Malice,** *wicked behavior,* issues from a defiled heart, summarizing the six previous problems.

The only slightly surprising term among those in the second group is **envy** (*ophthalmos ponēros*), literally, *an evil eye.* Collins (2007, 360) draws attention to Sir 14:8-10: "The miser is an evil person; he turns away and disregards people. The eye of the greedy person is not satisfied with his share; greedy injustice withers the soul. A miser [*ophthalmos ponēros*] begrudges bread, and it is lacking at his table" (NRSV). The evil eye marks not only an envious person but also one with a miserly spirit. Greed and covetousness are closely related.

Folly is more than stupidity. In Scripture the fool and the wicked are regularly linked (so France 2002, 293). In summary, Jesus states that "all these evil things come from within, and they defile a person" (NRSV). It is clear, therefore, that defilement is more than a ritual issue. Jesus is addressing moral defilement, which may also be ritually defiling (see Collins 2007, 362, citing Klawans 2000, 150).

FROM THE TEXT

This debate between Jesus and his opponents still has important lessons for contemporary readers:

First, and most obvious, is the comment that Mark makes about food and purity. While the debate over defiled hands in 7:1-5 might conceivably be construed as a halakic dispute between Jesus and his opponents, Jesus' more general comments in 7:14-15 lead inexorably to Mark's interpretation in v 19*b.* This leaves no doubt that followers of Jesus are no longer obliged to adhere to dietary rules as a matter of religious observance.

But does this mean that Jesus sets aside the Torah? Clearly not. In making his case, Jesus makes explicit reference and implicit allusion to the Torah. For Jesus, the Torah is encapsulated in the Great Commandments (see 12:28-34). This dispute is over the interpretation of Torah and its application to God's holy people.

Nor are ritual purity and moral purity separated in Torah itself. Even Lev 1—18, which sets out purity regulations, is placed in the context of Lev 19:2. The command to be holy is detailed in terms of just and righteous relationships within and outside the community. This dispute "should not be seen as [Jesus'] rejection of all Jewish ritual laws (or of the Law in general), nor does he disagree with all Jewish groups or even with all Pharisees" (Donahue and Harrington 2002, 228). But Jesus' pronouncement in 7:15-23 offers a reading of Torah radically different from most of Jesus' contemporaries.

But if this is so, why is this debate still alive in the church in the latter part of the first century? Many scholars argue that the language of Mark reflects a later situation and that his wording represents the view of the more liberal (Pauline) wing of the church. But this need not be the case. The remarkable slowness of the church to draw out the implications of Jesus' teaching is due to "the instinctive conservatism of almost all religious communities which tend to resist any change to fundamental traditional values until there is no other option" (France 2002, 279).

Whatever the case—and scholars are clearly divided on this—by the time Mark wrote, it is clear to most Christians that defilement is not a dietary issue. Whatever scruples some continue to hold about food or drink (see Rom 14) cannot appeal for support to the teaching of Jesus.

Second, it is clear from this debate that a concern for holy living can lead to different conclusions on micro-ethical issues. At one level, this is a healthy possibility. It is almost inevitable that differences in what constitutes the standards of holy living will vary according to cultural contexts. Discussion between people with differing perspectives on the practical implications of Christian holiness in the daily lives of people is important.

But in this debate it is important that perspective be maintained. Emphasis always needs to focus on the inner intentions of people, not on external identity markers. Holiness people then and now have been notoriously preoccupied with identity markers, whether dietary rules or matters of dress. The true identity of the holy people of God cannot be determined by culturally conditioned micro-ethical standards. Cherished traditions should never be elevated so as to possess the authority of the Scripture.

Third, this passage is a very clear warning to holiness people against legalism of any form. The bane of holiness people at all times and in all places is legalism. The traditions of the elders that build up around holy living, be they the halakah of the Pharisees or the helps to holy living of holiness churches of today, quickly and easily become crystallized into legal codes. When that happens, the performance of duties and the avoidance of proscribed vices become the criteria by which holiness is measured. This soon degenerates into an external performance code in which an unsavory hypocrisy and judgmentalism become characteristic of supposedly holy people. The problem is, as Jesus so acutely observes, that this sort of conformity to the traditions of the elders misses the heart of God's good purposes. Indeed, it entirely fails to understand the holiness of God and his purposes.

Fourth, holiness is a matter of the heart, which issues in behavior that reflects the will of God (→ 3:31-34). Those who see it essentially as separation and performance are at risk of adhering to codes instead of attending to mission. The Pharisees miss the big picture. Legalistic holiness people do as well. The truly holy people of God are on the mission of God.

That requires a heart that is set on the direction of God's purposes and considers holiness to be contagious. That is not, of course, to say that ethical issues do not matter. On the contrary, the heart set on God produces a life that is consistent with God's goodness and mercy toward others rather than merely external conformity. But the source of evil, according to Mark, is the heart turned away from God, rather than defilement that comes from casual contact with the unclean in the marketplace.

H. Healings on the Fringes (7:24-37)

I. The Syrophoenician Woman (7:24-30)

BEHIND THE TEXT

A decisive shift occurs in the narrative. Although Jesus has already been in Gentile territory to exorcise Legion (5:1-21), that was a unique event, bounded by two sea crossings. Jesus now moves to Gentile territory for a sustained period that will come to an end only when the journey to Jerusalem begins following the confession at Caesarea Philippi. The first story takes place in the region of Tyre, part of Phoenicia, hostile Gentile territory (Josephus, *Ag. Ap.* 1.13). Much of the agricultural produce of rural Galilee ended up on the tables of Tyre, while the Galilean peasants went hungry (Marcus 2000, 462).

Intertextual links in this story connect it to the Elijah/Elisha stories in 1 Kgs 17:8-24 and 2 Kgs 4:18-37. In both, an Israelite prophet restores life to the child of a Gentile widow. A miraculous feeding follows the second story.

IN THE TEXT

■ **24** The debate about purity precedes this section in which Jesus begins a foray into Gentile territory culminating in his feeding of four thousand Gentiles (8:1-10). Jesus abolishes the boundary markers separating Jews and Gentiles in his proclamation of good news. Contact with Gentiles does not threaten his purity, since nothing external can defile. Thus, his declarations in 7:15-19 (→) pave the way for this entrance into Gentile territory. The sequence resembles Acts 10:9-16, in which a vision prepares Peter for his contact with Cornelius. But the difference is noteworthy. In Acts, Peter receives a vision from God; in Mark, Jesus speaks for God.

This new stage in Jesus' ministry is signaled by the emphatic opening words: *And he got up from that place* (compare 10:1, another geographical transition). He goes *into the region of Tyre.* Some MSS add "and Sidon" (an assimilation to the || in Matt 15:21). Given the hostility between Tyrians and Galileans, this is not a promising place for a Jewish prophet.

Mark mentions no disciples. Jesus wants to be alone. So he **entered a house and did not want anyone to know it.** He wishes to avoid publicity, a common theme in Mark. But privacy is as impossible here as elsewhere: **he could not keep his presence secret.** People from Tyre have been present at his healings (3:8), so this is not surprising. This action has a superficial link to the Elijah story when the prophet is directed by God to go to Zarephath escaping from drought-ravaged Israel.

■ **25** Mark's characteristic *but immediately* (*all' euthys*) drives the story forward. He is accosted by **a woman whose little daughter** (*thygatrion;* → 5:23) has **an unclean spirit** (*pneuma akatharton*). Perhaps Mark first uses **unclean** here instead of "demon" (7:26, 30) to connect this to the previous discussion (→ 7:1-23). The woman **came and fell at his feet,** as had Jairus in 5:22 and the woman with the bleeding disorder in 5:33.

■ **26** The woman's need is the same as that of Jairus—a little daughter in dire straits, but with a different affliction. And this **woman was a Greek.** Mark's only use of the term *hellēnis* here could mean **Greek;** but it almost certainly means *Gentile* here. Mark often gives full descriptions for emphasis: she is a Syrophoenician. This distinguishes her from the Libyaphoenicians, as one born in the Roman province of Syria, perhaps of a Phoenician-Syrian intermarriage (Marcus 2000, 462-63). **She begged Jesus to drive the demon out of her daughter.**

It is no surprise that the fame of Jesus has spread to Tyre. What is surprising is that a Gentile woman with a daughter possessed by an unclean spirit approaches an observant Jewish holy man. Three issues make this contact risky: woman, Gentile, unclean. As in the case of the gynecologically impure woman, Jesus talked with her, and healed her daughter. This is "typical of his unconcern for convention when it stood in the way of his mission" (France 2002, 297). The good news of the kingdom ignores boundaries. But this story is more complex than this might suggest.

■ **27** Jesus' initial response is unexpectedly hostile and offensive: **"First let the children eat all they want, . . . for it is not right to take the children's bread and toss it to their dogs." Dogs,** even *little dogs* (*kynariois* here probably refers to feral, scavenger dogs), were not viewed with the same affection they are in the West today.

Some interpreters take this as Jesus' initial response, but that the woman persuaded him to change his mind (Marcus 2000, 468). Others suggest that, since tone of voice and facial expressions are hidden to readers, this was Jesus' way of testing the woman. If so, Mark gives no hint of it. Of course, it is impossible to know whether Jesus deliberately uses irony to provoke a response. Irony is frequent in Mark's passion narrative. But it is not clear here. The only ameliorating textual hint here is the word **First** (*protōn*). This may well reflect the chronological priority of Jews over Gentiles in the economy of God's saving purposes (so Marcus 2000, 469).

■28 In light of Jesus' insult, the woman's robust response is astonishing. Mark signals its importance by the phrase **But she answered and says to him.** The answer begins, **"Yes, Lord"** (the MS evidence for including **Yes** is divided; France [2002, 295] reads it; Collins [2007, 364] and Metzger [1975, 95] omit it as an assimilation to Matt 15:27). She recognizes Jesus' authority and right to deny her plea. But this is no cowering response; she counters Jesus' earlier **it is not right** (France 2002, 295).

She responds to his statement with her own parabolic observation: **even the dogs under the table eat the children's crumbs.** Alluding to the obvious (that Jesus is a Jewish healer), she does not question the priority of **the children** (the Jews). Her theologically potent assertion implies that Jesus has sufficient resources for Gentiles as well. She enters into Jesus' metaphor, accepts the priority of the Jews, but turns it to her advantage. There is more than enough even for the Gentiles. This may remind readers of the leftovers from the feeding of the five thousand. At the conclusion to this section, in 8:1-10, Jesus demonstrates the truth of her insight, feeding four thousand Gentiles. But "the 'dog talk' in this pericope is symbolic of a deeper cultural gap between Jews and Greeks" (Donahue and Harrington 2002, 234).

■29-30 Jesus' comeback is as astonishing as the woman's. It has dramatic tension, **Because of this statement, go.** At first, it is unclear whether he is dismissing her for her impertinence. But then comes the good news: **the demon has left your daughter.** "The liberation from evil that was promised to the 'children' is now to be available for non-Jews" (Donahue and Harrington 2002, 237).

As in the case of the woman with the flow of blood, this woman's persistence with Jesus brings about deliverance. The exorcism occurs without Jesus going to her house, only heightening his miraculous power. The woman returns home and confirms the exorcism: **and the demon** had **gone.** This woman is the "model of the outsider—the woman who challenges readers against setting limits to those who would be called sons and daughters of God" (Donahue and Harrington 2002, 238).

2. The Deaf and Mute Man (7:31-37)

BEHIND THE TEXT

This story of Jesus' healing of the deaf mute man has several noteworthy features:

First, the itinerary of Jesus in 7:31. Jesus appears to move north to Sidon, then east, then south to the Sea of Galilee, then east into the Decapolis. The shortest route would have been southeast from Tyre. Explanations for this are as varied as their plausibility:

- Mark's geography is suspect.
- Mark uses this to locate his readers.
- This implies an extensive ministry of Jesus in Gentile territory.

That Mark might not have precise geographical knowledge is not surprising. Few people have anything close to exact cartographic knowledge. That this locates his readers presumes the unlikely view that Mark is written in Syria rather than Rome. That Jesus has an extensive Gentile ministry is plausible; but Mark does not comment on it (Marcus 2000, 33-37). Nonetheless, the third seems to be the most likely explanation of his compressed and roundabout geographical reference (contrast 5:1-20). Jesus' sustained mission includes this miracle and the feeding of the four thousand (against Stein 2008, 357-59).

Second, this story, like the healing of the blind man in Bethsaida (8:22-26), is unique to Mark. If Matthew and Luke know it, they omit it. We can only speculate that they were put off by its quasi-magical nature or the use of saliva as a technique.

Third, the story has many similarities to the healing in Bethsaida, which follows the feeding of the four thousand. Some suggest that the two stories were together in Mark's source but were separated for narrative reasons. Both stories have strong intertextual links with Isa 35:5-6. The setting in Isaiah describes the eschatological hope of the people of God who return to Zion through the wilderness on the way of holiness (→ 1:2 on the way of the Lord motif).

Fourth, this story repeats the secrecy demand (→ 1:34, 44; 3:12; 5:37, 43) followed by its typical opposite effect—widespread disclosure. This seems to be a literary device: The command is given only to be broken (Collins 2007, 374). If so, it coheres with Mark's view that what is hidden will be disclosed (→ 4:22).

IN THE TEXT

■ 31 A collection of previously introduced locations is used in this transition statement. Jesus' journey takes him from *the region of Tyre, through Sidon.* Some MSS have "the region of Tyre and Sidon" (e.g., NKJV), which is almost certainly an attempt by a later scribe to resolve the geographical problems. Jesus ends up somewhere *in the middle of the Decapolis region.* The **Decapolis** is not a location but an ill-defined region of *ten cities,* predominantly populated by Gentiles. Mark places Jesus in the same mixed Jewish-Gentile setting as in 5:1-20 (but see Stein 2008, 359).

■ 32 People brought to Jesus **a man who was deaf and could hardly talk. Deaf** (*kōphos*) could refer either to his inability to speak or to hear. Gentiles are sometimes associated with deafness in the Scriptures (see Isa 42:17-19; 43:8-9; Mic 7:16; so Marcus 2000, 472).

Hardly talk (*mogilalos*) refers either to the man's inability to speak properly or to speak at all. Since the cure results in the man being able **to speak plainly** (v 35), the problem is likely a speech impediment. The word *mogilalos* only occurs here and in Isa 35:6 in the Greek Bible. **They begged him to *lay his hand*** [*cheira*—singular] **on the man** (see Collins [2007, 368] on the textual variant).

■ 33 Up to this point, the crowd who brought the man to Jesus has been an anonymous *they*. Jesus takes the man away from the crowd to heal him in private. This prevents those not involved to see the power of God at work (Collins 2007, 370). The sufferer is not merely a prop in a traveling healing show. Jesus has compassion on this man. But on a secondary level, this healing story, like the others, is still revelatory to Mark's readers.

Mark discloses what Jesus did in private: he **put his fingers into the man's ears** and he spat **and touched the man's tongue. Touch** is regularly associated with Jesus' healings in Mark (→ 1:31, 41; 5:23, 41; 6:2, 5). But here (and in 8:23, 25) he touches the specific areas requiring healing and uses spittle, although it is unclear how (compare John 9:6). "Spittle was extremely popular as a folk remedy in antiquity and was even highly regarded by 'professional' physicians" (Marcus 2000, 473; see Collins 2007, 370-71).

■ 34 Jesus **looked up to heaven** (→ 6:41). This might be understood as a prayer, but this is unusual since in the later exorcism (9:14-29) Jesus does not himself pray. The action here is linked with his **deep sigh.** Explanations for the sigh vary:

- part of a magical technique linked to the repetition of **Ephphatha;**
- a sigh of compassion, despair (see 9:19), or anger (see 1:41);
- appeal to God for the power to heal (Marcus 2002, 474). Stein calls it "an emotional prayer-like gesture" (2008, 360).

The use of the expression, *"Ephphatha!"* is not a magical incantation (→ 5:41). Rather, it simply preserves the Aramaic word, confirmed by Mark's translation, **Be opened.**

■ 35 Mark's description of the healing reverberates with intertextual echoes. This is God's action—the man's ears are opened and his tongue is loosened. The language of Isa 35:5-6—"Then the eyes of the blind shall be opened, and the ears of the deaf unstopped; then the lame shall leap like a deer, and the tongue of the speechless sing for joy" (NRSV)—is crucial for understanding the passage. Mark gives some clues that he is alluding to this passage, particularly in his use of the word *mogilalos* describing the man's speechlessness.

Mark uses Isaiah's marvelous picture of the return of God's people from exile to explain the significance of Jesus' ministry to the Gentiles, his journey through the wilderness, and his activity in restoring hearing, speech, and sight (in 8:22-26).

Isaiah 35:8-10 particularly influences Mark's narrative. This way shall be a pure and holy way. It shall be for all, because they are the gathered and restored people—no longer scattered, afflicted with feeble knees or blind or lame or deaf. Instead, they are on the journey with songs of joy on the way of the Lord to Zion. The evocative nature of this picture compels Mark to include these stories about the transformation of those unable to travel on the way into the gathered people of God.

■ **36** We have already noted that the command from Jesus **not to tell anyone** is a command to be broken. Indeed, **the more he did so, the more they kept talking about it.** In some ways, this is another odd command. It seems that "the spread of the good news about Jesus is an act of God, and no one can stop it—not even Jesus himself!" (Marcus 2000, 480). The good news must be proclaimed (*ekērysson*) even in the Decapolis.

■ **37** As a result, **people were overwhelmed** *beyond all measure* (*hyperperissōs*, only here in Greek). Mark's double superlative language leads to a summary statement: **he has done everything well.** Further intertextual echoes may be heard from Isa 29:18 and 32:4, but the key link is to Isa 35. "The acclamation of the people indicates the eschatological fulfillment of the prophecies of the Jewish Scriptures" (Collins 2007, 376).

FROM THE TEXT

These two healing stories speak of radical boundary breaking. Jesus, the Jewish prophet and healer, has gone outside his expected place of ministry to meet the needs of Gentiles. The Gentile woman offers a profound insight into the implications of Jesus' teaching. "The liberation from evil that was promised to the 'children' is now to be made available to non-Jews" (Donahue and Harrington 2002, 237). The man afflicted by deafness and a speech impediment is restored to wholeness, echoing the promise of Isa 35. What was in its original context a promise to the exiled Jews, here is applied to a Gentile who is restored for the journey to Jerusalem. In Jesus' ministry, the unclean have been made clean, the lost redeemed, and the broken made whole.

From our distance, it is difficult to understand how profoundly Jesus challenged the Jewish understanding of holiness. Both of these stories insist that the good news of the gospel breaks conventional boundaries and transforms the excluded into the people of God. The intertextual link to Isa 35 illustrates how this transformation enables the formerly excluded to walk in the holy way.

These two stories challenge followers of Jesus to be boundary breakers, to engage in the transformation of the marginalized so that they may become part of the redeemed people on the holy way with the Holy One.

I. Feeding the Four Thousand Men (8:1-9a)

BEHIND THE TEXT

This is the second miraculous feeding reported in Mark (→ 6:34-44). While there are significant differences in detail between the two, there are more similarities:

- Jesus' **compassion** for hungry people (6:34; 8:2);
- setting in a **remote place** (6:35; 8:4);
- the disciples' question indicating their sense of helplessness in the face of difficulties (6:37; 8:4);
- Jesus' question to the disciples (6:38; 8:5);
- the distribution of the food by the disciples (6:41; 8:6);
- the satisfaction of the people (6:42; 8:8); and
- the collection of the leftovers (6:43; 8:8).

Both feeding stories are told in Matthew (14:14-21; 15:32-39). Luke (9:13-17) preserves only the first. John reflects aspects of both in his version of the feeding of the five thousand in 6:1-14.

Does Jesus feed two multitudes or are these two accounts of the same event? If there were two feedings and Mark and Matthew preserve both for historical reasons, why don't Luke and John? But if there was only one feeding, why do Mark and Matthew tell such similar stories twice? Answers vary:

- Some think two versions of the same event circulated independently in the oral tradition. Mark and Matthew used both. But oral tradition normally preserves significant details, while minor points change. But the opposite seems to be true here (France 2002, 306).
- Other scholars think Mark created his second account from the first for narrative reasons. But the second account contains many unique words, not easily explained from Mark's editorial activity (Stein 2008, 365). Such proposals could be dismissed as overly skeptical. But in the second feeding, the disciples, who had just participated in the first, oddly express identical misgivings. How could they?

Mark has no difficulty including both stories and apparently thinks they happened. But this has little to do with historical accuracy. Rather, he uses both to advance his narrative purpose. That is our focus.

If Mark's reason for including both stories is narratological, then the sequence should provide some reasons:

- First, the theme of the disciples' blindness has been building since ch 4. It reaches a climax in the boat ride following the second feeding. It brings to a close the unveiling of Jesus' identity and the obtuseness of the disciples.
- Second, the sequence seems to end a series of mighty works in Gentile territory. This opens with Jesus' foray into the Decapolis to exorcise Legion, who spreads Jesus' story widely.

In Mark's sequence, Jesus is again in the Decapolis. There Gentiles are fed by the Jewish Messiah, just as the Jewish crowd was earlier. But here, there are no militaristic overtones—no setting of the proclamation of the kingdom by disciples, no ordered groupings, no hasty dismissal of the disciples (→ 6:30-46).

IN THE TEXT

■ **I-2** This story begins with the phrase "In those days" (NRSV), indicating an important event that links it directly with the preceding healings. Mark signals that this story should be read in light of the earlier feeding: **another** [*palin*] **large crowd** has **gathered** together. The description is less full, with no reference to Jesus' teaching nor to their harassed condition. He notes only that **they had nothing to eat,** because they had been with Jesus for **three days**—a long time. Mark does not explain why they are there. He assumes that Jesus is announcing and enacting the good news of the kingdom, this time outside Jewish territory.

As in the previous story, Jesus calls his disciples to him and announces his concern for the people. His reason is identical: "I have compassion for the crowd" (NRSV). In this story he focuses on their physical needs only.

■ **3** Marcus proposes a plausible intertextual link to Ps 107:2-5 (2002, 487). This psalm provides the background in Mark 4:35-41 (→). The link is suggestive rather than precise: those gathered in Ps 107 are exiled Jews, not Gentiles. But some come from **a long distance** (see Ps 107:3), as here. Marcus (2002, 487) points out that "non-Jewish nations are often describes as 'far away' (Deut 28:49; 29:22; 1 Kgs 8:41, etc.), whereas Israel is 'near' to God (e.g. Ps 148:14)." A similar contrast between Jews and Gentiles in "near" and "far" terms appears in Eph 2:17.

In Ps 107, the people were near collapse, but the Lord heard their cry and led them out of the wilderness. Here Jesus refuses to send them home lest they **collapse on the way** (*en tē hodō*). The phrase **on the way** becomes more prominent in the next section of Mark.

The general setting of this feeding is important but difficult to locate precisely. The narrative sequence suggests somewhere in the Decapolis, the scene of the previous healing. The desert setting and the proclamation of the good news there by the exorcised Legion (→ 5:20) suggest that the crowd was predominantly Gentile. Mark 8:10 has Jesus get into a boat immediately after the feeding. This indicates that the feeding occurs near the sea. But it could point to the narrative connection between the feeding and the discussion on the boat trip that follows. This reading suggests that the feeding occurs in Gentile territory, significantly developing Mark's inclusion of Gentiles as followers of Jesus.

But Collins thinks that 7:31 is in Jewish territory and locates the feeding in Galilee (2007, 378). Stein also places it in Galilee on the west side of the lake, in the otherwise unidentified Dalmanutha (8:10), where the Pharisees confront Jesus (8:11; Stein 2008, 368).

But these arguments for Galilee are unpersuasive. If the healing of the deaf man is in Gentile territory, then this aspect of Jesus' ministry concludes in Gentile territory. This geographical conclusion provides a coherent narrative explanation for including this feeding story: There are enough resources in the kingdom for Gentiles as well as for Jews.

■4 Jesus' expression of **compassion** for the Gentile crowds in v 3 prompts the disciples' question: **where in this remote place can anyone get enough bread to feed them?** This demonstrates that they still understand little about the identity of Jesus. From our perspective, this seems odd—have they not understood anything about Jesus? In narrative terms, however, it starkly emphasizes their incomprehension. This is extraordinary blindness. They are chosen by Jesus, act on his behalf, and see his divine activity. But their lack of faith is in marked contrast to the two preceding stories in which Gentiles exercise faith. The enormity of the problem of feeding a crowd in a desolate place overwhelms everything they have learned about Jesus. Their situation and response is similar to that of the Israelites in the wilderness (see Exod 16:3).

■5 Jesus' response to their question is exactly as in the earlier narrative. He asks, **How many loaves do you have?** And they reply, **Seven.** France detects a humorous undertone in the repetition that soon turns to exasperation by Jesus. The symbolic significance of the number seven has given rise to many suggestions:

- the seven deacons of Acts 6:3;
- the Noahic commands given to the whole world (Gen 9:4-7);
- the multiple of seven in the seventy peoples of the world or the seventy disciples (Luke 10:1-20);
- a general sense of completeness (Stein 2008, 369). This seems the most likely (so Marcus 2000, 489), although it is difficult to be certain.

6-7 The language used to describe Jesus' action here is strikingly similar to the earlier feeding and to the Last Supper, as the table below shows. If this is a Gentile feeding, Mark suggests that Gentiles are welcome at the table of the Messiah. He treats famished Gentiles as he does hungry and helpless Jews.

Both feeding stories have strong Eucharistic overtones. However, neither directly corresponds to the early church celebration of the Lord's Supper. Although the fish are blessed separately in this feeding, nothing is made of them in the subsequent narrative.

The key element is the bread. It is the repeated term Mark uses to make his point throughout this section. The collection of broken pieces after each meal followed by a discussion of the significance of bread in 8:14-20 is rich in Markan symbolism. In contrast, only after the theme of suffering emerges in 8:31-32 and the passion predictions in 9:30-31 and 10:32-33, does the blessed "cup" (replaced by the fish here?) figure in the story (10:35-45; 14:23-24).

The Three Feedings
(adapted from Stein 2008, 370)

Feeding of 5,000 6:41	Feeding of 4,000 8:6-7	Last Supper 14:22-23
taking the five loaves [labōn tous temte artous]	taking the seven loaves [labōn tous hepta artous]	taking the bread [labōn arton]
he blessed [eulogēsen]	having given thanks [eucharistēsas]	having blessed [eulogēsas]
he . . . broke [kateklasen]	he broke [eklasen]	he broke [eklasen]
he was giving [edidou]	he was giving [edidou]	he gave [edōken]
	having blessed [the fish] [eulogēsen]	having given thanks [the cup] [eucharistēsas]

8-9a As with the earlier feeding, **the people ate and were satisfied.** Considering the serious hunger of the crowd (v 3), this emphasizes the sufficiency of the miracle. Again, there is more than enough to go around, so that they are able to collect leftovers—**seven basketfuls.** Mark uses a more general term for basket here (*spyris*), not specifically the Jewish basket used earlier (→ 6:43), which supports the view that this occurs in Gentile territory.

The **seven basketfuls** correspond to **the seven loaves.** While the "twelve loaves" in the earlier story may have a symbolic connection to the whole regathered people of God, here a connection of seven with Gentiles is difficult to sustain. More likely it simply emphasizes the power of Jesus (Collins 2007,

380) or the fullness of the provision (Marcus 2000, 489). In this instance, **there were about 4,000 people.** In the previous feeding, the five thousand were specifically identified as men. Here, the **four thousand** likely refer to people of both genders and all ages.

FROM THE TEXT

This story has several important lessons:

First, it reveals Jesus as the messianic provider for all people. This scene closes the mission of Jesus in Gentile territory that began in 7:24 (but see Hooker 1991, 188, and Stein 2008, 371). Because it parallels a story in which Jesus meets the spiritual and physical needs of Jews, it shows that Gentiles are abundantly served as well. The announcement and effecting of the kingdom is good news for all.

Second, the question the disciples ask Jesus is profound—and one that modern-day disciples ask as well: "Where, in the vast desert of this world, is the spiritual nourishment to be found that can meet the hunger of the multitudes? Who can provide this 'bread of life'?" (Marcus 2000, 496). The answer, as in John 6:1-14, is that Jesus is the life-giving bread of heaven. This bread of life is in continuity with God's provision for his people in the Exodus. But it is different. This is provided by the Holy One in their midst.

Third, the few Eucharistic hints in both feeding stories are a poignant reminder that at the table of the Lord there are no divisions. The tragic history of schism in the church over the celebration of the Eucharist, however, has damaged this claim. Churches are still separated from other churches at an ecclesiastical level. Even more problematic is the de facto denial of unity represented by the homogeneous complexion of so many local congregations. "The Eucharist should be the memory and food of Jesus that break down barriers between different groups" (Donahue and Harrington 2002, 247).

J. Hardened Hearts (8:9b-21)

1. Crossing the Lake to Dalmanutha (8:9b-13)

IN THE TEXT

■**9b-10** Although Jesus entrusts the distribution of the food and the collection of the leftovers to the disciples, he remains in charge. He **sent the crowd away,** then **got into the boat with his disciples.** In the previous feeding, he sent the disciples away as well, perhaps to get them out of the highly charged situation. Here, he embarks with his disciples on the journey to the **district** [*ta mere*] **of Dalmanutha** immediately after the feeding. Mark does not explain such ready availability of a boat. Nor does he explain why Jesus returned by boat immediately after landing.

There are two sets of variant readings here. Some manuscripts have a synonym for **the region**—*ta horia* instead of *ta merē*—used in Matt 15:39. Others substitute better known place names for **Dalmanutha** (e.g., Magdala or Mageda), also assimilating to Matt 15:39. The most likely explanation for these variant readings is that Dalmanutha is otherwise unknown. It disappeared from memory and history soon after the time of Jesus (Metzger 1975, 381).

■ **11** When Jesus returned to the Jewish territory of Dalmanutha, **Pharisees came and began to question Jesus.** The Gospel's picture of the Pharisees has gradually become bleaker. In their first appearance, they engage Jesus in a halakic discussion about Sabbath observance. Unsatisfied with his perspective, debate deteriorates into a deadly conspiracy. They join forces with the Herodians on a plan to eliminate Jesus (3:6). The present brief incident confirms their negative role. By placing this discussion at the conclusion of his report of Jesus' Gentile mission, Mark suggests that they want independent divine confirmation that his work among the Gentiles is the activity of a holy person (compare 2:16). So, they ask Jesus for **a sign from heaven.**

They do not specify what would satisfy them. They are not seeking understanding; they are simply making a negative challenge—**To test him.** Jesus' last **test** (*peirazontes*) in Mark was initiated by Satan in the wilderness (1:12-13). This **test** similarly challenges Jesus to authenticate his identity and authority to act as he does. The Pharisees not only reprise Satan's role but also behave like the grumbling wilderness generation, who witness many divine signs but keep demanding definitive confirmation (see Exod 17:2, 7; Deut 32:20) that God is with them (Collins 2007, 384).

■ **12** Jesus "sighed deeply [*anastenazas*—only here in Mark] in his spirit" (NRSV). Is he exasperated? "What more do they need?" Is this ironic? "They have already seen mighty works, but fail to comprehend them or what they imply about me."

The intertextual echoes of the disbelieving Israelites in the wilderness are intensified by Jesus' question: **Why does this generation ask for a . . . sign?** Each of the four uses of **generation** in Mark (8:38; 9:19; 13:30) is negative and refers to unbelieving people (as in Deut 32:5, 20; Pss 78:8; 95:10).

Jesus prefaces his response to their question with a solemn declaration: **Amen, I say to you** (→ 3:28-30 on the unforgivable sin). The form resembles a Semitic oath, with the unexpressed apodosis, "May God do [so and so] to me, if . . ." This prepares for his emphatic negative statement: **No sign will be given to it.** Jesus implied that God would punish him if he performed a miracle intended only to persuade the unbelieving generation.

■ **13** The sole purpose of this short episode in Mark's narrative, involving two boat trips (8:10, 13), seems to be to report Jesus' confrontation with the Pharisees. Its conclusion is that **he left them** (*apheis autous*). This could be read as a simple statement announcing his departure. The word **left** is used repeatedly with no technical sense (Stein 2008, 377). But it could imply a more formal disassociation (Collins 2007, 385; France 2002, 313).

Since this episode is superfluous to Mark's story, his inclusion of it needs an explanation. It seems to be an opportunity spurned by the Pharisees. They reject Jesus' invitation to participate in his mission. So he **got back into the boat and crossed to the other side**—the eastern side—of the lake. From this point onward, his teaching turns more directly to his followers.

2. The Leaven of the Pharisees and the Missing Bread (8:14-21)

BEHIND THE TEXT

The difficulties in this small pericope require some attention: First, the details seem to be somewhat inconsistent. The disciples have **one loaf** with them; but they discuss having **no bread**. Second, what is the **leaven** of the **Pharisees and . . . of Herod?** Third, why is **Herod** Antipas mentioned in this story? Fourth, what is the unexplained relevance in this story of the number— **Twelve** and **Seven**—of **basketfuls** of bread collected after the two feedings.

These problems, however, are not an issue in Mark's narrative. First, readers should note the heavy use of irony in this passage. The lack of bread is juxtaposed to the miraculous feedings. This is not just about symbolism. But even on the physical level, the concern about the lack of bread here is puzzling.

Second, the Pharisees have apparently finally written Jesus off because of his refusal to provide a sign from heaven. Now the disciples don't get it either. Their lack of perception elicits a warning from Jesus, essentially: "Do not allow the Pharisees' agenda to pollute your commitment to my mission."

Third, the lengthy intrusion into the narrative of Herod's execution of John (→ 6:14-29) prefigures that of Jesus by the authorities. Herod's claim to authority and kingship lies behind his treatment of John. Jesus will warn that the disciples will also be arraigned before the temporal powers (13:9).

Fourth, the followers of Herod, the Herodians, have already joined with the Pharisees in a conspiracy against Jesus (3:6). Later Judas will conspire against Jesus. Mark says nothing about the Pharisees or the Herodians taking the lead in Jesus' crucifixion (14:10-11).

This story is the concluding episode in Mark's open revelation of Jesus' identity to the crowd along with the disciples. The first feeding should have brought understanding (see 6:52). But it didn't. Neither did the feeding of the four thousand.

Alongside Mark's development of the picture of Jesus' open and wide-spread announcement and effecting of the kingdom runs a parallel development. That is the escalating theme of the rejection, misunderstanding, and incomprehension of Jesus. The Pharisees want a sign from heaven; the disciples have had several. No wonder the pericope ends with an exasperated Jesus asking the dull disciples, **Do you still not understand?**

IN THE TEXT

■ **14** Mark's opening seems surprising. Why does it matter that **the disciples had forgotten to bring bread?** Why do they not ask Jesus for any explanation of his dispute with the Pharisees (→ 8:9b-13)? Why are they preoccupied with bread? The Gospel elsewhere says nothing about the arrangements for food Jesus and his disciples make. The concern at this point seems slightly banal.

This may indicate how little the disciples grasp about the significance of what has been happening around them. After distributing food to thousands, they have almost nothing for themselves. Would Jesus perform a miracle for the disciples? Mark does not give an answer.

The story mixes the literal and the symbolic. The disciples continue to struggle to understand what is going on and who Jesus is. He and they seem to talk past each other.

They were without bread **except for one loaf they had with them in the boat.** This information is completely gratuitous, unless Mark intends it to have symbolic value.

Some interpreters see this note as an attempt to tie the two previous stories to this one. In each case, the supply of bread has been inadequate and the disciples do not understand the provision of Jesus (see Stein 2008, 381; France 2002, 315).

But others see the **one loaf** (*hena arton*) as an allusion to the presence of Jesus himself on the boat. Mark's next use of *artos* in the singular is at the Last Supper.

The latter view is the more persuasive. By the time Mark is written, the symbolism of the **one loaf** would be widely known (see 1 Cor 10:17; 11:23-34). Readers would have no difficulty seeing this as symbolic of the presence of Jesus with them on the boat. Indeed, this is an excellent example of effective irony.

Whether or not this **one loaf** language carries a veiled reference to the Eucharist is uncertain. If the two feeding stories have such veiled language, it is possible here. But this may press the metaphor too far.

■ **15-16** Jesus picks up the bread theme in an unexpected way. He cautions the disciples: **Be careful, . . . Watch out for the yeast of the Pharisees and that**

of Herod. The imperfect tense of **warned** and the present tense of the command suggests that this is not a unique warning (*diestelleto—he was warning them*). The double **watch out, look out for** is similar to some other warnings (in 1:44; 4:24; 12:38; 13:5, 9, 23, 33).

Yeast often has negative metaphorical connotations as a morally corrupting agent that pollutes the entire batch of dough (Donahue and Harrington 2002, 252). It is to be eliminated from Jewish households at Passover (see 1 Cor 5:7-8; Gal 5:9). Yeast is connected with defilement in both Jewish and Greco-Roman culture (Collins 2007, 386). The **yeast of the Pharisees** follows naturally from the breach between Jesus and the Pharisees already noted in the previous dispute. But the translation **yeast** is an anachronism. **Leaven,** fermented dough (as in the starter for sourdough), would be more accurate.

But **the leaven of Herod** is more difficult to identify. Had Mark said Herodians (an early scribal change in light of 3:6 and 12:13; Metzger 1975, 98), the reference would have been clearer: Avoid succumbing to the collusion against Jesus. The reference to Herod may prepare for the setting of the confession at Caesarea Philippi. This was Antipas' capital and the center of Pan worship. But that is probably overly subtle (→ FROM THE TEXT above). Perhaps both warnings point to the corrosive impact of the questioning and ultimate rejection of God and his purposes explaining the rejection of Jesus as the Messiah. Both the Pharisees and Herod present a threat to Jesus' life (France 2002, 315).

The sum of the disciples' discussion following Jesus' warning is almost comic in its banality: *He is saying this* **because we have no bread.** They confuse the literal and the metaphorical, a common literary device used frequently and effectively in John's Gospel (e.g., John 3:3-4; 4:10-11; 7:35, 41-42; 11:50). This allows authors to explain metaphors for the benefit of their readers.

■ **17** The disciples' misunderstanding lets Jesus ask them questions. As always, Jesus knows their thoughts even though they attempt to conceal them from him. So seven penetrating questions follow, six before the disciples are able to respond. The first five are rhetorical, really implicit accusations.

The first is, **Why are you talking about having no bread?** There is a hint of exasperation in Jesus' tone. Instead of asking questions about the meaning of the **leaven of the Pharisees and . . . Herod,** they miss Jesus' point entirely.

The disciples' problem becomes apparent in Jesus' rapid-fire series of questions. They allude to a variety of incidents Mark reports earlier in the Gospel. They point to their failure to see beneath the metaphorical surface and their more basic failure to understand the identity of Jesus. They have been with Jesus, participating in his mission, but they **still** (*oupō*) do not know his identity (vv 17 and 21).

8:15-17

The second question is, **Do you still not see** [*noeite*, ***comprehend***] or understand [*syniete*; see v 21]? Both verbs indicate that the disciples fail to grasp the meaning of Jesus' metaphor. Both words imply insight rather than mere intellectual knowledge. The second is linked to 6:52, in which the disciples do not get the significance of the loaves. On this earlier occasion, the statement that their hearts were hardened is a Markan comment.

Here, Jesus asks his third question: **Are your hearts** [*kardia*, ***heart***] **hardened?** This is a "radical intensification of the theme of the misunderstanding of the disciples begun in 6:52" (Collins 2007, 387). Donahue and Harrington prefer to keep the singular ***heart***, translating the question, "Is the heart of all of you still hardened?" This highlights the disciples' collective failure (2002, 252; → 3:5 on "hardness of heart").

This stinging critique aligns Jesus' followers with those who have opposed him since 3:1-6 (→ 4:13-20). Their obduracy of heart comes at the end of a long process revealing Jesus' identity. The main difference between his earlier opponents and the disciples is that the disciples are still with him. His rebuke assumes that their hardness of heart is not a permanent condition. They can change.

■ **18** Jesus' fourth question is no less pointed: **Do you have eyes but fail to see, and ears but fail to hear?** The irony is that the disciples have been with Jesus for the whole journey and have seen and heard it all. But they fail to grasp what is going on. It is ironic that the immediately preceding healing has been of a deaf and dumb man (7:32-35) and the immediately following story has Jesus restore sight to a blind man (8:22-26). This incomprehension prefigures the passion in which those around the cross see but do not comprehend and hear but do not understand (15:28-36).

The language here is that of Jer 5:21. Jeremiah laments the state of the people because they prefer to follow blind guides. The use of sense organs to symbolize failure to perceive is "a recurrent theme of the OT" (France 2002, 317). Deuteronomy 29:2-4 offers a telling parallel. Israel had seen all the signs and wonders on the way to the promised land. But they did not have "a mind to understand, or eyes to see, or ears to hear" (Deut 29:4 NRSV). Clearly, the disciples will grasp the identity of Jesus only through his extraordinary touch, symbolized in the next healing story.

Jesus' fifth question introduces the rest of the discussion: **And don't you remember?** Of course, they don't. If they did, they would not be asking such irrelevant questions.

■ **19-20** Consequently, Jesus asks the disciples to recall the feedings. The focus is not on the multiplication of the loaves and fish or their miraculous distribution, but upon the abundance of the leftovers. Jesus' sixth question is:

How many basketfuls of pieces did you pick up? His remaining questions are no longer rhetorical.

He asks about each feeding; and the disciples give a response, which seems sheepish in light of their earlier worry about their one loaf. The search for a symbolic understanding of the numbers **Twelve** and **Seven** continues. The most likely reason for the questions and the answers is to remind the disciples of the abundance of provision Jesus offered the needy—both Jews and Gentiles. The distinctive terms for the baskets from the two stories are retained (→ 6:43; 8:8).

■ **21** Jesus asks his seventh and final question, which is left hanging unanswered. On the one hand, this is a story of Jesus, the master teacher, disgusted with these dull disciples. They are worried about bread when the One who supplied bread in abundance is with them. Surely they will have enough.

But at a deeper level, this sums up the whole sequence from the call of the Twelve to be with him in 3:13-15 through the miraculous feedings. They have been rescued from a storm in which Jesus demonstrated his mastery over the sea. He came to them when they were alone on the sea and in distress. They should have an answer to their own question—Who is this one? The evidence is before their eyes. But they still do not understand. His response is a combination of sorrow and wonder: "You still don't get it, do you?"

FROM THE TEXT

First, this story emphasizes the failure of the disciples to grasp Jesus' identity despite their participation in his mission and their firsthand experience of his command over nature, the demons, and the acts of power. They fail to see and trust. Like the Pharisees, they demand evidence and have already received plenty. The temptation to write them off as extraordinarily dull should be resisted, however. As we try to think our way back into their context, we must remind ourselves of our own extraordinary failure to see and trust.

Second, while Jesus is concerned by their hardness of heart, the good news for those who read on in the Gospel is that Jesus is not finished with them yet. He has more to teach them. The disciples find themselves in the position of Jesus' opponents because they refuse to understand. They cannot help themselves, however. Their hardness of heart and blindness of insight will be removed only by an extraordinary touch of grace.

V. DISCIPLESHIP: TEACHING ON THE WAY: MARK 8:22—10:52

The preceding section of Mark finishes on a somber note—even the followers of Jesus fail to grasp his identity and message. Despite his teaching, exorcisms, healings, command over nature, miraculous provision of food, and despite the evidence that this story is far bigger than a Galilean sideshow, the disciples do not understand. The section concludes with Jesus' warning against the agenda of the Pharisees and Herod, a dark warning of foreboding that goes unheeded by the disciples.

But all is not lost. Jesus, the Holy One, is still on his mission. He is on the way, a motif that emerges strongly through this central section of Mark. Mark's narrative now takes a significant move forward.

First, Mark tells the story, unique to his Gospel, of the two-stage healing of a blind man from a village near Bethsaida. Then, with the disciples, he goes to Caesarea Philippi, near the northern extreme of his mission. From there he begins his long journey that ends in Jerusalem.

At the beginning of this journey, Jesus asks the leading question: **Who do people say I am?** (8:27). The answer is varied. But to Peter's own apparent surprise, when pressed about their understanding, he confesses: **You are the Messiah**. This is a quantum leap in the disciples' understanding. Indeed, Matthew's account explicitly identifies this as a point of revelation, not something that has finally dawned on them.

Jesus immediately forbids the use of the language of Messiah. Instead, he reinterprets his identity as a Son-of-Man-must-suffer kind of Messiah. This theme recurs throughout the remainder of Mark. This emphasis upon suffering is too much for the disciples. They protest against it. But Jesus expressly notes that the way of the Messiah and his followers leads to the cross.

Jesus and his followers continue on the journey—Mark makes this point explicit in his narrative. The journey ends as Jesus approaches Jerusalem from Jericho. There he is met by blind Bartimaeus. Jesus heals him, and Bartimaeus joins Jesus on the journey into Jerusalem.

Among the noteworthy features of Mark's narrative are:

First, he encloses this final journey between two healings of blind people (8:22-26; 10:46-52). The story of Jesus and the disciples on their journey to Jerusalem occurs between these bookends. This is a journey from a pagan cultural center in Gentile territory to the heart of 2TJ. Between the outset and destination of this journey, Jesus teaches the disciples about the meaning of his messiahship and of discipleship. The two stories are chosen and placed with great care and precision. They address Mark's most significant themes. This is more than a geographical journey.

Second, the journey is also theological. "On the way"—a key phrase in this central section of Mark—the disciples confess that Jesus is the Messiah. And they discover what that means for Jesus, and what it means for those who would follow him. Jesus becomes ever more explicit in teaching about his fate, drawing the disciples into the story. They, in turn, continue to follow, but without clear understanding. Only when Bartimaeus is healed and he follows Jesus on the way do we see how the revelation of Jesus' identity becomes clear. And that revelation is at the cross (15:39).

A. The Blind Man at Bethsaida (8:22-26)

BEHIND THE TEXT

This miracle story comes after the final boat ride Jesus takes with his disciples (8:9b-21). That pericope summarizes the entire previous section, which ends with Jesus' exasperated question: **Do you still not understand?** (8:21). Mark gives the impression that the disciples are at a pivotal point. Are they going to stay with Jesus or follow the Pharisees and the others arrayed against him? Will they remain blind with hardened hearts (see 6:52; 8:17) or will they somehow begin to understand?

Mark doesn't directly answer this question. But he does include this story. At the story level, this healing is unique as the only instance in the Gospels in which a cure by Jesus is not effected immediately. Perhaps Matthew and Luke do not preserve it for fear it might suggest a limitation to Jesus' power. But Mark shows no signs of embarrassment about it. Nor does he seek to minimize the problem. The peculiarities of the story point firmly to its authenticity. This is not the kind of story one cobbles together out of a variety of sources; it's just too embarrassing.

The story includes the use of touch (→ 1:31) and saliva (→ 7:33). We are not told much about the man's blindness. From his ability to identify both people and trees, we infer that Mark's statement, **his sight was restored** (8:25), means that he regains lost sight.

We are not told why Jesus leads the man outside the village to perform the healing. It cannot be in the interests of privacy, since the man sees people after being healed. Does Jesus perceive some connection between the man's environment and his blindness? After the healing, he sends him home and commands him not to return to the village. But this is far from certain. The usual explanation for this odd command attributes it to Mark's secrecy motif (→ 8:26).

A plausible imaginative scenario might be constructed as follows: This man, who lives near Bethsaida, has made his living begging in the village. Once healed, Jesus sends him home rather than to his usual place of begging. Far from secrecy, this is a witness to the change this healing brings (so Gundry 1993, 419-20).

A possible literary solution might be considered. When Mark changes a scene and requires a crowd in the next scene, Jesus gives (an unheeded) injunction to secrecy (see 1:43-44 and 2:1-2; 7:37 and 8:1-8). But when he wishes to signal a change of location, he closes the scene with a command to go home (see 5:43 and 6:1-6a; Guelich 1989, 435).

Apart from these features, the story is unremarkable. It is unnecessary on the historical level. Mark must have other reasons for including it. The healing itself takes place in Galilee outside Bethsaida, an ethnically mixed territory. Jesus is the Messiah of Jews and Gentiles.

But this is probably not the primary reason. Mark has already established this point. Nor is it because this particular blind man receives his sight in two stages. Rather, the story is pivotal because of its narrative location. Its importance is literary and theological.

First, the story functions as a transition between two major sections in the Gospel. It concludes a section emphasizing Jesus' ongoing process of revealing his identity through a series of clues open to those with eyes to see (8:18). It also opens a section that concludes with the healing of blind Bartimaeus in 10:46-52. These two healings are a prime example of Mark's use of bracketing. Between them, Jesus and his disciples are on a lengthy journey from Caesarea Philippi (8:27) to Jericho (10:46).

Second, it is an "acted parable" (Hooker 1991, 198). It provides theological insight into the events beginning at 4:35. Although the exact terms of the parable should not be pressed, it is broadly allegorical. The blindness of the disciples is illustrated by the blind men Jesus heals. He is the source of the cure for their blindness and the slowness of them to see clearly. They have eyes but cannot see and ears but do not hear (8:18). Mark's story suggests that understanding will require a touch from Jesus.

Third, the story parallels the earlier healing of the deaf and dumb man (7:32-37). Both of these stories have rich intertextual echoes. According to Isa 29:18-19, "On that day the deaf shall hear . . . and . . . the eyes of the blind shall see. . . . and the neediest people shall exult in the Holy One of Israel" (NRSV).

The identity of Jesus as "the Holy One of God" (→ 1:24) is important to Mark. He uses passages such as this to confirm Jesus' identity. Intertextual echoes of Ps 146 may be heard: the Lord "gives food to the hungry [and] . . . opens the eyes of the blind" (vv 7-8 NRSV). He adds further complexity to Mark's picture of Jesus with links to Isa 35:5-6: He leads the people through the wilderness in a new exodus / new return from exile (→ 1:2-3; 7:32-37). Jesus' identity is plain to those whose eyes are open and ears are attentive to heed the will of God (→ 3:35).

This story aptly illustrates that the disciples have seen but not really understood who Jesus is, despite the repeated opportunities to do so since 4:35. The two-stage restoration of sight to the blind man parallels the coming to sight of the disciples. First, they realize that Jesus is the Messiah, but only dimly. Their understanding is clouded by their distorted cultural connotations of Messiah (→ 8:33). Second, they only gradually grasp the cost of following the Father's will for Jesus (→ 14:32-42) and of discipleship (→ 8:34).

If this analogy is correct, to what events in the lives of the disciples does Mark allude? The first almost certainly refers to Jesus' call and their response to it, which culminates in their confession of Jesus as Messiah (8:29). But any event pointing to their restoration to full sight is less clear. Although the disciples gradually gain insight into Jesus' identity and their call to be his disciples, this clearer insight does not lead them readily to accept cross-bearing discipleship.

The only hint in Mark seems to occur in 13:11. There the disciples are promised that they will be able to face trial because of the presence of the Holy Spirit in their lives. Had they been present at the cross, they too might have seen it as the clarifying revelation of Jesus' identity. Alas, clarity of vision is promised but occurs only outside Mark's narrative. That is, the disciples come to full sight only in the continuation of the story after the resurrection, ascension, and Pentecost.

IN THE TEXT

■ **22** Their last boat ride is over as Jesus and his disciples arrive at **Bethsaida** on the northeast shore of the Sea of Galilee. One textual variant has Bethany, which probably corrects Mark's geography. He mistakenly describes Bethsaida as a **village** (*kōmē*, vv 23, 26). It was, in fact, a fortified city (*polis*, see the lls in Matt 11:20-21 and Luke 9:10) recently renamed Julias by Herod Philip. Perhaps it retained its village organizational structure (Guelich 1989, 432; Stein 2008, 390) or the story occurs in a village on the fringes of Bethsaida.

Some people brought a blind man and begged Jesus to touch him. This is the first healing of a blind man in Mark. There is an obvious link to the previous story, in which Jesus asks the disciples about their blindness. People beg Jesus for healing (see 1:40; 5:23) and the story of Legion sees the demons, the townsfolk, and the healed man all entreating Jesus centered on this exorcism (5:10, 12, 17, 18). And healing by touch has occurred before (1:41; 3:10; 5:27-30; 6:56; 7:33). But this story is unique because the healing takes place in two stages.

■ **23** Jesus **took the blind man by the hand and led him outside the village.** Mark offers no explanation for the setting outside the city, apart from his secrecy motif. If this is the motive, as usual, Jesus' wish to avoid publicity goes awry.

As in 7:31-37, in this healing Jesus uses spit and puts his hands **on the man's eyes** (*ommata*). This more poetic term for **eyes** is sometimes used to point to spiritual sight (Marcus 2009, 593). The action seems almost magical. But Jesus engages the blind man in dialogue, asking him, **Do you see anything?**

8:22-23

Seeing in Mark

In this story, Mark uses five different verbs of "seeing" (see Johnson 1978). The first (*blepeis*) is the simple verb translated **Do you see?** The second (*anablepsas*) is translated in most versions **he looked up,** but it usually means *he saw* connected with blindness. The third (*horō*) is a synonym for the simple verb *blepō*. The fourth (*dieblepsen*) is translated **his eyes were opened.** This verb contrasts the man's initial hazy sight with his clear vision after Jesus' second touch. Thus, it may be translated, *he looked intently,* emphasizing the complete restoration of his sight. Mark reuses *anablepsas,* this time translated **his sight was restored,** confirming the completeness of the restoration of his sight. Finally, (*eneblepen*) **he saw . . . clearly** conveys a penetrating insight. This verb can also mean "look at, in a spiritual sense" (see BDAG). The richness of Mark's vocabulary here points to the highly symbolic purpose of this story.

■ 24 After this first touch, the man **looked up**. This could be translated *regained sight*. Both translations are possible in this context and both nuances may be intended, perhaps *looking up and beginning to see again* (Marcus 2009, 594). He **sees people**, but this is not clear sight, because **they look like trees walking around**. Although the Greek is awkward (lit., *I see people that as trees I see them walking*), the meaning is obvious. The man can now see, but not clearly. That he can distinguish people from trees suggests that he was not blind from birth (but see Stein 2008, 391).

This is the only two-staged healing in the Gospels. Whether this story came to Mark in this form cannot be known with certainty. But the partial sight of this blind man has symbolic meaning connected with the blindness of the disciples. Its precise referent is less clear (→ BEHIND THE TEXT above).

The simile of people like trees walking may have literary precedents. A pagan healing story tells of a blind man who, after a vision of Asclepios touching his eyes, sees trees in the temple. Judges 9:7-15 is a fable of walking trees (Marcus 2009, 595). But none of these alleged parallels is convincing.

■ 25 The second touch from Jesus is effective. The combination of verbs leaves no doubt about the profound restoration of sight. The man *saw with unimpeded vision, his sight was completely restored and he was seeing* [the imperfect form *eneblepen* gives a sense of continuing effect] *everything clearly*.

On the one hand, the man's physical healing is complete, but Mark intends more. This man's partial sight is fully restored to clarity of vision, emphasized by *plaugōs* (**clearly**). This work of Jesus is God's work, implied by the divine passive *apekatestē*, **was restored.**

But the point of the story has little to do with the blind man. It is an implied promise that God will remove the blindness of his people, symbolized by the obtuseness of the Twelve. Restoration will be a process, but the result is not in doubt, only its precise timing. It gradually occurs on the journey to Jerusalem. It probably comes to completion after Mark's story ends, with the regathering of the disciples in Galilee (16:7).

■ 26 Unless it continues with the standard Markan theme of concealment, the command to the cured man to go home but **Don't go into the village** is puzzling. The NIV marginal reading, **Don't go and tell anyone in the village,** follows the majority of texts. But it is almost certainly an assimilation to 1:44. The NIV text is to be preferred as the simpler reading.

Most commentators consider this story as symbolic of the condition and cure for the disciples' blindness (but see Stein 2008, 392-93). The evidence is overwhelming:

First, this story is unique. Whatever its origin, Mark is the only Evangelist who preserves it. If the others know it, they choose not to tell it. Perhaps, they are put off by its apparent limitation of Jesus' power. It does not enhance their story of Jesus. On the historical level, Mark does not need this story either.

Second, when the notions of narrative sequence and intratextuality are considered, the point of the story becomes clear. Juxtaposed between Jesus' exasperated comment on the blindness of the disciples and the open confession of Peter in 8:27-29, the story prepares readers for the opening of the eyes of the disciples but also for their failure to see clearly. Their eyes are gradually opened along the journey from 8:27 to 10:52, but they still do not see clearly. Mark seems to believe they will have clarity of sight only when they understand the significance of the cross and the resurrection. And that comes outside the horizon of Mark's text.

FROM THE TEXT

The story of the disciples takes a dramatic turn here. They have been with Jesus and have been part of his mission. They have been successful exorcists, ministering in his name and with his authority. But they still don't understand who he is and what this means for them.

But the light is about to dawn on them—Jesus is the Messiah. Matthew considers this a work of God (Matt 16:17); Mark implies the same. Jesus' touch restores sight to them. It presses the details too much to suggest that they once had seen clearly but are now blind. Mark's story is more complex than that. The disciples have moments of insight followed by days of dullness.

It is tempting to be overly critical of the disciples—they seem so dull. But we need to remember that we have huge advantages over them. We know the end of the story; we look back to the resurrection. We know that God's victory was won on the cross and that the powers of evil have been decisively defeated. We know that Jesus through the Spirit remains with us.

But is there any sense in which the Twelve reflect our own discipleship? We know better than they. But is it possible that a range of concerns and problems similarly interfere with our vision, as it did the disciples'?

This story helps us to acknowledge our blindness and to admit that only the touch of Jesus, the work of God through his Spirit, can remove our cataracts and correct our myopia. Along the way, following Jesus, we listen and learn, sometimes understanding, sometimes following without understanding. We may well require the touch of the Master again and again along the way. There is hope for the inwardly blind and for those with distorted vision.

Two gracious touches by Jesus occur. It may be tempting to press that detail too far, however, and to read it as support for a Markan ordo salutis. This

MARK

8:22-26

225

ignores the other restoration of sight in Mark, in which blind Bartimaeus has his sight restored completely with one touch. The point is, rather, that God through his mercy and grace touches the blind and restores their sight in a variety of ways. It is all of grace, a reminder that we can no more win our own salvation than these blind men could restore their own sight.

B. Confession and Identity (8:27-30)

BEHIND THE TEXT

All scholars recognize that this short section is pivotal. The reasons are numerous:

First, it comes near the middle of a narrative that has been building to this point. The key question heretofore has been the identity of Jesus. The opening line (1:1) tells the reader who Jesus is. The voice from heaven, heard only by Jesus, confirms this identity (1:11). The unclean spirits grudgingly make their own confession (1:24; 3:11; 5:7). The miracles add their mute testimony to his identity. The sequence concludes with a repetition of a miraculous feeding of the crowds.

These gradually but relentlessly unveil Jesus' identity as the Holy One of God in the midst of his renewed people. The crowds are aware that someone extraordinary is in their midst. So are the disciples. But to this point they are still asking the rhetorical question, "Who then is this?" This section takes the question of Jesus' identity to another level.

Second, immediately before this pericope, Mark places a remarkable healing story in which a blind man has his sight restored in two stages. He includes this story because it illuminates both of the previous stories and those that will follow. The disciples' eyes and ears have been blind and deaf to his message and identity. The two-stage restoration of the blind man's sight by the touch of Jesus prefigures the metaphorical coming to sight of the disciples. But their insight into Jesus and the purposes of God comes only gradually. And it is by revelation, not their own acuity.

Third, Mark now has Jesus travel near the northern extremity of his geographical territory, to the villages of Caesarea Philippi (formerly Panias, modern Banias). It is situated about forty kilometers (twenty-five miles) north of the Sea of Galilee at the foot of Mount Hermon, near one of the sources of the Jordan River. Augustus assigned the region to Herod the Great, who constructed there a temple dedicated to Augustus. Philip inherited it from his father and built Caesarea Philippi, made it his capital, and renamed it Caesarea Philippi in honor of the emperor. Panias, an ancient pagan center for worship of the god Pan, was becoming a center for the Imperial cult.

This is a curious setting for the identification of the Jewish Messiah—pagan center, emperor cult, and Philip's capital. Luke does not place the confession in this unexpected location for such a central part of the story. The suggestion by some interpreters that Mark created the story seems counterintuitive. The recognition of Jesus, the healer and teacher from Galilee, in this context would have been "provocative, perhaps disturbing, even controversial among Jesus' own following" (Evans 2001, 10). The story's symbolic value does not diminish its historical plausibility. Others suggest that its oddity supports its historical verisimilitude—remembered history (Collins 2007, 399-401).

Here begins the journey to the Mount of Transfiguration and south to Jerusalem. The journey is certainly geographical, but it is also the way on which the disciples receive crucial teaching from Jesus. The text serves as a useful opening to the teaching of the disciples culminating in 10:45. Jesus' identity is established and clarified. He teaches the disciples what kind of Messiah he is and the cost of following him on this path. The journey is challenging and somber with three passion predictions relentlessly drawing Jesus and his followers on the way to Jerusalem and the inevitable conclusion of the journey in his death.

IN THE TEXT

■ **27** The introduction to this new section is marked by a change of scene. **Jesus and his disciples left Bethsaida and** went . . . **to the villages around Caesarea Philippi.** The journey seems deliberately planned. It could be only a retreat from the crowds and the opposition. But Mark indicates that this is an important journey: Jesus leads the disciples **to the villages around Caesarea.** Apparently, they do not enter the city itself.

Collins explains the significance of the location:

- Both the confession and the transfiguration on a high mountain (9:2) occur in a sacred region. The god of Mount Hermon was thought to be an oracular deity, a fitting context for Peter's divinely revealed confession (explicit in Matt 16:15-17).
- Jesus' implicit contrast with other rulers is enhanced by this setting. The confession of Jesus as Messiah in the context of the Imperial cult gives the confession added power, especially to Roman readers. Jesus the Messiah, the Anointed One, is Lord, not Caesar.

The net effect "is to place the Christian reverence for Jesus in competition with pagan religious belief and practice and to co-opt the sacredness of the locality" (Collins 2007, 401).

At one level, the phrase **on the way** simply indicates that Jesus questions the disciples while they are on the journey to their destination. It suggests teaching by probing questions. But the phrase takes on greater significance when it becomes the way of Jesus and his disciples to Jerusalem. This is the way to the cross, a destination Jesus would soon embrace and make explicit to the disciples. On this journey, **he asked them, "Who do people say I am?"** In one sense, this question is about the cumulative effect of Jesus' ministry.

■ **28** The disciples' answer confirms the impressions of Jesus already expressed by the people in 6:14-15 (→). Some identify Jesus as the martyred prophet **John the Baptist,** no doubt dearly beloved by the common people because of his confrontation with Herod. **Others say Elijah.** Jesus makes the connection explicit between the two in 9:11-13 (→ 15:33-38; see Mal 4:5-6; Sir 48:10). But in Mark the people fail to make the connection between John and Elijah. The hope for **one of the prophets** may build upon Deut 18. Jesus is popularly perceived as a prophet. This is not incorrect, but it is inadequate.

■ **29** The question now probes their own understanding: **But what about you [plural]?** Peter responds as the spokesperson for the Twelve: "You are the Messiah" (NRSV). Some MSS add *the Son of God* or *the Son of the living God,* both assimilations of Matt 16:16.

Both *masiah* (Heb.) and *christos* (Gk.) mean "anointed one." Given the disciples' lack of understanding noted in 8:21, Peter's response is unexpected. Several points are noteworthy:

First, Mark considers this confession correct: Jesus is the Messiah. His whole story is about Jesus Messiah (1:1). Now, for the first time, the disciples make this identification. In a sense, this confession is the culmination of everything up to this point; it is also the opening statement for the rest of the narrative. This is a "watershed" moment in the narrative.

Second, according to Matt 16:17-19, Peter's response came through divine revelation. Mark does not make that point explicit. But he makes a similar point by inserting the two-stage healing in 8:22-26. This correct confession is the result of a miraculous opening of the disciples' blind eyes (but see France 2002, 329). Further divine intervention will follow.

Third, for Peter and others in this period, "Messiah" carried extensive and varied connotations. Some of them are part of Jesus' agenda; others are not. Most expected the Messiah to be a military leader who would lead a popular revolution against the Romans and reestablish the kingdom of David (see *Pss. Sol.* 17:21-22, 26-32; 1QS 9:11). But other views existed: "For the Lord will observe the devout, and call the just by name, and upon the poor he will place his spirit, and the faithful he will renew with his strength. For he will honour the devout upon the throne of eternal royalty, freeing prisoners, giving sight to the blind, straightening out the twisted" (4Q521 2:5-8; Martínez 1994, 394). Peter's messianic understanding was probably of the more militaristic variety.

■ 30 Jesus "sternly ordered" (NRSV) the disciples **not to tell anyone about him.** Mark uses the same term for "sternly ordered" (*epitimēsen*) that he often uses in Jesus' orders to the demons (1:25; 3:12; 4:39; 9:25).

Why the command to silence? This verse is the only direct evidence for the so-called messianic secret in Mark, although the command to silence occurs on a number of occasions.

First, the reason is unlikely to be the so-called messianic secret as originally proposed by Wrede or modified by others. Recent scholarship has quite rightly drawn back from this thoroughgoing historical skepticism while retaining a proper interest in Mark's theological purposes.

Second, it is not because this is an incorrect identification. It is because it is correct that Jesus enjoins silence. But it is capable of misunderstanding.

Jesus' message and ministry have created huge crowds and heightened expectations. Were he to be proclaimed as Messiah, the consequences would be greater. But an open proclamation of Jesus as Messiah would be completely misunderstood by most of the populace in a generally militaristic sense. The announcement that the Messiah has arrived could fan nationalistic and violent expectations.

Jesus seems to be aware of this potential (see 6:45; John 6:15) and has no interest in fanning those particular embers. If the disciples harbor such views (see 10:35-44; Acts 1:6), how much more the crowds?

If one claimed to be a messiah in the late 2TP, "his listeners would as a matter of course have assumed that he was referring to the Davidic Redeemer and would have expected to find before them a person endowed with the combined talents of soldierly prowess, righteousness and holiness" (France 2002, 331 n. 42, citing Vermes 1983, 134). The term "Messiah" was becoming "a convenient repository for a range of eschatological hopes and concepts derived from or developed out of the OT" (France 2002, 331). Still, it is remarkable that "the central truth, which alone makes sense of the story so far, is nevertheless to be kept secret" (France 2002, 330).

FROM THE TEXT

The identification of Jesus as Messiah is foundational for the Christian faith. It confirms that God has acted in Christ to rescue his ancient people and to fulfill his covenant promises. In Jesus as Messiah, the hopes and purposes of Israel are brought together and the rule of God is firmly established.

Peter's confession, then, is the foundation on which the gospel rests. Jesus is the Messiah of God, who gathers in himself all the promises and purposes God has for Israel. He acts as the representative and anointed Messiah of Israel, Son of David. But God's purposes embrace the entire created order. And it is through Jesus Messiah that all these purposes are accomplished.

The next pericope begins to reveal how God intends to act in and through the incongruity of a suffering and dying Messiah. Humans cannot apprehend that profound insight apart from a miracle—sight to the blind.

The confession of Jesus as Messiah is only the end of the beginning of the journey to unclouded vision. The meaning of his messiahship for would-be followers is not yet clear. Confession of Jesus as Messiah needs to be matched by commitment to his way—the way of the cross.

C. Teaching on the Way: First Passion Prediction (8:31—9:29)

Once the disciples confess Jesus as Messiah, it is as if a dam has burst. Now the meaning of messiahship and discipleship are ready for exposition. A concentrated period of revelation and teaching directed to would-be followers of Jesus dominates the narrative from 8:31 to 10:45. Within this central section of the Gospel, between two accounts of the healings of blind men, Jesus unveils the content of his messiahship and the discipleship it requires for still partially blind disciples.

The task is urgent. Mark quickly moves the scene of the confession of Jesus as Messiah to the first passion prediction. This seems so incongruous to Peter that he challenges Jesus, to set him straight. Then Jesus invites any who would follow him to take up the cross after him, to lose their lives in order to gain true life.

The appearance of Elijah and Moses with Jesus, when he is transfigured before the disciples' eyes, is accompanied by a voice from heaven who confirms the divine identity of the suffering-Son-of-Man Messiah Jesus claims to be. When he calls disciples to come and die, the voice commands that they listen to him.

There is a measure of repetition in the stories. They are structured around the three passion predictions in 8:31-33; 9:31; and 10:32-34. The disciples hear but only vaguely grasp what he predicts. But they still follow.

I. The Son of Man Must Suffer (8:31-33)

IN THE TEXT

■ **31** Jesus demands silence about his messianic identity, but he does not deny it. Rather, he **began to teach** (*ērxato didaskein*) his disciples **that the Son of Man must suffer.** His language suggests the opening of sustained teaching rather than a onetime lesson. Its content is completely unexpected. Jesus does not explain the "Messiah." Instead, he reinterprets it and fills it with new meaning: Jesus as a suffering-Son-of-Man kind of Messiah.

This is the first of Mark's suffering-Son-of-Man sayings. The term has links to Dan 7:13, although the precise connection is not entirely clear. Four points seem to be important here:

First, the Son of Man does not seem to be an off-the-shelf christological title, already filled with meaning. On the contrary, it is an open symbol, developed from Dan 7:13, but filled with content by Jesus' mission.

Second, the intertextual connection in Dan 7:13 importantly contributes to the meaning of the term. In the vision, the one like a son of man represents the oppressed but vindicated holy ones of the Most High God (see Dan 7:27).

Third, as a representative figure, the one like a son of man embodies the people of God.

Fourth, the idea of vindication present in Daniel's vision is sustained in this prediction in the expectation that the Son of Man will rise again after three days.

Jesus' teaching begins by emphasizing that the suffering of the Son of Man is a divine necessity (*dei*). This kind of messiahship accords with the purposes of God. Jesus' death is not due to human perversity alone, although this does not absolve the human perpetrators from responsibility. Mark notes the complex interplay of divine purposes and human responsibility in all three passion predictions (→ esp. 14:21).

The **many things** Jesus will **suffer** are not detailed here, but they begin to emerge in the next two passion predictions. The theme of rejection reflects the righteous-sufferer psalms, which significantly shape the gospel passion narratives. The rejected stone of Ps 118:22 is also important in Mark. Other influential OT texts include especially the Servant Songs of Isaiah.

Those Jesus predicts will reject the Son of Man include **the elders, chief priests and teachers of the law.** This list comprises the three main groups that make up the Sanhedrin. The elders are laypeople; the other two are priestly or part of the priestly establishment. The statement separates **be rejected** from **be killed,** probably because the Sanhedrin did not have the power to execute. That resided with the Romans.

The phrase **after three days rise again** may echo Hos 6:2. This intertextual link points to national restoration. It may also reflect Jesus' use of Hos 6 to support the hope of general resurrection (Evans 2001, 18).

Mark is clear that Jesus predicts his own resurrection. But the disciples must hear it in terms of the general hope of Israel's restoration (see Ezek 37; John 11:24). It does not seem to allay their dismay at the announcement of his forthcoming suffering and death. The connection between Jesus' resurrection and the resurrection of believers becomes clear in early Christian thought. Similarly, Paul connects suffering and hope (see Rom 8:17). But these connections are only implicit here.

Both Matthew and Luke have "on the third day" (*tē tritē hēmera*) rather than Mark's **after three days** (*meta treis hēmeras*). Mark's phrase in Jewish usage means "the day after tomorrow." But it could be misunderstood as a mistaken prediction. All four Gospels agree on a period of about thirty-six hours between Jesus' burial and the discovery of the empty tomb (see France 2002, 337).

■ **32** Mark carefully notes that Jesus **spoke plainly.** This is the opposite of his demand for silence on Peter's understanding of Messiah. The suffering-Son-of-Man Messiah is to be announced clearly as the word (*ton logon*), the heart of the good news of God and his purposes.

This is too much for Peter (and the other disciples), whose insight into Jesus did not leave room for a suffering figure. This is "a shocking inversion of the standard expectation of the messiah and his deeds" (Collins 2007, 403). So **Peter took him aside,** apparently in a private conversation. There he attempted to correct Jesus' unconventional understanding of messiahship. That he "began to rebuke" (NRSV, *epitiman*) Jesus suggests that the conversation was long and unpleasant. This is the verb Mark uses to describe Jesus' rebuke of unclean spirits. Here, the verb heightens the sense of shock that Jesus' teaching causes his followers. Suffering and messiahship are incompatible in their view.

■ **33** Peter is clearly the spokesperson for the Twelve, because **Jesus turned and looked at his disciples.** This explains why Jesus **rebuked** [*epetimēsen*] **Peter** in a somewhat public setting. His language chosen is strong: **Get behind me, Satan!** Jesus is not calling Peter Satan. That is clear from the elaboration of Peter's problem: "You are setting your mind not on divine things but on human things" (NRSV). Peter's views are locked into the common, militaristic expectation of the Davidic Messiah.

There is a huge gulf between the divinely ordered way of the cross and the human desire for power and authority. Human resistance to God's way aligns humans with the side of cosmic opposition to God's rule, which lies behind the confrontation between Jesus and Satan in his temptation in the wilderness (→ 1:13-14) and in his exorcisms. Jesus will face again the temptation to take the easier way in Gethsemane (14:32-41). Matthew's and Luke's temptation narratives have Satan attempt to give Jesus an easier option (see Matt 4:1-11; Luke 4:1-13). For Jesus, this is one in the series of temptations to abandon God's way.

FROM THE TEXT

The question, Who is Jesus? continues to face all those who encounter Jesus today. The answers are myriad—and the expectations surrounding each answer are diverse. His identity inevitably becomes the sticking point in interfaith dialogue. Jesus is one of the prophets and a holy man. But, for Christians, he is much more. Neither Muslims nor Jews can subscribe to the central claims of Christianity about Jesus' identity.

Christians affirm his messianic identity. But they can easily graft their own connotation onto it. We find it much easier than Peter to accept Jesus' passion prediction. After all, we know the end of the story. But all too frequently we find ourselves thinking human rather than divine thoughts.

It would be grossly unfair to see Peter as extraordinarily dull. His amazing articulation of Jesus' identity already has connotations in his culture. His resistance to Jesus' teaching, then, is completely understandable. The divine plan is often significantly different from what we would expect or find comfortable.

2. Cross-Bearing Discipleship (8:34—9:1)

IN THE TEXT

Following the disciples' confession of Jesus' identity and his first passion prediction, his teaching on discipleship begins. His kind of messiahship has implications for his followers. This may explain Peter's rebuke of Jesus. If the Messiah is going to suffer and be executed, what might be the fate of his followers?

The answer to that question is not long in coming. The sudden appearance of a crowd around Jesus and the disciples seems unexpected, given the semiprivate scene of the confession in v 30. Mark brings them on the scene not just to witness Jesus' teaching, but to receive it. This is for all would-be followers.

This entire section is arranged in a chiastic (X-shaped) fashion. Confession of Jesus' messiahship is tied to his suffering as the Messiah. Likewise, the suffering of his followers is tied to the triumph of the Son of Man and the vindication of those who follow him. Within the section, there are three couplets: double exhortations to follow Jesus (vv 34-35), double emphases on saving life (vv 36-37), and double predictions of the future (8:38—9:1; see Marcus 2009, 623). Thus, the theme of suffering and vindication is pervasive throughout the passage.

■ **34** After correcting Peter's views, Jesus takes the main point one significant step further. His teaching is for the crowds as well as the disciples. In Matt 16:24 the crowd is omitted; Matthew treats it as teaching for disciples, not would-be followers.

In Mark, the presence of the crowd is not incidental. Jesus *summons* the crowd, urging them to come to him: *anyone who wishes to follow me.* This teaching is "not a special formula for the elite, but an essential element in discipleship" (France 2002, 339).

Anyone who would follow Jesus **must deny himself and take up his cross**. The masculine singular in Greek emphasizes the personal character of the call, not that this call is for men only. English makes it difficult to maintain the personal and direct character of the demand in a gender-neutral way, without resorting to awkward language or the plural (as in the NRSV). The call is shocking: It is tempting to maintain its jarring effect by translating *she must deny herself and take up her cross*. However, the point is that Jesus' summons to the crowd implies that his call is indiscriminately personal—to each and every would-be follower, male and female alike (→ 3:31-35).

Jesus has just announced that the Son of Man is to be killed. Now, he mentions for the first time the **cross**. He notes that followers must take up a cross after him, strongly alluding to the manner of his coming execution as crucifixion.

The **cross** was an instrument of state execution normally reserved for slaves and revolutionaries. It was intended as a deterrent to terrorize people who might be tempted to challenge Roman hegemony. The phrase **take up his cross** could mean to carry the crossbeam on which one would be crucified to the place of execution (see 15:21).

While this phrase is primarily metaphorical (clear in Luke 9:23), Mark's readers and Jesus' hearers would be all too familiar with the literal—the grisly spectacle of condemned people on their way to execution carrying the cross. This is not, therefore, a reference to the ordinary suffering common to humanity. It refers to the painful imposition of lethal persecution, the cost of following Jesus on his mission to deliver humanity from evil and oppression. Jesus predicts his own fate. And he informs those who would share in his proclamation of the kingdom that it is costly. Dietrich Bonhoeffer notes that "when Christ calls a man, He bids him come and die" (1959, 79).

■ **35-37** The proverbial sayings here bring home the potential for literal loss of life that may come as a result of following Jesus. They follow Jesus' prediction of his own death—a real physical death involving a substantial cross. Following Jesus may call for more than abandoning selfishness and personal aggrandizement.

The meaning of the first two proverbs depends on how one understands **life** (*psychēn*). It might mean physical life, but if it does, how will loss of physical life lead to regaining it? If it means *soul*, it is difficult to see how it emerges out of the call to bear a cross. The structure of the passage helps to clarify its meaning:

First, to save physical life leads to the loss of true life in the future. To retain a hold on life against the confession of Jesus and the gospel leads to loss of true life in the future.

Second, the suffering following Jesus' demands is not for its own sake. It is part of the announcement and effecting of the kingdom: Jesus insists, this is **for me and for the gospel.**

This point is crucial and confirmed throughout the Gospel narrative. The cross-bearing that is part of the path of discipleship—the cruciform character of their lives—has to do with the cost of proclaiming the good news to intransigent people and resistant societal structures.

The words *emou kai,* **for me,** do not occur in some of the earliest MSS. Evans (2001, 26) thinks they should be omitted since the focus in Mark has been consistently on the gospel. Others, like the NIV, follow Metzger (1975, 99) and include them.

Third, the language is paradoxical, seen in the play on the word *psychē.* All who want to save their physical life will lose their eternal life. But all who lose their physical life will gain eternal life (so France 2002, 340; Collins 2007, 409). This may appear to promote martyrdom. But it is far more. Jesus calls would-be followers to give their lives **for me and for the gospel.** They are to be more than mere martyrs for a cause. They are to be participants in the announcement of the good news along with Jesus (Brower 2007b).

The second and third sayings are rhetorical questions that repeat the sentiments of the first statement. But they do so with a more metaphorical, even hyperbolic, tone. Both of these contrast a safety-first, profit-now approach with a long-term view. By hyperbole, both place infinite value on the human soul, which is more than one's physical life or power. What is the long-term value for one who might **gain the whole world, yet forfeit his soul** (→ 4:17-19)? **Or what can a man give in exchange for his soul?** Disciples have only one life; what they do with that life has serious, eternal consequences.

Mark's use of these sayings is challenging. Because Jesus is talking about his own physical death, he is, in the first instance, implying that following him may indeed lead to death. This does not come as a surprise to some of Mark's first readers, or even to some Christians today in various parts of the world. But it seems only a remote possibility to Christians in the West. We find martyrdom as unthinkable as did those first listening to Jesus. But it reminds us that the good news brings ultimate reversal and that the end is not death.

■**38** The cost of denying Jesus is expressed in terms of shame and honor. Death on a cross was unimaginably shameful in Jesus' context. Early Christians, who claim that Jesus is the Messiah, first have to explain the incongruity of a crucified Messiah. That claim is scandalous in an honor-shame society.

Mark's narrative acknowledges that Jesus' disciples deny him in an attempt to save their lives (see 14:52-72). Early Christians, especially church leaders, faced this prospect regularly. To retain honor or position or family might require renunciation of the Christian faith (see 13:9). The shame of the cross, then, is primary, but it extends to the message of Jesus.

Jesus said that if people are **ashamed of me and my words . . . , the Son of Man will be ashamed of** them. He refers to rejection of both himself and his gospel. The issue is more than simply external shame. To be ashamed of Jesus is to fail to embody the mission of the Son of Man and his God-given mission to the world. In the OT, shame is related to God's judgment. His adversaries and faithless Israel will experience disgrace (see, e.g., Ps 44:7, 9). Thus, Mark's Son of Man shares in the divine judgment.

The saying is enigmatic. Why does Jesus say **ashamed of me . . . the Son of Man will be ashamed**? Who is this Son of Man? Does Jesus refer to someone other than himself by using **Son of Man**? Debate over this question has been vigorous and inconclusive. Some argue that this is an authentic saying of Jesus but that he refers to someone other than himself. The Son of Man is an enigmatic figure developed in apocalyptic Jewish thought, developed from Dan 7 and 1 Enoch. Others see this saying as developing from an original saying of Jesus. He simply states that those who acknowledge him will be favorably acknowledged by God in the final judgment. It developed into two different forms, the form of this passage and that of Matt 10:32-33.

Considered in its narrative setting, it becomes clearer. The audience has shifted from disciples (8:27-33) to disciples plus crowd (8:34—9:1). The disciples know the connection between Jesus and the Son of Man. The wider audience has not heard this explicit connection. Hence, the ambiguity of the identification is plausible as part of Jesus' identity hidden from the crowds.

This is the only NT reference to **this adulterous and sinful generation.** It picks up a number of OT images including Isa 1:4 (Judah as turned away from the Holy One) and Hos 2:4 (Israel as illegitimate children of adultery). Mark does not make an explicit connection to the days of Noah as does Matt 24:37, "For as the days of Noah were, so will be the coming of the Son of Man" (NRSV). But his point is much the same. The unbelieving people who reject God's end-times message and messenger turn their backs on the Holy One in their midst.

But what is **this . . . generation**? Was Jesus' expectation a time-bound reference to those who lived during his earthly ministry? The saying clearly points to the triumph and vindication of the Son of Man. But what is the horizon of this future?

Later Christian reading usually sees this as a reference to the Parousia, the return of the Son of Man in triumph and glory at the end of time. But if this is Mark's meaning, it seems that Jesus is mistaken: The Parousia and final judgment did not occur in the lifetime of his contemporaries—**this . . . generation.** Luke may attempt to avoid this problem by omitting **in this adulterous and sin-**

ful generation. His more general statement removes the time-bound horizon of Jesus' saying (see Luke 9:23). Some interpreters suggest that **this . . . generation** in Mark has a timeless reference to all who reject Jesus whenever they do so. But this seems a desperate attempt to avoid the apparent dilemma posed by the text (→ 9:1).

The verse has rich intertextual links with Dan 7. There the "one like a son of man" is vindicated by the Ancient of Days. But the details are different. In Dan 7:13, the "one like a son of man" *"comes to the Ancient of Days (= God) in heaven and is given glory by him in a celestial enthronement scene, which is later connected with judgment"* (Marcus 2009, 620, his emphasis).

Mark 8:38 seems explicitly to link **Son of Man** and Son of God: **the Son of Man . . . comes in his Father's** [*tou patros autou*] **glory.** The christological title Son of God is rare but crucial in Mark. God as the Father of Jesus is not prominent, only occurring here and in 13:32 and 14:36. The **holy angels** likely are the heavenly entourage (see Rev 3:5) expected to accompany Jesus at his Parousia. But in light of the allusion to Dan 7, this could include the saints of the Most High God (see Dan 7:27).

Matthew 16:27 uses the saying but changes the emphasis to one of retributive justice. In the judgment the Son of Man will repay each according to what he or she has done. A similar saying is used in Matt 10:32-33 ‖ Luke 12:8-9. But in this instance a positive response to Jesus is rewarded by a positive commendation to the Father, while a negative response leads to condemnation.

■ **9:1** The preceding warning continues with prediction, introduced with a solemn opening. Both the expression, **And he said to them,** and the introductory words, **I tell you the truth,** point to the importance of what follows. There Jesus states categorically **some who are standing here will not taste death before they see the kingdom of God come with power.** Marcus calls this "one of the most troubling verses in the NT for those who hold that Jesus was infallible" (2009, 620).

The problem is straightforward. In isolation, this statement seems to suggest that Jesus' mission leads to the glorious appearance of the vindicated Son of Man. Through his coming, God's rule will come in power within the lifetimes of some of Jesus' original audience. This statement implies that the designation, "this . . . generation" (→ 8:38) is not a timeless or generic reference to any and all unbelievers who oppose God's rule. It must refer to the people alive during Jesus' time.

But if this refers to the Parousia, the prophecy fails: the Son of Man did not come before the death of some of Jesus' listeners. Either he was mistaken or the saying was inserted by later editors, who were mistaken. Their (well-meaning?) attempt to comfort their audience disillusions later readers (Marcus 2009, 621). Neither of these alternatives is satisfactory.

First, it is difficult to imagine how the insertion of a saying into the story that would cause such confusion would survive unaltered in the course of transmission. This saying is too awkward for it to be anything other than a remembered saying of Jesus.

Second, Mark consistently pictures Jesus as One whose prophecies are fulfilled (see esp. 11:13-14, 20; 14:30, 66-72). It is highly unlikely that he would retain a saying that is not fulfilled. Mark must think this prediction refers to an event fulfilled within the lifetimes of some of those who were then listening to Jesus. He could, of course, believe that as he wrote the Gospel, the end was imminent. But that leaves a failed prophecy of Jesus beyond Mark's horizon.

What if Mark is not referring to the Parousia? What does it mean to see **the kingdom of God *having* come with power** (*elēluthuian en dynamei*)? Many scholarly proposals have been offered, including seeing it as predicting the resurrection, the coming of the Spirit at Pentecost, the fall of Jerusalem in A.D. 70, the recognition that the kingdom has arrived in Jesus' life and ministry, the miraculous growth of the church, the transfiguration, or the crucifixion (Brower 1983; Bird 2003; Marcus 2009, 622; Stein 2008, 411). Each of these proposed alternatives has strengths and weaknesses. The preferred solution should be the one that makes the best sense of the saying in its narrative context.

First, this saying is parallel to 8:38. Together they serve as the counterpoint to the predicted suffering and death of the Messiah and his followers. In that sense, it confirms that the announcement of the good news of the kingdom will come to fulfillment, despite appearances to the contrary. Suffering and death is not in a hopeless cause. Rather they are part of the grand purposes of God in which he will finally put all things right.

Second, Mark's narrative has already shown the inbreaking of the kingdom in the mission of Jesus. There have been small but unmistakable hints of the rule of God in power—the exorcisms, the healings, the feedings. But the opposition is also strong. And Jesus will go to his death in apparent weakness and failure. The irony is that this is only apparent weakness, because his journey to the cross is God's means of fulfilling his purposes.

Third, some have seen the transfiguration as prefiguring the coming of the kingdom in power. The three disciples who witness it have a glimpse into the future. They see the resurrected Jesus in all his radiance. This solution has much to commend it. But the point of the transfiguration story for Mark is different. Mark places the transfiguration six days later than this affirmation: Jesus' solemn statement that some will not taste death is less than extraordinary if it is fulfilled within a week.

Fourth, a more comprehensive reading is possible. This section marks the beginning of the journey to Jerusalem, which ends at the temple (11:1-11).

There, Jesus performs a prophetic representative act that symbolizes its fate (11:12-23). Then he spends days teaching in the temple, culminating in the prediction of 13:2: "Not one stone here will be left on another; every one will be thrown down."

Jesus' increasing conflict with the religious authorities extends to his arrest and trial. It reaches its climax when he appears before the Sanhedrin in 14:53-65. There Jesus prophesies that they "will see the Son of Man sitting at the right hand of the Mighty One and coming on the clouds of heaven" (14:62). This, too, points forward to an ultimate triumph of the Son of Man.

At the crucifixion, some of Israel's religious leaders mock Jesus by saying, "Let this Christ, this King of Israel, come down now from the cross, that we may see and believe" (15:32). The irony of the situation is unmistakable. Precisely as he is being mocked for his weakness, Jesus is acting as the savior of Israel, king of the Jews, and agent of God. He is now the center of God's presence and activity. The temple is no longer the locale. The temple veil is "torn in two from top to bottom" as Jesus dies (15:38). And the revelation of the full glory and power of God is seen, paradoxically, in the Crucified One.

Thus, within the narrative of Mark, the culmination of God's revelation occurs precisely at the crucifixion of Jesus, when the centurion announces that "surely this man was the Son of God!" (15:39; see Brower 1980 and 1997; Bird 2003).

It stretches the evidence too far to suggest that the crucifixion narrative exhausts the prediction of 9:1. But for Mark it is the central revelatory event. There the power of God is paradoxically manifest. It marks the end of Jesus' journey and, for Mark, the end of the temple-system as the locale of God. The resurrection of Jesus vindicates this act of God in Christ, as does the destruction of the temple (→ ch 13). The triumph of the Son of Man and the powerful reign of God is the ultimate consummation of all things (Brower 1997).

FROM THE TEXT

These are some of the most challenging words in Mark. The breadth of the call is inescapable. Readers then, and now, cannot act as if there were two levels of discipleship—those who are the inner circle for whom cross-bearing is expected, and the rest of us, who require a far less demanding level of commitment. Mark eliminates such excuses. Discipleship calls for the total commitment of the entire person to Jesus and his message of all who would follow him.

This is not, however, a masochistic call to martyrdom of the sort that actively seeks death in imitation of Christ. Suffering and death are not ends in themselves, despite the long tradition of radical martyrdom in the church (see Middleton 2006). On the contrary, this is an open and unreserved commitment to the mission and person of Christ. If we intend to participate in the mission of the Son of Man, we cannot set arbitrary limits.

The temptation to avoid entering into the cruciform calling of Jesus is elaborated further in Mark's next section. But here, the collision between the divine path of redemptive suffering and human resistance to this prospect continues. Christians today, particularly in the affluent West, continue to resist the radical nature of God's redeeming activity, and our place within it.

The NT is clear—the path of the Messiah calls for participation in his mission of cross-bearing servanthood. This path is set out in stark colors as Jesus and his disciples journey from Caesarea Philippi to Jerusalem.

Mark knows no half-discipleship. To follow Jesus demands the commitment of the whole person to the journey. Discipleship means following Jesus with the equivalent of a signed blank check.

This discussion has concluded with the view that the primary fulfillment of 9:1 is, paradoxically, to be seen in the power in abject weakness of Jesus dying on a Roman cross. But the crucifixion is not the end of the story. It is the end of the beginning (see Brower 1997). The consummation of all things will come when the reign of God is visible and present, when his good purposes are fulfilled for the created order. That final triumph awaits its manifestation.

3. The Transfiguration (9:2-8)

This short episode, given greater prominence in the Eastern than the Western church, is a vital part of the narrative identity of Jesus. Tight sequential connections continue in this section. This event occurs a week after the confession at Caesarea Philippi. Together with the confession, it forms two matching story panels (8:27-38 and 9:2-9) that disclose Jesus' identity and reveal the direction of God's good purposes.

Lee (2004, 11) draws attention to the "procession of voices" that progressively disclose Jesus' true identity. This is finally revealed to the three disciples by the voice from the cloud. Readers, of course, already know this. But Mark tells the story from the perspective of the disciples. The three should have known Jesus' identity as well. But they have not perceived what they have seen nor understood what they have heard.

No Gospel offers a specific geographical setting for the transfiguration. This is less important than the event itself and its setting on a high mountain. The next geographical note occurs in 9:30, after the exorcism of 9:14-29. There Mark states that "they left that place and passed through Galilee."

Tradition from the third century locates the transfiguration on Mount Tabor in Galilee. But this is unlikely, since a military installation seems to have been located on its summit during the time of Jesus. Tabor stands alone on the plain of Esdraelon in Galilee, but it is only a hill, not a mountain (Stein 2008, 416).

A more plausible guess is Mount Hermon. It is not far from Caesarea Philippi (→ 8:27-30), the scene of the confession. Both were centers of the pagan worship of Pan. And Hermon easily qualifies as a high mountain.

The transfiguration story itself has a "bewildering array" of possible literary parallels/antecedents (see Marcus 2009, 1108-18): epiphanies of gods in human form, deifications, metamorphoses, apotheoses, and ascents to heaven. Intertextual echoes can be heard of the stories of Adam, the Messiah, and Moses. The story best fits the genre of OT theophanies and Hellenistic epiphany stories (so Collins 2007, 416).

Many scholars draw particular attention to Moses imagery. The opening words, **after six days,** link the event with Moses' ascent to Sinai in Exod 24:15-16. Both texts mention the presence of God in a cloud and the voice from the cloud.

The heavenly voice's command for the three disciples to **listen to** Jesus closely resembles Deut 18:15. There God charges the people of Israel to listen to a promised prophet like Moses. Marcus concludes that "the most important backgrounds for the Markan transfiguration are traditions about Moses, the Feast of Tabernacles, and royal epiphanies" (2009, 1118).

But there are differences as well. A theophany of *God* does not explain why *Jesus* is transfigured. The voice from the cloud speaks, but all attention is focused on Jesus. Moses' face shone when he descended from Sinai, but this "text seems to imply that Jesus' transfigured state is part of the revelation, rather than a result of it" (Collins 2007, 417). Mark considers Jesus more than a new Moses or Moses-like prophet, as the appearance of Elijah and Moses with Jesus confirms. Jesus is more than Moses (3:13-15); the transfigured One is of an order different from Moses: He is God's beloved Son.

Some scholars see the transfiguration as Mark's replacement for a resurrection appearance. Jesus appears with the deathless figures, Elijah and Moses. His shining clothing also points in that direction. There are other connections with the resurrection of Jesus: the transfiguration reveals the ultimate triumph of God's purposes in the suffering, death, and vindication of his Son. But there are compelling reasons why this is unlikely to replace an otherwise missing resurrection appearance in Mark (see Stein 2008, 413-14).

Questions about what happened are impossible to answer. The scene is otherworldly—for instance, the whiteness of the clothes is beyond any possible cleanliness. The appearance and disappearance of Elijah with Moses and the cloud are also ethereal. But Peter thinks this is more than a shared vision: he wishes to build tabernacles for the three figures. Mark, however, dismisses Peter's comment as foolish.

9:2-8

■ **2-3** The transfiguration is crucial to the disclosure of Jesus' identity to the disciples and Mark's readers. Mark ties it closely to the preceding confession and teaching by the time-reference **after six days.** This begins the second half of the identity of Jesus introduced in 8:27. It introduces and confirms several key points. But it also partially fulfills the prediction in 9:1 that some of the disciples will see the kingdom of God coming with power (→ 9:1). The transfiguration may be a proleptic glimpse of the heavenly glory of Jesus, foreshadowing the Parousia when Jesus will come in great glory (see Stein 2008, 417). But it cannot be its complete fulfillment.

The solemn assertion that "some who are standing here will not taste death" in 9:1 is curious if it refers to an event a week later. It does tie the two scenes together, but the time reference probably echoes the account of Moses' ascent to Sinai after six days in Exod 24:16, the first of several symbolic allusions to Moses tradition here (Marcus 2009, 637).

At crucial points (5:36; 14:33) Jesus takes **Peter, James and John with him.** Now he **led them,** indicating Jesus' command of the situation, **up a high mountain.** The mountain is probably Hermon, but Mark's interest lies elsewhere. This is a mountain of God, a "thin place," as a metaphor of Celtic spirituality would call it, "at the boundary between heaven and earth, 'on the outskirts of heaven'" (Lee 2004, 15). The four are **all alone.** The revelation the disciples are about to receive is a glimpse beyond the apparent weakness of the suffering Son of Man and the fear of cross-bearing discipleship. It will allow them to see the bigger picture of God's ultimate purposes. The story is told from their perspective.

The **high mountain** adds to the sense that something extraordinary is about to happen in the realm of the supernatural. High mountains were often thought to be sacred. Israel's God (Exod 24) appears with Elijah and Moses in the company of Jesus. This is a reminder of the continuity of Jesus' mission with God's purposes from the beginning. It places Jesus' identity in the divine realm; he is more than a prophet or a new Moses.

Jesus is **transfigured** (*metamorphōthē*; see Rom 12:2; 2 Cor 3:18) before them. The verb is passive, indicating divine responsibility for the transformed appearance of Jesus. The exact nature of the transformation is not clear. It could be understood in two ways: Either Jesus' true nature is being displayed before their eyes or his future glory as the resurrected One is temporarily open to the eyes of the three disciples (Collins 2007, 421). In 2 Kgs 6:17 and Rev 4:1 human eyes are opened to a dimension beyond the mundane. In favor of the first alternative is the revelatory character of the narrative. In favor of the second is the subsequent discussion in which the experience is understood in light of the resurrection. Both views are possible and complementary.

Mark refers only to the change in the appearance of Jesus' **clothes** (Matthew and Luke mention changes in his physical appearance as well). Mark also says that Jesus was transfigured, but he does not say what this entails. His clothes **became dazzling white** with a numinous character beyond anything mundane, such that *no launderer could clean them.* This description resembles other biblical descriptions of God (Dan 7:9; Ps 104:2). The young man at the empty tomb (Mark 16:5) is dressed in white; but Jesus' appearance surpasses that.

■ **4** After Jesus is transfigured, **there appeared before them Elijah and Moses.** This is the biblical language for angelic appearances (see Gen 12:7; 17:1; 18:1) and other supernatural events. Mark gives no hint as to how they are recognized.

Both their appearance and unusual order requires some explanation. Many argue that Elijah and Moses together represent the Law and the Prophets. Others note that both received visions of God (Evans 2001, 36). But neither explanation accounts for Mark's order; and both are unlikely. The chronological and logical order would be Moses and Elijah (as in Matt 17:3). Two other possibilities should be considered:

First, both figures may prefigure the resurrection, since both are popularly thought to be deathless. Elijah was taken to heaven in a whirlwind (2 Kgs 2:11). And according to some traditions (despite Deut 34:5-6), Moses was also taken to heaven without dying. Elijah was more prominent in eschatological contexts (Marcus 2009, 637).

Second, the emphasis upon Elijah is strong in Mark. John the Baptist fulfills the role of Elijah in popular expectations based on Malachi. Mark reports John's execution (6:14-29). But John-Elijah's work is already complete when he is arrested. During John's ministry "the whole Judean countryside and all the people of Jerusalem went out to him" (1:5), an amazingly comprehensive statement. But John is then executed. If John fulfills the role of Elijah, the narrative sequence demands that he be removed from the scene before Elijah appears here.

The importance of Elijah is emphasized by the discussion as Jesus and the inner circle make their way down the mountain. Nothing more is said of Moses. It is Elijah's name that is mistakenly heard at the cross (15:33-39). Elijah's work is also more prominent than Moses' in the LXX of Mal 3:22-24, where Elijah's work is set before Moses' work. Malachi 3 and 4 are important background texts for Mark (3:1 in Mark 1:2).

Mark describes **Elijah and Moses . . . talking with Jesus** but gives no information about the conversation. The significance of Jesus is heightened by the presence of these two prominent figures from Israel's past. Luke 9:31 makes explicit what Mark only implies: that "they spoke about his departure, which he was about to bring to fulfillment at Jerusalem."

■ **5-6** The verb in **Peter said** (*apokritheis*) is usually used in responses to questions. But here it is Peter's response to the situation (so France 2002, 353). Peter addresses Jesus as **Rabbi (*teacher*)**. This seems inadequate here (but see Marcus 2009, 633), but it may be more honorific than *didaskalos* (see 4:38). His inadequate address is followed by an assertion: **it is good for us to be here.**

Peter proposes, **Let us put up three shelters—one for you, one for Moses and one for Elijah.** Perhaps he thinks this is the fulfillment of 9:1, a sort of new Exodus to be celebrated by a renewed feast of booths (so Evans 2001, 37). Or he may have thought of establishing a permanent shrine at the scene of a theophany (Collins 2007, 424). But Mark is highly critical of this suggestion. It is completely wrongheaded, like much else Peter has said since his confession in 8:29. France kindly comments, "The proposal is simply the clumsy way for a practical man to express his sense of occasion" (2002, 354). Peter once again speaks for everyone. The occasion for his suggestion comes because **they were so frightened** at this overwhelming event.

■ **7** The appearance of Elijah and Moses talking with Jesus is important. But the central event is that **a cloud appeared and enveloped them.** The overshadowing cloud of glory demonstrates that Jesus' ultimate rescue from death is in God's hands (Marcus 2009, 639). It also alludes to the appearance of Yahweh to Moses in a cloud after six days on Sinai (Exod 24:15-18; see Exod 40:35). This is the presence of God.

According to Exod 24:16, "The LORD called to Moses from within the cloud." He also speaks to Moses from a cloud in Exod 19:9. He tells Moses what to say to the people so that they can live as God's holy people (Exod 19:6).

Significantly, the voice does not address Jesus, but the three disciples. Jesus is not a new Moses. The voice from heaven has already confirmed his identity for readers in Mark 1:11. Now, the voice confirms Jesus' identity to the disciples: **This is my Son, whom I love.** They are emphatically commanded: **Listen to him!** The episode makes a number of important points:

First, this confirms that the path announced by Jesus is God's intended purpose. Thus, when Jesus states that the Son of Man must suffer, and when he calls would-be disciples to take up the cross after him, he is making clear the way of God, not any human direction.

Second, it confirms that the confession of Jesus as Messiah and suffering Son of Man is correct. Peter's address of Jesus as "Rabbi" in 9:5 falls short of the identity of Jesus he grasped a week earlier.

Third, the suggestion that they stay on the mountain in booths is at odds with the call to cross-bearing. They cannot stay on the mountain and also go to Jerusalem where Jesus is to die.

Fourth, the scene is a reminder that Elijah and Moses are important in the divine scheme. But Jesus, as the beloved Son, is qualitatively different from and superior to them (→ 12:1-12).

Fifth, the transfiguration clearly confirms that the identity of the suffering Son of Man, who will be the Crucified One, and the glorious, beloved Son of the Father are identical. The transfiguration is clearly linked to the cross, where the identity of Jesus as Son of God is finally disclosed. He is also the one hanging on a Roman cross. "Mark's point is not just that Jesus engages radically with human suffering but rather that the beloved Son, revealed in heavenly glory and beauty on the mountain, is the harbinger of God's future, and the suffering Son of Man, dying in desolation on the cross, are one and the same person" (Lee 2004, 32).

■ **8 Suddenly** the scene returns to an earthly setting. The divine voice has spoken. Jesus' divine identity has been made clear to the three. And the primary purpose of the episode is fulfilled. Elijah and Moses are gone. The cloud has disappeared. And **they no longer saw anyone with them except Jesus.** "Only Jesus, not the great prophet Elijah or the great lawgiver Moses, can accomplish God's redemptive plan" (Evans 2001, 38).

FROM THE TEXT

The content and location of the transfiguration give it immense importance for Mark. The focus is on Jesus, with his identity sharply defined. Here is the "sign from heaven" that the Pharisees demanded in 8:11, but it is not given to "this generation" (8:12). Rather, it comes to his followers. The crowds may think he is John the Baptist or Elijah or one of the prophets (8:28). But he is none of these. In Mark, John fulfills the role of Elijah, and he appears on the mountain. A prophet like Moses was expected, but Jesus is neither Moses nor the prophet like Moses. He is, as Peter said (→ 8:29), the Messiah.

But Jesus' messianic identity must be nuanced. Peter speaks for all the disciples when he rejects Jesus' Son-of-Man-must-suffer kind of Messiah (8:31-33). Jesus' announcement and effecting of the kingdom is good news. But this good news is accomplished through the suffering and death of the proclaimer. Furthermore, Jesus' way of the Messiah is the way for would-be disciples.

All this is confirmed by the voice from the cloud. But the voice is not for Jesus. It's for the three disciples. Jesus announces the coming of God's rule, however unexpected its character turns out to be. Disciples of Jesus need to heed his interpretation of Messiah, because he is the beloved Son who announces the will of God (see 3:31-35).

The gospel looks forward to God's good purposes for the future being accomplished. The glorification of Jesus offers a glimpse of the glory he has with the Father (see John 17:5). The cross is not the end. Vindication will come as well: The Son of Man "must be killed and after three days rise again" (Mark 8:31). The death is the means to the end of the coming of God's kingdom with power.

The transfiguration may offer one further important lesson for God's holy people. We might like to enjoy "mountaintop" experiences with Jesus permanently. But if we are to be like Jesus and to share in his mission, we will need to return to the valley, where the situation is far different. The holiness of God is not only manifest in the luminous experiences of the mountaintop but also present in the cross and in the dark valleys where the work of the Holy One of God is occurring. Holy people cannot stay within the glowing circle of light sheltered in their booths. We must go to where the consequences of evil are manifest everywhere and where bleeding people and a broken world await the ministry of the Holy One and his followers.

4. The Return to the Valley (9:9-13)

IN THE TEXT

While the overall meaning of this passage can be determined in its wider narrative context, it is not particularly clear on its own. It starts with the now familiar call from Jesus for secrecy on the one hand, and the disciples' lack of understanding on the other. But the question they ask has to do with Elijah and his coming, not their puzzlement about the resurrection. Jesus' response is cryptic as well. He confirms that Elijah must first come to restore all things (Mal 4:5).

But then Jesus asks a question: Why does Scripture say **the Son of Man must suffer?** Apart from the fact that no scripture actually says this, the connection between the two comments is not immediately apparent. When Jesus returns to the Elijah theme, he solemnly announces that Elijah has come. And **they have done to him** as **they wished,** as foretold in Scripture. But the meaning of this statement is also far from clear.

Such problems have challenged scholars to try to determine whether this section is a Markan composition or a pre-Markan tradition. There is no consensus. Fortunately, this debate is not crucial. Whatever its origin and composition, it is better to make sense of it through the available intertextual and intratextual links.

■9 Now the significance of the transfiguration is made clear to the disciples. On the way down the mountain (compare Exod 34:29), **Jesus gave them or-**

ders not to tell anyone what they had seen until the Son of Man had risen from the dead. The command to secrecy here is specifically tied to the resurrection rather than simply a general command, but it otherwise parallels the command in 8:30. In that context, the secrecy was primarily about the suffering of the Messiah. Here it is his divine identity and anticipation of his triumph that the three disciples have been privileged to witness (→ 5:35).

Clearly, the transfiguration has something to do with the resurrection. But it is not a misplaced resurrection appearance. Rather, the resurrection is both the vindication of the suffering Son of Man and the confirmation of the turning of the ages, the presence of the kingdom, in the sense of firstfruits.

■ 10 Earlier, Jesus' commands to silence were universally ignored. But here, the disciples kept the matter to themselves. They are, however, confused about what "rising from the dead" meant. Mark's wording suggests that they struggle with the whole idea of resurrection (France 2002, 357). But many Jews (the Sadducees are an exception) believed in a general resurrection (see John 11:24). Thus, the disciples are more likely struggling to relate the resurrection to Jesus' earlier words (Marcus 2009, 643). Mark's readers know that Jesus has been raised. But as Paul emphasizes, Jesus' resurrection is out of sync. That is, Jesus is the firstfruits of the general resurrection; his resurrection is the key element in the beginning of the consummation of all things.

■ 11 The connection between the disciples' question about Elijah and their puzzlement over resurrection is not immediately clear. But when the widespread belief in the return of Elijah before the Day of the Lord (see Mal 4:5-6) is taken into account, it becomes clearer. Some early Christians associated the Day of the Lord and the resurrection. Their query—Why do the teachers of the law say that Elijah must come first?—must refer to Elijah's return preceding the resurrection/Day of the Lord.

■ 12 Jesus' response could be construed as either a question or a statement. Marcus thinks it makes better sense as a question, "since the continuation, which speaks of the suffering of the Son of Man, does not confirm the references to Elijah's restoration of the world but contradicts it. If Elijah had already restored everything before the Messiah came . . . what need would there be for the Son of Man's suffering" (2009, 645; see also Hooker 1991, 220)?

But Jesus's words can be taken as a statement (Evans 2001, 43; Stein 2008, 425): Elijah does come first, and restores all things. This expands Elijah's expected work in Mal 4:6. On this reading, Jesus confirms that the work of Elijah is finished. Mark implicitly connects John and Elijah in a number of ways. But the disciples have not recognized the connection (see 8:27: "some say John the Baptist; others say Elijah"). According to Matt 11:14-15, the connection is open only to those with ears to hear.

If this is so, then the implication is that the disciples thought the sequence of Elijah then Day of the Lord/resurrection was in the future. But Jesus says the future has already begun. Inaugurated by the coming of John, the Day of the Lord/resurrection is in the process of arriving. Perhaps they thought the arrival of Elijah with Moses on the mount marked the beginning of Elijah's work. But Jesus wants them to know that this is the end of Elijah's work, not the beginning of it.

If John fulfills the role of Elijah-who-is-to-come, and if his role has been preparatory, then Mark gives ample support for this view in 1:1-14. This concludes with the opening of Jesus' ministry "after John was arrested" (1:14 NRSV). The lengthy account of his beheading shows clearly that John is out of the picture, preparing the way for the appearance of Elijah with Moses in 9:5. In Mark's view, John's = Elijah's work is finished.

The next part of Jesus' answer is a rhetorical question. It reminds the disciples about the necessity of his death (so Stein 2008, 426). But the difficulty with the statement is that it is nowhere specifically **written** in the Scriptures **that the Son of Man must suffer much and be rejected.** This formula is used for a conflation of scriptures here and in 14:21 and 49. A constellation of OT suffering figures (the righteous sufferer of the psalms, the servant in Isaiah, and others) is coalesced in the suffering Son of Man in Mark (Marcus 2009, 645).

■ **13** This statement—**But I tell you, Elijah has come, and they have done to him everything they wished, just as it is written about him**—directly confirms that Elijah's role is finished. He has suffered as a holy and righteous man (6:20). And, by implication, the Son of Man will suffer the same fate, because it is written in Scripture.

5. Missional Failure (9:14-29)

BEHIND THE TEXT

The final episode after the first passion prediction is Mark's longest exorcism story. It is significantly longer than the parallels in Matthew and Luke. It is the only healing/exorcism that occurs between the healings of the two blind men, which surrounds this section like bookends. This section is devoted to teaching the disciples about messiahship and discipleship. Thus, the extensive descriptions, the dialogue in public and private, and the action of Jesus teach lessons on Jesus' identity and the importance of faith.

The geographical setting of the healing is unclear. The presence of the scribes and a large crowd suggests that this is Jewish territory, probably in northern Galilee. But this conflicts with the preferred location for the transfiguration on Hermon, in Gentile territory. There is no reason why scribes could not travel outside Jewish territory. Regular contact with the large Jewish community in Damascus is assumed in Acts 9:1-2. And Hermon is not far from Dan, the traditional northern limit of the land of Israel.

One interesting textual issue is raised in 9:29. The vast majority of MSS add "and fasting" (*kai nēsteiai*) here. But it is omitted in the earliest and generally best MSS (→ 2:18-20). The most probable early reading lacks the phrase. Its addition is readily explained by the increasing emphasis on fasting in the early church (see Metzger 1975, 101). But the words could just as easily have been omitted "to discourage a current overemphasis on fasting, or perhaps because a scribe felt them to be incompatible with the dismissal of fasting in 2:19" (France 2002, 361). On strictly textual grounds, the decision is finely balanced. But there are other sound narrative reasons for omitting (→ IN THE TEXT below).

IN THE TEXT

■ 14 The scene that greets Jesus and the three disciples when they **came to the other disciples** is one of chaos and dispute. The disciples have **a large crowd around them** and the scribes are **arguing with them.** The disciples themselves play no further role in the story until the end (9:28-29). Within the narrative, this lengthy story is part of the teaching on discipleship begun in 8:34.

Mark does not explain why the scribes are here. But their presence gives the story a hostile air. It is unclear whether they are arguing with the crowd or the disciples. And the cause of the dispute is unstated. They are probably discrediting the failed disciples (so Marcus 2009, 657). They are part of the faithless generation (9:19) Jesus condemns (Collins 2007, 437).

■ 15 When Jesus appears on the scene, the crowd is **overwhelmed with wonder and** runs **to greet him.** Why were they so awestruck? If the transfiguration evoked the story of Moses on Sinai, then it might be the lingering luminous effects of the transfiguration. But Mark gives no other hint that this is his point. If Mark evokes the story of Moses, we would expect the people to be fearful, making it necessary for Jesus to cover his face. But here the people come to welcome him. This seems to be Mark's preferred "literary device to highlight the significance and authority of Jesus" (Collins 2007, 437; see 1:27).

■ 16-18 When Jesus asks about the commotion, a **man in the crowd answered.** He addresses Jesus as **Teacher** (see 1:27 is designated "teaching . . . with authority") and begins his story: **I brought you my son.**

This is significant. The man is coming to Jesus because Jesus is widely known as an exorcist. But Jesus is absent, so the man asks the **disciples to drive out the spirit, but they *did not have the strength to do so*** (*kai ouk ischysan*). Despite the disciples' earlier success as exorcists (→ 6:13, 30), this time they are failures. Only later do the disciples understand why.

The symptoms of the boy **who is possessed by a spirit** are severe. They are similar to the symptoms of epilepsy, which were well known in antiquity (see Collins 2007, 435). But all three Gospels label this as an exorcism of a demon rather than a healing from epilepsy.

■ **19** Jesus' sharp response—**O unbelieving generation**—is probably addressed to the entire crowd, not only to the man and his son or the scribes or the disciples. Marcus (2009, 659) thinks that **unbelieving generation** in the first instance is directed to the disciples. But the phrase echoes God's exasperation with Israel in the wilderness expressed in Num 14:11 and Deut 32:20.

A central theme in this story is faith. The response of the father in Mark 9:24 indicates that he considers Jesus' comment to apply to him. The term "generation" (*genea*) in 8:12, 38, and 13:30, however, suggests a more general ascription. That the disciples are included is indicated by Jesus' rhetorical questions, **How long shall I stay with you? How long shall I put up with you?** The disciples are far from ready to carry on his mission.

■ **20-22** The boy is brought to Jesus and, recognizing Jesus, **the spirit . . . threw the boy into a convulsion.** That this is a long-standing affliction, **from childhood,** highlights the immediate deliverance affected by Jesus. The malevolence of the demon and the severity of the affliction are also highlighted. The combination of this and the disciples' failure to deal with the spirit explains why the father pleads with Jesus with a degree of uncertainty: **If you can do anything, take pity on us and help us.** He asks Jesus to go beyond the humanly possible (Collins 2007, 439). There are liturgical echoes in the cry for **pity on us,** normally directed toward God (Marcus 2009, 660).

■ **23** Jesus' response challenges the words of the father: **If you can?** The phrase is grammatically difficult, giving rise to various textual emendations; but it is clearly an ironic repetition of the father's words (see Metzger 1975, 100). Jesus then comments, **Everything is possible for him who believes.** This might be a statement about the power of the divine in Jesus. Or, it could emphasize the importance of faith for the petitioner. "Jesus has the ability to heal because of his faith, and the healing may be expected to be granted in response to the faith of the petitioner (as in 2:5; 5:34, 36)" (France 2002, 368). But what is at stake here is Jesus' power to heal because of his identity (Marcus 2009, 661).

■ **24** The response of the father is swift; the cry is one of deep pathos. On the one hand, the father's action so far indicates sincere belief—**I do believe.** This is evident in his approach to Jesus. He is confident that all things are possible to the one who believes, not because of the power of faith, but because of the inexhaustible power of God. But the condition of his son is dire and the failure of the disciples obvious. So he cries, **Help me overcome my unbelief!**

This man is much like the disciples in Mark. They exhibit the same mixture of belief and doubt. It also "captures the tortured self-doubt of many sincere prayers" (France 2002, 368). The simplistic connection sometimes made between the degree of the faith of the petitioner and the outcome of the petition is exposed as false in this story. The boy is healed despite the unbelief the man acknowledges. While unbelief (*apistia*) limits the effectiveness of Jesus' ministry in Mark (→ 6:1-6a), it does not prevent him from acting either there or here. The difference between this man and the Nazareth crowd is significant, however. Here this man acknowledges his need for faith; there the people reject Jesus.

■ **25** The exorcism follows as soon as Jesus sees that **a crowd was running to the scene.** He **rebuked the *unclean* spirit.** Jesus **rebuked** the demon in 1:25, the storm in 4:39, and Peter in 8:33. The term can be used for an ordinary reprimand.

The **spirit** is ***unclean*** because it is part of the cosmic opposition to God's reign. Jesus addresses the ***unclean*** spirit, because during an epileptic-like seizure the sufferer is unable to hear or speak. The spirit is driven out in emphatic language (*egō epitassō soi*). This draws attention to the authority of Jesus, which is qualitatively different from the disciples'. Theirs is a derived authority; his is intrinsic to his identity.

The demon is forbidden from ever returning, an essential point if this is understood along the lines of recurring epileptic seizures. But it also presupposes the common view that demons needed embodiment in some physical being in order to wreak their havoc (→ 5:11-13).

■ **26-27** The exorcism itself is described in the same terms as 1:26. The result is that **the boy looked so much like a corpse that many said, "He's dead."** As in the raising of Jairus' daughter (5:35-43), **Jesus took him by the hand and lifted him to his feet, and he stood up.** Both stories highlight Jesus' identity and authority. In both, unbelief surrounds the story—the laughing mourners (5:40) and ambivalence of the father (9:24). The language also hints at resurrection, but this boy is not dead.

■ **28-29** The exorcism occurs in public, but at its conclusion Jesus and the disciples enter a house, where they ask him in private: **Why couldn't we drive it out?** The ineffectiveness of the disciples shocks them, since they were successful exorcists earlier (see 6:7, 13, 30). Jesus' appointment of the Twelve included authority over the demons (3:15; 6:7). No wonder they are surprised.

The answer comes in Jesus' reply: **This kind can come out only by prayer.** The answer is puzzling. First, are exorcisms categorized by their degree of difficulty? Are some demons particularly strong? This might "accord with ancient conceptions that saw epilepsy as a disease that could be healed only by a god or someone with divine power" (Marcus 2009, 664). Are there weak demons that may be exorcised by disciples without prayer?

Second, Mark does not report that Jesus prayed before this exorcism (or any others). Nor does he tell us the disciples prayed when they were successful exorcists in ch 6. But if "and fasting" is read with it, prayer and fasting could be taken as an exorcistic technique.

Marcus suggests that an answer may be found in seeing this story as describing an incident in the life of Jesus, but contemporizing it for his readers. Thus, while Jesus exorcised the demon without prayer, current readers will discover that demons such as this require prayer, since Jesus is no longer with them (2009, 665).

A more plausible answer that is consistent with the developing narrative is simply that this story continues Mark's teaching on Jesus' identity and the path of discipleship. That Jesus does not pray in this story has the same significance for Mark as it does in the calming of the sea episode. Jesus does not pray because he is acting as God. His authority over the demons is his by virtue of who he is, another subtle but unmistakable clue in the mounting cumulative evidence of Jesus' identity. The response of this demon is implicitly that of the others: this is the Son of God (see 3:11).

Mark may make another important point. The disciples may have imagined themselves as independently empowered exorcists, who possessed in themselves and in their own right, authority over the unclean spirits. The dispute a few lines later (9:38-41), when the disciples forbade an unknown exorcist from acting in the name of Jesus, subtly hints they believed they were his equals in this ministry. If so, their failure and Jesus' explanation reminds them that their authority is derived and utterly dependent upon their connection with Jesus, the source of their authority. Prayer is not a technique, but a symbol of their derived authority. It always signals faithful and utter dependence of the petitioner on divine authority.

The phrase *touto to genos*, **this kind,** is not a class of evil spirits. It is a statement that evil in any form cannot be confronted successfully without faithful dependence on God.

> The disciples' problem, on this understanding, has been a loss of the sense of dependence on Jesus' unique *exousia* [**authority**] which had undergirded their earlier exorcistic success. They have become blasé and thought of themselves as now the natural experts in such a case, and they must learn that in spiritual conflict there is no such automatic power. Their public humiliation has been a necessary part of their re-education to the principles of the kingdom of God. (France 2002, 370)

FROM THE TEXT

First, this healing gives no warrant for treating epilepsy or similar disorders in the twenty-first century as demonic manifestation. Such assumptions in the past led to tragic consequences. Twenty-first-century readers should avoid two extremes: "the reductionist assumption that all biblical accounts of demon possession are merely primitive ways of describing malfunction of the brain, and . . . the simplistic attribution of epilepsy as we know it to demonic causes" (France 2002, 363).

Second, this episode reminds us that our effectiveness in ministry depends on our connection as disciples to the Master. The temptation to forget the source of strength in ministry is subtle and not restricted to exorcists. The story of the church is littered with the tales of leaders and others who began to see themselves (their ministry, their program, their personalities, their hard work, their education) as the basis for any apparent success. All too often their tragedies have had a widespread effect. Disciples are always disciples, always dependent; they are never Lord.

D. Teaching on the Way: Second Passion Prediction (9:30—10:31)

This is the second of Jesus' three predictions of his passion in Mark, the shortest of the three. It contains only the essentials of betrayal, death, and resurrection. Misunderstanding follows each of them, but in this instance the resistance is due to incomprehension rather than opposition. Jesus follows each of the predictions with teaching that startles the disciples because it challenges so many of their assumptions, primarily their understanding of Messiah. He also introduces the shocking link between following him and cross-bearing and between the reality of his identity and their future hope. He reminds them of the essential connection between their authority and their attachment to Jesus.

Following his second prediction, Jesus teaches about the meaning of true greatness in the kingdom: the first are last and servants of all. Disciples are not equal partners in this ministry. What matters is Jesus' name, not theirs. Mark gathers a series of sayings that relate to the behavior of disciples in the kingdom. Jesus gives attention to rights in the kingdom (in the divorce pericope), the status of those who enter the kingdom (as a child), and security (the rich man). In all of these discussions, expected patterns are reversed.

I. The Son of Man Will Be Betrayed (9:30-32)

IN THE TEXT

■ **30-31** The setting here is imprecise. Jesus and the disciples leave the unidentified place where the exorcism occurred and **passed through Galilee.** This marks the end of Jesus' public ministry in Galilee: From this point, **Jesus did not want anyone to know where they were, because he was teaching his disciples.**

Nothing new is added to the first prediction (8:31-33). But in this instance, Mark notes that "the Son of Man is to be betrayed into human hands" (NRSV). Here, "human hands" is a metonym for all that was involved in his arrest (see 14:46). There are sinister connotations to falling into merciless human hands (see Sir 2:18). But "fall[ing] into the hands of the living God" is also dreadful (see Heb 10:31; Marcus 2009, 669).

A form of the verb chosen here, *paradidotai* (**be betrayed**), in 1:14 describes the arrest of John. There the passive voice suggests that the arrest was according to the purposes of God. Here it refers to the handing over of Jesus. As a consequence, **they will kill him.** But it also connotes that the purposes of God are nonetheless accomplished. Mark emphasizes the action of Jesus' killers by continuing, **and when he has been killed,** after three days [*meta treis hēmeras*] **he will rise.** Some later MSS have **on the third day** (*tē treis hēmera*). But this is probably an assimilation to texts that bring the saying closer to the traditional confession of the church: "on the third day he arose from the dead."

■ **32** The disciples are still unable to understand the saying (*to rhēma,* see 14:72). This failure will ultimately lead to betrayal (Myers 2008, 261). This time, however, they do not attempt to dissuade Jesus from his way. Instead they **were afraid to ask him about it.** The reason for the fear is not explained. They could simply be reluctant to challenge Jesus again. More likely they fear for their own implied fate: Jesus' followers must take up their crosses as well. They have already heard enough (8:34-37) and would rather not hear it again. They are still unprepared to share Jesus' fate.

2. Who Is the Greatest? (9:33-37)

This episode is placed in Capernaum and sets the scene for a series of sayings linked thematically through catchwords or a verbal chain (see Myers 2008, 259). The series is compiled with Mark's audience in view, whatever the origin of the sayings in Jesus' teaching. It ends with an acted parable in which Jesus cradles a child and establishes a link between receiving such a child and receiving himself. This sets the literary stage for the interplay of "little child" and "in my name." At the heart of the series is discipleship teaching in the face of their obtuseness.

■ **33** This is the third time **Capernaum,** Peter's (and Jesus'?) home in Mark, features in the story. Once they arrived, Jesus asks them a pointed question, to which, Mark implies, Jesus already knows the answer: "What were you arguing about on the way?" (NRSV). The question is laden with irony. They are on the way from Caesarea Philippi, the place of confession, to Jerusalem, the place of crucifixion. Jesus has already announced to them his fate—twice. His way is leading to a cross; the disciples prefer a path that promises position and power.

■ **34** It is little wonder, then, that "they were silent" (NRSV), implying that they are aware of the dissonance between their debate and Jesus' teaching.

"On the way [deliberately repeated for emphasis] they had argued with one another who was the greatest" (NRSV). Their discussion shows that their way is not the way of the Lord. They dispute high status, not lowly servanthood. They continue thinking human rather than divine thoughts (see 8:33). Their concerns mirror those of their culture. But for Jesus, true greatness is true humility, living in his way. Jesus gives the first lesson on greatness; the last is the model Jesus sets as servant of all (10:45).

■ **35** Jesus deliberately "sat down" (NRSV) to teach, signaling the importance of this teaching (see also 4:1-2), foundational for his followers. He is again overturning the conventional wisdom. He **called the Twelve.** They represent the new people of God in Mark; they also symbolize its leadership.

The general focus of Jesus' teaching is clear: *Whoever wishes to be first, that one must be last of all and servant of all.* The character of leaders and all followers within the new people of God is different from existing cultural standards. This is more than a style of leadership, as if it could be taught by a management guru. Rather, this represents the transformed character of a person who has spent time with Jesus, on his mission, under his authority (→ 10:43-45).

■ **36** To illustrate, *Jesus took a little child* [*paidion*, also meaning *servant*] *and put it in the midst of them.* He does not use the child as an example (as in 10:14). Rather, he *took the child* in his arms. If this does not symbolize adoption (so Marcus 2009, 675), at the least it is an embrace.

The status of children in first-century culture was lowly—they were nonpersons. But Jesus' treatment of the child is warm and familial. He is sitting. Perhaps he puts the child on his knee. Jesus treats his followers as his fictive family (→ 5:34; 3:31-35).

■ **37** Jesus makes no explicit comment on status here. His point is that *whoever receives one such as this in my name receives me.* Two lines of interpretation may be possible:

First, this could be symbolic and apply to the childlike followers of Jesus who, when they are on mission and are welcomed, are actually being received as if it were Jesus himself (→ 10:13-15). This is consistent with the practice and teaching of the early church. The further discussion on children and Jesus' name also offers support for this reading.

Second, this may refer to actual children. The phrase *one such as this* suggests this meaning. In a cultural context in which infanticide was an accepted practice and children (especially girls) were often abandoned, the welcome and care of children would be important. Early Christians were known for their hospitality to orphans and abandoned children. They learned from Jesus' example "the sort of humble, everyday service to others [he] has just called for (9:35) and that is the antithesis of the self-serving attitude that the

255

disciples have just displayed (9:34). . . . Jesus really is present, in some mysterious way, in the needy child who lands on the Christian's doorstep" (Marcus 2009, 682).

Mark links the key phrases, **little child** and **in my name,** here. This prepares for the remainder of this collection of sayings. But the conclusion to the saying returns to a key theme in Mark: Jesus' mission is from God, **the one who sent** him. It is also a reminder of Jesus' divine identity—receiving him is receiving **the one who sent** him.

3. Whoever Is Not Against Us Is for Us (9:38-40)

BEHIND THE TEXT

The placement of this story and the sayings that immediately follow seem to have more to do with Mark's purposes in highlighting the authority of Jesus and teaching his readers than to historical concerns. No story setting is given. But it follows naturally from the exhortation that to welcome the least is to welcome Jesus. The inclusiveness of Jesus' mission with its welcome to the least and the outcasts has already been boundary-breaking. It has also been in contrast to the exclusiveness of the disciples.

Jesus reminds the disciples that their own authority comes from his. The irony of John's report to Jesus is stark, especially juxtaposed to the disciples' recent failed attempt to exorcise a demon (→ 9:24-32). There they should have learned that they are not independently empowered exorcists. Now they are to learn that the key to their mission is connection with Jesus, not whether the person is "one of us." France aptly titles this "A Warning Against Cliquishness" (2002, 375).

There are three major textual variants here. They may safely be ignored here, because the meaning is not affected by one's choice of readings.

IN THE TEXT

■ **38** John appears in Mark as a spokesperson only in this story. He tells Jesus about an exorcist **driving out demons in** Jesus' **name.** Acts reports healings and exorcisms in the name of Jesus (3:16; 16:18). The foiled exorcism in Acts 19:13-17 involved would-be exorcists who attempted to use Jesus' name but had no connection with him. Here the unnamed exorcist seems to be successful.

In Mark's story so far, Jesus has authorized only the Twelve to exorcise demons (3:15; 6:7). That partially explains why they **told him to stop.** But the problem may be greater than this. The link between their previous failure (9:29) and their recent debate about greatness (9:34) suggests that the Twelve imagine that they possess independent authority for exorcising demons. As

Jesus' mission partners, they challenge the other exorcist "because he was not following us" (NRSV).

Another, less likely explanation is that the incident was shaped to address Mark's readers. If this is so, the Lord challenges claims to exclusiveness that soon emerged in the early church.

■ **39-40** Jesus' response allows for either explanation. He echoes the open-minded response of Moses to Joshua's concern about Eldad and Medad in Num 11:26-29. But Jesus is not a new Moses figure in Mark. This is not just about misplaced loyalty. Jesus' point is that the exorcism is in his **name,** not that this unnamed exorcist fails to follow the disciples.

My name links this discussion with the previous story, referring to a child being received "in my name." There is also a play on words in Greek with the noun *dynamin* (*a work of power*) and the verb *dynēsetai* (*be able*). The proverbial **for whoever is not against us is for us** is reversed in Matt 12:30 ‖ Luke 11:23, although both passages focus on Jesus.

4. Reward and Punishment (9:41-50)

BEHIND THE TEXT

This section includes a series of sayings that are generally related to the theme of judgment, present or future. Connections to the wider narrative are remote. This difficulty might account for some of the many variant readings and other questions:

First, the textual issues:

- In v 41, the NRSV adopts the preferred reading "because you bear the name of Christ," while the NIV adopts a secondary reading, **in my name because you belong to Christ.** Either could be original.

- In v 42 both the NIV and NRSV read **believe in me,** while recent editions of the Greek text include **in me** in square brackets, as a secondary assimilation to Matt 18:6 (so Metzger 1975, 102). Collins (2007, 443) defends its originality.

- In Mark 9:43 and 45 the phrases *eis tēn geennan, eis to pyr to asbeston* (*to Gehenna, into unquenchable fire*) are variously represented in the textual tradition. The decision by the NIV to retain both phrases in v 43 and only the first (**into hell**) in v 45 is fully justified.

- Recent Greek texts omit both vv 44 and 46, because the words are missing in important early texts. Most scholars agree that these are "an early expansion of the text based immediately on v. 48 and ultimately on Isa 64:23 LXX, to which v. 43 also alludes" (Collins 2007, 443; see Metzger 1975, 103; France 2002, 379; Marcus 2009, 691; Stein 2008, 452). Recent translations (except NKJV) concur.

- Finally, Mark 9:49 has three main forms in the MSS. The most difficult (for this reason adopted by most Greek editors and the NIV and NRSV) is: **everyone will be salted with fire** (see Metzger 1975, 102-3).

Second, what is the precise nature of the sins to which the warning verses in vv 43-48 refer? Deming argues that Mark 9:42—10:12 and Matt 5:27-32 (and *b. Nid.* 13b) reflect the first-century discussion of adultery being extended to include all sexual activity outside of a heterosexual marriage and applied to women as well as men (1990, 141). That Matt 5:27-32 refers to sexual sin and uses similar vocabulary is "quite striking, for in both passages the eyes serve (1) to 'scandalize' and (2) should be plucked out in order (3) to avoid being thrown into hell" (Stein 2008, 448).

Deming (and most other scholars) thinks **one of these little ones** in v 42 refers to Jesus' followers. If so, the present form of Mark 9:42-48 is not explicitly about sexual sin. Collins thinks the phrase refers back to v 37 and that "vv 42-48 have sexuality as their primary referent" (2007, 450).

This perspective has not commended itself to most recent commentators. The language simply means "the *hand* is the instrument for the commission of sin, the *foot* is the means of transport to the place of its commission, and the *eye* is the means by which the temptation to commit it enters in." Marcus persuasively shows that the injunctions are against "the increasing inwardness of sin in general." He sets out his conclusions in the following table (2009, 697):

"If your *hand* offends you . . .":	Don't commit sins! (9:43)
"If your *foot* offends you . . .":	Don't *go anywhere* where you may commit sins! (9:45)
"If your *eye* offends you . . .":	Don't even *think* about committing sins! (9:47)

Third, the structure of the text is challenging. It shows clear signs of Greek catchword composition. This could point either to pre-Markan oral transmission (Donahue and Harrington 2002, 290) or Markan composition. The threefold synonymous parallelism of hand, foot, and eye is held together by other words ("stumble" [NIV 2011], **fire,** and **salt**), which bind individual sayings into a literary unit focused on rewards and warnings for disciples.

IN THE TEXT

■ **41** The phrase **in my name** connects this with the preceding section. Matthew 10:42 gives a mission context, not obvious in Mark, to the hospitable act of giving **a cup of** cold **water.** Its solemnity is enforced by the phrase **I tell you the truth** (thirteen times in Mark). It reaches its climax in the disclosure of the name **Christ.**

The disciples have already confessed Jesus as **Christ** (8:27-30). Here Jesus reminds the Twelve that their mission is Christ's. The cup of water matters because the missionaries belong to Christ. "It is *that* name which gives this kind act its specific significance and justifies the reward. This is not mere benevolence, but the demonstration that a person is *hyper hēmōn* [*one of us*] by means of the practical help given specifically to those who belong to Jesus" (France 2002, 378). This is the only instance of the word **reward** in Mark. The end-times flavor of the passage is confirmed by the eschatological punishments mentioned in the next sayings.

■ **42** Dire warnings follow: If anyone acts in a way that damages **one of these little ones,** the punishment is severe. But who are **these little ones?** Collins argues that they are literal children (as in 9:37) who are part of the community **who believe in me.**

If Jesus refers to children, what offense did he have in mind? The unusual active form of the verb *skandalizō*—"if any of you put a stumbling block before" (NRSV)—is noteworthy. The active verb *skandalizō* occurs elsewhere only in *Pss. Sol.* 16:7. There it alludes to sexual seduction (Deming 1990, 135). Thus, the statement, *if anyone acts scandalously toward one of these little ones,* would refer to taking sexual advantage of a child (Collins 2007, 450).

Most scholars, however, take **these little ones** to refer to followers of Jesus. The active verb may describe the result of causing a believer's "downfall" (France 2002, 380). On either reading, this is a serious matter (→ BEHIND THE TEXT above).

The sentence continues with an unreal condition. It would be **better if the millstone of a donkey** (as distinct from a smaller grinding stone used by women) were **tied around** the **neck** of the offender before his or her being **thrown into the sea.** In Collins' reading, "it would be better for a person who molests a child to die the horrible death described than to face the final judgment without having been punished for the sin already" (2007, 450).

■ **43-48** Warnings are given about three parts of the body: **hand, foot,** and **eye.** If your **hand** or **foot** should cause **you to sin, cut it off;** . . . **if your eye causes you to sin, pluck it out.** While all of the unreal conditions in vv 42-48 are hyperbolic and are not literally to be carried out, they indicate the seriousness of these sins.

But why the **hand,** the **foot,** and the **eye?** In the only OT instance of a command to cut off the hand, Deut 25:11-12 requires a woman's hand to be cut off if she seizes the genitals of another man while defending her husband during a fight. Collins (2007, 450-54) notes that **hand** (Heb. *yad* = hand) is a euphemistic replacement for the penis in Isa 57:8-10 and Song 5:4. And **foot** (Heb. *regel* = foot) is a euphemism for adultery. The erotic gaze lies behind the eye that causes sin (see Matt 5:28).

While these are possible meanings, **hand, foot,** and **eye** more likely have the metonymous references described by Marcus (→ BEHIND THE TEXT above). The wisdom tradition regularly refers metaphorically to parts of the body that lead to sin (Prov 6:16-19; Job 31:1, 5, 7). In each instance, a temporal punishment occurs that apparently allows entry to eternal life in a maimed condition. But the text says nothing about how this occurs.

Jesus continues, **It is better for you to enter life maimed** than to be thrown into Gehenna. This seems to be curious advice, but "the logic seems to be that punishment in this life is better than eternal punishment" (Collins 2007, 450). Perhaps the implication is that restoration will occur for maimed persons after they enter eternal life. But without earthly repentance and punishment, such offenders may not gain eternal life. They will suffer punishment in the afterlife.

It is difficult to build a more general doctrine of reward and punishment on the basis of these texts. It is impossible to determine the fate of the unrepentant on the basis of such difficult texts. The texts clearly point to some sort of post-mortem eschatological judgment, a biblical theme that cannot be avoided (see Wright 2007, 187-96).

Gehenna is the common name for the place of eternal punishment in 2TJ. It comes from the Aramaic and Hebrew words meaning the Valley of Hinnom. This is a valley running south-southwest from the city of Jerusalem. In OT times it served as a cultic shrine where child sacrifices were made to Molech and Baal. The "sacred" site was later desecrated by turning it into a rubbish dump. Continuous smoldering fires there may have given rise to this metaphorical image of never-ending fire. Gehenna is used twelve times in the NT, seven of them in Matthew (these sayings and four others), once in Luke, and once in James.

It is of utmost importance to stress that Jesus never expected his followers literally to amputate any part of their bodies as a solution to overwhelming temptation, whatever the precise nature. Self-mutilation cannot deal with human sinfulness. The Markan Jesus has already argued that purity is an inward matter (7:21-23). Stein argues that the point of these sayings is that "there is no sin worth going to hell for. Better to repent no matter how painful that repentance might be, and follow Jesus, whatever the cost, than to perish in hell" (2008, 449). But this passage is not so much about repentance as about punishment. The point of these sayings is general encouragement to follow Jesus and, conversely, warning against attempting to turn people away from Jesus.

The phrase **their worm does not die, and the fire is not quenched** is similar to Isa 66:24. There it describes the fate of the corpses of those who turn away from God.

■**49-50** The final two verses in this section are enigmatic. Three aphorisms are gathered together under the rubric of **salt.** The connections may be formal when these verses are considered in isolation. But they function as a suitable conclusion to this section. In effect, they close the debate about who is the greatest (9:34).

The first saying, **everyone will be salted with fire,** may mean that disciples will be tested. Some will perhaps even attempt *to scandalize* them (vv 43-47). The outcome may be either positive or negative, because fire has both destructive and purgative connotations in scripture.

France offers an alternative explanation that derives from the connection between the use of salt in covenant rituals and sacrifice in Lev 2:13. "To be 'salted with fire' seems then to evoke the image of temple sacrifice, but the victims who are 'salted' are now the worshippers themselves" (2002, 383). But it is unclear how this explains this saying.

The next statement, **Salt is good,** simply connects with the previous statement through the term **salt.** In the narrative it is directed to the disciples. Luke 14:34 has the same saying with only minor changes; Matt 5:13 explicitly points the saying to Jesus' audience in the Sermon on the Mount: "You are the salt of the earth." This strengthens the likelihood that here it is intended to be directed to the disciples.

Disciples are the good salt, but if *the salt becomes tasteless, how can you recover its seasoning character?* This metaphor now applies the seasoning properties of salt to the disciples. They are God's holy people in the midst of an unbelieving generation. This holy character is to be theirs if they are to be effective agents of Jesus' mission. If the disciples lose their distinctive character and take their agenda from their culture, they deny their reason for existence as disciples.

They need to retain their character, to *have salt within them.* This is to be who they are, God's holy people. Their inward goodness should not allow them even to contemplate turning away from the path to which they have been called. But Jesus offers one corrective: They are called to **be at peace with each other.** This is particularly poignant in light of their earlier debate about who is the greatest. That sort of individual self-elevation is the antithesis of the peaceable life to which they are called together.

FROM THE TEXT

Jesus' second passion prediction shows that the disciples have not yet accepted Jesus' direction or their own, if they wish to follow him. But this time, their resistance is twofold: They are silent because they are afraid to answer Jesus. So instead, they disregard his teaching and debate about which of them is the greatest. This prompts further teaching on discipleship. Important lessons are taught, both overtly by Jesus and through the narrative sequence.

First, disciples may know the destination and the cost of discipleship. They may even be on the journey, going in the right direction, following Jesus. Even so, they may still be unable to accept the character of his path. It is easy to be caught up in cultural systems in which dominating power is respected and prized, and greatness is measured by how many people one controls. But Jesus turns all this on its head. He claims that true greatness has nothing to do with power or status. It involves lowly service, an oddity in most societies.

Second, following Jesus involves the transformation of the character of his followers. The disciples are followers on the outside, but their character and identity are still being transformed on the journey as Jesus teaches them in word and deed. They are still looking out for themselves, seeking honor rather than being **at peace with each other.**

Third, God's purposes are far bigger than we imagine. The disciples tried to stop someone who was delivering people from oppression in the name of Jesus. "This may be the first time, but certainly not the last, in which ecclesiastical leaders have sought to hinder those who would minister in the name of Christ independently of their authority. . . . [They fail to recognized that] what is important is 'he/him' not 'we/us'!" (Stein 2008, 446). Christians need to hold fast to the absolute centrality of Christ in mission and identity. But they must reject an exclusiveness that fails to see the work of God occurring even through those who are not "one of us."

Fourth, the mission of God includes care of needy individuals as well as the deliverance of people from oppression. "Social ministries"—a cup of water for little ones—are not an ancillary part of the church's mission. This *is* mission "in the name of Christ." We minister because of, for the sake of, and as Christ.

Fifth, the intrinsic reward of participation in God's ultimate purposes and triumph is promised. As followers of Jesus, we must keep God's mission ever before us, lest we become discouraged in the midst of costly discipleship. This passage reminds us that those who do not participate in or resist God's purposes are self-excluded from his triumph, unless we repent and amend our ways.

5. The Rights of Divorce (10:1-12)

Chapter 10 brings Jesus' teaching toward its climax. Three episodes, public and private, occur on his journey to Jerusalem and the cross. The journey is a powerful symbol of the disciples' theological journey. As they follow, they learn about the nature and character of the Messiah, the kingdom of God (most frequent in this chapter), and the life of discipleship to Jesus.

MARK

10:1-12

Each of the episodes in ch 10 overturns conventional cultural wisdom. In 10:1-12, the first contrasts Jesus' radical understanding of marriage among the people of God with the widespread cultural acceptability of divorce. Its reminder is that the rights and responsibilities of the people of God are not gender-specific. They are also countercultural. Jesus addresses women as well as men on the subject of divorce and remarriage.

In the second episode, 10:13-16, Jesus insists that entry into God's kingdom is predicated on childlike reception of it as a gift given solely on the basis of love. In a culture that attached little value on children, Jesus announced an upside-down kingdom.

The third episode, 10:17-31, recounts the lengthy story of the wealthy man who seeks eternal life. In it Jesus challenged generally held assumptions associating wealth and piety. He poses some difficult questions for all who would follow Jesus.

Each of these stories pushes disciples outside their comfort zone. Jesus' statement in 10:27, **all things are possible with God** only partially explains. Each story has a plausible place in Jesus' mission, but their inclusion and placement here seems to be Mark's work.

Divorce and remarriage are not only first-century Jewish issues but also pressing issues for Mark's readers, then and now. The place of children in the Greco-Roman world—low status, few rights—is linked to the language of the kingdom. Jesus' words must be heard against the backdrop of an all-powerful Roman Empire, in which lowliness is scorned and weakness exploited. His announcement that entrance into God's kingdom demands divestment of power and privilege must have seemed breathtakingly naive. The sad story of the wealthy would-be disciple, juxtaposed to Jesus' welcome of children, gives it added poignancy. Wealth, widely attributed to the blessing of God, proves to be an insurmountable obstacle to following Jesus when the last is first and the first last.

BEHIND THE TEXT

The question of the grounds for divorce was a live issue in the 2TP. Deuteronomy 24:1-4 was at the center of a robust debate reflected in two leading strands of rabbinic thought. The key phrase is "something indecent about her" (Deut 24:1).

Hillelites interpreted the phrase as allowing a man to divorce his wife for any reason that displeased him. It seems unlikely that a woman could initiate a divorce (but see Instone-Brewer 2002, 59-132).

The Shammaite view was that divorce was allowed only for sexual misconduct, such as adultery. Adultery in the late 2TP "is defined as a man having intercourse with a woman married or betrothed to another man. Adultery is

263

the violation by one man of the marriage of another [man] (Deut 22:22-24; Lev 20:10). In Greek and Roman cultures, the situation was similar. Unconditional fidelity was required of the woman alone" (Collins 2007, 469).

The application of this double standard meant that a woman might commit adultery against her husband, but a husband could not commit adultery against his wife. The Hillelite view became the norm, with divorce allowed for any displeasure a woman might cause her husband. Changes in divorce law in late 2TP Judaism "added up to greater rights for women but also greater instability of marriage. Divorce became more common" (Instone-Brewer 2002, 84-85).

Given such contemporary interest, the dispute between Jesus and the Pharisees is plausible and fits the pattern of halakic dispute already encountered in Mark 7. In both instances Jesus' halakah penetrates beneath the external traditions or concessions to God's intentions, "from mere regulations to ethical principles" (France 2002, 387).

The debate features in Matt 19:1-9 in expanded form and in Luke 16:18 in abbreviated form. The differences among the discussions of divorce in the NT (see 1 Cor 7:10-16) suggest that Mark's uncompromising teaching was nuanced within the early church (see Matt 19:9 and 5:32 for the Matthean exception clauses).

There are several textual variants within the passage:

- In Mark 10:1, both readings differently identify the same geographical setting of this pericope. The NIV reading is undoubtedly the earliest. The other is likely an assimilation to Matt 19:1.
- In Mark 10:2, the NIV (so Stein 2008, 460 and Marcus 2009, 700) prefers the longer reading, **Some Pharisees came and tested him** (*kai proselthontas Pharisaioi epērōtōn auton*). But a shorter reading omits the phrase *proselthontas Pharisaioi*. This could have been borrowed from Matt 19:3. If so, Mark 10:2 would be translated *people asked him* (so Collins 2007, 457, and France 2002, 387).
- In Mark 10:7, a third variant omits the words **and be united to his wife** from the quotation of Gen 2:24. The fuller reading is preferred (France 2002, 387; see also Metzger 1975, 104, and Collins 2007, 457).

IN THE TEXT

Mark places Jesus' teaching to his disciples in a combination of public and private settings. He mentions private explanations in 4:10-12, 34; 7:17-23; and 9:28-29. The halakic dispute about divorce and remarriage begins in a public setting (10:1-9) but is amplified in private (10:10-12).

Jesus continues to teach his disciples on the way. Mark employs the journey motif as the progressive theological unveiling of the suffering Messiah and his relevance for disciples. Thus, Jesus' teaching is not simply in a series of discourses in one location (contrast the "Final Discourse" in John 13—17). Rather, it is on the way to Jerusalem and the cross.

■ 1 The precise geographical location is unclear. Mark states that **Jesus then left that place** (*ekeithen*)—apparently Capernaum (9:33)—**and went into the region of Judea and across the Jordan.** This is the usual journey from Galilee to Jerusalem, avoiding Samaria. **Crowds of people came** and Jesus continues to teach **as was his custom** (emphasized by Mark's double **again** [*palin*], included in the NRSV).

■ 2 The appearance of the **Pharisees,** his avowed enemies from the beginning (→ 3:6), and their desire "to test him" (NRSV) give this pericope a hostile tone. In Jesus' most recent encounter with them, their intent was "to test him" (see 8:11). This prompted Jesus to warn the disciples about the Pharisees (8:15).

The Pharisees' question seems odd: **Is it lawful for a man to divorce** [*apolusai*, **send away** or **dismiss**] **his wife?** Some Jews were hostile to divorce (see Mal 2:11-16). But all known first-century Jewish groups considered divorce lawful. It was "an accepted fact of life" in the Greco-Roman world (Collins 2007, 465).

Perhaps they try to force Jesus to side with the conservative groups that forbade divorce. But their question may be even more sinister. The Pharisees were conspiring with the Herodians on how to destroy Jesus (3:6). John's arrest and execution are due to his criticism of Herod's unlawful marriage (→ 6:14-29). Perhaps the Pharisees' strategy was to get Jesus to make a similar political statement in the hopes that Herod would arrest him (see Culpepper 2007, 328).

The debate in 2TJ was over the grounds for divorce, not divorce itself (see BEHIND THE TEXT above). Hence, the addition in Matt 19:3 "for any cause" (NRSV) makes explicit what was implied by any question such as this (see Instone-Brewer 2002, 134; against France 2002, 390). The heart of the debate rested on whether Deut 24:1 meant "for any cause" or "for any indecency." The former made divorce easy to justify—a woman needed merely to displease her husband and he could put her away.

According to the later rabbinic tractate on bills of divorce (*m. Gittin*), the essential statement to be included in any certificate was "You are free to marry another." A man was obliged to give his divorced wife this certificate freeing her from obligation to him and allowing her to marry another man. This tractate probably elaborates on halakah from the late 2TP.

■ 3 Jesus' response, **What did Moses command you?** is also interesting. It is possible that **command** is an attempt to restrict the debate to the issue of divorce. If so, Jesus invites his questioners to make the same exegetical moves that he himself will later make in the debate. He in effect argues that "the books of Moses" mandated lifelong, monogamous marriage. Other interpreters suggest that this was an attempt to contrast what God commanded with (the inferior) command of Moses (see Collins 2007, 466). But that is unlikely. Jesus' earlier halakic dispute equates God's command with Moses' (→ 7:8-13). More probably, Jesus is simply forcing the issue by a question in response to their question.

■ **4** Their retort is carefully worded: **Moses permitted a man to write a certificate of dismissal and send her away** ("divorce her" [NRSV]). But this response misses the point. Deuteronomy 24:1-4 does not address the question of whether or not divorce was permitted. Divorce is assumed (but not commanded). Rather, Deuteronomy prohibits a man from remarrying his divorced wife. The certificate regulates what happens after a divorce has occurred. It implies that a woman has the freedom to remarry, offering her some protection. In effect, the dismissal certificate releases the wife from her obligations to her former husband. It meant that a man who might subsequently marry the divorced woman was not committing adultery against her former husband.

■ **5** Jesus' response differentiates a divine command from a concession due to human stubbornness. He argues that this entire section on divorce and remarriage in Deuteronomy should be understood as a concession to the hardheartedness of the people in general rather than divine (or even, Mosaic) approval of divorce. But he still designates the Deut 24 passage as a command (*entolē*) prohibiting a man from remarrying his former wife.

Divorce and remarriage were, and are, human realities. But they are not God's intention for humans. The "hardness of heart" (NRSV) is a general comment about Israel's response toward God. It is not specifically directed against the Pharisees (but see Stein 2008, 457) or a critique of the way men treat their wives. A contrast between God's will and Moses' concession is implied. But that is not to suggest that Moses doesn't speak for God (see 1 Cor 7:12).

■ **6-9** Jesus now returns to the debate about divorce. He uses Moses in the broader sense to highlight the divine intention for marriage. Here he combines texts from Gen 1:27 and 2:24: **But at the beginning of creation God "made them male and female."** In citing this text, Jesus implies that gender differentiation is the Creator's design from **the beginning** and thus takes precedence over any subsequent statements. It does not comment on marriage itself. Hence, Jesus moves to the second creation narrative, which shows the essential unity of man and woman in marriage: "they were designed for each other by God" (Marcus 2009, 704). **For this reason a man will leave his father and mother and be united to his wife, and the two will become one flesh.**

The first citation does not directly relate to marriage. It simply insists that both male and female are created in the image of God, and that together as male and female both form the human being (Heb. = *hadam*). Combined with Gen 2:24, the reason for the gender difference becomes apparent. "The threefold pattern of Gn. 2:24, leaving parents, union with wife, and man and woman becoming *mia sarx*, provides the essential basis for marriage" (France 2002, 392). The conclusion of this union is that **they are no longer two, but one.** As Collins notes, "It is because God made man and woman as a unit that a man shall cling to his wife" (2007, 467).

The conclusion Jesus draws is sharp: **what God has joined together, let *no one* separate.** The intention of God takes precedence over a human concession. This may imply something of a God vs. Moses or Genesis vs. Deuteronomy contrast. But the deeper contrast is God vs. humanity. Divorce is not the divine intention. The Markan Jesus is distinctly countercultural in this. No other mainstream Jewish group forbade divorce during the 2TP.

■ **10-12** The radical nature of Jesus' teaching raised questions for his disciples. Jesus' response amplifies his teaching in two ways:

First, he redefines adultery: **Anyone who divorces his wife and marries another woman commits adultery against her.** The phrase *ep' autēn* (**against her**) probably refers to his first wife, since he was joined to her as one flesh initially. But it could refer to his prospective second wife. This is a significant change in the understanding of divorce. The typical 2TP view was that a man who has sexual relations with a betrothed or married woman commits adultery against *her fiancée* or *husband*, not against the woman. But Jesus makes the offense against the first wife, a significant reevaluation of a woman in this case.

Second, the conditional supplement is also important: **if she divorces her husband and marries another man, she commits adultery.** There was never any doubt that by infidelity a woman committed adultery against her husband. But this statement elevates the woman's responsibility to the same level as that of the man.

FROM THE TEXT

This text is part of the teaching on discipleship. Its uncompromising character is of the same order as the demand to the would-be disciple in 10:21. But there are four perspectives that need to be taken from this passage:

First, in cultural contexts in which divorce is common, such as the first-century Greco-Roman world or the twenty-first-century West, this passage offers an uncompromising statement of principle about the intention of marriage in the Creator's purposes. Marriage is to be a lifelong, monogamous, heterosexual relationship. The termination of a marriage for whatever reason is not an alternative pattern with the same divine intention. Divorce and remarriage are always deviations from God's ideal. Christians endorse the sanctity of marriage.

Second, the passage is also a reminder that things are often not the way they should be in this world. And this is due to hard hearts—human deviation from God's intentions, including for marriage. Divorce is an admission that something has gone wrong in a marriage relationship that renders it beyond repair. Divorce may bring great relief to an intolerable situation—such as spousal abuse of any kind or repeated infidelity. Divorce in such cases merely confirms that the trust necessary for a marriage no longer exists. But the reason for divorce is not a matter of celebration. Divorce as a last resort is merely the lesser of two evils.

Third, the victims of the tragedy of a broken marriage with its dashed hopes and severed relationships are among the last and the least that are the focus of Jesus' mission. They are in desperate need of the love, restoration, forgiveness, and healing that comes from God and through his people. This is important when religious instincts tend toward legalism and harshness.

Fourth, in this episode Jesus places men and women at the same level of responsibility and ethical standards. He insists that adultery applies equally to men and women as victims and perpetrators. He couples this egalitarian understanding with the citation of Gen 1:27 as the foundation of male and female relationships. Gender inequality has no place in the people of God.

6. The Status of a Child (10:13-16)

This episode is important for two reasons:

First, it continues Jesus' teaching on discipleship and the good news of the kingdom.

Second, it shows Jesus' attitude toward children, which has shaped the views of the church in a variety of ways. As in 9:36-37 (→), Jesus elevates the status of children—among the least in his culture—to the place of importance. This episode is more elaborate. Again, however, the story shows that the disciples have not grasped either the significance of Jesus' earlier teaching nor the implications of the kingdom in their midst.

IN THE TEXT

■ **13** The pericope begins with anonymous **people** (probably parents) **bringing** [*prosepheron, carrying*] **little children** [*paidia*] **to Jesus.** Their passivity confirms that they are **little** (so Marcus 2009, 714). The people want Jesus to **touch** their children. Only here in Mark is Jesus' touch for anything other than healing. They apparently come for his blessing. From the parents' perspective, this might simply be "folk religion" (so France 2002, 396). But it could treat Jesus as their fictive parent (see Gen 48; Marcus 2009, 717).

The disciples, however, **rebuked them.** Mark does not explain why. As in 9:33-35 (→), they assume the role of gatekeepers, at once screening Jesus from the unworthy and guarding their own privileged access to him. In doing so they resist the kind of kingdom he proclaims. Their view of children reflects their cultural assumptions. The language of rebuke is the same as that used in exorcisms (see 1:25; 3:12; 4:39; 8:30, 32-33; 10:48).

■ **14** Jesus' response, in turn, is strong: **he was indignant** with the disciples—a phrase omitted by the parallel stories in Matthew and Luke. Jesus' anger with the disciples "covers both irritation at their failure to learn and repugnance at their attitude itself" (France 2002, 396). They should not prevent people from coming to him, but rather welcome all, especially the last and the least. Jesus demonstrates again his care for children (→ 9:33-37) and tells the disciples to **let the little children come to me, and do not hinder them** (→ 9:42).

Jesus' next statement could be read in different ways. He could mean that **the kingdom of God belongs** to those who receive it with childlike joy and acceptance, not depending on their status or security. Or he could refer to actual children who participate in the kingdom. Perhaps both are correct. He welcomes actual children into his arms. But they represent the last and the least (see France 2002, 397).

■ **15** Jesus emphatically restates the previous verse: **I tell you the truth, anyone who will not receive the kingdom of God like a little child will never enter it.** This solemn saying may have circulated independently of the story. The kingdom of God must be received as a child receives a gift, without presumption.

That point connects this story to the next. The self-satisfied rich man, with his flawless performance and great possessions, is unable to follow Jesus. He cannot divest himself of his self-earned rights and security. His is the opposite of childlike reception. Paradoxically, "one cannot enter the dominion of God unless one first receives it" (Marcus 2009, 719).

■ **16** The tender scene ends with Jesus taking **the children in his arms** (→ 9:36), placing **his hands on them** and blessing them. His fatherly tenderness embodies God's love. Those near Jesus are his fictive family, as were the "daughters" in 5:25-43 (→).

FROM THE TEXT

The examples of Jesus' welcoming care for children highlight his concern for the last and the least, those who will receive him in contrast to those who will not. They illustrate that God's kingdom is received by those who have nothing to offer in return. But does the story offer other points to consider?

First, this story about Jesus' inclusion of children supports the practice of infant baptism. In one sense, it is slender support. But it is equally slender support for the later ecclesial practice of infant dedication.

Clearly, this incident shows that children have a prime place within the people of God as children. They are not excluded because they have nothing to offer or to say. And they are not excluded until they have achieved a rite of passage—whether their bar mitzvahs, age of accountability, first Communion, or confirmation. They are included simply because Jesus welcomes those with nothing to offer. He receives them without any statement of belief or any particular practice. And they receive God's kingdom as a gift.

If this is correct, the passage offers strong indirect support for the sacrament of infant baptism. Children brought to Jesus are included in the kingdom, the people of God independent of anything they do or understand. The gracious provision of God is not contingent upon one's comprehension of the way of salvation or articulation of a conversion experience. Intellectual ability is not a threshold for entrance into the people of God.

This point applies equally to the severely disabled. Those with profound autism, for instance, should not be excluded because they have not "reached the age of accountability" or cannot say "the sinner's prayer," much less understand its meaning.

All of us enter the people of God as infants. There is no other way than utter dependence upon the unmerited love of God and his gracious acceptance of us. All of us, regardless of our age or intellect or knowledge, are baptized as "infants." Welcome into the people of God is restricted to **little children.**

Second, more generally this passage supports the church's care for children through orphanages, child sponsorship, and similar means of ministering to their needs. Such social ministry is a legitimate implication of the love of God in Christ. Followers of Jesus do not hinder the children. They welcome them on the journey with Jesus, take them in their arms, and carry them until they are ready to walk.

7. The Security of Riches (10:17-31)

The story of the rich man (called a young man in Matt 19:16-22 and a ruler in Luke 18:18-25) is the third episode in this series of pericopes. Its placement here is significant, immediately after Jesus tells his audience that the kingdom can be entered only by "children." The story itself is followed by extensive and challenging teaching on wealth. Luke may have more to say about wealth than Matthew or Mark. But the teaching here is just as uncompromising. Readers should not seek ways to ameliorate the absoluteness of Jesus' demand and the impossibility of the wealthy entering the kingdom of God.

BEHIND THE TEXT

There are four noteworthy textual variants in this story and the teaching that follows it:

- In v 19, some MSS omit the command **Do not defraud**, either because it is not in the Decalogue or as an assimilation to Matthew and Luke, who omit it. But it should be retained here.

  The verb translated **defraud** (*aposterēsēs*) is used in the LXX only in Exod 21:10, "If he marries another woman, he must not deprive [*aposterēsei*] the first one of her food, clothing and marital rights." The bill of divorce in postbiblical Judaism was intended to prevent husbands from exploiting their divorced wives (→ Mark 10:1-12).

If "defraud" deliberately replaces "covet" (*epithumeoe*) in the Decalogue (Exod 20:17):

First, it might allow one to claim not to have legally defrauded anyone and honestly claim to have kept all the commandments (see Geddert 2001, 245). That claim would be hard to prove if stated as "Do not covet."

Second, this might be the weak point in the rich man's obedience. This verb "is often used in contexts suggestive of social oppression, especially keeping back a hireling's wages (see, e.g., Deut 24:14; Mal 3:5; Sir 4:1; Jas 5:4). This and similar types of exploitation frequently characterized the landed aristocracy in first-century Palestine" (see Marcus 2009, 721-22).

- In Mark 10:21 many later MSS add **having taken up your cross** as a "'moralising' expansion" (France 2002, 399).

- In v 24, some MSS modify this absolute statement about the difficulty of entering the kingdom by adding *the rich man* or *those who put their confidence in possessions.* Such additions make v 24 better fit the context of vv 23 and 25. So they are likely later additions.

- In v 25, a few later MSS replace **camel** (*kamēlon*) with **rope** (*kamilon*). This could be an error or "an attempt to 'improve' Jesus' bizarre comparison" (France 2002, 398).

IN THE TEXT

■ **17** Mark begins this story by reminding his readers that **Jesus** is **on his way.** His journey to Jerusalem concerns more than geography. It is about the path of discipleship even if their presence with him is not explicit here. On this theological journey, **a man ran up to him and fell on his knees before him.** Mark gives no further description at this point. He is simply *someone* (*heis*), rather than a "young man" (Matthew) or "rich ruler" (Luke). Mark tells us he is rich only at the end of the story (→ v 22), the end-stress literary device highlighting the issue.

He **ran** to Jesus. In 9:15, people overwhelmed with awe run to Jesus. Mark gives no further explanation in either instance. The man's level of interest is emphasized by his posture—he **fell on his knees before** Jesus (→ 1:40). On their own, these points are merely descriptive. Together, they highlight the identity of Jesus and the cost of discipleship.

The conversation begins with the man's request to be instructed on how to **inherit eternal life.** He addresses Jesus as **good teacher** (*didaskale agathe*). Jesus is frequently called **teacher,** but this is the only instance in which **teacher** is combined with **good.** It seems to be an address of esteem and honor. If so, it indicates the man's sincerity and that his question should not be interrupted negatively (Stein 2008, 468). Beneath his address lies a further unveiling of Jesus' identity in Mark.

The man requests authoritative teaching on what one must **do to inherit eternal life.** The OT background points to land as the inheritance of the people of God (e.g., Gen 15:7; 22:17; 28:4). Later traditions expand the language to include the whole world. "Disappointments of such hopes on the worldly level led to their transposition into an eschatological key (see, e.g., Isa 60:21; *1 En.* 5:7; Matt 5:5) and the frequent substitution of 'eternal life' and related phrases for an earthly inheritance" (Marcus 2009, 720).

The question is loaded with overtones of favored places in the future. Eternal life has a future orientation here and in v 30. Some interpreters suggest that the question, **What must I do . . . ?** should be understood as if the issue were faith vs. works. If so, Jesus' response in v 21 advises the man what he must *do* to **have treasure in heaven.** The notion of reward for obedience is presumed throughout the teaching of Jesus.

■ **18-19** The response of the Markan Jesus is unexpected: **Why do you call me good?** Indeed, Matt 19:16 shifts the emphasis from the good teacher to good deeds: "Teacher, what good thing must I do . . . ?" But here the attention is drawn explicitly to the adjective.

Jesus continues with a forceful statement: **No one is good—except *one,* God.** It alludes to the Shema in Deut 6:4: "The LORD our God, the LORD is one." "The Shema implies the uniqueness of divine attributes as well as of the divine existence" (Marcus 2009, 721).

The goodness of God is frequently tied to his steadfast love for Israel, especially in the Psalms. It is frequently in contrast to the character of humans. Thus, the statement could mean:

- "God only is good, so by definition I cannot be good." In this superficial reading, Jesus eschews a direct connection with God. He acknowledges an inseparable gulf between God and humanity and that he is fully human. But only a radical pessimism "places all humanity on the opposite side of the ledger sheet from God (see 8:33)" (Marcus 2009, 726). Jesus is much more optimistic about the transformation grace can effect in human character.

- "Why are you worrying about my goodness? You should be concerned with yours, not mine." This reading is more remote, since it fits only the first part of Jesus' retort. Jesus explicitly frames the question in terms of divine identity.

- "If you call me good you must also acknowledge that this is a confession of my identity" (see Geddert 2001, 245). In light of the continual literary unveiling of Jesus' divine identity in Mark, this reading should be preferred.

At the level of the event, the man's address to Jesus is excessively deferential flattery. At the narrative level, however, Jesus seems to challenge the man to consider the implications of what he is saying. Through this Mark reveals more of Jesus' identity: "If you call me good, you are making a statement about my identity."

The response, **You know the commandments**, focuses on the Ten Commandments. Although **commandments** could refer to oral halakah, the debate in Mark 7 over the traditions of the elders makes this unlikely here. Furthermore, Jesus continues with a recitation from the second table of the Decalogue, the section concerned with human relationships: **Do not murder, do not commit adultery, do not steal, do not give false testimony, do not defraud, honor your father and mother.** The order of commands seems not to have been firmly fixed at this time. They follow neither the MT nor the LXX.

Honor your father and mother is at the head of the second table in scripture. Here it is last. Failure to keep this command was at the center of the Corban dispute in 7:10-12 (→). This may explain its emphatic final location here. Perhaps this man was free from the Corban scandal Jesus had earlier condemned. But the temptation to invoke this technicality may have been particularly tempting to the wealthy, who are drawn to "loopholes." It is also a reminder that family ties are important in Mark. In this section children are featured twice (→ 9:36-37; 10:13-16). Marcus suggests that this "highlights the position of Jesus as the father, in association with God, of a new Christian family" (2009, 727).

■ **20-21** The man's response indicates his self-assessed upright way of life: **all these I have kept since I was a boy** (*neotētos*), presumably since his bar mitzvah. (There is no hint that he is a *young* man in Mark as in Matthew.) Jesus does not respond as if he evaluates his answer as economical with the truth. By his own definition of obedience, he has been flawless. Indeed, **Jesus looked at him and loved** [*ēgapēsen*] **him.** He treats the man's question and response with seriousness.

The remainder of the discussion suggests that the rich man has deprived someone of justice. He has honored the Law, but missed its point (→ 7:6). Jesus, with characteristic perception and "an intuition guided by fatherly affection" (Marcus 2009, 727), points to the central issue: **One thing you lack. . . . Go, sell everything you have and give to the poor, and you will have treasure in heaven. Then come, follow me.**

In light of the previous story, Jesus' demand graphically illustrates the full commitment the kingdom required. One cannot enter encumbered with possessions, but only in the utter dependence of a child. As the classic hymn "Rock of Ages" has it, "Nothing in my hand I bring; / simply to thy cross I cling."

■ **22** The radical demand of Jesus' call to follow and its cost to this man are quickly perceived: *Upon hearing this word, he was shocked and went away in great sorrow.* The pathos in this statement is high, especially juxtaposed to v 21. This is a failed call story, heightened by the remark: "Jesus looked at him and loved him." There is an implicit contrast to others who left all to follow (→ 1:16-20; 2:13-14).

Mark simply explains the failure: *he went away grief-stricken because he had great estates* (*ktēmata polla*). Most translate *ktēmata* "possessions" (e.g., NRSV). The term can point specifically to property (see Acts 5:1), which might be appropriate here. Regardless, his value system and self-worth are challenged by Jesus' radical demands.

The man's reluctance to follow Jesus, given the cost of discipleship, is heightened by the fatherly love Jesus has for him. But it goes further. "Jesus' outreach to the rich man" manifests "divine power and mercy." The Shema affirms "the unique goodness of God." When "Jesus demonstrates a godlike beneficence, he is not acting through a human capacity but through the eschatological power of God" (Marcus 2009, 728).

■ **23-24** Jesus generalizes the implications of this episode. These emphasize a number of Markan themes: the reversal of cultural norms, "the deceitfulness of wealth" (→ 4:19), and the impossibility of entering the kingdom apart from childlike dependence upon God (10:13-16). The contrast between children without legal possessions and the rich is sharp (see Collins 2007, 480).

Jesus **looked around** (*periblepsamenos*) at his disciples. This verb also occurs in 3:5, 34; 5:32; and 11:11. Here as there, he makes a startling countercultural pronouncement, made even more poignant by the dramatic and disappointing outcome of his encounter with the rich man. He emphasizes the difficulty of entering the kingdom, not its impossibility: **How hard** [*dyskolos*] **it is for the rich to enter the kingdom of God!**

Wealth was conventionally understood as blessing from God and, therefore, an advantage (see Deut 28:1-14; Prov 10:22). It was always convenient to ignore less favorable assessments (see, e.g., Prov 11:28; 22:1). The warnings of Jesus were reflected in some Cynic teaching in the Greco-Roman world, but with striking differences (Collins 2007, 479-80).

The disciples were amazed at his words. Their perplexity continues the theme of their lack of comprehension. They are following Jesus and have left their families and possessions behind (as they will remind Jesus shortly; v 28). But their perception is still distorted.

Then Jesus further generalizes the statement. He addresses the disciples as **Children** (*tekna*, only here in Mark), giving them a strong affirmation, akin to the look of love for the rich man. **Children,** he says, **how hard it is to enter the kingdom of God!** Entering into the redemptive purposes of God, into God's activity, is far from easy. It demands a total change in orientation.

■ **25** Jesus' hyperbolic saying here moves entry into the dominion of God from difficult to **impossible.** But the extreme formulation of the proverb, **It is easier for a camel to go through the eye of a needle than for** *one who is rich* **to enter the kingdom of God,** creates problems. Not the least of these are the exceptional rich people who do enter the kingdom. Attempts to soften the impact of Jesus' radical claim abound.

One common, but baseless, explanation involved a purported gate in the walls of Jerusalem called the Eye of a Needle, through which camels could only pass on their knees. This fictional gate "offers rich homiletical possibilities. . . . [but has] its effect in actually undermining the point of the proverb. That which Jesus presented as ludicrously impossible is turned into a remote possibility: the rich person, given sufficient unloading and humility, might just possibly be able to squeeze in. That was not what Jesus' proverb meant, and it was not how the disciples understood it (v 26)" (France 2002, 405; → BEHIND THE TEXT above).

Another prominent response is to note that this demand is directed to this person alone, not to every disciple. On this reading, Jesus penetrates to this man's need, perceives his distorted priorities, and offers him a way forward.

Others argue that this call to "sell everything" (v 21) is specific to the first disciples only, not to all disciples after them (Collins 2007, 481). Still others suggest that all Jesus demanded was a *willingness* to divest oneself of everything, not the demand to do so.

■ **26-27** Jesus' statement leaves the disciples **even more amazed.** So they ask **each other** [some texts have *ask him*], **"Who then can be saved?"** This shows their misunderstanding. Jesus has already told them quite pointedly that one enters God's rule as a child (→ 10:15). Their focus, however, has been dazzled by this eminently suitable candidate—obedient, earnest, loved by Jesus, and blessed by God with great wealth. If this rich man cannot enter the kingdom, who can? To be **saved** (*sōthēnai*) here means to enter the kingdom (see also 13:13).

In response, **Jesus looked** *intensely* **at them,** as he had the rich man (v 21). His penetrating insight is followed by another unexpected statement. Instead of saying "only a few" or "only the poor" can enter the kingdom, he replied, **With** *humans* **this is impossible, but not with God; all things are possible with God.** His comment is theologically profound, giving rise to several potential meanings.

- It could have the general sense that humans cannot enter the kingdom apart from grace. This is true. But in this context it seems banal.

10:23-27

- It continues Mark's tension between possessions and following Jesus. Does it mean that God will somehow squeeze the rich into the kingdom despite their wealth? Or does it imply that God can so change the rich that they will be able to abandon the security of their possessions for the incomparably greater security of the kingdom?

Neither of these solutions is conclusive. The Gospels and church history give evidence that wealthy people can follow Jesus with the abandonment of a child. But the tension between wealth and discipleship cannot be ignored. Wealth is a clear and present danger to disciples and would-be disciples of Jesus.

Jesus' statement is primarily about wealth. But more generally it summarizes all the seeming impossibilities Jesus has just outlined in the narrative to this point: welcoming children, abandoning the exclusive rights of the Jewish male to easy divorce, abandoning the status of an adult for the nonstatus of a child, and abandoning all security for the sake of the kingdom.

■ **28-31** Peter again speaks in behalf of all the disciples when he reminds Jesus that they **left everything to follow** him. Peter and Andrew still have homes (1:29) and perhaps boats (see 1:20; John 21:3). But Mark emphasizes the immediateness and totality of the response of the disciples to Jesus' call (1:20; 2:14). If there is an undertone of excessive spiritual pride on the part of the disciples here (see also 9:38; 14:29), Jesus does not address it.

Jesus simply accepts Peter's claim and responds with a solemn assertion, **I tell you the truth,** about the incomparable security of his followers. The statement has two long clauses set out in symmetric fashion. The first sets out what the disciples have abandoned for him: **home or brothers or sisters or mother or father or children or fields.** For everything they abandoned, the second clause sets out its replacement: **homes, brothers, sisters, mothers, children and fields.** Note the omission of "fathers."

Everything they abandon will be replaced "a hundredfold" (NRSV), with the apparent exception of "fathers." Explanations for this omission include a reminder that servanthood is the shape of leadership in this community and an antipatriarchal shape to the new community goes too far. More probably the implication is that God (or Jesus) is Father in this new community in which God rules. God's fatherhood of his people is deeply rooted in Israel's self-understanding (see Exod 4:22; Hos 11:1). Thus, with the exception of "father," the list seems comprehensive and includes both human and material resources. The point is that "nothing of consequence will be lost through discipleship" (Marcus 2009, 737).

This declaration seems surprising because it promises extraordinary compensation (**a hundred times as much**) that will occur **in this present age.** The theme of the inbreaking of God's rule (→ 1:14-15) is the backdrop of this promise. The signs of the kingdom are already present. They can be seen in

10:26-31

Jesus' re-creation of the people of God as those who do the will of God (→ 3:35).

But what is the content of this promise? "Disciples and missionaries have not generally been conspicuous for their material gain" (France 2002, 408). We must not take this promise in individualistic or materialistic terms. Still, the inclusion of **fields** in the list points to a material dimension to the counter-cultural life. In the early Christian community, goods and income were freely shared as need arose (Acts 4:35-36).

If this were not enough, Jesus adds that **in the age to come** his followers will receive **eternal life**. This phrase refers back to the request of the rich man to inherit **eternal life** (see Mark 10:17). The irony is that by abandoning all his security (see 8:34-38), the thing he most desires would have been his as well: eternal life.

The abundance of the compensation should not obscure the radical demands of discipleship set out here:

First, the demand to leave family and possessions calls for the radical abandonment of everything else that matters in order to announce the good news. Rejection and the severance of family ties may come as a consequence of following Jesus. But the point here is that the disciples have already left everything (1:20).

Second, the list points directly to Jesus and his mission: **for me and the gospel** (→ 8:35). This explains the meaning of the paradox about losing and saving life.

Mark adds a phrase that significantly tempers Jesus' promise of reward: **with . . . persecutions** (→ 4:17). The phrase is missing in the parallels in Luke 18:29-30 and Matt 19:28-29. Mark continues Jesus' teaching about the cost of discipleship. In ch 8 the reward is essentially eschatological. Here the emphasis falls on the present reality of the inbreaking good news that is occurring *now in this age.* God's ultimate purpose for his people, **eternal life,** will not be realized until **the age to come.**

The whole sequence is summed up with Mark's repetition of the reversal set out already in 9:35: **But many who are first will be last, and the last first.** There the statement is directed specifically at would-be disciples. Here it is a general statement, which includes disciples gloating over their superiority to the rich man. The countercultural call is clear.

FROM THE TEXT

Mark's teaching on wealth is particularly striking in its absoluteness. As a result, two temptations confront interpreters.

First, throughout church history, some have attempted to reduce the starkness of Jesus' demand through various expedients. The typical attempts to soften his demand must be abandoned. They fit neither the world of the story nor Jesus' historical reality. Jesus does not say that the rich can somehow enter the kingdom by kneeling before the cross.

Second, others have recast Jesus' startling saying into a general piece of holy law, which excludes the rich from the kingdom of God. On this reading, divestment of all possessions is the prior condition for entry into the people of God.

Commonality of goods seems to have been practiced at Qumran; the early church itself had all things in common (Acts 2:42-47). But this practice was not sustained. Arguably it evolved into a two-tier discipleship: Vows of poverty were a part of some monastic orders. Ordinary believers were considered exempt.

The Gospels remind us that wealthy people followed Jesus and supported his ministry (see, e.g., Luke 8:3). Even in earliest days, not all divested themselves of their riches. But the nagging suspicion is that those who are concerned about how to avoid selling all and giving the proceeds to the poor are precisely those for whom this challenge is most pertinent. This whole section should be taken seriously in all its countercultural aspects.

First, money—wealth and possessions—along with sex and power are still hindrances to joining Jesus' mission (Foster 1985). They are demonic-like forces in our society that enslave those who have them or only desire to have them. In Matt 6:24, Jesus bluntly states: "You cannot serve both God and Money."

Second, discipleship demands a wholehearted and unreserved commitment to Jesus. Divided loyalties are incompatible with single-minded love for God and neighbor. The demand to sell all, give to the poor, and come follow Jesus is specific to the rich man in this story. Perhaps, the episode of the rich man teaches readers that followers of Jesus should "voluntarily cultivate a simple lifestyle in the service of the apostolic mission" (Donahue and Harrington 2002, 307). But once the discussion becomes generalized, it is clear that the demands of discipleship are for all on the mission of God who are followers of Jesus. Those who would follow cannot have anything else that takes precedence—neither family nor possessions.

But those who follow Jesus are reminded of the incomparable security to be found in the people of God, the new family who do the will of God. The people of God are characterized by love that issues in Godlike generosity and hospitality. Within the family of those who do the will of God (3:35) this becomes manifest.

The love Jesus describes is not an emotional high. Rather, it brings outsiders into the family, welcomes sinners, gives generously to the undeserving. This love cannot be "worked up." It is the love of God poured out in our heart through the Spirit (Rom 5:5), the perfect love that no longer fears (1 John 4:18).

It is no accident that kinship language is preferred to describe mutual relationships within the NT church. Jesus' promise to those who abandon family ties might seem on the surface to countermand the command to honor one's parents (→ Mark 7:10; 10:19). But this is not a question of dismissing family ties as insignificant. It merely relativizes them in light of the primary allegiance to the purposes of God. "What is proposed is not an alternative social pattern to replace the household but alternative households to compensate (and more so) for those left behind" (Barton 1994, 107).

No wonder one of Wesley's favorite terms for the holy life was "perfect love." Happy indeed are those who find themselves serving and being served in a congregation that has no human explanation for its health but is wholly based on the love of God poured out in them. In such a community human barriers of race, class, gender, and economics do not matter.

E. Teaching on the Way: Third Passion Prediction (10:32-52)

1. The Son of Man Will Be Handed over to the Gentiles (10:32-34)

IN THE TEXT

10:32-34

The central section of Mark is about the journey of Jesus and his disciples to Jerusalem. It is organized around three passion predictions interspersed with other teaching and action. This third prediction is the most elaborate. Its details correspond closely to those of the passion narrative.

This has given rise to a debate: Is such precision due to the prediction being constructed subsequent to the events? Or, is this a true prophecy? The debate cannot be settled and it misses Mark's point. But "there is no compelling reason not to believe that the essence of the prediction derives from Jesus" (Evans 2001, 107; but see Culpepper 2007, 342).

In Mark's portrayal of Jesus, the emphasis has regularly been on Jesus' penetrative insight and his awareness of the Scriptures. According to Mark, Jesus has deliberately embarked on this journey to Jerusalem in full awareness of the fate that awaits him.

■32 The emphasis on the journey is strong in this prediction. Jesus and his followers are on *the* way up to Jerusalem. Jerusalem is important for Mark because it is the locale of the temple (Brower 1997, 122-23). Geographically going up to Jerusalem is apropos since at 750 meters (2,500 feet) above sea level. The elevation rises almost 1,000 meters (3,300 feet) above Jericho.

But this journey is also near Passover (14:1), and going **up to Jerusalem** conveys the idea of pilgrimage as well. Passover was the annual celebration of Yahweh's deliverance of Israel from their Egyptian oppressors. The way of the Lord theme has become the way of Jesus. Thus, "the Markan description of Jesus' ascent to Jerusalem, with bands of followers trailing in his wake, is redolent of other scenes of ascent and divine triumph that were alive in the hopes, living memories, and hallowed traditions of Israel" (Marcus 2009, 744).

Jesus is *going ahead of them.* He is pictured as a trailblazer, in front, resolutely **leading the way** (see Luke 9:51). Similar language in Mark 14:28 and 16:7 refers to Jesus going ahead of the disciples into Galilee. Mark is unclear about who comprises the group headed to Jerusalem. The NIV suggests three groups: **the Twelve,** the wider group including other **disciples,** and the more loosely defined sympathizers **who followed.** The Greek is far from clear (see Marcus 2009, 742). If **the disciples** are to be equated with **the Twelve,** there are just two groups (so Stein 2008, 479). We know from 15:41 that there were women among these followers.

Jesus alone is in control and focused on their destination. **The disciples were astonished** (*ethambounto*; → 1:27; 10:24) probably at his resolve, rather than by anything he says (but see Evans 2001, 108). **Those who followed were afraid** (*ephobounto*; see 9:32). Is their fear a sense of foreboding at the direction Jesus is taking? Or, is it awe in his presence (as in 4:41; so Evans 2001, 108)? There is little to distinguish between amazement and fear here. Mark is clear, however, that Jesus' followers do not abandon him. Not yet. They seem to cherish the hope that he will avoid the fate he predicts and will instead come *into his glory* in Jerusalem (10:37). Again he teaches **the Twelve** privately (→ 10:1-12 IN THE TEXT above) and *began to tell* them what was **going to happen to him.**

■ **33-34** Jesus does nothing to calm his followers. Instead, he offers graphic and explicit details about what will happen to the Son of Man: he **will be betrayed to the chief priests and teachers of the law.** The allusion is undoubtedly to Judas' betrayal. But behind that lies the divine necessity (→ 14:21).

Although the religious leaders cannot execute him, they **will condemn him to death** at a night trial of dubious legality. They will then **hand him over to the Gentiles,** the Romans, **who will mock him and spit on him.** This language echoes Isa 50:6 and Ps 22:7, both of which figure prominently in the Passion Narrative. They are used to picture Jesus as the righteous sufferer who goes to his death according to the Scriptures.

Jesus predicts that they will **flog him,** a common practice before executions, **and kill him.** The whole episode with its repeated echoes of scripture shows that Jesus' journey and destination are within the purposes of God. Jesus deliberately goes up to Jerusalem. Although the people of power, both

Jewish leaders and Roman oppressors, imagine that they have determined the outcome when they kill him, Jesus once again becomes the subject in the last phrase: "after three days he will rise" (NRSV).

2. True Leadership (10:35-45)

BEHIND THE TEXT

Immediately following the most explicit of Jesus' statements about the fate that awaits him in Jerusalem comes the most egregious example of misunderstanding by the disciples. It takes the form of an audacious request made by his earliest disciples.

The Twelve have heard teaching and seen examples that have pointed to the nature of discipleship. They have watched the rich man turn away and heard warnings about the encumbrance of possessions. Peter, in turn, has asserted that they left everything to follow. But Jesus pricks Peter's self-congratulatory pride with a blunt reminder that many who are first will be last; and last, first. Perhaps the disciples thought that the first-last paradox applied only to others—the rich, the powerful, the Pharisees, the Gentiles—rather than to themselves. Whatever the case, they do not grasp it.

Jesus' response to James' and John's request for preferential places when he comes into his glory is cryptic but clear. The other disciples, who were angry at the Zebedee brothers, also need to hear the lesson again: the standards of the people of God are radically different from those who are not. They are to be slaves of one another, a graphic metaphor in a society in which 60 percent of the population were slaves. **Even the Son of Man did not come to be served, but to serve.** Jesus sums up the destination of his journey as the cross and resurrection with the pregnant phrase **and to give his life as a ransom for many.**

Mark 10:45 has attracted huge attention from scholars. Evans (2001, 120) summarizes the issues: (1) the unity of this saying and its relationship to the preceding story; (2) its intertextual background; and (3) its authenticity. While the issues are intertwined, serious interpretation must begin with its Markan context. Intertextual links are crucial for a commentary devoted to the text of Mark rather than to the history of the tradition.

Readers of Mark across the centuries have used Jesus' statement in 10:45 in the development of atonement theology. The theologically potent word *lytron* (**ransom**), although infrequently used in the NT, has been used as one scriptural support for a model of the atonement especially associated with Anslem of Canterbury. But *lytron* must be understood within its specific Markan context.

■35 If Jesus' statement in 10:31 is an implied criticism of Peter's self-righ-teousness, **James and John** take this is as an opportunity to make their claim for primacy in the group to Jesus. Peter's voice is often heard (8:29, 32; 9:5; 10:28; 11:21; 14:29). John's only independent statement is in 9:38. James and John are usually part of a threesome (5:37; 9:2; 13:3; 14:33). They have already been identified as the sons of Zebedee (in 3:17), where they are also called "Sons of Thunder."

Although Mark makes it appear that they are within earshot of the oth-ers, their approach seems to be surreptitious. They make an outlandish and open-ended request: *Teacher, we wish that you might do for us whatever we might ask of you.* Matthew 20:20-21 attempts to ameliorate the embarrassing request by having their mother serve as their intermediary.

■36-37 Jesus' response is straightforward, but without any commitment: **What do you want me to do for you?** Collins compares the extravagant prom-ise of Herod (6:22), implying that this request is equally thoughtless (2007, 495). Some suggest that Jesus deliberately avoids agreeing to their request. More likely Jesus waits to see what, if anything, the disciples have learned from his teaching to this point (→ in 8:14-17).

Jesus' response to the two brothers is the same as that addressed to Bar-timaeus in 10:51. The irony is in the different responses of the pair and the blind man. In 10:37, James and John ask for position and power; in 10:51 Bar-timaeus says, "I want to see." Because of his faith he is healed and joins Jesus on the way. These two want to dominate their fellow disciples and have the prime leadership places in the coming kingdom.

Their reply, **Let one of us sit at your right and the other at your left in your glory,** shows how poorly they have understood Jesus' teaching about the last and the least. They wish to have the first places. The right hand would be the highest place of honor (see Ps 110:1), while the left would be the second place, even if the left side on its own would be considered unlucky. And there would be no place for Peter.

Their request might point to a future fulfillment, when "the Son of Man . . . comes in his Father's glory with the holy angels" (→ 8:38). But the two disciples may hope Jesus is not serious about his impending death. They hope that, instead, he will be enthroned as the Messiah-king in the holy city (see Matt 19:28). If so, they want to be in the prime places.

The irony would not be lost on Mark's readers that on the right and the left of Jesus at his crucifixion are two brigands (15:27). It is unlikely that James and John envisaged that prospect.

■ **38** But Jesus does. His response is blunt: **You don't know what you are asking.** If they want to reign with him in glory, it can only be via his path of suffering, death, and resurrection. Jesus' messiahship is a suffering-Son-of-Man messiahship (→ 8:31), and his followers must take the same path after him.

Jesus asks the penetrating question: **Can you drink the cup I drink?** The cup metaphor is often used in the OT. Sometimes it's the cup of blessing (Pss 16:5; 23:5; 116:13). But more often it is a bitter cup, the experience of God's wrath (Ps 75:8; Jer 25:15-29; Lam 4:21; Ezek 23:32). In Mark Jesus' acceptance of pain and anguish is the cup he must drink to follow the Father's will (14:36; see also 14:23).

The meaning of **the baptism I am baptized with** is less clear. John's baptism for the forgiveness of sins has featured prominently in Mark. Luke uses baptism as a metaphor for Jesus' destiny (Luke 12:50). Both metaphors connote the notions of vicarious suffering and death on behalf of others. The metaphor may allude to Ps 69:1-2, 14-15. This psalm posits a righteous sufferer sinking in water that threatens to overwhelm him. In this light, "the account of Jesus' death should therefore be read against it primary image, that is, of being overwhelmed by a flood of troubles. His death is his baptism" (Bolt 2004, 68-69).

■ **39-40** Surprisingly, the two answer, "We are able" (NRSV). Their incomprehension runs deep. But Jesus also gives a surprising response: **You will drink the cup I drink and be baptized with the baptism I am baptized with.**

This statement cannot refer directly to the journey they are currently on to Jerusalem. At the end "everyone deserted him and fled" (14:50), even after their latest overly self-confident response (→ 14:31).

Neither does it refer to the martyrdom of both James and John. According to Acts 12:2, James was executed by the sword, probably beheading, a more respectable form of execution. The fifth-century historian Philip of Side reported that the second-century bishop Papias wrote that both James and John died as martyrs, "slain by the Jews" (cited in Culpepper 2007, 347). This is likely a late interpretation of Mark 10:38. Jesus' statement probably refers to the post-Easter church in which persecution and death awaits all the disciples, including these two.

The cup Jesus' followers drink is not independently redemptive apart from his death and resurrection. The suffering endured by his followers is not merely in imitation of Jesus, but also participation with him. Some interpreters argue that the disciples "will share in the *form* of Jesus' death but not in its *meaning.*" But Mark's picture is that they participate in its *meaning* as well (Collins 2007, 497). That is, by their suffering, disciples enter into the afflictions of the Messiah (see Col 1:24). They participate in the cruciform life of Christ in the world.

283

The call to suffering servanthood running through the NT is more than the inevitable outcome of discipleship, simply to be endured. Rather, it is participation in the redemptive purposes of God. Disciples enter into the redemptive sufferings of the Son of Man, the Messiah (Brower 2007b, 177-208).

Jesus confirms their participation in his mission but denies their request: **to sit at my right or left** [*euōnymōn*, a euphemism for left] **is not for me to grant.** We are not told who will occupy these places: It is **those for whom they have been prepared,** presumably by God.

■ **41-44** Not surprisingly, when the rest of the disciples learn what the Zebedee brothers have requested, **they became indignant.** Mark gives the impression that their irritation is not due to the inappropriateness of the brothers' request. Rather, the two seek an advantage they want for themselves.

Dissension results. So **Jesus called them together** to remind them—once more—about the true nature of discipleship. This time he talks about the contrast between the hierarchical structures of society alienated from God and the organization of life in his new community.

Jesus' statement could hardly be clearer. Their Gentile oppressors **lord it** [*karakyrieuousin*] **over them, and their *great ones* exercise *tyrannical* authority over them.** "Greatness was defined in Jesus' day as power, coercive power" (Evans 2001, 118). Jesus highlights the pattern of ruthless power, manipulation, intrigue, and coercion by their Roman oppressors. He could just as easily have pointed to the corruption of the Herodian family or the high priestly family of Annas.

Jesus is blunt. This kind of leadership, modeled on the patterns of their oppressors, is wrong. *It shall not be so among you.* Jesus' saying has influenced 1 Pet 5:3, "Do not lord it over those in your charge" (NRSV), which uses the same Greek verb (*katakyrieuō*) to warn church leaders against coercive and manipulative leadership.

Jesus' pattern of leadership for the people of God is the opposite at every point. The statement is made twice, the second absolutizing the first. The pairs are:

> **great** (*megas*) = **your servant** (*hymōn diakonos*)
> **first** (*prōtos*) = **slave of all** (*pantōn doulos*)

The idea of service might not have been abhorrent in the Jewish world (see Evans 2001, 119). But by drawing the contrast with Gentiles, Jesus reminded his disciples of their experience of oppression (reflected in Matt 5:41). For Mark's Greco-Roman readers, such slave-like leadership would have seemed not only distasteful but impossible.

■ **45** The supreme model for servanthood is **the Son of Man.** "To be great in the kingdom of God will require a willingness to suffer (vv 37-38) and a willingness to serve (vv 43-44), and the prime example of one who is willing to serve and to suffer is the 'son of man'" (Evans 2001, 120). This statement gathers up the narrative in a theologically rich conclusion:

First, in Dan 7:14, 27 the one like a son of man and "the saints . . . of the Most High" are given authority and power. The nations/Gentiles (Dan 7:14) shall worship him. Vindication follows oppression in Daniel. But Mark's saying is not about vindication. Here the Son of Man does not **come to be served, but to serve.**

Second, the interpretation of the vision in Dan 7:15-27 shows that the one like a son of man represents the saints of the Most High God. He "is an ideal figure and stands for the manifestation of the Kingdom of God on earth in a people wholly devoted to their heavenly King" (Manson 1935, 227). Mark uses **Son of Man** as a self-designation of Jesus. He represents his followers, whose lives, like his, will include suffering and cross-bearing. They share fully in his own mission.

Read in the context of Mark's Gospel, the conclusion is inescapable: Jesus "and his followers *together* should share that destiny . . . that he and they *together* should be the Son of Man, the Remnant that saves by service and self-sacrifice, the organ of God's redemptive purpose in the world" (Manson 1935, 231; Brower 2007b, 188-89).

This does not minimize the uniqueness of Jesus' death as the means of redemption. Without his death there is no redemption or redemptive story. But it does take seriously the call to cruciform living that dominates and gives meaning to this central section of Mark.

Third, "the inter-textual background of this passage combines the 'one like a son of man' in Daniel 7:13, the figure who represents the people, the holy ones of the Most High (Dan 7:17-27) with the suffering figure of Isaiah 52:13—53:12" (Brower 2007b, 187). Most scholars acknowledge that a direct allusion to Isaiah in 10:45 is difficult to establish. But the Isaianic servant motif shapes Jesus' whole ministry and mission, a mission that is the restoration of the people of God (see Edwards 2006; cited in Brower 2007b, 187).

Many readers of Mark conclude that the phrase **ransom for many** evokes the whole "of God's basic activity in saving his people and establishing them *as* his people. . . . What these words in Mark 10:45 affirm, then, is not that Jesus' death saves certain individuals, but that it is the saving action by which God establishes his new people" (Hooker 1994, 55-56).

Mark insists that Jesus is the locus of God's presence (see 1:10-11). The Son of Man image has already been evoked, occurring twelve times in Mark. In this passage, Jesus as the Son of Man gathers up in his being the holy people of God.

Fourth, the intertextual echoes of Dan 7 and Isa 40—55 illuminate the clause **and to give his life as a ransom for many.** The quest for identical wording here and in Isa 53:10-12 obscures the bigger picture. Echoes of Isa 53:11 occur in **serve** and of Isa 53:10-12 in **give his life** and **ransom for many.** The identity of the servant of Yahweh in Isaiah oscillates between a person and Israel. This offers further support for the combination of personal and corporate reading of this passage.

Fifth, the intertextual and intratextual context of *lytron* is also rich. While commentators disagree on the precise background (Hooker 1994 vs. Evans 2001), several images illuminate our passage.

In the first instance, *lytron* is used primarily in the LXX to refer to the freedom of slaves and frequently to a price paid for freedom (see Exod 21:30; 30:12; Num 3:12-51). This fits the context well because, unlike the tyrants who lord it over their underlings, Jesus gives himself for them.

The cognate verb *lytroō* (*redeem*) occurs frequently in the LXX describing Yahweh as the Redeemer (see Isa 41:14; 43:14; 44:24), who rescues his people (see Isa 43:1; 44:22-23). This summarizes well Jesus' goal to create a new people around himself. In gathering the new people of God together and rescuing them, Jesus brings the purposes of God's holy people in Isaiah to fulfillment in his life and mission. In Christ, God is rescuing and redeeming his people that they might fulfill their mission as a light to the nations. The ransom/rescue/redemption has the mission of God as its goal for the people of God.

That is not to dismiss the notion of sin-bearing. Although *lytron* never translates *asham* (= sin offering) in the LXX, at a secondary level it does have connotations of a ransom for sin in late 2TJ. In 1 Tim 2:6, Jesus is the One "who gave himself as a ransom [*antilytron*] for all" (*hyper pantōn*). Collins concludes that "the implication would be that the death of Jesus is a substitute for the deaths of many others" and that "the term *lytron* (ransom) in v. 45 is a synonym of *hilastērion* ('expiation' or 'propitiation')." Ransom "is thus analogous to the saying over the cup in 14:24, according to which the blood of Jesus was poured out for many" (2007, 502).

Jesus' death is atoning in some way. "At the heart of the ransom idea is the concept of exchange" (Bolt 2004, 72), in which one takes the place of the many. This notion of ransom for many is the ultimate service of the Son of Man. It is more difficult to answer the question, Ransom from what? Sin, death, wrath, and the devil all have limitations (Bolt 2004, 71-75).

But the primary focus here is on creating a holy people for the mission of God (→ 14:24). Jesus' death creates a new community and it is atoning. These ideas are complementary in Mark's Gospel: The baptism of John is for the forgiveness of sins understood as the restoration of the people (1:5); "the Son of Man has authority . . . to forgive sins" (2:10); and the new covenant is being established through his "poured out" life (14:24).

Mark devotes the story so far to establishing Jesus' identity and mission. He describes the creation of the renewed holy people of God who join Jesus on this mission. This concluding statement about **the Son of Man** giving **his life as a ransom for many** draws the whole story together. It challenges the followers of Jesus to enter fully into the mission of God.

Who are **the many**? This could be taken to refer to a limited number (see Marcus 2009, 750, who sees it referring to the elect community). It might also be a Semitism meaning "all" in contrast to "one" (see Isa 53:6, 12). Therefore, it could refer to humanity as a whole (as in 1 Tim 2:6). Even if Marcus is right, the point is that "although Jesus died for all, not all accept his death on their behalf" (Culpepper 2007, 350).

FROM THE TEXT

This short exchange between Jesus and his disciples is one of the most potent stories in Mark because it directly challenges the way we do things. This applies to the congregational level, where our lives together as the holy people of God are to reflect the unreserved self-giving of the servant Messiah to each other.

But it offers its greatest challenge at the structural and organizational level of the institutional church. In its bluntest terms, it demands that the business or corporate models adopted by denominations be brought continuously under the scrutiny of the gospel. All too often ecclesiastical structures simply mirror the power structures of corporate life in the secular world. Corporate image, business models, management structures, and so on, can become determinative of the way things are done in the church. Power is exercised in ways that are closer to the command structures of the corporate boardroom or the military than to the model of genuine servanthood offered by Jesus.

All too often, the powerless and voiceless are carelessly treated while those in leadership exercise power in ways that are barely distinguishable from the models applied in the world. To be sure, all of this is done for the sake of "the mission." But to try to sanctify worldly practices by baptizing them in the font of "the mission" can be a subtle temptation to betray the servant Messiah's model, and so the greatest risk of all.

The text may not directly demand examination of our practices as Christians in the secular workplace. But it might be worth asking if our identity as God's holy people on God's mission in his world affects our way of being in the wider community. Do our practices reflect kingdom values or are we indistinguishable from those whose values are antithetical to these outlined by Jesus?

At the very least, Jesus' statement, **Not so with you,** demands that we constantly reexamine our models. Wherever our structures and practices are closer to the hierarchical structures and practices of the secular sphere than to the organic life of the holy people of God, repentance and reform should be the order of the day. "The only kind of power that shall characterize the disciple community is the power of servanthood, of slavery, of sacrificing oneself for others" (Geddert 2001, 257).

3. Blind Bartimaeus (10:46-52)

BEHIND THE TEXT

The last leg of the journey from Caesarea Philippi to Jerusalem has arrived. This is a climactic story for several reasons. First, this is the second restoration of sight (see 8:22-26), acting as the closing bracket of this teaching-on-the-way section of Mark. Second, Bartimaeus is pictured as the ideal disciple. His sight is restored, he sees clearly, and he follows Jesus on his way. Third, he cries out to Jesus, abandons all, and is determined to follow the Lord. He is both compared and contrasted to the rich man, who approaches Jesus but does not follow, and to the other disciples, who follow Jesus but whose vision is still metaphorically clouded. Fourth, he is named, but his name never appears again. It may be that his name is well known among the disciples (France 2002, 422). But his name may have significance beyond this simple identity.

Jericho is about twenty kilometers (twelve miles) east of Jerusalem in the Jordan valley just a few kilometers (a mile) north of where the river enters the Dead Sea. Its elevation is also about 1,000 meters (3,300 feet) lower than Jerusalem. So the journey from Jericho to Jerusalem is a steady climb up a better than 5 percent grade. The city is warm in winter, making it a pleasant place to escape the cool and damp of Jerusalem. But summer temperatures can be oppressively hot.

IN THE TEXT

■ **46** The end of Jesus' teaching journey occurs in **Jericho.** Mark says nothing about what happens in Jericho (see Collins 2007, 486-93). A **large crowd** of pilgrims bound for Jerusalem to celebrate Passover accompany Jesus and his entourage. This then describes the continuation of the journey.

As they are **leaving the city,** they come upon a blind man, the **Son of Timaeus.** It is difficult to determine whether the name is Greek or Aramaic (Collins 2007, 508-9). **Bartimaeus** is Aramaic in form; **Son of Timaeus** in Greek means *son of honor* (Marcus 2009, 759). The unusual Greek word order is missed in English: **Son of Timaeus** precedes the name **Bartimaeus.** France sees no significance in this, putting it down to "Mark's prolixity" (2002, 423). But emphasis falls on this man, **Son of Timaeus, Bartimaeus,** who shouts out *hui Dauid Iēsou,* **Son of David,** *Jesus,* emphasizing **Son of David.**

"This text is about shame and honor" (Geddert 2001, 253). This son of honor is blind and **sitting by the roadside begging.** He is pictured as one of the last and least. He may have had a better past, but now he lives by begging. Some Qumran texts consider blindness defiling and exclude the blind from the new people of God. This may be another reversal of values. Jesus transforms the impure and excluded into God's holy people. This healing enables Bartimaeus to join Jesus on his way to Jerusalem and the temple (Marcus 2009, 759).

■ **47** Bartimaeus hears that *Jesus the Nazarene* is coming. But he identifies him as the **Son of David, Jesus.** Since he is blind, this may be presented as a revelation (Collins 2007, 510). This, Mark's first use of the title **Son of David,** prepares readers for the next episode, when Jesus enters Jerusalem.

This entry and this name have clear nationalistic associations. Passover was always a concern for the Romans with its potent imagery of deliverance from oppression. Mark considers this to be a proper identification of Jesus (see 10:52): he is **Son of David.** But as becomes clear in 12:35-37, it inadequately accounts for the full identity of Jesus.

10:46-51

The blind man's plea for healing, **Have mercy on me!** resembles petitions to kings requesting a special favor (see *Pss. Sol.* 17:34; Evans 2001, 132). This cry is regularly on the lips of those utterly dependent upon God. No doubt, Bartimaeus has often called out for alms in just these words (Geddert 2001, 253). But this time, he is expecting far more.

■ **48-49** All attempts to silence Bartimaeus are futile. They serve only to strengthen his shouts and confidence in the **Son of David.** The word translated **rebuked,** *epetimōn,* is regularly used in exorcisms. But this does not suggest that the crowds played a demonic role, attempting to keep him by the road and off the path of Jesus (but see Marcus 2009, 763). **Jesus *stood still* and said, "Call him."** Now, the crowd facilitates the blind man's healing by giving him encouragement: *Take heart, get up; he summons you.*

■ **50-51** The response is dramatic. Bartimaeus *abandons his cloak,* **jumped to his feet and came to Jesus.** The picture is graphic and potent. "Suddenly we realize that this is not only a healing narrative: it is a 'call story'" (Geddert 2001, 254). This man, like the earlier disciples, abandons everything to follow Jesus. It isn't much but it is all, like the widow in 12:44 (Collins 2007, 511). His response gives visible expression to his **faith** (v 52): He refused to be silenced in his pursuit of Jesus. A blind man, **throwing his cloak aside** into the darkness, does not expect to return from his encounter with Jesus blind or to return to his old life as a beggar (see Culpepper 2007, 354-55).

Jesus' question to him is the same as to James and John in 10:36: **What do you want me to do for you?** Their answer was grasping and self-seeking. Bartimaeus' is simple and direct: **Rabbi** [*rabbouni;* see John 20:16]**, I want to**

289

see **again** (*anablepsō*; see Isa 61:1). The word might imply that he had once been able to see. At a symbolic level, the language is of encouragement to disciples whose eyes have been blinded that they can be restored to full sight.

■ **52** The response of Jesus is immediate: **Go, . . . your faith has *saved* you.** Jesus sees the blind man's **faith,** not through some clairvoyant insight, but through the man's tangible expression of trust in Jesus' ability to heal. In this respect, this story resembles the earlier accounts of the healing of the paralytic (→ 2:5) and of the woman with the gynecological disorder (→ 5:34).

Jesus dismisses the healed blind man, as he has other would-be followers (see 5:19; 8:26). But Bartimaeus is different: **Immediately he received his sight and followed Jesus *on the way.*** He joins Jesus on the road up to Jerusalem and the temple. But he also offers hope to failed disciples then and now. Sight can be regained. They can be restored and can follow on the way to the cross (4:4, 15; 6:8; 8:3, 27; 9:33-34; 10:17, 32, 46).

FROM THE TEXT

Bartimaeus is the ideal disciple. His is the second of two healing stories of blind men. In the first we also see a symbolic representation of the disciples, who know Jesus' identity (→ 8:27-30) but cannot grasp its significance for Jesus or its implications for themselves. Here we see a blind man, whose sight is fully restored and who follows Jesus on the way without question. "Jesus asks no more or no less of any would-be disciple. Rich or poor are asked to give up only one thing, *everything*" (Geddert 2001, 256).

The picture, of course, is idealized. We know nothing of Bartimaeus' subsequent story. But we do know that all those who are following Jesus forsake him and flee (14:50). He is, nevertheless, the picture of a true disciple. We cry **have mercy on me** and in his mercy he calls us to himself and heals our brokenness and removes our blindness. And we respond by following Jesus on the way—a way that includes redemptive suffering and death.

VI. JESUS IN JERUSALEM AND THE TEMPLE: MARK 11:1—13:37

A. The First Entry into Jerusalem (11:1-11)

1. Bethphage, Bethany, and the Mount of Olives (11:1-6)

BEHIND THE TEXT

Jerusalem and the temple now take center stage in the story. Until now, people have come to John (1:5) or to Jesus (3:8, 22; 7:1) from Jerusalem. Initially, people from Jerusalem are viewed positively (1:5). But the picture darkens when scribes come from Jerusalem and accuse Jesus of demonic activity (3:22) and enter into halakic dispute with him (7:1). In the last and most detailed passion prediction Jesus tells his disciples he is going to Jerusalem (10:33), where the religious leaders will join forces with the Romans to kill him.

Relationships between Jesus and the religious establishment and the Pharisees deteriorate throughout the Galilean ministry. By holy week, we are not surprised when the Pharisees conspire with the temple authorities to secure Jesus' death. But it is the temple establishment—the high priest, chief priests, and scribes—who deliver Jesus to Pilate (see Brower 1997).

The journey from Caesarea Philippi is over. It has been a theological as well as a geographical journey for the disciples, framed by the healings of two blind men. The disciples have moved from rejecting the notion of suffering messiahship and cross-bearing discipleship (8:32-33) to a willingness to die with Jesus (14:31). The shift is dramatic, even if failure lurks in the wings, and clarity of vision will come fully only outside the Gospel narrative after the resurrection. Jesus, his disciples, and a crowd with them are about to climb the 1,000-meter (3,300-foot) ascent from Jericho to Jerusalem.

The journey culminates in Jerusalem, with the events pictured as occurring within just one week. Even during this week, Jerusalem is important primarily because of its temple and religious establishment. For Mark, these three are inseparable and equally critiqued.

This entire section from 11:1 to 16:8 is full of irony. It is particularly apparent in the passion narrative (chs 14—16). People in the drama act and speak in ways that have significance beyond their awareness or understanding. But perceptive readers, with eyes to see and ears to hear, detect what is happening.

IN THE TEXT

■ **1-3** The journey is nearly over. Significantly, Mark implies that this last section of the journey is in the company of many people. Since the calendar is approaching Passover, the people are probably Galileans and other pilgrims. **As they *approach* Jerusalem,** they come first to **Bethphage (*house of figs*),** somewhere between Jerusalem and **Bethany (*house of dates*).** **Bethphage** is not mentioned again. But **Bethany** figures in the story in 11:11, 12; and 14:3. Here Jesus eats at the home of Simon the leper. But Mark says nothing of Jesus' friends Mary, Martha, and Lazarus who live there (see John 11:1, 18; 12:1).

At the story level, mention of **the Mount of Olives** is redundant. Both Bethphage and Bethany are within the outskirts of Jerusalem. But the Mount of Olives has significance beyond its location. Jesus predicts the temple's fate from there in 13:3. Thus 11:11, with its location in Bethany, frames Jesus' teaching in the temple.

This also is the first of several intertextual echoes of Zechariah that inform Mark's theology. Zechariah 14:4-5 features the Mount of Olives in the last judgment: "On that day his feet will stand on the Mount of Olives, east of Jerusalem . . . Then the LORD my God will come, and all the holy ones with him." In Mark's scheme, this future day of the Lord is already underway, and judgment is about to occur on another hill, even if the final judgment is still to come.

With this evocative setting, **Jesus sent two of his disciples** with instructions to bring a colt to him. The instructions are specific and the disciples acquire the colt precisely as Jesus said. Some interesting historical explanations have been given for this:

First, this was not Jesus' first trip to Jerusalem according to the Gospel of John as it is in Mark. Thus, Jesus prearranged this with its owner. Or, perhaps he owned the colt, having purchased it on a previous trip to Jerusalem. In either case, Jesus consciously staged the event to evoke the tradition of Zech 9:9.

Second, perhaps the phrase, **the Lord** [*ho kyrios*] **needs it,** reflects the Jewish use of **Lord** as a divine title. This donkey is being conscripted for God's service (see France 2002, 431-32).

Third, this episode is an example of Jesus' prescient knowledge, since Jesus has not yet been to Jerusalem. This is probably Mark's view.

This is a **colt** [*pōlon* of a donkey or horse] . . . , **on which no one has ever sat.** Mark does not cite Zech 9:9 as Matt 21:2-7 does. But his language echoes the LXX of the passage (Marcus 2009, 772). That passage is important for understanding this one: "Rejoice greatly, O Daughter of Zion! Shout, Daughter of Jerusalem! See, your king comes to you, righteous and having salvation, gentle and riding on a donkey, on a colt, the foal of a donkey."

That this is an unbroken animal "echoes the special value placed in the OT on a hitherto unused animal for religious purposes (Num 19:2; Deut 21:3; 1 Sam 6:7), and perhaps, too, the convention that no one else may ride the king's mount (*m. Sanh.* 2:5)" (France 2002, 431). Matthew 21:3 woodenly takes the parallelism in Zechariah to refer to two animals, a colt and a mare.

Jesus instructs the disciples as to how they are to deal with potential objections to their taking the colt: **Tell *them*, "The Lord needs it."** This is ambiguous on the historical level: **Lord** could mean its master/owner. Its owner is commanding the keepers to release it for his use. At the readers' level, it points to Jesus. **Lord** could signal his messiahship. But, if so, this is Mark's only use of **Lord** in this fashion.

■ **4-6** Just to show the prescient character of Jesus' instructions, Mark repeats the details of the episode.

2. Entering Jerusalem (11:7-10)

IN THE TEXT

■ **7-8** When the disciples had **brought the colt to Jesus and threw their cloaks over it, he sat on it.** The accompanying crowds **spread their cloaks on the way** (*eis tēn hodon*). At a superficial level this simply means **the road.** But at the close readers' level, it refers to the way of Jesus on which Bartimaeus has recently embarked.

The **many people** (see 10:45) are almost certainly fellow pilgrims and followers of Jesus from Galilee. The **branches** (*stibados*) are leafy branches **cut in the fields.** Matthew 21:8 has *kladous*, a term closer to palm branches, cut from trees. Only John (12:13) explicitly mentions "palm branches" (*ta baia tōn phoinikōn*) in the Palm Sunday procession.

■ **9-10** The picture of the entry is full of joy. The language is drawn from Ps 118:26, the final Hallel psalm (113—118) recited by pilgrims at Sukkot (Tabernacles), Hanukkah (Lights), Pesach (Passover), and Shavuot (Weeks) in Jerusalem. **Hosanna** transliterates a Hebrew word meaning *Please, save us.* By the 2TP, it was simply a note of praise, comparable to "Hallelujah." Mark concludes with **Hosanna in the highest!** alluding to the heavens, the home of God and angelic hosts (see Luke 2:14).

The echo of Ps 118 continues with an exact citation of Ps 118:26: **Blessed is he who comes in the name of the Lord!** The words were ordinarily chanted by those already in the temple to welcome arriving pilgrims: "From the house of the LORD we bless you" (Ps 118:26b). This is not cited. Here, the language has messianic overtones.

Mark continues with an echo of 2 Sam 7:14: **Blessed is the coming kingdom of our father David!** This passage was widely used in messianic terms during the 2TP (see 4QFlor = 4Q174). It expressed popular longings for the restoration of the throne of David. The language here is of the arrival of the kingdom of David (not the kingdom of God). The sentence explicitly lends a nationalistic or political tone to the arrival. Jewish revolutionaries may have exploited the link between Ps 118 and 2 Sam 7 (Marcus 2009, 780). The pleading cry of Bartimaeus, Jesus' response in healing him, and the ascription of "Lord" to Jesus in securing the use of the donkey are all wrapped up in this outburst of praise from these pilgrims. Jesus is Son of David and Lord, and this language points directly to him in ways that those calling out scarcely grasp.

3. Entering the Temple (11:11)

■ **11** According to 11:1, Jesus is approaching Jerusalem. Now, at last, the destination has been reached and **Jesus entered Jerusalem.** The story builds up to this point from the confession in Caesarea Philippi. Jesus' way has come to its destination. The "Son of David" (10:47) and "Lord" (11:3), terms used in the immediate context, is coming into Jerusalem. But this is the place where the Son of Man must suffer. The passion predictions on the journey south give sense of purpose to Jesus' determined path.

After entering Jerusalem, Jesus **went** directly **to the temple.** In Matthew and Luke, the clearing of the temple follows his first entrance. But Mark tells the story with a significant difference. Jesus **looked around** [*periblespamenos*

3:5, 32; 5:32; 9:8; 10:23] **at everything.** He perceived what was going on in *his* temple. This was a proprietary gaze.

Readers might have expected climactic action or great acclaim to follow. The time has arrived and Jesus has come into Jerusalem, especially if we gild this arrival with great fanfare. But the story seems to come to an astonishing anticlimax: **but since it was already late, he went out to Bethany.** Jesus noted the time, realized it was time to quit work for the day, and left. And **the Twelve** went with him. What's going on?

First, Jesus' identity as the Messiah and Lord is clearer to the readers than to the participants in the event. No one in the temple sings Hallel psalms to welcome or acclaim him as Messiah. He has ridden into Jerusalem on the back of an unbroken donkey, not a warhorse. He and his followers are on pilgrimage to Jerusalem for Passover with thousands of others. On the historical level, his entry is far less extraordinary than we sometimes imagine. Jesus is not entering Jerusalem to liberate the temple from the Romans.

Second, Mark sets the scene for an altogether more dramatic story about Jesus' action in the temple (11:15-18). Jesus leaves Jerusalem so he can enter again. His reentry is bracketed by the cursing of the fig tree (11:12-14, 20-21).

Jesus' first entry to Jerusalem is rather anticlimactic, on the surface. But Mark's telling of the story proves to be deceptively dramatic and effective.

B. The Second Entry into Jerusalem (11:12-19)

BEHIND THE TEXT

This is one of the most important stories in Mark. Jesus' second entry to Jerusalem and its consequences are highlighted through Mark's intercalation style: setting a story between literary bookends. The prophetic action in the temple is set between the two parts of a curious episode about the curse Jesus pronounced on a fig tree.

The stories pose historical questions. Did Jesus really act this way? What was going on in the temple that so incensed Jesus? And when did this occur? John 2:13-22 places the event at the beginning of Jesus' ministry. Such questions are interesting but, beyond some basic comments, they cannot detain us here. Much more challenging and important are other questions.

First, what are we to make of Jesus' curse on the fig tree? The action appears "destructive . . . spiteful . . . discreditable . . . petty" (France 2002, 439). These are all fair characterizations. But if the event is so embarrassing, why does Mark include it? Most scholars think Mark has constructed "one of his most original and revealing compositions" (Marcus 2009, 788). The clue to its meaning lies in the significance Mark attaches to the inner relationship between the stories of the temple and the fig tree. When the fig tree is understood as a metaphorical symbol, the reasons for including it become clearer, even if unanswered questions remain.

Second, what is Jesus doing in the temple? His action in the temple must have significance beyond the temporary disruption of temple traffic. In 13:1 the disciples comment accurately on the magnificence of the temple. It was probably the largest such site in the world, occupying an area of about thirty-five acres (fourteen hectares). It had four concentric sections, the largest, the outer Court of the Gentiles marked its perimeter. Walled off within were three inner courts—the Court of Women, the Court of Men, and the holy place—and the holy of holies in the center (see Stein 2008, 515).

Third, what is the connection between this "interpretative envelope" (Marcus 2009, 788) and 11:20-25? The commentary attempts to answer these questions.

I. Cursing the Fig Tree (11:12-14)

IN THE TEXT

■ **12-14** Jesus and his disciples spend the night in **Bethany.** Mark gives no further details but places this episode on **the next day. Jesus was hungry.** Mark's failure to mention their accommodations suggests that this story is a metaphorical narrative, perhaps relocated from elsewhere (Collins 2007, 525; but see Stein 2008, 512).

Jesus came to **a fig tree in leaf.** Mark paints an inviting picture of a healthy tree, so Jesus **went to find out if it had any fruit. When he reached it, he found nothing but leaves.** "It was the leaves, visible from a distance, which promised fruit, and it was the finding of no fruit but *only leaves* that triggered Jesus' violent reaction" (France 2002, 439).

Our first impression is of a tree that should have fruit, but does not. But Mark immediately explains, **because it was not the season for figs.** Matthew 21:19 omits this explanation, perhaps to soften Jesus' apparent petulance. Mark's explanation is botanically plausible. In Israel fig leaves appear in March. But the early fruit does not develop until the end of June (see 13:28). This story is set just before Passover, when the fig trees would be in leaf but not yet bearing fruit.

Mark's explanation of the barrenness of the fig tree alerts readers that there is more to be considered than simply Jesus' annoyance. This is not about a literal fig tree at all. Often used to symbolize people (see Marcus 2009, 789), here the tree likely points to the faithless leaders and the doomed temple, not to Israel as a whole.

An intertextual connection provides illumination. In Mic 7:1-4, the prophet's laments, "I have become like one who, after the summer fruit has been gathered, after the vintage has been gleaned, finds no cluster to eat; there is no first-ripe fig for which I hunger" (7:1 NRSV). The reason is that "the faithful have disappeared from the land" (7:2a NRSV). Jesus has just been acclaimed as the Coming One on his entrance to Jerusalem, but the leaders have not welcomed him. The leaves "correspond to the acclamations of the crowd, and the lack of fruit corresponds to the missing welcome from the leaders" (see Mark 11:18; Collins 2007, 526).

Jesus' curse of the tree is boldly stated: **May no one ever eat fruit** [*karpon*] **from you again** (see Stein 2008, 513 n. 6). The choice of **fruit** instead of "figs" may invoke "the biblical motif of fruitfulness or fruitlessness as a symbol of spiritual health or disease" (Marcus 2009, 782). This appears to be an acted parable (see Hooker 1991, 262), or a prophetic-representative action. It is significant in itself; and it illuminates the next event, the clearing of the temple.

Jesus' words seal the fate of the fig tree and its symbolic counterpart, the temple. If it points to the leaders, it signifies that "their role as leaders is forfeit," because they failed to recognize in Jesus the coming of their Messiah (Collins 2007, 526). It may also serve as a reminder that Jesus' messiahship has not fully arrived. The suffering and death, vindication and triumph of the Son of Man are still unfolding in this drama. The actual fate of the temple and its leadership has been signaled but not fully accomplished. Like other prophetic representative actions, the event and its interpretation participate in the action to which it points. This is best illustrated at the Last Supper (14:22-25). The important point is that **his disciples heard him say it.**

2. Prophetic-Symbolic Act in the Temple (11:15-19)

BEHIND THE TEXT

The importance of the temple can scarcely be exaggerated. This was the national shrine for the Jewish people, the central place of worship and of continual sacrifice, and the destination of pilgrims. The defilement of the temple in 164 B.C. under Antiochus IV Epiphanes led to the Maccabean Revolt. The restoration of temple service, after the cleansing and rededication of the temple was celebrated in Jerusalem as Hanukkah.

The temple was Israel's central treasury, a major part of the economic existence of Jerusalem. It generated great commercial activity, providing animals for sacrifice and massive building projects. Herod the Great knew its political worth. He attempted to win the support of his Jewish subjects through a massive rebuilding program, begun in 20 B.C. and completed only in A.D. 63, just before its destruction by the Romans in A.D. 70.

■ **15-16** Jesus and the disciples came to **Jerusalem** and **entered the temple area.** The Gospel has given significant hints that the Jerusalem authorities want nothing to do with this Galilean prophet. But nothing overly hostile happens until now. Jesus inspects the temple (11:11), but Mark says nothing about his response to what he sees. In this short episode, the ambience changes. Hostility now colors the story, which culminates in the crucifixion of Jesus as an enemy of the state and the temple.

When they enter the temple, Jesus finds people buying and selling, and a flourishing currency exchange. They probably had the approval of the temple authorities, since they provided essential services to worshippers. Each year every Jewish male paid a half-shekel temple tax (see Exod 20:11-16). This required Tyrian coinage, which used no forbidden images. Sellers supplied doves for the offerings of poor people and unblemished livestock for other sacrifices. Business was especially brisk during the Passover season. This business could just as easily have been conducted outside the temple precincts.

To what did Jesus object in the temple? The precise location of the **tables** he **overturned** is not clear. But they would likely be in the Court of the Gentiles. This seems to be the problem—the Court of the Gentiles was designed as a place of prayer for the nations (v 17, citing Isa 56:7), not the marketplace for temple trade. His clearing of the temple could be a protest at the avarice and corruption of the temple system. Ample evidence documents the discontent among the people toward the temple establishment. But Jesus' actions in the temple cannot have been more than a symbolic gesture: He acts alone against a massive enterprise. This suggests that the problem is more than temple corruption. It is better to picture this as a prophetic-representative action, symbolizing and anticipating the destruction of the temple, which Jesus explicitly prophesies in Mark 13.

Whatever the reason, Jesus **began driving out those who were buying and selling there. He overturned the tables of the money changers and the benches of those selling doves.** That he "would not allow anyone to carry anything [*skeous* = **vessel,** a "weapon"] through the temple" (NRSV) is puzzling. It could allude to Zech 14:21: In the eschatological temple there will be no longer any need for traders supplying ritually pure containers because all the vessels will be holy. Or, *skeous* could refer to **weapons** as in Gen 27:3; 2 Kgs 11:8, 11; and 2 Chr 23:7. Some scholars plausibly prefer the latter meaning in light of the reference to "a den of robbers" in Mark 11:17.

■ **17** Jesus may teach more than Mark reports. Mark distills the point of his teaching in the citation of Isa 56:7 LXX: **Is it not written: "My house will be called a house of prayer for all nations"?** Matthew 21:13 omits **for all nations,**

MARK

11:15-17

298

thereby missing the point Mark draws from the quotation. It is ironic that Jesus criticizes the Jewish temple authorities instead of expelling the Romans and the Gentiles from the temple (Stein 2008, 517).

Jesus contrasts the purpose of the temple with what is actually occurring there. Instead of a place of worship, he charges its caretakers with malfeasance: **you have made it a hideout of brigands** (*spēlaion lēistōn*). This alludes to Jer 7:11: "this house, which is called by my name, [has] become a den of robbers in your sight" (NRSV). Jeremiah concludes with the statement: "You know, I too am watching, says the LORD" (NRSV). Ultimately judgment falls on the temple in Jeremiah, just as he had predicted. Mark may have had this allusion in mind in 11:11, which reports that Jesus, the Lord of the temple, is watching.

If the problem in the temple is simply one of greed and financial corruption, then the phrase *spēlaion lēistōn* could mean simply **den of robbers.** This allusion fits well the dysfunctional high priestly family of Annas during the days of Jesus. Josephus notes that the temple became a Zealot stronghold and safe house in the years preceding its final destruction, A.D. 66—70 (Collins 2007, 531).

■ **18-19** The opposition is important. **The chief priests and the teachers of the law** (not the Pharisees) are listening and begin **looking for a way to kill him** (see 3:6). But at this point, the **whole crowd** is **amazed** at his teaching. In 1:22 Jesus' teaching is contrasted with that of the **teachers of the law** (6:2; 7:37; 10:26), which raised the fears among the leaders that they would lose control. Here, they plot but take no action against Jesus yet. **When evening came,** Jesus and his disciples **went out of the city.**

C. The Withered Fig Tree (11:20-26)

IN THE TEXT

■ **20-21** No reference is made to the evening destination of Jesus and his disciples. Rather, they depart so that they can return **in the morning** to see that **the fig tree** Jesus **cursed has withered** *from the roots.* This expression would convey the leaders' loss of power (Collins 2007, 534). If so, the withering fig tree symbol applies solely to the corrupt leadership, not to the temple. But the developing hostility of all the leadership to Jesus leads to the destruction of the temple (→ 13:2). The temple and the sacrificial system are rendered obsolete (→ 15:38).

■ **22-23** Jesus uses the dead fig tree to teach the disciples. His solemn comment, **if anyone says to this mountain, Go, throw yourself into the sea** and **believes** it **will happen,** probably alludes in the first instance to the temple itself, situated on the Temple Mount (see Stein 2008, 520; against France 2002, 449). It continues his radical critique of the temple and overturns expectations that in the coming kingdom the temple would be exalted, rather than cast down (Marcus 2009, 787).

The sayings themselves are transitional in Mark. They likely existed independently of and prior to Mark's use of them here (see Matt 17:20 || Luke 17:6). The Markan Jesus generalizes on the episode as a model for dependence upon God in faithful prayer. Mark postpones any direct discussion of the temple's fate until ch 13.

The connection to the temple may not be wholly lost, however. Since it has been judged to have failed in its function as the house of prayer, Jesus' community becomes the locus of God's activity and the place of prayer (see France 2002, 448).

■ **24-25** The first statement is categorical: **Whatever you ask for in prayer, believe that you have received it, and it will be yours.** The statement depends upon the locus of God's presence being in Jesus and the inauguration of the kingdom. On its own, it seems magical. But even within Mark's narrative, Jesus' apparently unanswered prayer in Gethsemane (14:36) tempers any sense of manipulative prayer. Furthermore, 11:25 links this effective prayer to forgiveness. Belief is central, but so is forgiveness.

The teaching is the same as in Matt 6:14-15. Forgiveness of the other is essential **so that your Father in heaven may forgive you your sins.** This is the only occasion in Mark in which the heavenly Father (*ho patēr hymōn ho en tois ouranois*) is connected to the disciples. These words would be particularly apt in a context in which a prayer for revenge might be contemplated, but personal revenge is excluded (Marcus 2009, 796).

■ **26** Verse 26 in the KJV is omitted in modern translations because it is not found in the earliest MSS of the Greek NT. Its inclusion here is best explained as an assimilation to Matt 6:15.

These words pose a problem to devout Christians whose prayers do not seem to be answered. They can be prey to a "name it and claim it" view that has overtones of magic. When this seems to happen, well and good. But when prayer is apparently unanswered, the anxiety of prayer being unanswered due to "lack of faith" is deeply distressing. The picture of God that emerges from this perspective is actually unattractive and capricious, not like the God revealed in Jesus.

But these words (and others like them) cannot be taken in isolation and treated in a promise-book fashion, either as a means to "remind God of what he said" or to heap guilt on the petitioner for lack of faith when prayer appears to go unanswered. Nor must they be read in a prosaic fashion. This is hyperbole, exaggeration for effect, which "grasps the imagination and encourages the fainthearted to imagine what they could accomplish by trusting in God"

(Collins 2007, 535). Scripture and experience tell us that unanswered prayer is also part of the life of devout followers.

D. The Third Entry into Jerusalem (11:27—12:44)

This third visit to Jerusalem and the temple has a series of opponents of Jesus coming to question him. First, the temple authorities (the chief priests, the scribes, and the elders) issue a hostile challenge to Jesus to prove his right to carry out his prophetic act and to speak as he is doing. They are in charge of their temple, and Jesus has usurped their authority (11:27-33). Then Jesus gives the parable of the vineyard, which they rightly perceive is directed at them (12:1-12). Next, the Pharisees and the Herodians (see 3:6) arrive to entrap him on loyalty to God or Caesar (12:13-17), followed quickly by the Sadducees with a riddle intended to show the absurdity of resurrection belief (12:18-27). This brings the parade of hostile debaters to an end.

The tone of the encounter with a single **teacher of the law** concerning the great commandments (12:28-34) is entirely different. It serves as a summation of the message Jesus is bringing about the Law and the temple system. Mark signals the importance of this short story by concluding: **from then on no one dared ask him any questions** (v 34).

The debates are over, but Jesus continues to teach. First, he shows the acceptability and inadequacy of Son of David as a title (12:35-37). Then he warns people to beware of the wealthy and unscrupulous scribes, and contrasts the commitment of other rich people to the temple compared to the abandonment of all by a poor widow (12:38-44).

1. Debate: By Whose Authority? (11:27-33)

IN THE TEXT

■ **27-28** The third entry follows nicely from v 19 suggesting that Mark has elongated the return by inserting some teaching in vv 20-25 into an earlier continuous unit. Thus the entrances to Jerusalem and the temple in v 15 and v 27 form a bracket around the prophetic action of vv 17-18.

Whatever its origin, Jesus and the disciples **come again into Jerusalem,** a reminder that this has been the predicted place of suffering (10:32-33), and go directly back to the temple. Jesus is walking in the **temple courts** (*hieron*), probably teaching (see 11:17-18) with no apparent concern for his own safety. The impression already gained by Jesus' look around the temple in 11:11, his prophetic action, and his spellbinding teaching is one of veiled but unmistakable **authority.** Mark has already drawn attention to Jesus' divine authority (1:22, 27; 2:10), and the disciples derive any authority they have from him

(3:15; 6:7). Marcus comments on the "sovereign unconcern with which Jesus walks around the temple" (2009, 799).

Jesus is challenged by **the chief priests, the teachers of the law and the elders** (see 8:31). This same collection of temple establishment, who are the Sanhedrin (see 14:55; 15:1), will be assembled against Jesus in 14:53. As far as Jesus and the Essenes at Qumran are concerned, the problem with the temple is that the establishment is hopelessly corrupt. For the Essenes, the solution would be a new temple; for Jesus the transformation is more radical. The new locus of God's dwelling among his people is now himself and the temple itself is doomed (but see Collins 2007, 527-28, 535).

The leaders confront him with the question of his right to act and teach in the temple, much like a hostile demand for a police permit. They are probably referring to the previous day's events: **these things** (*tauta*). The second question is more specific: **who gave you authority?** with the implication that no one in the establishment has done so.

Marcus suggests that this story is the midpoint of a sequence starting from the entry and concluding with the debates about taxes and the resurrection in ch 12. The issue is the authority of Jesus vis-à-vis the authority of the temple establishment. Mark further highlights this particular episode by placing it between the parabolic story of the fig tree and the parable of the vineyard (2009, 798).

■ **29-32** Jesus responds by stating that he will answer their question if they first answer his: **John's baptism—was it from heaven . . . ?**—a circumlocution for God (see Matthew's "kingdom of heaven" = Mark's "kingdom of God") "or was it of human origin? Answer me" (NRSV). Jesus has employed this technique in debate before (see especially 10:3), and somewhat surprisingly, they do not challenge this display of Jesus' authority but recognize the conundrum he has set for them. Either answer will be problematic. Their refusal to heed John will be seen as refusal to obey God, including his preparation of the way for the One who would come after him (1:2-9) and hence his witness to Jesus. But if they dismiss John as merely a self-appointed and misguided irrelevance, the people will be furious because **everyone held that John really was a prophet** and therefore from God. Mark has already confirmed the widespread influence of John in Jerusalem and Judea (see 1:4-5).

■ **33** They take the only way out: they admit they **don't know.** Their strategy backfires, however, because Jesus then refuses to confirm to them his authority: **Neither will I tell you by what authority I am doing these things.** But the problem is worse than that. These religious leaders are the ones who should know, yet they admit that they know neither John nor Jesus. The Sadducees, who were the chief priests, are confronted with their lack of piety combined with ignorance in 12:24: they "know neither the scriptures nor the power of God" (NRSV).

2. The Parable of the Vineyard (12:1-12)

BEHIND THE TEXT

The dominance of Isaiah as Mark's primary intertext continues with this story. The OT regularly uses metaphors of the vineyard and the vine to describe Israel and her people (e.g., Ps 80:8-18; Isa 3:14; 27:2-6; Jer 2:21; 12:10; Hos 10:1). The Johannine Jesus uses the metaphor to describe his new community (John 15:1-6, see Kunene 2010, 170-95). But the closest connection to this passage is Isaiah's Song of the Vineyard (Isa 5:1-8). It is likely that Jerusalem scribes and elders would recognize the allusion, but even if they don't, the meaning is clear enough.

This parable has many realistic elements within Jesus' Galilean social context, where absentee landlords were common. But like most of Jesus' parables, it has extraordinary elements as well. As in Mark 4:1-9, this parable is allegorical. Previous generations of scholars quite properly warned against overinterpretation of parables through excessive allegorization. But this parable, like 4:1-9, cannot be interpreted at the reader's level without some recourse to allegory. Following 4:1-9 Jesus explains the allegory in private. Here there is no need for interpretation. Those against whom it is directed find its meaning all too obvious.

The parable occurs in all three Synoptics as well as the *Gospel of Thomas* (65). Scholars have attempted to identify its earliest form. Some argue that *Thomas*'s form is earlier, because it lacks the allegorical elements present in Mark's version and fits the socio-agrarian context of Galilee, in which the fertile land was now held in large estates with tenants (Kloppenborg 2006, 38-41).

But this does not exclude an allegorical interpretation from its earliest form (Evans 2001, 216-19). The combination of realism, extraordinary aspects, and interpretative application is typical of the Markan Jesus. Arguments against its authenticity on the questionable assumption that Jesus could not have used allegory in his parables are simply implausible (see Snodgrass 2008, 276-99; Brooke 2005).

IN THE TEXT

■I Jesus continues his dispute with the temple authorities by speaking **in parables.** This may simply signal the literary form of the following story. Or it may indicate that this is one parable selected from several in Jesus' teaching in the temple. Mark hints that the teaching is ongoing (11:17).

This parable features **a vineyard,** a highly evocative metaphor in Israel's story. Through Yahweh's rescue of Israel from Egypt, it becomes the vine of his planting (Ps 80:8). But the closest intertextual allusion is Isa 5:1-2. There the prophet sings the Song of the Vineyard: "My loved one had a vineyard on a fertile hillside. He dug it up . . . built a watchtower in it and cut out a winepress as well."

The metaphorical language in the DSS and related 2TP literature suggests that "the vineyard is Jerusalem, Israel in miniature, the tower is the sanctuary and the winepress is the altar and its drainage system which can take on various eschatological significances" (Brooke 2005, 251).

■ **2-5** If Jesus' listeners are expecting a simple retelling of Isa 5, predicting disaster for the vineyard, he takes an unexpected turn. This vineyard is fruitful; the owner wishes to have his proper share when the time is right (*tō kairō*). At one level, this is a horticultural point: Vineyards take up to four years to produce grapes. But at an eschatological level, "the time has come" (Mark 1:15) for its purposes to be realized. But the temple is not delivering its expected fruit.

The owner sends a *slave* [*doulon*] to the tenants to collect his share of the profit. But the tenants seized him, beat him and sent him away empty-handed. The story pattern of threes escalates. The second servant is beaten about the head (*ekephaliōsan*—the only occurrence of this word in Greek literature; Collins 2007, 540). This is probably not an allusion to the beheading of John in 6:14-29. They kill the third slave.

Jesus adds that the owner of the vineyard also **sent many others; some of them they beat, others they killed.** Jerusalem is often the place where prophets meet their destiny (see Matt 23:37 || Luke 13:34).

In Isaiah, the vineyard fails to produce good fruit. In Mark, the problem is that the tenants of the vineyard refuse to provide the master with the vineyard's fruit. This may echo Isa 3:14: "The LORD enters into judgment against the elders and leaders of his people: 'It is you who have ruined my vineyard; the plunder from the poor is in your houses.'" Yahweh's complaint against Judah's leaders draws attention to their social injustice (see Isa 5:7). That is reflected in Mark 12:38-44. Mark's critique is directed explicitly against the Jerusalem authorities: They are the problem.

The fate of the vineyard in Isaiah is destruction (Isa 5:5-7). In Mark, the vineyard is given to new tenants. This change is significant. In Mark, the emphasis falls on God's continuation of the good news announced and effected by Jesus and his followers. The purpose of the vineyard to bear fruit for the owner will be realized under new tenants. The current leadership is doomed.

Isaiah explicitly identifies the vineyard and the owner: "the vineyard of the LORD Almighty is the house of Israel, and the [people] of Judah are the garden of his delight" (Isa 5:7). In Mark, such interpretation is unnecessary: The leaders know the story is directed at them. Perhaps, the "Jerusalem leadership, who were *in fact* the absentee landowning class, appear as *tenants* of an absentee landlord—that is, Yahweh" (Myers 2008, 308). This possibility is enhanced by the biting criticism of the scribes in Mark 12:38-40.

■ **6-8** There is no reason, apart from gracious optimism, for the owner to think the tenants **will respect** his **son**. Nevertheless, he has **one left to send, a son, whom he loved.** The Jerusalem authorities probably grasp Jesus' none-too-subtle self-reference. He has already challenged their practice (11:17) and authority by refusing to answer their question (11:33). Mark's readers, of course, know that the beloved son is Jesus (see 1:11; 9:7).

Mark's readers hear an eschatological note as well. This is the fullness of time (see 1:15), the last opportunity to forestall the loss of the vineyard. The owner **sent him last** (*eschaton*). For some reason, the tenants think that if they kill the son **the inheritance will be** theirs. Their extraordinary stupidity is exceeded only by the extravagant patience of the landowner.

Not surprisingly, **they took** the son **and killed him, and threw him out of the vineyard.** Mark's hearers certainly took this as disgraceful treatment—not even a proper burial. It may also allude to Jesus' crucifixion outside the walls (explicit in Heb 13:13).

■ **9** Jesus asks a question, expecting an answer: **What then will the owner** [*ho kyrios*; see Mark 12:1: *anthrōpos*] **of the vineyard do?** The word *kyrios*, Lord, indicates Jesus in 11:3 and 9. It could allude to the Son of Man as the Lord and Judge. But it probably refers to God, who will execute judgment, as in Isa 5:5-7. Jesus answers the question himself: "He will come and destroy [*apolesei*] the tenants" (NRSV).

The choice of "destroy" (NRSV), rather than **kill** or another verb, "conveys a more ominous message: this is not just the penalty for murder in the story, but the destruction of all that the old régime has stood for" (France 2002, 461; see Stein 2008, 537). That is, the unworthy leaders will be removed (Collins 2007, 547). They lead the people astray and pervert the proper use of the temple. They presume to own it and use it for selfish ends. Hence, they bring God's judgment on the corrupted temple system and themselves (see Mark 11:15-19; 13:1-37; 15:38).

The owner will then **give the vineyard to others.** But who are they? Mark seems to refer first to the leaders. But the people are victims of these leaders. And the leaders represent the people and ultimately turn the crowd against Jesus (15:8-15). Not surprisingly, significant differences exist among contemporary scholars as they attempt to identify the **others:**

12:2-9

- Collins thinks this refers to new leadership that will emerge "among those who accept Jesus as the messiah" (2007, 547), perhaps the Twelve (3:13-15).

- Donahue and Harrington think it refers to Jesus and his Jewish disciples, rather than the Gentile church (2002, 342).

- Geddert insists that the parable "is *not* about 'unfaithful Israel'" or God's rejection of "Israel in favor of the Gentiles" (2001, 283).

- Marcus thinks the parable means "Israel has lost its status as the people of God—as symbolized by its catastrophic defeat in the war [A.D. 66-70]—and has been replaced by the church. Our parable thus moves in the direction of supersessionism but that does not mean that present-day Christian readers are required to follow it there" (2009, 814).

- Snodgrass concludes, "What is taken from the tenants is the privilege of being engaged with the purposes of God, or in other words, election and the promises of God" (2008, 293).

- Brooke argues that "the parable is about how the leaders of Judaism have abused their privileged role in Jerusalem and its temple, the centre of worship of God. It is the significance of all of that which will be passed to others" (2005, 253).

■ **10-12** The explanation continues with an exact quotation of Ps 118:22-23: **The stone the builders rejected has become the capstone; the Lord has done this, and it is marvelous in our eyes** (Matt 21:42 ‖ Luke 20:17; Acts 4:11; 1 Pet 2:7). Scholars draw attention to a possible play on words in Hebrew (and Aramaic) between son, stone, and builders (Marcus 2009, 808). But this "would be lost on many of Mark's readers," who were Greek-speaking (France 2002, 463).

Mark introduces the quotation with Jesus' rhetorical question: **Haven't you read this scripture . . . ?** But the cited Psalms passage does not seem to be related to the parable at all (see also Mark 2:25; 13:26). The challenge Jesus offers is forthright: He reads the foundational intention of Scripture as a whole with authoritative penetration. The temple authorities may have read the Scriptures, but they have missed their application to Jesus. The texts cited would not spring readily to mind. They "involve a creative transfer of a biblical text to a different setting" (France 2002, 462), possibly connected through the wordplay noted above (so Collins 2007, 548).

Is the rejected **stone,** which has become the ***head of the corner*** (*kephalēn gōnias*), a reference to the **capstone** on the pinnacle of the temple (so Stein 2008, 538) or to "the foundation stone of the corner at which a building is begun, fixing its site and orientation" (Collins 2007, 548)? Either is possible, but the latter is closer to the rare Hebrew phrase translated *kephalēn gōnias* in the LXX.

Mark intends his readers to identify the builders as the temple authorities and the stone as the beloved Son, Jesus. In its original context in Ps 118, the rejected stone is a corporate metaphor, referring to Israel. Its rescue is marvelous in their eyes. As part of the psalm of ascent cited already in Mark 11:1-10, it expresses gratitude to God for his preservation of Israel. They were rejected by the nations, but God has made them the cornerstone of his entire redemptive project.

Clearly, Mark's meaning is radically different. The builders are not those who oppose the nation from outside, but Israel's leaders. The rejected stone is not Israel, but Jesus, the Son the temple leaders reject. Here the language echoes Isa 5:24: The people "rejected the law of the LORD Almighty and spurned the word of the Holy One of Israel." And the cornerstone is no longer the central place Israel holds within God's purposes, but Jesus, the Israelite par excellence, who is "consciously taking on the task of Israel" (Snodgrass 2008, 294). The parable is "a prophetic indictment of the leaders. . . . The people would indeed have to decide who to follow, but this parable is not anti-Semitic and is not a rejection of the Jewish nation" (Snodgrass 2008, 297).

The point of the citation is primarily to describe the outcome of the parable, outside Mark's story itself. The story does not end with the son's body eaten by the dogs outside the vineyard, but with vindication. The future vindication of the Son of Man is already announced in the passion predictions (8:31; 9:31; 10:33). The building imagery in which Christ is the cornerstone of his new community features prominently in the NT. The people of God in Christ form a living temple built into Christ (see 1 Cor 3:10-17; 2 Cor 6:16; Eph 2:19-22; 1 Pet 2:4-7).

The response from the temple authorities is understandably hostile. They wish to **arrest him because they knew he had spoken the parable against them.** But the crowd for now continues to be on his side. So the leaders **left him and went away.**

FROM THE TEXT

This parable raises the broader question of supersessionism, or "replacement theology." The term is used pejoratively today to describe those who do not see a continuing special and separate place for ethnic Israel in God's purposes. If Marcus is correct, this parable lends biblical support for supersessionism. Not all scholars agree on this, of course. Others believe Jesus predicts only a change in leadership (see Snodgrass 2008, 296). But is this so?

First, according to Marcus' reading, the vineyard will be given to others, which Mark's readers would naturally hear as the Gentile church. This would mean an end to the place of Israel in the purposes of God. But this goes too far. The parable does not indicate who the others are. This parable is consistent with the rest of Mark: Responsibility for the rejection of Jesus and his message rests firmly on the leaders, not the people as a whole.

Second, the overall picture of the NT is that all of God's good purposes for his created order come to rest in Jesus. Jesus is the embodiment and fulfillment of God's promises to Abraham and the patriarchs that all the nations would be blessed (see Gen 12:1-3). Through Jesus, the NT argues, that is exactly what happens. This is good news to Jews, who see their purpose being fulfilled in Jesus Messiah, and to Gentiles, who are brought into the people of God through following and participating in the death and resurrection of Jesus, the Jewish Messiah. He inaugurates a new covenant in his sacrificial death that is for all, Gentile and Jew alike. Those who wish to be part of the new covenant community can only do so through participation in Christ (see John 6:53). "In terms of Israel as a whole, some rejected Jesus and some accepted him. It was precisely the same with the Gentiles who subsequently heard the good news" (Geddert 2001, 295).

But is there still a separate path for God's "chosen people" (by whom some mean Israel)? The question is further complicated by confusing the modern secular state of Israel with the "chosen people." In doing so, they ignore that the only NT reference to "chosen people" is in 1 Pet 2:9. There Peter refers to the newly created people in Christ without regard to ethnicity.

The NT writers are all adamant that the only way to be part of God's holy people is in Christ, not through a two-covenant arrangement, one for Gentiles and the continuation of the old covenant for Jews. All people who are part of the new holy people of God, both Gentiles and Jews, are so because they are in Christ. There is no other way for either Jews or Gentiles. And that is so, whether or not salvation in Christ is acknowledged.

All interpreters of this text and others must vigorously resist any anti-Semitic reading. There is no place for anti-Semitism in the people of God. But the solution is not a two-covenant arrangement that bypasses participation in the life, death, and resurrection of Jesus, the Jewish Messiah, as the only way for salvation on offer in the NT.

3. Herodians and Pharisees: Caesar and God (12:13-17)

BEHIND THE TEXT

Roman taxation in Judea was vexatious. From A.D. 6 when the ethnarch Archelaus was deposed, Judea became an imperial province, administered from Damascus. When Quirinius, the legate in Syria, conducted a census for poll tax purposes in A.D. 6, it led to an uprising under Judas the Galilean, perhaps the founder of Zealotism (see Bruce 1984, 257). Paying tribute to

Rome was doubly distasteful because it symbolized the subjugated condition of Judea as well as the tacit acknowledgment of Caesar's lordship. The question posed by Jesus' questioners is a live issue, especially in Jerusalem.

While the circulation of denarii may not have been as widespread as locally minted copper coins (without the image of Caesar imprinted on them), enough coins have been discovered to confirm the plausibility of this confrontation. Most scholars think that "the denarius that Jesus looked at had been minted by Tiberius in the 20s. Its legend probably read: *TI CAESAR DIVI AVG F AVGVSTVS*, 'Tiberius Caesar Augustus, Son of Divine Augustus'" (Evans 2001, 247; see Hart 1984, 241-48).

This story shows the gathering opposition to Jesus from the religious establishment. It brings back the Herodians in combination with the Pharisees (see 3:6). Perhaps they were on opposite sides of the question (so Evans 2001, 244; but see Bruce 1984, 251): "Should Jews pay the poll tax to the Romans?" The Herodians would undoubtedly answer, "Yes." But the stance of the Pharisees is less clear. All that held the two groups together was their shared opposition to Jesus.

IN THE TEXT

■ **13-14** The third confrontation of the temple authorities with Jesus begins. Apparently, at the instigation of these leaders—**they,** the Pharisees and Herodians—attempt to entrap Jesus, using flattery and hypocrisy. Mark regularly conveys the truth about the character and mission of Jesus through the words of his opponents (see 1:24; 3:11; 5:7; 15:2, 18, 26-32). 12:13-14

The antagonists' approach is laden with irony: Jesus is indeed a **Teacher,** "sincere, . . . show[s] deference to no one, [and does] not regard people with partiality" (NRSV). The last characterization is a Semitic idiom reminiscent of 1 Sam 16:7: Jesus does not look at the face of a person (*ou gar blepeis eis prosōpon anthrōpōn*). Instead, Jesus teaches **the way of God in accordance with the truth.** Mark, of course, considers their insincere words to be actually correct. Opposition to Jesus' teaching from the Pharisees is notorious.

The big question is this: **Is it *permissible*** [*exestin,* **lawful** (Bruce 1984, 257)] **to pay taxes to Caesar or not?** If Jesus' teaching is **in accordance with the truth,** what halakah would he offer an observant Jew? Is it lawful to give the *kēnsos,* **the poll tax,** to Caesar? The Pharisees thought it tacitly acknowledged the lordship of Caesar. But the issue is beyond the simple question about taxation (Bruce 1984, 251-57).

His questioners place Jesus in an awkward position. Anything he might say seems certain to alienate one or more groups in his audience. If he says, "No," the Roman authorities will have cause to end his career abruptly, and their worries are over. If he says "Yes," the crowds who have been spellbound by his teaching will think he has sold out to the hated Romans and his popularity will plummet.

■ **15-16** "To pay or not to pay?" that is the question. The question is insincere, despite the flattering words that preceded it. But Jesus is not fooled by their flattering **hypocrisy** (*hypokrisin*—only here in Mark). His retort is perceptive: **Why are you trying to trap** [*peirazete*] **me?** His actions have implicitly already caused anxiety for the temple authorities: Is their security and that of the temple at risk? Is Jesus' action and teaching at Passover and in the temple a revolutionary plot?

Jesus asks that they **bring** him **a denarius.** He apparently does not have one at the moment. There is no implication that he has never seen one. But he is certain they do have one of these coins, which was equivalent to a daily wage for a day laborer (→ 6:37). His question to them is direct: "Whose image [*eikōn*] is this?" (v 16 NIV 2011). Their response is clear: **Caesar's.**

The word *eikōn* refers to images that are worshiped (Rom 1:23). Revelation 13—15 uses the term in its description of the idolatrous worship given to the beast and its image within the Imperial cult. The NT uses the expression positively to describe Christ as the visible expression of God (2 Cor 3:18; 4:4; Col 1:15; 3:10), to which believers are to be conformed. Strictly speaking, the image on the coin was blasphemous.

So offensive, because of the breach of the Second Commandment involved, was a human image on a coin in the sight of some strictly orthodox Jews that the exceptional holiness of a third-century rabbi, Nahum ben Simai, is illustrated by the fact that never in his life did he allow his eyes to look at the portrait on a coin. (Bruce 1984, 259)

■ **17** Jesus' response is deliberately enigmatic: **Give to Caesar what is Caesar's and to God what is God's.** Taken out of context, this verse may support a view that Caesar has a realm and rights. Thus, everyone should pay the taxes they owe. God has his realm too. And everyone owes him his due, whatever it may be. Some interpreters argue that Jesus' response challenges the zealotic tendency to resist the Roman colonial rule by refusing to pay the poll tax. Such refusal featured prominently in the First Jewish Revolt of A.D. 66—70. Similar resistance might seem particularly expected during Passover, which celebrates the liberation of Israel at the Exodus.

But this statement may set out Jesus' alternative agenda. Citing 1 Macc 2:66-68, the Markan Jesus issues a similar coded message, which *could* have been heard as revolutionary. But the context suggests that Mark was "not advocating compromise with Rome; but nor was he advocating straightforward resistance of the sort that refuses to pay the tax today and sharpens its swords for battle tomorrow" (Wright 1996, 505).

The Markan context is decisive. The previous parable highlights the refusal of the wicked tenants to give God what rightfully belongs to him. "They are robbing God! The ultimate concern of Jesus is not whether the correct number of coins end up in Caesar's treasury. It is whether those entrusted with God's vineyard are faithful tenants" (Geddert 2001, 286). In Jesus' view, they are manifestly not. The remainder of this series of confrontations simply adds to the evidence.

FROM THE TEXT

This text has been used widely to illuminate church-state relationships, as if it supported the notion of two distinct spheres. This can lead to a compartmentalized faith, in which one's Christian life is practiced at church, but the ethical and moral standards of the secular world define other aspects of life. At the opposite extreme is the utopian, theocratic ideal. Within this worldview, the ethical standards of the followers of Christ are imposed upon the state, if possible.

But this passage supports neither perspective. Compromise with the empire is rewarded with limited power. When the people of God align themselves too closely with any empire, accommodation silences their prophetic voice. The Sadducees had long since abandoned this voice. But when resistance to the empire is seen as an end in itself, the politicized people of God are at risk of adopting the tools of power they resist. Here, the Pharisaic holiness movement collaborates with the Herodians, whose agenda was far different from theirs.

This passage deals with a specific tax, not the authority of God or the state.

> Jesus' final ambiguous answer gives "Caesar" no ultimate authority, either beside God, or under God. . . . [Rather it] suggests that Rome has *some* authority in *some* matters, but God has *final* authority in *all* matters. . . . Faithfulness to God's reign means living by values different from those of the political rebels but also different from those of the collaborating politicians. (Geddert 2001, 298-99 emphasis original)

The people of God can ill afford to surrender their prophetic voice in exchange for an easy accommodation to any state.

4. Sadducees: The Seven Brothers (12:18-27)

BEHIND THE TEXT

The name "Sadducees" is usually thought to come either from the adjective *saddiq* meaning "righteous" or, more probably, from *sādōq*, the priest (LXX: *zaddouk* in 2 Sam 8:17). Here they make their only appearance in Mark and their first literary appearance in any extant texts. Outside the NT, the other ancient source of information about them comes from Josephus, who has an apologetic reason for supporting the Pharisees. All indisputable literary remains from the Sadducees have disappeared, so they are known only from the writings of their opponents. They ceased to exist following the fall of Jerusalem in A.D. 70.

Traditionally, scholars identify the Sadducees as the wealthy priestly aristocracy. But not all Sadducees were priests, nor were all priests Sadducees. According to Ezek 44:15, "The priests, who are Levites and descendants of Zadok and who faithfully carried out the duties of my sanctuary when the Israelites went astray from me, are to come near to minister before me." If the Sadducees did, in fact, trace their lineage to Zadok, then passages like this would give warrant for their leadership.

During the second century B.C., the high priesthood was usurped by the Hasmoneans (the Maccabees). But if Josephus is correct, they still exercised considerable influence under direct Roman rule (A.D. 6-66). Sadducean high priests served for thirty-four years of this sixty-year period. They included Annas and his son-in-law Caiaphas (see Marcus 2009, 1121-23). They were certainly part of the ruling elite who were quite detached from the ordinary people.

We know Sadducean beliefs only from their opponents' reports. They were accommodating to the hellenization of Jewish culture. But they were conservative in rejecting innovation in religious beliefs, preferring views that could be established from the Pentateuch alone. Some scholars argue that they accepted *only* the Pentateuch (like the Samaritans). But Marcus concludes that they considered only the legal aspects of Scripture binding: "One was free to argue about or even to disbelieve in matters of *haggadah* (narrative), such as angels, spirits, and the resurrection" (Marcus 2009, 1123).

The dispute here is how the law of levirate marriage could play out in the speculative (from the Sadducean perspective) doctrine of personal resurrection. The notion of levirate marriage is based on Gen 38:8; Deut 25:5; and Ruth 4: A man whose married brother has died without offspring is obliged to marry his sister-in-law and father children by her to secure his brother's posterity and property rights. But the Pentateuch expressly forbids such unions (in Lev 18:16; 20:21). Some scholars argue that "the law of levirate marriage had been generally abandoned by the first century" (Instone-Brewer 2002, 123). The ceremony of *halitzah* (Deut 25:7-10) released a man from this obligation.

Some usually reliable MSS of v 23 lack the phrase *hotan anastōsin*, **when people rise from the dead.** But most scholars (e.g., Metzger 1975, 110-11; Collins 2007, 557; Marcus 2009, 827) argue that the words are probably original, based on Mark's prolix style and the difficulty of explaining their addition.

■ **18** The appearance of the **Sadducees** in the parade of Jesus' questioners has a clear narrative purpose. It fits within "the rich and explosive mixture of politics and theology that forms the climax of the synoptic narrative" (Wright 2003, 419). They represent the elite temple establishment, especially if Caiaphas is one of their number. They are also a foil in the continuing demonstration that Jesus is the authoritative teacher and interpreter of Scripture. Mark identifies them by their conservative theological belief: they say **there is no resurrection.** Most Second Temple Jews held some notion of afterlife (extrapolating from Isa 26:19; Ezek 37:1-14; Dan 12:2; Pss 16:9-11; 49:15; 73:23-26; Job 19:26). The minimal scriptural indicators were insufficient to persuade the Sadducees. They restricted their belief in the afterlife to a shadowy existence in Sheol.

■ **19-23** The Sadducees' question is hostile. They make no attempt at flattery, although they respectfully address Jesus as **Teacher.** Their question gives the impression that it is a well-rehearsed conundrum, used as the clinching argument in debates before. The scenario is absurd and makes resurrection sound absurd.

A similar story occurs in Tob 3:7-15. But the seven marriages in it were never consummated. This story demands that each of the seven marriages be consummated, but **none of the seven left any children.** Each marriage was thus a lawful levirate marriage. Jesus addresses the question of marriage and divorce in Mark 10:1-9, but this is a different situation. It does, however, portray "the patriarchal nature of Jewish marriage law, in which men are active agents and women are passive" (Marcus 2009, 827). With this improbable setup, the question is: **At the resurrection, *when they rise,* whose wife will she be, since the seven were married to her?**

■ **24-27** Jesus' extended reply criticizes the Sadducees on two fronts. They are **in error** (*planasthe* = possibly ***been deceived***) because they **know** neither **the Scriptures** nor **the power of God.** These are strong accusations. These are predominantly the religious leaders of the people. They should know the Scriptures well (see 12:10-12). But they have been deceived. Mark doesn't say by whom (Marcus [2009, 833] suggests "demonic interference"). Jesus implies that they oppose the reign of God and, therefore, oppose God.

Jesus' accusations directly challenge the assumptions of the Sadducees. Their conception of the afterlife, and hence, of the resurrection is wrong. Resurrection life "is no mere continuity of the present life. Whereas marriage on earth is for the purpose of procreation," in the future, when death is no more, procreation will be unnecessary (Stein 2008, 554).

MARK

12:18-27

Rather, those raised from the dead **will be like the angels in heaven.** This language has been responsible for a range of popular quasi-theological views of the afterlife. But, as Wright points out, to be **like the angels** is not to suggest that resurrected ones are "in the *ontological* sense . . . the same sort of creature as the angels." Nor, are they identical "in the *locational* sense that they are sharing the same space" **in heaven.** The similarity applies only "in the *functional* sense that the angels do not marry," nor do resurrected humans (2003, 422).

The first problem of the religious leaders is their surprising ignorance of Scripture. Jesus does not support his assertion about being **like the angels** directly from Scripture. He makes a case for the resurrection in general. Since the Sadducees would conduct any debate on the basis of the Pentateuch, Jesus meets them head on. He asks if they are unaware that **in the book of Moses, in the account of the bush** (Exod 3:6), God identifies himself as **the God of Abraham, the God of Isaac, and the God of Jacob.** Of all the passages they should understand, they misunderstand this important one. Jesus insists that this statement implies that the dead patriarchs are now living.

Jesus does not explain why this assertion is correct. Some interpreters point to God's everlasting covenant with the ancestors (France 2002, 472; Stein 2008, 550). If God is the God **of the living,** there is life after death. The Sadducees' view of no life after death is wrong because **He is not the God of the dead, but of the living.**

But this does not prove Jesus' specific point about the resurrection. It might support the Sadducean view that "the dead are *not* raised, but only live on in post-mortem disembodiment of whatever sort" (Wright 2003, 425). The patriarchs continue to be in relationship with the living God and, therefore, are still alive. On the basis of similar rabbinic debates, Wright argues that the argument is clear to all parties in the confrontation. "The patriarchs are still alive, and therefore will be raised in the future. Prove the first, and . . . you have proved the second" (2003, 425; see Collins 2007, 563).

The second problem is that they know nothing about **the power of God.** "Jesus doubts that the Sadducees have ever experienced God's power and that they therefore have any insight into what scripture reveals" (Evans 2001, 254). They are so locked into the way they think God can and should act that they restrict his creative power to their ability to understand and conceptualize it. Jesus argues that if God can create, and if he can enable the dead to live beyond the grave, they can be raised from the dead in a transformed existence in the age to come. This will be "a new way of being in communion with God" (Donahue and Harrington 2002, 350).

In the life and mission of Jesus, the power of the age to come has already been inaugurated. The scribes from Jerusalem (including some scribes of the Sadducees?) reject this, however (see 3:22-30). None of the evangelists appeal

12:24-27

to Jesus' own resurrection as the basis for the resurrection of believers. But Paul does. Jesus, raised from the dead "before time," has become the firstfruits of all those who await the general resurrection from the dead (1 Cor 15:23).

With Jesus' accusations of the religious elite still ringing in their ears, he concludes with the stinging words: **You are badly mistaken!** (lit., *greatly deceived*). With this, the debate concludes. Within the wider context, this could conclude Jesus' disputes with all the establishment groups that oppose him: They are all badly mistaken in their assessment of Jesus and his mission.

FROM THE TEXT

Two important lessons emerge from this story:

First, Christian faith in life after death is not based upon the unbiblical notion of innate human immortality, but solely upon resurrection from the dead as the gift of God. The sure and certain hope of the resurrection is based upon the resurrection of Jesus as firstfruits.

But the picture of resurrection hope in this passage is troubling. It seems to make the future life "a bloodless existence where the warmth of human relationships has ceased to matter" (Hooker 1991, 284). If the intimacy of marriage is not part of the resurrected life, is this really a blessed existence? But this passage does not address this question. It insists only that there is no need for procreation in the resurrected life.

Not every question about the afterlife can be answered from this passage. Only a general answer can be given. The resurrection life is far more than a continuation of this life. It is immeasurably richer and unimaginably fuller. To be raised with Christ and in Christ is the glorious hope of those in Christ. It is not to cease to be human or to be transformed into angels.

Second, Jesus' stinging critique of his conservative religious opponents is a reminder that knowledge of God is more than an article of faith that affirms its scriptural authority. Scripture needs to be read, absorbed, and interpreted before pronouncements are made. It is also more than adherence to literalist readings of sacred texts and resistance to anything that does not fit that reading.

Knowledge of God is a relational knowledge possible only through the revelation of the triune God within his people. These people experience the power of God in the most unexpected places, in unexpected ways, and through unexpected people. An understanding of Scripture that is faithful to the Wesleyan heritage combines faithful reading of Scripture illuminated by the Holy Spirit and openness to the transforming and creative power of God at work beyond any narrow reading of the text.

Peter has to be dragged kicking and screaming into a broader understanding of how God is at work in the world in ways that directly contradicted Peter's prior understanding of God's explicit commands (see Act 10:10-16).

Similarly, only through the illumination of the Spirit are we able to discern how God may be at work in our world. The Sadducees had God defined and confined. Unfortunately, their God turned out to be a diminished God, not the God of the living.

5. The Teacher of the Law: The Great Commandments (12:28-34)

BEHIND THE TEXT

The series of hostile questions challenging Jesus' authority ends with the Sadducees, symbolically representing the pinnacle of the religious establishment. This questioner, who is a scribe, is not portrayed as hostile. Thus, Mark differs from the parallels in Luke 10:25-28 || Matt 22:34-40, where he is a *nomikos*, **lawyer.** If they are following Mark, they may have read his story as portraying a hostile approach. More probably, they have a slightly different reason for writing it in their own fashion.

The two commandments are regularly a discussion in this period and later, although their succinct combination in Mark may be explicit for the first time. Philo similarly combined piety and holiness (*eusebeia* and *hosiotētos*) toward God and righteousness and kindness (*dikaosynē* and *philanthrōpias*) toward humans as the two main virtues that sum up the Law (*Spec.* 2.15 §63; cited in Collins 2007, 568). After considering the available ancient evidence (including *T. Iss.* 5:2; *T. Dan* 5:3; *Jub.* 7:20; 20:2; 36:7-8; and Philo), Collins concludes that "the formulation of two most important or summarizing commandments in terms of love in Mark or the tradition to which the evangelist was heir was at least distinctive, if not original" (2007, 569; see 566-70).

The narrative connection between this story and the preceding ones is deliberately drawn by Mark. First, the scribe observes the dispute between Jesus and the Sadducees, or perhaps, the whole series of disputes. This pericope ends with the telling comment: ***After this no one dared to ask him any further questions.***

IN THE TEXT

■ **28** The narrative connection between this story and the previous one is explicit. Perhaps the scribe (**one of the teachers of the law**) is initially part of the entourage coming to question Jesus. Hostility would be the expected outcome of an encounter with scribes, judging from the earlier challenge from the legal experts from Jerusalem (3:22-28). But this **one** (*heis*) is different and stands out from the rest, symbolizing what might prefigure the minority of those in the religious elite who support him (so France 2002, 476, 478; see 15:43).

He grasps the quality of Jesus' answer, so he asks Jesus: **Of all the commandments, which *has primary importance* [*prōtē*]?**

A debate over the most important commandment was standard fare for expert rabbis in the 2TP. Later rabbis divided the 613 commandments in the Torah into 248 positive and 365 negative. So a discussion of the most important command would be expected.

■ **29-30** Jesus' response begins with Deut 6:4, the first words of the Shema. This designation for Israel's central creed is taken from the first Hebrew word in Deut 6:4. The Shema as the classic Jewish expression of its identity combines three OT quotations (Deut 6:4-9; 11:13-21; and Num 15:37-41). It was recited twice daily by pious Jews in the temple (*m. Tamid* 5:1; cited by Marcus 2009, 837).

The opening words in Deuteronomy are "Hear, O Israel: The LORD our God, the LORD is one." The inclusion of the introduction to the commandment is significant. The debate has been over Jesus' authority and identity. Thus, in its Markan context

> to love "the Lord our God" with all one's heart, soul, mind and strength . . . is at the same time to love and follow Jesus—as this scribe seems nearly ready to do. Mark thus foreshadows a daring Christian reinterpretation of the Jewish idea of divine oneness, a reinterpretation that implies a unity between God and Jesus. (Marcus 2009, 843)

Deuteronomy 6:5 summarizes the first table of the Ten Commandments: "Love the LORD your God with all your heart and with all your soul and with all your strength [*dynameōs*]." Mark's version has minor variations from the LXX of Deut 6:4. First, Mark has four elements: In addition to **heart**, **soul**, and **strength**, he adds **mind**. Second, Mark uses *ischys* for **strength.** Both the LXX and Mark use the preposition *ek* (***out of***) rather than *dia* or *meta* (**with**) to describe the fourfold origin of love for God. This better captures the inward source of this love for God that issues in action (Marcus 2009, 837).

The Great Commandment urges love for God with the entire person. It does not divide humans into three or four discrete parts. Rather it calls for single-minded and comprehensive devotion to God, involving every aspect and dimension of being. The **heart** (*kardia*) is the center of thinking and affections (contrast 7:6). The **soul** (*psychē*) often refers to *life* itself (as in 8:34-37); but it can overlap with *kardia* as the center of emotions and desires. **Mind** (*dianoia*) refers to intelligence and can also overlap with *kardia*. It may have been added because of greater attention to the things of the "mind" during Hellenistic times (so Donahue and Harrington 2002, 355). **Strength** (*ischys*) is the power to act. The relational language of **love** (*agapaō*) is fundamental to the God of Scripture.

■ 31 Significantly, Jesus does not stop with the "vertical" command to love God. He continues by citing Lev 19:18: "You shall love your neighbor as yourself" (NRSV). This is a call to give the same care for others as one does for oneself. It is not a call for self-love "as a pre-condition for loving others. Self-love is assumed" (Marcus 2009, 839). For Jesus the command to love God cannot be divorced from love of neighbor. Together these commandments summarize the entire law: **There is no commandment greater than these.**

This inevitably raises the question: Who is my **neighbor**? In the OT, the neighbor is a fellow Israelite. Later Hellenistic Judaism moves in a more generalized, all-inclusive direction. Some NT passages could be read in a restrictive sense as applying only to fellow believers (see 1 John 4:20-21). But the clear teaching of the Lukan Jesus confirms that **neighbor** includes even enemies (Luke 10:29-37).

■ 32-33 The scribe commends Jesus for his perceptive answer, offering his own summary by repeating Jesus' teaching with some additional points:

First, he adds the clause **there is no other but him,** which echoes Isa 45:21-22. This language was frequently used against Christians by Jews who were suspicious of their claims about Jesus. But this statement "implies that the Shema's affirmation of divine oneness is compatible with reverence for Jesus" (Marcus 2009, 844).

Second, these two commands are combined into a single commandment: **is more important than** (*perissonteron estin* is singular). Isolating one part of the Great Commandment "from the other can lead to a religious mysticism that ignores the needs of one's neighbor or to a humanistic concern based on a false sentimentality" (Stein 2008, 562).

Third, the scribe elaborates on the importance of this combined command by stating that it is more important than **all burnt offerings** [the sacrifices that were burnt entirely on the altar] **and sacrifices** (those that were partly burnt on the altar and partly consumed by priests and worshippers). This, too, echoes Scripture (1 Sam 15:22; Isa 1:10-17; Jer 7:22-23; Hos 6:6). It should be noted that the setting for this discussion is the temple, where burnt offerings and sacrifices are made. The temple establishment is trying to destroy Jesus. Such an explicit affirmation of Jesus' teaching, which relativizes the entire sacrificial system, is remarkable. It is also courageous, given the murderous intentions of Jesus' opponents.

■ 34 The expressions of mutual admiration continue. Mark explicitly reports Jesus' commendation of the scribe's perceptive answer: **You are not far from the kingdom of God.** This statement is remarkable.

First, we know tantalizingly little about this man. Is he a leader like Joseph of Arimathea, who is "waiting for the kingdom of God" (15:43)? Or might he be Joseph? We are not told.

Second, it reminds readers that the religious establishment was not universally opposed to Jesus. This one is close to the **kingdom,** if not in it. Mark contrasts this man with the man in 10:17-22, who leaves sorrowfully. This man seems to have understood the path of Jesus like few others. But did he join Jesus on the way? We are not told.

The conclusion to the episode is also extraordinary. It brings the whole debate to a close: **from then on no one dared ask him any more questions.** But it is more. It signals that the pinnacle of Jesus' teaching about the new people of God reiterates God's purposes for his ancient holy people from Exod 19:6. Jesus' re-creation of Israel, centered on himself as the Holy One of God in their midst, penetrates to the heart of the life the renewed people of God are to live. Their entire beings focus on their covenant relationship with God. This issues in the love of neighbor that characterizes God's love for the entire created order.

Such a renewal of focus on doing the will of God is not seen chiefly in the temple rituals of burnt offerings and sacrifices in the priestly tradition. Rather it is to be found in that righteousness and justice called for by the prophets. This succinctly characterizes Jesus' proclamation and practice of the reign of God in their midst. He lives in obedience to the Father and offers his life-giving sacrifice for the many.

The love Jesus calls for is no sentimental feeling of casual friendship or pious phrases. The heart of being God's holy people is articulated in this command: Love God with the entirety of one's being and one's neighbors as God loves them. Such love is costly. Vindication is assured through participating in the way of Jesus, following Jesus in God's rescue plan for his creation.

FROM THE TEXT

Christian holiness has all too often been confused with rule-keeping and meritorious performance. Israel sometimes confused holiness with the elaborate rituals and performances of sacrifices and offerings. The prophets rail against this confusion of the means and end. The system was not to be an end in itself. It was, rather, the means of keeping and restoring the people to the appropriate covenant relationship with God.

If the meaning of holiness has become clouded, Jesus redefines it here by recalling his followers to the heart of God's purposes. They are to be the means by which God will bless all nations, so that God's good purposes will be fulfilled in all the world. This single-minded devotion to God and selfless love of neighbor is the essence of Christian holiness in the Gospels (see Brower 2005, 101). This is indeed how John Wesley succinctly defined what he meant by holiness of heart and life (Wesley 1979, 5:278-79; 7:38).

6. Messiah and David (12:35-37)

BEHIND THE TEXT

This complex pericope resembles a riddle. It raises a question no one asks and leaves the last question unanswered. In v 36 the ancient MSS tradition offers two alternatives: *hypopodion* (***footstool***) or *hypokatō* (**under**). France (2002, 482) tentatively opts for ***footstool,*** because the rest of the verse follows the LXX and most NT citations of Ps 110:1 do so as well. Evans (2001, 270) and Collins (2007, 577) opt for **under,** arguing that ***footstool*** is either an independent assimilation to the LXX or to the parallel text in Luke 20:43.

IN THE TEXT

■ **35** The Greek text of this story begins with *kai apokritheis* (***and answering***) omitted in most translations as either redundant or idiomatic. Mark uses a similar phrase earlier (3:33; 7:28), but within a story. Here, its usage suggests to some that this is "a fragment of a controversy" (Evans 2001, 271).

Whatever its origin, a narrative reason is plausible. The preceding pericope ended with Mark's comment that "no one dared ask [Jesus] any more questions" (12:34c). Hence, there is either no questioner in this story or Jesus responds to the silence of his questioners (Marcus 2009, 846).

The setting of the section that begins in 11:27 has been **in the temple,** which ties this story to those that precede it. The last story has a scribe who is not far from the kingdom. This story returns to a confrontational motif: ***How is it possible for the scribes to say that the messiah is the son of David?*** Here Jesus takes the offensive in a somewhat opaque argument.

The issue is: How is Jesus' identity as the Jewish Messiah to be understood? In 2:25, Jesus appealed to the example of David to justify the Sabbath activities of his disciples. There, he implies that he is greater than David. His identity as the Messiah has been important since 8:27-30—the great confession at Caesarea Philippi. His identity as the Son of David first becomes explicit in 10:47-48 in his response to Bartimaeus. There he tacitly accepts the title. In 11:10, the acclamation of Jesus by the crowds as he enters Jerusalem and the temple is in Davidic terms. But this acclamation is not given by the temple establishment. Jesus does not reject the phrase Son of David, although it does not reappear in Mark after this pericope.

The connection between Messiah and Son of David is not explicitly made in Scripture. But it is certainly implied in numerous passages (see Isa 11:1; Jer 23:5; 33:15; Zech 3:8; 6:12; *Pss. Sol.* 17:21) and in rabbinic literature. ■ **36** Jesus answers his own question. The answer depends on several assumptions held in common by Jesus and the scribes: David is the author of Ps 110; **Lord** refers to the Messiah, and **Lord** is superior to **son** (France 2002, 483).

David himself [*autos* is emphatic], **speaking by the Holy Spirit** [prophetically, so Evans 2001, 273], **declared: "The Lord said to my Lord: 'Sit at my right hand until I put your enemies under your feet.'"**

Recent translations correctly follow the variant reading **under.** Older translations follow the LXX, in which the enemies are made *a footstool* (→ BEHIND THE TEXT above). In the late 2TP, these enthronement psalms were understood as prophecies of the establishment of God's reign through his Messiah (Marcus 2009, 846).

■ **37** Jesus asks another equally cryptic question. The argument is that: Since **David himself** [again emphatic] **calls *the messiah* "Lord,"** and not son, **How then can he be his son?** On its own, this suggests that the Messiah is David's lord not David's son. But this text must be read in Mark's wider context. *First*, Mark has not rejected the **son of David** title for Jesus. A great deal in the narrative supports the notion that Jesus is the Davidic Messiah. This becomes part of the early church tradition (see Rom 1:3-4; 2 Tim 2:8). *Second*, the "overwhelming OT and Jewish expectation that the Messiah is to be a descendant of David" (Marcus 2009, 846) is significant. Then how is this passage to be interpreted? Several alternatives are possible:

First, this addresses a view that Jesus was not from David's line and, therefore, is not the Messiah. Such a question may be addressed in the birth narratives in Matthew (1:1, 6, 17, 20) and Luke (1:27, 32, 69; 2:4, 11; 3:31). Christian tradition has always affirmed that Jesus is of Davidic descent.

Second, Jesus accepts the title but shows its inadequacy. Clearly he is much more than **the son of David.** He is also Son of Man, the favorite self-designation of the Markan Jesus (see further 8:31).

Third, Jesus avoids any hint that he is a military Son of David, about to be enthroned in Jerusalem, despite his entrance and parabolic activity in the temple.

A combination of the second and third possibilities offers the best solution: Mark affirms and qualifies the title Son of David with respect to Jesus. On its own, it is inadequate and dangerously close to a revolutionary perspective Mark rejects. Jesus is not merely David's son. He "far surpasses David's greatness reigning over an entirely different order" (Geddert 2001, 292). The Markan "Jesus' identity is not defined so much by his relationship to David as by his relationship to God" (Marcus 2009, 850). **The large crowd listened to** Jesus **with delight,** but the temple authorities did not.

7. Warning Against Scribes (12:38-44)

IN THE TEXT

■ **38-40** Jesus' continuous teaching in the temple concludes with an attack on the scribes followed by a story of contrasts between the rich and the poor.

He warns the crowd: **Watch out for the *scribes*** (see the similar warning in 8:15). Clearly, this is not directed at all scribes—see the recent commendation of a scribe, so this critique is something of a caricature. According to Collins (2007, 583), who cites Sir 39:4-11, the social standing of scribes was already high well before Jesus' time. Sirach 38:34 contrasts the life of the artisan with that of the scribe: "How different the one who devotes himself to the study of the law of the Most High" and then lauds the life of a scribe.

But the picture here is far from flattering. These scribes **like to walk around in *long*** flowing robes that make a statement about the wearer. They like to **be greeted in the marketplaces** as important celebrities. They like to have **the *top* seats** [*prōtokathedrias*] **in the synagogues**—those up front, facing the congregation. They expect ***the premier couches*** [*prōtoklisias*] **at banquets.**

The language would resonate with Mark's Greco-Roman readers in their honor-shame society, in which outward appearance was highly valued. But these scribes' extravagance is falsely based and ill-gained: **they devour widows' houses** (either homes or estates; see Isa 10:2; Jer 49:11; Mal 3:5). This was quite the opposite of the biblical commands about the care of widows (e.g., Deut 14:29; 16:11, 14). The lot of widows was better than it had been before the 2TP. But traditionally they are among the poorest of the poor. This is reflected in Jesus' characterization of the widow in Mark 12:41-44. Stein suggests six ways in which corrupt scribes may have defrauded widows (2008, 575).

Corrupt business dealings did not stop these dishonest scribes from praying at length for the sake of public appearance. But Jesus "unmasks the brutal reality that beautiful robes and impressive-sounding prayer may conceal" (Marcus 2009, 856). The combination of ostentatious self-promotion and ruthless treatment of the marginalized "will be punished most severely" (NIV 2011; *perissoteron*—a comparative adjective used with superlative force).

■ **41-42** The second picture has Jesus **sitting,** watching people make their contributions to the temple. Jesus' sitting in the temple is controversial since, according to some later rabbinic texts, sitting there is reserved for the Davidic king, or forbidden even to him (see Marcus 2009, 857). At the least, it seems presumptuous and is another signal of Jesus' authority.

The ***receptacle*** **where the offerings were put** (*gazophylakion*) is usually thought to refer to the thirteen trumpet-shaped metal offering boxes mentioned in the Mishnah for various offerings (see Evans 2001, 283). If so, someone sitting near the receptacles would hear the coinage strike the sides when **many rich threw in** [*eballon*] **large amounts.** The contrast is with one **poor widow who came and put in two very small copper coins** [*lepta*], **worth only a fraction of a penny** (*kodrantēs*). A lepton was worth less than 1 percent of a daily wage (a denarius).

■ 43-44 In response to this scene, Jesus calls the disciples and makes a solemn pronouncement. His assessment is perceptive. He does not comment on the amounts being given but upon the value of the gift: she contributed more than all the others combined because **They all gave out of their wealth.** They still have plenty left in their pockets. But her gift was **all she had to live on** (*holon ton bion autēs*).

Traditionally, this has been viewed as a solemn commendation of the widow's generosity in contrast to the great amounts given by the rich. But the context of the story allows for another possibility. Jesus is in the temple after having already prophetically enacted its downfall in 11:17-18. He has seriously disputed with the temple establishment (12:1-27). He has just castigated the rapacity of the scribes (12:38-40). And in 13:2 he will explicitly predict the downfall of the temple.

It is in this context that a poor woman gives everything she has to this corrupt and doomed temple system. The religious establishment is fleecing the poor. And Jesus offers judgment upon this action. Jesus' observation is a lament, not a commendation. "At the very least, attention to the Markan context leaves open whether the widow is presented as a model to be imitated for her sincerity and generosity or as someone to be pitied as a victim of religious exploitation" (Donahue and Harrington 2002, 365).

FROM THE TEXT

The scribes in this story are the trusted interpreters of Scripture, the experts in the Law, the ones who uphold the Torah. The scribe who questions Jesus knows the greatest commandment—and also knows that the outward performance of religious duty cannot substitute for obedience. The scribes who receive Jesus' condemnation love neither God nor their neighbors. Two clear points are important to note from this passage:

First, this story is not a blanket condemnation of all scribes, much less of all of Judaism. The scribes as a class are not particularly prone to fraud. But some apparently are. This episode has nothing at all to say about Judaism in general. Careless Christian readers sometimes point to passages like this to support the view that late 2TJ was morally and spiritually bankrupt. But this would be a grave injustice to Judaism. Jesus is a Jew critiquing some of his fellow Jews for their moral failures.

Second, the treatment of pious widows in this story is made immeasurably worse by the rapacious scribes, who abuse their positions of trust, power, and honor. They betray that trust while maintaining an outward show of great personal piety.

In recent years, the scandal of child abuse by priests, pastors, and religious leaders has been exposed. In each of these proven cases, a breach of trust has occurred that has destroyed the lives of children and families, and has fanned a culture of cynicism and distrust of all Christians. The vast majority of priests and ministers are not guilty of such heinous crimes against children and families. But all have been tainted by the stench of betrayal of a few.

If the story of the widow's offering is a commendation of her willingness to entrust her entire existence to God, then she is an example of the kind of discipleship required in 8:34-37. Traditionally, the poor widow is held up as an example of sacrificial giving that should be emulated by all followers of Jesus. Frequently, it is spiritualized in terms of giving one's whole life to God.

But if it is a continuation of the rebuke against the temple establishment, it serves as a perpetual reminder to the church about the need for vigilance in resisting the trappings of power. Leaders who become accustomed to corporate lifestyles and expense accounts need to remember the sacrificial giving of the faithful. Sadly, the history of the church has been disgraced by the accumulation of obscene wealth. This may be seen in the vast wealth of the Vatican. But it is equally visible in the corporate images projected by the pastoral staffs of many evangelical churches.

Few religious leaders dare follow the more contextual interpretation too far. The financial exploitation of the vulnerable by religious entrepreneurs is well known and widely deplored. A contextual reading offers a severe critique of the predatory practices of the pretentious pious. More respectable churches need to hear this as well and watch their practices.

E. The Fate of the Temple (13:1-37)

This chapter is one of the most difficult to interpret and, therefore, has always given rise to a range of interpretations (see Oden and Hall 1998 for early examples). Its character is distinctive enough to raise questions about how it fits with the rest of the Gospel. Apocalyptic imagery is widespread with an apparent other-worldly tinge. Old Testament imagery is also prominent. Indeed, the chapter is almost unintelligible without an understanding of Mark's scriptural background. Its sheer size underlines its importance for Mark.

The language is explicitly prophetic, although the time scale of the prophetic oracle is ambiguous (Collins 2007, 594). Its worldwide, even cosmic, scope belies the initial focus on the temple. This apocalyptic journey takes us to multivalent parables of watchfulness only to be bring us back abruptly to the earthiness of the Passion Narrative.

Such observations lead some interpreters to suggest that ch 13 is a Markan composition or a pre-Markan tradition. He has inserted it here as the only suitable setting allowing Jesus to offer hope for the future.

The central interpretive problem in ch 13 arises from the assumption that it predicts the return of Christ (the second coming). Jesus solemnly declares that "this generation will not pass away until all these things have taken place" (v 30 NRSV). If Mark 13:5-37 predicts the return of the Son of Man (v 26), and if by this the text refers to the second coming of Christ, the two millennia separating the prediction and its nonoccurrence present an almost unresolvable interpretive problem. Next to this, the issue in 9:1 (→) is comparatively small.

One solution is to accept that, quite simply, Jesus was mistaken. Many shy away from such a conclusion on theological grounds. But the text acknowledges that **no one knows about that day or hour, not even the angels in heaven, nor the Son, but only the Father** (v 32). And yet this explanation ignores the many signs of the times that Jesus has already given in the discourse. This approach probably creates more problems than it solves.

Some solutions are more plausible than others, but none has commended itself to the majority of scholars. The most widely known and still curiously popular solution is the "Little Apocalypse" theory of Timothée Colani (1864; see Beasley-Murray 1954, 1993). It postulates that this chapter existed independently as a Jewish-Christian apocalypse and was incorporated into Mark. It does not go back to the historical Jesus. Rather, it is a tract (Collins 2007, 594) constructed from apocalyptic material in light of the impending fall of Jerusalem. This thesis absolves Jesus of error by pushing the problem to the early Christian community.

Furthermore, this thesis presupposes that Jesus could not or would not use apocalyptic material—something that is unlikely in light of his use of Scripture and his reputation as a prophet. Despite the distaste of some modern readers for apocalyptic imagery, there is nothing intrinsically improbable about Jesus' use of it.

The approach of this commentary is resolutely literary. We interpret the text as we have it. Our questions are: How does this text fit into the narrative flow of the Gospel? What does it contribute to the whole picture? Questions about the historical Jesus, Mark's possible sources, or the tradition history are relevant here only as they illuminate the full story. "It is not possible to reconstruct earlier oral or even written traditions used by the evangelist in this chapter with a reasonable degree of certainty" (Collins 2007, 600). This commentary tries to show how each part of the narrative fits together and contributes to Mark's overall picture.

Perhaps as much as anywhere, the weight we assign aspects of Mark's narrative to this point influences our interpretation. The preceding parts of the narrative set the literary context for this chapter. The meaning and significance of 8:27—9:13 are important, with 8:38—9:1 crucial. The journey to Jerusalem leading to Jesus' prophetic action in the temple is followed by a large section in which he teaches in the temple and engages with the temple leadership. This is the immediate setting of ch 13. It must be important for interpreting the chapter within the flow of Mark's narrative.

Stein (2008, 584-85) provides a helpful chart, outlining ways in which 13:5-37 has been interpreted and the presuppositions interpreters bring to the task. The first two treat the text as a prophetic prediction culminating in the second coming of Christ as the Parousia of the Son of Man. The last two focus primarily on the fall of Jerusalem and the destruction of the temple. Option 3 treats the end of the chapter as a warning against predicting the end while encouraging watchfulness. Option 4 focuses exclusively on the fall of Jerusalem.

My approach comes closest to Option 4. On this reading, ch 13 is not about the second coming of Christ, or, at least, not primarily about it. Rather, the chapter needs to be read as part of the developing narrative. Its setting is Jesus' sustained engagement with the temple authorities and their implacable opposition to him. The disciples witness this conflict and note Jesus' prophetic-representative action in the temple juxtaposed to the withering fig tree (11:11-19). After Jesus' startling pronouncement in 13:2, the question on their minds is the fate of the temple and how it relates to Jesus himself. The answer is that "the Temple's destruction would constitute his own vindication. Once grant this premise, and the nightmare of puzzled textual reconstruction is in principle over" (Wright 1996, 342).

This approach accepts a measure of prophetic polyvalence. There is sufficient prophetic ambiguity (see Geddert 2001, 303) in the text to suggest that its meaning is not exhausted by its application to A.D. 66-70 (see Brower 1997). "Sadly, those who come to Mark 13 with a specific eschatological timetable in mind usually find a way to use the ambiguities of this chapter to make it support their preconceived views" (Geddert 2001, 325).

Nevertheless, the text within its intertextual and intratextual contexts makes coherent sense. It points primarily to the fate of the temple (France 1971 and 2002; Wright 1996; and Kernaghan 2007). This perspective removes "at a stroke the single most embarrassing feature of chapter 13 for traditional interpretation, the quite unequivocal and very emphatic statement in v. 30 that the events just described will take place before this generation has passed. They did!" (France 2002, 501).

Option I

13:5-23	The destruction of the temple and Jerusalem	A.D. 30-70
13:24-27	The coming of the Son of Man	Parousia
13:28-31	The lesson of the fig tree	A.D. 70
13:32-37	The unknown time of the end	Parousia

Option 2

13:5-13	The destruction of the temple and Jerusalem	A.D. 30-70
13:14-23	The great tribulation before the Parousia	Parousia
13:24-27	The coming of the Son of Man	Parousia
13:28-31	The lesson of the fig tree	A.D. 70
13:32-37	The unknown time of the end	Parousia

Option 3

13:1-31	The destruction of the temple and Jerusalem, the coming of the Son of Man, and the lesson of the fig tree	A.D. 30-70
13:32-37	The unknown time of the end	Parousia

Option 4

13:1-37	The destruction of the temple and Jerusalem	A.D. 30-70

1. Not One Stone upon Another (13:1-2)

BEHIND THE TEXT

Joel Marcus calls ch 13 an interlude in the form of a farewell discourse between the story of the woman who devotes her entire living to the temple and the story of Jesus who gives his life a ransom for many (Marcus 2009, 864-67). But this is unlikely.

This section is much closer to a prophetic discourse in which Jesus looks beyond his death to events that lead to his ultimate vindication as the Son of Man. Two questions may be posed. First, does Jesus leave discourse on the temple at any time in this chapter to turn to predictions of the end? Second, does he speak about the end of the time-space universe? The view taken here is a qualified "No" to both questions.

The reasons for this view are straightforward. The temple has been the scene of a series of confrontations between Jesus and a gallery of opponents centered on the temple. His prophetic-representative action (11:15-18) foreshadowing the demise of the temple is now made explicit. The temple, which has been the center of Israel's faith and God's purposes, will no longer hold this place.

Jesus himself, the Holy One of God, is now the locus of God's being and action, as has been gradually unveiled in the narrative to this point. Luke 13:34-35 and 19:41-44 give the impression that the fate of Jerusalem and the temple could have been different had Jesus been welcomed. Mark does not speculate on what might have been. Rather, the events set in motion in 11:15-

18 will work their way out in history. Jesus' earlier prophecy, given in symbolic form and confirmed parabolically by the fate of the fig tree, and his assertion about the mountain cast into the sea, will find fulfillment.

IN THE TEXT

■ 1 The setting remains the temple and the focus remains on Jesus: **he was leaving the temple.** In one sense, this is a simple change of scene; in another, this is symbolic: Jesus abandons the temple to its fate. It is his final departure. This may imply an act of divine judgment (Marcus 2009, 871), which will come to fuller exposition in 15:38 in the rending of the temple veil. Jesus' departure becomes the occasion for **one of his disciples** to make a comment. This opens the way for Jesus' teaching.

The **massive stones** and **magnificent buildings** of Herod's temple were truly impressive. Even allowing for Josephus' penchant for hyperbole, the sight must have been glorious: "Now the outward face of the temple . . . was covered all over with plates of gold of great weight, and, at the first rising of the sun, reflected back a very fiery splendor, and made those who forced themselves to look upon it to turn their eyes away, just as they would have done at the sun's own rays. But this temple appeared . . . like a mountain covered with snow; for as to those parts of it that were not gilt, they were exceeding white" (Josephus, *J.W.* 5.5.6 §222).

■ 2 The response of Jesus, then, is chilling: **Do you see all these great buildings? . . . Not one stone here will be left on another; every one will be thrown down.** The destruction of the temple in A.D. 70 did not destroy the foundations, but the building itself was completely razed. Scholars have discussed whether this is properly predictive or whether it was composed after the destruction of the temple. The fact that some of the chapter predicts the fall of the temple in general terms that do not conform to the details of the events suggests that this is not simply *vaticinia ex eventu*, a prophecy after the event. This is of minor significance in this commentary, but the historical evidence points to other near-contemporary predictions against the temple.

More importantly, as several scholars note, is the intertextual connection to Hag 2:15, the only other use of the phrase *lithos epi lithon*, **stone upon stone.** This then becomes a reversal of the building of the second temple (see Collins 2007, 602). Indeed, the whole chapter is full of language, "not from descriptions of battles and sieges in the field, but from scriptural predictions of catastrophic judgments on this or that city" (Wright 1996, 340).

2. Warnings to Be on Guard (13:3-23)

BEHIND THE TEXT

According to Mark, Jesus exercises prophetic insight into the direction the Jewish nation is going and offers his predictions of what would happen in the First Jewish War of A.D. 66-70. There is nothing improbable about Jesus speaking this prophetic oracle. In fact, the reason Mark includes this lengthy section is "the appearance of popular prophets and claimants to messianic status during this war" (Collins 2007, 603; see 603-5 for examples):

- In the summer of A.D. 66, the Zealot leader Menahem seized arms from Masada and laid siege to the palace.
- He was executed by followers of Elazar, another Zealot leader, who opposed the Romans at every stage for the four years of the war. He never united all the Jews in opposition to Rome.
- John of Gischala, another Zealot leader, set up his power base in the temple.
- He was opposed by Ananus (the former high priest and leader of the pro-Roman faction during the war) and Jesus, son of Gamalas.
- Simon, son of Giroas, like John, was also a guerilla fighter who emerged as a messianic leader.

These are the most likely candidates for the **Many** of Mark 13:6. The evidence is not always clear from our main source, Josephus, because he has his own specific apologetic agenda. But it seems clear that a bitter civil struggle between various messianic pretenders characterized this period.

IN THE TEXT

■ **3-4** After his stunning observation, Jesus sits, the customary posture for teaching, **on the Mount of Olives opposite the temple.** The location is historically plausible and geographically likely. But Mark's explicit reference to the Mount of Olives may have more significance (France 2002, 507). According to Ezek 11:23, when the Shekinah departs from the first Temple: "The glory of the LORD went up from within the city and stopped above the mountain east of it." Zechariah 14:4 is also particularly important (so Marcus 2009, 869).

The three disciples **Peter, James,** and **John** are often grouped (see 5:37; 9:2; 14:33). But here **Andrew** is added (see 1:16-20). Peter, the usual spokesperson for the Twelve, asks Jesus **privately** [*kat' idian;* see 4:34; 9:28] **when will these things happen?** Jesus regularly explains puzzling statements to the disciples (see 4:10; 7:17; 10:10, 23-31). Here **these things** refer to the razing of the temple.

The second question, **what will be the sign that they are all about to be fulfilled** [*synteleisthai*]? allows for Jesus' response. The disciples want to know how they will know that the cataclysmic event of the temple's demise is unfolding. Shockingly, fulfillment here refers to the accomplishing of God's purposes in the destruction of the temple. Unlike Matt 24:3, Mark does not make the second question point explicitly to the coming of the Son of Man as a postdestruction prospect. Rather he focuses only on the destruction of the temple (France 2002, 505-6).

■ **5-6** Jesus' response is "a classic piece of reworked apocalyptic" (Wright 1996, 346) with images drawn from the OT. He first warns them to be aware of *deceivers.* This sets the stage for one of the leading reasons why Mark includes this chapter. It is to foster Christian alertness—to be watchful, awake, discerning. Rather than stoking the flames of second-coming fervor, Mark dampens the enthusiasm.

Matthew and Luke use this material in different ways. Even Matthew's more eschatological reading does not seem to detach the second coming from the temple's fall or make it the opening act of the final drama. More than the other Evangelists, Luke explicitly points to the temple's destruction rather than to any specific occurrence at an unknown future time.

The deception Jesus warns against concerns either false claims to be the Messiah or to act in his behalf. The Greek is ambiguous, but the NIV chooses the better contextual option: **Many will come in my name, claiming, "I am he."** The disciples must not succumb to the blandishments of the many who claimed authority and kingship in the years leading up to A.D. 70.

■ **7-8** Mark continues with the "non-signs" (Stein 2008, 598). Wars are the inevitable and grotesque signs of human sinfulness and alienation, not signs of the end. In fact, Mark insists: **wars and rumors of wars . . . must happen.** This may allude to Dan 2:28-29, indicating that the events in Nebuchadnezzar's dream are coming to pass (Collins 2007, 605).

Other "non-signs" include some standard formulae: **Nation will rise against nation, and kingdom against kingdom** (see *4 Ezra* 13:31, noted by Marcus 2009, 876). Mark's wording may be shaped by current events near his time. We know that **earthquakes in various places** were common during the decade in which he wrote: Philippi in A.D. 61, Pompeii in A.D. 62, and Jerusalem in A.D. 67. And **famines** were widespread during the reigns of Claudius and Nero (A.D. 41-68; see details in Marcus 2009, 877).

Many scholars explain **the beginning of birth pains** as referring to the rabbinic notion of the birth pangs of the Messiah associated with the coming of the new age. But the parallels are not exact. This language metaphorically describes great suffering in many contexts, including that attached to cities (see esp. Isa 13:8; Jer 6:24; 22:23; Mic 4:9-10; France 2002, 512). The phrase often conveys a sense of divine judgment (Marcus 2009, 877-78).

■ **9** Jesus next warns the disciples to **be on your guard** for opposition. Opposition to him and his mission builds throughout the narrative. This escalation of violence will be their fate as well. Indeed, the paradigmatic call in Mark 8:34-37 has already alerted them to the severity of the persecution "for me and for the gospel" (8:35).

He offers specific examples of the kinds of suffering the disciples may expect: "They will hand you over [*paradōsousin;* → 1:14] to councils; and you will be beaten in the synagogues; and you will stand before governors and kings because of me, as a testimony to them" (NRSV). This "testimony" could be understood as **witness** to them or *against* them. In the latter case it is their persecutors who are on trial rather than the disciples.

The disciples' path is the same as Jesus'. He will soon be before the Sanhedrin; they will be before local sanhedrins. He will be flogged by the high priest's temple guard; they will be beaten in synagogues. He will stand before Pilate and Herod; they will also stand before governors and kings. Acts may illustrate the fulfillment of this prediction. But even this personal persecution is a "non-sign" of the end of the temple. The end, although imminent, is not immediate.

■ **10-11** Either before the destruction of the temple or before they are arrested, **the gospel must first be preached to all nations.** Popular interpreters sometimes take this verse out of context and treat it as an explanation for the "delay of the Parousia." But if the chapter is really *not* about the Parousia, this reading falls to the ground. A related problem is the false notion that the spread of the gospel and the arrival of God's future is dependent upon human effort. Jesus emphasizes "that proclamation is not really a human activity but the work of the Spirit" (Marcus 2009, 886).

The passage should not be read through twenty-first-century spectacles, as if the Evangelist (or Jesus) anticipate spreading the gospel to the 195 nations of the world through the missionary movement, the Internet, or international teleconferencing.

Mark's view is that "the temple will not be destroyed (and with it the central role of Israel in God's purposes will come to an end) until the good news has already gone out beyond Israel to *panta ta ethnē,* and so the new 'temple' which replaces the physical building will not be a solely Jewish institution" (France 2002, 516). This view ties in with the opening line of the Gospel—"the beginning of the good news about Jesus Christ." This story will be good news outside of Judaism (see also 14:9). It is the gospel for all nations: "the good news for the Jews has [also] become the good news for the Gentiles" (France 2002, 517).

By the time Mark writes his Gospel, the gospel has arrived in Rome, the symbolic center of the world. The disciples have been witnesses from Jerusa-

13:9-11

lem and Judea to the ends of the earth (see Acts 1:8). The disciples are to be confident before their accusers in persecution. They do not need to prepare their defense since the response they are given are the words of **the Holy Spirit.**

■ **12-13** The disintegration of normal blood ties is viewed more or less positively in Mark 3:32-35. But here Jesus pictures active betrayal (echoing Mic 7:6; see Isa 19:2; Ezek 28:21). This is an "example of an entire passage being evoked by a single reference" (Wright 1996, 348; see also 15:34). In Micah, the people endure persecution from Babylon but hope for Yahweh's vindication. In Mark, Jesus recasts the story in light of his own mission. "The great city that oppresses them, from whose imminent judgment they must flee, is not Babylon. It is Jerusalem" (Wright 1996, 348). It is his disciples, if they stand **firm to the end,** who **will be saved.**

■ **14** What or who is **the abomination that causes desolation** (*to bdelygma tēs erēmōseōs*)? And what does the enigmatic phrase **let the reader understand** mean?

The interpretation of the **abomination** must cohere with the plot development in Mark to this point and meet four criteria (France 2002, 520). It must:

1. connect with Dan 9:27; 11:31; 12:11; and 1 Macc 1:54, 59 and, therefore, involve the temple and the cult.
2. be recognizable in Judea, so that it actually serves as a warning sign.
3. occur while escape is still possible.
4. refer to a person rather than a thing, because the word **standing** (*estēkota*) is a masculine participle normally referring to a man.

Stein (2008, 603) lists eight proposed interpretations. Each commends itself to some scholars. But only the first three seem plausible to me:

1. Caligula's attempt to erect a statue of himself in the temple in A.D. 39-40. This failed because Caligula died before it could be carried out, but rumors did cause huge turmoil in Judea.
2. The attempt by Pontius Pilate to have Roman soldiers march into Jerusalem displaying their standards. This is unlikely, because it is too early.
3. The atrocities committed in the temple by John and Elazar in A.D. 67-68.
4. Titus' entry into the temple sanctuary in A.D. 70.
5. The victorious Roman soldiers setting up their standards and offering sacrifices to the emperor in the temple. Both 4 and 5 leave insufficient time for escape.
6. The events leading up to the siege. But this is too general and cannot explain "standing where *he* ought not to be."
7. The destruction of the temple itself is too late to serve as a warning.

8. An event involving an antichrist that precedes the Parousia. This simply does not fit the narrative context concerning the destruction of Jerusalem and the temple.

Snow draws attention to the importance of Jer 7 in identifying the "corrupt and fraudulent activity of the temple leaders themselves" in the chaotic period leading up to the Jewish War. Vitriolic attacks against the temple found in the Dead Sea Scrolls give a similar perspective on the perverse state of the temple (2010). Jeremiah 7, the most biting temple critique in Scripture, featured significantly in the cleansing episode (→ Mark 11:15-18).

Since this is to warn **those who are in Judea** to **flee to the mountains,** it needs more specificity. The irony of this command is inescapable. The place of safety, the temple sanctuary, has now become the place of danger. Snow's view could be combined with Stein's third possible interpretation. The Zealot leaders are merely the latest of those who desecrate the temple. In Mark's construction of Jesus' historical context, the temple is doomed; and it is the fault of the leaders.

Another viable solution is proposed by Collins. She sees this as a prediction that the Romans would actually set up a statue to "the divinized emperor or the deity he claimed to be or to represent" in the temple (2007, 610). *Bdelygma* is used widely to refer to the image of a god (Collins 2007, 610; citing Deut 7:25-26; 27:14-15; 29:15-16; 32:16-17; Isa 2:8, 20; 44:19). The phrase itself alludes to Dan 12:11 or a tradition developed from it (Collins 2007, 608). These words anticipate the likely outcome of the rebellion. On either view, the temple is doomed because it is hopelessly corrupt.

What does the enigmatic phrase **let the reader understand** mean? It appears to be an aside or parenthesis. This could direct the oral performer of this Gospel to signal the audience that Jesus' words are directed to more than the first disciples (Collins 2007, 608). France, however, suggests that "the aside is an N.B."—note well! More probably it is "a warning that the meaning is not on the surface" (2002, 524). Echoes of Dan 9:27 and 12:11 may hint that the destruction of the temple is the fulfillment of that prophecy.

The statement may alert the oral reader to give careful attention to the masculine "standing where *he* ought not to be. . . . The effect of mismatched words that are heard is harder to ignore" (Kernaghan 2007, 254). If so, it could refer to the illegitimate investiture of Phanni as high priest.

■ **15-23** The images in this section speak of haste: Get out now while one can! But the conditions of flight from the city will be harsh: **pregnant women and nursing mothers** (Mark 13:17) will especially suffer, and more so if it happens to be **in winter** (v 18). The language fits well Josephus' account of the siege of Jerusalem. The Roman campaign was a relentless progress through the countryside to Jerusalem, but comparatively swift. Jesus' forewarning could apply to those in the city before the siege or to people in the countryside ahead of the advancing armies.

The section points to unprecedented suffering: **Those will be the days of distress unequaled from the beginning, when God created the world, until now—and never to be equaled again.** It is unlikely that this refers to some indeterminate future tribulation divorced from the fall of Jerusalem, as some think. The closest language is Dan 12:1b. Mark strategically changes Daniel's "until that day" (LXX) or "until that time" (Theodotion) to **until now.** Daniel's predicted future has arrived.

Nothing in Mark's language compels readers to think beyond the destruction of Jerusalem. Much of it is best explained in that framework. Stein points to its idiomatic and hyperbolic nature (2008, 606). This is not the end of all things but the focal point of the prophecy. Several other OT passages are also evoked (see Exod 9:18; 10:14).

As a prediction of Jerusalem's fate, it has a rich OT background. Wright draws attention to the bleak prophecies against Babylon (Isa 13:6, 9-11, 19; 14:4, 12-15; 34:3-4; Ezek 32:5-8). They all "tell a story with the same set of motifs: YHWH's victory over the great pagan city; the rescue and vindication of his true people who had been suffering under it and YHWH's proclamation as king" (1996, 356-57).

But here "Babylon is not the focus—Jerusalem and the temple are the real enemy of the people of God" (Wright 1996, 361). The application of these images to Jerusalem is startling. But it coheres with the gradual ramping up of the consequences of the temple leadership's failure to welcome Jesus and his followers.

The distress is so severe that the Lord limits it or else "no one would be saved" (NRSV; see Dan 12:1b). All is under the providential control of **the Lord,** who has not abandoned his people. **Lord** is ambiguous here, but as in Mark 1:3 the term that originally referred to Yahweh is applied to Jesus. The repetition of **for the sake of the elect, whom he has chosen** (*tous eklektous hous exelexato*) is emphatic. The foreshortening of the suffering is for the sake of Jesus' followers.

Mark has not used the term **the elect** previously. But he does not mean what it came to mean in later theological categories. He refers to the Twelve (see 3:13-15), the vanguard of the new people of God gathered around Jesus (3:32-25), and those who take up their crosses in following him (8:34-37).

The term **elect** has rich antecedents. The Qumran sect called themselves "the elect." That is, they considered themselves God's righteous remnant (Marcus 2009, 893). A similar sentiment is expressed here. The elect are the re-created people of God.

A warning against deceivers parallels the earlier warning in vv 5-6. Now these false messiahs are connected directly with the destruction of Jerusalem. Most scholars cite Menahem, son of Judas the Galilean, who had messianic pretensions, as the referent (see Josephus, *J.W.* 2.433-48). No doubt, as Kernaghan observes, there would be false prophets and messianic pretenders who would proclaim that "God would save Jerusalem in a fruitless attempt to rally the inhabitants of Judah to its defense" (2007, 261). But Jesus' warning here is specifically for the elect against these deceivers (France 2002, 529).

Despite **signs and miracles,** deception would likely fail (*ei dynaton, **if possible***). To avoid deception, the disciples should **keep their wits about them** because Jesus has told them **everything ahead of time.** The fate of Jerusalem has already been announced: The temple will be destroyed (see France 2002, 530) and Jesus' followers will experience persecution (so Stein 2008, 608). Collins argues that this summary statement shows that it is only up to this point—before the coming of the Son of Man—that humans have the opportunity to choose a course of action (2007, 614).

3. Watching: Be on Guard for the Coming of the Son of Man (13:24-37)

BEHIND THE TEXT

Most commentators are agreed to this point in the chapter. Now diver- gences increase. The majority argue that this section, which includes a cosmic cataclysm, the appearance of the Son of Man in glory (vv 24-27) and the gathering of the elect, points to the Parousia (see Collins 2007, 614-15; Stein 2008, 615; Marcus 2009, 906). In popular Christianity, these events follow closely on the heels of the great tribulation in vv 14-23, and occur in a short space of time (see Kernaghan 2007, 263).

A significant minority, however, maintain that this section is better understood in connection to the destruction of the temple (e.g., Wright 1996, 360-65; France 2002, 530-37; Kernaghan 2007, 262-70). The decision flows from three related points: First, this is coherent with the narrative to this point. Second, the cosmic language in vv 24b-25 seems to refer not to the coming of the Son of Man at the Parousia, but to be a metaphorical description of the catastrophic destruction of Jerusalem in A.D. 70 (Stein 2008, 612). Third, the image evoked in v 26 of the Son of Man evokes Dan 7:13 and echoes the language of Mark 8:38 and 9:1.

The majority take this passage as referring to the Parousia as the vindication of the Son of Man and the gathering of his followers, living and dead, from the nations. Evidence supporting this view includes: First, the NT does not understand the vindication of Jesus as the Son of Man as the destruction of Jerusalem but the resurrection. Second, outside the Gospels there is little attention to the fall of Jerusalem. Can this localized event bear the weight of cosmic fulfillment? Third, Matthew explicitly takes this to refer to the Parousia. Fourth, Mark's readers "would have been predisposed" to interpret 13:26 as referring to the Parousia, not the fall of Jerusalem (Stein 2008, 613-15).

But a sizable minority of commentators are not persuaded. France argues that the alternative view depends upon

> our willingness and ability to hear the prophetic imagery as it would have been heard by those in Jesus' day who were at home in OT prophetic language, rather than as it is "naturally" heard by Christian readers for whom the "coming of the Son of Man" has since gained a different connotation through its association with the idea of *parousia* (a word which is conspicuously absent from this discourse in Mark). (2002, 531)

The case is put forcibly by N. T. Wright. He argues that the coming of the Son of Man does not refer to the Parousia, because this does not fit the meaning in Dan 7:13 nor the teaching of Jesus. In that light, the Greek word *erchomenon*, translated **coming** in Mark 13:26, could equally mean *going*. In Dan 7 the one like a son of Man "comes *from* earth *to* heaven, vindicated after suffering" (Wright 1996, 361). Mark 13:26 employs "good first-century metaphorical language for two things: the defeat of the enemies of the true people of god [*sic*], and the vindication of the true people themselves" (1996, 362).

Wright anchors his reading of the cosmic phenomena securely on their widespread use in Scripture. There they do not refer to the end of the world (e.g., Isa 13:10; 34:8-13; Ezek 32:7-8). Rather, they are "part of the description of a complete realignment of the power structures of that era" (Kernaghan 2007, 264). "They are regular Jewish imagery for events that *bring the story of Israel to its appointed climax.* . . . [Thus,] the promises to Jerusalem, to Zion, are now transferred to Jesus and his people" (Wright 1996, 361-63).

This minority perspective makes much better sense of the narrative as a whole. It sees Mark 13 as a coherent part of Mark's theological explanation of God's purposes in Jesus' life and death. Furthermore, it maintains the narrative focus on the relentless progress to the cross.

IN THE TEXT

■ **24-25** Once the distress is over, cataclysmic events follow. **But** (*alla*) signals a change—to a new stage moving from "preliminaries, horrible as they may be, to the climax of Jesus' vision of what is to come" (France 2002, 532). The time frame is the same: **in those days, following that distress,** that is, the event discussed in v 19. Following this is a series of cosmic disturbances expressed in "a pastiche of OT eschatological prophecies" (Marcus 2009, 906). In contrast to the earlier (v 22) "false" signs, these are the true signs: **the sun will be**

darkened, and the moon will not give its light; the stars will fall from the sky, and the heavenly bodies will be shaken. But these must be understood in the light of their OT antecedents (see Isa 13:10; 24:21, 23; 34:4; Ezek 32:7-8; Joel 2:10, 31; 3:15; Amos 8:9).

The imagery of Isa 13:10 is similar in an oracle against Babylon: "For the stars of the heavens and their constellations will not give their light; the sun will be dark at its rising, and the moon will not shed its light" (NRSV). Actual celestial disasters are not the point: "It is not about the collapse of the universe" (France 2002, 533). It simply recognizes the fall of Babylon as "an earth-shattering event!" (Wright 1996, 354). What is shocking in Mark is not the cosmic metaphors well known from the prophets, but the startling reversal of images: Jerusalem has now taken Babylon's place.

Mark's cosmic language signals the end of the Jerusalem temple leadership and the fall of the temple, not the end of the world. These may seem minor in global perspective. But the destruction of Jerusalem and the second temple shaped the subsequent history of Judaism as surely as the Exodus had shaped Israel and the exile had shaped Second Temple Judaism. It also profoundly affected early Christianity and its relations with Judaism.

If this language refers to cosmic collapse—and few argue for a literal reading of apocalyptic images, it must point to something more earth-shattering than the end of 2TJ. Marcus suggests that it might portray a return of the created order to chaos or (his view) the victory of God and Jesus over Satan and the demons, symbolized by the demise of sun, moon, and stars: "one supernatural power displacing another" (2009, 908).

■ **26** Answers to two questions may further illuminate this passage: Who will see this and what will they see? There is no direct antecedent for the pronoun *they* implicit in the Greek verb *opsontai*, **they** will see. Options must be supplied from the context. Some suggest "the elect" (v 20). But the elect are not yet gathered (Kernaghan 2007, 266). Marcus suggests the personified powers in heaven (2009, 908). France opts for people in general (2002, 535 n. 18), as in the 2011 NIV: "people will see." But none of these is satisfactory.

The closest parallel in Mark is 14:62. There Jesus predicts that the high priest and his entourage "will see the Son of Man sitting at the right hand of the Mighty One and coming on the clouds of heaven." Similarly, 9:1 identifies those who will see "the kingdom" having "come with power" as the witnesses of the paradoxical revelation of God's power in the crucifixion of Jesus (see Brower 1980; Bird 2003).

In light of this, Hatina (2005) argues that it is the opponents of the Son of Man who will see the coming of the Son of Man in 13:26. Jesus' shift in pronouns is crucial to Hatina's interpretation. Most of ch 13 directly addresses the disciples in the second person (vv 5, 9, 23, 33, etc.). But in v 26, "they will see" (NRSV) is in the third person plural. "They" likely refers to his antagonists, the opponents Jesus addresses directly as "you" (*opsethe*) in 14:62—the chief priests, scribes, and elders. They will see this (Hatina 2006, 29-30; see also Kernaghan 2007, 266).

The second question is: What will **they** literally see when **they** metaphorically **see the Son of Man coming in clouds with great power and glory?** If **they** refers to "personified powers," they will see the descent of the Son of Man through their realm (so Marcus 2009, 908). If **they** is "the elect," they will experience "eschatological divine intervention" through the Son of Man, that is, the Parousia (see 1 Thess 4:13-18; Collins 2007, 614-15).

But if **they** refers to "Jesus' opponents," then they will witness the enthronement of the Son of Man as the embodiment of Israel and its destiny. God vindicates the Son of Man in the resurrection of Jesus (see Mark 8:31; 9:31; 10:34). Visual confirmation of the coming of the Son of Man in judgment will be the destruction of the temple. This judgment upon it has been predicted since 11:15-17. The judgment of the Son of Man's oppressors comes in two stages: first, the rending of the temple veil in 15:38; and second, its destruction predicted in 13:2 (see vv 23-24). Jesus' oppressors will see both.

The irony is that "the chief priests and the teachers of the law," who taunt Jesus on the cross, claim that if he will "come down . . . from the cross" and "save himself," they will "see and believe" (15:31-32). They do see, but what they see is darkness at noon and the temple veil torn in two from top to bottom. Both symbolize God's inaugurated judgment.

■ **27** When the Son of Man is vindicated, **he will send his angels** (*angeloi*, messengers; see 1:2) to **gather his elect** (*tous ekletous* [*autou*]). Whether or not **his** (*autou*) is original, the meaning within Mark's narrative is **his elect.**

The **elect** will be gathered **from the four winds, from the ends of the earth to the ends of the heavens.** This language echoes the gathering of the scattered exiles in Deut 30:4; Isa 11:11-12; 43:5-6; Ezek 39:27-28; Hos 11:10-11; and Zech 2:6. In the reading that sees Mark 13:26 as the Parousia, this appears to be an end-time event as in 1 Thess 4:13-18. When the Son of Man appears, the elect will be gathered to him.

But if this section continues to refer to the fall of Jerusalem, the gathering of the elect as the people of God from all the nations is the result of the universal proclamation of the gospel (Mark 13:10). The temple failed in its role as "a house of prayer for all nations" (11:17). Jesus ironically reverses the OT gathering to include the nations within the people of God rather than extracting ethnic Israel from the nations (France 2002, 536).

The **elect,** the new people of God, are comprised of all the followers of Jesus the Messiah, the Son of Man, without regard to their ethnicity. Kernaghan argues that these verses describe "three interrelated events: the destruction of the temple as an obstacle to God's purposes, the vindication of the Son of Man, and the sending of messengers to do what the temple did not accomplish" (2007, 268).

■ **28-29** Jesus now gives a **lesson from the fig tree** (see 11:12-14, 20): The horticultural signs of spring mean that **summer** [*theros*, **harvest;** so Marcus 2009, 910] **is near.** The lesson is clear even if the seasonal details are not.

Does *tauta*, **these things,** refer to the cosmic phenomena of vv 24-27 or to the whole series of events leading up to this statement in vv 14-25? Marcus argues for the series of events that alert readers the Parousia is near. If so, **all these things** in v 30 include the destruction of heaven and earth, which indicates that the Parousia has arrived (2009, 911). But France takes **these things** to refer to the events in vv 14-22. Then, **all these things** respond to the question of v 4 (2002, 538-40) about the fall of Jerusalem.

The translation of *engys estin*, **it is near** or "he is near" (NRSV), is pivotal in determining the sense of the passage. It is also difficult. Grammatically, either "he" or **it** is possible. If "he" is correct, it refers to the coming of the Son of Man in the Parousia. If **it** is correct, it refers directly to the fate of the temple.

> *Engys* is an adverb, not a masculine adjective, so that the phrase means "he/she/it is near" leaving the identification of the "he/she/it" to be determined by the context. And here the context leaves little room for doubt. The disciples had asked when the temple would be destroyed and how they would know the time. Jesus' reply . . . now homes in directly on the latter part of their questions: this is how you will know that it (the destruction of the temple, the subject of your question and of the whole discourse so far) is near; this is the *sēmeion* you asked for. (France 2002, 538)

If so, **it is near** is the better translation. It has the advantage of being able to accommodate both views (as Parousia or as fall of the temple). But "he is near" narrows the meaning to the Parousia of the Son of Man without grammatical warrant. An event **right at the door** is imminent.

■ **30-31** In contrast to the prophetic character of the previous sections, Jesus' solemn statement, **I tell you the truth** (*Amēn legō hymin*—used twelve times in Mark), is "emphatic and authoritative" (France 2002, 538). Jesus asserts: **this generation will certainly not pass away until all these things have happened.** The assurance is enforced by **certainly not** and an equally strong promise: **Heaven and earth will pass away, but my words will never pass away.** This challenges interpretations that do not focus on the destruction of the temple.

The text is clear: These words should govern interpretation of the entire chapter. **This generation** must refer to those who are listening to Jesus and, perhaps, Mark's first readers. They will not all die before **all these things have happened.** Those who argue that ch 13 as a whole (with the possible exception of vv 32-37) refers to the destruction of the temple have little difficulty with this statement. Those, however, who read this as about the Parousia have considerable explaining to do (France 2002, 501-2).

If ch 13 is about the Parousia, and **this generation** refers to Jesus' generation, one explanation is that Jesus and Mark are wrong. The Parousia has not happened. For some readers, this is not a problem. The text simply shows that Jesus' (and Mark's) end-time prediction proved to be mistaken.

Interpreters anxious to protect Jesus and Mark from error offer a variety of ingenious explanations. Some suggest that **generation** refers to the Jewish people (reading *genea* as if it were *genos*, **race**). Others think it refers to Christians as a generation who will see the fulfillment of all the prophecies. Others think of the human race as a whole, with the fulfillment of all occurring before the destruction of the earth. Some dispensational premillennial interpreters speculate that it applies to those who were alive when the modern secular state of Israel was created in 1948.

None of these is persuasive. "There is no need to seek some esoteric interpretation of this expression, once we realize that the event being referred to by 'these things' and 'all these things' in 13:29-30 is the same as 'these things' and 'all these things' in 13:4—Jesus's prediction of the destruction of Jerusalem in 13:2" (Stein 2008, 619; but see Collins 2007, 616).

This approach reads this text in line with its intratexts in 8:38; 9:1; 13:26; 14:62; 15:32 (→). The cumulative evidence is that **this generation** refers to those living as Jesus speaks; they are those who will see the coming of the Son of Man in glory. In each of these texts, the shadow of the crucifixion is very near to hand. Throughout Mark the irony is that Jesus is most clearly revealed as Son of God on the cross (→ 15:38).

■ **32** A change occurs between vv 31 and 32. Note the contrast between **no one knows** in v 32 and the "resounding certainty" of v 31 (France 2002, 541). Many scholars who read 13:1-31 as referring to the fall of Jerusalem, therefore, interpret v 32 as a reference to the Parousia.

Stein thinks vv 24-27 and 32-27 refer to the Parousia (2008, 621). But if that is so, the certainty of Jesus about the events leading up to it in vv 24-27 is seriously qualified by this statement. The explanation is usually that "Jesus and Mark (according to this view) know in which generation the Son of Man will return; the only thing they do not know is the exact day and hour [on which] it will occur" (Geddert 2001, 318).

But for the minority of interpreters who see all of ch 13 connected to the fall of Jerusalem, the saying is uncomplicated. The Markan Jesus has given a prospectus about the path to the fall of Jerusalem. Jerusalem's fate is certain and imminent. But Jesus is unable to state exactly when it will occur.

Determining which perspective is better here is difficult. The opening words, *Peri de tēs hēmeras ekeinēs*, give the impression of a new topic: **Now concerning** that day. The discussion is about **that day,** possibly an allusion to Dan 12:1. The phrase is certainly in the same semantic field as "the day of the Lord." **That day** occurs in Mark 2:20 where it alludes to the grim day of crucifixion. Its future orientation is clear. The Parousia is largely outside Mark's concern. But Jesus' followers clearly anticipated it with great hope (Kernaghan 2007, 273).

However, if ch 13 is focused exclusively on the temple, it simply means that Jesus does not know the exact timing of the end of the temple. No one apart from God **the Father** knows the timing of whatever event is being described. This includes **the Son.**

This verse has given comfort to Arians and caused consternation for the orthodox. The problem might have been noted rather early since Luke 21:29-36 omits it. By the fourth century a variety of explanations attempted to avoid the view that Jesus was merely human or the Son subordinate to the Father. Mark uses this absolute sense of the Son only here (without the qualification "of God"). And, ironically, here it is juxtaposed to the statement about the Son's lack of knowledge. Mark seems oblivious to the difficulties the statement might cause later christological formulations (→ Mark 1:5). But, christologically sound answers are near to hand—primarily in the kind of understanding Paul has of the incarnation (see Phil 2:5-11).

Mark's interest lies elsewhere: Human calculations about the future are futile. Such knowledge is restricted to **the Father.** This saying opposes all efforts to calculate "the date of the end and even . . . the impulse to do so." It is unclear whether Mark responded to his audience's "impulse" or merely "attempts to prevent it from arising" (Collins 2007, 617).

■ **33-37** The responsibility of disciples is to **Watch out** [*blepete*]! (→ Mark 8:15; 12:38; 13:5, 9—all referring to the opposition they will receive from the religious establishment; → 13:23). The asyndeton—here, two imperatives unconnected with a conjunction—emphasizes both: **Watch out! Keep alert!**

The reason for this call to vigilance is that calculations are futile and self-deceptive: Disciples **do not know when that time** [*kairos*] **will come.** The time may refer to the Parousia (so most scholars). It could refer to the coming of the kingdom as in 1:15, which is how Luke 21:31, 34 reads it. They are, therefore, urged to keep their eyes open to understand coming events already manifest in their midst. Jesus refers to the startlingly counterintuitive coming of "the kingdom of God" (→ Mark 9:1) in the crucifixion, which culminates in an empty tomb and the destruction of the temple.

Jesus illustrates by a simile: **It's like a man going away: He leaves his house and *gives* his servants *authority,* each with *an* assigned task, and tells**

the one at the door to keep watch. The simile ends without an explicit comparison. But the implication is clear. The disciples are to keep awake as well, because they **do not know when the *lord* of the house will come**. A state of constant alertness is onerous—this doorkeeper is to be awake at all hours of the night.

The owner of the house may return at any time, but only the night watches are noted: **evening, or at midnight, or when the rooster crows, or at dawn**. The demand is formidable—constant alertness. But the mention of the night watches and the statement, **If he comes suddenly, do not let him find you sleeping,** achieves a subtle shift.

Just a few verses later—in 14:34, 37, and 41—Jesus will invite Peter, James, and John to watch and pray with him in Gethsemane. He comes three times and finds them asleep. Here the Markan Jesus speaks, first to the disciples, then to his wider audience of readers: **What I say to you, I say to everyone: "Watch!"** (13:37).

Within the narrative, this statement is directed to the disciples and this generation. However, Mark also uses it as a message to all Christian readers—the unpredictability of the end, first in terms of the fall of Jerusalem, and ultimately in terms of the consummation of all things in the final triumph of God.

FROM THE TEXT

13:24-37 Mark 13 has been used to support an incredible range of eschatological theories. Many of them extract the chapter from its Markan context. But the chapter makes sense when read as an integral and deliberately connected part of Mark's narrative. It is part of the continued escalation of conflict between Jesus and the Jerusalem elite. They have been arrayed against Jesus one after another in ch 12. Now Jesus predicts the sad consequence of their rejection of his teaching: the destruction of the temple and the fall of Jerusalem. There are several sound reasons for adopting this view.

First, it is relatively simple. It does not depend upon theories explaining its origin as a pre-Markan independent tradition. It does not require exegetical gymnastics to explain (away) Jesus' solemn assertion in 13:30-32. Rather, ch 13 smoothly connects ch 12 to ch 14. Mark brackets it between two stories of generous women (12:42-44; 14:3-9), employing his typical intercalation technique. The first features sacrificial giving to a doomed institution; the second, giving to Jesus.

Second, it addresses the question with which it begins, namely, the fate of the temple (13:2). The chapter opens with Jesus addressing the disciples in response to their question; it closes with a challenge to them, extended to all. The temple suffers because the religious authorities lead the people astray. By their actions they have rendered the temple obsolete. It will soon no longer be the dwelling place of God (see 15:38). Rather, the dwelling of God among his re-created people will be centered on Jesus, the Holy One of God, and those gathered around him. Jesus will shortly inaugurate the new covenant in his blood (14:24).

Does this mean that ch 13 has nothing to say to readers now about the future? Far from it. Its message is as relevant now as it was in the first century.

First, this chapter is a call to faithfulness to God and confidence in the good news even in the face of appalling circumstances. It calls Christians to hold their nerve despite false leaders on the one hand and unprecedented suffering on the other. Contemporary Western Christians know something of the former; they know little of the latter. But their brothers and sisters in other parts of the world know all too well that faithfulness to Christ and hope in God's future is often met with persecution and hostility. This chapter encourages Christians whatever the challenge to faithfulness. Jesus assures us that the Spirit will be with us however we are betrayed (v 11).

Second, human predictions of the future—including the time and the date of the consummation of all things—are futile. The dampening of speculation is important both then and now. This chapter warns against "the sort of superficial impressions of 'fulfilment' which have been the bane of students of apocalyptic and eschatological literature ever since" (France 2002, 508). The history of Christianity is littered with the failed predictions of those who claim to be able to unlock the mystery of Mark 13 and similar passages, read the signs of the times, and forecast the return of Christ. Scripture repeatedly and explicitly warns against this: "It is not for you to know the times or dates the Father has set by his own authority" (Acts 1:7).

This chapter is a reminder that, despite appearances to the contrary (oppression and suffering, corrupt religious leaders, false prophets, and false messiahs), the goal and future of God's creation is within his control. His ultimate good purposes will triumph. Opposition to God's reign may be fierce. But his good purposes will be accomplished. That end is never in doubt.

VII. THE PASSION NARRATIVE: MARK 14:1—15:47

A century ago the Gospels were characterized as Passion Narratives with extended introductions. That is certainly wrong—the narrative to this point is essential for understanding the good news (1:1, 15)—yet without these three chapters there would be no good news. Indeed, the shadow of the Passion Narrative has lain over the whole narrative. The allusions to "that day" (2:20), the plots against Jesus almost from the start (3:6), and his explicit predictions of suffering and death (8:31; 9:31; 10:33) have all driven the story forward to this point.

There has been an inevitability about this process. First, in Mark's view, all of this is according to the ultimate purposes of God as set out in Scripture and understood by Jesus. Mark makes this an explicit part of his story. Second, hostility between Jesus and the Jerusalem authorities has escalated. His entry into Jerusalem and his prophetic representative action in the temple are followed by sustained teaching in which Jesus set out his uncompromising opposition to the way the religious authorities are leading God's people.

345

The exploitation of the latent tension between the ruling elite and the ordinary people through his denunciation of the abuse of the temple system has ended all dialogue with the leaders. The consequence, set out in stark terms, is that "Not one stone [of the temple] will be left on another" (13:2). As France comments, "All this is now inevitable. It is guaranteed by the indestructible word of Jesus. Within the generation it will all have taken place" (2002, 547). If the entry into Jerusalem was the beginning of the end, the Passion Narrative and ch 13 mark the end of the beginning (see Brower 1997, 125-43).

The Passion Narratives in all four Gospels are similar but not identical. Scholars discussing the literary relationship between them have attempted to answer three questions. First, if Mark's Gospel is first, was there a pre-Markan Passion Narrative that has been used by Mark? And what was the source of this tradition? Second, did the other three Gospels use Mark or the pre-Markan tradition or independent sources? The literary relationship between them becomes especially interesting in this section. Matthew stands closest to Mark, but there are significant variations. John may also have connections with Mark, but the differences are greater than in the case of Matthew. Luke seems to be quite different in detail from the other three.

Third, how can one account for the historical divergences between the accounts? This may well be the most complex of the issues, complicated by presuppositions surrounding Scripture.

Each of these questions is of great interest in its own right. But this commentary is concerned primarily with Mark itself rather than the development of the tradition. Extensive treatments of each of these questions are readily available (see Collins 2007, 621-38; Evans 2001).

A. From Bethany to Arrest (14:1-52)

1. The Meal at Bethany (14:1-11)

BEHIND THE TEXT

Mark reports Jesus making one visit to Jerusalem; and it occurs at Passover. This is crucial for Mark. The historical connection between Jesus' death and this feast has always been granted, so this is at least a historical note. But this dating evokes much more.

Passover (Pesach) is mandated in Scripture (Num 9:2-14) as the annual celebration in the month of Abib/Nisan of God's deliverance of Israel from Egypt (Exod 11:1—13:22). Ideally, it was one of three feasts celebrated in Jerusalem (Deut 16:1-8). Hence, during Passover the city's population swelled to many times its normal size of about 60,000 (see Reinhardt 1987, 263) to perhaps half a million (Marcus 2009, 939). But Jeremias' estimate of under 200,000 may be more realistic (France 2002, 548).

Passover was a time of great business opportunity—the thousands of lambs slaughtered demanded a huge supply from the surrounding countryside. The sacrifice must have required thousands of priests collecting the blood of about 12,000 lambs on the day of preparation. The logistics are difficult to conceive: How could so many lambs be slaughtered within the temple confines at the appropriate time on 14 Nisan? Speculation is rife; evidence, scarce. Housing for pilgrims was daunting as well. Hence, the surrounding territory, including Bethany and the Mount of Olives, was officially designated as "Jerusalem" for the Passover season.

Passover and Unleavened Bread had been combined into a single feast well before this period. Both celebrated the exodus, Israel's founding story, and lent themselves to nationalist fervor. During the Roman occupation, the combined feast was a particularly potent flashpoint, since it celebrated liberation from oppressors. In fact, Josephus (*Ant.* 20.5.3) reports an incident at Passover in A.D. 50 in which more than 20,000 died attempting to escape the Roman soldiers.

All four Gospels have stories of Jesus being anointed by a woman (compare Matt 26:6-13; Luke 7:36-50; John 12:1-8). Matthew's account probably abbreviates Mark's. Luke's is significantly different in substance and setting. Matthew, Mark, and John set the story at Passover and connect the anointing with Jesus' burial. There are differences:

	Mark 14	John 12
Time before Passover	two days (v 1)	"Six days" (v 1)
Host	Simon the Leper (v 3)	"Lazarus" (vv 1, 2)
Woman	Anonymous woman (v 3)	"Mary" (v 3)
Anointed	Jesus' head (v 3)	"Jesus' feet" (v 3)

Most scholars argue that there are two separate traditions and probably separate incidents that have become closer in transmission (see France 2002, 550; Collins 2007, 640; Stein 2008, 630; Marcus 2009, 938) rather than three separate traditions.

The Last Supper and Passover

The problems surrounding the time and character of the Last Supper are complex. Data in the Gospels is insufficient to be definitive and difficult to co-ordinate. All four Gospels agree that Jesus was crucified on the day before the Sabbath, that is, between sunset on Thursday and on Friday. Beyond that, the issues become complicated. Was Jesus crucified on Passover, as implied (though not stated) by the Synoptics, or on the day of preparation, when the lambs were slaughtered, as stated by John? And was the Last Supper a Passover celebration or a special pre-Passover meal? Several factors need to be considered (see Brown 1994, 1350-78; Stein 2008, 640-43):

First, Jews in the 2TP disputed the proper calendar. Some sectarian groups (Qumran, the Essenes, and the author of *Jubilees*) used the solar calendar with intercalation to coordinate it with the lunar calendar. This dispute might explain why Qumran covenanters separated from other Jews who followed a lunar cycle (VanderKam 1998, 97-101). The beginning of Nisan depended upon the sighting of the new moon; Passover was celebrated at full moon.

Second, how were hours counted, from sunrise or from midnight? Both possibilities existed within 2TJ. Countless ingenious explanations attempt to resolve the questions. They can be placed into three groups: (1) Both the Synoptics and John are historically correct. They can be harmonized (with great difficulty) or the Last Supper was not a normal Passover meal (Marshall 1980, 75; Wright 1996, 554-56). (2) One account is more historically accurate than the other: Most scholars prefer John's chronology. (3) Neither is historically correct (Brown 1994, 1369).

Wright revives an older view that the Last Supper was an irregular Passover celebration: "The meal in question was *some kind of* Passover meal," but probably not on the officially appointed day (Wright 1996, 555; see Bruce 1969, 191-92). This coheres at the narrative level: Mark considers it a Passover meal. The solution is historically plausible for calendric and practical reasons.

This meal was almost certainly without a lamb. "That would be no bar to treating the meal as a proper Passover, since it was after all what happened in the Diaspora (and, of course, what was to happen throughout the Jewish world after AD 70)" (Wright 1996, 556). It seems best to assume "that Jesus held a Passover meal earlier than the official Jewish date and that he was able to do so as the result of calendar differences among the Jews" (Marshall 1980, 75). But "no truly satisfactory explanation has come forth" (Stein 2008, 642).

The second story of an extravagant woman brackets Jesus' teaching on the destruction of the temple (12:38-42; 14:3-9). The first gives all her living to the temple, which is doomed; this one anoints Jesus for his death. Both will be "destroyed." The temple will be razed; Jesus, raised to become the center of the new people of God.

IN THE TEXT

■ **1-2** The setting of the Passion Narrative during **the Passover and the Feast of Unleavened Bread** gives the story a significant and deliberate context. "It is hard to imagine a greater contrast than the one between the prophecy Jesus had just delivered about the destruction of Jerusalem and the nationalistic dreams associated with the Feast of Unleavened Bread" (Kernaghan 2007, 275). This compressed story can be understood properly only in the context of Passover.

348

By continuing to call attention to the opposition to Jesus, Mark compels us to understand this week against the background of Roman oppression and the political collaboration of religious leaders who have betrayed their people. This bleak background prepares us to expect a new exodus and deliverance.

Jesus' death and resurrection are not only saving events but also "eschatological events" (Marcus 2009, 939). His entry to Jerusalem (ch 11), the growing conflict with the religious leaders (ch 12), the inevitable demise of the temple, and his instructions to watch (ch 13) belong in this end-times framework.

Now, the time is **only two days away** (*meta duo hēmeras*). The Jewish reckoning of days was from sunset to sunset (1800 to 1800 or 6:00 P.M. to 6:00 P.M.). Mark's phrase is ambiguous. If *after two days* is understood inclusively, it refers to 13 Nisan. If understood exclusively, it is 12 Nisan (Stein 2008, 631-32).

Mark gives a short statement about the opposition to Jesus. From this point forward, the **chief priests** figure in every description of those arrayed against Jesus. They represent the religious leadership as a whole, not the Jews in general. The Pharisees disappear from the narrative after 12:13.

The opposition to Jesus has become murderous. Not only do they wish **to arrest Jesus** and keep him quiet during the festival, but they want to **kill him.** He is a threat to their power and risks damaging their collaboration with the Romans. While Jesus has repeatedly predicted his death, this is the first time Mark explicitly identifies their intent to **kill** him.

Their only misgiving about their plot is not to carry it out **during the Feast** lest **the people . . . riot.** The people are looking for deliverance, and the Romans would hold the leaders accountable for any disturbance centered on a messianic pretender. They know, therefore, that it would have to be done *by stealth* (*en dolō*). This already hints at the dubious legality of their actions. There is also a possible link to Ps 10:7-8. Such righteous-sufferer psalms are a key intertextual background for the whole Passion Narrative.

The Righteous-Sufferer Psalms and the Markan Passion Narrative

From this first quiet echo in Mark 14:1 to the crescendo in the crucifixion scene itself in 15:40, events in Mark's Passion Narrative are illuminated by Psalms of the righteous sufferer. These echoes and citations may come to Mark largely from his sources, but he uses and enhances their application to the passion of Jesus. Marcus (1993, 174) offers this table of possible allusions:

Mark		Psalms
14:1	by cunning, to kill	10:7-8
14:18	the one eating with me	41:9

14:34	very sad	42:5, 11; 43:5
14:41	delivered to the hands of sinners	140:8
14:55	sought to put him to death	37:32
14:57	false witnesses rising up	27:12; 35:11
14:61; 15:4-5	silence before accusers	35:13-15
15:24	division of garments	22:18
15:29	mockery, head shaking	22:7
15:30-31	Save yourself!	22:8
15:32	reviling	22:6
15:34	cry of dereliction	22:1
15:36	gave him vinegar to drink	69:21
15:40	looking on at a distance	38:11

It is clear from this table that Ps 22 is particularly important for the crucifixion scene. Its direct citation in 15:34 evokes other echoes of the psalm. It also suggests that Mark's text cannot be properly treated in isolation from its pattern in this psalm in which vindication is the conclusion. In the late 2TP, the pattern of suffering and eschatological vindication has already been a well-established development of the righteous sufferer theme (Marcus 1993, 177-82; see Brower 1978). Richard Hays states,

> The distinctive hermeneutical move of early Christianity was to see the sufferings of Israel in these psalms (or . . . the sufferings of the kings who represent Israel) as having been accomplished in an eschatologically definitive way by Jesus on the cross, *and* to see the vindication of Israel accomplished proleptically in his resurrection. (2005, 111)

That pattern is the same in Mark's Passion Narrative.

■ **3** The opening bracket (vv 1-2) concluding with Judas' offer (vv 10-11) is typical Markan style. He surrounds the anointing story (vv 3-9), heightening the tension within the narrative. The story within the brackets is set in **Bethany,** about three kilometers (two miles) east of Jerusalem. But it was probably considered to be within "greater Jerusalem" for the purposes of Passover. Jesus is **reclining at the table,** standard posture for formal meals in the Gospels.

Jesus has already demonstrated his boundary-challenging behavior and does so again: He is **in the home of . . . Simon the Leper.** Simon probably did not have leprosy at the time of the event. **Simon** was such a common name that **the Leper** would distinguish him from other Simons. But the appellation reminds people of his previous condition of impurity. Speculation about his identity ranges from someone healed by Jesus, the father of Mary, Martha, and Lazarus, or someone who later contracted leprosy. Lepers may have been housed east of Jerusalem (see 11QT[a] 46:17-18, cited in Evans 2001, 359).

Then an anonymous **woman came** into the room. The presence of an unattached woman who anoints Jesus with expensive perfume "increases the hint of scandal" and "culpable luxury" (Marcus 2009, 933, 940). In contrast to the widow of 12:42-44, this woman is apparently wealthy. She has **an alabaster jar,** a container made of alabaster stone, usually with a long neck and a stopper of some sort (Marcus 2009, 934). It contained **very expensive perfume, made of pure nard.** *Myron nardou pistikēs* is difficult to translate. *Myron* means ointment; so it probably refers to an oil-based perfume. A word-for-word translation would be *ointment of nard faithful.* **Nard** is derived from spikenard, which originates in India. Instead of removing the stopper and pouring a few drops, **She broke the** neck of the **jar and poured** all of **the perfume on** Jesus' **head.**

■ **4-9** This extravagance causes consternation among **some of those present** (identified in Matt 26:8 as "the disciples" and in John 12:4 as "Judas Iscariot"): **Why this waste?** *Apōleia,* **waste,** normally means *destruction* or *death.* This usage may foreshadow the link between **perfume** and Jesus' death in Mark 14:8 (Marcus 2009, 935).

On the eve of Passover, **the poor** were remembered with alms. So the expressed concern might have been topical. This was worth **more than a year's wages** of a laborer—three hundred denarii (→ 6:37, where the disciples estimated that it would require two hundred denarii to feed five thousand). So the onlookers **rebuked her harshly,** reacting much like the scribes did to Jesus in 2:6-7 (Marcus 2009, 935).

Jesus responds, **She has done a *good work*** (*kalon ergon*). This might be interpreted as an act of kindness, but Jesus explains further: **The poor you will always have with you, and you can help them any time you want.** The first part of this statement might appear to be dismissive of the poor. But it actually echoes Deut 15:11, which appears within the regulations governing the Year of Jubilee. Read in that context, it offers no comfort to those who think social justice is not part of the gospel of the kingdom.

Deuteronomy continues: "I therefore command you, 'Open your hand to the poor and needy neighbor in your land'" (NRSV). Far from being dismissive, the care for the poor is to be part of Israel's very fabric: "Remember that you were slaves in Egypt and the LORD your God redeemed you. That is why I give you this command today" (Deut 15:15). In Mark, however, the explanation is different:

First, the emphasis on **the poor** becomes important throughout the Passion Narrative as Jesus' oppression and death are explained in terms of the righteous-sufferer psalms. In these psalms the righteous sufferer is often described as **the poor** one. In Mark 15:34, Jesus, the poor one par excellence goes to his death as the righteous sufferer of the psalms, with the words of Ps 22:2 on his lips.

14:3-9

Second, two other passages (Mark 10:21; 12:42-43) also show Jesus' concern for the poor. This statement does not diminish the expectation of care for the poor. But once a year at Passover scarcely counts as care for the poor. For the moment, this unnamed woman has ministered to Jesus. His reminder, **But you will not always have me,** refocuses the passage on Jesus rather than the woman. **She did what she could,** and in doing so anticipated and participated in the conclusion to the messianic story: She prepared Jesus' body **for** his **burial.**

Overtones of anointing the Messiah—oily ointment on the head—are possibly present (see Evans 2001, 361; Marcus 2009, 936). Lightfoot observes that Mark "puts into his readers' hands, as it were, the means whereby they may best approach and understand the narrative which follows. The *passion is the supreme act* of the Messiah, and conversely the Messiahship of Jesus is the explanation of the passion" (Lightfoot 1935, 141, my emphasis). If so, this messianic anointing is full of irony. Again Mark reinterprets messiahship in terms of suffering (→ 8:31). Jesus reigns from the cross, and he is never more Messiah than when he does not come down from the cross (15:28-32).

No wonder, then, that **wherever the gospel is preached throughout the world, what she has done will also be told, in memory of her.** This anonymous woman plays a crucial role in the passion story. God's good news will prevail, and her story will be told. God remembers her name, even if we are never told it. Jesus knows what is going on in these events and exactly where he is headed. He also knows that the outcome will transcend his burial (see 14:28).

The good news throughout the world is also poignant within this context of nationalistic fervor. To people who expected "the kingdom of God would see the Jewish people elevated to a position of supremacy over the nations, that would have been a profoundly disturbing thought" (Kernaghan 2007, 280).

■ **10-11** Meanwhile, in contrast to the woman who *came in* (*ēlthen*, v 3), **Judas Iscariot . . . went out** (*apēlthen*). He, too, is essential to the story (→ 14:21). He has already been identified in 3:19 as **one of the Twelve** selected to be with Jesus and on his mission. But Mark is not particularly interested in Judas per se, unlike the other Gospels. Judas will soon become the focus of the betrayal of Jesus and has the sobriquet of *betrayer* (Luke 6:16). This developing Judas tradition reaches its full flowering in grotesque medieval portrayals (see Klassen 1996, 1-10). In Mark, except for this episode (see also 14:43-45), Judas is a minor character. He has been with Jesus almost from the beginning and has exercised the authority given by Jesus.

Now, **Judas** leaves Jesus for **the chief priests to betray** [*paradoi*] **Jesus to them.** Mark makes no attempt to assign a motive, nor does he attribute this to Satan's influence. Perhaps, he takes seriously that Judas is not alone in abandoning Jesus. Rather, he is part of the wider notion that the delivering up of Jesus nonetheless fulfills the purposes of God (→ 1:14; 8:31; 9:31; 10:33).

Since the chief priests were wishing to seize and kill Jesus by stealth (14:1), they are **delighted to hear this.** This is the breakthrough about which they could only dream. In addition to providing information about Jesus' whereabouts and identity on the night of betrayal, Judas may well have given insider information about Jesus' teaching (France 2002, 557). That he is given money "reduces Judas, whatever his motive may have been, to the indignity of a paid informer" (France 2002, 558).

FROM THE TEXT

The Passion Narrative now enters its final phase. Mark deliberately encloses the story of Jesus' anointing between the desires of the religious leaders to see Jesus killed before Passover and the gift of betrayal Judas gives them. These two texts read together are powerful. The unnamed woman who comes to Jesus is contrasted to the named disciple who goes out and betrays Jesus. She participates in his death by anointing him, perhaps as the coming Messiah, before his burial. Judas participates in Jesus' death by collaborating with Jesus' enemies. The haunting words of Jesus are coming true: "Brother will betray brother to death" (13:12; → 3:31-35).

The anointing story is all too often remembered solely for the citation from Deut 15:11—"the poor you have with you always." Few verses have suffered worse at the hands of interpreters. Some read them as comfort to the comfortable and powerful: They need not be overly concerned about poverty and the poor. The underclass of society will always be with us. An offering for the poor at major festivals will suffice. More subtly, the verse is sometimes taken to mean that the gospel is only about the salvation of souls, not about the inequities of society. Any attempt to critique the systemic evil of society that requires an underclass is viewed as outside the gospel.

This distortion runs completely counter to the comprehensive character of the good news of the kingdom announced in Mark. Jesus has been re-creating Israel to be Israel as God intended it should have been. The Twelve are to be the vanguard of this re-created holy people. The marginalized are brought to the center; the sick and the demoniacs are healed; the excluded sit at table with Jesus. Jesus' welcome of the marginalized is the paradigm of what the people of God are to be like. He demonstrates the unequivocal welcome of God to all his lost creation. Any casual dismissal of care for the marginalized simply does not express the depth of transformation and the breadth of good news that is the message of the kingdom.

The lingering question, however, is this: What does Jesus' death have to do with the poor? Kernaghan (2007, 281-82) draws two helpful conclusions:

First, "the death of the Son of God at the hands of the ruling elite in Jerusalem exposed the bankruptcy of social hierarchies." Second, it "implies the leveling of all human structures" because Jesus' conception of the kingdom is "in stark contrast to any system of privilege." This "is a new picture of society with a broadened view of the family and a radically restructured relationship between people and property." In short, Jesus' death condemns the old order and creates a new one in this age (see Mark 10:29-31).

2. Preparing for the Last Supper (14:12-16)

IN THE TEXT

The days leading up to Passover are over, according to Mark's scheme. From here to 15:47, the narrative flows as one connected and compressed sequence in which the whole story comes to focus. This story (14:12-16) has clear parallels to 11:1-10, in which Jesus sends his disciples to get a colt for him to ride into Jerusalem.

■ **12** Mark's time notation confuses modern readers, largely because we are uncertain about how Mark reckons the time (→ 14:1-11 BEHIND THE TEXT). But Mark's point is clear: The feast has begun. Furthermore, the meal that Jesus will celebrate with his disciples is to be understood in connection with Passover. Whatever the precise historical details, this connection occurs before Mark early in the Christian tradition (see 1 Cor 5:7).

This is the day *when they were slaughtering* the **Passover lamb.** If Jewish customs were being followed, Jesus would be in the temple. As the "head" of his family, he "would have slit the animal's throat, its blood would have been drained into a silver or gold basin held by a priest, and the priest would have taken the basin to the altar where he would have sprinkled the blood at the base of the altar" (Evans 2001, 373).

If this is so, Jesus' command to the disciples, **Go into the city,** makes little sense. This suggests that he is not in the city at this time. Most of the city would have been west of the Temple Mount. But it is coherent with the assumption that Jesus' feast was without a lamb, an irregular Passover meal (→ Mark 14:1-11 sidebar, "The Last Supper and Passover").

Although **Jesus' disciples** take the initiative in asking where they should **make preparations for . . . the Passover** meal and are involved in all that takes place, the focus is on Jesus. This preparation is *so that* you [singular] *might* **eat the Passover.** This Passover meal together will not only be a feast of contemporary remembrance of the exodus, however important that would be. It would be a significant reinterpretation of the whole exodus event in light of Jesus' broken body and his poured out new covenant blood.

■ **13-16** This next section has remarkable parallels to 11:1-6. Jesus sends **two of his disciples** (→ 11:1). As there, he gives explicit details as to what they will see and what they should do. All happens as predicted. They are to **go into the city** where they meet **a man carrying a jar of water.** Most scholars consider this unusual (but see Marcus 2009, 945). Perhaps the man was from a celibate Essene community in Jerusalem, where there were no women to fulfill this stereotypical gender role (see Capper 1995, 350 n. 98). But this tantalizing speculation is inferential rather than evidential.

The note that they will meet him may imply a previous arrangement for a clandestine rendezvous. But the following statement raises a question about that. They are to **follow him** to **whatever house he enters** (*hopou ean eiselthē*), language that suggests this is not a previously arranged location. They are to ask a question on behalf of **The Teacher** (*ho didaskalos*, used twelve times in Mark referring to Jesus; contrast 11:3, in which "the Lord" is used).

The question, **Where is my guest room . . . ?** may indicate this is not Jesus' first journey to Jerusalem (e.g., France 2002, 565). If he is aware of the plot to kill him, he may want a private place **where** he, as the leader of this "family," **may eat the Passover with** his **disciples.** Mark does not indicate how many participate. It certainly includes the Twelve, maybe more, even women and children (Evans 2001, 574).

The place where they are going will be **a large** [*mega*] **upper room.** Some houses would have two stories, with the ground floor used for a variety of domestic purposes including water storage (see Marcus 2009, 946). The second story would be the living space, reached by an indoor ladder or outdoor staircase. Only wealthier households would have a large guest room. This one is **furnished and ready.** That is, the room was already prepared for a meal: "the rugs, carpets, cushions, and couches for reclining were arranged, and short tables for the food were set up. All that was lacking was the food itself, and this the disciples were to prepare" (Stein 2008, 647).

Everything turned out **just as Jesus had told them.** The same questions arise here as in 11:1-6: Did these events occur because of Jesus' prearrangement, or not? This would be both prudent and plausible: Jesus knows he is a wanted man. He also wants to celebrate the Passover (see Luke 22:15); so he needs a safe house. Opportunities for this to be carried out in the gaps of Mark's narrative are conceivable, even if Jesus makes only one trip to Jerusalem. But if this is so, it is not Mark's point. Once again, Mark uses this story to show that Jesus is completely in control of the situation: All of this is occurring according to the purposes of God.

So they prepared the Passover. The meal would include "the Passover lamb (slaughtered, skinned, cleaned, and roasted over a fire), unleavened bread, a bowl of salt water, a bowl of bitter herbs, a fruit puree or haroseth, and enough wine for each participant to drink four cups in celebration of

God's fourfold blessing in Exod. 6:6-7" (Stein 2008, 647; but → 14:1-11 sidebar, "The Last Supper and Passover").

3. The Last Supper (14:17-25)

a. Betrayal Predicted (14:17-21)

BEHIND THE TEXT

All four Gospels include the Last Supper. John's is in the lengthy upper room discourse (chs 13—17), but without the Passover theme and the so-called words of institution at the heart of the Synoptic accounts.

The notion of a Suffering Messiah, resisted by Peter when first predicted (8:32), is now anticipated with Jesus' prophetic-representative action at the table. Jesus thereby participates in his own death. The use of scriptural citations, allusions, and echoes increases from this point until the end of the narrative in 16:8. A whole constellation of OT suffering figures is now related to Jesus' passion. In doing so, Mark continues to transpose Israel's story and key symbols in light of Jesus' story.

The central theme, the righteous sufferer of the Psalms, is the overall metaphorical figure. The theme is introduced in the story of the betrayer's identification. But to that figure is grafted the righteous poor, the servant of Yahweh from Isa 40—55, and the smitten shepherd of Zech 9—13. All of these fill out the notion of the Son of Man's suffering and vindication according to the Scriptures. By this means, Mark makes explicit the theme of the rejected Righteous One that has been implicit from the movement of the scribes away from Jesus in ch 2, and made clear in the reference to the rejected stone in 12:10-11 (so Collins 2007, 648-49).

The first part of the story is the bleak characterization of Jesus' betrayal. The second part is the reconstitution of the covenant community. This renewed and new community is now centered on Jesus, the Holy One of God. Thus, he is both the covenant maker and the covenant itself for his followers who participate in the new covenant. All this occurs at Passover, the celebration of the foundational event of Israel as a covenant people. Now, the foundation event becomes the broken body and poured out blood of the new covenant maker. The new covenant people of God celebrate their participation in the new covenant community through this reenactment at the Lord's Table.

IN THE TEXT

■ **17-21** The first sign that Mark considers this a Passover meal is its timing: **When evening came.** Despite the importance of the Passover context, a great deal more attention is given to the betrayal, the broken bread, and shared cup than the Seder itself. **Evening** could also have a symbolic significance, since the whole betrayal and abandonment sequence occurs at night: "the cosmic darkness of the time of eschatological trial is looming" (Marcus 2009, 953). During this festive and formal meal—**reclining at the table** was to celebrate the leisure of liberty, Jesus made a jarring and solemn announcement (*amēn legō hymin*) to **the Twelve** . . . "**one of you will betray me**" (*paradōsei me* = hand me over [to death]).

Jesus told the Twelve: My betrayer is **one who is eating with me** (v 18). Mark does not use this allusion to Ps 41:9 to identify the betrayer, but to call attention to the enormity of the betrayal and to identify Jesus as the OT righteous sufferer (see Brower 1978). "Even my close friend, whom I trusted, he who shared my bread, has lifted up his heel against me" (Ps 41:9; cited in John 13:18). The parallel in Matt 26:23-25 identifies Judas as the betrayer and omits the allusion to Ps 41. Mark identified Judas as the betrayer in 3:19 and 14:10.

The surprise of the Twelve is indicated by their individual responses: **Surely not I** [*mēti egō*]? The form of this rhetorical question in Greek expects a No answer. That they asked him **one by one** emphasizes the disingenuousness of the betrayer. This is another feature of the enemy of the righteous sufferer in the Psalms (e.g., Ps 109).

Jesus confirms that **it is one of the Twelve.** The emphasis on the shared meal continues—this betrayer is one of his most intimate and trusted friends. He **dips bread into the bowl with me,** that is, he shares at Jesus' table. The parallel structure of the section intensifies this sense:

14:17-21

v 18	v 20
one of you will betray me	**one of the Twelve**
one who is eating with me	**one who dips bread into the bowl with me**

Mark's statement in 14:21 makes explicit the connection between the Son of Man and the righteous sufferer. The righteous sufferer who is betrayed by his intimate companion is the Son of Man. This builds on Jesus' earlier pronouncements about the fate of the Son of Man (→ 8:31; 9:12, 31; 10:33, 45). Here, Mark's point is that **the Son of Man will go just as it is written about him.** That is, he will both suffer and be vindicated by God.

Scripture nowhere explicitly states that the Son of Man must suffer. But Mark's allusion to Ps 41:9 provides a specific instance of betrayal by an intimate friend as the initiation of Jesus' approaching death. Thus, a whole constellation of OT righteous sufferers within Mark's Passion Narrative contribute to his scriptural depiction of the suffering Son of Man. The assured vindication of the Son of Man shows that the betrayer's actions, far from thwarting God's purposes, actually serve to further them.

The *men . . . de* construction in Mark 14:21a and b—**On the one hand
the Son of Man will go . . . , *but on the other hand,* woe to that man who betrays the Son of Man!** (emphasis added)—is rare in Mark. It indicates that the
two parts must be held in tension. Thus, the fulfillment of scripture emphasizes that the purposes of God are being accomplished on the one hand; but
on the other hand, the betrayer is fully culpable for his dastardly deed. Jesus'
desolate word about the betrayer—**Woe to that man. . . . It would be better for
him if he had not been born**—is not a curse, but a cry of anguished sorrow at
the starkness of being betrayed by a friend.

FROM THE TEXT

Mark 14:21 is a troubling text. It affirms the good purposes of God being
accomplished in the death and resurrection of Jesus, the Son of Man. God acts
sovereignly in the events lying behind the death and resurrection of Jesus, who
is fulfilling his destiny (see 1 Pet 1:20). That picture is coherent and as long as
it does not impose a determinism on human choices, we are content.

But the other half of Mark 14:21 does not give us this luxury. The betrayer is fully responsible for his choice to betray Jesus. Did Judas have a real
choice? Could he have avoided playing his role in the divine drama?

Mark makes no attempt to resolve the paradox of divine sovereignty and
human responsibility. They are simply held in tension. Both are affirmed by
Mark; and therefore, both are legitimately affirmed by believers. The com-
plexities of the relationship between free will and determinism are not resolved by preferring one over the other. What can be clearly asserted is that
the choices of humans, for good or ill, cannot thwart the ultimate purposes of
God. The future is not open-ended. It has already been signaled in the raising
of Jesus from the dead in what Paul calls the firstfruits (1 Cor 15:20-24).

b. Body and Blood (14:22-25)

BEHIND THE TEXT

This important section in Mark bristles with questions beyond the concerns of this commentary:

First, there are three other versions of the Last Supper in the NT (1
Cor 11:24-25; Matt 26:26-29; Luke 22:15-20), none of which is identical (see
Marcus 2009, 972). How can this variety be explained?

Second, the question of whether the words go back to the historical
Jesus in some form was of considerable interest during the heyday of form
criticism. Several scholars expressed doubts. Such historical skepticism is far
less prominent today. Marcus opines that "the church *may* have retrojected
its own Eucharistic ceremony onto Jesus, but then again, it may have gotten

the rudiments of the Eucharist from the memory of what Jesus had done 'on the night in which he was turned over,' as Paul says he did" (2009, 963). The precise wording, however, is difficult to determine. These words come to us in Greek, while Jesus likely used Aramaic or Hebrew (see Jeremias 1966, 138-203; Marshall 1980, 40-56).

Third, many MSS read the *new* [*kainēs*] covenant in v 24. But the earliest MSS do not have *new*. Clearly, the word *new* attached to this cup saying is earlier than Mark: It is already called "the new covenant" in 1 Cor 11:25. The word coheres with the significance of this passage in light of Jesus' death and resurrection. But it probably is a scribal assimilation from Luke 22:20 or 1 Cor 11:25 (Metzger 1975, 113).

IN THE TEXT

■ **22** The form of the Passover Seder (see Stein 2008, 650-51) may lie behind this account in Mark (even more so in Luke). That implied context is essential for understanding the Last Supper. But the emphasis here is upon the two action statements of Jesus. There are other meals in Mark, but this is the only one in which Jesus acts and explains his actions. He appropriates the implicit Passover setting and reinterprets it completely.

At this communal occasion, Jesus acts as the host, or the "father" of the family, welcoming his disciples. These almost certainly included the Twelve, but perhaps up to thirty people (see France 2002, 562). It is **while they were eating** that Jesus took *a loaf of* bread, **blessed, broke,** and **gave it to** *them, and said,* "Take . . . : this is my body." The language recalls the feedings in 6:41 and 8:6.

Every part of these word-actions is of interest. First, this is in the context of a Passover meal: **While they were eating.** The first word-action probably occurs after they were reminded of the traditional significance of this family celebration—the liberation from oppression of their ancestors. Significantly, the Passover celebration was always understood as more than a remembrance—it was to be celebrated as if they themselves were delivered from Egypt, not just their ancestors (see Exod 13:8; Deut 16:3). The words of Jesus, then, acquire an implicit context and import from the Passover celebration. He then *blessed* (*eulogēsas*) God for the bread (see Stein 2008, 650).

Then Jesus departs from the script. He speaks an unexpected word in connection with the breaking and distributing of the bread to his disciples. This is a prophetic-representative act, a performative word that not only predicts his own death but participates in it. By this action, Jesus freely accepts his own death. Jesus takes the **bread** (*artos* can refer to either leavened or unleavened bread—Evans 2001, 389), blesses God, and breaks the bread. Breaking the **bread** is essential for distributing it and for the communal sharing of

14:22

the one loaf (see 1 Cor 10:17). It could also signal the violence of his death. His earlier call for disciples to take up their own crosses and his passion predictions already anticipate this violence.

Jesus makes an implicit messianic claim if this bread is understood as the *aphikoman*, a portion of the unleavened Passover bread set aside for the Messiah to eat when he returns to Israel. On this reading, "Jesus has identified himself as the *aphikoman*, that is, as 'he who comes,' the Messiah. In accepting and eating the *aphikoman*, thus identified, the disciples demonstrate their faith in Jesus as the Messiah" (Evans 2001, 390). The bread eaten at the table may also symbolize the coming redemptive results of Jesus' death (Marcus 2009, 964).

Of the bread, Jesus tells them in the starkest of words: **this is my body.** Debate over the phrase *touto estin to sōma mou* has been fierce. The crux of the problem is the word *estin*: What does **is** mean? Ironically, the verb would probably have been unexpressed in Aramaic, leaving any exegetical answer risky. Furthermore, the language is "metaphorical and symbolic rather than propositional or metaphysical" (Collins 2007, 655). Thus, in the final analysis, answers tell more about one's prior theological convictions about the Eucharist (e.g., transubstantiation, consubstantiation, etc.) than about this passage. "Whether one interprets the words of institution as implying total identification, mere symbolism, or something in between will depend on larger doctrinal and hermeneutical considerations that cannot be decided by exegesis" (Marcus 2009, 965).

■ **23** The bread is followed by **the cup.** The term in 10:38-39 and 14:36 signals the death of Jesus. The **cup** contains wine—which is clear from v 25 (**the fruit of the vine**). Attempts to distinguish alcoholic vs. nonalcoholic wine cannot be supported from this or any other text. Jesus **gave thanks** (*eucharistēsas*). This Greek word accounts for the term the "Eucharist" as one of the names for the Lord's Supper. The interchangeability of the terms "thanksgiving" and "blessing" in the other traditions reflects normal Jewish practice in this period.

Jesus then **offered it to them, and they all drank from it.** In Mark, they drink from the cup before Jesus explains it. That they **all** [*pantes*] **drank** emphasizes the communal character of their cross-bearing as well as Jesus' death. In 10:38 Jesus promises the Zebedee brothers that they will drink from the cup. Now all the disciples share in it. Thus, the bread and wine become the medium of their intimate fellowship and participation in Jesus' actions. Then Jesus explains the action.

■ **24** The explanation is brief but profound and even more startling than the bread saying. This shared wine is **my blood of the covenant.** The power of these words comes from its OT antecedents. The primary referent is to Exod 24. There the people of Israel ratify the covenant with God based on God's gracious saving activity on their behalf (Exod 19:3-6). The covenant is enacted in two ways.

First, Yahweh invites Moses, the three other leaders, and the seventy elders to a meal on Sinai (Exod 24:1-2, 9-11). Now, in Mark 14:17-25 the representatives of the new and re-created Israel, the Twelve, are eating a meal that is hosted by the Holy One of God. This is explicitly interpreted as a covenant-making or covenant-renewal meal.

Second, Moses sprinkles "the blood of the covenant [*to haima tēs diathēkēs*]" on the people (Exod 24:8). This is the only OT instance in which "the blood of the covenant" is clearly connected with sacrifice *and* unequivocally called "the blood of the covenant," as in Mark. Both aspects are important. This meal is hosted by Jesus, and the disciples eat the broken bread as a participation in him. Then they all drink from one cup, which he explains as **my blood of the covenant, which is poured out for many.**

There may be an OT allusion to Jer 31:31-33, in which the new covenant is promised: "'The time is coming,' declares the LORD, 'when I will make a new covenant with the house of Israel and with the house of Judah.'" While the word *kainēs* (**new**) is probably not original in Mark, the concept of a new covenant is implicit in the addition of the word **my**. This is in "conscious relationship to the older covenant" (Taylor 1966, 176). But it is not simply a repetition of the old covenant. This is indeed a new covenant (see Heb 8:6—9:20). Jeremiah 31 is likely behind the longer version in Luke 22:20 and is explicit in 1 Cor 11:25. It is cited in Heb 8:8-12. It may have influenced the addition of the words "for the forgiveness of sins" in Matt 26:28, since forgiveness was a crucial part of Jeremiah's new covenant promise (see Jer 31:34).

There may be another possible allusion to Zech 9:9-11, which links the Last Supper to Jesus' entry to Jerusalem (Mark 11:1-10). "See, your king comes to you, . . . gentle and riding on a donkey" in v 9 is followed in v 11 by the words, "As for you, because of the blood of my covenant with you, I will free your prisoners." These words of liberation evoke the theme of a new exodus.

A final OT allusion to the Suffering Servant Song in Isa 52:13—53:12 may be present in the words **which is poured out for many** (*hyper pollōn*). Isaiah 53:11-12 in particular makes repeated use of "many." **Many** can mean "some, but not all" or "all." In this context, however, it is a reminder that the new **covenant** Jesus establishes is "inclusive, not restricted to one group of people. It is not restricted to the Jewish people, nor does it exclude them. It is for all the nations" (Kernaghan 2007, 290).

This part of the saying has sacrificial overtones. "Although the phrase 'for many' (*hyper pollōn*) is not a technical term in the sacrificial tradition, the idea that a sacrifice can be performed on behalf of a specific group was widespread, and the preposition used by Mark, *hyper* ('for' or 'on behalf of'), is used elsewhere to express this idea" (Collins 2007, 656). The notion of an atoning sacrifice is conveyed by the idea of pouring out (→ Mark 10:45, which echoes Isa 53).

■ **25** The solemn statement here is paradoxically both foreboding and an implied promise. The day has arrived when feasting and celebration have ended (→ Mark 2:20). But the promise of the resurrection and the future is explicit. Jesus will not drink wine again because he goes to his death. But he will drink it **anew in the kingdom of God.** There will be suffering (cross) and vindication (empty tomb), just as he said. And it will happen for them all—he will share wine with them in the kingdom.

FROM THE TEXT

The rich texture of this passage can easily be missed in a perfunctory celebration of the Lord's Supper, whether the liturgy is elaborate or simple. The kaleidoscope of images evokes Mark's whole narrative reinterpretation of Israel's story. This is a new exodus, the fulfillment of Israel's hopes and dreams. It inaugurates a new relationship between God and his people.

The passages to which Jesus alludes are given greater color from the context in which he utters the words and performs the actions. Each of them should enhance our celebration of Holy Communion: Passover; the divine host at his covenant meal; the broken body of the righteous sufferer; the shared bread and cup by which Jesus predicts and participates in his own death and through which the disciples become participants in this event and are shaped into a new covenant community; the sacrificial and vicarious pouring out of the life of the obedient Servant on behalf of the many. All of these images are evoked to a greater or lesser degree in this Last Supper. If this complex of images is lost, then distortion is possible.

These words in their context should shape our understanding of Holy Communion. The invitation comes from Christ: He is the host, and it is an open invitation for the many not just the few. The elements do not have magical properties—after all, the betrayer also participated in the feast. But for those who come to the feast, there is unconditional welcome. The meal context should prevent covenant from being malformed into a legal category or contract instead of a dynamic relationship into which people are invited to participate by the divine host. This is a grace-full invitation by Christ to be transformed into God's holy people together through the power and presence of the crucified and risen Christ.

Thus, when we take Communion, it is certainly in remembrance of this event in an upper room that was full of foreboding. Like Passover celebrations, somehow we are there, once again participating in the death and resurrection of Christ in this meal, and being transformed into his likeness as his cruciform people. And so it becomes more than a celebration of a past event, like a birthday party. In a way that is mysterious, it becomes a means of grace to us. This accounts for Wesley's sermon, "The Duty of Constant Communion" (Wesley 1986, 427-39).

4. The Mount of Olives (14:26-31)

BEHIND THE TEXT

Jesus' ministry begins in Galilee, where he received a positive response. By contrast, his reception from the Jerusalem authorities has been universally hostile. Anticipating his execution in Jerusalem, in 14:28 Jesus comments, **But after I have risen, I will go ahead of you into Galilee.** This raises the question about the place of Galilee in the mission of Jesus.

France considers Galilee the "natural place for a future hope to be located" (2002, 578). Some have even argued that it "is destined to be the *locale* of the ingathering of the exiles and the appearance of the Messiah" (Wieder 1962, 21). This would suit 14:28, but the evidence against it is overwhelming (see Brower 1978, 239-46; Collins 2007, 658-67). Galilee could symbolize the mission to the Gentiles. But if so, it is coincidental to the simple view that Mark or his sources know of appearances of the risen Lord in Galilee as promised in this passage.

The sequence of passages here is important. In characteristic Markan style, the Last Supper (vv 22-25) is bracketed by two betrayal predictions (vv 17-21, 26-31), highlighting their similarities and differences. Both the betrayal and the denials are according to Scripture (vv 21 and 27). Both emphasize vindication at the end (the raised Son of Man implied in v 21; the risen stricken shepherd in v 28). But the difference between conclusions is dramatic—the betrayer has a grim fate (v 21), the others will be gathered again in Galilee (v 28).

An analysis of 14:18-72 shows how the dual themes of betrayal and fulfillment play out in the narrative (adapted from France 2002, 574). Within this narrative pattern other literary techniques are also used to convey meaning, especially in vv 53-72:

A	14:18-21	*Prediction* of betrayal by one disciple
	14:22-25	Last Supper
B	14:26-28	*Prediction* of desertion by all of them
C	14:29-31	*Prediction* of denial by Peter
	14:32-42	Garden of Gethsemane
A¹	14:42-49	*Fulfillment* of Judas' betrayal
B¹	14:50-52	*Fulfillment* of desertion by all

363

C¹   14:66-72   *Fulfillment* of Peter's denial

Some MSS omit *dis* (**twice**) in 14:30, probably by assimilation to the parallels in Matt 26:34, Luke 22:34, and John 13:38, which omit it (see Metzger 1975, 114).

IN THE TEXT

■ **26-28** The supper ends with **a hymn,** possibly Ps 136, which recounts God's constant love. Usually, however, the Hallel Psalms (Pss 113—118) would be attached to Passover (see Evans 2001, 399). Jesus and his disciples then return to **the Mount of Olives** (→ Mark 11:1; 13:3). Zechariah 9—14, which is the source of the citations and allusions in this section, has this same geographical setting. Marcus summarizes these connections (1993, 157):

Mark		Zechariah
14:24	My blood of the covenant	9:11
14:25	That day, kingdom of God	14:4, 9
14:26	Mount of Olives	14:4
14:27	Strike the shepherd, scatter the sheep	13:7
14:28	Resurrection and restoration of scattered sheep	13:8-9

It is difficult to tell from the citation in Mark 14:27 of Zech 13:7 whether the shepherd is one of Israel's false leaders (see Ezek 34) or a good shepherd. Since Zech 13:7 is so close to Isa 53:10, a canonical reading suggests that the shepherd in Zechariah is to be understood as the shepherd-king who suffers for and in solidarity with his people. Thus, "the judgment meted out upon the shepherd and his flock results in the ultimate salvation, through fiery trails, of a remnant" (Brower 1978, 252).

The language is subtly changed in Mark. In the LXX of Zech 13:7, the verb is imperative: "Strike the shepherd." Yahweh commands the sword to execute judgment on the people and the shepherd. In Mark the verb becomes **I will strike the shepherd.** This could simply be a necessary adaptation, since there is no reference to "the sword" here (so France 2002, 575). But it could confirm Mark's view that the events surrounding Jesus' death are part of God's purposes. The disciples' flight is inevitable because **it is written** (see Mark 14:21). But it also shows that Jesus is in control.

They **will all fall away** (*skandalisthēsesthe*). The word is used eight times in Mark, most significantly in 4:17. The irony is that the description of shallow followers there is now explicitly pointed to the disciples: those who have

MARK

14:26-28

received the word—the gospel—but "when trouble or persecution comes because of the word, they quickly fall away."

The citation of Zech 13:7 is used to predict the denial of the disciples. "I will strike the shepherd, and the sheep will be scattered" (*diaskorpistēsontai*). Jesus is the Shepherd, but the focus is on his followers as the representatives of Israel who will, once again, be scattered.

This disheartening prediction is followed by another prediction in Mark 14:28: **But after I have risen, I will go ahead [*proaxō*] of you into Galilee.** This is Mark's strongest statement so far of Jesus' vindication through resurrection. The story does not end in tragedy: Not only will Jesus die, but he will rise. *Proaxō* may suggest that "as their commander, Jesus will continue to lead his disciples in Galilee" (Evans 2001, 402). More probably this simply means that "Jesus will precede them into Galilee and there await them" (Stein 2008, 655). The predicted denying of Jesus, which leads to the scattering of his disciples, will be reversed in Galilee. Scattering is "a temporary undoing of the messianic task of gathering the sheep, the lost, and the exiles of Israel" (Evans 2001, 401).

14:26-31

■ **29-31** The disciples were rocked by the earlier prediction of betrayal, but that applied to one person only. Now failure is predicted of all. Their erstwhile spokesperson, Peter, however, now wishes to distance himself from the rest. He states with apparent confidence: **Even if all fall away, I will not.** While he no longer rejects the death of Jesus, "he still lacks understanding concerning who Jesus is and how great the test will be to which the Twelve will be subjected. . . . [It] implies a lack of self-knowledge as well" (Collins 2007, 671). This failure of solidarity with the other disciples affirms his loyalty to Jesus. This assertion heightens the tragic irony of his denial just hours later.

Jesus, however, knows Peter will fail spectacularly. He solemnly and emphatically tells him **today—yes, tonight—before the rooster crows twice you yourself will disown me three times.** Mark alone has the **rooster** crowing **twice.** The other Gospels refer more generally to the time when the rooster crows, just before dawn. The best answer may be simple: Roosters never crow just once (as any farm child would know)!

The verb ***deny*** (*aparnēsē*) means to be ashamed, the opposite of confessing. Earlier the Markan Jesus has called all would-be followers to self-denial (8:34). The irony is that his follower Peter is about to deny Jesus. Peter strenuously (*ekperissōs*) contradicts Jesus: **Even if I have to die with you, I will never *deny* you.** This "may be well intended, and his profession of a willingness to die (see 2 Macc 6-7) may have been sincere, but his professed superiority over the other disciples . . . is shameful" (Stein 2008, 655). **And all the others said the same.** Just hours later, ***they all abandoned him and fled*** (14:50). And Jesus' prediction comes true (14:66-72).

Mark tells his readers a great deal about the identity of Jesus by his appeal to Zech 9—14. He is the stricken Shepherd and eschatological King as well as the Suffering Servant on God's mission. His followers are still with him in this journey to rejection, suffering, and death. But ultimately Jesus will be rejected even by his followers.

The sadness of Judas' betrayal is compounded by the denial of the rest of Jesus' intimate followers. One can only imagine the anguish of the first disciples when they heard these stories recited every Holy Week after that first Easter. The pain of failure, the remorse of denial, and their unworthiness as failed disciples would haunt them. Nevertheless, this story of failure is part of the gospel. Its inclusion advances the theme of rejection and suffering of the righteous sufferer. But it is also vital for understanding discipleship. Some comfort may be taken by noting that the purposes of God are not thwarted by disciples' failure. But that never absolves them of the consequences of failure.

5. Gethsemane (14:32-42)

BEHIND THE TEXT

The scene shifts to **Gethsemane,** east of Jerusalem across the Kidron Valley. The name probably comes from the Aramaic *gath shemanim,* **oil press,** which would be appropriate for its location on the Mount of Olives. It was considered within Jerusalem for the purposes of Passover, and so acceptable for pilgrims to stay there for Passover night. Its designation as a garden (only in John 18:1) implies that it was a walled enclosure.

John 18:2 explains that this place was well known to Judas, "because Jesus had often met there with his disciples." Luke (21:37; 22:39) indicates that they stayed on the Mount of Olives every evening while they were in Jerusalem. Mark does not make this clear (see 11:12, 19-20). This tranquil setting is the scene for "a study in human weakness" (France 2002, 580) and of Jesus' relationship with his Father.

The connections between this passage and ch 13 are impressive but often obscured because Mark 13 is thought to refer only to the Parousia. But the four night watches in 13:35 are used by Mark to organize the time on this last night. In the evening watch (1800-2100; 6:00-9:00 P.M.), Jesus eats his Passover meal with the disciples and the ominous predictions of betrayal and denial are given. Now in the midnight watch (2100-2400; 9:00 P.M.-12:00 A.M.) Jesus goes to Gethsemane, with his arrest and betrayal (0000-0300; 12:00-3:00 A.M.) following in the cockcrow watch. The trial (0300-0600; 3:00-6:00 A.M.) occurs in the dawn watch (see Geddert 2001, 345).

The midnight watch is particularly poignant. In 13:37 Jesus urges all his followers to "watch" so as not to get caught sleeping and miss the hour (see also 13:33, 35, 36). Now, he again urges the disciples to stay awake—his last attempt to avert their failure. But he finds them asleep three times.

The reference to *the hour* in 13:32-35 has to do with the eschatological fulfillment of the purposes of God. Now Jesus prays that **the hour might pass** (14:35), but at the end of his profound wrestling in prayer with his Father, Jesus announces that **the hour has come** (14:41).

IN THE TEXT

Nothing in the narrative so far prepares us for Jesus' anxiety. His resolution to accept his death has been unshakable in his confrontations with the religious authorities and the unseen world. He has expressed his clear understanding of the Father's will. He is the beloved and obedient Son. But now, as the reality of his scriptural destiny looms, he is put to the test. The Markan Jesus experiences a profound tension between his Father's will and his own desire to avoid death. Nevertheless, the alignment of wills occurs and the Son of Man fulfills scripture (14:21).

■ **32-34** After the somber events of the evening, Jesus retreats with his disciples to **Gethsemane** to **pray.** We know Jesus prayed on other occasions (1:35; 6:45), but here alone Mark gives us the content. Once again, he takes **Peter, James and John along with him** and leaves the others some distance away (v 32).

On previous occasions, these three witness "Jesus' life-giving power" (5:37-43) and "transcendent glory" (9:2-9). "Now they become observers of his human frailty" (Marcus 2009, 983). Jesus knows the end is near: His predictions are unfolding as he speaks. Although Mark does not tell us, one of the Twelve is apparently missing or slips away while Jesus is praying and the others are sleeping.

Mark does not shield us from Jesus' anguish. **He began to be deeply distressed and troubled** (v 33, echoing Ps 42:5). The righteous-sufferer psalms plumb the depths of human anguish; they also contain notes of hope and trust in God. "Jesus' complaint about his depression thus stands within a biblical context of ultimate trust in God's purposes" (Marcus 2009, 984). They eminently suit this context as they will in Mark 15:34 (see Brower 1978, 268).

The words **deeply distressed and troubled** (*ekthambeisthai kai adēmonein*) add to the sense of Jesus' agony, only amplified by his own statement: *I am* [= **My soul is**] **overwhelmed** [*perilypos*] **with sorrow to the point of death.**

Misguided attempts to diminish Jesus' fear by implying that his anguish is solely because he will bear the sins of the world or will be separated from his Father during the crucifixion dehumanize Jesus. Rather, here "the true humanity of Jesus comes dramatically and stunningly into view" (Brower 1978, 269). But Jesus' humanity alone is also insufficient to explain this passage.

The identity of Jesus as the Holy One of God and the beloved Son are crucial to Mark's portrait of Jesus. This is the time when the ultimate purposes of God are being fulfilled. Christology must always maintain the tension of a Jesus who is fully human and fully divine. Thus, "it is not a question of either fear of physical death or abandonment by God; it is both, which is precisely why the depth of anguish and sorrow expressed plumbs the extremities of human suffering" (Brower 1978, 271).

Jesus instructs the disciples to **stay** behind **and keep watch.** They are to provide Jesus support in his hour of need (so Collins 2007, 677). Their failure only deepens the sense of Jesus' rejection. But they also fail to grasp the significance of these events. This continues Mark's mixed portrait of them as uncomprehending followers.

■**35-36** Jesus goes **a little farther** from the disciples. Does he remain within earshot (France 2002, 583) or seek privacy (Collins 2007, 677)? That he falls to the ground—the normal posture for prayer is standing—indicates the depths of his emotion. Mark summarizes the content of his prayer "that, if . . . possible, the hour might pass from him" (NRSV). But his petition is not granted (v 41).

When the Markan Jesus directly addresses God, he does so in an intimate and distinctive fashion: *Abba,* **Father.** Mark transliterates the Aramaic *Abba* (→ 5:41 and 15:34) and provides the translation **Father.** *Abba* is not an adjective, nor is *Abba* Father one name. The suggestion that *Abba* was Jesus' unique address to God, expressing a childlike intimacy comparable to the English "Daddy," goes beyond the evidence. Still, Jesus' addressing God as Father is distinctive and remembered in the church (see Rom 8:15; Gal 4:6). But it is not unique. The address expresses both the intimacy of family relationships and filial obedience (see Evans 2001, 412-13).

His petition to the Father mirrors his teaching in Mark 9:23; 10:27; and 11:24. His confidence in God is strong: **everything is possible for you.** His prayer assumes God can **take this cup from** him. **This cup** is the experience of suffering and death (→ 10:38). But it could also allude to the cup of judgment and wrath (see Isa 51:22). If so, drinking the cup "suggests that Jesus, though innocent, will take upon himself the wrath that others deserve" (Collins 2007, 680).

The key to Jesus' petition occurs in the next clause: **Yet not what I will, but what you will.** He is willing to align his will with God's redemptive purposes. He has come announcing and effecting the arrival of God's kingdom. But bringing God's rule to its fullness entails embodying in himself the destiny of Israel, including the suffering figures of Scripture. Jesus' prayer expresses his willingness to align himself with God's purposes and to follow the path he has chosen. He will be the perfectly obedient and beloved Son.

■ **37-38** When **he returned to his disciples, he found them sleeping.** Jesus addresses **Peter** as **Simon,** asking him specifically, **Are you asleep?** *Didn't you have the strength to* **keep watch for** *even an* **hour?** A double irony occurs here: First, Peter, who claimed he would remain loyal to Jesus whatever the other disciples did (→ Mark 14:29, 31), sleeps with the others. Second, Mark does not explain why Jesus renames Simon in 3:16. But his reversion to Peter's old name here is ironic. "Peter is in danger of slipping back into the old age where Satan holds sway" (Marcus 2009, 987; → 8:33).

Jesus addresses all three of the inner circle, urging them, **Watch and pray so that you will not fall into temptation** [*peirasmon:* "the time of trial" (NRSV)]. The temptation the disciples face is to save their lives by denying Jesus in the hour of trial (→ 8:34-37). Jesus will soon be on trial for his life before the religious authorities (14:53-65). Peter will also be on trial (14:54, 66-72), but his accusers will be a slave girl and bystanders. The others will flee the scene (14:50-52).

■ **39-42** Jesus prays a second time and returns to find the disciples again are **sleeping, because their eyes were heavy** (*katabarynomenoi:* **weighed down**). They are tired, but they are also weighed down with eyes that cannot see (→ 8:18). And **they did not know what to say to him** (→ 9:6). Mark offers no further details about Jesus' third prayer. His focus is on the disciples when he returns **the third time.** They are **still sleeping and resting** (v 41).

The words *apechei ēlthen hē hōra,* **Enough! The hour has come,** together with **Are you still sleeping and resting?** are difficult to construe. They are usually taken as heavily ironic questions or indignant statements. They might imply that Jesus is finished praying and no longer needs them to stay awake, but this is inconsistent with his next command to get up because the betrayer is at hand (France 2002, 588). The more common use of *apechei* is "far away." In this context, it may be better to translate Jesus' response as a series of questions: "*Still sleeping and taking your rest? Still thinking the end is far away? Actually, the hour has come*" (Evans 2001, 416-17).

However one construes the words before it, the phrase, **the hour has come,** is clear. This not only refers to the immediately preceding events, but to the entire drama from 1:15, in which Jesus announces the arriving of the reign of God, and in 9:1, in which he speaks of the kingdom coming in power. The time of fulfillment is now.

The passion predictions (8:31; 9:31; 10:33-34) are now unfolding. Judas' betrayal sets these events in motion. The **Son of Man is betrayed** (*paradidotai,* **handed over**). The passive voice may be a "divine passive" akin to 1:14. Just as

John is arrested (according to the purposes of God), so Jesus' betrayal by Judas (see 3:19; 14:21) is according to God's purposes.

Jesus will be betrayed **into the hands of sinners** (*hamartōloi*). But why **sinners**? It is ironic that those he has come to transform align themselves with "this adulterous and sinful generation" (→ 8:38; Evans 2001, 417). Earlier passion predictions describe those who crucify him by their occupations or humanity; "here they are described by their moral character, as sinners" (Stein 2008, 665). But a better solution may be a reversal of what was normally expected for the eschaton. It "expresses the same basic thought as 10:45 and 14:24, and that Paul points to when he speaks about Christ being 'made sin' for humanity's sake (2 Cor 5:21)" (Marcus 2009, 991).

Jesus' words, **Rise! Let us go! Here comes my betrayer!** "indicate Jesus's acceptance of the will of God" (Stein 2008, 665). They also point to Jesus' prescience. "Ironically, it is Jesus who announces the arrival of the betrayer (v 42), not his feckless disciples who were supposed to be keeping watch" (France 2002, 418).

FROM THE TEXT

The starkness of Mark's narrative troubled Christians from the beginning. All of the other Gospels more or less soften it. Matthew is closest to Mark, with minor differences in 14:35. Luke's account is significantly different, omitting references to Jesus being overwhelmed with anguish and reducing the three prayers to one. The Johannine Jesus says, "Now my heart is troubled, and what shall I say? 'Father, save me from this hour'? No, it was for this very reason I came to this hour" (John 12:27). "Subsequent Christian interpreters have often followed in the footsteps of these later Gospels by toning down the rough edges of the Gethsemane tradition through ingenious exegesis" (Marcus 2009, 987).

Contemporary Christians still ask why Jesus experienced such anguish. Some commentators argue that "it is not the physical sufferings he will have to endure that trouble Jesus. Rather, it is that he would become sin for us even though he knew no sin (2 Cor 5:21) and a curse for us (Gal 3:13) that we might escape the wrath of God" (Stein 2008, 663). Others point to Mark 15:34, suggesting that it "is this abandonment that Jesus fears most" (Evans 2001, 411). Still others see Jesus' agony as significant "precisely because it shows him to be human. . . . And because Jesus is shown here to share in human weakness, he is also a model for the way in which feeble and wavering Christians may be strengthened through the grace of God" (Marcus 2009, 986).

The author of Hebrews, probably referring to this same scene (see Heb 5:7) holds these points in creative tension: "Although he was a son, he learned obedience from what he suffered" (Heb 5:8). Jesus learned the cost of following the Father's will in his human condition. Nowhere is that shown with greater power than in Mark's Gethsemane story.

France comments,

> Jesus' appeal to his Father is based on the twin assumptions that on the one hand *panta dynata soi* [**everything is possible for you**, Mark 14:36], but on the other hand God has a will which is to be accepted rather than altered by prayer. It is the blending of these two convictions which gives all prayer its mysterious dynamic, and frustrates any "quick-fix" approach. . . . Prayer, so understood, consists not in changing God's mind but in finding our own alignment with God's will. (2002, 585)

6. Betrayal and Arrest (14:43-52)

BEHIND THE TEXT

Mark notes that a **crowd armed with swords and clubs, sent from the chief priests, the teachers of the law, and the elders** came to Gethsemane to arrest Jesus (v 43). It is more likely that this was an organized force than a random mob of vigilantes. The Roman occupation forces were in overall control, including the religious authorities. The high priest's vestments were under Herod's control (Josephus, *Ant.* 18.4.3). And Herod or the Romans reserved the right to appoint high priests (Josephus, *Ant.* 20.10).

Josephus and other sources demonstrate that armed thugs worked for the ruling priestly elite in the late 50s and 60s. This Jerusalem elite sent tithe collectors to the threshing floors in the country to gather the tithes for the temple that should have gone to the local priests. They had a deserved reputation for corruption and arrogance. "The arrest of Jesus attests a similar strong-armed enforcement. . . . [It] fits this pattern of intimidation and violence" (Evans 2001, 424-25). Mark already hints at this in 12:38-40.

IN THE TEXT

The story now begins its relentless progress to the crucifixion. Jesus, who has been speaking frequently up to now, is increasingly silent. The events unfold as God wills, and Jesus' determination to follow his Father's will is no longer a commitment in the abstract. The betrayal by Judas is followed by the flight of the rest of the disciples. A short intervening speech by Jesus (14:48-49) reminds readers of the place of these events in the grand scheme.

■ **43-46** Jesus' control of the situation is stressed by the immediate appearance of **Judas,** now named as **the betrayer** (v 44). Mark adds to the enormity of his betrayal by noting that he is **one of the Twelve.** He is one of those chosen to be a representative of "a repentant and restored Israel, the foundation for a new beginning" (Evans 2001, 424). But he is also one of the intimate group around Jesus (3:33-35), who even shared his food (14:17-21). He now aligns himself with the religious opposition to Jesus.

The **crowd armed with swords and clubs** are enforcers used by the Jerusalem religious elite, **the chief priests, the teachers of the law, and the elders.** It is almost certain that the leaders paid these thugs to carry out their dirty work. They had money available to offer for his services. All that prevented them from acting earlier was their fear that the masses might riot, if the arrest was done in a public setting, like the temple (→ 12:12).

Judas **had arranged a signal** to identify Jesus to those who came to **arrest him and lead him away:** Judas would greet Jesus with a **kiss** (v 44). This would not have been unusual in the eastern Mediterranean cultural context. An affectionate kiss between family members was common in antiquity (Collins 2007, 684). This may help explain the "holy kiss" mentioned by Paul (Rom 16:16; 1 Cor 16:20; 2 Cor 13:12; 1 Thess 5:26; see 1 Pet 5:14). Early Christians perceived themselves as a fictive family (Marcus 2009, 997). A kiss could also be a sign of affection between a disciple and his rabbi.

Judas went at once to Jesus and said **"Rabbi!"** and kissed him (v 45; see Geddert 2001, 352). The horror of betrayal is heightened by this hypocritical display of respect and affection. Jesus offers no resistance. **The men seized Jesus and arrested him** (v 46).

■ **47-49** The violent intervention of **one of those standing near** Jesus is surprising. Mark does not identify who is responsible or why he has a **sword.** Luke 22:49-50 indicates that the disciples have two swords (Luke 22:38). John 18:10-11 identifies Peter as the one who used his sword to cut off the ear of Malchus, **the servant of the high priest.** Whoever he is, his attempt to defend Jesus by cutting off the servant's *earlobe* (*ōtarion*) is laughably ineffective.

Jesus speaks for the only time in this episode. His question is full of irony. They have acted as if he were a *brigand* (*lēstēn*). But if that was so, why had he not been arrested earlier? He was teaching in the temple **every day.** There he had accused the temple authorities of making it *a den of brigands* (*lēstōn*; 11:17).

Jesus' final statement in 14:49, however, raises the perspective beyond the immediate action. This arrest happens *so that the Scriptures might be fulfilled.* The nearest text in Mark is Zech 13:7, which is about to be fulfilled. But the plural suggests that his reference is more general, to God's will expressed in Scripture.

■ **50-52** The solidarity solemnly vowed by the disciples in v 31 evaporates under pressure: **Then everyone deserted him and fled** in panic. The emphatic placement of *pantes*, *all,* at the end of the sentence, gives it the sense: *And abandoning him, they fled—every last one of them.*

Mark gives a detail that has always tantalized readers. Who is this **young man** [*neaniskos*], **wearing nothing but a linen garment,** who escapes **naked, leaving his garment behind?** Suggestions have ranged widely (see Collins 2007, 688-92; Geddert 2001, 354-55):

1. It fulfils OT prophecy (Amos 2:16; Gen 39:12).
2. It symbolizes the shame of the disciples.
3. It shows the extent of the disciples' failure: They have nothing left.
4. It symbolizes Jesus' passion, his shame in death, and the glory of his resurrection.
5. It symbolizes Christian baptism.
6. It is the young man of Mark 10:17.
7. It is an angel as in 16:5.
8. It is John Mark himself.

Geddert considers the last the best solution. Whatever its attraction as a solution, evidence is lacking. Collins concludes that "the young man is best interpreted as one whose flight and abandonment of his linen cloth contrast dramatically with Jesus' obedience in submitting to being arrested, stripped, and crucified" (2007, 695).

Evans (2001, 427-29) considers these and other options before concluding that Mark's point is both simpler and more profound: "Whereas *Jesus* was prepared for the temptations and dangers that lie ahead, his *disciples* are not. . . . One strikes at the high priest's servant, all flee, and then a young man, perhaps a would-be follower, narrowly escapes, fleeing in utter disgrace" (429).

Perhaps Amos 2:16 ("'Even the bravest warriors will flee naked on that day,' declares the Lord") is echoed here (→ Mark 15:33, citing Amos 8:9). Meanwhile, Jesus' predictions are coming true to the letter.

B. Jesus and Peter on Trial (14:53—15:20*a*)

BEHIND THE TEXT

This section is devoted to the trial of Jesus, first before the Sanhedrin in a quasi-official arraignment, then before the Roman prefect Pilate. The narrative is quickly reaching its climax. While the death of Jesus is the focus of the divine activity, the key christological statement is in Mark 14:61-62. There Jesus confirms his identity before the high priest. After this he is deemed worthy of death. Most scholars agree that the Sanhedrin, whatever its shape and composition, did not have the authority to sentence people to death. Only the Romans could do that. They used crucifixion as an instrument of state terror, predominantly against the underclass, "slaves, violent criminals and unruly elements in rebellious provinces, not least in Judaea" (Hengel 1986, 179).

14:53—
15:20*a*

The key protagonists in the trials are the high priest, the chief priests, and the elders who are assembled against Jesus, and the slave girl and the bystanders who question Peter. The chief priests and Pilate enter the trial only in part two. The term "chief priests" (*archiereis*) refers "to the high priest, any former high priests, and the adult male members of their elite families. . . . [The high priest] was the most prestigious religious authority in Second Temple Jewish Palestine, being the supreme officiant at the Jerusalem Temple and the head of its vast economic, social, and political power" (Marcus 2009, 1102).

Interwoven with Jesus' arraignment before the Sanhedrin is what we call the "trial" of Peter. These two stories are deliberately juxtaposed in typical Markan fashion. Mark notes first the arrest of Jesus and the assembling of his opponents. Then he sets the scene for Peter's unofficial examination in the courtyard of the high priest's house. Then he switches back to Jesus' ordeal before the high priest and assembled leaders.

The parallels between Jesus and Peter are fascinating:

Jesus	Peter
High priest's house (v 53)	Courtyard of high priest's house (v 54)
Assembled power brokers (v 53)	Assorted guards and servants (v 54)
No evidence (v 55)	Evidence (vv 67, 69, 71)
Faces false testimony (vv 56-59)	Faces true testimony (vv 67, 69, 71)
Silent (v 61)	Denies (vv 68, 70, 71)
Mocked as false prophet (v 65)	Fulfills Jesus' prophecy (v 72)

One indication of the importance of this interwoven episode to Mark's story is the number of OT citations and allusions woven throughout (→ 14:57, 61b-64, 65; 15:5, 16, 19-20). Its pinnacle is one of the richest theological sections in the Gospel: 14:61-62.

Each Gospel has trial scenes. They agree in general terms:
- Jesus is arrested and arraigned before the high priest
- the high priest condemns him as deserving of death
- he is sent to Pilate, who ultimately commits Jesus to his death by crucifixion

But differences also occur. These differences, combined with the apparent lack of eyewitness testimony, raise historical questions about the details of these events. Two questions arise.

First, what actually happened? Scholarly literature on this topic is vast. Most scholars agree that there was some sort of arraignment before the Jewish religious authorities. Some disagree, seeing this as historically unnecessary since the death penalty was reserved for the ruling Roman authorities. They assume it is inserted as part of Mark's polemic against the Jerusalem leadership.

Many of the details in Mark point to a trial that would be illegal under rules in *m. Sanh.* 4—7. This is hardly surprising—the trial is portrayed as "a kind of preliminary hearing to determine if Jesus was as dangerous as the leadership sensed and whether he could be credibly sent to Rome" (France 2002, 602, citing Bock 1998, 191). They needed to formulate charges sufficient to convince the Roman prefect to execute Jesus. This explains the night trial, the false witnesses, the attempt to formulate a threat of temple destruction, the abandonment of this charge followed by a summary condemnation of Jesus on the grounds of blasphemy, and the abuse of the prisoner by the high priest's guards. These details point to the haste and extraordinary character of this event; they do not make it unhistorical. In short, this seems not to have been a formal trial, but an informal hearing (Stein 2008, 680).

Some scholars question whether a great Sanhedrin existed in the late 2TP. The evidence strongly suggests that something akin to "the Sanhedrin" existed. But its description in the later Mishnaic tractate *Sanhedrin* may be an idealized picture of the pre-A.D. 70 period. In Jesus' time it is unlikely that its membership was formally fixed at 70 or 71 (Marcus 2009, 1102). Questions about Mark's sources of information can also be raised: How would he know about details of Jesus' trial before the Sanhedrin? None of these objections is insurmountable (see Brown 1994, 357-92).

Second, how did Jesus blaspheme? There are several possibilities. The questioning seems initially to attempt to charge him with blasphemy against the temple. It could be for false prophecy connected with the temple, evidenced by the mockery. But the charge seems finally to have been confirmed by Jesus' confession of his identity (→ 14:63-65).

Some scholars have noted that the charge seems not to fit the provisions of the Mishnah tractate *Sanhedrin*. But nothing in Mark is inconsistent with Jewish literature before and contemporary with Mark's account (Evans 2001, 456). "Jesus committed blasphemy when he claimed . . . to be the 'son of God' in the highest sense. . . . He also committed blasphemy by implicitly threatening the high priest at the time he came to judgment" (Evans 2001, 456). The charge "is not to be found in any narrowly defined misuse of language but in a total claim to which the whole of Jesus' public life and teaching has been building up" (France 2002, 601).

The entire Passion Narrative is full of irony. Narrative irony lies in the two simultaneous trials of Peter and Jesus. In point after point, the "meanwhile in the courtyard" juxtaposing of the events surrounding Jesus and Peter adds poignancy to the interwoven stories. That Jesus is finally mocked as a

14:53—
15:20a

false prophet precisely when Peter is fulfilling Jesus' prophecy to the letter signals that his prophecy about his fate, that of the temple, and the future of the disciples will all be fulfilled.

Another irony is that the false witnesses assembled against Jesus could not agree on their stories. And yet, with further irony, their testimony was a mixture of truth and falsehood. The confession of Jesus before the high priest, the spiritual leader of the people, is immediately followed by his preemptory rejection of Jesus' identity.

IN THE TEXT

1. Jesus Before the Assembled Leaders (14:53)

■ **53** The story moves swiftly forward. The guards who arrest Jesus in behalf of the temple authorities **took Jesus to the high priest,** almost certainly to his house (see v 54). This house may have been the mansion (excavated in 1970) or one much like it, overlooking the Temple Mount. It was "a large Herodian structure of nearly two thousand square feet built on the ruins of a Hasmonean dwelling on the eastern slopes of the Upper City" (Marcus 2009, 1001). Jesus is brought to this location rather than any formal chamber. This implies that this is not a formal trial. Mark does not name the chief priest, but he was likely Caiaphas (A.D. 18—37), or, perhaps, his father-in-law, Annas (see Luke 3:2; John 18:12-14).

Those who opposed Jesus while he taught in the temple gather together in the high priest's house. **All** is Markan hyperbole (→ Mark 1:5) signaling the solidarity of the religious elites against Jesus. They have likely been individually summoned by the high priest. The Pharisees and the Herodians, who first plotted to destroy Jesus (→ 3:6), however, are noticeably absent. Mark sets the stage for the remainder of this interwoven story of Jesus and Peter.

2. Peter Warming Himself (14:54)

■ **54** The scene abruptly shifts to **the courtyard of the high priest**'s house. Peter, who has followed Jesus **at a distance** (*apo makrothen*; see 15:40), probably for his own safety, has entered the courtyard. Mark does not explain how he gained entrance (see John 18:15-16).

Peter is *sitting with the servants* [*hypēretōn*] *and keeping warm by the blazing fire* (*phōs*). The servants could be **guards,** but the Greek word need not mean this. The presence of a slave girl in vv 66-67 points to a general meaning here, although it probably means **guards** in v 65. The unusual word for fire, *phōs*, **light,** explains how the maid is able to recognize him (v 67).

The stage is set for comparisons and contrasts between Jesus and Peter. Jesus is now in the high priest's house with the high priest and all the religious elite assembled against him. Peter is in the courtyard warming himself with the servants of the high priest (and, perhaps, some of the servants of the assembled leaders).

3. Jesus Accused and Mocked (14:55-65)

■ **55-59** Mark points out the dubious character of the "trial" by having the **chief priests and the whole Sanhedrin** act as prosecutors, **looking for evidence against Jesus.** They pervert justice by deciding the desired outcome in advance. They simply need enough evidence to support their call for the death penalty (see 14:1).

This does not make Mark's picture historically implausible. That religious authorities could act in extraordinarily perverse ways would surprise only the most naive of twenty-first-century readers. Democratically elected governments have resorted to worse extrajudicial and illegal actions under the guise of state security.

Despite the difficulties of assembling **the whole Sanhedrin** for an event between midnight and dawn, Mark's language shows the united opposition to Jesus by the temple elite. This united front would be important, if the Romans were to execute Jesus. They needed to act promptly, while Jesus was away from the crowds (see 11:18; 12:12).

Mark tells us that **many testified falsely against him** (*epseudomartyroun kat' auton*). The imperfect tense of the verb may indicate that false testimony against Jesus continues the earlier testimony against Jesus. The authorities have long sought to discredit and eliminate Jesus. But it could refer simply to the parade of witnesses assembled for this occasion. Regardless, **their statements did not agree** under examination. Mark does not indicate what these charges were. He only states that the leaders **did not find any** evidence that could plausibly lead to Roman execution.

In v 57, a specific accusation against Jesus is mentioned. They accuse Jesus of saying, *I will destroy this temple made with hands and in three days I will build another not made with hands.* Mark makes no attempt to discredit their testimony. He simply comments: **even then their testimony did not agree.**

Clearly, the Markan Jesus has predicted the demise of the temple. But nowhere does Jesus make the explicit claim that *he* would destroy the temple. In 13:2, Jesus' "divine passives" signify that its destruction is God's doing. The accusation against Jesus, however, is emphatic: He said, **I will destroy** (*egō katalysō*).

The accusation distinguishes the temple "made with hands" (*cheiropoiēton,* NRSV) and another "not made with hands" (*acheiropoiēton,* NRSV). Jesus does not condemn the temple specifically because it is made by humans (see Acts 7:47-51). Nor does he predict the rebuilding of the temple buildings in Mark 13, although that might have been a reasonable expectation (see John 2:19). Some

14:54-59

evidence suggests the eschatological Messiah was expected to rebuild the Jerusalem temple (see 2 Sam 7:13; Zech 6:12).

The accusation would undoubtedly rankle the guardians of the temple. In Jewish polemic something "made with hands" (NRSV) is often equivalent to an idol (see Lev 26:1, 30; Isa 2:18; 10:11; 16:12; 19:1; 21:9; 31:7; Jdt 8:18; Wis 14:8). The language negatively assesses the temple (compare Acts 7:47-51), perhaps even associating it with idolatry (Evans 2001, 446). The temple is "an idol, a weak caricature, a humanly devised substitute for the 'holy place' it was intended to be" (Geddert 2001, 358).

The Markan Jesus does not state *and after three days I will build another.* Mark does not explicitly make the connection between a rebuilt temple and the resurrection of Jesus as does John 2:19-22. But the irony is unmistakable to Mark's readers who know the passion predictions, who recognize Jesus, the Holy One of God, as now the locale of God's presence among his people, and who know that Jesus has made them his new covenant community.

A subtle but highly significant difference occurs in the Greek terms used for temple in Mark 13:1 (*hieron*) and 14:58 (*naos*). In 13:2, Jesus predicts the destruction of the entire temple. Here, the accusation is that Jesus will destroy the *naos*, the inner sanctuary—the holy place and the holy of holies. Jesus does not make that claim. But ironically, Mark's readers soon learn that at Jesus' death the veil of the inner sanctuary is torn from top to bottom (15:38).

Mark seems reticent to counter these charges. His description of the false witnesses echoes Ps 27:12. The righteous aufferer of the psalms endures false testimony; these witnesses are false because they testify against the righteous sufferer, regardless of what they say. Their accusations are full of irony because their words are close to the truth.

It is not uncommon in Mark that those who oppose Jesus (e.g., the demons) often convey profound truths beyond their comprehension. Hence, the accusations are chosen carefully to show that, while they are false, strictly speaking, at a deeper level, they advance Mark's theology. Mark "has woven into the (false) charge a (true) statement" (France 2002, 607). The physical temple will not be rebuilt. But another, "not made with hands" (NRSV), will be built after three days. This will be fashioned by God. It will be preceded by judgment, which will be the action of God. Only after darkness at noon (15:33) and the torn veil (15:38) will the new temple arise.

■ **60-61** Mark notes that their testimony did not agree, but the **high priest** nonetheless **asked Jesus** to respond to it. The hearing has reached its decisive stage, because the high priest sees a clear link between the confused testimony and Jesus' guilt. **But Jesus remained silent.**

It might be that Jesus refuses to dignify their false testimony by a response. But his silence is also part of the Righteous Sufferer motif that builds throughout the Passion Narrative (see Pss 38:12-15; 39:9; Isa 53:7). For Mark, Jesus is being accused by false witnesses whose testimony is true in ways his accusers cannot imagine.

In response to Jesus' silence, the **high priest** takes the initiative and asks him directly: **Are you the *Messiah*, the Son of the Blessed One?** This turns out to be the critical question. Mark's way of expressing it (lit., *he asked him and says to him*) takes the high priest's question as a statement (Marcus 2009, 1004). It is also emphatic: **Are you the *Messiah*?**

This question, asked by the religious authorities, gathers up the whole narrative-identity of Jesus. It is connected to the previous testimony, especially if the priests perceive that there is indeed some truth in the accusations and if there is an expectation that the Messiah would rebuild an eschatological temple.

The phrase **Son of the Blessed One** is a Jewish circumlocution for "Son of God," which circumspectly avoids pronouncing the divine name. It "heightens the irony of the high priest observing theological niceties by avoiding using the sacred name for God (Lord or YHWH) while unjustly condemning Jesus to death" (Stein 2008, 683).

The phrase **Son of the Blessed One** may well be an explanatory expansion of the term "Messiah." At the story level, the high priest probably thinks in conventional terms. He assumes that Jesus is simply another deluded messianic pretender. Son of God was already a well-established messianic title in the late 2TP (see Juel 1977, 162-72).

But at the reader's level, Mark gives more significance to the question. In the opening line of the Gospel, *Messiah* and "Son of God" identify Jesus. This is the content of the good news: Jesus is the Messiah and Son of God (→ Mark 1:1). Now these two terms come together again for the first time within the story. This is a crucial point in Jesus' public identity.

Jesus answers this question. He has not explicitly claimed to be the Messiah before (but → 9:41); nor has he rejected the claim. His identity as Son of God has been given by the demons. Jesus has given only a parable in 12:1-12 and a riddle in 12:35-37 that point in this direction. Importantly, readers know that Jesus' identity as God's beloved Son is twice confirmed by the voice from heaven (1:11; 9:7).

■ **62** Jesus' response, **I am,** ends any messianic secret. Israel's highest religious authorities now know Jesus' identity. Once again, he prefers to speak about his messiahship in terms of the Son of Man. In 8:27-31, Jesus tacitly accepted the identity as Messiah but forbade any mention of it by the disciples. Now that his fate is sealed, he accepts the title. But he elaborates it in terms that could easily be perceived as a threat.

Most scholars agree that the shorter reading, *egō eimi*, is the earliest recoverable form (Collins 2007, 696). Marcus (2009, 1007-8) defends the poorly attested longer reading: *sy eipas hoti egō eimi*, **You say that I am he**. I am is simply an affirmative response by Jesus to the question. John makes the very utterance of the phrase pregnant with significance (see John 18:6). But most do not press Mark in this direction.

Clearly, at the story level, these words are simply affirmative. But "on the second level, as discerned by the readers, and, according to Mark, by Jesus himself, it may also have had the reverential connotation of a close relationship of Jesus with God" (Brower 1978, 359). In the end, however, this matters little. It is the continuation of the statement that causes such consternation by the high priest and leads to the charge of blasphemy. Jesus adds a challenge to the high priest in which almost every word is significant:

First, **you will see** (*opsesthe*, plural). Jesus implies that those present will see what he describes: **the Son of Man sitting at the right hand of the Mighty One and coming on the clouds of heaven.** Most scholars see the sequence of sitting and coming as referring to separate events, the exaltation and the Parousia (Stein 2008, 685). But this is neither the obvious reading of this text nor is it necessary: "To understand the saying as referring solely to a future, rather undifferentiated, and, in any case, probably somewhat incomprehensible parousia is to rob the verse of any real significance in the trial scene itself" (Brower 1978, 367). Jesus' Sanhedrin audience will be the ones who will see this event. The words need to be explained primarily by reference to these priests.

Second, Jesus again interprets the term "Messiah" in light of **the Son of Man.** But this time, the picture is not of suffering but of vindication and authority (→ Mark 8:38). This is achieved by combining two texts, Ps 110:1 and Dan 7:13. Both have already played a significant role in Mark. This time, **the Son of Man** will be **sitting at the right hand of the *Power* and coming *with* the clouds of heaven.**

The NT frequently quotes or echoes Ps 110:1 with one primary goal: to symbolize Jesus' ultimate status as the Messiah (see Hay 1973, 155). Jesus continues to refuse to claim to be a political Messiah (→ Mark 12:35-37).

Daniel 7:13 adds the notion of suffering. In a great reversal, the oppression Daniel's Son of Man receives from the Gentile oppressors of Israel, Jesus receives from Israel's religious leaders (see Snow 2010).

The combination of a **seated** and **coming** Son of Man results in imagery those who read the two verbs as sequential find difficult to interpret. But if both are metaphorical, both refer to the vindication and sovereign authority Jesus—the Son of Man, Messiah, Son of the Blessed One—will exercise before the eyes of the watching religious authorities (France 2002, 612-13). God will assign him a position of ultimate authority **at his right hand.** Here *Power* is another circumlocution for God (→ Mark 14:61: **Blessed One**). But when will they see this?

The rich irony may provide a clue. This is a judgment scene. Presently, the whole religious establishment is sitting in judgment on Jesus. But Jesus predicts a complete reversal: Those who judge will be judged. For Mark, that judgment is about to begin, with the darkness at noon (15:33) and the rending of the veil (15:38). It will be continued in the destruction of the temple and the gathering of the people of God (→ ch 13).

Jesus' claim to such authority, of course, is patently absurd given his perilous state. He has been delivered into the hands of his enemies, and he is nothing but a deluded messianic pretender. And yet, for Mark's readers, the picture is plain. As will be seen later (15:33-39), God is acting behind the scenes throughout the crucifixion from beginning to end. Jesus is seen most clearly as Son of God as he dies (15:39).

This is a complete reversal of traditional messianic expectations. While the chief priests mocked and demanded that Jesus come down from the cross so they might "see and believe" (15:32), they fail to recognize that by remaining on the cross, Jesus is exercising authority in a way beyond their comprehension. They see, but they fail to believe. Power is present in the midst of weakness.

■ **63-65** The high priest considers Jesus' response to be a self-incriminating statement. He **tore his clothes,** an action that has deep roots in the OT and is expressed in later judicial rulings in the Jewish Mishnah (*m. Sanh.* 7.5). There it signals a guilty verdict by the high priest (Stein 2008, 685).

14:62-65

In this setting, the entire priestly establishment witnesses **the blasphemy.** This was the moment they were waiting for. Earlier attempts to entrap him had failed (12:14-17). This time they **all condemned him as worthy of death.**

Mark does not say whether anyone defended Jesus. That **all condemned him** gives the impression of a unanimous decision. That may have excluded people like Joseph of Arimathea, "a prominent member of the Council" (15:43).

Why was Jesus' answer blasphemy? Most scholars agree that a claim to messiahship was not blasphemous. In the later formalization of blasphemy (*m. Sanh.* 7.5), pronouncing the divine name would qualify. But Mark does not have Jesus do so, unless his **I am** response was so construed. At the historical level, this is unlikely. Mark reports that Jesus used the divine circumlocution *the Power* to avoid mentioning God by name.

Recent scholarship agrees that the range of offenses classified as blasphemy was broader than those preserved in the later Mishnah. And these were applied by the Sadducees in a particularly strict manner. Jesus' statement fits

Philo's definition of blasphemy as an insult to God involving "a human being claiming a greater degree of authority and power than he has the right to do and, directly or indirectly, claiming divine status for himself" (Collins 2007, 706).

This is precisely what Jesus' statement seems to do. He implicitly claims divine status: He will be seated at God's right hand (Ps 110:1). As the Son of Man, he will exercise universal and public authority by coming with the clouds of heaven (Collins 2007, 706). Jesus claims a special relationship with God (France 2002, 615). "Jesus did not claim a mere honorific title 'son of God,' which might be applied to a Davidic Messiah. He claimed to be God's 'son' in heavenly terms" (Evans 2001, 456). Once again, the irony is palpable—what is blasphemous for the Sanhedrin is simply the truth for Mark and his readers.

The mockery of Jesus through spitting and beating by some members of the Sanhedrin echoes Isa 50:6 and the experience of the Suffering Servant (→ Mark 10:34; 15:19). The mockery Jesus undergoes throughout the Passion Narrative reinforces the Righteous Sufferer motif. Ironically, Jesus is mocked as a false prophet precisely when his prophecies are being fulfilled in a general sense, and specifically with respect to Peter.

4. Peter's Denial (14:66-72)

Much like a film director, Mark now turns his lens toward Peter. He is still in the courtyard, still at the fire. Mark evidently intends readers to see that the prophecy of Peter's denial occurs at the same time as Jesus is on trial before the Sanhedrin. This fulfills Jesus' predication in 14:30 exactly. Furthermore, the increasingly close scrutiny of Peter is matched by the escalating intensity of his denials. The sequence ends with Peter remembering Jesus' prediction and his bitter remorse at his failure.

■ **66-68** Peter, in the high priest's courtyard, is first challenged by a **servant girl** (*paidiskōn*) who **saw Peter warming himself** by the blazing fire. **She looked intently** [*emblepsasa*; see 8:25; 10:21, 27] **at him,** and asked rhetorically, **You also were with that Nazarene, Jesus, weren't you?** The Greek question serves as an accusation.

While Jesus is being challenged by the powerful high priest, Peter is challenged by his powerless female servant. While Jesus confirms his identity, Peter **denied** (*ērnēsato*) understanding her question or knowing the person she is talking about.

At this point, Mark gives no explanation as to how she identifies Peter (→ 14:69-71). He would be a previously unknown figure at the high priest's house. The extraordinary event of Jesus' arrest and interrogation might explain why both she and he were in the courtyard.

Her query is couched in disdainful terms: **that Nazarene.** Peter's response to this private question is excessive: **I don't know or understand what**

you're talking about. Once Peter issues this denial, he goes "out into the fore-court" (NRSV). Peter moves away from Jesus.

The phrase, **and the rooster crowed** (NIV margin), in some MSS of v 68, is textually uncertain. The dramatic effect Mark is creating is heightened if it is read as a warning to Peter (→ v 72).

■ **69-71** The second approach of the female servant to Peter results in an escalation of the tension. This time she speaks **to those standing around** and identifies him. Peter is **one of them**—a follower of the Nazarene. There is no overt hostility in either statement of the maidservant. But the location and series of events is ominous. To be identified as an associate of the defendant on trial in the high priest's house carries a latent threat. Peter fears for his safety. So, **again he denied it.** His response is not specified.

The third denial follows **after a little while.** This time, his accusers are *the bystanders* (*parestōtes*), who will also play an important role in the death scene (15:35, 39). They now challenge Peter: **You must be** one of them, **for you are a Galilean** (v 70). Mark does not indicate how Peter was identified as a Galilean. But it must almost certainly have been from his Galilean dialect (see Matt 26:73; Acts 4:13).

Peter "began to curse, and he swore an oath [*ērxato anathematizein kai omnynai*]" (NRSV). This is difficult to translate without interpreting the passage, since the object of his curse is not stated. It seems unthinkable that he should curse Jesus. To this point, he has not mentioned Jesus' name, so as not to be found out. Even here he refers to **this man you're talking about** rather than to "Jesus." But "his cursing, or anathematizing" may, in fact, be "directed against Jesus. At the very least he has called down curses on himself" (Evans 2001, 466). Marcus concurs: "Since Peter has been asked about his association with Jesus, the object of his curse is probably also Jesus" (2009, 1020).

The 1984 NIV translation decides the case for its readers: **He began to call down curses on himself, and he swore to them.** But the 2011 NIV omits **on himself.** Grammatically, "the natural object to be understood is Jesus, so that Mark portrays Peter as voluntarily doing what Pliny was later informed that 'real Christians' could not be compelled to do (Pliny, *Ep.* 10.96.5), cursing Jesus" (France 2002, 622).

■ **72** For Mark's readers, then and now, the next verse is haunting. Mark's **immediately** simply confirms that the awful prediction of denial in 14:30 has happened and **the rooster crowed the second time.** Only Mark mentions this small detail, which emphasizes the accuracy of Jesus' prediction. Now Peter hears and **remembered the word** (*ho rēma*; → 9:32) of prophecy **Jesus had spoken to him.**

The description of Peter's remorse is given in three Greek words: *kai epibalōn eklaien.* Both the NRSV and NIV translate this: **And he broke down**

14:66-72

and wept. The difficulty is the meaning of *epibalōn*. Mark's usage in 4:37; 11:7; and 14:46 do not help much. Several possible meanings include "and beginning," "and when he thought," "and covering his head," "and rushing outside" (Evans 2001, 466-67; see Marcus 2009, 1020-21). The precise meaning is unclear, but the general tone is not. Peter is filled with remorse, goes away from Jesus into the dark and weeps. Matthew and Luke both capture Mark's sentiment: "And he went outside and wept bitterly" (Matt 26:75 ‖ Luke 22:62).

FROM THE TEXT

Perhaps as clearly as anywhere in Mark's narrative, the stories of the two trials plead to be read together. Jesus' arraignment inside before the religious authorities and Peter's dissembling outside in the courtyard are shocking, challenging, and (ironically) encouraging.

Mark's readers know that the public disclosure of Jesus' identity before hostile opposition confirms what has been building from the Gospel's opening line. He is the Righteous Sufferer, par excellence, who embodies in himself the anguish of God's people. But his suffering is linked with the assurance of vindication and ultimate triumph. Jesus is also the Messiah, the Son of God, in a way that moves well beyond the usual understandings of those two terms in his time. The high priest states far more than he intends in his sarcastic question to Jesus. Instead of a denial, Jesus acknowledges the truth of the question. But then he raises the temperature considerably by implying that these terms, understood correctly, signal his divine status and authority.

If Jesus is who he seems to claim to be, the grim continuation of this trial and mockery, culminating in his crucifixion, seem odd. If he has divine status, why is he embodying the suffering of OT suffering figures? The answer awaits the end of the death scene, but it is anticipated here. God's power is displayed in weakness. And Jesus is most clearly shown to be Son of God in his death on the cross. For Mark, that is the end of the beginning of the final establishment of God's kingdom in strength and the creation of the new covenant community in his blood.

The picture is grim on the surface. Jesus seems powerless in the face of false witnesses and overwhelming religious authorities. God seems to have abandoned him. The rejection and abuse that has been anticipated throughout the narrative is now a reality.

And yet, Mark is clear that events are unfolding just as Jesus predicted. Jesus goes to his death within the will of God. After Gethsemane, the purposes of God unfold in breathtaking fashion.

As a counterpoint to Jesus' story, Peter's story is particularly poignant. All the disciples have forsaken Jesus and fled (14:50). But Peter continues to follow, albeit from a distance, right up to the fringes of Jesus' interrogation and

14:53-72

condemnation. He is, to the best of his ability, honoring his commitment to Jesus. But then he is confronted by a slave girl—a slave girl—and his courage and resolve melt away in fear. His denial of Jesus follows, just as Jesus had warned. And Peter is left outside, away from Jesus, in the anguish of self-knowledge. Several important points emerge from these intertwined stories.

First, this story reminds us that it is one thing to confess our loyalty and commitment in the safe surroundings of the community of faith—in a closed room or on the mountaintop with Jesus. It is quite another when confronted with the reality of life. Mark has already noted that self-reliance and self-sufficiency are incompatible with being one of Jesus' followers. Rather, denial of self and of self-reliance are expected of Jesus' disciples (8:34-37). Self-reliance regularly comes up short in the circumstances of life. Failure can and sometimes does follow. Then we remember—and go out and weep (14:72).

Second, the good news of the gospel in this story must be heard clearly as well. Peter remembers the prediction of Jesus that he will fail miserably. But in that prediction is also the promise that Jesus will gather the scattered disciples and remake them into his people. This is good news indeed: The gospel is also for failed disciples. The risen Christ awaits us on the other side of failure. If we go to meet him again, he is there to welcome, just as he said (see 16:7).

Third, the earliest readers of Mark's Gospel almost certainly were undergoing persecution of some sort. Within a few decades of Jesus' trial, his followers would be arraigned before powerful authorities and would face abuse, rejection, and even death. Today's readers in some parts of the world find it difficult to put themselves in such a situation.

But that is not so for many followers of Jesus in other parts of the world. They know the reality of illegal seizures, of trumped-up charges and false witnesses, of illegal trials and summary convictions. They know the humiliation and rejection that comes from acknowledging that they are followers of Jesus. They also know the temptation to reject their discipleship and save their lives. They know the risk of losing life for his sake and the gospel's.

These stories offer hope to them as well. They know that vindication and life will surely come after suffering because God is sovereign and his purposes are being accomplished even in unpromising situations. Jesus can be their model of courage borne of doing the Father's will. But Peter can also be a model for them, whether through his failure or the gracious forgiveness and restoration that links his story with that of Jesus. There is hope even for failed disciples.

5. The Verdict of the Temple Leaders (15:1)

IN THE TEXT

■ I The story of Peter's denial interrupts the flow of the narrative of Jesus' "trial." But Mark shows that the process continues unabated with a "meanwhile back in the court"-type of opening to the scene. It is set at the conclusion of the fourth night watch, **very early in the morning** (*prōi*; see 13:35). This continuation of the arraignment follows hard on the heels of the second cockcrow.

Although the language is unclear, this is not a reconvening of the Sanhedrin for a second hearing. Rather the **chief priests,** who take the lead throughout the rest of the story, **reached a decision** *in consultation with the elders, the teachers of the law and the whole Sanhedrin.* The implication is that this decision has been confirmed by all who are present. Jesus is guilty, so they **handed him over** [*paredōkan*] **to Pilate.**

The polyvalent *paradidōmi* (see 1:14; 9:31; 10:33) once again shows that all that is occurring is within the purposes of God for his servant. Marcus goes so far as to suggest that the parallelism in the trials shows that "the same inimical power that masterminded Jesus' condemnation by the Jewish authorities is now bringing about his condemnation by the Gentiles in a strikingly similar manner. Behind that power of evil, however, lies the overarching will of God" (2009, 1032).

Mark has a tight three-hour pattern from trial to burial, yet another indication that the events are the fulfillment of God's purpose (see 1:15). A great deal occurs on the one day—the whole summary execution from arrest to burial occurs within eighteen hours.

The Day of the Crucifixion

14:17	Evening	Last Supper
14:26		Mount of Olives
[13:35]	Midnight	Arrest and Sanhedrin trial
14:72	Cockcrow	Peter's denial
15:1	Daybreak	Delivery to Pilate
15:25	The third hour	Crucifixion
15:33	The sixth hour	Darkness at noon
15:34	The ninth hour	Cry and death
15:42	Evening	Burial

(France 2002, 626)

6. The Trial Before Pilate (15:2-15)

BEHIND THE TEXT

Part two of Jesus' trial is before Pilate, who alone could sanction the execution of Jesus. It has several similarities to the arraignment before the high priest, including the questioning of Jesus by Pilate, Jesus' response to Pilate's question, his silence in the face of his accusers, and mocking treatment by his custodians.

In this scene, Mark shows that responsibility for the charge and the demand for crucifixion do not originate with Pilate. If Mark's first readers were in Rome, this would be no bad thing: Jesus was no threat to the empire. He was an innocent victim of the Jewish temple leadership. Pilate quickly comes to the conclusion that the accusation brought against Jesus is vexatious and spiteful.

Pilate initially seeks to bring the trial to an end, but seems too weak to control matters. His self-serving attempt to curry favor with the crowd by offering to release the innocuous, if deluded, Jesus of Nazareth backfires spectacularly. The crowd spurns his offer and chooses the release of Barabbas, a convicted insurrectionist. Having miscalculated on that gambit, he yields to the demands of the crowd. Although he could have acted with justice, he thinks it is in his best interests to mollify the crowd by sending an innocent person to be crucified. He colludes with the ruling priests in Jesus' death to keep the peace. As the face of Roman justice in Judea, his actions bring him no credit whatsoever.

This is the first and last mention of Pilate in Mark. Contemporary evidence indicates that Tiberius appointed Pilate (his surname Pontius is not mentioned) as the "prefect" (military governor) of the troubled Roman province of Judea (A.D. 26-37). He was not the procurator, a later office concerned with civic and financial affairs (Evans 2001, 476-77). He usually resided in Caesarea Maritima on the Mediterranean coast, coming to Jerusalem for festival days, where he stayed in one of Herod's palaces in Jerusalem. Apparently he had a good working relationship with Caiaphas, the high priest. Indeed, when Pilate was removed from office in A.D. 37, Caiaphas was also removed from the high priesthood shortly thereafter. The available evidence about Pilate from Philo and Josephus is neither flattering nor unbiased (see Evans 2001, 477). Pilate effectively maintained "Roman order in the province without recourse to undue aggression" (Bond 1998, 93).

No evidence survives in either Jewish or Roman law for the so-called Passover pardon through which Barabbas is released. Some take this to indicate that this story is historically unreliable. Others find it difficult to see how such a story could enter the tradition without some basis in fact. However, ad hoc amnesty at festal occasions is not unknown then or now.

IN THE TEXT

■ **2-5** Pilate immediately asks the bound, perhaps hooded, and battered Jesus: **Are you the king of the Jews?** It is the first time this designation occurs in Mark (see also vv 9, 12, 18, 26). The absurdity of the situation—Pilate in control, Jesus bound and bloodied—makes the question seem sarcastic on Pilate's lips but ironic in Markan terms (but see France 2002, 628).

Mark intends readers to infer that the question forms the basis of the allegations laid before him by the chief priests. Jesus admitted to being Messiah—for Gentile ears, that would be "king of the Jews." This is a serious charge—there had not been a "king of the Jews" since the death of Herod the Great in 4 B.C. and talk of a claimant to kingship would trouble imperial Rome and get the attention of the Roman prefect.

Jesus' response lacks any deferential tone and may be ironic: **Yes, it is as you say** (*sy legeis*), despite all appearances to the contrary. It might imply that this statement is correct, but not in the way Pilate imagined—a "your words, not mine" answer.

To this question, the **chief priests** added many other accusations. Pilate again invited Jesus to respond, but Jesus' next words will be from the cross in 15:34. His silence continues the theme of the Righteous Sufferer, which lies behind the entire Passion Narrative, echoing Isa 53:7 and developed in Wis 2:10-20. It again shows "Jesus' sovereign self-possession" (Marcus 2009, 1034).

Mark once again places on the lips of an antagonist a statement that displays a facet of Jesus' identity. So far he has already assembled a range of identities for Jesus including Messiah, Son of God, Son of Man, Suffering Servant of God, and Righteous Sufferer, primarily through narrative sequence and intertextuality. Now the designation King of the Jews joins the rich tapestry.

■ **6-11** The story of **A man called Barabbas** is now inserted into the drama. There is no evidence outside the Gospels for Mark's claim that **it was the custom at the Feast to release a prisoner whom the people requested.** His interest in Barabbas has little to do with the amnesty. He is interested only in comparing and contrasting the two men.

Nothing is known of **Barabbas** outside the Gospels, nor is it possible to determine what is meant by **the uprising.** His name is "son of the Father" in Aramaic. He was **in prison with the insurrectionists who had committed murder.** Matthew identifies him as "Jesus Barabbas" (27:16-17 NRSV). Mark does not state that he was a murderer, but Luke 23:19 does. Mark identifies these prisoners as *stasiastōn* (**insurrectionists**). The term seems to be synonymous with *lēstēs*, **rebel** or **brigand** (see John 18:40). According to Mark 15:27, Jesus is crucified between two *lēstas*, probably some of Barabbas' cohorts.

The **crowd** returns to the scene in an entirely negative role. These are not necessarily the same people who had acclaimed Jesus a few days earlier in the temple (11:18; 12:12, 37) nor attended his arrest (14:43). They request that Pilate **do for them what he usually did.**

Pilate sees this as an opportunity to exercise his cynical leadership. He could please the crowd and honor the tradition by releasing a harmless pretender, the battered, self-confessed **king of the Jews.** Mark tells his readers that Pilate knew **it was out of envy** that Jesus had been turned **over to him** and that the chief priests were attempting to manipulate him. The **envy** probably stemmed from the perceived threat Jesus' popularity presented their privileged position (see Bond 1998, 110).

But Pilate's cunning plan is frustrated by the chief priests who **stirred up the crowd to have Pilate release Barabbas instead.** The text does not suggest that that option was offered initially. But it may indicate that the chief priests were privy to the impending crucifixions of three insurrectionists, including Barabbas, the leader.

Mark's curious way of introducing Barabbas into the narrative suggests that the name was was a pseudonym with a certain pretentiousness to it, or that he was notorious (see Matt 27:16), even if unknown to modern readers. The story compares and contrasts Jesus and Barabbas. Both are bound before Pilate; both are perceived to be threats to the state; Jesus has prayed to his Father just verses earlier—"*Abba*, Father" (14:36); Barabbas is son of the father. "Barabbas is an insurrectionist and a murderer, whereas Jesus bestows health and life . . . and does not pose a threat to the *pax Romana* (see 12:13-17). One 'son of the father,' then, has tried in vain to usher in the heavenly *Abba*'s dominion through revolutionary violence against the Romans; the other succeeds in doing so by dying on a Roman cross" (Marcus 2009, 1036).

■ **12-15** Pilate's strategy fails miserably. Abdicating all sense of leadership and justice, he asks the crowd what he should do with Jesus, as if he were determining the life or death of a gladiator. But he could scarcely have been ready for the vehemence of the response. His feeble attempts to release Jesus are met with increasing frenzy: **they shouted all the louder: "Crucify him!"**

Mark describes the motive for Pilate's capitulation: **Wanting to satisfy the crowd, Pilate released Barabbas to them.** Marcus detects a demonic character to the scene: "under the influence of malignant spirits" throughout the narrative, opposition to Jesus arises (2009, 1036-37). This is a reminder that for Mark the problem for Israel is not primarily the Romans, or even their false shepherds. The battle is supramundane. Mark does not explicitly note the powers of evil in his betrayal story as do Luke (22:3, 31) and John (13:27). But the opposition to God's rule is present, nonetheless. And it is embodied in the religious leaders, the crowd, and in Pilate and Jesus' executioners.

Pilate has **Jesus flogged.** This probably involved a whipping with leather thongs equipped with sharp objects designed to cause deep lacerations and tear the flesh to the bone. It was a gruesome prelude to the most awful of deaths: Pilate **handed him over** [*paredōken*] **to be crucified.** Jesus' prediction in 10:33 has come true: "There is more at work in the death of Jesus than political intrigue. Jesus died in the final analysis because it was the will of God for him to die" (Kernaghan 2007, 326).

7. Jesus Mocked (15:16-20a)

The mockery Jesus undergoes is similar to that he endured at the hands of the high priest's guards. But events have moved on. Jesus has been flogged by Roman soldiers and is probably near death. He endures spitting and hitting. In the first instance, he is mocked as a false prophet. Then, his prophetic words come true as he absorbs the abuse. He is mocked as a pathetic claimant of kingship. The irony is rich: Mark's readers know that Jesus is king.

■ **16-20a** Marcus proposes a textual emendation: Changing *praitōrion* to *praitōriou* allows him to translate "the soldiers led him away, into the courtyard—that is, of the praetorium" rather than **the soldiers led Jesus away into the palace (that is, the Praetorium).** The existing text requires *aulēs* and *praitōrion* to be treated as synonyms meaning "palace." The advantage of this speculative change is that it is easier to imagine the rest of this scene occurring in the courtyard of the palace than in the palace itself. There is no Greek MSS evidence supporting this change, but the Vulgate and some Latin texts support it (Marcus 2009, 1039). The NRSV reads: "the soldiers led him into the courtyard of the palace (that is, the governor's headquarters)," which is close to the emendation.

The **soldiers** now control Jesus. They are Gentiles under Roman command. These soldiers **called together the whole *cohort.*** Mark probably means only that part of the cohort on duty at the time, rather than all 600 men in a typical ***cohort*** (so Donahue and Harrington 2002, 435).

The sorry state of the **king of the Jews** is fit only for mockery. A **purple robe** probably signified royalty and the **crown of thorns** adds to the absurdity of the scene. The thorns may well have been part of the torture, but they could also be a mocking symbol of rays emanating from Jesus' head. The sadistic ridicule continues: **they struck him on the head with a *reed* and spit on him *and knelt before him.*** Of course, all this was in mockery: the purple robe and crown of the king, the royal scepter of authority in the hands of his tormenters, and the pretended obeisance before him (see Collins 2007, 723).

Much of this echoes the language of the abuse heaped on the Suffering Servant of Yahweh. Isaiah 50:6, "I offered my back to those who beat me, my cheeks to those who pulled out my beard; I did not hide my face from mocking and spitting," has particular resonance here (and in Mark 14:65). The irony is rich: Those who think they are in control are only bit players in the drama. Jesus is the Righteous One, the Suffering Servant, the Son of Man who goes as it is written of him.

FROM THE TEXT

From the time in the garden, when Jesus aligns his will with that of the Father, the direction is sealed and Jesus goes as it is written concerning him. But nothing in the story is at it seems.

At the one level, the story is of a disaster. Within a few days, a man hailed by the crowds is humiliated. Jesus is reduced to a pitiful spectacle crucified in public as a warning to any would-be leaders. The deterioration is relentless. Although Jesus perceives an impending crisis and tries to prepare his closest followers for it, they are not ready when it comes. He is arrested after one of his trusted followers betrays him. All of the others promptly abandon him, probably fearing for their lives.

Jesus is arraigned before the most powerful civic and spiritual leaders of his own people, who have delegated authority in many matters from the ruling Romans. He is accused of a range of delusional predictions—such as building a temple not made with hands in three days—to which he has no answer. But in the end, he admits his self-described messianic identity to the high priest, who immediately has all the evidence he needs to shape a charge of treason that would get the attention of the Romans. Jesus is mocked as a false prophet, beaten, and bundled off to the courtyard of Herod's palace to face the Roman governor. Pilate shrewdly recognizes the political intrigue behind this charge, considers Jesus innocent, but finds it expedient to appease the crowd and order the death penalty for the insurrectionists to proceed. He has Jesus flogged, mocked, and sent to his crucifixion.

But Mark's readers see the irony in all this: Behind these events lie Jesus' earlier predictions that this was the way events would unfold. Mark makes this clear to readers by skillfully interweaving OT themes into the Passion Narrative. This intertextuality increases and reaches its crescendo in the death scene. Jesus gathers up in himself and embodies all the suffering figures of the OT and the inscrutable divine purpose in suffering.

Jesus goes as it is written concerning him, but those who participate in his betrayal remain culpable and responsible (14:21). His predictions are fulfilled at every step in the story. This is seen most sharply in the betrayal by Judas, the abandonment of Jesus by his followers, the threefold denial of Peter, and the brutality he endures—all as he predicted earlier.

The question of who killed Jesus, however, is fraught with complexity. Mark's picture "divides the responsibilities for Jesus' condemnation and subsequent execution between the Jewish chief priests and other leaders on the one hand, and the Roman prefect Pilate and the soldiers under him on the other hand. The Jewish leaders in Jerusalem (not the whole people!) put the

MARK

15:2-20a

process into motion, but the ultimate legal responsibility lay with Pilate and the Romans" (Donahue and Harrington 2002, 439).

The tragedy of the Christian interpretation of this founding story over the centuries is that it has aided and abetted anti-Semitism. The Jews as a people are not responsible for the death of Jesus. Since the Holocaust, all Christians are under a permanent obligation actively to ensure that anti-Semitism in any form is never acceptable at any level in society but especially among the people of God.

In a deeper sense, Mark portrays the death of Jesus as a ransom for many (10:45). Through it a new relationship between God and his created order is possible (14:24). Jesus dies because it is the will of God. And he dies in the confidence that God will vindicate him and bring the good news of the kingdom of God to completion.

C. The Crucifixion (15:20b-39)

I. The Road to Crucifixion (15:20b-22)

IN THE TEXT

■ **20b-21** The relentless path to the cross continues. The horror of crucifixion is vastly understated: **they led him out to crucify him.** Crosses were of several types: Some were upright poles (Latin: *stipes*) with a crossbeam (Latin: *patibulum*) on top like a "T." Others used crossbeams secured part of the way from the top like a "✝." Others took the form of an "X," with victims spread-eagled. People could be crucified in any position, although vertically, with their heads up, was most common.

Death by crucifixion was slow and, on occasion, deliberately prolonged to inflict the maximum humiliation on its victims. Their arms were normally tied to the crossbeam or nailed to it through the wrists. This might be done before they reached the cross, so that victims carried their crossbeam to the pole. Once they arrived at the pole, victims would be hoisted by the crossbeam to the appropriate place on the vertical pole, and left naked and exposed to public gaze. A peg or a rudimentary seat (Latin: *sedile*) was sometimes inserted into the upright on which the suspended and immobile victim was placed, not to ease the pain but to prolong the agony.

Crucifixions were done in public spaces as a warning to passersby of the fate that awaited those who challenged the authority of the state. The poles may have been a semipermanent installation as a constant visual reminder of state power. A notice (Latin: *titulus*) attached to the victim's body or the cross was an additional warning. Bodies left hanging after death became food for carrion birds and wild dogs.

As Jesus makes his way from the courtyard to the crucifixion site on **Golgotha,** he would be expected to carry his own crossbeam—part of the disgrace the condemned person was to face. Apparently Jesus' weakened condition from the scourging and other abuse made it impossible for him to carry it. So the soldiers compelled a **man from Cyrene, Simon, . . . to carry the cross** (but see John 19:17). Soldiers could press-gang any person to do their bidding.

Mark gives enough information about **Simon** to be tantalizing, but insufficient to reach any conclusions. Was he a Jew or a Gentile? The names of his sons are Greek names, but these names were also used by Jews. He is entering Jerusalem from the country, but why? Was he a pilgrim for Passover coming from Cyrene, a major Greek colony with a substantial Jewish community (Collins 2007, 736) and located near Shahat in modern Libya? Was he a long-term resident in Jerusalem's hinterland and part of a synagogue that included Cyrenians (Acts 6:9)?

Mark identifies Simon as **the father of Alexander and Rufus.** The most plausible explanation for this gratuitous information is that these names were known to his first readers. Some speculatively connect Rufus with Rom 16:13.

■ **22** The soldiers **brought** [*pherousin*, ***carried***] Jesus . . . **to Golgatha.** The location was likely outside the oldest city wall. Two locations have vied for recognition: Gordon's Calvary and the place on which the Church of the Holy Sepulcher was built, which has ancient tradition behind it. There is little to commend Gordon's Calvary—a nineteenth-century attribution (Brown 1994, 936-40). **Golgotha** may refer to an outcropping of unexcavated rock in the ancient quarry that lay west of the city, outside and north of the first wall and outside and west of the second wall, near a road and the Gennath Gate (Collins 2007, 740, following Taylor). Why it was called **The Place of the Skull** (Latin: *Calvaria*) is difficult to determine. Was it because it had a reputation as a place of execution or because it was a barren hill that somehow resembled a skull?

2. The Crucifixion (15:23-27)

IN THE TEXT

■ **23-24** It is not stated who offers the **wine mixed with myrrh.** Bystanders may have mercifully offered it, perhaps echoing Prov 31:6. But the mixture's analgesic properties are uncertain (see Evans 2001, 501). Some thought myrrh enhanced the taste of some wines. Matthew 27:34 eliminates the allusion to Proverbs. Instead he makes an explicit connection to Ps 69:21 (which Mark uses in 15:36), but Matthew thereby misses the connection to Proverbs where bystanders come to the victim's aid.

Here, however, it seems that the soldiers are offering the wine. More likely it is another attempt at mockery (so Evans 2001, 501). It could also have been further torture: myrrh made the wine undrinkable, only "frustrating the great thirst of the person being executed" (Collins 2007, 742). Some see his refusal linked to Mark 14:25; others that he needed to experience the full pain as part of the cup of suffering (so Brown 1994, 942). These might explain why **he did not take it.** All are plausible, but Mark does not say.

The short journey from Pilate's headquarters to Golgotha (three hundred meters [under one thousand feet]; France 2002, 642) is completed. Again, Mark tells us that **they crucified him** without any details (for details, see Brown 1994, 945-53). More attention is given to the soldiers who are **dividing up his clothes**—all his clothing, leaving Jesus naked on the cross. They are *casting lots to see who gets what.*

The language itself comes from Ps 22:18 at the end of a series of descriptions of a suffering figure who endures all kinds of insults, humiliation, and rejection.

> The soldiers, in their actions, are totally oblivious to the deeper significance of their custom. . . . No doubt they divided the garments of other victims in precisely the same way. But to Mark and his readers, much more is happening, for the soldiers are carrying out their part in a much greater drama, whose final act had already begun by the words, "But let the scriptures be fulfilled" (14:49). Their action confirms that Jesus is the righteous sufferer. (Brower 1978, 423)

At this point, Mark begins an extensive use of Ps 22 to interpret the death of Jesus. Like other psalms of lament, it follows the pattern: address, lamentation, confession of trust, petition, and praise. Their internal transition means that lamentation and praise are always juxtaposed (Westermann 1974, 26).

Psalm 22 has as its end the deliverance of God. It also has the tension, present from the first verse, between complaint and confidence. It emphasizes the humiliation of the sufferer. This is easily linked to Jesus, who is now left completely exposed to ridicule, especially when the *titulus* reads THE KING OF THE JEWS (v 26). But Ps 22 as a whole shows that Jesus' passion is within the purposes and activity of God. It serves both as a quarry for citations and a palate for color to tell the story of Jesus' death.

■**25** Mark notes that it **was the third hour when they crucified** Jesus, the first in a series of explicit time markers (→ 15:19). Matthew and Luke omit this reference. Mark is internally consistent, showing "how carefully God took care of the events surrounding the death of the Son" (Brown 1994, 960). But Mark conflicts with John 19:14, in which Pilate sentences Jesus at "about the sixth hour." Attempts to resolve the discrepancy (e.g., Stein 2008, 713) are largely unsuccessful. After an exhaustive treatment, Brown concludes, "Both [Mark and John] may be theological; one may be chronological and the other theological or liturgical; but both cannot be chronologically exact" (1994, 959).

■ **26** Mark includes the **written notice of the charge against** Jesus. While Mark does not tell us, the traditional picture that this is attached to the cross as a public warning as well as humiliation is plausible. Similar placards are attested in antiquity (see Evans 2001, 504). Its place above his head and crossbeam are also plausible. The notice of Pilate's condemnation is inscribed upon the placard: THE KING OF THE JEWS. "Placed over a man dying in agony and disgrace it was both a cruel joke and a powerful deterrent" (France 2002, 646).

■ **27** Three people are crucified that day: ***And with him they crucify two brigands, one on the right and one on his left.*** This passage echoes Isa 53:12: "because he poured out his life unto death, and was numbered with the transgressors," adding to the cumulative case for the Righteous Sufferer motif. Mark does not identify the brigands. But they could be those awaiting execution with Barabbas. What we do know is that they are not James and John (→ Mark 10:37), who have fled. "The places of honor [they sought] are filled with men who are unworthy" (Collins 2007, 748). The irony of the situation in light of the Zebedee brothers' request is unmistakable.

Jesus is in the center. While he is undergoing the same cruel death as they, Mark is clear that Jesus is different. Suffering does not make the brigands righteous sufferers nor does execution at the hands of the Romans make Jesus an insurrectionist.

3. Mockery (15:29-32)

IN THE TEXT

■ **29-30** The concentrated threads of OT motifs woven into Mark's narrative add color to the actions of Jesus' opponents. Here, Jesus is rejected by bystanders, the chief priests and scribes, and the two brigands. He dies reviled by all. Again nothing is said about the crucifixion details. The mockery continues with some standard language of abuse.

The abuse by passersby begins: **hurled insults** (*eblasphēmoun*) and **shaking their heads.** The irony of blaspheming Jesus is probably not lost on Mark's first hearers (Hooker 1991, 373; France 2002, 714). But here it simply means "insult" or "ridicule." This echoes Ps 22:7: "All who see me mock me; they hurl insults [*exemyktērisan*], shaking their heads," and Ps 109:25: "I am an object of scorn to my accusers; when they see me, they shake their heads." Neither passage is cited exactly, but the language of abuse of the Righteous One adds to the picture. **Shaking their heads** may also allude to Lam 2:15 (→ Mark 15:31-32 sidebar, "The Righteous Sufferer in the Book of Wisdom," on Wis 2:17-20).

The words of mockery on the lips of the passersby reflect the testimony of the false witnesses in Mark 14:58. They would be better placed on the lips of the priests, although the allegations may have been widespread. The by-standers throw Jesus' claim back in his face: One dying on a cross was unlikely to make good on this prediction of temple destruction (15:29). Their taunt is: **Come down from the cross and save yourself!** This pitiful figure could not even save himself, much less destroy the temple.

■ **31-32** *Similarly, the chief priests with the scribes were mockingly saying to one another, "He saved others, but he is unable to save himself!"* The basis for this mockery is obvious in chs 1—8, in which Jesus' deeds are described using *sōizō* (3:4; 5:23-34; 6:56; 10:52). Scribes from Jerusalem oppose him (3:22; 7:1).

But the whole Markan narrative reinterprets the notion of messiahship and power. Thus, "the Messiah, the King of Israel" (NRSV) who is apparently dying in disgrace, and powerless to save himself, is fulfilling the purposes God has established for saving others. He cannot **come down now from the cross.** The biting mockery of a powerless king who cannot command anyone and a messiah without followers is, of course, deeply ironic. Mark's readers know that it is precisely by staying on the cross that Jesus exercises ultimate author-ity, serves others, and re-creates the new covenant people of God (→ 10:45; 14:24).

The mockers have no expectation that Jesus will come down from the cross, of course. Priests and brigands alike think Jesus is a failed visionary. But Mark's readers know that Jesus is indeed "The King of the Jews" (v 26), that precisely by staying on the cross and giving His life, He is actually saving it (15:30, see 8:35) and that His power to save others is demon-strated in the cross itself (15:31). He is indeed "The Messiah, the King of Israel" (15:32a) and in the crowning irony of all, the religious leaders ask to see so that they might believe at the precise moment when they are seeing, but failing to believe (15:35b). (Brower 1997, 128)

The Righteous Sufferer in the Book of Wisdom

The Book of Wisdom, one of the so-called apocryphal books, was re-garded as scripture by most Christians in the second century A.D. and may well have been known by some of the NT writers. It was probably written in Greek in Alexandria in the first century B.C.

Wisdom's picture of the righteous sufferer obviously reflects the Servant Songs of Isa 40—55 and the psalms of lament, such as Ps 22. In this it resembles Mark's Passion Narrative. In Wisdom, the righteous man is opposed by ungodly men who reason that, if he is truly God's Son as he claims (Wis 2:13, 16), deliver-ance will come from God. Consider Wis 2:17-20:

> Let us see if his words are true, and let us test what will happen at the end
> of his life; for if the righteous man is God's child, he will help him, and will
> deliver him from the hand of his adversaries. Let us test him with insult

and torture, so that we may find out how gentle he is, and make trial of his forbearance. Let us condemn him to a shameful death, for, according to what he says, he will be protected. (NRSV)

A similar idea plays a part in Mark 15:33-39. Some of the language and the overall theme of Wisdom resemble Mark. Mark probably did not use this source. It seems to represent a parallel but distinct development of the tradition of the righteous sufferer.

4. The Death (15:33-39)

BEHIND THE TEXT

"That day" (2:20) has arrived. The explicit timing that Mark uses throughout the Passion Narrative is significant:

First, Mark has a fondness for threes. In Gethsemane Jesus prays three times and finds his three disciples asleep three times. He predicts that Peter will deny him three times. He is mocked by three groups. The crucifixion is divided into the two three-hour intervals.

Second, the precision in time is a strong signal that all of this is in the Father's control. According to 13:32, only the Father knows "about that day or hour." Now this is the day and the hour; all is within the purview of God.

But Jesus is dying on a Roman cross after suffering abuse from passersby, religious authorities, and the state. The story so far ends with the mocking statement of the chief priests and scribes: "Let the Messiah, the King of Israel, come down from the cross now, so that we may see and believe" (NRSV). They clearly do not expect this will happen. Gradually, and irrefutably, Jesus is being shown to be a fraud. He will die as a blasphemer against God and the temple, and as an enemy of the state. Where, then, is God in this bleak scene?

The answer Mark gives is complicated. The story at one level is unremittingly grim, with the darkness and cry of dereliction in v 34 plumbing the depths. But, Mark's story is told on two levels. All the action occurs and the participants perceive the meaning of their actions at the dramatic level. But Mark and Jesus (according to Mark) function at the readers' level. They know "what is going on in what is happening." This two-level narration is particularly obvious in the widespread use of irony and parody in the Passion Narrative.

This section of Mark is structured carefully to illuminate the meaning of Jesus' death. Like so much else in the Passion Narrative, the death of Jesus is not what it seems on the surface—the confirmation of Jesus' self-delusion. Mark makes no attempt to minimize the death or to deny it. Rather, the death is surrounded by events that shed light on its meaning.

The simple questions, "What is happening?" "Who is doing it?" and "What is going on?" form the basis for a nontechnical analysis (adapted from Brower 1983, 89-90).

	Verse	Actor(s)	Action	Motif
A	33	God	Darkness	Judgment
B	34	Jesus	Cry	Righteous Sufferer
C	35	Bystander	Elijah	Misunderstanding
D	36a	Bystanders	Wine offered	Righteous Sufferer
C¹	36b	Bystanders	Elijah	Misunderstanding
B¹	37	Jesus	Death cry	Righteous Sufferer
A¹	38	God	Temple veil	Judgment
E	39	Centurion	Confession	Son of God

This analysis calls attention to several points that aid in understanding the death scene:

First, the action of God brackets everything that happens on that day. The darkness at noon is over the whole earth, according to Mark; so this could only be a divine activity. Similarly, the rending of the temple veil from top to bottom can only be a divine activity. If this is correct, the whole scene must be interpreted in terms of God's action, demonstrating the coherence of this story with Paul's assertion that "God was in Christ reconciling the world unto himself" (2 Cor 5:19 KJV).

Second, the death cry of Jesus (either one cry reported in Mark 15:34, 37, or two cries) should be understood in the context of the righteous sufferer. Furthermore, that it cites from Ps 22 and constitutes the only words Jesus says after his response to Pilate indicate their seriousness. The undeniable Righteous Sufferer motif is confirmed by Mark 15:36a, a probable allusion to Ps 69:21.

Third, this structure helps explain the apparently gratuitous (and difficult) misunderstanding about Elijah in Mark 15:36. The death scene could move smoothly from v 34 to v 37 without this detail. But Mark's inclusion of it raises the question, why?

Fourth, the conclusion of the narrative with the confession of the centurion is ambiguous on the narrative level, but on the reader's level is clearly a true statement.

IN THE TEXT

■ **33** For Mark the death of the Messiah, the king of the Jews, is demonstrably an act of God. **At the sixth hour** [noon] **darkness came over the whole land** [*holēn tēn gēn*] **until the ninth hour.** Time notations are vital for Mark (→ 15:1), with the striking parallel to ch 13 continuing (see Lightfoot 1950, 53). This darkness lasts for the three hours of Jesus' agony.

There is little point in seeking a rationalistic explanation of this darkness as a blinding dust storm, a solar eclipse (which would never cause total darkness for three hours nor occur at Passover), or some other local and otherwise inexplicable phenomenon. Mark's point is different.

First, this almost certainly alludes to one or more OT texts: Exod 10:21-23; Isa 13:10-11; Jer 15:6-9; Joel 2:31; or Amos 8:9-10. Of these, the closest is Amos: "'In that day,' declares the Sovereign LORD, 'I will make the sun go down at noon and darken the earth in broad daylight. I will turn your religious feasts into mourning. . . . I will make that time like mourning for an only son and the end of it like a bitter day.'"

If this is correct, it implies that the darkness is an act of God. This is confirmed by Mark's claim that the darkness covers **the whole *earth*** and occurs at noon. These phenomena in Amos are part of "the day of Yahweh." In Amos, this is a day of darkness and not light (Amos 5:18-24) in which Yahweh judges his people who have been perverting justice while maintaining an elaborate religious facade. "That day" is already alluded to in Mark 2:20. Now, the high feast of Passover is turned into "mourning for an only son" (Amos 8:10). Jesus is called God's "beloved Son" in 1:11 and 9:7 (KJV and NKJV). At the end of this scene, in Mark 15:39, the centurion will confess that Jesus is "the Son of God."

These echoes resonate in the darkness at noon. Its main thrust is judgment. Some suggest that this is judgment on Jesus, especially in light of the cry of dereliction that follows. On this view, Jesus vicariously absorbs the judgment of God in himself as the ransom for many (→ 10:45). But it could also be seen as judgment against Israel's leadership. Jesus' opposition from the Jerusalem religious elite has been part of the narrative explicitly since 3:22. Jesus has spoken prophetic words and acted against the temple establishment especially since his entry to Jerusalem. Others suggest that the darkness symbolizes the demonic presence in the Passion Narrative.

But Mark uses this motif in his own way. It is judgment, to be sure, but this is the judgment of the cosmos, including humanity, symbolized by darkness **over the whole land.** In the depth of the darkness, one can see the act of God. His judgment is occurring in the cross of the Crucified One. "Mark sees this as a climactic day for all peoples and the whole earth" (Brown 1994, 1036). The view is essentially the same as in John 12:31-33.

■ **34** Just as the darkness would seem to go on forever, and the one on the cross is reaching the end, at the **ninth hour** [1500; 3:00 P.M.] **Jesus cried out in a loud voice** (*phōnē megalē*). The phrase **loud voice** is used in 1:26 and 5:7 of the cry of demons. On this reading, the crucifixion becomes for Mark the ultimate result of demonic hostility and Jesus expels a demon with this loud cry (Danker 1970). No doubt the crucifixion does represent Jesus' climactic conflict with evil and the demonic—it is certainly understood by Paul in these

15:33-34

399

terms (see Col 1:20; 2:15). But to suggest that this is an expulsion of a demon is highly unlikely (see Brower 1978, 482-85). The great voice is better understood as an expression of the suffering Jesus experiences (see the prayer of the martyrs in Rev 6:10).

As he does elsewhere when Jesus speaks at crucial moments (most recently in Gethsemane), Mark includes the transliterated Semitic phrase, **Eloi, Eloi, lama sabachthani,** and provides a translation. In Gethsemane Jesus addresses God as *"Abba,"* Father. Now he cries out in Aramaic (or Hebrew?), **My God, my God, why have you forsaken me?** While the intimacy of the **Abba** is gone, this difference should not be overplayed. This is still **My God** (but see France 2002, 652).

Jesus' haunting question occurs only in Mark and Matthew. Why does Mark include it? Luke and John can tell the passion story without it. At the dramatic level, these words express the agony of death. Jesus experiences death to the dregs (see Heb 2:9, 14-15). While we cannot know exactly what Jesus experienced, it should not surprise us to find the words of Ps 22 on his lips. These words are "passionate, expressing both the loneliness of intense suffering and a bold and demanding challenge addressed to God . . . quite different from the idealized accounts of the deaths of the later martyrs" (Collins 2007, 754).

But Mark's reason for including these words is more obvious at the readers' level. His readers are encouraged to grasp the full sense of Jesus' abandonment. Stein lists several suggestions: some emphasize Jesus' intense suffering, others see this as the decisive moment in his struggle against evil, and still others highlight the depths of his emotion—expressing the feelings of forsakenness experienced by Jesus (2008, 715).

Stein prefers to read Jesus' death cry as have many exegetes and theologians: It points to Jesus' "complete self-identification with sinners, [which] involved not merely a felt, but a real, abandonment by his Father" (Stein 2008, 716, citing Cranfield). France, however, rightly argues that interpreting these words in light of later doctrines of atonement, Christology, and Trinity presses Mark's language too far. "He wants us to feel Jesus' agony, not to explain it" (2002, 653).

Mark also wants readers to take seriously the origin in Ps 22 of this cry from the cross. Psalm 22 ends in vindication. So it reflects the tension between complaint and confidence, which must be maintained. Mark places this saying *after* the darkness at noon and *before* the rending of the temple veil. These are divine actions. Thus, far from giving the impression that God is absent from the scene between noon and 1500 (3:00 P.M.), the three hours are enclosed in divine action. At the conclusion of this period of darkness is the confession

15:34

that Jesus "was the Son of God" (Mark 15:39). This is Mark's conclusion to the immediate episode and to the entire Passion Narrative.

France rejects any attempt to hear vindication in Mark's use of Ps 22. He opines that Jesus' choice of this quotation on this occasion, "rather than one expressing a trusting relationship with God, [speaks] for itself. . . . Jesus feels abandoned by God" (2002, 652). Marcus goes further, arguing that the situation "is one of real forsakenness" (2009, 1064).

We are not compelled to take one view or another. These views of Jesus' death cry are not mutually exclusive. "Jesus is not questioning the existence of God or the power of God to do something about what is happening; he is questioning the silence of the one whom he calls 'My God'" (Brown 1994, 1046). He is taking on himself the full role of the servant (see Mark 14:22-25), while maintaining his confidence in the will of God. "The words at once show the agony and despair of this unique suffering, and the ultimate hope of vindication. . . . The words epitomize the unfathomable paradox of the cross" (Brower 1978, 489).

■**35-36** These verses are unnecessary for the flow of the narrative. Indeed, without this intervening section, v 37 could refer directly to v 34. Mark must, therefore, have a reason for including them.

The story is clear enough in general. Someone near the cross—Mark does not say who—hears *"Eloi, Eloi"* and misunderstands the words as a call for **Elijah.** This is surprising at the story level because (beyond the first two letters) the terms are not particularly close in Hebrew, Aramaic, Greek, or English.

The mishearing presupposes some knowledge of Jewish legends that Elijah would come in critical times to protect the innocent and rescue the righteous. This suggests that some bystander, not a soldier, heard Jesus' words. Although Elijah is "prominent in popular expectations of the endtimes" (Brown 1994, 1062), direct evidence for this legend is sketchy. However, "It would be impossible to portray such a misunderstanding unless at that time Elijah was regarded as a helper sent from heaven in cases of distress" (Schweizer 1971, 353).

Someone lifts **a sponge with wine vinegar, . . . and offered it to Jesus to drink.** Whether this is an act of kindness or more cynical mockery is unclear at the story level. Mark does not say whether or not Jesus accepts it. But the bystander wishes to see if Elijah will hear his cry and **take him down** from the cross. To no one's surprise, Elijah fails to show. So, Jesus is not a Righteous One. He dies as he deserves, mocked and disgraced, having failed the final opportunity to come down from the cross to show his bona fides. At the readers' level, however, things are different:

First, behind this story is an allusion to Ps 69:20-21. The richness of this psalm contributes to the color of Jesus' passion. The psalmist laments the absence of comforters: "I looked for sympathy, but there was none, for comforters, but I found none." Even God is silent. Then his enemies "put gall in my food and gave me vinegar for my thirst." The vindictiveness of the psalmist's enemies knows no bounds. At the readers' level, this is the latest and last in a long series of mocking and rejection events of the righteous sufferer, all according to Scripture.

Second, the misunderstanding of *"Eloi"* is more than a problem of faulty hearing. Readers know Elijah comes before the day of the Lord to prepare the way (see Mal 4:5). They also know that Jesus has told them that Elijah has already come and fulfilled all things (→ Mark 9:12). The Baptist fulfills the role of the Elijah in the messianic drama. They also know that John is dead. The misunderstanding, then, is profound and deeply ironic (see Collins 2007, 755; but see Evans 2001, 508). "It extends to their total ignorance of the true character of Elijah's role and their failure to discern its completion in the Baptist" (Brower 1983, 93; Marcus 2009, 1065). Just as all were wrong about John, they are wrong about Jesus.

Elijah does not come because he has already "returned" as the Baptist and his role has already been completed. He has prepared the way for the Lord and has been delivered up (1:14) as a righteous man (see 6:20). In Mark's view the day has arrived, Elijah has played his role, and the messianic drama now focuses on Jesus alone. The irony of the desire to **let us see . . . Elijah** simply enhances the picture. They are seeing the pinnacle of God's revelation as they look upon the crucified Jesus. But they fail to see it, as surely as do the mockers in 15:28-32.

■ **37** The death of Jesus is signaled by **letting out** [*apheis*] **a great cry,** the same phrase used in v 34. No words are mentioned here, however. He **exhaled his last breath** (*exepneusen*) is the death itself. Evans implausibly suggests this shows his power: "the release of his spirit is awesome" (2001, 508).

■ **38** At the precise moment when Jesus dies, **The curtain of the temple was torn in two from top to bottom.** Mark's insertion of this statement is central to the culmination of all that has happened. This event takes place some distance away from Golgotha. Therefore, it does not figure directly in the scene at the cross. Mark gives no indication that the centurion connected the rending of the temple veil and his confession.

Whether **the curtain of the temple** (*to katapetasma tou naou*) is the outer curtain separating the sanctuary from the courtyard or the one within the sanctuary before the holy of holies is unclear. In either case, this is presented as an act of God, since the inner curtain was nearly ten meters (thirty-two feet) high. The outer curtain was about twenty-five meters (eighty-two feet) high.

Some interpreters argue that it must have been the outer curtain, since only that could be seen by the centurion. But the traditional location of Golgotha with respect to the temple makes it highly improbable that the centurion could have seen even this curtain. Mark shows no interest in this connection. In favor of the inner curtain is the use of *naos* for temple, which usually (but not always) refers to the inner sanctum.

The insertion, then, is for readers. They are to understand its significance (see Collins 2007, 760). Geddert thinks at least five of the many proposals explaining its significance are plausible (2001, 380-81). This number can further be reduced to three:

First, this is God's action. Like the darkness at noon, this cannot be understood as other than a divine action. It is significant that divine activity opens and closes the death scene. The (divine) passive **was torn** (*eschisthē*) confirms this view. The verb is the same as that describing the tearing open (*schizomenous*) of the heavens when the Spirit descended on Jesus (in 1:10). The cry in 15:34, the mockery, and the death of Jesus are all enclosed within these two actions of God.

Thus, God is present throughout the entire death scene. Questions about the apparent absence of God are answered in narrative form. "By the violent rendering (*schizein*) God responds vigorously, not only to vindicate Jesus whom God has *not* forsaken, but also to express anger at the chief priests and Sanhedrin who decreed such a death for God's Son" (Brown 1994, 1100).

Second, this is divine judgment. If the opening darkness was judgment on the whole cosmos, this action is God's judgment on a temple that has been rendered obsolete by its ruinous leadership, on the one hand, and the creation of the new covenant community by Jesus' death (14:24), on the other.

The prophecy of Jesus in 14:62—"you will see the Son of Man sitting . . . and coming"—is being fulfilled in a way the high priest and the Sanhedrin did not anticipate. They see the beginning of the end for the temple. That will finally come to conclusion in A.D. 70 when **there will not be one stone left standing on another** (13:2). They also "see the kingdom of God come with power" (9:1) in quite the reverse of what they had expected. Their sarcastic mockery calling on Jesus to come down from the cross so that "they might see and believe" is ironically true. They will see, only too late, that the holiest place is now open to view.

Third, the fact that the torn curtain leaves the holy of holies open to view has a range of possible theological implications. It could signal that Jesus has "entered the Most Holy Place," as Heb 9:12 reads it. But this is less likely in Mark who has been establishing that the locale of God's dwelling among his people has been Jesus, the Holy One of God in the midst of his followers. The locale of God among his people is no longer the holy of holies. It is Jesus and the new community sealed with his blood.

■ **39** The interpretation of this verse is controversial, mainly because of the disputed meaning of the words spoken by **the centurion.** The term refers to a

15:38-39

noncommissioned Roman army officer who has risen through the ranks to become the commander of one hundred men. This centurion commands the detail charged with Jesus' execution. If the usual location for Golgotha is correct, he could not have witnessed the rending of the temple veil as he **stood there in front of Jesus.** To assume otherwise presents insurmountable geographical problems. Mark does not link the centurion's confession to the phenomenon of the torn curtain. In fact, the torn veil is strictly unnecessary to the story. His cultural background would have led him to consider the darkness at noon as an omen of some sort (Collins 2007, 765).

The different descriptions of what the centurion witnessed that led to his confession—**heard his cry** and "saw that in this way he breathed his last" (NRSV)—are due to the translation of different MS traditions. Both are early and certainty are impossible. The meaning of the phrase **saw how he died** is ambiguous and open to speculation.

The translation of the centurion's confession is open to debate. The same Greek words *alēthōs houtos ho anthrōpos hious theou ēn* could be translated definitely: **Surely this man was the Son of God!** as in the NIV, or "Truly this man was God's Son!" as in the NRSV. But the crucial phrase could also be translated indefinitely as "a son of a god."

Three main arguments have been raised against the definite reading:

First, there is no article modifying **Son.** But Greek phrases may be definite without the article. Debates between grammarians cannot settle this issue.

Second, since this is the only time the words occur on the lips of humans, the centurion is an unlikely candidate to give such a lofty confession. This is a strong argument only on the story level.

Third, the centurion would simply not have the religious background to point to Jesus as the unique Son of the one true God. This, too, is problematic on the story level (see Brown 1994, 1146-50).

The best answer is to recognize that this story operates on two levels. On the story level, the term is ambiguous. The centurion could mean no more than "Surely this was a righteous man," as Luke 23:47 reports his confession. That would give it an ironic twist and, like so much else in Mark's Passion Narrative, be true in a way he could not possibly imagine.

A decision is hardly crucial. For Mark and his readers, the second level, there can be little doubt that, whatever the centurion said or meant, this is the true confession: Jesus is the Son of God. This is the nodal point to which the whole narrative has been building.

Mark ties the confession closely to the rending of the temple curtain because this judgment by God involves both the ending of the temple's place in God's purposes and the concentration of God's purposes in his Son, who is now the dwelling place of God among his people.

The confession is ironic in that it is a centurion who utters these words: A lackey of the hated oppressors sees and believes, offering the greatest human confession in the Gospel. In contrast, the high priest witnesses the same thing but rejects Jesus' true identity as **Messiah, Son of the Blessed One** (14:61-63) as blasphemous.

This high christological reading is supported by the literary brackets of Mark 1:1 and 15:39. It is also confirmed by 1:1-15 and 15:38—16:8. In 1:9-11, after Jesus' baptism, God rends the heavens and announces: "You are my Son, whom I love; with you I am well pleased." In 15:38-39, God again acts when Jesus finishes his fatal mission (14:36). "This time, however, the confession is not the prospective announcement by God stating Jesus' being and mission, but the retrospective confirmation that Jesus has been precisely the Son of God in the whole gospel story and supremely so in the death scene. Jesus was never more truly Son of God than when He died" (Brower 1997, 233).

FROM THE TEXT

The crucifixion of Jesus Messiah on a Roman cross is the central datum of Christian theology. In this shameful death, Christians see and believe that the good purposes of the redeeming Father are fulfilled. Mark does not offer a full view of the atonement but does offer us several points for reflection:

First, Jesus dies as the Righteous Sufferer. He embodies in himself the whole plethora of OT suffering figures. All of these are how Mark defines what it means to be Messiah, the Son of God (1:1; 14:62; 15:39). The death of the Messiah gathers up all the alienation and pain that is the human condition. In his death, he experiences this in himself. God's power is displayed supremely in weakness and humiliation in the obedience of the Son to the Father. He becomes the ransom for many (10:45) and the basis and means through which God's new covenant with his re-created holy people is established.

Second, Jesus' death has consequences for the religious establishment. They seek to preserve their privilege and position in the face of what God is doing in Jesus. The destruction of the veil that opens the holy of holies follows the creation of this new covenant community. It also confirms that the temple is no longer the locale of God's dwelling on earth. This is now centered on Jesus, the Holy One of God, and the new community, created by his death. Instead of a holy place in a holy land, the holy people of God become a sort of walking temple. It is an open community, welcoming all who would take up their crosses and follow.

Third, the horror of Jesus' death is neither denied nor embellished. Cross-bearing is real, not just for Jesus, but for his followers. Suffering and death for the sake of the gospel continues to be the experience of countless followers of Christ around the world. They suffer rejection, mockery, impris-

15:33-39

onment, and even death because of their confession of Christ. The pattern of Jesus, then, becomes a source of strength in the midst of this suffering: He himself has gone before them to his death and has been vindicated.

Fourth, the silence of God in the midst of suffering is not the same as the absence of God. Even when Jesus is driven to utter those haunting words, "My God, My God. Why have you forsaken me?" readers know that Jesus is never abandoned by the Father.

Christians in despair and anguish, haunted by doubts and fears, know this utter sense of forsakenness, just as Jesus did. They can cry to God and experience nothing but silence, as Jesus did. This story reminds us that even in our darkest moments, when we neither see nor experience God's presence, we are not abandoned.

"This passage presents the search for a faith that knows that God is real even in times that the believer feels forsaken and when the resources for thinking and experience have been exhausted" (Schweizer 1971, 353). Jesus' experience is all-important for his followers who are hanging on by their fingernails.

Fifth, the cross is the reversal of all human expectations and pretensions. The Messiah should not die. And the forces of evil should not triumph. Kings are powerful. But the Messiah dies; and evil seems to triumph.

The irony is that Jesus is confessed as the Son of God, a title that Caesar claims for himself, by a Roman centurion. "A pagan from a distant land becomes the first human in the gospel to grasp the height and depth of Jesus' identity. In doing so, he unwittingly fulfills the triumphant ending of the psalm whose searing words have punctuated the Markan death scene (cf. 15:24, 29-32, 34)" (Marcus 2009, 1068).

D. The Burial (15:40-47)

BEHIND THE TEXT

The introduction of named women into the story at this point is pivotal for several reasons.

First, were it not for this passage, we would not know that women were part of Jesus' entourage in Galilee. France calls it "a remarkable shift in the gospel's emphasis." It is only at this point, when all the other disciples "have fallen by the wayside, that Mark lets us know that all the time there has been a female element to Jesus' entourage, who are now ready to pick up where the men have left off" (2002, 661-62). That they have been with Jesus from the beginning, and continue to observe the whole events from crucifixion to empty tomb, gives them a role that actually exceeds that of the male disciples, to whom they are to convey the good news.

Second, Mark compares and contrasts the female and male disciples. Both follow Jesus, both are associated with his ministry in Galilee, and both go up to Jerusalem. But "these women are linked with Jesus' own ultimate act of service, his death (10:45). The service of women thus brackets the entire Gospel (see 1:31)" (Marcus 2009, 1069).

Third, a likely background to this passage is an allusion to Ps 38:11 in which the psalmist laments, "My friends and companions avoid me because of my wounds; my neighbors stay far away." The fact that the only other reference to "from afar" (*apo makrothen*) in Mark is Peter's location in 14:54 suggests that this allusion is still part of the comprehensive Righteous Sufferer motif.

Fourth, Mark's failure to name any women in Jesus' entourage previously has a clear narrative function. Their introduction gives particularly strong emphasis to their key role in the story as the link between Jesus' death, burial, and resurrection. "Put simply, their sole task and literary function in these scenes is to witness what happens" (Hurtado 2009, 8).

The service of **Joseph of Arimathea** is also unexpected. Members of the Jewish religious elite, like he, to this point have uniformly opposed Jesus. Arimathea (*Harimathaias*), the birthplace of Samuel (1 Sam 1:1), is located in the hill country of Ephraim, fifteen kilometers (nine miles) northeast of Lydda and thirty kilometers (eighteen miles) east of Joppa. Joseph came from Arimathea but probably lived in Jerusalem, since he had a tomb there (Collins 2007, 777).

The remainder of Mark's story after the centurion's confession has the character of denouement. But some crucial loose ends remain. The torn temple curtain was an indirect vindication of Jesus, but Jesus predicted he would rise from the dead (8:31; 9:31; 10:33). He has also promised that he would gather his scattered flock (14:28).

IN THE TEXT

Particular aspects of this text are also crucial for Mark's conclusion, including the eyewitness testimony of the women and the burial of Jesus, confirming the reality of his death.

■ **40-41** Mark introduces **some women** who **were watching from a distance.** They have both positive and negative attributes. Like Peter, they are following in a semidetached manner. But they are watching and witness the whole process culminating in Jesus' burial. Mark names three for the first time in his Gospel:

Mary Magdalene was probably from Magdala, on the northwest shore of the sea of Galilee, five kilometers (three miles) north of Tiberias (probably modern Migal). She is mentioned in all four Gospels. Here she witnesses the crucifixion of Jesus (15:40), the place of his burial (15:47), and the empty tomb (16:1-7). This makes her the critical witness to the resurrection. Later traditions embellish her story, making her a former prostitute from whom Jesus exorcised seven demons.

Mary the mother of James the younger and of Joses may refer to Jesus' mother. But if it is she, this is an odd way of identifying her. More likely she is the mother of James, the son of Alphaeus (3:18). **Salome** is otherwise unidentified in Mark. But Matthew seems to identify her as the mother of James and John (Matt 27:56).

Mark surprises his readers, mentioning here for the first time that women were among Jesus' disciples from the beginning: *When Jesus was in Galilee, these women were following* [*ēkolouthoun*] *him and were ministering* [*diēkonoun*] *to him, and many other women who came up with him into Jerusalem were also there* (Mark 15:41). In retrospect, they could well have been present in 2:15; 6:1; and possibly the "daughter" in 5:34. Mark says no more about their service but uses the same verb for the assistance angels gave Jesus in the wilderness (1:13). It also describes the service of Peter's mother-in-law (1:31) and significantly, the Son of Man (10:45). Here, the women perform another crucial role—witnessing the death, burial place, and empty tomb.

■ **42-46** Mark's next time notation, referring to the burial of Jesus, is complex: *And since it was already evening, when it was Preparation Day, which is before the Sabbath.* Clearly his burial required great haste, since he died a mere three hours before sunset, by which time the burial would have to be completed. Deuteronomy 21:23 required that corpses be removed before sunset to prevent pollution of the land.

So as evening approached, Joseph of Arimathea took action. He is otherwise unknown, but was **a prominent member of the Council** (probably the Sanhedrin; Donahue and Harrington 2002, 453). Joseph's concern was "an act of piety in obedience to the law" (Collins 2007, 776).

Mark says nothing of what happened to the others crucified with Jesus. Pilate's surprise that Jesus **was already dead** suggests that they were still alive on their crosses. If they were also dead, they were probably removed and put in a common grave near the crucifixion site. This would have been in obedience to the Law as well. Mark shows no interest in their burial.

Mark describes Joseph as a sympathetic hearer of Jesus (so France 2002, 666) because he **was himself waiting for the kingdom of God.** Nevertheless, Mark shows no need to modify the earlier statement that all the Sanhedrin was against Jesus (15:1). Joseph may have had ready access to Pilate as a member of the Sanhedrin. But it was at some risk to himself that he **went boldly to Pilate and asked for Jesus' body.** Once Pilate confirmed from **the centurion** that Jesus was dead, *he released the corpse to Joseph.*

The description of Jesus' burial implies standard practice, "the absolute minimum one could do for the dead" (Brown 1994, 1246). No mention is made of washing or anointing the body. Significantly, at Jesus' anointing in Bethany (→ 14:1-9), he said of the woman, "She has anointed my body beforehand for its burial" (14:8 NRSV). Perhaps, this made up for its absence now. No spices are mentioned either: this was a hasty affair (contrast John 19:38-42). Spices were to be added on the first day of the week. Mark gives no information about the tomb—that it was Joseph's (Matt 27:60) or that it was a new tomb (Luke 23:53). In fact, "Mark's account is singularly lacking in elements that would suggest an honorable burial for Jesus" (Brown 1994, 1244).

The necessary haste is shown in the verbal sequence: he **bought . . . took down . . . wrapped . . . placed,** all completed before sunset. The **linen cloth** (*sindona*) was a large piece of cloth like a sheet. This is the same word describing the garment the naked young man left behind in Gethsemane in Mark 14:51. Mark does not enhance his description at all.

According to Collins, the use of the term in both contexts implicitly contrasts the young man and Jesus. "Whereas the young man escaped death by fleeing . . . and shamefully leaving the *sindōn* behind, Jesus did not flee when he was arrested . . . so that, at the end of his ordeal, his body was wrapped in a *sindōn*" (2007, 778). But this might stretch the narrative connection too much. Joseph placed Jesus' wrapped body **in a tomb cut out of rock.** Mark gives the impression that this is a tomb built into the walls of a quarry, since Golgotha may have been on a knoll above a quarry (so Brown 1994, 1247). The tomb itself probably had an entrance at ground level into a cave-like chamber. A number of configurations were current then (see Brown 1994, 1248-51). Once the body was in the tomb and placed either in a burial tunnel or on a bench (Mark does not say), **he rolled a stone against the entrance.** Joseph was probably assisted by his servants, since it is difficult to imagine one person doing all of this alone (John 19:39-42 mentions Nicodemus).

■ **47** Mark then gives a key bit of information: The two Marys ***were watching where he was laid.*** They took in the whole event (see Donahue and Harrington 2002, 455).

FROM THE TEXT

Mark emphasizes four important points here: First, Jesus is really dead. This has been observed by the women, tested by Pilate, and confirmed by a centurion. Second, the women witness the entire sequence of events—crucifixion, death, confession, removal from the cross, and burial. These women are guarantors of a crucial part of early church tradition—"that he was buried" (1 Cor 15:4). Third, from the beginning women were followers of Jesus, a remarkably countercultural dimension of Jesus' ministry. That the veracity of

15:42-47

these events depends on the constant watch given by these women is particularly noteworthy in a cultural context that discounted the testimony of women. Fourth, at the least, one named member of the Sanhedrin was an earnest seeker after God's reign, even if Mark does not say he is a follower of Jesus.

15:40-47

VIII. THE EMPTY TOMB: MARK 16:1-8

BEHIND THE TEXT

This scene is immensely powerful but full of ambiguities for modern readers. It is further complicated by the major textual problem of the Gospel's ending. Does it end with 16:8 or 16:9 or 16:20, the three most likely options? Almost all now agree that the added shorter and longer endings are not the earliest recoverable form of the text, which ends at 16:8. The evidence is both textual and contextual:

First, the long ending (16:9-20) occurs in the vast majority of manuscripts (including the Textus Receptus, on which the KJV and many other translations were based). But it does not occur in the two oldest surviving MSS.

Second, the vocabulary and style of vv 9-20 are strikingly different from the rest of the Gospel. The connection between the parts is awkward and difficult to explain. In short, it bears all the features of an addition from a scribe who has pieced together a pastiche of ideas and events from the other Gospels and other parts of Scripture. The longer ending has little to commend it (Metzger 1975, 122-28; Marcus 2009, 1088-96).

But if this is not the ending, is "for they were afraid" (v 8 NRSV) an appropriate close to this story? While 16:9-20 is manifestly secondary, it does show that fairly early in transmission, someone did not regard v 8 as adequate. Did Mark actually intend to add more but didn't? Has the original ending been lost? Or, did he actually intend to end at 16:8?

Perhaps Mark did intend to add more but for whatever reason was unable to do so—illness, persecution, death, etc. Perhaps a page or a leaf was accidentally torn from the codex in the earliest stages of transmission. Both of these suggestions are plausible, but far from certain.

Third, maybe Mark did intend to end with 16:8: **They said nothing to anyone, because they were afraid** (*ephobounto gar*). A few other books similarly end with the conjunction *gar* (see Collins 2007, 798-801).

If Mark intends to end his Gospel this way, what could this mean? Is it an opened-ended story written in a sort of bleak postmodern way that allows readers to continue the story? This suggestion is popular in many circles that agree that this is the intended ending (Collins 2007, 798-801). There is considerable evidence that the ending as it stands invites us into the story (Marcus 2009, 1088-96). But, is there an alternative view? If this is the intended ending, is there a better way to understand this sentence that makes the story more coherent and better fits the continuation of the story known to Mark's readers?

First, I consider Mark 16:1-8 the earliest recoverable version of Mark. Therefore, it is the subject of this commentary. Mark 16:9-20 contains material that can be found elsewhere in the NT. If people insist that snake-handling or speaking in tongues are essential signs of the kingdom, they can find limited biblical support elsewhere.

Second, Mark intends to end his Gospel in 16:8. There is no need, therefore, to postulate how the Gospel was shortened or what might have been lost. This is where Mark stopped. Other endings are later scribal additions. That leaves the commentator wrestling with **for they were afraid** as the end of the Gospel.

IN THE TEXT

1. The Women Come to the Tomb to Anoint the Body (16:1-4)

■ 1 Sabbath ended at sunset, so the women (→ 15:40-41) are able to buy spices **to anoint Jesus' body.** The pressure of time between death and burial on the day of preparation (15:42) meant that this was not possible earlier. Mark is at particular pains to show the reality of Jesus' death (see 15:43-45); this event simply confirms that.

These women bought spices because Jesus was dead. However, "that they thought in terms of anointing at all suggests that . . . they have simply not taken seriously his expectation of rising again after three days" (France 2002, 677). That should cause little surprise. Those in late 2TJ who believed in resurrection thought of a future and primarily a corporate resurrection of Israel. The trauma of the past six days may have eviscerated hopes and dreams (see Luke 24:18-24). But they had served him in life; now they would serve him in death.

This is the third time the women have been named, indicating the extraordinary significance Mark assigns them. They are named as the only followers of Jesus who witnessed the crucifixion, who saw his burial, and who witness the empty tomb. They bring spices to anoint the body of Jesus, so they guarantee Jesus' actual physical death and burial, the location of his tomb, and that his tomb was empty. They observe the whole scene. Their silence highlights this role (Hurtado 2009, 8).

■ **2-4** Mark's syntax is confusing here, because the first and second parts of the sentence seem to be contradictory. The problem is that *prōi* refers to the fourth watch of the night (so 13:35), while *anateilantos tou hōiou* usually means "the sun having risen."

Evans speculates that a word, *oupō* ("not yet") has dropped out of the text or that **just after sunrise** should be taken with **they asked each other** (2001, 534). While this is plausible, it is speculative, and without MSS evidence. Stein, however, simply suggests that Mark was not intending to be precise. Mark repeats a phrase for emphasis (see 1:32-34; 14:12), leaving a redundant phrase (2008, 729).

As they journeyed, the women remembered **the stone, which was very large** (v 4). The size is emphasized in Mark. This would be a formidable object to move without proper equipment or enough people. It was probably shaped like a disk and over a meter (three feet) in diameter, sufficient to cover the **entrance of the tomb.** But when the women **looked up** [*anablepsasai*], **they saw that the stone . . . had been rolled away.** Mark mentions no tools for leverage nor does he place any men at the scene. He gives the impression that this stone could not be shifted easily. He perhaps hints at something extraordinary by having the women look up, not simply look. He also uses the passive voice: **the stone . . . had been rolled away** (*apokekylistai*). Who moved it remains a mystery. This is their first clue to the extraordinary sight that will greet them in the tomb.

2. He Is Risen (16:5-8)

■ **5** Since the women know in which tomb Jesus was buried, and now see that it is open, they enter it. Now comes the crucial part of their witness: The tomb is empty. They are looking for the body of Jesus but see **a young man dressed**

in a white robe. "The women do not see the risen Jesus, but the young man communicates to them his resurrected status, both in words and in his person" (Collins 2007, 795). Mark does not have the vivid and explicit description of Matt 28:3-5. But Mark's **young man** is probably an angel as well. He certainly isn't the young man of 14:51-52. If he were, Mark would have written "the young man" (so Collins 2007, 795). This young man is **sitting on the right side,** presumably right of where the body of Jesus had been placed. The response of the women is unsurprising: **they were alarmed,** first by the appearance of the young man, but possibly also at the empty tomb.

■ **6** In several reported appearances of angels to humans in Scripture (see, e.g., Matt 1:20; Luke 1:13), the first words are calming: **Don't be alarmed.** But the central words here are next: *You seek Jesus the Nazarene, the crucified one.* The women are in the right place. And they are looking for the right person. But the news is unexpected: **He has risen!** This aorist passive emphasizes that this action has just occurred on the third day since his crucifixion, as he predicted (Mark 8:31; 9:31; 10:33). It also establishes this as God's action. To confirm the obvious, he states: **He is not here.** He commands them to believe their own eyes: **See the place where they laid him.**

Each part of this announcement is laden with significance. The slightly formal language may reproduce an early creedal confession making these essential points (Marcus 2009, 1085). The young man tells the women in effect, "Jesus, the flesh and blood Nazarene that you remember, and whose crucifixion, death, and burial you saw, this man is risen. His body is not here. See the place where they laid him. This is no ghost story. The risen Jesus is the same Jesus who was crucified."

■ **7** The women are not allowed to stay. *Instead,* they are commanded to **go, tell his disciples and Peter.** They are to tell the story of the empty tomb (and perhaps the crucifixion, death, and burial) to which they alone among his followers are witnesses. They are also to tell them, **He is going ahead of you into Galilee. There you will see him, just as he told you.** A number of important points emerge:

First, the phrase **his disciples and Peter** is deliberate. Peter has a crucial future beyond the story as one of the first witnesses to the resurrection: **you will see him.** But it also reflects the memory of Peter's cowardly betrayal (14:71), despite his protestations to the contrary (14:29, 31). Now, the angel implies that Peter will be restored to discipleship and will share this good news. Marcus captures the nuance and ambivalence of Peter's situation well: this message is *especially* to Peter and *even* to Peter (2009, 1086). And the rest of the **disciples,** who had abandoned Jesus, are to follow Jesus into Galilee as well.

414

Second, this is a final tying up of Jesus' prophecies. So far, all of them have been fulfilled, including the beginning of the end for the temple (13:2; 15:38). Now the promise of gathering the scattered flock (14:28) is being arranged, **just as he told you.** Jesus will be in Galilee to await them and the mission will resume (→ 14:28). Jesus has been raised and will be appearing to his disciples in Galilee. Mark's readers can have confidence in Jesus' words.

■ **8** **Trembling and bewildered, the women went out and fled from the tomb.** This, too, is understandable. The next line, however, is problematic. Mark writes, **They said nothing to anyone, because they were afraid** (*kai oudeni ouden eipan ephobounto gar*). Most scholars read this as direct disobedience to the young man's command, due to the women's fear. Others suggest that this is a temporary disobedience that is later rectified by telling all. Hurtado (2009, 1-45), however, proposes an alternative reading:

First, he argues that Markan usage of the phrase *kai oudeni ouden eipan* can be taken as indicating, "not a complete failure to communicate, but that the women spoke to *no one else* beyond those to whom they were directed" (Hurtado 2009, 23). In 1:44 Jesus uses the same phrase to the cleansed leper: Say nothing "to anyone. But go . . . to the priest." He gives a similar command to those at the scene of his healing of the deaf mute in 7:36, which they promptly disobey.

Second, a *kai*-consecutive construction introduces the statement. If Mark wished to show their disobedience, an adversative particle would have been expected (Hurtado 2009, 23).

Hurtado contends that the intention of 16:8 is to reinforce "the numinous significance of the scene" by focusing attention on the immediate effect it had on the women: "The final words, *ephobounto gar*, are not the author's parting shot at the women, but a concluding reference to their agitated state brought on by the numinous 'youth' and the astounding news of Jesus' resurrection" (2009, 24). They do not tell anyone *"other than those to whom they had been sent"* (Hurtado 2009, 24, his emphasis).

This is exactly how the other Evangelists understand the events.

Mark does not really end on a note of failure and uncertainty. Instead, Mark 16:1-8 forms a fully satisfactory climactic episode that was designed to thrill and empower intended readers to follow Jesus in mission, through opposition and even their own potentially violent death, confident in an eschatological vindication by resurrection for which Jesus' resurrection was the inspiring model. (Hurtado 2009, 35)

FROM THE TEXT

And so, Mark's story of Jesus comes to an end. The section has several important points. Above all is the empty tomb—**He has risen! He is not here!**

(v 6). Without those words and the reality of the empty tomb, Jesus' death is a disaster for his disillusioned followers and a dismal failure for a deluded Jesus. But the suffering-vindication pattern that Jesus announced repeatedly for himself and his followers comes true. It is both fulfillment for Jesus and promise for his followers. God's good news ultimately will triumph. With the reality of the empty tomb, the whole direction of God's future purposes as announced by Jesus—the kingdom of God has arrived—is guaranteed. These words are the heart of the good news.

Second, the promise in 14:28 to the soon-to-be-scattered disciples is already in the process of realization. All that Jesus has promised has occurred. The disciples can have confidence that **He is going ahead of you into Galilee. There you will see him, just as he told you** (v 7). He will continue to lead his disciples into the future—a future that is open-ended—and into a story that continues. But he will be with them on the journey and on the mission to which he has called them.

Third, this is a message of forgiveness and restoration. The good news of the gospel is that Jesus welcomes failed disciples back into the mission if they go to him. For the ten disciples who had turned tail and fled, this is good news indeed; for Peter, the one who promised never to forsake Jesus whatever the cost—and then denied he knew Jesus just a few hours later, it is even more powerful. Mark goes out of his way to name Peter—**Go, tell his disciples and Peter**—as a powerful message of forgiveness and restoration even for the Peters among Jesus' followers. Those prominent, up-front, and somewhat unself-aware disciples who are Peter-like in their ability to see off the big threats but are blindsided by the little things may take hope. This is good news indeed.

Fourth, the rest of the story becomes open-ended. The women play a crucial role in this ending. Contrary to the usual reading of this passage, but in accordance with the reading by Matthew and Luke, they do tell the disciples and Peter. But readers then and now know that the story continues. Just as Jesus' first disciples were invited to join him again in Galilee, so readers then and now are drawn into the story and asked to participate in it, to become followers of the Crucified and Risen One. They do so in the confidence that the risen and ascended Jesus is Lord, that through his Spirit he leads his followers on his mission into the world, and that the ultimate good purposes of God will prevail.